Netherlands Yearbook of International Law

Volume 53

Volume Editors

Otto Spijkers, Faculty of Governance and Global Affairs, Leiden University, Leiden, The Netherlands

Julie Fraser, Faculty of Law, Economics and Governance, Utrecht University, Utrecht, The Netherlands

Emmanuel Giakoumakis, Faculty of Law, University of Oxford, Oxford, United Kingdom

Managing Editor

Carl Emilio Lewis, T.M.C. Asser Institute, The Hague, The Netherlands

As a double-blind peer-reviewed publication, the Netherlands Yearbook of International Law offers a forum for the publication of scholarly articles of a conceptual nature in a varying thematic area of public international law. In addition, as of 2012 each Yearbook includes a section entitled 'Dutch Practice in International Law', which replaces the section previously dedicated to Documentation. Part of the Documentation is still available online (since 2011) here: www.asser.nl/nyil/documentation. The NYIL has been published under the auspices of the T.M.C. Asser Instituut since 1970.

Otto Spijkers · Julie Fraser ·
Emmanuel Giakoumakis
Volume Editors

Netherlands Yearbook of International Law 2022

Reparations in International Law: A Critical Reflection

ASSER PRESS

Springer

Volume Editors
Otto Spijkers
Faculty of Governance and Global Affairs
Leiden University
Leiden, The Netherlands

Julie Fraser
International and European Law
Utrecht University
Utrecht, The Netherlands

Emmanuel Giakoumakis
Faculty of Law
University of Oxford
Oxford, UK

ISSN 0167-6768 ISSN 1574-0951 (electronic)
Netherlands Yearbook of International Law
ISBN 978-94-6265-626-0 ISBN 978-94-6265-627-7 (eBook)
https://doi.org/10.1007/978-94-6265-627-7

Published by T.M.C. ASSER PRESS, The Hague, The Netherlands www.asserpress.nl
Produced and distributed for T.M.C. ASSER PRESS by Springer-Verlag Berlin Heidelberg

This T.M.C. ASSER PRESS imprint is published by the registered company Springer-Verlag GmbH, DE, part of Springer Nature
The registered company address is: Heidelberger Platz 3, 14197 Berlin, Germany

Board of Editors

Aims and Scope

The Netherlands Yearbook of International Law (NYIL) was first published in 1970. As a double-blind peer-reviewed publication, the NYIL offers a forum for the publication of scholarly articles of a conceptual nature in a varying thematic area of public international law. In addition, each Yearbook includes a section *Dutch Practice in International Law.* The NYIL is published under the auspices of the T.M.C. Asser Instituut

T.M.C. Asser Instituut

Located in the 'international zone' of The Hague—the City of Justice, Peace and Security, the T.M.C. Asser Instituut is a leading, inter-university research institute operating in the broad field of international law.

Founded in 1965, the Institute's international community of scholars is engaged in research, postgraduate training and dissemination of knowledge in furtherance of the purposes and principles of international law. This inter-university institute cooperates closely with and supports the Dutch universities' activities in the relevant disciplines. The academic fields covered by the Institute are Private International Law, Public International Law, Law of the European Union, International Commercial Arbitration, International Humanitarian Law, International Criminal Law and International Sports Law.

The Institute enjoys an excellent reputation at both a national and an international level for its development, organisation and hosting of conferences and academic meetings, demand driven postgraduate programmes and training. Its ancillary Websites and data collections all contribute to a coherent and integral strategy in the area of knowledge transfer.

The Institute has its own publishing house, T.M.C. Asser Press. T.M.C. Asser Press not only serves the publishing needs of the T.M.C. Asser Instituut, but also those of academics and practitioners worldwide in the fields of International and European Law.

T.M.C. Asser Instituut
Institute for Private and Public International Law
International Commercial Arbitration and European Law

Institute Address:
R. J. Schimmelpennincklaan 20–22
2517 JN The Hague
The Netherlands

Postal Address:
P.O. Box 30461
2500 GL The Hague
The Netherlands
Tel.: +3170 342 0300
Fax: +3170 342 0359
Email: NYIL@asser.nl
Internet: https://www.asser.nl

Contents

Chapter 1
Introduction: New Frontiers in Reparations since *Factory at Chorzów*

Julie Fraser, Emmanuel Giakoumakis and Otto Spijkers

Contents

Abstract Almost a century has passed since the judgment in the case concerning the *Factory at Chorzów* by the Permanent Court of International Justice in 1928. This judgment provided the principle for reparations under international law that is still applied today. This volume of the Netherlands Yearbook of International Law examines this case and subsequent developments to study the development of reparations around the world. It focuses particularly on the influence of international humanitarian, criminal, and human rights law on reparations and the shift from a State to a victim-centric approach. The chapters in the volume include traditional legal research as well as empirical studies that bring to light views of victims/survivors in places like Cambodia and Senegal. The chapters reveal the difficulty of reparations in practice and the need to reinvest in fulfilling the rights of victims to a remedy.

Keywords Reparations · Human rights · Historical wrongs · International law

---

J. Fraser (✉)
Utrecht University, Utrecht, The Netherlands
e-mail: J.a.fraser@uu.nl

E. Giakoumakis
Faculty of Law, University of Oxford, Oxford, United Kingdom
e-mail: emmanouil.giakoumakis@sant.ox.ac.uk

O. Spijkers
Leiden University College, The Hague, The Netherlands
e-mail: o.spijkers@luc.leidenuniv.nl

O. Spijkers et al. (eds.), *Netherlands Yearbook of International Law 2022*, Netherlands Yearbook of International Law 53, https://doi.org/10.1007/978-94-6265-627-7_1

1.1 Introduction

Almost a century has passed since the much-celebrated judgment on the merits was delivered in the case concerning the *Factory at Chorzów*. In this 1928 judgment, the Permanent Court of International Justice (PCIJ) affirmed the essential principle of reparation contained in the actual notion of an illegal act. It held that 'reparation must, as far as possible, wipe out all the consequences of the illegal act and re-establish the situation which would, in all probability, have existed if that act had not been committed'.[1] The principle of 'integral' or 'full reparation' was subsequently accepted by the International Law Commission (ILC) as the basic tenet governing the consequences of internationally wrongful acts in Articles 34-39 of the ILC Articles on Responsibility of States for Internationally Wrongful Acts of 2001 (ARSIWA),[2] and has since been applied by international courts and tribunals in a wide range of disputes.

Still, the precise contours of this normative proposition on reparations remain unclear, not least because of the profound transformations since the rendering of that judgment. Like all judgments, *Factory at Chorzów* is a child of its time, reflecting the strictly bilateral nature of the international legal order in the inter-War period and the State-centric character of international law at that time. As such, reparation in the judgment is focused on the loss sustained by the injured State and is intended to reinstate the *status quo ante* without much regard to additional considerations or to the interests of stakeholders other than the States involved. Moreover, the normative foundations underlying the standard of reparation propounded in *Factory at Chorzów* proceed from a close analogy with municipal private law governing torts: the responsible State is assimilated to a private tortfeasor whose transgression of responsibility generates consequences on the international plane. Yet, this construction does not sit comfortably with the public interests protected by the international legal order, or the legal consequences stemming from serious violations of international law, in particular human rights, humanitarian, and criminal law.

The rules governing reparation enunciated in the *Factory at Chorzów* have traditionally been dealt with by the ILC and academic scholarship as 'secondary' norms in the Hartian sense, governing the consequences of wrongfulness independent of the primary norms setting out States' rights and obligations. Whilst this classification may have been a useful analytical instrument for the purposes of the ILC's codification work, the ILC itself was cautious in not ascribing to it an intrinsic normative value. It affirmed that the content of the primary rules, as well as broader normative considerations and structural features of the international legal system, may inform the scope and content of the secondary norms governing responsibility.[3] As a result,

---

[1] PCIJ, *The Factory at Chorzów (Germany v. Poland)*, Merits, 13 September 1928, p. 47.

[2] ILC 2001, chap. IV.E.1.

[3] See, for example, ILC 2001, art. 41(3) and commentaries (13)–(14), which suggest that the gravity of the breach in question may inform the obligation to provide reparations and that international law may provide further obligations flowing from the commission of serious breaches of international law within the meaning of Article 40.

the precise scope and meaning of the rules governing reparation are in a constant state of dialogue with the primary rules to which they attach.

Since the judgment in *Factory at Chorzów*, the world has experienced remarkable changes with the creation of the United Nations (UN) as successor to the League of Nations, the prohibition on the use of force, the obligation to settle international disputes peacefully, and the adoption of the Universal Declaration of Human Rights in 1948[4] and treaties on the topic of international human rights law. Other significant developments include the progressive independence of formerly colonised states, the women's movement, globalisation, and the increasing role of non-State actors including corporations, intergovernmental organisations, and civil society. These structural changes have resulted in a gradual shift in the attention of the international community from (purely) power dynamics to a rule-based legal system, where the consequences of responsibility are articulated in norms and principles aimed at ensuring an equitable balance of interests between the various State and non-State actors. In this context, the rules governing reparation have evolved into a nuanced instrument of promoting compliance with international norms, ensuring accountability for potential violations, and caring for those harmed.

Moreover, the practice of awarding reparations has undergone a profound evolution—even predating the *Factory at Chorzów* judgment. International practice since the conclusion of the Treaty of Jay between the United States and Great Britain in 1794[5] was dominated by direct negotiations for the (more-or-less peaceful) settlement of claims or inter-State arbitration aimed at bringing about an 'appropriate' settlement of disputes. The 1919 Treaty of Versailles[6] following the First World War was influential regarding reparations and, in fact, was part of the rich legal background to the *Factory at Chorzów* dispute. This treaty, with the catastrophic consequences of the 'Carthaginian Peace' it imposed through the infamous 'guilt clause' against Germany, revealed the potential risks inherent in the strict adherence to the rules of reparation and the potential scope for abuse against vanquished or weaker nations.[7]

The period following the Second World War confirmed States' reluctance to resort to strict-liability mechanisms for the apportionment of responsibility and was marked by a general distrust of international legal institutions as a means for the settlement of international disputes. It therefore comes as no surprise that most international claims were typically settled diplomatically through inter-State lump sum agreements. Reparations were provided to war victims/survivors *inter alia* by establishing public compensation schemes, through the restitution of property, or by way of satisfaction through criminal trials, the erection of monuments, and the creation of national days of remembrance. However, following the creation of the Iran-US

---

[4] Universal Declaration of Human Rights (adopted 10 December 1948 UNGA Res 217 A(III).

[5] Treaty of Amity, Commerce, and Navigation, between His Britannic Majesty and the United States of America (signed 19 November 1794; entered into force 29 February 1796).

[6] Treaty of Peace with Germany (Treaty of Versailles) (signed 28 June 1919; entered into force 10 June 1920).

[7] Van Hoogstraten et al. 2017.

Claims Tribunal though the Algiers Claims Settlement Declaration in 1981,[8] and the establishment of the UN Compensation Commission by the UN Security Council[9] a decade later, reparation rules have increasingly been interpreted, applied, and reinforced as a means for ensuring the effectiveness of international norms. The end of the Cold War and the progressive embedding of the multilateral international legal system has resulted in renewed interest in and opportunities for the rules governing reparation. In this context, the development of new rules reflecting broader community interests such as human rights and the environment, and legal constructs such as peremptory norms (*jus cogens*) and obligations *erga omnes*, have had a profound impact on the articulation of the consequences of responsibility.

In response to such developments, scholars and practitioners have argued that the principles in *Factory at Chorzów* no longer adequately serve the needs of the international community and require recalibration to account for the structural shifts in international society and international law. This raises questions such as: what scope is there for a modern interpretation of the rules relating to reparation, and what should these modern rules be? Or, how to account for harm that can never be 'wiped out'? Should the *status quo ante* even be a goal of reparations? As we near the closing of a century since the PCIJ's dictum in *Factory at Chorzów*, it is important to re-examine the normative premise and appositeness of the principle to our 'brave new world'. In light of the structural, normative, and axiological changes in international law, this special volume of the Netherlands Yearbook of International Law critically assesses the practical application of the reparations principle and its limitations. It approaches this issue from three different angles: (1) the practice of international human rights law in international and domestic courts; (2) the role of international (or internationalised) criminal courts; and (3) the role of de-colonisation in the practice of reparations.

1.2 The Role of International Human Rights Law in the Development of Reparations

A key development in the evolution of the rules governing reparation at the international level was the wide range of mechanisms established after the Second World War to administer reparations beyond the strictly inter-State paradigm and the gradual recognition of reparation as part of a victim's right to a remedy.[10] The codification

[8] Declaration of the Government of the Democratic and Popular Republic of Algeria Concerning the Settlement of Claims by the Government of the United States of America and the Government of the Islamic Republic of Iran, 19 January 1981.

[9] United Nations Security Council resolution 687 (1991), 8 April 1991.

[10] See for example Art 2(3) of the International Covenant on Civil and Political Rights (1966) United Nations, Treaty Series, vol. 999, p. 171; Basic Principles and Guidelines on the Right to a Remedy and Reparation for Victims of Gross Violations of International Human Rights Law and Serious Violations of International Humanitarian Law, UNGA Res 60/147 (16 December 2005) UN Doc A/RES/60/147.

of human rights law has had a significant influence on reparations, providing normative foundations for the obligation to repair individual victims/survivors of human rights violations or international crimes. The established mechanisms—including UN treaty bodies, regional human rights courts, and specialised criminal courts—have further developed and elaborated upon reparative norms in practice. Chapter 2 in this volume by Deborah Casalin illustrates how international law on reparations has shifted from State-centricity to victim-centricity and the role of human rights law as a catalyst in this process. She does this by charting the emergence in the last century of a right not to be displaced in international law as well as attendant rights for victims to receive reparations that may take different forms based on the needs of those displaced.

This reparative practice has been complemented by private, domestic, or hybrid mass-claims programmes aimed at repairing historical wrongs, such as public compensation schemes, the restitution of looted property or dormant accounts, or the establishment of numerous truth and reconciliation commissions. Particularly across the Americas, a wave of reparation measures was implemented as part of transitional justice processes in numerous States, including Argentina, Chile, and Colombia. Chapter 3 in this volume by Jemima García-Godos and Lisa Laplante focuses on reparations in the context of transitional justice, tracing the dilemmas, debates, and new directions. Based also on empirical insights, they note the distance travelled since *Factory at Chorzów* and the prevailing understanding now that harm often cannot be (simply) repaired or 'wiped-out'. When individuals are the victim of a wrongful act, restitution is almost always impossible, and even financial compensation may be inappropriate in cases. There is thus a need for more creativity from courts, States, donors, and all other stakeholders involved. Indeed, reparative bodies should be open to all forms of reparation as long as they are adequate, effective, prompt, and proportional to the gravity of the violations and the harm suffered.

Among the existing human rights mechanisms, the Inter-American Court of Human Rights (IACtHR) is generally recognised for its progressive approach to reparations.[11] In Chap. 4, Edward Perez examines the role of the IACtHR as a policy maker and concludes that the IACtHR has intervened in policy cycles through agenda setting, policy formulation, and ordering policy implementation or requiring policy evaluation (favouring the second of these alternatives). His chapter shows how various factors have influenced the Court's decision regarding how to design its structural remedy. These factors include the year the decision was issued, the State that is held responsible, and the participation of certain victim's counsel, among others. The chapter concludes by calling for further research on possible public policy tools that the Court could incorporate when issuing structural remedies, the role of the litigating parties in incorporating a policy perspective into their legal strategies, and possible alternatives to the Court's practices for improving policy intervention.

Chapter 5 in this volume by Pietro Sferrazza Taibi and Francisco Bustos examines the influence of international human rights law on Chilean case law on civil claims for crimes committed during Augusto Pinochet's dictatorship (1973–1990). It argues

[11] Contreras-Garduño and Fraser 2014, p. 175.

that, due to the inadequacy of reparations granted by the Chilean government, victims have taken their struggle to courts demanding compensation. A significant obstacle to be overcome was the statute of limitations. International human rights law provided the basis for national courts to conclude that all claims derived from crimes against humanity were not subject to the statute of limitations, regardless of their nature. This chapter shows how the application of international human rights law can lead to progressive developments at the national level towards achieving justice, truth, reparation, and guarantees of non-repetition. The 'domestication' of State practice on reparations is an interesting development, as such practice may provide valuable evidence of State practice and *opinio juris* for the purposes of tracking and ascertaining the existence of customary norms in the field of reparations in the future.

Two chapters in the volume relate to recent developments in the Netherlands as well as human rights. They serve a dual function: they are part of the Yearbook devoted to reparations, but they also constitute the part of the Yearbook that is traditionally reserved for a discussion of the 'Dutch Practice in International Law'. Chapters in this part of the volume seek to bring Dutch practice across the borders and to the attention of the wider international community, and as is custom, form the final part of the yearbook. The first of these (Chap. 13) relates to accountability for the 1995 genocide in Srebrenica. The second (Chap. 14), addresses the interaction between the international and domestic Dutch legal order in the context of reparation claims.

Chapter 13, by Alma Mustafić and Niké Wentholt, is entitled: 'Finding the Truth but Ending the Conversation: How Dutch Civil Court Cases on the Srebrenica Genocide Shaped the Space for Reparation'. The authors describe what efforts were made to seek reparation before, during, and after these Dutch national legal proceedings. They show that, whilst much academic attention was paid to these cases, much less attention was paid to the wider societal impact of these cases on the reparation process. They demonstrate that civil court cases hold potential for subsequent wider political and societal reparation, and detail various initiatives by the Bosnian-Dutch community including commemoration, an art movement, and a theatre play. These were creative means through which the Bosnian-Dutch community 'spoke back' to imagine and reinvigorate the reparation process. Where Dutch politics and society had failed to take up the court cases' potential the first time around, they were thus provided with a second chance to design and implement an inclusive and participatory reparation process. The chapter argues that both the Bosnian-Dutch community and Dutch society as a whole, deserve such reparation for their shared history of Srebrenica.

Anneloes Kuiper-Slendebroek's Chap. 14 is entitled 'No 'Effective Remedy' Without National Enforcement: A Dutch Perspective on the Obstacles for Application of the Right to a Remedy in Tort Law Cases'. It examines the interaction between international rules and the domestic legal order, with the Netherlands as a case study. National courts play an important role in ensuring adequate protection of individual rights based on international law, including the rights in the European Convention on Human Rights (ECHR). Central to the cooperative relationship between this regional human rights treaty and the Dutch domestic legal system is Article 13 ECHR, which provides a right to an effective remedy. According to the author, for this cooperative relationship to succeed, the self-executing character and prevailing nature of ECHR provisions must be acknowledged, and national courts must be allowed to play a principal role in the enforcement of these rights. The Netherlands is an interesting case study because the Dutch Constitution gives priority to self-executing norms of international treaties over conflicting domestic law—even the Constitution itself[12]—and, as demonstrated by analysing some high-profile public interest cases including *Urgenda*,[13] because human rights are often implemented in the Netherlands through the open norms of tort law.

1.3 The Role of International Criminal Law in the Development of Reparations

Some of the most recent developments in the international law on reparations come from the branch of international, or internationalised, criminal law. The Rome Statute of the International Criminal Court (ICC) has been hailed as a highpoint for victim's rights in that victims can both participate in the criminal trial as well as apply to receive reparations from convicted persons.[14] This marks a sharp (and welcome) turn from the approach of the two *ad hoc* tribunals created by the UN Security Council in the 1990s to prosecute international crimes in the former Yugoslavia and Rwanda that did not include a role for victims. Much contemporary scholarship has examined the reparations regime unfolding in the ICC's jurisprudence at the horizontal level (i.e., between the victims of international crimes and the perpetrator of such crimes). Less attention has been paid to the complementary reparative obligations of States[15] and State organs involved in the perpetration of international crimes.

In Chap. 6, Meagan Wong focuses on the ICC's power to award reparation in the event of a crime of aggression under Article 8*bis* of the Rome Statute. This provision is quite exceptional, insofar as the wrongful conduct by a State (an act of aggression) constitutes an essential component of the definition of a crime. As the ICC is not an inter-State court, a question arises as to whether the ICC has the power to determine the legal consequences of responsibility arising from an internationally wrongful act as between the aggressor and aggressed State. The question is a direct emanation of a lesser known aspect of the *Factory at Chorzów* judgment, that a

[12] Fraser 2024.

[13] Netherlands Supreme Court, Judgment of 20 December 2019 in the case between the State of the Netherlands (Ministry of infrastructure and the environment) and the Urgenda foundation. English translation available at: http://deeplink.rechtspraak.nl/uitspraak?id=ECLI:NL:HR:2019:2007 (Urgenda Supreme Court Judgment). See Spijkers 2020, pp. 192–206.

[14] See for example ICC, *The Prosecutor v Thomas Lubanga Dyilo*, Appeals Chamber, Judgement on the Appeals Against the 'Decision Establishing the Principles and Procedures to be Applied to Reparations' of 7 August 2012 with Amended Order for Reparations (Annex A) and Public Annexes 1 and 2 ICC-01/04-01/06-3129 (3 March 2015).

[15] See for example Moffett and Sandoval 2021.

'decision whether there has been a breach of an engagement involves no doubt a more important jurisdiction than a decision as to the nature or extent of reparation due for a breach of an international engagement'.[16] Wong argues that whilst the ICC does not have the authority to determine restitution and compensation at the inter-State level, the States Parties to the Rome Statute have conferred upon the ICC the authority to award satisfaction at the inter-State level for the crime of aggression. Tracing international practice on reparation, Wong argues that this may include—apart from the acknowledgement of a breach—the institution of penal proceedings, an apology, or collective reparations for the victims of aggression. Whilst the ICC has yet to be seized in a case involving the crime of aggression, the analysis introduces a new dimension in the conduct of criminal proceedings where the interests of one or more sovereigns are involved, and raises the question how the Court can safeguard those interests in a procedurally fair manner.

The remedy of satisfaction is particularly relevant to the present volume, as it was not mentioned by the PCIJ in its much-celebrated dictum on reparations in *Factory at Chorzów*. Yet, the remedy has been repeatedly affirmed in diplomatic and judicial practice, and the ILC expressly included satisfaction in the forms of remedies available under customary international law.[17] In Chap. 7 Alice Ollino reappraises the role of satisfaction twenty years after the adoption of ARSIWA in light of inter-State judicial practice. She demonstrates that inter-State courts and tribunals award satisfaction as a form of reparation for internationally wrongful acts, but they do so in a way that does not necessarily reflect the principles in the ARSIWA and may occasionally appear controversial. Ollino considers that international courts tend to minimise the afflictive element of satisfaction and the 'private' character of the dispute, adopting a more 'public' dimension to the dispute, utilising satisfaction as an instrument to reaffirm the validity of primary obligations in a forward-looking manner.

Returning to criminal justice, it is important to note that the practice of reparations for victims of international crimes is by no means limited to the framework of the ICC. The chapter in this volume by Christoph Sperfeldt (Chap. 8) as well as Chap. 9 by Alina Balta, Mijke de Waardt and Marola Vaes examine reparations by the internationalised hybrid criminal courts in Cambodia and Senegal: the Extraordinary Chambers in the Courts of Cambodia (ECCC) and the Extraordinary African Chambers (EAC). These two chapters present vital empirical insights into how victims experience participating in criminal trials, the reparations process, and outcome of awards. Both chapters highlight the necessity of such insights and call for more empirical research with victim communities to complement the wide-ranging normative scholarship on the topic. In a way, these chapters are sobering reminders of the reality of reparations in practice and the extent to which they fall short of victim's expectations (and rights). While reparation awards or orders are often lauded in scholarship, most of them are un- or under-implemented in practice due to limited

[16] *Factory at Chorzów*, Jurisdiction (1927) PCIJ Ser A No 9, 23.
[17] ILC 2001, art. 37.

funding and political will.[18] As Sperfeldt notes, victims of Hissène Habré are yet to receive anything from the landmark award by the EAC of almost US$140 million, and most Cambodian civil parties were unaware or had limited knowledge of the ECCC's reparation projects. Ultimately, reparation orders by both courts are to be funded via donations—mirroring the experience of victims at the ICC.

In this context, it is noteworthy that several chapters in this volume emphasise the importance of victim/survivor participation and consultation in the reparations process—what Balta, de Waardt and Vaes recognise as the procedural part of reparative justice. Laplante and García-Godos in Chap. 3 similarly argue that victim consultation is part of the reparative process and 'is the constitutive act that restores full citizenship'.[19] The authors recommend consultations with victims to find answers to the question of what they need to *feel* repaired and encourage the development of new and different types of reparation based on cultural contexts and worldviews, urging that the process matters just as much as the outcome. In their study of the ECCC, Balta, de Waardt and Vaes reveal the role of culture (including religion) in designing reparations and the importance of understanding how victims give meaning to their lives, understand their (mental) health, and envisage/relate to their lost loved ones in the afterlife. The chapters in this volume reiterate the importance of tailoring reparations measures to the context in every situation.

1.4 De-colonialisation and the Law of Reparations

Another important aspect of the *Factory at Chorzów* judgment lies in its Western-centric focus. Indeed, the case dealt with a European dispute and the majority of judges were European. The chapters of this volume attempt to deconstruct this narrative by widening our perspective on the *international* practice of reparations. By looking at the practice of States, courts, and tribunals in Asia, Africa, and Latin America many chapters in this volume attempt to de-centre Europe/the West as the epistemic sites for developing international law, and seek to enhance the legitimacy and representative character of our understanding of reparations.

As noted above, decolonisation in the second half of the 20th century greatly impacted international law, but it has also given rise to new claims for reparations. Today, there are increasing calls for European States (including the Netherlands)[20] to pay reparations to former colonies for injuries caused by acts of oppression, the exploitation of natural resources, and enslaving people. This is an area where the law of reparations has been underdeveloped, but there is a growing interest amongst several States to pursue this issue.

In Chap. 10, entitled 'A Century on from the *Chorzów Factory*: Reparations, National Wars of Liberation and the Limits of Wiping out the Consequences of

[18] McGonigle Leyh and Fraser 2019, p. 52.

[19] Laplante 2013.

[20] See for example van den Herik 2012 and Immler 2022, Article 8.

Armed Conflicts', Luke Moffett focuses on the practice of reparations in settling claims after armed conflict, in particular those emerging from colonialism and occupation. Moffett discusses the challenges of redressing the harm caused to victims and examines the limits of international humanitarian and human rights law in providing a legal basis and (often) a forum for victims' claims. After a comprehensive assessment of international practice, he concludes that in the past century, reparations for violations have been inadequate and in many cases absent. This has been particularly acute in wars of national liberation that marked the mid-twentieth century and recent neo-colonial conflicts in the Middle East by Western powers. On that basis, he argues for a more rigorous implementation of the right to a remedy for the victims of armed conflict as an instrument for restoring a more enduring peace.

The most common objection to claims for repairing historical wrongs is the difficulty of identifying the relevant norms that were applicable at the time of the act—also known as the issue of intertemporal law. Karina Theurer's chapter in this volume (Chap. 11), entitled 'Racism as an Obstacle to Reparations for Colonial Crimes? The Doctrine of Intertemporal Law in the German-Namibian Context' addresses this issue. Theurer looks at the controversial aspects of the doctrine of intertemporal law and argues that, when this doctrine is applied in the context of past events, we should ask: which laws *really* were in force at the time and which law do we apply to assess the lawfulness of these actions? Focusing on the example of the Ovaherero and Nama reparation claims, Theurer traces the extent to which the application of the doctrine of intertemporal law may be situated between the reproduction of colonial racism and the decolonisation of our retrospective perception of the laws at the time of German colonialism. She sketches what a decolonised application of the doctrine of intertemporal law might look like as well as its impact on reparations. Theurer argues that reparations for colonial crimes should consist of deconstructing colonial racism, refraining from reproducing it, and finding ways of overcoming it. This in itself is a form of reparation.

In this regard, lessons can be learned from the case-study of Sweden. In Chap. 12, Ebba Lekvall explores the process initiated by the Church of Sweden (itself a State institution) to repair colonial abuses against Sweden's indigenous people—the Sami. As the Church played an important role in the colonisation and oppression of the Sami (the effects of which are still felt today), it has worked since the 1990s to address its role in these abuses and embark on a path towards reparation and reconciliation. Lekvall provides a critical analysis of the lack of participation by the Sami in the process and of the limits of the Church's approach to reparation. She discusses whether the process can be a catalyst for adequate reparation for colonial harms to the Sami in Sweden. She argues that while there have been some good faith efforts on the part of the Church, more is needed for the process and substance of reparation to be adequate and effective.

1.5 Testing the Limits of *Factory at Chorzów* and Tracing New Frontiers

The present volume seeks to test the limits of the *Factory at Chorzów* standard of reparation and to flesh out the new frontiers in contemporary legal practice. The volume offers a diversified approach, focusing on new areas of growing importance to assess how the reparation standard has been interpreted, applied, and modernised. The chapters are situated in different legal contexts, and many are linked to efforts—often led by survivors—to come to terms with particularly problematic episodes of international, regional, or local history. Nevertheless, the volume does not profess to be comprehensive and some important areas of the modern practice of reparation are not included, such as the developing practice on environmental reparations and climate justice, or the intricate jurisprudence of international arbitral tribunals in the law governing the protection of foreign investments.

A consistent theme across the contributions in this volume is that reparations in modern international law should strive to adopt a more tailored, victim-centred approach. When reparations are not seen as (just) a consequence of a wrongful act, but as the right of a victim/survivor, this fundamentally changes the lens through which violations are viewed: the focus shifts from the wrongfulness of the perpetrators' conduct to the harms suffered and potential measures to respond to that harm, victims/survivors themselves must be involved in this (creative) process and help identify appropriate reparative measures, which may go beyond restoring the *status quo ante* or may fall far short of it. In practice, all reparations for serious violations of international law are ultimately symbolic. This does not mean, however, that adequate political, financial, and human resources should be not dedicated to the task. It must nonetheless be noted that this proposition is not free from ambiguities or complexities. On the contrary, it raises a wide spectrum of legal, moral, and political considerations and calls into question the very essence of the rules governing reparation. While not resolving these issues, we hope that this volume provides a source of discussion and further reflection.

In closing, we would like to thank the editors of the Netherlands Yearbook of International Law for their valuable assistance throughout the preparation of this edition—in particular the managing editor Carl Lewis—as well as the peer reviewers for performing the double-blind review process, and the authors for contributing to this project.

References

Contreras-Garduño D, Fraser J (2014) The Identification of Victims before the Inter-American Court of Human Rights and the International Criminal Court and Its Impact on Participation and Reparation: A Domino Effect? Inter-American and European Human Rights Journal (2014) 7(1–2)

Fraser J (2024) Bringing the Law to Life: Judicial Operationalisation of International Human Rights Law, in the Domestic Sphere. In: Riyadi E, Tømte A (eds) Human Rights and Legal Methodology in Indonesia. Routledge, Milton Park

ILC (2001) Draft Articles on Responsibility of States for Internationally Wrongful Acts (Nov 2001) Supp No. 10 (A/56/10)

Immler NL (2022) The Netherlands-Indies; Rethinking post-colonial recognition from a multi-voiced perspective. Wacana, Journal of the Humanities of Indonesia, 23:3

Laplante L (2013) Negotiating Reparation Rights: The Participatory and Symbolic Quotients. Buffalo Human Rights Law Review 19:217–250

McGonigle Leyh B, Fraser J (2019) Transformation reparations: changing the game or more of the same? (2019) Cambridge International Law Journal, Vol. 8 No. 1

Moffett L, Sandoval C (2021) Tilting at windmills: Reparations and the International Criminal Court. Leiden Journal of International Law (2021) 34:3 749–769, https://doi.org/10.1017/S092215652100025X

Spijkers O (2020) The Case Between Urgenda and the State of the Netherlands. In: Szabó M (ed) Hungarian Yearbook of International Law and European Law, Volume 8, Issue 1 (2020)

van den Herik L (2012) Addressing 'Colonial Crimes' through Reparations? Adjudicating Dutch Atrocities Committed in Indonesia. (2012) Journal of International Criminal Justice 10:3 693–705

van Hoogstraten S, Schrijver N, Spijkers O, de Jong A (eds) (2017) The Art of Making Peace: Lessons Learned from Peace Treaties. Brill, Leiden

Julie Fraser is an assistant professor at Utrecht University, The Netherlands

Emmanuel Giakoumakis is affiliated to the Faculty of Law at the University of Oxford, United Kingdom, and is an associate lawyer at Steptoe & Johnson LLP

Otto Spijkers is a lecturer at Leiden University College, The Netherlands.

Part I
The Practice of International Human Rights Law in International and Domestic Courts

Chapter 2
Reparations for Displacement since *Chorzów*: Moving from the 'Problems of Displacement' to the 'Problems of the Displaced' via International and Regional Human Rights Bodies

Deborah Casalin

Contents

Abstract At the time the Permanent Court of International Justice was deliberating on the principles of reparation in the *Chorzów* case, mass displacement of people from their homes was not yet broadly recognized as wrongful in international law. The few displacement situations proscribed internationally were seen as affronts to state sovereignty or stability. The interests of displaced individuals and communities were not the main object of international legal protection, and reparation claims would have been an interstate matter. Since then, two major evolutions in international law

D. Casalin (✉)
Principal Research Fellow, Law and Development Research Group, University of Antwerp Law Faculty, Prinsstraat 13, B-2000 Antwerp, Belgium
e-mail: deborah.casalin@uantwerpen.be

Department of Public Law, Nelson Mandela University Law Faculty, Gqeberha, South Africa

O. Spijkers et al. (eds.), *Netherlands Yearbook of International Law 2022*, Netherlands Yearbook of International Law 53, https://doi.org/10.1007/978-94-6265-627-7_2

on displacement have reflected and epitomized the broad shift in the international law of reparation from addressing state interests to addressing impacts on individuals and communities. These are: (1) recognition of a broader range of internationally unlawful forms of displacement; and (2) elaboration of various forms of reparation addressing the harms of displacement for individuals and communities. This chapter charts and analyses these two evolutions and demonstrates the important role of international and regional human rights bodies' decisions in response to the claims of displaced people. Given the particular tensions among the interests of states, individuals, and communities in resolving mass displacement, developments on this issue offer salient illustrations of the movement away from state-centricity in the international law of reparations. The role played by human rights bodies also offers a significant example of how actors beyond the state have contributed to this shift.

Keywords Displacement · International/regional human rights bodies · Normative development · Reparations · State responsibility · Victims

2.1 Introduction

In resolving situations of mass displacement, particular tensions arise between the macro-level political 'problems of displacement' and the human-centred 'problems of the displaced', with the former frequently taking precedence over the latter.[1] For example, a state may offer restitution to promote displaced people's return to their areas of origin, without reference to their own interests and choices. This could allow the state to consolidate territorial claims, relieve pressure on host communities, or address inter-group tensions. Alternatively, a state may have an interest in displaced people accepting compensation so that the housing or land they left behind can be made available for other uses, such as resource extraction. These tensions have manifested prominently in post-conflict situations. However, they can also be observed in cases of development-induced displacement, where often marginalized communities must make way for projects which will supposedly benefit the economic development of the country as a whole. In disaster situations, such as flooding, displaced people may also be under pressure to accept compensation and resettlement so that their land can be used for other purposes. As such, displacement is a particularly salient issue to illustrate the more general tension in international law on reparations between state and individual/community interests.

This chapter analyses two main legal developments regarding displacement since the time of the *Chorzów* judgment. These are: (1) the recognition of a broader range of internationally unlawful forms of displacement; and (2) the elaboration of various

[1] The terms 'problems of displacement' and 'problems of the displaced' are from Johansson 2019, p. 139.

forms of reparation which specifically address the harms of displacement for individuals and communities. These two developments reflect the broader shift in international law on reparation from safeguarding the interests of states to addressing impacts on individuals and communities. The main objective of this chapter is to demonstrate how the decisions of international and regional human rights bodies (such as the regional human rights courts/commissions and UN treaty bodies) have played a particularly important role in these normative developments in response to the claims of displaced people. This exemplifies how actors beyond the state—i.e. the human rights bodies and the rights-holders approaching them—have contributed to shaping international law on reparations in a more victim-centric manner.

For the purposes of this chapter, displacement is broadly defined as forced, involuntary, or coerced population movement, with lack of voluntariness as the key defining element.[2] This allows the analysis to trace how a growing range of such situations have been recognized as violations of primary rules of international law, giving rise to an expanding range of context-specific forms of reparation. In principle, no distinction is made between internal and cross-border displacement, as the destination of displaced people generally does not have a bearing on the lawfulness of their initial displacement, and therefore their entitlement to reparation. However, in Sects. 2.3 and 2.4, it will be seen that particularly internal displacement has gained prominence as a matter of international concern and as the subject of reparation claims. This in itself reflects how the focus of international law has evolved from regulating relationships among states to addressing situations within states. It also reflects the particular role played by international and regional judicial and quasi-judicial human rights bodies, where affected individuals or communities may advance their claims for reparation without requiring the diplomatic protection of a state.

Section 2.2 outlines the state of international law regarding displacement around the time of the *Chorzów* judgment. It focuses on conflict displacement (Sect. 2.2.1), population transfers (Sect. 2.2.2), as well as observations on the lack of regulation of other forms of displacement (Sect. 2.2.3). The sections thereafter address two key legal developments since then, i.e. the recognition of a broader range of internationally unlawful forms of displacement (Sect. 2.3) and the elaboration of a range of more victim-centric and context-specific forms of reparation (Sect. 2.4). Sections 2.3 and 2.4 disaggregate the contributions of interstate processes (Sects. 2.3.1 and 2.4.1.) and the role of decisions by international and regional human rights bodies in response to displaced rights-holders' claims (Sects. 2.3.2 and 2.4.2). Finally, Sect. 2.5 draws conclusions on the significance of these normative developments on displacement in shifting international law on reparation from state-centricity to victim-centricity, as well as the role of international and regional human rights bodies in this process.

[2] See Stavropoulou 1994, p. 692.

2.2 Displacement in International Law at the Time of the *Chorzów* Case

In the 1920s, as the Permanent Court of International Justice (PCIJ) was deliberating on the principles of reparation for breaches of international law in the *Chorzów* case, the displacement of people from their homes was not yet broadly viewed as an injustice in international law, or even a matter of international concern. The few forms of displacement which had started to be proscribed internationally were mostly sanctioned as an affront to state sovereignty (e.g. deportation from occupied territory) or the stability of nation-states (e.g. expulsions in breach of minority protection treaties). The tolerance—or even formalization—of large-scale displacement was visible in contexts of armed conflict, population transfer treaties, and forced removals for an array of other purposes, including colonization. The legal position at the time on these three broad types of displacement will be examined in the sub-sections below.

2.2.1 Displacement in Armed Conflict

The only form of conflict displacement which had been explicitly addressed in international law by the time of the *Chorzów* judgment was deportation from occupied territory.[3] The prohibition on this practice was first articulated in the Lieber Code, drafted in the context of the American Civil War, through the injunction that '[p]rivate citizens are no longer ... carried off to distant parts'.[4] This provision was not explicitly carried over into the 1899 and 1907 Hague Regulations. Apparently, the practice of deportation was deemed to have fallen into disuse and its prohibition was considered too self-evident. Deportation from occupied territory would in any case have breached the occupying power's duties to maintain order and safety, as well as the prohibition of collective punishment.[5] However, the Hague Regulations proved inadequate to deal with deportations from occupied territories in the context of the First World War (WWI) in Europe. As a result, in the interwar period, the International Committee of the Red Cross began work on a draft convention on the protection of civilians. This would later form the basis for the Fourth Geneva Convention of 1949 (GCIV).[6]

[3] For an example of the contemporary relevance of this prohibition (regarding arrest warrants issued for the alleged deportation of children from occupied areas of Ukraine to Russia as from February 2022), see International Criminal Court 2023.

[4] Instructions for the Government of Armies of the United States in the Field, adopted 24 April 1863, accessed 31 August (Lieber Code), art 23.

[5] Katselli Proukaki 2018, pp. 5–6; Jacques 2012, pp. 22–25; Dawson and Farber 2012, pp. 48–50; de Zayas 1975, pp. 210–212.

[6] Arai-Takahashi 2012, pp. 61–62.

The law of occupation in the interwar period was strongly rooted in the conservationist principle, of which the primary rationale was not to protect civilians as such, but rather to preserve the underlying sovereignty of the occupied state and the social order established through private property rights.[7] It can thus be supposed that the prohibition on deportation also stemmed largely from this state-centric rationale. As can also be seen in the Lieber Code's explicit reference to the 'modern regular wars of the Europeans, and their descendants in other portions of the globe',[8] the prohibition on deportation was conceptualized in the context of conflicts amongst European states or settlers. Preserving the independence of colonized peoples and protecting them from displacement was not envisaged. Indeed, the pursuit of colonization was actively excluded from the paradigm of the law of occupation as developed and codified in Europe and the United States in this period.[9]

Outside situations of occupation, the League of Nations and the PCIJ were also called upon to take action on situations of conflict displacement which affected (mostly European and/or Christian) minorities. This endeavour was viewed as central to preserving the stability of the system of independent, sovereign nation-states in and around Europe.[10] For example, in response to the displacement of civilians from Eastern Carelia into Finland by Russia, the Finnish government invoked a minority protection treaty between the two countries before the PCIJ. Besides decrying its own economic difficulties in receiving the refugees, Finland emphasized that 'a national minority, which is in imminent danger of complete annihilation, stands in urgent need of all the guarantees and of all the direct assistance which the League of Nations can offer.'[11] However, the PCIJ declined to admit the case, as Russia did not consent to its jurisdiction or cooperate in the proceedings.[12] This may be contrasted with the later approach of the International Court of Justice (ICJ) following the advent of the UN Charter and the recognition of *erga omnes* obligations in relation to the right to self-determination, as well as the fundamental norms of international humanitarian law (IHL) as they later developed.[13]

Furthermore, the League's Fifth Committee was tasked with investigating reports on the situation of Armenian and Greek women and children who had reportedly been forced into adoption, marriage and/or service in Turkish households after being displaced during WWI and the Armenian genocide. On examining the reports, the Committee made recommendations which largely focused on humanitarian measures. These entailed recovering women and children from households and

[7] Ibid., pp. 53–61.

[8] Lieber Code, above n.4, art 25.

[9] Arai-Takahashi 2012, pp. 72–79.

[10] JR 1944, pp. 579–588; Watenpaugh 2010, pp. 1315–1339.

[11] Finnish Minister of Foreign Affairs 1921, pp. 29–30.

[12] PCIJ, *Status of Eastern Carelia*, Advisory Opinion, 23 July 1923, Series B No 5, pp. 28–29.

[13] ICJ, *Legal Consequences of the Construction of a Wall in the Occupied Palestinian Territory*, Advisory Opinion, 9 July 2004, ICJ Reports 2004, p. 136, para 155–160.

placing them in rescue homes, rather than measures to remedy their initial displacement from their homes and/or other associated harms. In any event, these recommendations were never implemented, as the Lausanne Convention (to be discussed in Sect. 2.2.2 below) subsequently superseded earlier agreements and arrangements regarding minorities in Turkey.[14]

2.2.2 *Population Transfers*

In the era of the *Chorzów* judgment, the form of displacement which was most prominently addressed in the practice of the League of Nations and the PCIJ was the mass cross-border transfer of members of minority groups in terms of bilateral treaties. This particularly concerned treaties concluded in the context of the dissolution of the Ottoman Empire, which were overseen by the League of Nations. Population exchange treaties generally aimed at allowing members of minorities to move to a state where the majority shared their ethnic and/or religious identity, thus further homogenizing the nation-states in question. These treaties—for example, the Convention of Neuilly concluded between Greece and Bulgaria after WWI—usually entailed agreements facilitating voluntary migration of members of minority groups in both directions and compensation for immovable property. However, the voluntary nature of migration in practice was often highly questionable, as minority communities were often directly or indirectly pressured to move.[15]

The Convention of Lausanne, concluded after Turkey prevailed in the Greek-Turkish War of 1919—1923, went a step further by mandating bilateral population exchange of Greek and Turkish minorities. While this exchange had grave consequences for the people involved, the practice of compulsory population exchange in terms of a treaty was not considered to be prohibited by positive law at the time. Indeed, member states of the League rather saw this as a solution to the perceived problem of heterogeneity within nation states and the resultant need to regulate the situation of minorities, in a context which was deemed too unstable to be dealt with by a minority protection treaty (as in Central Europe) but also not amenable to far-reaching intervention (as in the colonies).[16] The former type of treaty would have provided indirect protection from displacement, as the expulsion of members of minority groups from their homes and expropriation of their properties in a discriminatory manner would most likely have constituted a breach of the protections agreed to in the treaty. This was established by the PCIJ in connection with Poland's attempted expulsion of former German settlers (who had been granted Polish nationality) from their lands. Although Poland had adopted a law to this effect which was ostensibly neutral, the PCIJ found that the situation was governed by the

[14] Watenpaugh 2010, pp. 1323, 1333–1337.

[15] See JR 1944, pp. 579–585; Özsu 2015, pp. 3–12.

[16] Özsu 2015, pp. 4–5, 12; see also Katselli Proukaki 2018, p. 9; JR 1944, pp. 585–588.

Treaty of Versailles (which guaranteed the protection of minorities in Poland) and that the actions of Poland were not in conformity with the treaty.[17]

The PCIJ was called upon to settle disputes relating to the Conventions of Lausanne and Neuilly, and issued the relevant judgments in 1924 and 1925 respectively.[18] In these judgments, the legality of the population transfers (ostensibly voluntary in the first case and compulsory in the second) was not questioned, nor were issues of reparation raised. Rather, the PCIJ's role was confined to interpreting the treaties' scope of application and terms. Thus, the PCIJ did not associate these population transfers with the principles on reparation it was developing concurrently in the *Chorzów* case. Rather, it contributed to legitimating population transfers agreed between states, regardless of the actual conditions of implementation and their effects on the individuals and communities concerned.[19]

2.2.3 Other Forms of Displacement

At the time of the PCIJ's decision in *Chorzów*, besides minority protection treaties and a largely implicit prohibition on deportations from occupied territory, there were no explicit protections against or prohibitions of displacement in international law. Other contemporary forms of displacement, such as the forced removal and dispossession of colonized peoples in favour of settlers, appeared to meet with little reaction at the legal level and certainly not internationally.[20] Indeed, de Zayas highlights how displacement through colonial violence and dispossession, along with other forms of internal displacement at the time, was considered to be a domestic issue rather than a matter to be regulated by international law.[21] However, for purposes of applying the principle of inter-temporality, a further examination of dissenting legal opinions (including those of displaced peoples themselves) would be warranted to nuance this view and avoid perpetuating the 'standard of civilization' into the present day.[22] For example, Tzouvala points out that colonized peoples were at least considered to be owed the basic 'obligations of humanity' at the time and were in some cases also parties to treaties.[23] Nevertheless, internal displacement was largely unregulated in international law at the time owing to sovereignty concerns. This effectively remained the case well into the 20th century. The changing status of displacement in

[17] PCIJ, *German Settlers in Poland*, Advisory Opinion, 10 September 1923, Series B No 6.

[18] PCIJ, *Treaty of Neuilly, Article 179, Annex, Paragraph 4 (Interpretation)*, Judgment, 12 September 1924, Series A, No. 3; PCIJ, *Exchange of Greek and Turkish Populations*, Advisory Opinion, 21 February 1925, Series B No. 10.

[19] Katselli Proukaki 2018, pp. 6–7; Özsu 2015, p. 12.

[20] For examples roughly contemporary to the *Chorzów* case (in South Africa and Kenya respectively), see Schechla 1993, pp. 254–255; Veit 2011, p. 5.

[21] De Zayas 1975, pp. 250–251.

[22] See Tzouvala 2023.

[23] Ibid.

international law—from an inevitable by-product of international or internal affairs to a frequently wrongful act giving rise to reparation claims by displaced individuals and communities—is discussed further in Sect. 2.3 below.

2.3 From Inevitability to Wrongful Act: Recognition of a Broader Range of Internationally Unlawful Forms of Displacement

2.3.1 Interstate Processes

Since the 1940s, interstate legal processes leading to the progressive prohibition of a growing range of forms of displacement have proceeded along four largely concurrent and interconnected tracks.[24] The first track was the codification of further IHL prohibitions on certain forms of conflict-related displacement and their crystallization as rules of customary international law. The second was the accompanying criminalization of these forms of displacement as war crimes and/or elements of crimes against humanity or genocide. The third was the (mostly implicit) broadening of the prohibitions or legal limitations on displacement beyond contexts involving armed conflict and/or international crimes, via the adoption of global and regional human rights treaties. The fourth track entailed the coalescence and growing recognition of an emerging, overarching 'right not to be displaced', mainly via global soft law instruments and African regional treaties. These legal developments helped to move the focus of international law on displacement from state interests to the impacts on individuals and communities. However, a number of protection and accountability gaps remain, which are outlined briefly in this sub-section. Subsequently, Sect. 2.3.2 highlights how decisions on displaced rights-holders' claims before international regional human rights bodies have contributed to addressing these gaps regarding reparation for displaced people.

Regarding conflict-related displacement, the relevant body of IHL has developed via piecemeal prohibitions with differing material and personal scopes. These consist of the prohibitions on deportation from or forcible transfer within an occupied territory, or causing cross-border displacement or ordering internal displacement of civilians in non-international armed conflict.[25] The prohibition of deportation from occupied territories (see Sect. 2.2.1 above) is widely considered to have

---

[24] For extensive accounts of legal developments along these four tracks, as well as discussions of their relative limitations and gaps, see generally: Katselli Proukaki 2018; Moffett 2015; Morel 2014; Dawson and Farber 2012; Jacques 2012; Acquaviva 2011; de Zayas 1975.

[25] Convention (IV) relative to the Protection of Civilian Persons in Time of War, adopted 12 August 1949, 75 UNTS 287, entered into force 21 October 1950, art 49; Protocol Additional to the Geneva Conventions of 12 August 1949, and relating to the Protection of Victims of Non-International Armed Conflicts, adopted 8 June 1977, 1125 UNTS 609, entered into force 7 December 1978 (Additional Protocol II), arts 17 (1) and (2).

already become a rule of customary international law at the time of its codification in Geneva Convention IV.[26] Nevertheless, de Zayas notes a continuing ambiguity on cross-border population transfers, particularly post-conflict.[27] In this sense, both he and Katselli Proukaki highlight post-Second World War (WWII) mass cross-border transfers of Germans as a major inconsistency in state practice.[28] Today, such practices would likely fall within the scope of subsequent prohibitions on mass or collective expulsions in international human rights law. Partially owing to the political sensitivities around the transfer of German and other minorities in post-WWII Europe, these legal prohibitions were only endorsed and elaborated later, rather than in the context of concurrent discussions on the Universal Declaration of Human Rights.[29]

Furthermore, while many forms of forced displacement in non-international armed conflict were arguably covered by the concept of crimes against humanity and/or the prohibition on inhumane treatment, explicit prohibitions on forced displacement in such contexts were only adopted in the 1977 Second Additional Protocol to the Geneva Conventions.[30] While these provisions were viewed as pushing the boundaries of state sovereignty at the time, their content is now considered part of customary international law.[31]

Remaining protection gaps in IHL include regulation of displacement during conduct of hostilities or of states' own nationals in international armed conflict, and indirectly coerced internal displacement in non-international armed conflict. These gaps are not incidental, but reflect IHL's initial premise that displacement is an inevitable consequence of conflict, which is only to be prohibited or regulated exceptionally.[32] This also reflects the roots of IHL in interstate conflict and the privileging of state sovereignty concerns. In IHL, applicability of protection is tied to the nature of the conflict, which is usually self-defined by states and may allow for the deflection of concerns with non-intervention discourses. The scope of protection in international armed conflict may also depend on the nationality of the people involved, as those presumed to be protected by their own state do not benefit from IHL protection. While customary IHL may have the potential to bridge these gaps, it does not appear to have sufficiently developed in this direction yet.[33] Furthermore, while the uneven scope of application of IHL prohibitions is somewhat smoothed out regarding transfer as an international crime, the threshold for displacement to

[26] Jacques 2012, pp. 22–25; Dawson and Farber 2012, pp. 47–48; Meron 1998, p. 279.

[27] De Zayas 1975, pp. 225–227.

[28] Katselli Proukaki 2018, pp. 9–11; de Zayas 1975, pp. 230–242.

[29] Henckaerts 1995, pp. 8–9.

[30] Additional Protocol II, above n.25, art 17.

[31] Jacques 2012, pp. 69–71; International Committee of the Red Cross ('ICRC'), Customary International Humanitarian Law Database, Rule 129B, https://ihl-databases.icrc.org/customary-ihl. Accessed 31 August 2023.

[32] Casalin 2018a; Cantor 2012, pp. 841–842; Jacques 2012, pp. 19–21, 42–48; Willms 2009, pp. 547–565.

[33] Jacques 2012, pp. 72–76, 253–254; c.f. ICRC, Customary International Humanitarian Law Database, Rule 129, https://ihl-databases.icrc.org/customary-ihl. Accessed 31 August 2023.

constitute a crime against humanity is high, and subject to the strict interpretation and stringent standards of proof required in criminal law.[34]

Interstate procedures aiming to establish state responsibility for displacement have also been relatively few and far between. Relevant judgments only began to be handed down at the start of the 21st century by the ICJ,[35] as well as the European Court of Human Rights (ECtHR).[36] As these judgments largely related to situations of occupation, they have added little to the existing explicit prohibition on forcible transfer and deportation.

International human rights law has been viewed as a means of complementing IHL protections from displacement, as well as addressing the lack of clear protection in situations outside of armed conflicts or international crimes.[37] UN and regional human rights treaties concluded since WWII contain indirect protections against arbitrary displacement via, e.g., the rights to property, an adequate standard of living (including adequate housing), freedom of movement (including the right to choose one's residence and return to one's country), and freedom from arbitrary interference with the home.[38] Express prohibitions on displacement were only included in regional prohibitions on collective or mass expulsion and with regard to indigenous peoples.[39]

Since the 1990s, displacement-specific regional and soft law initiatives have sought to bridge remaining protection and accountability gaps by framing displacement—including internal displacement in particular—as a human rights violation in principle, for which reparation may be owed. This has been framed in terms of an emerging, comprehensive 'right not to be displaced', which entails the right of all persons not to be arbitrarily forced or obliged to leave their homes or places of habitual residence. This draws the focus to the situation of the (potentially) displaced rights-holder, rather than the interests of their state of nationality or residence.[40]

34 See Moffett 2015, p. 143.

35 ICJ, *Legal Consequences of the Construction of a Wall*, above n.13; ICJ, *Armed Activities on the Territory of the Congo (Democratic Republic of the Congo (DRC) v. Uganda)*, Judgment (Merits), 19 December 2005, ICJ Reports 2005, p 168; ICJ, *Armed Activities on the Territory of the Congo (DRC v. Uganda)*, Judgment (Reparations), 9 February 2022, ICJ Reports 2022, p 13.

36 ECtHR, *Cyprus v. Turkey*, Judgment (Merits), 10 May 2001, App no 25781/94; ECtHR, *Cyprus v. Turkey*, Judgment (Just satisfaction), 12 May 2014, App no 25781/94; ECtHR, *Georgia v. Russia (II)*, Judgment (Merits), 21 January 2021, App no 38263/08.

37 Jacques 2012, p. 48; de Zayas 1975, pp. 251–253.

38 See Morel 2014.

39 Protocol No. 4 to the (European) Convention for the Protection of Human Rights and Fundamental Freedoms, securing certain rights and freedoms other than those already included in the Convention and in the first Protocol thereto, adopted 16 September 1953, ETS 46, entered into force 2 May 1968, Article 4; African Charter on Human and Peoples' Rights, adopted 27 June 1981, 21 ILM 58, entered into force 21 October 1986, Article 12(5); International Labour Organization Convention No. 169 concerning Indigenous and Tribal Peoples in Independent Countries, adopted 27 June 1989, 1650 UNTS 383, entered into force 5 September 1991, Article 16.

40 See Adeola 2016; Morel 2014; Stavropoulou 1994; UN ECOSOC 1995, para 235.

More specifically, the 1998 Guiding Principles on Internal Displacement (GPID)[41]—which have been widely endorsed by states and incorporated into national legislation[42]—provide that '[e]very human being shall have the right to be protected against being arbitrarily displaced from his or her home or place of habitual residence.'[43] A right not to be displaced is similarly recognized in the London Declaration on Internally Displaced Persons (IDPs), adopted by the International Law Association (ILA) (2000),[44] and the Pinheiro Principles (2005), adopted by the UN Sub-Commission on the Promotion and Protection of Human Rights.[45] These two soft law documents address the situation of people displaced both within and across borders.

These global soft law instruments were followed by the adoption of binding multilateral treaties on displacement in Africa. The first to recognize states' responsibility to prevent arbitrary displacement and eliminate its root causes was the sub-regional Great Lakes Protocol on the Protection and Assistance to Internally Displaced Persons, adopted in 2006.[46] The most broadly applicable binding instrument is the African Union Kampala Convention,[47] adopted in 2009, which applies to any situation of internal displacement in states parties (numbering 55 at the time of writing).[48] It obliges states to '[r]efrain from, prohibit and prevent arbitrary displacement of populations' and recognizes a corresponding right to be protected from arbitrary displacement.[49]

As will be discussed in the next section, international and regional human rights bodies which allow victims to claim reparation (or at least obtain remedial recommendations) have consolidated and contributed to these important normative developments. In particular, they have done so by more explicitly interpreting and applying human rights treaty provisions to recognize a greater range of forms of displacement as internationally unlawful.

---

[41] UN Commission on Human Rights 1998.

[42] See Gaviria and Piper 2023.

[43] UN Commission on Human Rights 1998, principle 6(1).

[44] International Law Association 2000, Article 4(1).

[45] UN Commission on Human Rights ('Sub-commission') 2005, principle 5.

[46] International Conference on the Great Lakes Region Protocol on the Protection and Assistance to Internally Displaced Persons, adopted 30 November 2006, entered into force 21 June 2008, Articles 3(1)-(2).

[47] African Union Convention for the Protection and Assistance of Internally Displaced Persons in Africa, adopted 23 October 2009, entered into force 6 December 2012 ('Kampala Convention').

[48] African Union, List of countries which have signed, ratified/acceded to the African Union Convention for the Protection and Assistance of Internally Displaced Persons in Africa, https://au.int/en/treaties/african-union-convention-protection-and-assistance-internally-displaced-persons-africa. Accessed 31 August 2023.

[49] Kampala Convention, above n.47, Articles 3(1)(a) & 4(4).

2.3.2 *Displaced Rights-holders' Claims before Human Rights Bodies*

As a result of displaced people's claims, international and regional human rights bodies have extended the reparation principles in *Chorzów* to a broader range of displacement situations by recognizing these as the outcomes of violations of international law (rather than a normalized and permissible state of affairs) and confirming victims' rights to reparation. There are two particular ways in which human rights bodies have expanded the notion of displacement as a consequence of an internationally unlawful act or omission. The first has been the confirmation that causing displacement may give rise to human rights violations even in situations not otherwise addressed by express prohibitions. The second has been the articulation of positive obligations on states to prevent and/or remedy displacement brought about by non-state actors or natural/human-made disasters in certain circumstances.

Overall, international and regional human rights bodies have applied human rights treaty provisions to claims stemming from a broad range of displacement contexts. As a result, reparative measures have been ordered or recommended for several forms of displacement which were not explicitly addressed in binding, applicable international instruments. Examples include forms of conflict displacement not expressly prohibited by IHL;[50] development-induced displacement;[51] and forced evictions.[52] The confirmation of violations of international human rights law in these cases, as well as displaced persons' resultant right to reparation, breaks down presumptions of the permissibility of displacement in such situations.

Thus, the concept of a right not to be displaced has been further developed and strengthened, and a right to reparation for violations has been operationalized. While the Inter-American Court of Human Rights (IACtHR) and the African Commission on Human and Peoples' Rights (ACommHPR) have explicitly recognized the right

---

[50] Casalin 2018b. See e.g. ECtHR, *Selçuk & Asker v. Turkey*, Judgment, 24 April 1998, App Nos 23184–23185/94; IACtHR, *Mapiripán Massacre v. Colombia*, Judgment, 15 September 2005, Series C No. 134; HRC, *Vojnovic v. Croatia*, 30 March 2009, Comm No 1510/2006; ACommHPR, *Sudan Human Rights Organisation (SHRO) & Centre on Housing Rights and Evictions (COHRE) v. Sudan*, 27 May 2009, Comm No 279/03–296/05.

[51] ACommHPR, *Centre for Minority Rights Development and Minority Rights Group on behalf of Endorois Welfare Council (Endorois) v. Kenya*, 25 November 2009, Comm No 276/03; ACtHPR, *ACommHPR (Ogiek) v. Kenya*, Judgment, 26 May 2017, App No 006/2012.

[52] Forced evictions are not explicitly prohibited by any UN or regional human rights treaty. This includes the International Covenant on Civil and Political Rights ('ICCPR'), which guarantees the right to privacy of the home, and the International Covenant on Economic Social and Cultural Rights ('ICESCR'), which contains the right to adequate housing. Only in its General Comment 4 did the Committee on Economic Social and Cultural Rights ('CESCR') first expressly state that forced evictions are a *prima facie* violation of ICESCR ('CESCR' 1991, para. 18). For application of ICCPR and ICESCR to forced eviction cases, see e.g. HRC, *Georgopoulos et al. v. Greece*, 29 July 2010, Comm No 1799/2008; HRC, *Naidenova et al. v. Bulgaria*, 30 October 2012, Comm No 2073/2011; CESCR, *I.D.G v. Spain*, 17 June 2015, Comm No 2/2014; CESCR, *Ben Djazia & Bellili v. Spain*, 20 June 2017, Comm No 5/2015; CESCR, *López Albán v. Spain*, 11 October 2019, Comm. No. 37/2018.

not to be displaced,[53] similar effects have also been achieved via other overlapping legal concepts which focus on the situation of displaced people beyond property rights. This problematizes displacement in an overarching manner and shifts the onus of justification to duty-bearers. Such concepts include the right to development (applied by the ACommHPR) and the right to adequate housing (applied by the UN Committee on Economic, Social and Cultural Rights—CESCR).

Owing to their mandates based on human rights treaties, which establish states as the primary addressees of obligations, human rights bodies have primarily dealt with cases of displacement carried out by state agents. However, some cases have been handled where displacement was triggered by the activities of non-state actors or by disasters. In these cases, human rights bodies have elaborated on states' positive obligations and ordered or recommended reparative measures accordingly. For example, regarding displacement caused by armed groups, the ACommHPR has found the state to be responsible for reparation based on its failure to exercise due diligence to protect civilians and to provide prompt remedy to victims.[54] In such cases, the IACtHR has also found that there is a positive duty on the state to reverse the effects of displacement, regardless of whether the initial displacement was attributable to the state.[55] Outside conflict contexts, in cases of displacement by mob violence, the ECtHR has taken a similar line on states' positive obligations in relation to violence by private actors. It has found states responsible based on inadequate action to prevent, mitigate or investigate attacks; remove hindrances to investigation or domestic remedies; or address the living conditions of those displaced.[56]

In disaster displacement situations, the ECtHR has also found that inadequate risk reduction measures or responses may give rise to human rights responsibility of the state.[57] In such situations, the state must take action to acknowledge and redress the effects of violations.[58] Where physical integrity is at risk, the state also has a duty to ensure investigation.[59] In cases of environmental disasters stemming from activities of private companies, the ACommHPR has also urged the state to clean up affected land and rivers, and to regulate companies' activities to ensure non-repetition.[60]

[53] See e.g. IACtHR, *Mapiripán Massacre v. Colombia*, above n.50, para 188; ACommHPR, *SHRO & COHRE v. Sudan*, above n.50, paras 189–190.

[54] ACommHPR, *SHRO & COHRE v. Sudan*, above n.50, paras 168, 203–205.

[55] See IACtHR, *Mapiripán Massacre v. Colombia*, above n.50, para 179; IACtHR, *Ituango Massacres v. Colombia*, Judgment, 1 July 2006, Series C No. 148, paras 210–212; IACtHR, *Case of the Afro-descendant Communities displaced from the Cacarica River Basin (Operation Genesis) v. Colombia*, Judgment, 20 November 2013, Series C No 270, para 315.

[56] ECtHR, *Burlya and others v. Ukraine*, Judgment, 6 November 2018, App No 3289/10, paras 138–143; ECtHR, *Moldovan and others v. Romania (no. 2)*, Judgment, 12 July 2005, No. App Nos 41138/98 and 64320/01, paras 102–114.

[57] ECtHR, *Budayeva v. Russia*, Judgment, 20 March 2008, App No 15339/02; ECtHR, *Öneryıldız v. Turkey*, Judgment, 18 June 2002, App No 48939/99.

[58] ECtHR, *Öneryıldız v. Turkey*, above n.57, para 137.

[59] ECtHR, *Budayeva v. Russia*, 2008, above n.57, paras 163–165.

[60] ACommHPR, *Social and Economic Rights Centre (SERAC) and Centre for Economic and Social Rights (CESR) v. Nigeria*, October 2001, Comm No 155/96, para 53.

Thus, international and regional human rights bodies have played an important role in broadening the range of forms of displacement which violate international law and are therefore subject to reparation. This has mainly had implications for internal displacement situations, as these were less addressed by international law, and IDPs would not usually be eligible for diplomatic protection in an interstate procedure. This has contributed to developing international law on reparations from a state-centric to a more victim-centric approach, and allowed the interests and concerns of stakeholders beyond the territorial state to be taken into account. The following section highlights another aspect of this shift—namely, the recognition of various forms of harm experienced by displaced people and the development of a range of appropriate reparative measures.

2.4 From Safeguarding State Interests to Addressing Impacts: Developing a Range of Displacement-specific Reparative Measures

2.4.1 Interstate Processes

At the time of the *Chorzów* judgment in 1928, the state was generally recognized as the primary actor entitled to reparation at the international level. While individual and community rights to reparation were foreseen in minority transfer treaties, it was not unthinkable for community compensation under such a treaty to be offset against other state obligations.[61] The PCIJ was one of few forums for international reparation claims, which were exclusively interstate.[62] As seen in minority protection cases, the PCIJ's consideration of the situation of individuals and communities was purely incidental to its regulation in interstate agreements or in international law, which at that stage was largely concerned with relations among states.[63] Where violations were found, reparation for affected individuals or communities was not envisaged. The question of whether these injured persons would benefit from an interstate reparation order remained entirely at the discretion of the claimant state. This section outlines how interstate law-making processes—although still largely focused on state interests—have moved towards greater recognition of the impacts of displacement on individuals and communities, as well as their position as holders of a right to reparation. Both interstate litigation on displacement (Sect. 2.4.1.1) and interstate law-making processes (Sect. 2.4.1.2) are examined.

[61] See JR 1944, p. 580.

[62] Statute of the Permanent Court of International Justice, adopted 13 December 1920, entered into force 8 October 1921, Articles 34–35.

[63] Ibid., Article 36.

2.4.1.1 Interstate Litigation on Displacement: Growing Focus on the Situation of Individuals

Interstate procedures aiming to establish state responsibility for displacement before the ICJ, as well as the ECtHR, have continued to largely focus on occupied territories. In such situations, displacement has traditionally been linked to the occupied state's interest in preserving sovereignty, and the occupying state's interest in consolidating territorial control. Nevertheless, interstate cases before the ECtHR have addressed harm caused to displaced individuals on the merits, though this has not yet been reflected in corresponding reparation judgments.[64] The ICJ has also applied human rights provisions in displacement cases and paid greater attention to the harms caused to displaced persons. In its *Wall* opinion, no reparation order could be made owing to the advisory nature of the proceedings. However, the Court specified that natural or legal persons were to receive restitution of their lands, orchards, olive groves and immovable property which were seized, as well as compensation for any material damage they suffered as a result of the construction of the wall.[65] In its *DRC v. Uganda* reparation judgment, the Court's order was limited to monetary compensation awarded to the state. Nevertheless, the Court explicitly recognized that this reflected harm caused to individuals and communities. It therefore welcomed the DRC's intention to set up a reparation fund for victims, and encouraged reparative measures for the benefit of affected communities as a whole.[66] This can be contrasted with the ICJ's approach in *Diallo*, where it held explicitly that the compensation awarded to the state was intended to remedy injury to the individual beneficiary of diplomatic protection.[67] The less prescriptive approach in the former case may be connected to the mass nature of the reparation process to be undertaken, which is not uncommon in displacement situations.

2.4.1.2 Development of the Right to Reparation in Interstate Law-making Processes

Otherwise, international norms on state responsibility and the practice of intergovernmental bodies have also reflected a growing recognition of rights to reparation

---

[64] The only relevant just satisfaction judgment so far has been *Cyprus v. Turkey*, which did not award reparations relating to displacement even though related violations were found on the merits – see ECtHR, *Cyprus v. Turkey (just satisfaction)*, above n.36.

[65] ICJ, *Legal Consequences of the Construction of a Wall*, above n.13, para 153.

[66] ICJ, *DRC v. Uganda (Reparations)*, above n.35, paras 408–409.

[67] ICJ, *Ahmadou Sadio Diallo (Republic of Guinea v. Democratic Republic of the Congo)*, Judgment (Compensation), ICJ Reports 2012, p. 324, para 57.

beyond the state.[68] Certainly, this tendency has been strengthened by the development of international human rights law, in which the individual right to reparation (as part of the right to a remedy) has a well-established basis.[69] Recognition of an individual right to reparation has been furthered through its operationalization in the context of the International Criminal Court.[70] It has also been included in a range of international soft law instruments addressing the rights of victims.[71] These victim-centric instruments have supplemented the Articles on State Responsibility by elaborating upon the forms of reparation referred to in *Chorzów*—i.e. restitution, compensation, and satisfaction. They have expanded them to include measures more tailored towards individuals such as rehabilitation.

Displacement-specific soft law instruments have also detailed and contextualized displaced peoples' rights to reparation. The GPID recognizes the right of internally displaced people (IDPs) to an effective remedy, as well as a duty on competent authorities to assist internally displaced people in recovering their property and possessions (i.e. in effect, to ensure restitution).[72] Where restitution is not possible, authorities are to provide other forms of 'just reparation', including compensation, or assist displaced people in obtaining these.[73] Displaced persons' property must also be protected against destruction, illegal appropriation, or occupation.[74] A right to housing, land and property restitution, supplemented by other forms of reparation such as compensation, is more explicitly recognized in the ILA London Declaration on IDPs, the Pinheiro Principles, and the Basic Principles and Guidelines on Development-Based Evictions and Displacement.[75] The Pinheiro Principles focus on reparation in more detail than the GPID, including by setting out the actions that states must take to protect and realize the right to restitution.[76] However, when the GPID and the Pinheiro Principles were adopted, their articulation of a right to restitution for displaced people was deemed to be an aspirational element aimed at influencing the progressive development of international law.[77]

---

[68] UNGA 2001, Art. 33(2); Protocol Additional to the Geneva Conventions of 12 August 1949, and relating to the Protection of Victims of International Armed Conflicts, adopted 8 June 1977, 1125 UNTS 3, entered into force 7 December 1978, Article 91; Van Boven 2020, pp. 20–22; Shelton 2015, pp. 78–79, 115, 172; Rombouts et al. 2005, p. 368; Sandoz et al. 1987, pp. 1055–1057.

[69] Van Boven 2020, pp. 18–22; Rombouts et al. 2005, p. 368.

[70] Rome Statute of the International Criminal Court, adopted 17 July 1998, 2187 UNTS 3, entered into force 1 July 2002, Article 75.

[71] UNGA 1985, para 8, 12, 19; UNGA 2005, Principles 11(b), 15 & 18; UN Commission on Human Rights 2005, principle 31.

[72] UN Commission on Human Rights 1998, Principles 7(3)(f).

[73] UN Commission on Human Rights 1998, Principle 29(2).

[74] UN Commission on Human Rights 1998, Principle 21.

[75] International Law Association 2000, Article 9; UN Commission on Human Rights (Sub-commission) 2005, Principles 2 & 21; Human Rights Council 2007.

[76] UN Commission on Human Rights (Sub-commission) 2005, Principles 12–13, 15–16, 20.

[77] UN ECOSOC 1995, p. 107; Williams 2008, pp. 23–24; Phuong 2004, p. 64; Bagshaw 2003, pp. 378–380.

There has also been significant innovation on displaced people's reparation rights in African regional treaties. The Great Lakes Protocol on the Property Rights of Returning Persons incorporated the GPID's provisions on duties to ensure restitution and other forms of reparation, and explicitly extended them to refugees and resettled persons. It elaborated on more specific restitution and compensation measures to be taken and included noteworthy provisions on safeguarding the property rights of women, children, and communities.[78] The Kampala Convention also sets out a duty to ensure land restitution where possible for 'communities with special dependency and attachment to such lands'. It contains obligations on states to ensure effective remedies for displaced people; establish domestic legal frameworks to provide 'just and fair compensation and other forms of reparations'; and to make reparation to displaced people in case of failure to protect or assist them in disaster situations.[79]

2.4.2 Displaced Rights-holders' Claims before Human Rights Bodies

In spite of the normative developments outlined in Sect. 2.4.1 above, avenues for displaced individuals and communities to claim a right to reparation remain scarce, both at the domestic and international levels. International and regional human rights bodies have to some extent filled this gap by serving as relatively accessible forums for displaced individuals and communities to act independently of their state of nationality/residence and claim reparation where this is not available via domestic or interstate channels. This is often the case for internally displaced people, who feature in the majority of these cases.

This section highlights how, in the process of responding to displaced people's claims, human rights bodies have elaborated various reparation measures—which aim to address the particular harms experienced by displaced people in a particular context and reestablish their situation as far as possible. It firstly outlines the mandates of human rights bodies to order/recommend reparative measures and how these have contributed to any differences in approach (Sect. 2.4.2.1). This is then followed by an overview of how human rights bodies' decisions have overall contributed to the consolidation of a right to restitution (Sect. 2.4.2.2) and the elaboration of various forms of reparation to address the specific harms of displacement (Sect. 2.4.2.3).

[78] International Conference on the Great Lakes Region Protocol on the Property Rights of Returning Persons, adopted 30 November 2006, entered into force 21 June 2008, Articles 4–8.

[79] Kampala Convention, above n. 47, Article 12.

2.4.2.1 Human Rights Bodies' Mandates to Order or Recommend Reparative Measures

The regional and UN human rights bodies examined here are those of a judicial or quasi-judicial nature, to which states and intergovernmental organizations have delegated authority to examine individual or mass claims of human rights violations and make reparative orders or recommendations. The judicial bodies—empowered to make binding orders—are the African Court on Human and Peoples' Rights (ACtHPR), the ECtHR, and the IACtHR.[80] The quasi-judicial bodies, which may make non-binding recommendations, are the ACommHPR, the Inter-American Commission on Human Rights (IACommHR), and the UN human rights treaty bodies.[81]

The bodies' respective founding instruments do not go into detail on the types or scope of reparation which may be granted. Each body has largely developed its own practice in this regard. In displacement cases, the main differences in the bodies' approaches to reparations can be seen per human rights system (i.e. between regional systems and with the UN system) rather than according to the judicial or quasi-judicial nature of the body. However, in all systems, practices and precedents have developed which contribute to a more nuanced and detailed understanding of what reparations for displaced people may entail. Overall, the IACtHR, and to a growing extent, the ACommHPR and ACtHPR, have interpreted their mandates to grant reparations broadly. These bodies have accordingly developed the widest range of context-specific and structural forms of reparation for displaced people, and have directly ordered or recommended specific and detailed reparative measures going beyond monetary compensation.[82]

In contrast, the ECtHR does not typically issue such orders/recommendations and has mainly limited itself to awarding monetary compensation. However, similarly to the IACommHR,[83] it has endorsed structural remedial measures agreed to

---

[80] Protocol to the African Charter on Human and Peoples' Rights on the Establishment of an African Court on Human and Peoples' Rights, adopted 10 June 1998, entered into force 25 January 2004, Article 27(1); (European) Convention for the Protection of Human Rights and Fundamental Freedoms, adopted 4 November 1950, 213 UNTS 222, entered into force 3 September 1953, Article 41; American Convention on Human Rights, adopted 22 November 1969, entered into force 18 July 1978, Article 63(1).

[81] African Charter on Human and Peoples' Rights, above n.39, Article 58(2); American Convention on Human Rights, Article 50(3); Optional Protocol to the International Covenant on Civil and Political Rights, adopted 16 December 1966, UNTS 999 171, entered into force 23 March 1976, Articles 4-5; Convention Against Torture and Other Cruel, Inhuman or Degrading Treatment or Punishment, adopted 10 December 1984, 1465 UNTS 85, entered into force 26 June 1987, Article 22; Optional Protocol to the International Covenant on Economic, Social and Cultural Rights, adopted 10 December 2008, 2922 UNTS, entered into force 5 May 2013, Article 9.

[82] See e.g. IACtHR, *Mapiripán Massacre v. Colombia*, above n.50; ACommHPR, *SHRO & COHRE v. Sudan*, above n.50; ACommHPR, *Endorois v. Kenya*, above n. 51; ACtHPR, *Ogiek v. Kenya*, above n.51.

[83] See e.g. Inter-American Commission on Human Rights ('IACommHR'), *Community of San Vicente los Cimientos v. Guatemala*, Friendly settlement, Case 11.197, Rep No 68/03; IACommHR,

in friendly settlements of displacement cases, which may serve as examples of what integral reparation may entail.[84] The ECtHR's pilot judgment procedure, developed to address systemic human rights deficiencies, has also opened up possibilities to order more structural forms of reparation in mass displacement cases, including the establishment of claims mechanisms and guarantees of non-repetition. The seminal example in this regard is the *Broniowski v. Poland* case, which addressed the inadequate functioning of a compensation scheme for Polish people repatriated from territories ceded to the Soviet Union after WWII. The Court recognized that this constituted a systemic problem affecting approximately 80,000 people and called for general legal and administrative measures at the domestic level to remedy this problem and offer redress.[85] In *Xenides-Arestis v. Turkey*, general measures were also ordered in respect of people displaced from their homes by the Turkish invasion of northern Cyprus.[86]

As for the UN treaty bodies, their remedial recommendations in individual communications procedures relating to displacement have overall remained quite broad. However, the CESCR's crafting of remedial recommendations—particularly in forced eviction cases—can be considered notable, as it has recommended wide-ranging structural measures in addition to measures aimed at remedying the situation of the individual complainant.[87]

2.4.2.2 Consolidation of a Right to Restitution

One important normative contribution of human rights bodies on displacement reparations has been the confirmation of a right to restitution for displaced people. As outlined above (Sect. 2.4.1.2), this was previously articulated in soft law instruments such as the GPID and the Pinheiro Principles, but was deemed to be a point on which these instruments had anticipated the development of international law. The overall practice of the African and Inter-American human rights mechanisms has been to order or recommend restitutive measures on a relatively systematic basis, also in cases of mass displacement.[88] While the ECtHR has not directly made such orders,

---

Enxet-Lamenxay and Kayleyphapopyet (Riachito) Indigenous Communities v. Paraguay, Friendly settlement, 25 March 1998, Case 11.713, Rep No 90/99.

[84] See e.g. ECtHR, *Moldovan and others v. Romania*, Judgment (friendly settlement), 5 July 2005, App nos 41138/98 and 64320/01, paras 29.2 –29.3; ECtHR, *Broniowski v. Poland*, Judgment (friendly settlement), 28 September 2005, App No 31443/96, paras 39–42.

[85] ECtHR, *Broniowski v. Poland*, Judgment (merits), 22 June 2004, App No 31443/96, paras 189–194.

[86] ECtHR, *Xenides-Arestis v. Turkey*, Judgment (just satisfaction), 7 December 2006, App No 6347/99, para 37.

[87] Sun 2018, pp. 637–639; Krsticevic and Griffey 2016, pp. 331–333, 341–346.

[88] See e.g. IACtHR, *Plan de Sánchez Massacre v. Guatemala*, Judgment (Reparations and Costs), 19 November 2004, Series C No 116; IACtHR, *Moiwana Community v. Suriname*, Judgment, 15 June 2005, Series C No 124; IACtHR, *Mapiripán Massacre v. Colombia*, above n.50, para 313; IACHR, *Sawhoyamaxa Indigenous Community of the Enxet-Lengua people v. Paraguay*, Judgment,

it also recognizes a right to restitution in principle, including its prioritization where possible.[89]

In their approach, human rights bodies have also to some extent addressed previous criticisms of restitution in displacement contexts. The latter often related to the shortcomings of large-scale, domestic post-conflict restitution programs implemented with intensive international involvement. Firstly, though the Pinheiro Principles have been criticized as focusing insufficiently on customary or communal rights,[90] the mechanisms have recognized a right to restitution where claimants had a legitimate right to their home. This was done even where the right was collective and/or not previously recognized in domestic law, e.g. because of its customary nature. As for occupants without title, their requests for restitution as such have not been endorsed.[91] However, the ECtHR and UN treaty bodies have emphasized state responsibilities to ensure their access to effective remedy and adequate alternative accommodation, as well as recommending compensation.[92] Secondly, the degree of latitude left to states in implementing the mechanisms' decisions, coupled with the participation of rights-holders in the process and the legal preservation of individual choice, counters characterizations of restitution endeavours as being driven by external interests.[93] Indeed, judicial or quasi-judicial mechanisms –especially at the supra-national level—are not in a position to articulate detailed or complete programs of reparation beyond the claimants in a particular case.[94] Nevertheless, the mechanisms have taken broader contexts into consideration by setting standards to ensure the consistency of broader domestic reparations processes with human rights law, as well as complementing domestic mechanisms' orders where such consistency is not yet evident.[95]

2.4.2.3 Developing Forms of Reparation to Address the Specific Harms of Displacement on Individuals and Communities

In response to displacement claims, the regional and UN human rights bodies examined have interpreted their remedial mandates to order or recommend forms of reparation addressing the particular harms that displacement causes for individuals and

29 March 2006, Series C No 146, paras 230 – 233; ACommHPR, *SHRO & COHRE v. Sudan*, above n.50; ACommHPR, *Endorois v. Kenya*, above n.51; ACtHPR, *Ogiek v. Kenya*, above n.51.

[89] ECtHR, *Selçuk and Asker v. Turkey*, above n.50, paras 99–102, 125; ECtHR, *Chiragov and others v. Armenia*, Judgment (just satisfaction), 12 December 2017, App No 13216/05, para 59; ECtHR, *Sargsyan v. Azerbaijan*, Judgment (just satisfaction), 12 December 2017, App No 40167/06, para 42.

[90] See Smit 2015, p. 71.

[91] On the right to restitution's failure to address the situation of people displaced from informal housing, see García Amado 2016, pp. 80–83.

[92] HRC, *Georgopoulos et al. v. Greece*, above n.52; HRC, *Naidenova et al. v. Bulgaria*, above n.52; CESCR, *López Albán v. Spain*, above n.52; ECtHR, *Öneryıldız v. Turkey*, above n.57.

[93] See e.g. Ballard 2010, pp. 469–473, 487–489.

[94] See Sandoval 2017, p. 1193; Moffett 2017, pp. 4–6, 35–36; Van Der Auweraert 2012, p. 141.

[95] See Murray and Sandoval 2020, p. 9; Sandoval 2017, pp. 1196–1200; Capone 2018, pp. 200–207.

communities. In doing so, they have interpreted, adapted, and elaborated forms of reparation which were initially recognized in an interstate context, such as restitution, compensation, satisfaction, and guarantees of non-repetition. They have also applied more victim-centred forms of reparation, such as rehabilitation, in displacement contexts.

Regarding restitution, the African and Inter-American human rights bodies have developed or endorsed specific reparation measures to ensure restitution for displaced people in specific contexts. Such measures have included securing indigenous land rights through delimitation, demarcation, and mapping, or interim protection of housing, land, and property rights where these are at risk.[96] Regarding compensation, the ECtHR has recognized a range of pecuniary and non-pecuniary losses associated particularly with displacement and/or denial of return, and awarded compensation accordingly. Examples include the cost of alternative accommodation, the loss of land-based livelihoods, and the distress of losing one's home and way of life.[97] The IACtHR has also developed a range of displacement-specific measures of satisfaction and rehabilitation to complement restitution and compensation. These measures have aimed to address displaced persons' poor living conditions pending their return or resettlement, and ensure dignified and secure conditions at the site of return or resettlement.[98]

The regional mechanisms have also elaborated a range of measures aimed at guaranteeing non-repetition, which have been articulated and tailored to each context. These include legislative change and/or establishment of claims mechanisms to address structural causes of displacement or barriers to reparation; investigations and prosecutions of perpetrators in cases of violent displacement; and the provision of security guarantees to facilitate safe return. Finally, it is noteworthy that the consultation and participation of displaced people is often required in the implementation of these measures.[99] In response to repeated claims of forced eviction in the context of Spain's housing crisis, the CESCR has also recommended wide-ranging legislative and policy changes as guarantees of non-repetition.[100]

---

[96] See e.g. IACtHR, *Plan de Sánchez Massacre v. Guatemala (Reparations and Costs)*, above n.88; IACtHR, *Moiwana Community v. Suriname*, above n.88; ACommHPR, *SHRO & COHRE v. Sudan*, above n.50; ACommHPR, *Endorois v. Kenya*, above n.51, ACtHPR, *Ogiek v. Kenya*, above n.51.

[97] ECtHR, *Selçuk and Asker v. Turkey*, above n.50; ECtHR, *Esmukhambetov v. Russia*, Judgment, 29 March 2011, App no 23445/03, paras 207–216; ECtHR, *Xenides-Arestis v. Turkey (just satisfaction)*, above n.86.

[98] See e.g. IACHR, *Sawhoyamaxa Indigenous Community of the Enxet-Lengua people v. Paraguay*, above n.88, paras 230–233; IACtHR, *Mapiripán Massacre v. Colombia*, above n.50, para. 313; IACtHR, *Moiwana Community v. Suriname*, above n.88, paras 212–215; IACtHR, *Plan de Sánchez Massacre v. Guatemala*, above n.88, paras 105, 109–110.

[99] E.g. AfrCommHPR, *SERAC/CESR v. Nigeria*, above n.60; IACtHR, *Ituango Massacres v. Colombia*, above n.55, para 400; IACtHR, *Moiwana Community v. Suriname*, above n.88; IACtHR, *Plan de Sánchez Massacre v. Guatemala*, above n.88, para 98; ECtHR, *Chiragov v. Armenia (just satisfaction)*, above n.89, para 199; ECtHR, *Sargsyan v. Azerbaijan (just satisfaction)*, above n.89, para 238.

[100] CESCR, *I.D.G v. Spain*, above n.52; CESCR, *Ben Djazia & Bellili v. Spain*, above n.52; CESCR, *López Albán v. Spain*, above n.52.

It is pertinent that in the decisions in question, there is no clear distinction in the forms of reparation granted according to the cause or type of displacement (e.g. displacement related to conflicts, development projects, or disasters), or the destination of displaced persons (i.e. internal or cross-border). Rather, differences have been noted along the lines of the applicability of specific human rights norms (e.g. rights of indigenous peoples); displaced persons' ownership of or other legitimate right to the property; and whether violations resulted from the state's failure to respect human rights (i.e. state agents directly carrying out the displacement), or the state's failure to protect human rights (e.g. against third parties or in disaster situations).[101]

Overall, it is submitted that this recognition of context-specific harms of displacement would scarcely be possible without the claims of displaced people themselves being directly taken into account in human rights bodies' decisions. This has taken place via their testimonies, their representatives' pleadings, and/or their involvement in friendly settlement agreements. Thus, this normative development owes much to the agency and participation of displaced people in the proceedings of human rights bodies. This is particularly important for displaced people who lack domestic avenues to be heard (or the possibility of benefiting from an interstate claim), and are likely to have a strained or severed relationship with their state of nationality.[102]

2.5 Conclusion

This chapter has closely examined the development of international law on reparations since *Chorzów* through the lens of legal evolutions around displacement. It has focused on the decisions of international and regional human rights bodies in response to displaced people's claims. At the time of the *Chorzów* judgment, very few cases of mass displacement were considered to breach international law, let alone warrant reparation. Indeed, the PCIJ was concurrently legitimizing mass transfers of minority populations that had been agreed to by states but had serious consequences for the people involved. The PCIJ's parallel engagement with interstate population transfer agreements starkly illustrates the state-centric nature of international law at the time. This underlines how the situation of individuals and communities was viewed as simply an object of interstate agreements and relations. For a long time, the forms of reparation foreseen in the *Chorzów* judgment were viewed as means of redressing injuries to state interests, even if this is not how they were explicitly formulated in the judgment.

Two major shifts have taken place in international law on displacement which reflect and contribute to developments in the law of reparations. The first is recognition of a wider range of forms of displacement which are considered to be internationally unlawful acts or omissions giving rise to reparation. The second is the elaboration of various forms of reparation which more closely address the specific

[101] Casalin 2022, pp. 123–164.

[102] See Bradley 2015, pp. 351–352.

harms that displacement causes for individuals and communities in context. The development of international human rights law played an indispensable role in facilitating these shifts, as this drew international focus to the situation of people who are not adequately protected by their state of nationality or residence and recognized their right to a remedy (including reparation). The legal evolutions on reparation for displacement demonstrate how the principles enunciated in the *Chorzów* judgment have been operationalized and built upon in favour of individuals and communities, thus transcending the state-centric context from which they originated.

As shown in this chapter, largely interstate processes such as the conclusion of treaties, the development of customary international law, and endorsement of soft law instruments have played a role in curtailing the previously broad normalization of displacement and instead foregrounding the situation of victims. The establishment of human rights treaties and their associated monitoring and enforcement bodies was among the most important of these interstate processes. Furthermore, the engagement of displaced people and their representatives with the international human rights system has played a key role. This is evidenced by the wealth of decisions from the African, European, Inter-American and UN human rights bodies. These are among the rare avenues available for (particularly internally) displaced people to claim reparation beyond the domestic level. Through their decisions, the human rights bodies have consolidated these normative developments and made them concrete and operational in a broadening range of contexts. This is not only significant with regard to displacement, but serves as a highly relevant example of how the agency of individuals and communities has contributed to the development of international norms to address concerns beyond state sovereignty, as well as recognize and address a growing range of harms through various forms of reparation.

References

Acquaviva G (2011) Forced Displacement and International Crimes. UNHCR, Geneva

Adeola R (2016) The right not to be arbitrarily displaced under the United Nations Guiding Principles on Internal Displacement. African Human Rights Law Journal 16: 83–98

Arai-Takahashi Y (2012) Preoccupied with occupation: critical examinations of the historical development of the law of occupation. International Review of the Red Cross 94:51–80

Bagshaw S (2003) Property restitution for IDPs: developments in the normative framework. In: Leckie S (ed) Returning Home: Housing and Property Restitution Rights of Refugees and Displaced Persons. Transnational Publishers, Ardsley, pp 375–394

Ballard MJ (2010) Post-Conflict Property Restitution: Flawed Legal and Theoretical Foundations. Berkeley Journal of International Law 28: 462–496

Bradley M (2015) Implications for Research, Policy and Practice. In: Bradley M (ed) Forced Migration, Reconciliation and Justice. McGill-Queens University Press, Montreal, pp 345–358

Cantor DJ (2012) Does IHL Prohibit the Forced Displacement of Civilians during War? International Journal of Refugee Law 24:840–846

Capone F (2018) A Reflection on the Transformative Potential of Reparations: The Approach of the Regional Human Rights Courts. Human Rights & International Legal Discourse 12:200–207

Casalin D (2018a) Prohibitions on Arbitrary Displacement in International Humanitarian Law and Human Rights: A Time and a Place for Everything. In: De Hert P, Smis S, Holvoet M

(eds) Convergences and Divergences between International Human Rights Law, International Criminal Law and International Humanitarian Law. Intersentia, Cambridge, pp 223–257
Casalin D (2018b) A green light turning red?: the potential influence of human rights on developing customary legal protection against conflict-driven displacement. Human Rights and International Legal Discourse 12:62–78
Casalin D (2022) The role of international (quasi-)judicial mechanisms in ensuring reparation for arbitrary displacement. University of Antwerp Faculty of Law—Law and Development Research Group, Antwerp. https://hdl.handle.net/10067/1875990151162165141. Accessed 9 October 2023
Committee on Economic Social and Cultural Rights (CESCR) (1991) General Comment No. 4: Forced Evictions: The Right to Adequate Housing (Art. 11 (1) of the Covenant), UN Doc. E/1992/23
Dawson G, Farber S (2012) Forcible Displacement Throughout the Ages: Towards an International Convention for the Prevention and Punishment of the Crime of Forcible Displacement. Brill, Leiden
de Zayas AM (1975) International Law and Mass Population Transfers. Harvard International Law Journal 16:207–258
Finnish Minister of Foreign Affairs (1921) Letter to the Secretary-General of the League of Nations. https://www.icj-cij.org/public/files/permanent-court-of-international-justice/serie_C/C_03_05/C_03_03_avis_consultatif_No_5.pdf. Accessed 31 August 2023
García Amado P (2016) Connecting Tenure Security with Durable Solutions to Internal Displacement: From Restitution of Property Rights to the Right to Adequate Housing. International Migration 54:74–86
Gaviria P, Piper R (2023) Twenty-five years of the Guiding Principles on Internal Displacement: A Call to Action: Ending the curse of internal displacement. https://www.ungeneva.org/en/news-media/press-release/2023/04/twenty-five-years-guiding-principles-internal-displacement. Accessed 31 August 2023
Henckaerts J-M (1995) Mass Expulsion in Modern International Law and Practice. Kluwer Law International, The Hague
Human Rights Council (2007) Basic Principles and Guidelines on Development-Based Evictions and Displacement, Annex 1 of the report of the Special Rapporteur on adequate housing as a component of the right to an adequate standard of living, UN Doc. A/HRC/4/18
International Criminal Court (2023) Situation in Ukraine: ICC judges issue arrest warrants against Vladimir Vladimirovich Putin and Maria Alekseyevna Lvova-Belova. https://www.icc-cpi.int/news/situation-ukraine-icc-judges-issue-arrest-warrants-against-vladimir-vladimirovich-putin-and. Accessed 15 September 2023
Jacques M (2012) Armed Conflict and Displacement: The Protection of Refugees and Displaced Persons under International Humanitarian Law. Cambridge University Press, Cambridge
Johansson P (2019) Displaced persons as symbols of grievance: collective identity, individual rights and durable solutions. In: Bradley M, Milner J, Peruniak B (eds) Refugees' Roles in Resolving Displacement and Building Peace: Beyond Beneficiaries. Georgetown University Press, Washington DC, pp 132–149
Katselli Proukaki E (2018) The right not to be displaced by armed conflict under international law. In: Katselli Proukaki E (ed) Armed Conflict and Forcible Displacement: Individual Rights under International Law. Routledge, Abingdon, pp 1–45
Krsticevic V, Griffey B (2016) Remedial Recommendations. In: Langford M, Porter B, Brown R, Rossi J (eds) The Optional Protocol to the International Covenant on Economic, Social and Cultural Rights: A Commentary. Pretoria University Law Press, Pretoria, pp 327–358
Meron T (1998) Francis Lieber's Code and Principles of Humanity. Columbia Journal of Transnational Law 36:269–282
Moffett L (2015) Accountability for Forced Displacement in Democratic Republic of Congo and Uganda before the International Criminal Court. African Journal of International Criminal Justice 1:129–152

Moffett L (2017) Reparations in Transitional Justice: Justice or Political Compromise? Human Rights & International Legal Discourse 11:59–70
Morel M (2014) The right not to be displaced in international law. Intersentia, Cambridge
Murray R, Sandoval C (2020) Balancing Specificity of Reparation Measures and States' Discretion to Enhance Implementation. Journal of Human Rights Practice 12:101–124
Özsu U (2015) Formalizing Displacement: International Law and Population Transfers. Oxford University Press, Oxford
Phuong C (2004) The International Protection of Internally Displaced Persons. Cambridge University Press, Cambridge
JR (1944) The Exchange of Minorities and Transfers of Population in Europe since 1919. Bulletin of International News 21:579–588
Rombouts H, Sardaro P, Vandeginste S (2005) The right to reparation for victims of gross and systematic violations of human rights. In: De Feyter K, Parmentier S, Bossuyt M, Lemmens P (eds) Out of the Ashes: Reparations for Gross Violations of Human Rights. Intersentia, Antwerp, pp 345–503
Sandoval C (2017) Two steps forward, one step back: Reflections on the jurisprudential turn of the Inter-American Court of Human Rights on domestic reparation programmes. International Journal of Human Rights 22:1192–1208
Sandoz Y, Zimmermann B, Eberlin P, Gasser H-P, Wenger CF (1987) Protocol I: Article 91 – Responsibility. In: Sandoz Y, Swinarski C, Zimmermann B (eds) Commentary on the Additional Protocols of 8 June 1977 to the Geneva Conventions of 12 August 1949. International Committee of the Red Cross/Martinus Nijhoff, Geneva, pp 1053–1058
Schechla J (1993) Ideological roots of population transfer. Third World Quarterly 14:239–275
Shelton D (2015) Remedies in International Human Rights Law, 3rd edn. Oxford University Press, Oxford
Smit A (2012) The Property Rights of Refugees and Internally Displaced Persons Beyond Restitution. Routledge, Abingdon
Smit A (2015) Property Rights and Public Interests: Restitution, Transitional Justice and Post-Conflict Reconciliation. In: Bradley M (ed) Forced Migration, Reconciliation and Justice. McGill-Queens University Press, Montreal, pp 68–86
Stavropoulou M (1994) The Right Not to Be Displaced. American University International Law Review 9:687–749
Sun S (2018) Five Years after the Entry of Force of the Optional Protocol to the International Covenant on Economic, Social and Cultural Rights: Some Observations. Journal of Human Rights 17:625–639
Tzouvala N (2023) The Alibis of History, or How (not) to Do Things with Inter-temporality. https://cil.nus.edu.sg/blogs/the-alibis-of-history-or-how-not-to-do-things-with-inter-temporality/. Accessed 31 August 2023
UN Commission on Human Rights (1998) Report of the Representative of the Secretary-General, Mr. Francis M. Deng, submitted pursuant to Commission resolution 1997/39 (Guiding Principles on Internal Displacement), UN Doc. E/CN.4/1998/53/Add.2
UN Commission on Human Rights (2005) Updated Set of principles for the protection and promotion of human rights through action to combat impunity (Impunity Principles), UN Doc. E/CN.4/2005/102/Add.1
UN Commission on Human Rights (Sub-commission) (2005) Final report of the Special Rapporteur Paulo Sérgio Pinheiro: Principles on housing and property restitution for refugees and displaced persons (Pinheiro Principles), UN Doc. E/CN.4/Sub.2/2005/17
UN ECOSOC (1995) Report of the Representative of the Secretary-General, Mr. Francis M. Deng, submitted pursuant to Commission on Human Rights resolution 1995/57. UN Doc. E/CN.4/1996/52/Add.2
UN General Assembly (1985) Declaration of Basic Principles of Justice for Victims of Crime and Abuse of Power, UN Doc. A/RES/40/34

UN General Assembly (2001) Articles on Responsibility of States for Internationally Wrongful Acts, UN Doc. A/RES/56/83 (Annex)
UN General Assembly (2005) Basic Principles and Guidelines on the Right to a Remedy and Reparation for Victims of Gross Violations of International Human Rights Law and Serious Violations of International Humanitarian Law, UN Doc. A/RES/60/147 (Annex)
Van Boven T (2020) Victims' Rights to a Remedy and Reparation: The United Nations Principles and Guidelines. In: Ferstman C, Goetz M (eds) Reparations for Victims of Genocide, War Crimes and Crimes against Humanity: Systems in Place and Systems in the Making, 2nd edn. Brill, Leiden, pp 15-37
Van Der Auweraert P (2012) The Potential for Redress: Reparations and Large-Scale Displacement. In: Duthie R (ed) Transitional Justice and Displacement. Social Science Research Council, New York, pp 139–188
Veit P (2011) History of Land Conflicts in Kenya. https://doi.org/10.21955/gatesopenres.1115885.1. Accessed 31 August 2023
Watenpaugh KD (2010) The League of Nations' Rescue of Armenian Genocide Survivors and the Making of Modern Humanitarianism, 1920–1927. The American Historical Review 115:1315–1339
Williams RC (2008) Guiding Principle 29 and the right to restitution. Forced Migration Review GP10:23-24
Willms J (2009) Without order, anything goes? The prohibition of forced displacement in non-international armed conflict. International Review of the Red Cross 91:547–565

Other Documents

International Law Association (2000) Declaration of International Law Principles on Internally Displaced Persons

Treaties

Convention (IV) relative to the Protection of Civilian Persons in Time of War, adopted 12 August 1949, 75 UNTS 287, entered into force 21 October 1950, art 49
Convention Against Torture and Other Cruel, Inhuman or Degrading Treatment or Punishment, adopted 10 December 1984, 1465 UNTS 85, entered into force 26 June 1987
International Labour Organization Convention No. 169 concerning Indigenous and Tribal Peoples in Independent Countries, adopted 27 June 1989, 1650 UNTS 383, entered into force 5 September 1991
Optional Protocol to the International Covenant on Civil and Political Rights, adopted 16 December 1966, UNTS 999 171, entered into force 23 March 1976
Optional Protocol to the International Covenant on Economic, Social and Cultural Rights, adopted 10 December 2008, 2922 UNTS, entered into force 5 May 2013
Protocol Additional to the Geneva Conventions of 12 August 1949, and relating to the Protection of Victims of International Armed Conflicts, adopted 8 June 1977, 1125 UNTS 3, entered into force 7 December 1978
Protocol Additional to the Geneva Conventions of 12 August 1949, and relating to the Protection of Victims of Non-International Armed Conflicts, adopted 8 June 1977, 1125 UNTS 609, entered into force 7 December 1978 (Additional Protocol II)
Rome Statute of the International Criminal Court, adopted 17 July 1998, 2187 UNTS 3, entered into force 1 July 2002

African Charter on Human and People's Rights, adopted 27 June 1981, 21 ILM 58, entered into force 21 October 1986

African Union Convention for the Protection and Assistance of Internally Displaced Persons in Africa, adopted 23 October 2009, entered into force 6 December 2012 (Kampala Convention)

American Convention on Human Rights, adopted 22 November 1969, , entered into force 18 July 1978

(European) Convention for the Protection of Human Rights and Fundamental Freedoms, adopted 4 November 1950, 213 UNTS 222, entered into force 3 September 1953

International Conference on the Great Lakes Region Protocol on the Property Rights of Returning Persons, adopted 30 November 2006, entered into force 21 June 2008

International Conference on the Great Lakes Region Protocol on the Protection and Assistance to Internally Displaced Persons, adopted 30 November 2006, entered into force 21 June 2008

Protocol No. 4 to the (European) Convention for the Protection of Human Rights and Fundamental Freedoms, securing certain rights and freedoms other than those already included in the Convention and in the first Protocol thereto, adopted 16 September 1953, ETS 46, entered into force 2 May 1968

Protocol to the African Charter on Human and Peoples' Rights on the Establishment of an African Court on Human and Peoples' Rights, adopted 10 June 1998, entered into force 25 January 2004

Instructions for the Government of Armies of the United States in the Field, adopted 24 April 1863. (Lieber Code)

Statute of the Permanent Court of International Justice, adopted 13 December 1920, entered into force 8 October 1921

Table of Cases

ACommHPR, *Centre for Minority Rights Development and Minority Rights Group on behalf of Endorois Welfare Council (Endorois) v. Kenya*, 25 November 2009, Comm No 276/03

ACommHPR, *Social and Economic Rights Centre (SERAC) and Centre for Economic and Social Rights (CESR) v. Nigeria*, October 2001, Comm No 155/96

ACommHPR, *Sudan Human Rights Organisation (SHRO) & Centre on Housing Rights and Evictions (COHRE) v. Sudan*, 27 May 2009, Comm No 279/03–296/05

ACtHPR, *ACommHPR (Ogiek) v. Kenya*, Judgment, 26 May 2017, App No 006/2012

CESCR, *I.D.G v. Spain*, 17 June 2015, Comm No 2/2014

CESCR, *Ben Djazia & Bellili v. Spain*, 20 June 2017, Comm No 5/2015

CESCR, *López Albán v. Spain*, 11 October 2019, Comm. No. 37/2018

ECtHR, *Broniowski v. Poland*, Judgment (friendly settlement), 28 September 2005, App No 31443/96

ECtHR, *Broniowski v. Poland*, Judgment (merits), 22 June 2004, App No 31443/96

ECtHR, *Budayeva v. Russia*, Judgment, 20 March 2008, App No 15339/02

ECtHR, *Burlya and others v. Ukraine*, Judgment, 6 November 2018, App No 3289/10

ECtHR, *Chiragov and others v. Armenia*, Judgment (just satisfaction), 12 December 2017, App No 13216/05

ECtHR, *Cyprus v. Turkey*, Judgment (Merits), 10 May 2001, App no 25781/94

ECtHR, *Cyprus v. Turkey*, Judgment (Just satisfaction), 12 May 2014, App no 25781/94

ECtHR, *Esmukhambetov v. Russia*, Judgment, 29 March 2011, App no 23445/03

ECtHR, *Georgia v. Russia (II)*, Judgment (Merits), 21 January 2021, App no 38263/08

ECtHR, *Moldovan and others v. Romania*, Judgment (friendly settlement), 5 July 2005, App nos 41138/98 and 64320/01

ECtHR, *Moldovan and others v. Romania (no. 2)*, Judgment, 12 July 2005, No. App Nos 41138/98 and 64320/01

ECtHR, *Öneryıldız v. Turkey*, Judgment, 18 June 2002, App No 48939/99

ECtHR, *Sargsyan v. Azerbaijan*, Judgment (just satisfaction), 12 December 2017, App No 40167/06
ECtHR, *Selçuk & Asker v. Turkey*, Judgment, 24 April 1998, App Nos 23184–23185/94
ECtHR, *Xenides-Arestis v. Turkey*, Judgment (just satisfaction), 7 December 2006, App No 6347/99
HRC, *Georgopoulos et al. v. Greece*, 29 July 2010, Comm No 1799/2008
HRC, *Naidenova et al. v. Bulgaria*, 30 October 2012, Comm No 2073/2011
HRC, *Vojnovic v. Croatia*, 30 March 2009, Comm No 1510/2006
IACommHR, *Community of San Vicente los Cimientos v. Guatemala*, Friendly settlement, Case 11.197, Rep No 68/03
IACommHR, *Enxet-Lamenxay and Kayleyphapopyet (Riachito) Indigenous Communities v. Paraguay*, Friendly settlement, 25 March 1998, Case 11.713, Rep No 90/99
IACtHR, *Case of the Afro-descendant Communities displaced from the Cacarica River Basin (Operation Genesis) v. Colombia*, Judgment, 20 November 2013, Series C No 270
IACtHR, *Ituango Massacres v. Colombia*, Judgment, 1 July 2006, Series C No. 148
IACtHR, *Mapiripán Massacre v. Colombia*, Judgment, 15 September 2005, Series C No. 134
IACtHR, *Moiwana Community v. Suriname*, Judgment, 15 June 2005, Series C No 124
IACtHR, *Plan de Sánchez Massacre v. Guatemala*, Judgment (Reparations and Costs), 19 November 2004, Series C No 116
IACHR, *Sawhoyamaxa Indigenous Community of the Enxet-Lengua people v. Paraguay*, Judgment, 29 March 2006, Series C No 146
ICJ, *Ahmadou Sadio Diallo (Republic of Guinea v. Democratic Republic of the Congo),* Judgment (Compensation), ICJ Reports 2012, p 324
ICJ, *Armed Activities on the Territory of the Congo (Democratic Republic of the Congo (DRC) v. Uganda)*, Judgment (Merits), 19 December 2005, ICJ Reports 2005, p 168
ICJ, *Armed Activities on the Territory of the Congo (DRC v. Uganda)*, Judgment (Reparations), 9 February 2022, ICJ Reports 2022, p 13
ICJ, *Legal Consequences of the Construction of a Wall in the Occupied Palestinian Territory*, Advisory Opinion, 9 July 2004, ICJ Reports 2004, p 136
PCIJ, *Exchange of Greek and Turkish Populations*, Advisory Opinion, 21 February 1925, Series B No. 10
PCIJ, *German Settlers in Poland*, Advisory Opinion, 10 September 1923, Series B No 6
PCIJ, *Status of Eastern Carelia*, Advisory Opinion, 23 July 1923, Series B No 5
PCIJ, *Treaty of Neuilly, Article 179, Annex, Paragraph 4 (Interpretation)*, Judgment, 12 September 1924, Series A, No. 3

Chapter 3
Administrative Reparations Programs and Transitional Justice: Dilemmas, Debates and New Directions

Jemima García-Godos and Lisa J. Laplante

Contents

Abstract Non-judicial victim reparation programs developed within transitional justice processes challenge traditional legal approaches to ensure access to remedies and reparations for victims of human rights violations. Programs respond to a wider range of violations, with the hope of redressing a diversity of victims and their families. Drawing from their prior field work and scholarship over the past two decades, the authors discuss some of the primary dilemmas and debates in the field, while also signaling some significant new directions. Among others, some of the tensions arising with administrative reparation programs relates to the identity of victims and perpetrators; the overlap between collective reparations and development; the need

The authors would like to thank Eman Elshrafi for her editing assistance for this chapter.

J. García-Godos
Department of Sociology and Human Geography, University of Oslo, Oslo, Norway
e-mail: jemima.garcia-godos@sosgeo.uio.no

L. J. Laplante (✉)
New England LawI Boston, Boston, USA
e-mail: llaplante@nesl.edu

O. Spijkers et al. (eds.), *Netherlands Yearbook of International Law 2022*, Netherlands Yearbook of International Law 53, https://doi.org/10.1007/978-94-6265-627-7_3

for governments to create large scale programs while satisfying the victims right to reparation in a manner that meets their expectations and needs; and the limits to what a reparations program can do. In this way, victim reparation programs provide important opportunities to revisit the concept of repair, to explore the potential of transformative reparations and to bring more attention to measures of non-repetition if aiming to repair a whole society and assure lasting peace.

Keywords Transitional justice · Reparations · Administrative reparation programs · Human rights · Victims' rights · Transformation

3.1 Introduction

Victim reparations figure as a central pillar of transitional justice—a practice of countries resorting to a range of legal and political mechanisms to redress a violent and repressive past that leaves a legacy of large-scale human rights violations.[1] While aspects of transitional justice overlap with other areas of international law related to post-conflict reconstruction, peacekeeping, conflict resolution, human rights, and development, it was only in the 1990s that the field coalesced into an internationally recognized practice and field of study in which scholars have raised awareness of both best practices as well as areas of concern. Former United Nations (UN) Secretary-General Kofi Annan recognized this disciplinary overlap in 2004, issuing an important imprimatur of the field of transitional justice in a report to the Security Council.[2]

Certainly, the complexities of the field relate back to the ambitious goals of transitional justice which consist of establishing the rule of law, assuring accountability of perpetrators, building democratic institutions and a culture of rights, and fostering national reconciliation in order to assure lasting peace and the prevention of new cycles of violence.[3] At its core, transitional justice recognizes that reaching these aspirations requires addressing and redressing the harm of the past through judicial as well as non-judicial processes and mechanisms, including programs to provide reparations for victims and their families.[4] Indisputably, political violence and armed conflict lead to fractured societies comprised of not only families mourning loved ones who were killed or disappeared, but also survivors of torture, rape, and unjust imprisonment among other serious harms which constitute human rights violations.

[1] Arthur 2009, p. 321; Roht-Arriaza 2006, p. 2; United Nations Human Rights Council 2019, para 44(d).

[2] United Nations Secretary-General 2004.

[3] United Nations Secretary-General 2010; Paige 2009.

[4] Throughout the chapter we use the term 'victim' in its legal sense as someone who suffered a human rights violation. However, this chapter will discuss how the term victim can be contested as a general term of reference.

All such individuals and communities have the internationally recognized right to redress for these harms: the right to remedy and reparation.[5]

Yet, traditional avenues of justice, like courts, which provide a civil remedy or criminal prosecutions, may be foreclosed due to the breakdown of the rule of law and/or a weak judicial infrastructure that cannot handle hundreds, and even thousands, of cases.[6] This situation points towards one of the defining dilemmas of transitional justice in which governments seeking to redress mass atrocity must do so beyond traditional judicial mechanisms used in 'ordinary' times.[7] Thus, forming administrative victim reparation programs, often following the recommendation of a truth commission, has become one of the common approaches to ensuring redress in these challenging settings.[8] Indeed, according to the Transitional Justice Research Collaborative, to date, there have been approximately forty-five reparation programs established in thirty-one countries.[9] Responding to this notable trend, Priscilla Hayner observed in 2010, in the updated edition of her authoritative text on truth commissions, that there had been a significant increase in the creation of such reparation programs since the book's original publication in 2002.[10] Today, the field of reparations flourishes and is a firm and well-recognized area of practice, although it continues to face many of the same challenges observed in the early years of its development.

A primary cause of these challenges relates to the fact that victim reparation programs deviate from more traditional, legal notions of reparations, and often result in victims and their families being left feeling not fully repaired or redressed. The failures of reparation programs have been studied closely over the past several decades through empirical and ethnographic research, including by us, to reveal the ways in which reparations fall short of their goals as well as victim expectations.[11] Certainly, case studies of administrative victim reparation programs show how these approaches may deviate from the legalistic notions of reparations, and may even be challenged by victims and their families as falling below full repair. Sometimes these failings occur due to economic and political trade-offs, resulting in the priority of repair being ignored or minimized for political convenience. For this reason, some commentators worry that the reparation process could potentially re-victimize those it intends to repair and even lead to them rejecting reparation programming, thus undermining the aims of transitional justice.[12] Yet, despite these concerns, governments continue

---

[5] Laplante 2015.

[6] Benomar 1995.

[7] Hesse and Post 1999.

[8] Laplante 2015; Dixon 2017.

[9] Transitional Justice Research Collaborative, https://tjrc.tulane.edu. Accessed 27 March 2023. For further discussion of the database, see Olsen et al. 2010. For a short list of twenty-six reparation programs, see Van Der Merwe et al. 2009.

[10] Hayner 2002, 2010; Falk also notes that there has been a general lack of extensive study of reparations until recently: Falk 2006, p. 484-485.

[11] See, e.g., Johnston and Slyomovics 2009; Miller and Kumar 2007; Rubio-Marin 2006; Aguilar 2009.

[12] Fletcher 2009; Waterhouse 2009.

to resort to administrative reparation programs, which are often seen as better than doing nothing at all.[13]

In this contribution, we draw from our collective research over the last two decades to highlight some of the dilemmas and areas of tension that arise when governments resort to administrative reparation programs, while also highlighting how administrative reparation programs, if done well, may offer opportunities to expand the role of reparations to better ensure transformative justice. The aim of the chapter is therefore to provide an overview of what we consider to be the primary dilemmas, debates and new direction of reparations arising out of tensions with the traditional parameters of the law. Given the brevity of space, we provide references to where readers may find more in-depth discussions of these observations, especially in our previous scholarship. In drawing out these general themes, we also recognize that every transitional justice experience is context-specific and each new reparation program may encounter unique challenges and opportunities, thus acknowledging that there may be ideas that we have overlooked.

Following this introduction, Sect. 3.2 starts by establishing the normative framework for non-judicial remedies. Then, in Sect. 3.3, we discuss some dilemmas and tensions with victim reparation programs, while in Sect. 3.4, we address new directions and possibilities arising from the current practice of reparation programs. Finally, in Sect. 3.5 we conclude the chapter with some reflections about the possible way forward for victim reparation programs.

3.2 The Normative Framework of Non-Judicial Remedies

When governments establish national administrative reparation programs, they are technically taking steps towards fulfilling their international obligation to protect and guarantee the right to an adequate and effective remedy as recognized in most international human rights treaties.[14] For example, the *International Covenant on Civil and Political Rights* directs States Parties to protect the fundamental rights of individuals and to provide a prompt and effective remedy in the event that these rights are violated, although not necessarily limiting it to a judicial process.[15] These directives can also be found in the United Nations *Basic Principles and Guidelines on the*

[13] More recent examples of administrative reparation programs include Iraq's General Directorate for the Female Yazidi Survivors' Affairs and Northern Ireland's Troubles Permanent Disablement Payment Scheme, both established in 2021.

[14] The right to an effective remedy and reparations can be found in all major international human rights treaties, mirroring the provision of the Universal Declaration of Human Rights which provides, [e]veryone has the right to an effective remedy by the competent national tribunals for acts violating the fundamental rights granted him by the constitution or by law.' For an exhaustive list of international human rights treaties which include an 'effective remedy' provision, see United Nations General Assembly 2005, preamble, sec IX. See generally Shelton 2015.

[15] International Covenant on Civil and Political Rights, opened for signature 19 December 1966, entered into force 23 March 1976.

Right to a Remedy and Reparation for Survivors of Violations of International Human Rights and Humanitarian Law [*Basic Principles*] which the UN General Assembly approved in 2005.[16]The *Basic Principles* establish that 'a State shall provide reparation to victims for acts or omissions which can be attributed to the State and constitute gross violations of international human rights law or serious violations of international humanitarian law'.[17] Importantly, the Basic Principles clarify that it is not left to state discretion on whether or not to ensure the right to a remedy and reparations, but rather the law binds them to these norms which arise out of both treaty and customary international law.[18]

Yet, how a state fulfills this duty to repair may vary. As stated by Principle 12, an effective remedy may include administrative and other bodies '*as well as mechanisms, modalities, and proceedings conducted in accordance with domestic law*'. One such mechanism is administrative victim reparation programs that occur within the context of transitional justice. Indeed, the Inter-American Court of Human Rights (IACtHR), through the exercise of its contentious jurisdiction, has recognized that administrative reparation programs set up as a part of transitional justice may fulfill a State's duty to guarantee these rights.[19]

Pablo de Greiff's distinction on the way reparations are conceptualized in international law and in national administrative reparation programs can be useful at this point.[20] In international law, reparations refer to all sorts of reparatory measures implemented to address human rights violations. Thus, the available options are many, broad, and extensive, allowing adaptability to individual cases and different situations. In contrast, the context of designing specific reparation programs requires a more restrictive definition of reparations, usually with reference to specific target groups (victims) affected by specific types of crimes and human rights violations. For example, the IACtHR can reach a decision that includes not only monetary compensation for individual victims, but also the implementation of measures of satisfaction and guarantees of non-repetition, truth-telling and even call for institutional reform of the state involved. The repertoire of measures available for an administrative reparation program are far more restricted. Such programs are by necessity more operational and designed along two fundamental elements: the types of reparations to be provided (material and symbolic), and the forms of distribution to be taken (individual and collective). Reparation programs are thus constrained by the operational character of their portfolio and by the definitions of victim established by domestic laws.

---

[16] United Nations General Assembly 2005.

[17] Ibid., principle 15.

[18] The Inter-American Court of Human Rights (IACtHR) established this fact in its first contentious case of reparations. See IACtHR, Velásquez-Rodríguez v. Honduras, Reparations and Costs, 21 July 1989, (ser C) No 7.

[19] IACtHR, García Lucero et al. v Chile, Judgement, 28 August 2013, (ser C) No 267, para 67. The Court declared that "the existence of administrative programs of reparation must be compatible with the State's obligations under the American Convention and other international norms."

[20] De Greiff 2006, pp. 451 and 477.

Despite the constraints mentioned above, in many ways, administrative reparation programs may better meet the full and effective reparation envisaged by the *Basic Principles* given their flexibility. For example, they may offer the varied forms of reparations recognized in human rights law, such as restitution, compensation, rehabilitation, satisfaction, and guarantees of non-repetition.[21] These distinctions bring conceptual clarification into the field of victim reparations, contributing to the operationalization and design of specific measures in the context of reparation programs.

At the granular level, administrative programs often include both monetary and non-monetary reparations. The former can consist of lump sum payments, pensions, or funding for specific projects, while the latter can include mental and physical rehabilitation, housing, or scholarships to make victims and their families 'whole'.[22] While restitution aims to restore the victim to the original situation before violations were committed, compensation refers to economically assessable damages, and rehabilitation to medical and psychological care.[23]

However, in fulfilling the right to reparations, governments must do more than simply guarantee the deliverable outcomes mentioned above, rather they must adhere to the legal principles which inform whether reparations are effective. Here, international human rights law provides a framework that lays out specific legal contours of the right to reparations that includes: equal and effective access to justice; adequate, effective, prompt, and appropriate reparations for harm suffered; and access to relevant information concerning violations and reparation mechanisms.[24] In transitional justice practice such principles are commonly referred to as 'victims' rights to truth, justice and reparations' or simply 'victims' rights'.[25]

In this chapter, we suggest that it is these legal principles which, although protecting the interests of victims, often complicate the process of implementing successful reparation programs. At the same time, these same principles may be an invitation to innovate traditional approaches to reparations in ways that the ordinary judicial notion of repair may not fully deliver. In the next two parts, we first outline some of the common challenges in administrative reparation programs when scrutinized through both the legal framework and how it influences implementation; we then share ways in which these programs invite new innovations in reparation programming.

---

[21] United Nations General Assembly 2005.

[22] García-Godos 2008.

[23] Ibid.

[24] United Nations General Assembly 2005, principle 11.

[25] Sriram and García-Godos 2012; Buchanan et al. 2014.

3.3 Tensions and Dilemmas

Administrative reparation programs take into account specific national contexts and needs, yet they share some common challenges. Below we discuss four of these core issues, in particular those that relate to the definition of victim and the distinction between individualized or collective approaches to reparation. Finally, we also address the relation between reparations programs and development.

3.3.1 Inclusions and Exclusions of Victim Definitions

Reparation programs in transitional justice typically entail administrative programs to handle reparation claims from a wide range of individuals and communities. As a first step, governments must establish a registration process to determine the eligibility of claimants as victims before they can participate in reparation programs. Thus, the identification of victim status is vital to ensuring a person is entitled to whatever form of remedy or benefit that they are legally entitled to and which the government is obligated to provide.[26] Government officials use legal categories to identify the universe of victims to which a reparation program is addressed most often by reference to specific types of human rights violations. In that manner, the category of 'victim(s)' refers to all those who have suffered a specific type of violation, such as extrajudicial execution, kidnapping, torture, forced disappearance, sexual violence, mutilation, forced draft, and displacement among others. For example, following the Peruvian Truth and Reconciliation Commission's recommendations, the Peruvian government sought to create the Registro Único de Víctimas (Victims National Registry) to identify those who would qualify as victims and thus potentially be entitled to the reparation programs being established concurrently. This registration process constituted the gatekeeper of the overall reparation process in Peru's transitional justice process.

Because the identification of victims is the cornerstone of any victim reparation program, it is necessary to problematize how this status is used to both include and exclude people. Unique from a judicial process, the practice of most administrative reparation programs demonstrates an inclusive approach to the definition of victims, which usually extends not only to direct victims but also encompasses indirect victims, such as close relatives and dependents. For example, in cases involving death and disappearance, it is often the closest relatives who become beneficiaries of reparations programs. In most Latin American reparation programs, for instance, the parents, spouses, or children of the disappeared are entitled to be identified as indirect victims and therefore become beneficiaries of reparation programs. The amalgamation of time passed between the claim and the violation, and the degree of kinship/closeness to the direct victim can produce several surprising combinations when it comes to reparations. For example, land and property restitution in Colombia can

[26] Ibid.

deem second-generation descendants of families displaced during the armed conflict as beneficiaries; descendants may not even live in the country any longer, yet they are entitled to restitution.[27]

However, given that the eligibility of victims and beneficiaries always rests on a government first prescribing criteria and requirements, the claimant often carries the burden of proof to establish that they are truly a victim. Certainly, in the operational logic of reparation programs, it is very important to complete a proper eligibility assessment in order to avoid granting reparations to people not entitled to them. Yet, the demand for rigorous proof of victimization may, for some victims, challenge their ability to meet fixed requirements. Relevant identity documents can be lost and hard to recover, particularly if the bodies of the disappeared may still be missing.[28] Marriage and birth certificates might have been destroyed, and informal land tenure and family arrangements can be difficult to prove in the absence of what counts as formal documentation.

In terms of exclusion, one of the most problematic instances concerning victim status occurs when registries reinforce the dichotomy of victim and perpetrator. The human rights discourse that informs most transitional justice literature tends to reduce complex realities into these two identities to create neat, clear-cut, legalized categories.[29] As the armed conflicts across the world have demonstrated, the categories of victim and perpetrator do not cover the universe of actors that take part in armed conflict. Moreover, the boundaries of these categories are not always clearly delineated.[30] Rather, it is not uncommon to find that a single individual can have several roles; that is, be identified as a victim due to a raid of their village; and at the same time, as a perpetrator for participating in a raid against a neighboring village. Yet, if a person who experienced a human rights violation can also be considered a perpetrator, they may be excluded from a reparations program. Unlike in legal proceedings, an administrative reparation program may factor a person's innocence or guilt into whether they deserve to be repaired as well as to what degree they should be repaired.

Sometimes, determinations of a 'guilty' status may not necessarily be based on final criminal convictions, but only on allegations or even perceived allegiances and beliefs. This issue has arisen particularly in situations where a victim may be found to have any connection to a 'subversive' or 'terrorist' organization. Perhaps the clearest example of this can be seen in the Peruvian case, where the law creating the reparation program excludes former members of the Maoist guerrilla group, Shining Path, even

---

[27] García-Godos and Wiig 2018.

[28] Bermúdez Qvortrup 2021.

[29] Wilson 1997.

[30] Elster 2004. Elster identifies at least eight different types of agents relevant for transitional justice: wrongdoers (those who committed wrongdoings); victims (those against whom wrongdoings were committed); beneficiaries (those who benefited from the wrongdoing); helpers (those who helped victims); resisters (those who fought against wrongdoing); promoters (those who promote transitional justice processes); neutrals (neither wrongdoers, victims, helpers nor resisters); wreckers (those who obstruct transitional justice processes).

when their human rights may have been violated.[31] A similar practice can be seen in Colombia, where the Victims' Law of 2011 excludes members of illegal armed groups at the margin of the law from the category of victim.[32] This is the same law that recognized as victims those people affected by agents of the Colombian armed forces, who until then, were not considered legitimate victims by the Law of Justice and Peace that had been passed earlier in 2005. These examples show that 'national reparations programs have been shaped less by international standards or guidelines than by domestic notions of who is a 'victim' and by national understandings of what is possible and what is important.'[33]

Ultimately, the practice of exclusion amounts to a violation of the principle of non-discrimination which is inconsistent with human rights law.[34] The *Basic Principles* instruct that the determination and distribution of reparations cannot be based on discriminatory practices. Furthermore, states must 'provide those who claim to be victims of a human rights or humanitarian law violation with equal and effective access to justice … irrespective of who may ultimately be the bearer of responsibility for the violation.'[35] Dinah Shelton, a leading authority on reparations in international human rights law, explains that '[i]n general, the character of the victim should not be considered because it is irrelevant to the wrong and to the remedy, and implies a value judgment on the worth of an individual that has nothing to do with the injury suffered.'[36] The non-discrimination principle plays a central role in human rights law since it would otherwise create a 'two-class tier of right holders' in which 'delinquents' who become subject to state control could expect no protection from state harm.[37] As author Laplante wrote on this issue, '[g]iven that the overarching purpose of human rights protection is to curb state abuse, one could argue that carving out exceptions where human rights violations have no consequences presents a worrisome precedent.'[38]

As we have seen, victimhood and the experience of a violation itself are not enough to define a person as an eligible and legitimate victim entitled to reparation. Administrative victim reparation programs are established through national normative frameworks (such as national reparation laws passed in a political process) and they need to apply the definition of victim established by these laws. Arguably, the official acknowledgment of a person's victimhood as legitimate reflects not only a

[31] Law No. 28592: Law that Creates the National Integral Reparations Plan. Lima: Congress of the Republic of Peru, 20 July 2005, art 4. For discussion, see Laplante 2007a.

[32] Law 1448 of 2011: Establishing Comprehensive Measures of Attention, Support and Reparation to the Victims of the Internal Armed Conflict and Dictating Other Measures. Bogotá: Congress of the Republic of Colombia, 10 June 2011.

[33] Hayner 2010, p. 164; Moffett 2016, pp. 146-167.

[34] United Nations General Assembly 2005, principle 25.

[35] United Nations General Assembly 2005, principle 3(c).

[36] Shelton 2015, p. 151.

[37] Laplante 2009.

[38] Ibid., p. 66.

neutral legal norm, but also the popular sentiment towards specific groups of victims and non-victims in a given society.[39]

3.3.2 *Individualized Compensation or Lump Sums*

Even once a person qualifies as a victim for the purpose of a reparation program, one of the foundational challenges of implementing non-judicial reparation programs arises due to the impossibility of staying faithful to traditional legal principles used to calculate the actual award of damages. For example, in enforcing the right to remedy, national courts as well as international tribunals, such as the Inter-American Court of Human Rights and the European Court of Human Rights, adopt legalistic approaches to narrowly determine reparations in accordance with the damages suffered by plaintiffs bringing a claim.[40] Certainly, international judges, like their national counterparts, evaluate the harm suffered by the person or group whose rights were violated based on evidence submitted by the plaintiff or petitioner in order to determine the appropriate reparations, similar to how damages are calculated in tort lawsuits.[41]

In contrast to these judicial proceedings, administrative reparation programs established by governments to manage hundreds, if not thousands (even millions), of cases usually must resort to less individualized approaches to providing remedy. In doing so, governments often blame limited resources and competing social and economic issues that must be addressed also using public monies.[42] Thus, they may opt for predetermined reparation packages with fixed monetary amounts regardless of proof of harm and suffering. In this scenario, all qualifying victims receive the same amount.

For example, following the recommendations of the South African Truth and Reconciliation Commission, then-president Thabo Mbeki, implemented a one-time payment of ZAR 30,000 (approximately US$4,000) to the victims who testified before the TRC as a form of economic reparations for 18,000 people. This decision made in 2003 occurred only because of the ongoing lobbying of civil society and fell far short of the more generous recommendations of the Truth and Reconciliation

---

[39] For a discussion of different understandings of victimhood by state institutions, non-governmental organisations and victim organisations, see De Waardt 2016, pp. 432–450.

[40] Antkowiak 2008. This redress might include criminal prosecutions, reparations, truth, and even institutional reform to respond to the harms suffered by victims and to prevent the repetition of future violations. In cases of isolated incidents of violations, legal proceedings suitably attend to the justice demands of victims.

[41] Laplante 2004; Malamud-Goti and Grosman 2006, p. 540.

[42] In South Africa, the Parliament found the recommendations of the Truth and Reconciliation Commission to be "excessive" and settled on a much smaller amount justifying other competing social needs. Du Bois 2009, pp. 125-126. Governments often claim that reparations are not always economically feasible. See also Roht-Arriaza 2004, p. 124.

Commission.[43] These minimalist approaches ultimately set mostly symbolic sums of money that rarely match what would be awarded an individual judicial process.[44]

In contrast, those victims who do resort to courts, especially international courts, may receive a significantly higher economic reward, thus causing divisions within victims' groups who view the disparate amounts as inherently unfair. This situation arose in Peru when the Inter-American Human Rights Court in *Miguel Castro Castro Prison v. Peru* (*Castro Castro Prison*) ordered reparations for survivors and the families of victims who were killed and harmed during a 1992 state lockdown of a prison where the victims were detained on charges of terrorism, although some had not yet been convicted. Notably, these same individuals were excluded from the national reparation program due to their alleged connection to terrorism. Their receipt of a significant reparation package from the State, per the judgment of the international court, resulted in a significant domestic dispute, tension, and anger, especially among the victims registered with the national reparation program who received significantly less through the uniform sums.[45] This disparate treatment can undermine political support for reparation programming, while leaving many individual victims dissatisfied with the government response to their claims.

3.3.3 Individual and Collective Reparations: More than Monetary Compensation

While the presumption may be that monetary compensation forms the primary form of reparations, as it does in most judicial processes, administrative reparation programs usually include, and may even emphasize, non-monetary provisions. These provisions may be individualized to a certain extent, such as through access to health and education benefits, but include also collective measures, like community projects. Governments with limited resources tend to prefer collective and non-monetary reparation schemes for funding reasons as well as for easier administration. Arguments in favor of individual or collective forms of distribution are many, and include pragmatic, normative and philosophical considerations.[46]

One of the primary concerns relates to the provision of collective reparations and whether an individual victim of serious human rights violations receives the appropriate acknowledgment and redress they deserve (and need) through such schemes, as opposed to through individualized measures. Collective reparations can take many forms including monetary, non-monetary, tangible or symbolic, but in essence aim to repair a whole group or community. In Chile, for example, the Museum of Memory and Human Rights, inaugurated in 2010, is a form of collective reparations, providing

---

[43] Naidu 2013.

[44] Daly 2003.

[45] Laplante 2007a.

[46] For valuable contributions to this debate, see edited volumes by De Greiff 2006, De Feyter et al. 2005, Du Plessis and Peté 2007, and Miller and Kumar 2007.

acknowledgment and testimony to the massive human rights violations committed during the Pinochet regime (1973-1990).[47] Also in Chile, the Program for Reparations and Comprehensive Health Care (known as PRAIS for its Spanish name) provided individualized health services to survivors and relatives within the framework of a collective public service. The monetary pension that victims and beneficiaries receive in Chile as compensation is thus complemented by other forms of reparation that attend a variety of needs that victims have.[48]

While measures provided through collective reparation programs technically provide substantive redress, unlike in judicial processes they do not arise out of individualized assessments intended to return the plaintiff to the condition prior to a rights violation. This results often because reparation programs usually do not have the capacity to conduct an individualized assessment for every beneficiary, and as discussed above, they must resort to more uniform packages in their efforts to offer some form of reparation to victims. At the same time, collective reparations require a certain level of coordination and resources in order to reach victim groups and provide the services that are needed.

In Sierra Leone, five priority victim groups were identified based on their vulnerability: amputees; other war-wounded persons; children affected by war (orphans and child soldiers who had not benefited from the disarmament, demobilization and reintegration (DDR) program); war-wounded children; and sexually abused women and widows. Monetary compensation was provided to amputees and other war-wounded persons, skills training was offered to women and girls victims, while all priority groups received humanitarian relief.[49] An individual assessment of the victims in this case would have called for more comprehensive reparation measures, involving physical and mental health services, education and occupational training, social services, among other possibilities. Due to funding constraints and limited state capacity, collective reparations on health and education were not available to prioritized victims in Sierra Leone. Symbolic reparations in the form of commemoration ceremonies and an apology to Sierra Leonese women were also given.[50] However, because of the critical situation in which most prioritized victims lived, such symbolic collective reparations did not reach victims in a meaningful way.

3.3.4 Reparations and Development—Confusing the Causal Connection

Building off the last section, non-pecuniary reparations (both individual and collective), often resemble 'development', especially when they include programs and projects that build the social and economic infrastructure of local communities,

[47] Collins and Hau 2016.

[48] Ibid.

[49] Ottendörfer 2014.

[50] Langmack 2020.

whether they be related to education, health and other services. These measures may be met with resistance from victim-survivors and their advocates who argue that such measures correspond to pre-existing obligations of a government and do not adequately respond to the violation of civil and political rights.[51]

Here, reparation programs may be challenged by traditional legal concepts of 'causation' where damages are traced back to the exact harm from the violation of civil and political rights (CPR). Thus, if a community receives funds for a new school in a war-torn community that never had a school, it technically is repairing violations of Economic, Social, Cultural Rights (ESCR), and not CPR. Yet, most reparation programs claim to repair CPR and rarely include a remit to repair ESCR. In this situation, labeling development programs as forms of reparation risks confusion and even resentment, especially if they are open to other non-victims. For example, following the Peruvian TRC's Final Report in 2003, then President, Alejandro Toledo, presented his Plan de Desarrollo y Paz (Plan of Development and Peace) as the means for implementing the TRC's Plan Integral de Reparación (Comprehensive Reparations Plan). The initiative was met with resistance and was publicly criticized for confusing reparations and development.[52] Disgruntled communities pointed out that these were measures that corresponded to a separate obligation of governments regarding development and public services.

The blurring of reparations and development also risks not adequately acknowledging the harm of individuals who suffered serious harms, thus missing an opportunity for full repair. For example, the Peruvian government decided to implement its poverty subsidy program, *Juntos* ('Together'), beginning with the poorest regions of the country where the brunt of the war took place.[53] The program offered, to those who qualified, a set amount of money (100 soles) every month as long as their children attended schools. As a social program, the initiative was well received. The tension arose when the government framed this program as also a form of reparations, and yet it was open to all indigent people who qualified, regardless of whether they were victims of the war.[54] This approach not only created a dynamic in which the poor had to compete with 'the poverty-victims' in a struggle for limited resources, but it minimized the reparative effect of reparations as well.[55]

Additionally, the blurring between development and reparations is common in collective reparations programs. By 2016 in Peru, forty percent of the 5,712 local communities registered as affected by the armed conflict received collective reparations in the form of funding for community projects, such as basic infrastructure and productive initiatives, but also day-care centers, schools, and playgrounds. In fieldwork conducted by author García-Godos, she found that collective reparations in the form of local development projects were often welcomed as appropriate redress for the harm experienced. For community members who had endured displacement

---

[51] Laplante 2007b.

[52] Ibid.

[53] Ibid.

[54] Ibid.

[55] Ibid.

during childhood, a playground for the community's current children was considered as an appropriate form of reparation although it did not respond to their direct harm.[56]

Some of the challenges shared above have drawn attention from observers and led to a common observation that governments need to have better awareness of the intentions and aims of measures undertaken by government agencies and reparation programs to stay more focused on the legal criteria for reparations and at the same time do more to include victims and beneficiaries in establishing what is to be considered appropriate reparation. In the field of international development cooperation stakeholder participation has been an explicit element for many decades.[57] In transitional justice, stakeholder participation comes in the form of victim-centered approaches and victims' rights, yet appropriate ways to operationalize victims' participation in the design of transitional justice policies and programs are still a work in progress.[58] We return to this issue below.

3.4 Opportunities and New Directions

Although it is important to recognize the tensions, limits and dilemmas that administrative reparation programs cause, we believe it is important to give equal attention to some of the opportunities that these programs provide to move governments beyond traditional legal approaches to awarding reparations. Indeed, while reparation programs may cause tensions due to nonconformity with traditional legal notions of reparations, paradoxically this same ability to operate beyond the traditional legal parameters also allows for innovations that can offer a broader view of reparations. As mentioned earlier, while reparation programs are constrained by the operational character of their reparations portfolio and the definitions of victim established by domestic laws, programs are finding new and flexible ways to address the need to repair past harms. We address some new directions below, including taking a victim-centered approach, assuring meaningful participation, symbolic reparations, and transformative justice.

3.4.1 Victim-centered Approach

One way in which administrative reparation programs offer a more expansive approach is by bringing more focus on the victims it seeks to repair. Unlike in

[56] García-Godos 2018, p. 45.

[57] Sriram and García-Godos 2012; García-Godos 2013.

[58] García-Godos 2023.

court proceedings such as criminal trials or even civil suits, administrative reparation programs have more flexibility for innovation in how they integrate beneficiaries in the design, implementation and even evaluation of programs.[59] Indeed, the field of transitional justice prioritizes taking a victim-centered approach which invites different ways of imagining the framing of reparations.[60]Similarly, the *Basic Principles* instruct that reparations should be 'victim oriented'.[61]

This starting point has generated innovative theoretical models for conceptualizing and designing reparation programs. For example, while typical discussions about reparations implicitly rest on the basis of specific crimes identified in legal instruments, another approach with a much wider scope is to focus on the suffering of victims. Here, Jon Elster goes to the heart of the matter by asking 'what forms of suffering constitute victimhood?'[62] The answer to his question, in turn, informs who has the right to demand or deserves reparations. Elster distinguishes between three types of suffering: material, personal and intangible. *Material* suffering involves the loss of real or personal property, the loss coming about either by destruction or confiscation. By personal property, one refers to physical objects or financial assets. In some cases, the way the loss occurred may strengthen or delegitimize certain claims. For instance, the experience of violent internal displacement in Colombia can strengthen the claims of internally displaced persons (IDPs) for land and property substitution, while delegitimizing the claims of those causing or effecting the displacement. *Personal* suffering refers to harm to life, body or liberty, which can take place both during and outside conflict and/or repressive situations. *Intangible* suffering refers to the loss or lack of opportunities. These categories highlight different dimensions of victimhood and contribute to imagining alternative approaches to developing appropriate and effective reparations.

Another approach developed by author Laplante presents what she terms the *Justice Continuum of Repair* that is based on an individualized, pluralistic approach to redress that leads with the fundamental question: 'What does a victim need to *feel* repaired?'[63] As Laplante explains, '[t]his theory embodies the notion that justice in transitional justice rests on pluralistic values and ideals that reflect both local and individualized *felt justice needs.*'[64] Taking this subjective individualized approach helps to more accurately determine if reparations are truly adequate, effective, prompt, and appropriate based on a range of factors, including, not only rights violations, but other demographics and interests of the survivor.[65] It also allows for a broader

[59] Laplante and Reyes 2023.

[60] Laplante 2010.

[61] The Basic Principles includes in its preamble that "in adopting a victim-oriented perspective, the international community affirms its human solidarity with victims of violations of international law." United Nations General Assembly 2005, preamble.

[62] Elster 2004.

[63] Laplante 2015.

[64] Ibid.

[65] Of course, this approach may encounter challenges with regard to what interests will be considered legitimate. Thus, further elaboration on how to reach some parameters is necessary.

plural view of what justice means for victims through what Laplante terms a 'justice continuum' that includes the possibility of a focus on reparative, restorative, civil and socio-economic justice. While this approach to implementing reparations is more complex, it is more likely to succeed since it honors what the victims and beneficiaries need to feel fully repaired.[66] Recalling the above example from Sierra Leone, a justice continuum would be more likely to succeed in meeting the comprehensive and diverse needs of the prioritized groups of victims eligible for reparation.

3.4.2 Bottom Up or Top Down: Assuring Meaningful Participation

Importantly, to implement alternative models like those shared above, reparation programs often need to be more participatory. Administrative reparation programs are better positioned to involve victims in the design and implementation of reparation programs which leads to more effective redress. Ensuring meaningful participation in transitional justice reparation programs has come to be steadily recognized as a priority and also supports the victim focus explained above.[67] Indeed, former UN Secretary General Kofi Annan recognized in 2004 that 'most successful transitional justice experiences owe a large part of their success to the quantity and quality of public and victim consultation carried out.'[68] Then in 2011, Annan explained that[69]

> [r]obust national consultations are now understood to be essential prerequisites to ensure that transitional justice mechanisms reflect the needs of conflict-affected communities, including victims. There is also growing evidence that transitional justice measures that evolve over time and involve strong national ownership result in greater political stability in post-conflict settings.

The citizen-building aspect of ensuring full participation offers an inherent reparative effect given that it treats victims, who are often the traditionally marginalized members of society, as equal citizens under the law.[70] As theorized by author

---

[66] Laplante 2015. Similarly, Ramji-Nogales notes that "the effectiveness of transitional justice mechanisms [should] be measured by perceptions of legitimacy on the part of relevant actors." Ramji-Nogales 2010. Sirleaf argues that "perceptions of transitional justice mechanisms matter. The justice that people see and experience shapes the reality of what is. As a consequence, it is important to examine the way people most impacted by mass violence perceive transitional justice processes meant to provide redress." Sirleaf 2014. Doak opines, "it is vital that transitional justice theory sharpens its focus with regard to victims in order to be perceived as more accountable and legitimate." Doak 2011. Ford offers, "numerous studies by psychologists and sociologists have concluded that legitimacy is important to political and legal institutions because individuals are more likely to voluntarily adopt the norms of such institutions to regulate their own conduct when the institutions are perceived as legitimate." Ford 2012.

[67] Laplante and Reyes 2023.

[68] United Nations Secretary-General 2004, para 16.

[69] United Nations Secretary-General 2011, para 18.

[70] Laplante 2013.

Laplante, '[t]he act of being consulted is the constitutive act that restores full citizenship.'[71] Indeed, participation can be viewed as a 'reparative process' which goes towards a form of citizen restitution as it restores dignity, empowers the formerly voiceless, and restores the relationship between the government and the governed.[72] Given that it is often the same marginalization that made victims vulnerable to human rights violations in the first place, and that during the violation they were treated as sub-citizen and less than human, the importance of empowering them to have voice in the reparation process becomes all the more pressing. The intrinsic value of participation is matched by an instrumental value in giving beneficiaries of reparation programs a greater stake in the process while also enabling them to design programs that not only better meet their justice needs but may also result in a program feasible for the government to implement. Essentially, participation forms the cornerstone of 'transformative justice' processes that can lead to reformed political, social, and legal systems.[73]

The reparations unit within the Peruvian Truth and Reconciliation Commission recognized the importance of the effect of the *process* of implementing a reparations program and met with victims throughout the development of their recommendations to receive their feedback on the process. Eventually, the Commission adopted this same approach and called for 'the participation of the population in decision-making and definitions of their own process of social, cultural, economic and material construction and reconstruction.'[74] Subsequently, however, the government's efforts to implement the Commission's recommendations failed to adequately ensure victim participation, thus making the program arguably less effective.[75] Indeed, other transitional justice experiences report the same issues, which is often blamed for the failure of reparation programs.[76]

The issues may come down to a lack of knowledge and skill on how to best facilitate effective participation. Pamina Firchow and Yvette Selim, through an extensive review of literature, confirm the current consensus that reparation programs must include more victim participation, but observe that there is still a lack of depth in what it means to assure participation is 'meaningful'.[77] In Colombia, De Waardt and Weber show the limitations that institutionalized mechanisms of victim participation face, even with the best of intentions, by not taking into account spaces and forms of participation already existing and functional at the local level.[78] This resonates with Firchow and Selim's suggestion of the need to prioritize meaningful practices for

[71] Ibid.

[72] Laplante 2010; Laplante and Reyes 2023.

[73] Daly 2002, p. 100; Gready and Robins 2019.

[74] Comisión de la Verdad y Reconciliación del Perú (Peru's Truth and Reconciliation Commission) 2001, Vol. IX, Part 4, Ch. 2.2. [authors' translation]

[75] Laplante 2013.

[76] For example, Lydiah Bosire describes how the truth commission in the Democratic Republic of the Congo failed to adequately include the participation of victims. Bosire 2006.

[77] Firchow and Selim 2022.

[78] De Waardt and Weber 2019.

participants, not simply 'more participation'.[79] Therefore, the next stage of scholarship may begin to take a deeper dive into unpacking what it means to effectively engage victims in the design and implementation of reparation programs.[80]

3.4.3 Expanding the Notion of Repair: Symbolic Reparations and Memorialization to Ensure Satisfaction and Non-repetition

Symbolic measures form a central aspect of administrative reparation programs, which may even better facilitate localized and national symbolic reparations than individualized reparations awarded through a judicial proceeding. For example, a country can create a day of commemoration or remembrance to respond to the demands of victims, whereas individualized reparations through court orders typically do not. Indeed, reparation programs often include the establishment of places of memory and museums, erecting monuments, and changing the names of streets and public spaces as forms of symbolic reparations, even when they may involve tangible, material artifacts and facilities. Yet, although most symbolic reparations have a collective character, they can be designed to respond to the harms of individual victims as well. A letter of apology for crimes committed by the state against an individual is a symbolic restoration of the victims' dignity. Indeed, Principle 22 of the *Basic Principles*, referring to measures of satisfaction as a form of reparation, includes various examples of symbolic reparations, such as an official declaration or judicial decision restoring the dignity, reputation, and rights of the victims, public apologies (including acknowledgement of the facts and acceptance of responsibilities), and commemorations and tributes to the victims.

Although at first sight one can dismiss the relevance of symbolic reparations as just that, 'symbolic gestures' without much consequence, practice shows the contrary. Frank Haldemann sheds light on 'the significance of what we might call *reparatory symbolism* as a necessary additional step toward *acknowledging* wrongdoing, breaking with an atrocity and its legacy, and thus restoring the dignity of the victims as full-fledged, equal citizens.'[81] Here, economic reparations, even significant amounts, may lose their reparative value without symbolic elements of acknowledgment.[82] For example, Elazar Barkan describes how Japan's unwillingness to admit guilt 'depreciated the economic value of the compensation [for comfort women] and made it valueless.'[83] Trudy Govier terms the mistreatment associated with human rights violations as 'misrecognition' or 'non recognition',[84] which undermines healthy human agency

[79] Firchow and Selim 2022.

[80] Laplante and Reyes 2023.

[81] Haldemann 2008, p. 730.

[82] Daly 2002; Laplante 2013.

[83] Barkan 2000.

[84] Govier 2003.

and denies a person their very humanness especially when governments cover up or deny past wrongdoing.[85] In these situations, a 'second wounding' results '[w]hen recognition is withheld, victims of injustice are subjected to the symbolic injury of being ignored- of being rendered passive, powerless, voiceless, or simply invisible in matters that deeply affect them as human beings.'[86]

An important aspect highlighted by Margaret Urban Walker is the expressive function that reparations fulfill, conveying meaning and a message of acknowledgement while providing exemplification of the type of relationships that society values and aims for when reconstituting itself.[87] She argues that the expressive function is present in all forms of reparations, either material or symbolic, individual or collective, yet it is possibly in symbolic reparations that the expressive function takes center stage.

Significantly, while symbolic reparations play an important role in restoring individuals, it also serves the principle of non-repetition in a number of ways. In Argentina, the acknowledgement of victims of state terrorism led, among other things, to the establishment of a Memory Park in Buenos Aires and the building of a monument to victims of state terrorism inaugurated in 2001 as part of a public effort to take a clear stand against the atrocities committed during the military dictatorship and to prevent historical amnesia. In this way, the aim or purpose of the park and monument is to raise awareness among the younger generations about violations committed by the state and the need to ensure that it never happens again.[88] Symbolic reparations not only strive to provide satisfaction to victims, but also to offer guarantees of non-repetition.[89] However, as mentioned above, this outcome may not be achieved fully without the effective participation of the victims.[90]

3.4.4 Victim Reparations and Transformative Justice

Reparation programs have greater potential for ensuring that victims recover from past suffering and can contribute to improving their lives and future needs. This question is particularly relevant in societies with deep socio-economic inequalities, where socio-economic and political forms of distribution and access to power and resources are uneven. This type of consideration is the realm of distributive justice,

---

[85] Laplante 2007a.

[86] Bernstein 2005.

[87] Walker 2013.

[88] Balardini 2016, pp. 50-76; Monumento a las Víctimas del Terrorismo de Estado Parque de la Memoria, https://parquedelamemoria.org.ar. Accessed 9 October 2023. We need to be aware as well that public efforts through symbolic reparations can also provoke heated debates and be contested by different sectors of society for a multiplicity of reasons, including the expression of struggles for memory over the past, the ownership and the different versions of that past. For a Peruvian example, see Drinot 2009.

[89] Greeley et al, 2020.

[90] Reyes 2019; Reyes 2020.

and there is an ongoing debate on whether distributive justice ought to be an integral part of a transitional justice framework,[91] or if it belongs to the political sphere,[92] where it is complementary but not directly included in the 'mandate' of transitional justice mechanisms proper. There is an increased acknowledgement, however, of the complementary role of distributive justice if the overall objective of a transitional process is sustainable peace.[93]

The role or contribution of distributive justice to the field of transitional justice is often addressed as part of the concept of 'transformative justice,' referring to the transformative potential that transitional justice has to effect change in unequal societies and to protect and enhance the rights of people.[94] Applied to victim reparations, 'transformative reparations' call for a new look at the aim of reparations beyond bringing the victim back to the original situation, but instead aim to improve the victim's living standards, prospects for the future as well as to transforming the socio-structural conditions that fostered human rights violations in the first place.

In this way, transformative justice views reparations in transitional justice settings as having the potential to address a wider range of harms. In societies with deep socio-economic inequalities, a relevant entry point to an analysis would be examining the violation of socio-economic rights in past episodes of violence.[95] Here, Sandoval-Villalba traces the discussion on transformative justice back to the field of victim reparations, with attention given to the victim-centred focus that reparations have and the different forms of reparation available to address past violations.[96] She indicates that calls for gender justice in particular highlight the transformative potential of reparations to secure the rights of women, for example, through guarantees of non-repetition and consideration of the socio-economic and cultural context. The transformative aspiration of reparations has also been included in UN policy and operational guidance.[97]

The tangible nature of victim reparations brings up the immediate question as to how this transformative potential can be realised, how can it be operationalised? One way should be through the selection of the specific forms of reparations provided to individual victims through administrative reparation programs and to identify or design appropriate measures that will have a lasting, positive effect in the lives of individual victims. Options might include more generous monetary compensation or monthly pensions, participation in labour schemes and training programs, support to return to one's place of origin, and the restitution of abandoned property among other measures.

---

[91] Duthie 2008; Huggins 2009.

[92] For a critical view on reparations as means of structural change, see Walker 2016.

[93] De Greiff 2009.

[94] Gready and Robins 2014; Gready and Robins 2019.

[95] Waldorf 2012.

[96] Sandoval-Villalba 2017.

[97] United Nations Secretary-General 2014.

At the societal level, other forms of reparation may be better able to assure a transformative effect, such as guarantees of non-repetition. Among the five forms of reparations identified by the *Basic Principles*, measures of satisfaction and guarantees of non-recurrence are perhaps the ones with the most potential for transformative reparations and societal change, and at the same time, are the types of measures that fall outside the mandates and objectives of specific victim reparation programs. Satisfaction and non-recurrence involve broader actions and processes of institutional reform geared towards a higher societal, more structural level. For example, in Colombia, the debate on transformative reparations[98] has already made its way into the field of practice as one of the core principles guiding the current reparations and restitution programs implemented in the country since 2011.[99] Article 25 of Law 1448 of 2011, known as the Victims' Law, clearly established victims' right to reparations that are appropriate, effective and transformative, while Article 5 of its regulating decree (Decree 4800 of 2011) established a transformative approach as one of the main principles to guide the design and implementation of reparations programs. The goal is to work towards the elimination of conditions of discrimination and marginalization that contributed to victimization in the first place. The transformative approach comes more clearly forward in the collective reparations program, which addresses the needs of collective actors such as ethnic groups, peasant communities, labour unions, and political parties.[100]

While there is great potential and hope in the idea of transformative reparations, the challenge is how much leverage victim reparation programs actually have to influence policy change and reform at the macro-level. Administrative reparation programs cannot initiate, for example, security sector or judicial reform, yet they can promote agendas for change and institutional reform, either independently or by joining forces with other public institutions or stakeholders, such as victims' organisations. In spite of their legal basis, reparation programs are dependent on the government's political will and commitment to victims. Programs can be subject to budget cuts, influencing implementation. The expectations for change and effective implementation among victims and beneficiaries can turn into disillusion and frustration. Thus, currently, full realization of transformative justice remains mostly aspirational.

However, author Laplante suggests that one way to bring in a wider scope to reparations is to include economic, social and cultural rights in the mandates of truth commission which would better facilitate the initial framework for conceptualizing reparations.[101] This approach may also help to avoid some of the confusion related to causation issues between development and reparations discussed in Sect. 3.4. This practice is still uncommon with most Truth Commissions which historically tend

---

[98] On the transformative potential of reparations in the Colombian context, see Uprimny and Saffon 2009.

[99] García-Godos and Wiig 2018.

[100] Reparación colectiva. Unidad para las Víctimas, https://www.unidadvictimas.gov.co/es/atencion-asistencia-y-reparacion-integral/reparacion-colectiva/119. Accessed 20 August 2023.

[101] Laplante 2009.

to examine socio-economic causes and consequences of civil and political rights violation.

For example, the Peruvian Truth and Reconciliation Commission dedicated an entire volume on the causes of its nation's internal armed conflict to reveal the social, economic, and cultural inequalities that fueled the insurgency.[102] Moreover, the Commission documented that the war disproportionately impacted the already traditionally marginalized groups, namely *campesinos* and indigenous communities. Yet, because the mandate of the Commission did not include reference to the violation of such rights, its recommendations for reparations considered only civil and political rights, thus shaping the government's approach to reparations, although the current needs of those entitled to reparations often have roots tracing back to violations of both types of rights.

Reparation programs could embrace the indivisibility principle and consider both sets of rights to avoid the confusion and tension among recipients. This adjustment would also allow for more flexibility in honoring *how* victims need to feel repaired and moving closer to the transformative model discussed above. Indeed, victims often include measures that respond more to their current economic situation than to the specific harms they suffered from the violations of civil and political harms. Since many victims suffered economic and social inequalities before the violence, making them 'whole' requires a more expansive approach, especially as poverty, exclusion and other such conditions prevent a victim from achieving well-being. They may ask for health benefits and access to education, especially for their children even if born after the violence ended. They may seek other ways to improve their lot such as assistance with productive capacity (more farm animals, farm machinery, technical skills) even if these never existed before the violence.

3.4.5 Reparations for Historical Injustices

Although transitional justice traditionally responds to more immediate past episodes of violence, debates about the transformative potential of transitional justice to address structural inequalities have led both scholars and practitioners to inquire into the nature and root causes of these inequalities, especially historical episodes of colonialization and oppression. Colonialism as a system of domination and exploitation has been studied in many disciplinary fields, from history to development studies, political science to geography, cultural studies to economics. In the early 2000s, as the study of victim reparations was in its initial phases, the legacy of colonialism was addressed mainly by historians and in the framework of historical injustices.[103] As fields of inquiry, transitional justice and historical injustice have run parallel, the former focusing on civil and political rights violations in the context of conflict and

[102] Laplante 2007a.
[103] García-Godos 2008.

authoritarianism; the later, on historical processes of domination, such as slavery and various forms of colonial rule.

Over the past decade, however, as transitional justice moves in the direction of transformative justice, there are voices calling for a more direct involvement of transitional justice mechanisms in addressing the legacy of gross violations of human rights and international humanitarian law committed in colonial contexts. Initiatives both from civil society and state institutions are emerging in response to more awareness about the relationship between racial and ethnic discrimination as well as marginalization and criminalization of minority groups and indigenous peoples with structural patterns rooted in slavery and colonialism.

In response, a report by the Special Rapporteur on the promotion of truth, justice, reparation and guarantees of non-recurrence, in July 2021 examined the design and application of transitional justice measures to address violations committed in colonial contexts.[104] The point of departure for the report is that 'for transitional justice processes to be holistic and appropriately comprehensive, it is imperative to include the study of the colonial legacy, where appropriate'.[105] With this statement, the Special Rapporteur takes a clear stand on the debate about transitional justice's position with regards to structural inequalities, at least if we assume that these originate in colonial legacies. The report focuses on rights violations from colonialism in two contexts:

> (a) Settler States and other contexts of dispossession and oppression of indigenous peoples and people of African descent;
> (b) Former colonies that are now independent States. These contexts have a common denominator: Such rights violations have clear direct and indirect consequences today.[106]

The report explicitly discusses how various transitional justice measures can address human rights violations arising from colonial and historical injustices, highlighting the important role of dialogue and participation by victims of colonialism. Concerning reparations, the Special Rapporteur highlights the need for rehabilitation, the restitution of cultural heritage, public apologies accompanied by other measures of reparation, and compensation in the form of debt cancellation for former colonies. Memorialization initiatives and guarantees of non-recurrence, particularly those geared towards education and institutional reform, are also addressed.

The types of measures mentioned above can be effectively implemented by victim administrative reparation programs in terms of design and operations, if a state so decides. But it is necessary to ask whether this is actually the best way to address present inequalities, discrimination, and marginalization. Reparation programs require the identification of victims. If not of specific violations, to what extent can we consider the entire population of a former colony 'victims of colonialism?' How can victimhood be assessed? Perhaps the burden of proof in this

[104] United Nations General Assembly 2021.
[105] Ibid., p. 5.
[106] Ibid.

hypothetical scenario becomes superfluous, or even in the context of specific groups, such as indigenous populations in Canada, Australia, United States, Colombia or Chile, it can be taken for granted that all members of the group have experienced the legacies of colonialism and/or discrimination. At this stage in the debate, the field offers more questions than answers, forcing us to question our assumptions and to problematize the expansion of transitional justice.

3.5 Conclusion

This review of dilemmas, debates and new directions in the field of victim reparations has focused on the practice of administrative reparation programs. It is clear that these programs are well established in the transitional justice toolbox, undoubtedly given that they respond to legitimate and consistent needs and demands for reparative measures by the victims of human rights violations. While scholars (us included) may offer critical assessments of reparation programs, rejecting them is not an option. On the contrary, what both scholars and practitioners argue for is their continuous development and fine tuning to meet the diverse needs of victims, both individuals and collectives.

The tensions and dilemmas we find in administrative reparation programs are based on core issues that, more often than not, are decided outside of the programs, by legislative bodies and higher levels of government. This implies a limited room of maneuver in, for example, core issues such as the definition of victim or the budgets assigned to the program. What a program can do, is to identify and develop different forms of measures to address different kinds of needs and forms of victimhood. Beyond the specific measures, a program can also determine the 'how' of reparation programs, not only in terms of the form of distribution of different measures (individual or collective), but even more productively, about how the program is designed. This includes the desirable level of participation by victims and other stakeholders in the development, implementation and assessment of the measures. There is therefore a relation, a connection, between the inner tensions and dilemmas experienced in administrative programs and the opportunities and new directions that are emerging.

Yet tensions and dilemmas do not arise solely from the implementation of reparation programs, they also originate from outside the programs, in the societal and international contexts in which programs operate. Reparation programs are immersed in society, so it is not surprising that they too are influenced by larger debates, political contestation and struggles over memory and recognition. Transitional justice is a field of struggle and contestation, and victim reparations are part of that field. Societies' expectations of transitional justice do not leave victim reparations unaffected; instead, responses are demanded also from reparation programs. Calls for transformative justice touch upon reparation programs in a very direct manner, given that reparations are the most tangible forms of redress directed to the victims.

Yet, how realistic is it to expect institutional reforms as guarantees of non-repetition in the portfolio of measures offered by an administrative reparations program? Looking back at the normative framework of non-judicial remedies, particularly to the UN Basic Principles, it should be possible to differentiate between forms of reparation that fit within administrative programs, and those that are better seen as part of broader policies of acknowledgement and redress by states towards victim populations, particularly some measures of satisfaction and guarantees of non-repetition. The valuable contribution and potential of administrative programs rest in their ability to reach a large number of victims. It comes at a cost, of course, but fine-tuning the programs to better accommodate the interests and expectations of victims seem undoubtedly the best way forward.

References

Aguilar P (2009) The Timing and the Scope of Reparation, Truth and Justice Measures: A Comparison of the Spanish, Argentinian and Chilean Cases. In: Ambos K, Large J, Wierda M (eds) Building a Future on Peace and Justice. Springer, Berlin, pp. 503–529

Antkowiak T M (2008) Remedial Approaches to Human Rights Violations: The Inter-American Court of Human Rights and Beyond. Columbia Journal of Transnational Law 46:351–419

Arthur P (2009) How "Transitions" Reshaped Human Rights: A Conceptual History of Transitional Justice. Human Rights Quarterly 31:321–367

Balardini L (2016) Argentina: Regional Protagonist of Transitional Justice. In: Skaar E, García-Godos J, Collins C (eds) Transitional Justice in Latin America: The Uneven Road from Impunity towards Accountability. Routledge, London, pp. 50–76

Barkan E (2000) The Guilt of Nations: Restitution and Negotiating Historical Injustices. W.W. Norton & Company, New York

Benomar J (1995) Justice After Transitions. In: Kritz N J (ed) Transitional Justice: How Emerging Democracies Reckon with Former Regimes. United States Institute of Peace Press, Washington, D.C., pp. 32–41

Bermúdez Qvortrup N (2021) Finding Ways of Searching for the Disappeared: The Information Practices of the Families in Colombia. Journal of Documentation 78:1371–1388

Bernstein J M (2005) Suffering Injustice: Misrecognition as Moral Injury in Critical Theory. International Journal of Philosophical Studies 13:303–324

Bosire L K (2006) Overpromised, Underdelivered: Transitional Justice in Sub-Saharan Africa. Sur—International Journal on Human Rights 5:71- 107

Buchanan C, García-Godos J, O'Connell M, Widmer M (2014) Evolution of Victims' Rights and International Standards. In: Buchanan C (ed) Gun Violence, Disability and Recovery. Surviving Gun Violence Project, Xlibris, Sydney, pp. 31–53

Collins C, Hau B (2016) Chile: Incremental Truth, Late Justice. In: Skaar E, García-Godos J, Collins C (eds) Transitional Justice in Latin America. The Uneven Road from Impunity Towards Accountability. Routledge, London, pp. 126–150

Daly E (2002) Transformative Justice: Charting a Path to Reconciliation. International Legal Perspectives 12:73–183

Daly E (2003) Reparations in South Africa: A Cautionary Tale. University of Memphis Law Review 33:367–407

De Feyter K, Parmentier S, Bossuyt M, Lemmens P (eds) (2005) Out of the Ashes: Reparation for Victims of Gross and Systematic Human Rights Violations. Intersentia, Antwerp

De Greiff P (2006) Justice and Reparations. In: De Greiff P (ed) The Handbook of Reparations. Oxford University Press, Oxford, pp 451–477

De Greiff P (2009) Articulating the Links Between Transitional Justice and Development: Justice and Social Integration. In: De Greiff P, Duthie R (eds) Transitional Justice and Development: Making Connections. Social Science Research Council, New York, pp. 28–75
De Waardt M (2016) Naming and Shaming Victims: The Semantics of Victimhood. International Journal of Transitional Justice 10:432–450
De Waardt M, Weber S (2019) Beyond Victims' Mere Presence: An Empirical Analysis of Victim Participation in Transitional Justice in Colombia. Journal of Human Rights Practice 11: 209–228
Dixon P (2017) Reparations in the Transition from Violence to Peace. Oxford Research Encyclopedia of Politics
Doak J (2011) The Therapeutic Dimension of Transitional Justice: Emotional Repair and Victim Satisfaction in International Trials and Truth Commissions. International Criminal Law Review 11:263–298
Drinot P (2009) For Whom the Eye Cries: Memory, Monumentality, and the Ontologies of Violence in Peru. Journal of Latin American Cultural Studies 18:15–32
Du Bois F (2009) Reparation and the Forms of Justice. In: Du Bois F, Du Bois-Pedain A (eds) Justice and Reconciliation in Post-Apartheid South Africa. Cambridge University Press, Cambridge, pp 125–126
Du Plessis M, Peté S (eds) (2007) Repairing the Past? International Perspectives on Reparations for Gross Human Rights Abuses. Intersentia, Antwerp
Duthie R (2008) Toward a Development-Sensitive Approach to Transitional Justice. International Journal of Transitional Justice 2:292–309
Elster J (2004) Closing the Books: Transitional Justice in Historical Perspective. Cambridge University Press, Cambridge
Falk R (2006) Reparations, International Law, and Global Justice: A New Frontier. In: De Greiff P (ed) The Handbook of Reparations. Oxford University Press, Oxford, pp. 478–503
Firchow P, Selim Y (2022) Meaningful Engagement from the Bottom-Up? Taking Stock of Participation in Transitional Justice Processes. International Journal of Transitional Justice 16:187–203
Fletcher L E (2009) Institutions from Above and Voices from Below: A Comment on Challenges to Group-Conflict Resolution and Reconciliation. Law & Contemporary Problems 72:51-55
Ford S (2012) A Social Psychology Model of the Perceived Legitimacy of International Criminal Courts: Implications for the Success of Transitional Justice Mechanisms. Vanderbilt Journal of Transnational Law 45:405-476
García-Godos J, Wiig H (2018) Ideals and Realities of Restitution: The Colombian Land Restitution Program. Journal of Human Rights Practice 10:40–57
García-Godos J (2008) Victim Reparations in Transitional Justice–What is at Stake and Why. Nordic Journal of Human Rights 26:111–130
García-Godos J (2013) Victims' Rights and Distributive Justice: In Search of Actors. Human Rights Review 14:241–255
García-Godos J (2018) Victims and Victimhood in Reparation Programs: Lessons from Latin America. In: Druidolle V, Brett R (eds) The Politics of Victimhood in Post-conflict Societies. Comparative and Analytical Perspectives. Routledge, London, pp. 25–51
García-Godos J (2023) Abriendo Paso: La CVR a la Luz de las Comisiones de la Verdad en América Latina. In: Lerner S, Salmón (eds) Legados de un pasado irresuelto. El Informe Final de la CVR y la crisis de la democracia veinte años después. Instituto de Democracia y Derechos Humanos de la Pontificia Universidad Católica del Perú (IDEHPUCP), Lima, pp. 92–115
Govier T (2003) What is Acknowledgment and Why is it Important? In: Prager C, Govier T (eds) Dilemmas of Reconciliation: Cases and Concepts. Wilfrid Laurier University Press, Waterloo
Gready P, Robins S (2014) From Transitional to Transformative Justice: A New Agenda for Practice. International Journal of Transitional Justice 8:339–361
Gready P, Robins S (eds) (2019) From Transitional to Transformative Justice. Cambridge University Press, Cambridge

Greeley R, Orwicz M, Falconi J, Reyes AM, Rosenberg F, Laplante LJ (2020) Repairing Symbolic Reparations: Assessing the Effectiveness of Memorialization in the Inter-American System of Human Rights. International Journal of Transitional Justice 14: 165–192
Haldemann F (2008) Another King of Justice: Transitional Justice as Recognition. Cornell International Law Journal 41:675-737
Hansen T O (2011) Transitional Justice: Toward a Differentiated Theory. Oregon Review of International Law 13:1-46
Hayner P B (2002) Unspeakable Truths: Confronting State Terror and Atrocity. Routledge, New York
Hayner P B (2010) Unspeakable Truths: Confronting State Terror and Atrocity, 2nd edn. Routledge, New York
Hesse C, Post R (1999) Introduction. In: Hesse C, Post R (eds) Human Rights in Political Transitions: Gettysburg to Bosnia. Zone Books, New York, pp. 20–21
Huggins C (2009) Linking Broad Constellations of Ideas: Transitional Justice, Land Tenure Reform, and Development. In: De Greiff P, Duthie R (eds) Transitional Justice and Development: Making Connections. Social Science Research Council, New York, pp. 332-374
Johnston B R, Slyomovics S (eds) (2009) Waging War, Making Peace: Reparations and Human Rights. Routledge, New York
Langmack F-J (2020) Reparations in Sierra Leone: News from the periphery of transitional justice. Justiceinfo.net. 3 February.
Laplante L J, Reyes M A (2023) Measuring Up: A Dialogical Model for Assuring a Reparative Process. Law & Social Inquiry 1-30.
Laplante L J (2004) Bringing Effective Remedies Home: The Inter-American Human Rights System, Reparations, and the Duty of Prevention. Netherlands Quarterly of Human Rights 22:347–388
Laplante L J (2007a) The Peruvian Truth Commission's Historical Memory Project: Empowering Truth Tellers to Confront Truth Deniers. Journal of Human Rights 6:433–452
Laplante L J (2007b) On the Indivisibility of Rights: Truth Commissions, Reparations and the Right to Development. Yale Human Rights and Development Law Journal 10:141–177
Laplante L J (2009) The Law of Remedies and the Clean Hands Doctrine: Exclusionary Reparation Policies in Peru's Political Transition. American University International Law Review 23:51–90
Laplante L J (2010) Evaluating Truth Commissions and Reparations through the Eyes of Victims. L'Observateur des Nations Unies 28:167–176
Laplante L J (2013) Negotiating Reparation Rights: The Participatory and Symbolic Quotients. Buffalo Human Rights Law Review 19:217–250
Laplante L J (2015) Just Repair. Cornell International Law Journal 48:513- - 578
Malamud-Goti J E, Grosman L S (2006) Reparations and Civil Litigation: Compensation for Human Rights Violations in Transitional Democracies In: De Greiff P (ed) The Handbook of Reparations. Oxford University Press, New York, pp. 539- - 559
Miller J, Kumar R (eds) (2007) Reparations: Interdisciplinary Inquiries. Oxford University Press, New York
Moffett L (2016) Reparations for 'Guilty Victims': Navigating Complex Identities of Victim–Perpetrators in Reparation Mechanisms. International Journal of Transitional Justice 10:146–167
Naidu E (2013) Symbolic Reparations and Reconciliation: Lessons from South Africa. Buffalo Human Rights Law Review 19:251–271
Olsen T D, Payne L A, Reiter A G (2010) Transitional Justice in Balance: Comparing Processes, Weighing Efficacy. United States Institute of Peace Press, Washington D.C.
Ottendörfer E (2014) The Fortunate Ones and the Ones Still Waiting: Reparations for War Victims in Sierra Leone. Peace Research Institute Frankfurt
Paige A (2009) How "Transitions" Reshaped Human Rights: A Conceptual History of Transitional Justice. Human Rights Quarterly 31:321–367
Ramji-Nogales J (2010) Designing Bespoke Transitional Justice: A Pluralist Process Approach. Michigan Journal of International Law 32:1–72

Reyes A M (2019) The Monument to the Children of Villatina: Commemorating Innocent Child Victims in the Context of Lethally Stigmatized Youth in Colombia. Visual Communication 18: 379–398

Reyes A M (2020) Sites of Repair: Symbolic Spaces in Reparations. Latin American and Latinx Visual Culture 2:112–118

Roht-Arriaza N (2004) Reparations in the Aftermath of Repression and Mass Violence. In: Stover E, Weinstein H M (eds) My Neighbor, My Enemy: Justice and Community in the Aftermath of Mass Atrocity. Cambridge University Press, Cambridge, pp. 121–140

Roht-Arriaza N (2006) The New Landscape of Transitional Justice. In: Roht-Arriaza N, Mariezcurrena J (eds) Transitional Justice in The Twenty-First Century: Beyond Truth versus Justice. Cambridge University Press, Cambridge

Rubio-Marin R (ed) (2006) What Happened to the Women? Gender and Reparations for Human Rights Violations. Social Science Research Council, New York

Sandoval-Villalba C (2017) Reflections on the Transformative Potential of Transitional Justice and the Nature of Social Change in Times of Transition. International Center for Transitional Justice

Shelton D (2015) Remedies in International Human Rights Law, 3rd edn. Oxford University Press, Oxford

Sirleaf M (2014) Beyond Truth and Punishment in Transitional Justice. Virginia Journal of International Law 54:223–294

Sriram C L, García-Godos J (2012) Conclusions and Considerations for Practitioners. In: Sriram C L, García-Godos J, Herman J, Martin-Ortega O (eds) Transitional Justice and Peacebuilding on the Ground. Victims and Ex-Combatants. Routledge, London, pp. 255–268

United Nations General Assembly (2005) Basic Principles and Guidelines on the Right to a Remedy and Reparation for Victims of Gross Violations of International Human Rights Law and Serious Violations of International Humanitarian Law, UN Doc A/RES/60/147

United Nations General Assembly (2021) Promotion of Truth, Justice, Reparation and Guarantees of Non-recurrence: Note by the Secretary-General, UN Doc A/76/180

United Nations Human Rights Council (2019) Promotion of Truth, Justice, Reparation and Guarantees of Non-recurrence: Report of the Special Rapporteur on the Promotion of Truth, Justice, Reparation and Guarantees of Non-recurrence, UN Doc A/HRC/42/45

United Nations Secretary-General (2004) The Rule of Law and Transitional Justice in Conflict and Post-Conflict Societies: Report of the Secretary-General, UN Doc S/2004/616

United Nations Secretary-General (2010) Guidance Note of the Secretary-General: United Nations Approach to Transitional Justice

United Nations Secretary-General (2014) Guidance Note of the Secretary-General: Reparations for Conflict-Related Sexual Violence

United Nations Secretary-General (2011) The Rule of Law and Transitional Justice in Conflict and Post-Conflict Societies: Report of the Secretary-General, UN Doc S/2011/634

United Nations Security Council (2011) The Rule of Law and Transitional Justice in Conflict and Post-Conflict Societies: Report of the Secretary-General, UN Doc S/2011/634

Uprimny R, Saffon M P (2009) Reparaciones Transformadoras, Justicia Distributiva y Profundización Democrática. In: Díaz C et al (eds) Reparar en Colombia: Los Dilemas en Contexto de Conflicto, Pobreza y Exclusión [To Repair in Colombia: Dilemmas in a Context of Conflict, Poverty and Exclusion]. ICTJ, DeJusticia, Bogotá, pp. 31–69

Van Der Merwe H, Baxter V, Chapman A R (2009) Assessing the Impact of Transitional Justice: Challenges For Empirical Research. United States Institute of Peace, Washington D.C.

Waldorf L (2012) Anticipating the Past: Transitional Justice and Socio-Economic Wrongs. Social and Legal Studies 21:171–186

Walker M U (2013) The Expressive Burden of Reparations: Putting Meaning into Money, Words, and Things. In: MacLachlan A, Speight A (eds) Justice, Responsibility and Reconciliation in the Wake of Conflict. Springer, New York, pp. 205–225

Walker M U (2016) Transformative Reparations? A Critical Look at a Current Trend in Thinking about Gender-Just Reparations. International Journal of Transitional Justice 10:108–125

Waterhouse C (2009) The Good, the Bad, and the Ugly: Moral Agency and the Role of Victims in Reparations Programs. University of Pennsylvania Journal of International Law 31:257–294

Wilson R A (1997) Representing Human Rights Violations: Social Contexts and Subjectivities. In: Wilson R A (ed) Human Rights, Culture and Context: Anthropological Perspectives. Routledge, London, pp. 134–160

Laws

Decree 4800 of 2011, Ruling Law 1448 of 2011 and Establishing Other Legal Provisions. Bogotá: Ministry of Law and Justice, 20 December 2011

Law 1448 of 2011: Establishing Comprehensive Measures of Attention, Support and Reparation to the Victims of the Internal Armed Conflict and Dictating Other Measures. Bogotá: Congress of the Republic of Colombia, 10 June 2011

Law No. 28592: Law that Creates the National Integral Reparations Plan. Lima: Congress of the Republic of Peru, 20 July 2005

Jemima García-Godos Professor of Human Geography, Department of Sociology and Human Geography, University of Oslo.

Lisa J. Laplante Professor of Law, New England Law | Boston and Director, Center for International Law and Policy.

Chapter 4
Structural Remedies as Policy Making: Data, Rationales and Opportunities of the Inter-American Court of Human Rights

Edward J. Perez

Contents

Abstract This chapter provides an in-depth description of the Inter-American Court of Human Rights' role as a policy maker through its structural remedies, the alternative ways in which it intervenes from a public policy perspective, and the possible rationales that justify why it intervenes one way or another. Using the public policy cycle as a roadmap for this classification, the chapter concludes that the Inter-American Court has intervened in policy cycles through agenda setting, policy formulation, ordering policy implementation or requiring policy evaluation, favoring the second of these alternatives. The Court's rationales, on the other hand, are more elusive. It seems that variables such as the year the decision was issued, the State responsible, participation of certain victim's counsel, among others, contribute directly to the Court's decision of how it is going to design its structural remedy. These conclusions argue in favor of the need of further research on possible public policy tools that the Court could incorporate when issuing structural remedies, the role of the litigating parties in incorporating a policy perspective in their legal strategies, and possible alternatives to the Court's practices to favor an improved policy intervention.

E. J. Perez (✉)
University College of London, London, UK
e-mail: edward.perez.23@ucl.ac.uk

O. Spijkers et al. (eds.), *Netherlands Yearbook of International Law 2022*, Netherlands Yearbook of International Law 53, https://doi.org/10.1007/978-94-6265-627-7_4

Keywords Inter-American Court of Human Rights · Structural remedies · Reparations · Non-repetition · Public policy · Rationales

4.1 Introduction

This chapter addresses whether the Inter-American Court of Human Rights (hereinafter "IACtHR") is acting as a policy maker when issuing structural remedies (also known as measures of non-repetition). It will further address preliminary approximations as to what are the reasons in which the IACtHR decides to intervene in one step or another. The measures of non-repetition issued by the IACtHR aspire to transform situations of injustice that led to a case coming before the court, so that they do not occur again.[1] Therefore, these structural remedies provide a mandate addressed to the State to adopt and implement a measure aimed at execrating a situation of human rights violation that was being perpetuated.[2] Similar measures have been ordered not only by the IACtHR, but also by local courts, within the framework of their jurisdiction.[3] However, within the universe of international tribunals, the IACtHR stands out both for the number of non-repetition measures it has ordered and for the variety of their scope, as will be analyzed below.[4]

The research provides a mixed methods study of the 176 judgments containing such types of reparations that the IACtHR has issued up to 2021, where each structural remedy was codified and classified according to different types of policy intervention, as described in the public policy cycle described in this chapter. The data was further complimented and analyzed according to interviews made to personnel from the IACtHR.

As will be evidenced, the IACtHR's structural remedies are a form of policy making. Furthermore, the IACtHR has intervened in all stages of the public policy cycle through its structural reparations (agenda setting, public policy formulation, implementation and evaluation), although more recently it has directly favored influencing mainly the stages of policy formulation and implementation. Notwithstanding, reasons on why the IACtHR decided to intervene one way or the other were not as a clear.

This research builds upon the results of a dissertation presented before Universidad de los Andes's School of Government.[5] It complements other important studies such as those that study the impact of the judgments of the IACtHR[6] and those that

---

1 Krsticevic 2020.

2 America 1998; Roht-Arriaza 2003; Rubio-Marín 2012.

3 Cano Blandón 2015b, p. 111; Yáñez Meza 2014; Herrero 2011.

4 Saavedra Alessandri 2017.

5 Pérez 2022.

6 Londoño Lázaro 2019; Saavedra Alessandri 2017.

analyze the process of monitoring compliance with its decisions.[7] It also complements studies on the way in which the IACtHR designs reparations and their impact in specific contexts, particularly the difficulty of implementation, the need for inter-institutional coordination, or in some cases, the lack of political will.[8] In addition, this research contributes to the literature on courts intervention in public policy cycles. The literature on the role of the courts in public policy cycles has been limited to the study of national courts,[9] mainly constitutional courts.[10] In these cases, the courts assume a "transformative" role in society, becoming *policy makers through their* rulings.[11]

4.2 Relevant Considerations on the IACtHR's Jurisdiction to Issue Structural Remedies

The IACtHR maintains the jurisdiction to issue structural remedies (measures of non-repetition), that is, orders aimed at correcting structural flaws that contribute to the repetition of the human rights violations that occurred in the specific case under analysis.[12] These remedies seek to prevent repetition of the same human rights violations identified, through concrete interventions to address what IACtHR considered the structural causes of the problem were.[13]

There is no closed catalog of non-repetition measures. These orders have been very varied, including constitutional and legal modifications; the creation, modification or elimination of regulations; trainings; campaigns aimed at the dissemination of information, among other.[14] The degree of specificity with which each measure of non-repetition is provided also varies, there being on many occasions measures in which States are allowed a broader flexibility as to how they should comply with the measure of non-repetition, and other cases in which—on the contrary—the Court provides orders with a very detailed specificity[15]. The appropriateness of the greater breadth or specificity of the measure is disputed.[16]

The IACtHR's decision to order a structural remedy is associated, according to the literature, with the court being able to identify a causal link between the human rights

[7] Perez 2018; Sanchez de Miguel 2018.

[8] Murray and Sandoval 2020; Sandoval et al. 2020.

[9] Baum 1983.

[10] Cano Blandón 2015a; Yáñez Meza 2014; Herrero 2011; López Andrade 2017; Cano Blandón 2010; Martínez Pabello 2017.

[11] Otero Pilonieta 2018; Uprimny Yepes and Rodríguez Garavito 2005.

[12] Calderón Gamboa 2013.

[13] Saavedra Alessandri 2017.

[14] Saavedra Alessandri 2017.

[15] Murray and Sandoval 2020.

[16] Murray and Sandoval 2020.

violation identified and some structural deficiency that contributed to the noncompliance. Calderón Gamboa identifies that the IACtHR issues such reparations according to certain elements as the type of facts that occur, the violations declared in each case, the damages proven, and the outstanding characteristics of the victims. These guiding criteria do not respond to the form in which they intervene.

Measures of non-repetition are, in general, directed at the State as a whole.[17] Therefore, beyond the fact that they are of mandatory compliance as previously described, it is sought that all state bodies, within the framework of their competences, adopt the necessary measures to enforce the measure of non-repetition.

With the aim of promoting compliance with its orders, the IACtHR retains jurisdiction to monitor compliance of its decisions.[18] Thus, the case remains under its cognizance until it declares full compliance with the totality of remedies ordered.[19] In the framework of the supervision of compliance with the judgment, the Court can assess the degree of compliance of a specific remedy, guide the parties on alternatives to comply with the orders, promote spaces for interaction between States and victims to reach agreements on how to carry out the implementation, incorporate other interested parties in the process of implementation of these reparation measures, among other possibilities aimed at the ultimate goal of achieving compliance with the judgment.[20]

4.3 Public Policy, the IACtHR's Actions and Other International Human Rights Mechanisms

For the purposes of this research, public policy is understood as encompassing any state intervention that aims to solve a public problem.[21] The public policy cycle is a useful tool to identify the different stages of policy making and implementation. For the purposes of this study, a simplified version of the public policy cycle was used,

[17] IACtHR, *Artavia Murillo y Otros (Fecundación in Vitro) v Costa Rica*, Supervisión de Cumplimiento de Sentencia, 26 February 2016; Perez 2018.

[18] IACtHR, *Baena Ricardo y Otros v Panamá*, Competencia. Serie C No. 104, 28 November 2003.

[19] Sanchez de Miguel 2018.

[20] Perez 2018.

[21] Arellano Gault 2013; Torres-Melo 2013.

divided into four stages:[22] agenda setting,[23] policy formulation,[24] policy implementation[25] and evaluation.[26] This definition of the cycle is valuable because it is the one proposed by the Inter-American Commission on Human Rights in its studies on the relationship between public policy and human rights.[27]

Within the universe of problems that may be the object of a public intervention, many of them are constitutive of human rights violations, both by action and omission from the state.[28] Thus, public policies are tools that can also contribute directly or indirectly to the respect, guarantee or fulfillment of a human right.

Under contemporary Latin American constitutionalism, human rights have to play an important role in the public policy cycle. Recognizing these rights as constitutional norms, as is the case in most Latin American countries, and the recognition that they are goals to be achieved has provided them with an important role in the different stages of the public policy cycle.[29] The Inter-American Commission on Human Rights prepared a manual with proposals for *policy makers* to incorporate a human rights vision within the public policy cycle.[30]

These objectives articulate with article 2 of the American Convention. This rule provides that "the States Parties undertake to adopt, in accordance with their constitutional processes and the provisions of this Convention, such legislative or other measures as may be necessary to give effect to those rights or freedoms". Therefore, when faced with a public problem that constitutes a violation of the obligations set forth in the Convention, States are under an obligation to transform their legislation and practices to bring them into conformity with the Convention.[31]

Structural remedies aspire to generate a transformative impact, becoming a catalyst that uses the development of its own jurisprudence to achieve the objectives

22 Shiffman 2008; Torres-Melo 2013.

23 Agenda setting will be understood as the incorporation or pretension of incorporating a public problem within governmental priorities, as possible issues that should be the subject of a public policy. Torres-Melo 2013; Zahariadis 2016.

24 Policy formulation will be understood as any measure that is aimed at identifying the specific problem that will be the object of a public policy, analyzing possible alternatives for dealing with it, and with the objective of suggesting a proposal on how to deal with it. Torres-Melo 2013; Veselý 2017.

It shall encompass the process of finding, designing and defining the solution to a public problem. Howlett and Mukherjee 2017.

25 Policy implementation measure if its order implies carrying out a public policy decision that has already been adopted; Torres-Melo 2013.

26 Evaluation of a public policy if it seeks to determine the performance of a pre-existing policy; Torres Melo 2013.

27 Inter-American Commission of Human Rights 2018.

28 Inter-American Commission of Human Rights 2018.

29 Abramovich 2006; Courtis and Abramovich 2001; Hunt 2016; Pautassi 2017.

30 Inter-American Commission of Human Rights 2018, p. 50.

31 Ferrer Mac-Gregor and Pelayo Moller 2019.

provided for by the American Convention itself.[32] They are thus the ultimate means to achieve the transformational mandate the IACtHR understands it has.

This does not mean that structural remedies are the only means that the IACtHR or an international court may impact in policy making, regardless of whether they have a transformational mandate or not. The decisions of international human rights courts help to put on the agenda certain government and market problems that require attention,[33] regardless of there being a structural remedy. Likewise, the initiation of the processing of a case before the IACtHR, the holding of hearings (both in merits stages and in the stage of supervision of compliance with judgments), visits, and other procedural actions of the court, the issuance of advisory opinions, among others, may also have an indirect impact on the public agenda.[34] For example, these actions may be echoed in the media, promote actions from the non-litigant civil society, among others, which could have an impact on the public policy cycle.[35]

Other international human rights bodies may intervene as well in public policy processes, although to a very different extent. The European Court of Human Rights does not order measures of non-repetition similar to those ordered by the IACtHR. That court, in general, orders measures of financial compensation and, very exceptionally, some measures of a different nature. However, its jurisprudential developments serve as an agenda-setting mechanism for public policy issues.[36] The African Court on Human and Peoples' Rights retains jurisdiction to order guarantees of non-repetition in its respective cases. Despite the few precedents of the African Court, there are examples that reflect a wide variety of non-repetition measures, similar to that ordered by the IACHR Court.[37]

Within the United Nations system, treaty bodies such as the Human Rights Committee, the Committee on Economic, Social and Cultural Rights, and the Committee on the Elimination of All Forms of Discrimination against Women also have jurisdiction to issue structural remedies. However, in practice, it appears that their orders favor leaving room for the State to decide on how to implement.[38] In addition, it does not have a mechanism for supervising compliance with the decisions like that of the IACtHR, which accompanies the case until full compliance, but has one of lesser intensity.[39]

However, the IACtHR's extraordinary approach to structural remedies has been the subject of significant criticism. In 2019, five States requested the IACtHR "that

[32] Von Bogdandy 2020.

[33] Helfer and Voeten 2014.

[34] Sandoval et al. 2020. IACtHR, *Comunidad Indígena Sawhoyamaxa v Paraguay*, Supervisión de Cumplimiento de Sentencia, 14 May 2019.

[35] IACtHR, *Barrios Altos y La Cantuta v Perú*, Solicitud de Medidas Provisionales y Supervisión de Cumplimiento de Sentencia, 7 April 2022.

[36] Helfer and Voeten 2014.

[37] Kioko 2020, p. 163.

[38] Joseph et al. 2006. 'The Covenant on Civil and Political Rights - Description' (*Bayefesky.com*) http://www.bayefsky.com/complain/10_ccpr.php, Accessed 18 April 2022.

[39] Fox Principi 2020, p. 185.

the forms of reparation should maintain due proportionality and respect both the constitutional and legal systems of the States, as well as the requirements of the rule of law."[40] Throughout the process of selecting judges that took place during the year 2021, multiple concerns of the States referred to the extent to which the IACtHR was providing reparations, including structural remedies.[41] The impact of these concerns has yet to be studied in depth.

4.4 Methods[42]

As of 2021, the IACtHR had issued 448 judgments, of which 176 included structural remedies. Many of these 176 judgments contain more than one structural remedy. Eight judgments were excluded as they corresponded to friendly settlement agreements, where the IACtHR did not intervene substantially in the drafting of the structural remedy order.

Data collection was achieved through three stages: (1) preliminary data collected from twenty-three randomly selected decisions,[43] one per year in which a non-repetition measure had been identified. Randomization sought to ensure that all the Court's compositions were represented at least once; (2) thirteen semi structured interviews[44] were carried out to officials and former officials of the IACtHR in order to validate the categories identified in the prior stage with respect to the rationalities and, if possible, to identify new rationalities that had not been identified. The interviews provided "behind the scenes" information that officials wished to share that made visible factors that contribute to a decision being made that might normally be overlooked through strictly legal analysis.[45] The interviews contributed "subjective experiences, opinions, and motivations" that informed this research.[46] Finally, (3) all judgments with structural remedies were codified[47] under categories identified in the first two stages.

---

[40] Ministerio de Relaciones Exteriores de Paraguay 2019, https://www.mre.gov.py/index.php/noticias-de-embajadas-y-consulados/gobiernos-de-argentina-brasil-chile-colombia-y-paraguay-se-manifiestan-sobre-el-sistema-interamericano-de-derechos-humanos. Accessed 3 October 2021.

[41] Bernal 2021.

[42] Methods were approved by Universidad de los Andes's ethics committee (Colombia).

[43] The decisions with structural remedies were coded under a dummy variable. Stata® was used for randomization. The algorithm used sought to have the program identify a random sample by year of sentences ('count by') that contained non-repetition measures. It was excluded from the algorithm ('drop if') if the sentence did not contain at least one non-repetition measure.

[44] The selection of interviewees followed the following premises: (1) a snowball method was used, inviting those who were indicated by the first interviewees (Merkens 2004) (2) not all the people invited responded in time, (3) interviews were conducted between January and March 2022.

[45] Jaremba and Mak 2014.

[46] Busetto et al. 2020.

[47] Hall and Wright 2006.

Data analysis also had different stages. Each structural remedy within each judgment was identified and codified according to year of judgment, State involved, stage of policy cycle, association with context in the decision,[48] breach of article 2 of the Convention determined by IACtHR,[49] NGO/individual representing the victim; whether it was requested by the party;[50] expressed State willingness of the State to comply,[51] and data available on preexisting policies.[52] These categories were identified based on data obtained from interviews and the preliminary review of the remedies. They were grouped through axial coding.[53] Furthermore, they were codified according to the stage of the policy cycle proposed: agenda setting,[54] policy formulation,[55] policy implementation[56] and policy evaluation.[57]

---

48 Aims to justify, by means of a dummy variable (1 = affirmative; 0 = negative) whether within the chapter corresponding to the non-repetition measure it is explained which structural problem the sentence intends to correct with the measure. It should be noted that 0 does not mean that the measure does not seek to resolve a public problem identified in the sentence, but rather that the chapter corresponding to the non-repetition measure does not expressly state the problem it seeks to address.

49 The purpose is to make visible, by means of a dummy variable (1 = affirmative; 0 = negative), whether the chapter corresponding to the measure of non-repetition expressly states that the measure responds to a violation of Article 2 of the American Convention. Again, 0 does not mean that there is no violation of Article 2 in the case, but rather that the reasons for the measure of non-repetition are not expressly mentioned.

50 The purpose is to make visible whether the measure of non-repetition was requested by any party to the litigation by means of a dummy variable (1 = affirmative; 0 = negative). As the IACtHR has the power to formulate its measure at its discretion and to interpret the requests of the parties at its discretion, 1 is considered to the extent that there are substantial similarities between what was requested by the party and what was ordered by the Court.

51 This willingness must be expressed in the decision to qualify as affirmative.

52 The purpose is to analyze whether the IACtHR included in its motivation any data or reference to the public policy prior to its order, through a dummy variable (1 = affirmative; 0 = negative). Any reference to the public policy in force and on which it intends to intervene is included as 1, regardless of how detailed this reference is, and that it is referenced in the section on the non-repetition measure or to which it refers from that chapter. Any acknowledgement of the existence of the pre-existing public policy in the motivation within the judgment will be considered as affirmative.

53 Simmons 2017.

54 It will be classified as an agenda-setting structural remedy if it answers the following question in the affirmative: does the measure mandate the inclusion of a public or social problem among the government's priorities?

55 A structural remedy will be classified as a *public policy formulation* if it answers the following question in the affirmative: does the measure identify a specific alternative to be implemented, does it identify the failure that generated the human rights violation that must be modified, or does it require a specific action by the State aimed at addressing a public problem? Therefore, non-repetition measures that provide specific orders on how to address a public problem will fall into this category.

56 It will be classified as a structural remedy of *implementation* if it answers the following question in the affirmative: is it ordered to implement a public policy already existing or to exist in the State?

57 It will be classified as a measure of non-repetition of *public policy evaluation* if it answers the following question in the affirmative: is the State ordered to evaluate the performance of a pre-existing or to-be-existing public policy?

4.5 Results

4.5.1 Distribution of Structural Remedies According to Stage within the Public Policy Cycle

Between 1989 and 2021, the IACtHR has issued 301 judgments in which it has ordered reparations. As previously mentioned, of these, 176 judgments issued structural remedies. There are 8 judgments whose structural remedies derive from an approved friendly settlement agreement, and which were not included in this study. Taking into account the above, during this period of time, the IACtHR issued a total of 334 structural remedies, issued in 168 judgments. The study reveals that the IACtHR intervenes substantially in the different stages of the public policy cycle.

An aspect that must be clarified preliminarily is that the percentages available clearly do not total 100%. As argued before, many structural remedies imply interventions in more than one public policy stage. The percentages below show exclusively the percentages of the intervention in a determined policy stage, regardless of whether they intervene in other stages simultaneously. Thus, it is the number of structural remedies in one policy stage *vis-à-vis* the total number of structural remedies issued (334).[58]

151 of these remedies (45.21% of the 334 structural remedies) were identified as falling within the agenda-setting stage. In these cases, as opposed to simply referring to the issue in the judgment, the intervention of the IACtHR seeks to place the identified public problem on the public agenda. The IACtHR, in this way, becomes an agent external to the State that seeks to break (*punctuate*) the balance between policies within the internationally responsible State.[59]

For example, in the *Petro Urrego v. Colombia* case, the Court ruled in its 2020 decision that the State "shall, within a reasonable period of time, bring its domestic legal system into conformity with the parameters established in this Judgment."[60] This measure refers to paragraphs 111 to 116 and 154 of the judgment where it determined the incompatibility with international human rights law of the powers of the Office of the Attorney General of the Nation and the Office of the Comptroller General of the Republic in Colombia to disqualify a public official. Although the Court analyzed how certain norms contribute to perpetuate this situation, such as Article 277.6 of the Constitution, norms of the Single Disciplinary Code and Law 610 of 2000, the Court refrained from requiring the modification of such norms or

[58] The full database is available at: https://www.researchgate.net/publication/373999991_2022_04_26_Base_de_Datos_Final. Accessed 16 September 2023.

[59] Cairney 2020.

[60] IACtHR, *Petro Urrego v Colombia*, Excepciones Preliminares, Fondo, Reparaciones y Costas, 8 July 2020, Serie C No 406, para 156.

adopting any concrete measures.[61] It only limited itself to ordering as a structural remedy that the identified legal problem be resolved so that similar events would not be repeated. This had a direct impact on the Colombian public agenda. In 2021, Congress approved Law 2094, which sought to immediately address several of the requirements, despite the fact that the IACtHR considered that this reform did not meet the aspirations of the same judgment.[62]

242 structural remedies (72.46% of the 334 structural remedies studied) constituted policy formulation. There is a significant preeminence of these measures in the universe of remedies studied. However, just as the concept of formulation is quite broad, the ways in which the IACtHR intervenes at this stage also occur with degrees of strength.[63] Thus, there are cases in which the IACtHR orders the State to formulate public policy leaving the State with some degree of flexibility, while there are other cases in which the IACtHR formulates public policy entirely.

For example, the IACtHR in the 2018 *López Soto v. Venezuela* case ordered the State to "incorporate into the national curriculum of the National Education System, at all levels and educational modalities, a permanent education program under the name of 'Linda Loaiza'" aimed at "eradicating gender discrimination, gender stereotypes and violence against women in Venezuela, in light of international standards on the matter and the jurisprudence of this Court".[64] In this sense, it is observed that the Court made the decision on the name of the program, its territorial scope, and in general terms its content, leaving a limited margin for Venezuela to do something different. A public policy formulation of lesser force is found in the case of *Molina Theissen v. Guatemala*, where the Court ordered "to create an expeditious procedure to obtain the declaration of absence and presumption of death due to forced disappearance", without further specification.[65] The Court thus required Guatemala to formulate the required policy, only stating its objectives, and leaving a greater margin of action to the State to decide how to meet the challenge.

In those cases in which the formulation of a public policy is provided for through legislation, the IACtHR also reflects these differences in the forces of intervention. A greater force is observed in the case of *Urrutia Laubreaux v. Chile* of 2020, where the Court directly ordered the State to "abolish numeral 4 of Article 323 of the Organic Code of Courts" because of its impact on the independence of the judiciary.[66] A lesser degree of intervention is found in those cases where the legislative modification ordered gives room for maneuver to the State. For example, in the 2007 case of

[61] IACtHR, *Petro Urrego v Colombia,* Excepciones Preliminares, Fondo, Reparaciones y Costas, 8 July 2020, Serie C No 406.

[62] IACtHR, *Petro Urrego v Colombia, Supervisión de Cumplimiento de Sentencia,* 25 November 2021.

[63] Tushnet 2008.

[64] IACtHR, *López Soto y Otros v Venezuela,* Fondo, Reparaciones y Costas, 26 September 2018, Serie C No. 362, para 345.

[65] IACtHR, *Molina Theissen v Guatemala,* Reparaciones y Costas, 3 July 2004, Serie C No. 108, para 91.

[66] IACtHR, *Urrutia Laubreaux v Chile, Excepciones Preliminares, Fondo, Reparaciones y Costas,* 27 August 2020, Serie C No 409, para 150.

Chaparro Álvarez and Lapo Iñiguez v. Ecuador, the Court ordered "to modify within a reasonable period of time the Law on Narcotic and Psychotropic Substances and its pertinent regulatory resolutions, in order to stop charging for the deposit and handling of goods that are seized in accordance with said Law to persons who have not been convicted by a final judgment".[67]

169 structural remedies were identified in which the IACtHR intervenes in the policy implementation stage (50.59% of the 334 structural remedies). It is clear that the IACtHR, being an international court, cannot implement a public policy on its own. However, the IACtHR does issue orders for the State to implement a certain public policy. For example, in the cases of *Véliz Franco vs. Guatemala*[68] and *Velásquez Paiz vs. Guatemala*[69] the IACtHR took note of the existence of a public policy formulated in that State under which it undertook to implement "specialized jurisdictional bodies" and a "specialized prosecutor's office", provided for in the Law against Femicide enacted in 2008, several years before the issuance of those judgments. Thus, the public policy was already formulated in the law, but its implementation was pending. The IACtHR's structural remedy was to order that these bodies be put into operation.

Finally, the intervention of the IACtHR in the evaluation stage of a public policy, in contrast to the others, has been considerably scarce. Only two cases were identified (0.60%) in which the IACtHR intervened in some way in this stage of the cycle. The most prominent case is the judgment of *Fábrica de Fuegos Artificiales de San Antonio de Jesús v. Brazil* of 2020. In that case, the IACtHR ordered Brazil to submit a report "on the application of the National Guidelines on Business and Human Rights," requesting input on "the promotion and support of measures of inclusion and non-discrimination through the creation of incentive programs for the hiring of vulnerable groups" and "the implementation by companies of educational activities on human rights, with the dissemination of national legislation and international parameters and a focus on standards relevant to the practice of individuals and risks to human rights."[70] The IACtHR has yet to issue a ruling interpreting the scope of this measure and how far it will go in evaluating the policy, or how far it will require Brazil to make an evaluation of the policy.

It is important to clarify that the public policy cycle is very permeable, allowing for many structural remedies to be classified in more than one stage. For instance, 160 structural remedies intervened in both policy formulation and implementation

---

[67] IACtHR, *Chaparro Álvarez y Lapo Íñiguez v Ecuador*, Excepciones Preliminares, Fondo, Reparaciones y Costas, 21 November 2007, Serie C No. 170, para 269.

[68] IACtHR, *Véliz Franco y otros v Guatemala,* Excepciones Preliminares, Fondo, Reparaciones y Costas, 19 May 2014, Serie C No 277.

[69] IACtHR, *Velásquez Paiz y Otros v Guatemala*, Excepciones Preliminares, Fondo, Reparaciones y Costas, 19 November 2015, Serie C No. 307.

[70] IACtHR, *Los Empleados de La Fábrica de Fuegos de Santo Antônio de Jesus y Sus Familiares v Brasil*, Excepciones Preliminares, Fondo, Reparaciones y Costas, 15 July 2020, Serie C No. 407.

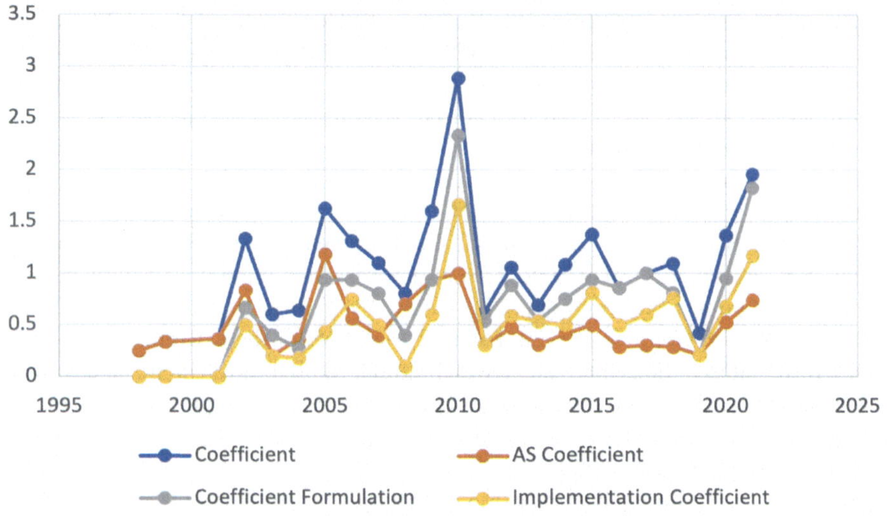

Fig. 4.1 Coefficient per stage of the cycle where it intervenes.[72] *Source* Perez 2022

(47.9%), meaning that the IACtHR formulates the policy but also orders its implementation. In the case of *Yarce v. Colombia*, for example, the Court ordered "to implement, [...] a program, course or workshop [...] to be offered by the corresponding state entities within the Comuna 13", adding, among other aspects, that the facts of that case should be included in its agenda "in order to exemplify the risks that the defense of human rights can entail and thus promote recognition of those who work in this task".[71]

4.5.2 *Rationalities Underlying the Decision to Intervene in Different Stages of the Policy Cycle*

This section will seek to explore some of the rationalities that possibly influence the decision on the stage of the public policy cycle. As previously anticipated, the analysis described here is based on both judgments and interviews. However, it is not intended to reflect an exhaustive list of potential rationalities.

First, it can be observed that over time the trends regarding the stage at which the IACtHR intervenes have changed (see Fig. 4.1).

---

[71] IACtHR, *Yarce y Otras v Colombia*, Excepción Preliminar, Fondo, Reparaciones y Costas, 22 November 2016, Serie C No. 325, para 350.

[72] Since the IACtHR issued a different number of judgments, the above can be measured using a coefficient that relates the number of structural remedies, classified by the stage of the cycle in which they intervene, with respect to the number of judgments issued, in order to standardize the data. The blue line shows the result of the number of structural remedies issued divided by the

The general trend until 2010 was to favor agenda-setting measures, while from that year onwards, structural remedies aimed at the formulation and implementation of the sentence began to be favored in a notorious way. The paradigm shift in 2009 may reflect an incorporation of a policy logic in its judgments. This conclusion finds further support. Interviews with IACtHR officials reflect a general perception about the need to develop more specific measures of non-repetition, which could be associated with formulation and implementation stages of the policy cycle. Furthermore, the *Campo Algodonero vs. Mexico* case was the case that began to give a public policy "logic" to non-repetition measures, as described in one of the interviews. In this decision, when analyzing the public policies that Mexico has carried out to combat gender-based violence, the IACtHR refrained of analyzing whether they were problematic "without information on the structural flaws in these policies, the problems in their implementation processes and their results on the effective enjoyment of rights by the victims of such violence", and without "outcome indicators regarding how the policies implemented by the State can constitute reparations with a gender perspective".[73]

Second, there was a general tendency among the interviews to argue that there can be a relationship between the States and the type of non-repetition measure ordered. This assertion also finds validation in the data collected for this analysis. As shown in the following figure (see Fig. 4.2 below), a clear trend can be observed: most of the States reflect a tendency whereby structural remedies associated with the formulation of public policies are the majority, followed by those corresponding to implementation.

Trinidad and Tobago, Venezuela, Dominican Republic and Haiti reflect a lower coefficient of implementation measures with respect to the others. This could be associated with the lower rates of interaction that these States have with respect to the Inter-American system. All four States have been identified as States that are in a position of serious non-compliance with the decisions of the IACHR Court.[74] Trinidad and Tobago and Venezuela have denounced the American Convention on Human Rights. A recent study argues that the probabilities of compliance by these are 0% for Venezuela, Trinidad and Tobago and Haiti, and 0.01% for the Dominican Republic.[75] The case of Barbados, on the other hand, may be justified in the substantial differences in the legal systems of continental Latin America with respect to the Anglo-Saxon system. Interviews stated that in this case the different legal systems favor an agenda-setting approach, a result confirmed with the data collected.

Third, several interviews sustained that there was perceived relationship between the representation of victims and the provision of a structural remedy at one or

number of cases decided overall. The orange, gray and yellow lines show the result of the number of structural remedies issued per stage of the public policy cycle divided by the number of cases.

[73] IACtHR, *González y Otras ("Campo Algodonero") v México*, Excepción Preliminar, Fondo, Reparaciones y Costas, 16 November 2009, Serie C No. 205, paras 495-496.

[74] IACtHR, *Niñas Yean y Bosico y Personas Dominicanas y Haitianas Expulsadas v República Dominicana*, Supervisión de Cumplimiento de Sentencias y Competencia, 12 March 2019; IACtHR 2020a, b, c.

[75] Pérez Liñán et al. 2019.

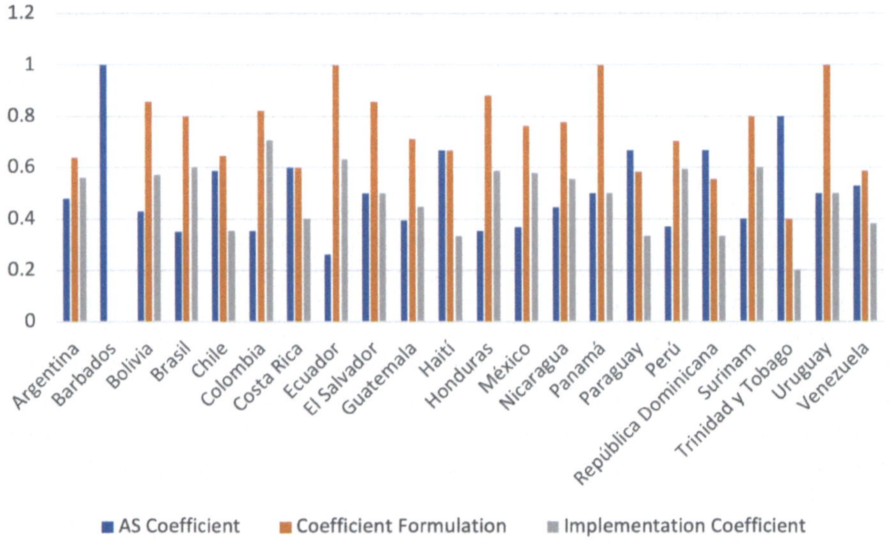

Fig. 4.2 Relation between intervention in public policy cycle and number of structural remedies per country.[76] *Source* Perez 2022

another stage of the public policy cycle. This perception also finds basis in the collected data. The Center for Justice and International Law (CEJIL) is the most assiduous user of the Inter-American Human Rights System throughout its history. It has participated in litigation that has resulted in 130 measures of non-repetition out of the 334 documented, representing 38.92% of all the measures of this nature ordered. Of these non-repetition measures, 57 were classified as agenda-setting, 100 were classified as formulation, and 69 were classified as implementation. Inter-American Public Defenders appointed for those cases in which the victims do not have legal representation have achieved 3 agenda-setting measures, 12 formulation measures, and 11 public policy implementation measures. Victims' representatives who have acted individually and not under the auspices of an organization have achieved 41 agenda-setting, 40 formulation, and 28 implementation measures.

It should be noted that the data on the total number of cases that CEJIL, the Inter-American Public Defenders, or any other organization has represented was not collected, so the information described in this paragraph should be analyzed with caution. This does not preclude that this information can serve as an indication of potential influence of the organization representing the victim with respect to the

[76] Given that each State also has a different number of sentences, a coefficient was be developed to try to standardize the data to be compared. This coefficient was generated as a function of the ratio between the stage in which it intervenes with respect to the number of non-repetition measures per country. Thus, the blue column reflects the division of the number of agenda setting measures divided by the number of cases per State. The orange column reflects the same with policy formulation measures, and the gray one reflects on policy implementation ones.

stage of the public policy cycle in which they intervene, as more experienced organizations may be able to achieve more formulation measures *vis-à-vis* less experienced representatives. Interviews validated this conclusion, arguing that there are certain organizations that have more technical expertise and experience in litigation before the IACtHR, and that, therefore, they make the requests and present the necessary evidence in a way that allows them to have sufficient elements to succeed.

Fourth, all of the interviews reflected that the determination of a violation of Article 2 of the American Convention on Human Rights influences the design of the measure of non-repetition. Of the 334 measures of non-repetition, 100 expressly included Article 2 of the American Convention as part of their reasoning. Of these 100, 81 were classified as agenda-setting measures, 62 as formulation measures, and 15 as implementation measures. Thus, it would appear that the violation of Article 2 of the American Convention could be related primarily to agenda-setting measures. These statistics may have an empirical basis in the IACtHR's case law, inasmuch as Article 2 application has been mostly oriented to require constitutional, legal and regulatory normative adjustments, but that following the precedents of the IACtHR, this norm exhorts that these objectives must be adopted in accordance with the constitutional procedures for the modification of the norms of each State.[77] The greater deference needed to achieve these objectives justifies that the measures derived from violations of Article 2 of the Convention are mostly subsumed within those of agenda-setting.

Fifth, 238 structural remedies (71.26%) make some reference to the context they seek to correct with the non-repetition measure, even if only superficially.[78] The context makes reference to "the historical, social or political context of the cases, since this allows 'situating the facts alleged as violating the American Convention in the framework of the specific circumstances in which they occurred' and characterizing 'the facts as part of a systematic pattern of human rights violations, as a practice applied or tolerated by the State or as part of massive and systematic or generalized attacks against some sector of the population'".[79] The relationship between the structural remedy and the context should be the causal nexus between them.[80] Of the structural remedies that makes some reference to the context within its reasons, 120 were classified as agenda-setting, 176 as formulation, and 111 as implementation of public policy. On the other hand, of those that do not refer to the context, 31 correspond to agenda setting, 66 to formulation, and 57 to implementation. These data seem to reflect that in those cases in which the context is directly linked to the motivation of the structural remedy, the probability that the measure will be classified as implementation decreases. However, no reason is identified either in the interviews or in the literature to justify this difference.

---

[77] Ferrer Mac-Gregor and Pelayo Moller 2019.

[78] A positive response for the purposes of this statistic is limited to a reference of the context the remedy was intended to respond to in the sections of the judgment corresponding to the structural remedies.

[79] IACtHR, *López Lone y Otros v Honduras*, Excepción Preliminar, Fondo, Reparaciones y Costas, 5 October 2015, Serie C No. 302; Paúl 2020.

[80] Calderón Gamboa 2013.

Sixth, interviews unanimously perceived that the IACtHR would intervene in different stages of the policy cycle according to the terms a similar remedy was requested by the parties of the litigation. In 242 out of 334 of the non-repetition measures that form part of this study, one of the parties proposed a structural remedy in terms reasonably similar to how it was granted. Therefore, the cases in which the measure was issued by the IACtHR *motu proprio motu* are exceptional. However, it should be noted that there are multiple examples where the request of the parties was subsequently modified in scope by the IACtHR itself. Therefore, it is difficult to identify from the judgments what was the degree of influence of the pleading.

For instance, in the *Petro Urrego* case, the Inter-American Commission and the representatives requested an order to modify "the Political Constitution and the Single Disciplinary Code, which respectively contemplate the power to remove and disqualify popularly elected officials by the Office of the Attorney General of the Nation in the exercise of its disciplinary power," requiring intervention with greater force than what the IACtHR Court ultimately ordered, which maintained the measure of non-repetition in the agenda-setting stage.[81] Thus, although it is perceived that there is some degree of relationship between the request for a structural remedy and the order issued, it would seem that the decision on the stage of the public policy cycle in which it intervenes is not so closely linked to the terms in which it is requested by the IACtHR Court. This situation, in turn, could be associated with the court's perception of aspiring to ensure that its decisions have a real impact and that its decisions are complied with.

Seventh, the interviews reflected a perception where the IACtHR, when it identifies that the respondent States reflect openness to adopt measures aimed at addressing public policies within their country, is more likely to order structural remedies in more advanced stages of the policy cycle. However, this perception of a favorable will tends not to be clearly visible in the judgments. Only 50 of them reflect some express reference to the good will of the State prior to the judgment, of which 31 provided for a public policy formulation measure, 26 for agenda-setting, and 21 for implementation. An emblematic example is the order of the Inter-American Court of Human Rights in the *Bedoya Lima* case,[82] in which the IACtHR ordered the creation of the "No es Hora de Callar Investigative Center", to contribute to the dignification of women victims of sexual violence during the armed conflict and as a consequence of the practice of journalism. The initial proposal to present this measure was presented by the Colombian State itself. However, the State's allegations that allow measuring its position with respect to reparations are little developed in the litigation process and the judgment. Thus, it is hard to identify the extent of this relation.

Finally, in only 172 of the measures of non-repetition analyzed (51.5%), the IACtHR directly or indirectly takes into consideration public policies with respect to the problem under analysis that preexist the judgment, and expressly states it in

[81] IACtHR, *Petro Urrego v Colombia*, Excepciones Preliminares, Fondo, Reparaciones y Costas, 8 July 2020, Serie C No. 406, paras 151-154.

[82] IACtHR, *Bedoya Lima y Otra v Colombia*, Fondo, Reparaciones y Costas, 26 August 2021, Serie C No. 431.

its reasons for issuing the structural remedy. Although there is no noticeable change in the distribution trends between the stage of the public policy cycle where they intervene, whether or not the existence of a public policy is reflected, the interviews do reflect the need for the IACtHR to receive information on these pre-existing policies to identify whether it is necessary to interfere within the public policy cycle, at all, and if so, how to intervene.

Specific reference must be made to the budget. None of the structural remedies make reference to the State's budgetary situation or the budgetary impact that any intervention ordered by the IACtHR will have. This, despite the fact that in many cases the parties have requested that the state budget be taken into account when defining the policies to be carried out.[83] The Court should deal with budgetary concerns when issuing structural remedies to improve compliance rates, as was stated by the people interviewed. They expressed the importance and the need to start taking the budget into account when deciding on a measure of non-repetition and determining the form of its intervention, as in many occasions the main obstacle to compliance is precisely inappropriate budgeting to achieve the goals of the topic.

4.6 Conclusions

Three clear conclusions are obtained from this chapter: (1) that the IACtHR intervenes in the public policy cycle of the States under its jurisdiction,[84] (2) that it has progressively intervened in more advanced stages of the public policy cycle, and (3) that rationalities on how the IACtHR intervenes are not necessarily clear in the judgments. Furthermore, there are elements that are perceived as factors that have an impact on the stage of the public policy cycle that the IACtHR intervenes in. It seems that the State that is the object of the decision, the representation of the victims and the identification of a violation of Article 2 of the Convention influence the outcome of the structural remedy issued.

On the other hand, there are some rationales that are perceived by the persons interviewed as relevant when issuing a structural remedy, but that are not as evident in the judgments. For instance, the relationship between the context and the order, the relationship between what was requested by the parties and what was ordered, the openness to change on the part of the responsible State, and the availability of information on existing public policies, on the other hand, were not so clearly identified within the decisions as factors that were determinant but were considered relevant within the interviews.

[83] IACtHR, *Gonzales Lluy y Otros v Ecuador*, Excepciones Preliminares, Fondo, Reparaciones y Costas, 1 September 2015, Serie C No. 298.

[84] Those interviewed maintained divided positions on whether it is desirable for the Inter-American Court to intervene in all stages of the public policy cycle. This discussion, however, was not discussed in depth in this research.

These results open opportunities for new research. Having established that the IACtHR intervenes at any stage of the cycle, and taking into account that the Court's intention, according to most of the interviews, is that its decisions generate a real impact, it could adopt a series of tools for the analysis of public policies (policy diagnostics, knowledge of budget availability, indicator development, dialogue with more actors than the parties in litigation, among others) to try to improve its impact. The results further favor a need to examine how the Court interacts with previously existing policies, as the data analyzed is a clear indicative that the Court wishes to intervene as a policy maker. Alternatively, the IACtHR could maintain a dialogue with members of the State and civil society with the capacity to carry out these analyses when defining what remedy it will issue.

A different idea that should be introduced is that of litigation with a public policy perspective. The entire judicial process before the IACtHR should seek not only to determine the responsibility of States, but also to generate opportunities to obtain information that will allow for an analysis of existing public policies and the reforms that are necessary. The current procedure before the IACtHR is mainly oriented towards determining the existence of human rights violations and making visible the structural problems that lie behind these violations. Therefore, all parties to the process tend to favor in time and effort their legal arguments, leaving at a lower level of importance the possibility of the IACtHR to order structural remedies, as is logical given that it has judicial review in its core.

Acknowledgement The author wishes to acknowledge the invaluable support of Dr. Juan David Gutiérrez for his valuable insights, feedback and support in the development of this chapter.

References

Abramovich V (2006) Una aproximación al enfoque de derechos en las estrategias y políticas de desarrollo. Revista de la CEPAL: 35–50. https://doi.org/10.18356/a48f3cca-es

America RF (1998) Reparations and Public Policy. The Review of Black Political Economy 26: 77–83

Arellano Gault D (2013) Políticas públicas y democracia. Instituto Federal Electoral

Baum L (1983) Understanding Courts as Policy Makers. American Bar Foundation Research Journal 8:241–250

Bernal C (2021) Tres Desafíos de Legitimidad Del Sistema Interamericano de Derechos Humanos [Three Legitimacy Challenges to the Inter-American System of Human Rights]. International Journal of Constitutional Law 19:1213–1217

Busetto L, Wick W, Gumbinger C (2020) How to Use and Assess Qualitative Research Methods. Neurological Research and Practice 2:14

Cairney P (2020) Punctuated Equilibrium Theory, Understanding Public Policy—Theories and Issues, 2nd edn. Palgrave Macmillan, London, pp 147–167

Calderón Gamboa JF (2013) La reparación integral en la jurisprudencia de la Corte Interamericana de Derechos Humanos estándares aplicables al nuevo paradigma mexicano. Instituto de Investigaciones Jurídicas Suprema Corte de Justicia de la Nación, Fundación Konrad Adenauer, pp. 1–75

Cano Blandón LF (2010) Eficacia de Los Derechos Sociales: Análisis de Las Sentencias de Tutela y de Las Políticas Públicas Para Su Protección En La Subregión Del Magdalena Medio Antioqueño. Estudios de Derecho 67:149

Cano Blandón LF (2015a) El litigio estructural en salud: un estudio comparado con base en casos de Sudáfrica, Argentina, India y Colombia. Revista Facultad Nacional de Salud Pública 33:111, pp. 111–120

Cano Blandón LF (2015b) La narrativa de las políticas públicas en la jurisprudencia de la Corte Constitucional colombiana. Papel Político 19:2, p. 435

Courtis C, Abramovich V (2001) Apuntes sobre la exigibilidad judicial de los derechos sociales. Cuadernos electrónicos de filosofía del derecho 4

Ferrer Mac-Gregor E, Pelayo Moller C (2019) Artículo 2. Deber de Adoptar Disposiciones de Derecho Interno. In: Steiner C et al. (eds) Convención Americana sobre Derechos Humanos: comentario, 2nd edn. Konrad Adenauer Stiftung, Bogota, pp 71–105

Fox Principi K (2020) Implementation of UN Treaty Body Decisions: A Brief Insight for Practitioners. Journal of Human Rights Practice 12: 185-192

Hall M, Wright R (2006) Systematic Content Analysis of Judicial Opinions. California Law Rev 96

Helfer LR, Voeten E (2014) International Courts as Agents of Legal Change: Evidence from LGBT Rights in Europe. International Organization 68: 77–110

Herrero Á (2011) La Incidencia de La Corte Suprema de Justicia En La Formulación de Políticas Públicas: Una Exploración Empírica Del Caso Argentino. Revista de Ciencia Política 49

Howlett M, Mukherjee I (2017) Policy Formulation: Where Knowledge Meets Power in the Policy Process. In: Howlett M, Mukherjee I (eds) Handbook of policy formulation. Edward Elgar Publishing, Cheltenham, 3–22

Hunt P (2016) Interpreting the International Right to Health in a Human Rights-Based Approach to Health. Health and Human Rights 18: 109–130

IACtHR (2020) Informe Anual 2020 https://corteidh.or.cr/docs/informe2020/espanol.pdf Accessed 16 September 2023

Inter-American Commission of Human Rights (2018) Políticas Públicas Con Enfoque de Derechos Humanos. OEA/Ser.L/V/II. 191

Jaremba U, Mak E (2014) Interviewing Judges in the Transnational Context. Recht en Methode in onderzoek en onderwijs https://doi.org/10.5553/REM/.000003

Joseph S et al. (2006) Seeking Remedies for Torture Victims: A Handbook on the Individual Complaints Procedures of the UN Treaty Bodies. OMCT, Geneva

Kioko B (2020) Perspective from the African Court on Human and Peoples' Rights. Journal of Human Rights Practice 12: 163-170

Krsticevic V (2020) El derecho común transformador: el impacto del diálogo del Sistema Interamericano de Derechos Humanos con las víctimas en la consecución de justicia. In: Von Bogdandy A et al. (eds) Cumplimiento e impacto de las sentencias de la Corte Interamericana y el Tribunal Europeo de Derechos Humanos. Instituto de Estudios Constitucionales del Estado de Querétaro

Londoño Lázaro MC (2019) Impactos Estructurales de La Corte Interamericana de Derechos Humanos: Una Mirada a Propósito de Sus 40 Años. In: Von Bogdandy et al. (eds) Cumplimiento e impacto de las sentencias de la Corte Interamericana y el Tribunal Europeo de Derechos Humanos. Instituto de Investigaciones Jurídicas, Universidad Nacional Autónoma de México, Mexico City.

López Andrade AR (2017) La Judicialización de Políticas Públicas: Caso Del Ministerio de Salud Pública En Ecuador En 2011 y Repercusiones En El Estado Constitucional de Derecho. Estado & comunes, revista de políticas y problemas públicos https://doi.org/10.37228/estado_comunes.v2.n5.2017.56

Martínez Pabello AC (2017) La influencia de la Función Jurisdiccional en la Implementación de Políticas Públicas Derecho Global. Estudios sobre Derecho y Justicia 2: 57-86

Murray R, Sandoval C (2020) Balancing Specificity of Reparation Measures and States' Discretion to Enhance Implementation. Journal of Human Rights Practice 12 : 101-124

Otero Pilonieta LM (2018) Control Judicial y Políticas Públicas En Colombia: Un Análisis Del Control Ejercido Por La Corte Constitucional En Las Políticas Públicas de Desplazamiento Forzado y Salud Para Los Periodos 2004–2012, 2008–2015. Universidad Autónoma de Bucaramanga, Bucaramanga

Paúl A (2020) El Relato de Los Contextos Históricos, Sociales y Políticos En Las Sentencias de La Corte Interamericana. ACDI—Anuario Colombiano de Derecho Internacional. https://doi.org/10.12804/revistas.urosario.edu.co/acdi/a.7647

Pautassi L (2017) La vinculación entre derechos y políticas públicas: nuevos abordajes en la enseñanza. Número extraordinario 2017. Anales de la Facultad de Ciencias Jurídicas y Sociales

Perez E (2018) La Supervisión Del Cumplimiento de Sentencias Por Parte de La Corte Interamericana de Derechos Humanos y Algunos Aportes Para Jurisdicciones Nacionales. Anuario de Derecho Constitucional 2018. Konrad Adenauer Stiftung, Bogota, pp 337–362

Pérez EJ (2022) La intervención de la Corte Interamericana de Derechos Humanos en el ciclo de políticas públicas a través de medidas de no repetición. Universidad de los Andes https://rgdoi.net/https://doi.org/10.13140/RG.2.2.10895.05288/1

Pérez Liñán A et al. (2019) Time and Compliance with International Rulings: The Case of the Inter-American Court of Human Rights. SSRN Electronic Journal. https://doi.org/10.2139/ssrn.3463105

Roht-Arriaza N (2003) Reparations Decisions and Dilemmas. Hastings Int'l & Comp. L. Rev. 27:157

Rubio-Marín R (2012) Reparations for Conflict-Related Sexual and Reproductive Violence: A Decalogue. William & Mary Journal of Race, Gender, and Social Justice 19: 69

Saavedra Alessandri P (2017) Algunas reflexiones en cuanto al impacto estructural de las decisiones de la Corte Interamericana de Derechos Humanos. In: Ferrer Mac-Gregor E et al. (eds) Ius constitutionale commune en América Latina: Textos básicos para su comprensión. Instituto de Estudios Constitucionales, Querétaro, pp. 457–502

Sanchez de Miguel L (2018) Supervisión de La Ejecución de Sentencias. Un Análisis Comparado de Los Sistemas Europeo e Interamericano de Derechos Humanos. Anuario de Derecho Constitucional 2018. Konrad Adenauer Stiftung, Bogota, 275-309

Sandoval C (2021) The Power of Hearings: Unleashing Compliance with Judgments at the Inter-American Court of Human Rights. http://www.bristol.ac.uk/media-library/sites/law/hric/2021-documents/2.%20The%20power%20of%20hearings_Sandoval%20ENG.pdf. Accessed 16 September 2023

Sandoval C et al. (2020) Monitoring, Cajoling and Promoting Dialogue: What Role for Supranational Human Rights Bodies in the Implementation of Individual Decisions? Journal of Human Rights Practice 12: 71-100

Shiffman J (2008) Agenda Setting in Public Health Policy. In: Heggenhougen H (ed) International Encyclopedia of Public Health. Oxford Academic Press, Oxford, pp. 55–61

Simmons N (2017) The SAGE Encyclopedia of Communication Research Methods. https://sk.sagepub.com/reference/the-sage-encyclopedia-of-communication-research-methods/, accessed 20 March 2021

Torres-Melo J (2013) Introducción a las políticas públicas: conceptos y herramientas desde la relación entre Estado y ciudadanía. IEMP Ediciones, Bogota

Tushnet M (2008) Weak Courts, Strong Rights. Princeton University Press, Princeton

Uprimny Yepes R, Rodríguez Garavito C (2005) Constitución, Modelo Económico y Políticas Públicas En Colombia: El Caso de La Gratuidad de La Educación Primaria. https://repositorio.idep.edu.co/handle/001/2149, accessed 3 October 2021

Veselý A (2017) Problem Delimitation in Policy Formulation. In: Howlett M, Mukherjee I (eds) Handbook of Policy Formulation. Edward Elgar Publishing, Cheltenham, pp. 81–95

Von Bogdandy A (2020) El mandato transformador del Sistema Interamericano de Derechos Humanos. Legalidad y legitimidad de un proceso jurisgenerativo extraordinario. In: Von

Bogdandy A (ed) Transformaciones del derecho público: fenómenos internacionales, supranacionales y nacionales, 1st edn. Instituto Max Planck de Derecho Público Comparado y Derecho Internacional Público, Querétaro, pp 95-126
Yáñez Meza DA (2014) Las Órdenes de La Corte Constitucional: Su Papel y Límites En La Formulación de Políticas Públicas. Estudios de Derecho 71
Zahariadis N (2016) Setting the Agenda on Agenda Setting: Definitions, Concepts, and Controversies. In: Zahariadis N (ed) Handbook of Public Policy Agenda Setting. Edward Elgar Publishing, Cheltenham, pp 1–22

Table of Cases

IACtHR, *Chaparro Álvarez y Lapo Íñiguez v Ecuador*, Excepciones Preliminares, Fondo, Reparaciones y Costas, 21 November 2007, Serie C No. 170.
IACtHR, *López Lone y Otros v Honduras*, Excepción Preliminar, Fondo, Reparaciones y Costas, 5 October 2015, Serie C No. 302.
IACtHR, *Artavia Murillo y Otros (Fecundación in Vitro) v Costa Rica*, Supervisión de Cumplimiento de Sentencia, 26 February 2016.
IACtHR, *Niñas Yean y Bosico y Personas Dominicanas y Haitianas Expulsadas v República Dominicana*, Supervisión de Cumplimiento de Sentencias y Competencia, 12 March 2019.
IACtHR, *Comunidad Indígena Sawhoyamaxa v Paraguay*, Supervisión de Cumplimiento de Sentencia, 14 May 2019.
IACtHR, *Petro Urrego v Colombia,* Excepciones Preliminares, Fondo, Reparaciones y Costas, 8 July 2020, Serie C No 406.
IACtHR, *Urrutia Laubreaux v Chile, Excepciones Preliminares, Fondo, Reparaciones y Costas,* 27 August 2020, Serie C No 409.
IACtHR, *Petro Urrego v Colombia,* Supervisión de Cumplimiento de Sentencia, 25 November 2021.
IACtHR, *Baena Ricardo y Otros v Panamá*, Competencia, 28 November 2003, Serie C No. 104.
IACtHR, *Barrios Altos y La Cantuta v Perú*, Solicitud de Medidas Provisionales y Supervisión de Cumplimiento de Sentencia, 7 April 2022.
IACtHR, *Bedoya Lima y Otra v Colombia*, Fondo, Reparaciones y Costas, 26 August 2021, Serie C No. 431.
IACtHR, *Gonzales Lluy y Otros v Ecuador*, Excepciones Preliminares, Fondo, Reparaciones y Costas, 1 September 2015, Serie C No. 298.
IACtHR, *González y Otras ("Campo Algodonero") v México*, Excepción Preliminar, Fondo, Reparaciones y Costas, 16 November 2009, Serie C No. 205.
IACtHR, *López Soto y Otros v Venezuela*, Fondo, Reparaciones y Costas, 26 September 2018, Serie C No. 362.
IACtHR, *Los Empleados de La Fábrica de Fuegos de Santo Antônio de Jesus y Sus Familiares v Brasil*, Excepciones Preliminares, Fondo, Reparaciones y Costas, 15 July 2020, Serie C No. 407.
IACtHR, *Molina Theissen v Guatemala*, Reparaciones y Costas, 3 July 2004, Serie C No. 108.
IACtHR, *Velásquez Paiz y Otros v Guatemala*, Excepciones Preliminares, Fondo, Reparaciones y Costas, 19 November 2015, Serie C No. 307.
IACtHR, *Véliz Franco y otros v Guatemala,* Excepciones Preliminares, Fondo, Reparaciones y Costas, 19 May 2014, Serie C No 277.
IACtHR, *Yarce y Otras v Colombia*, Excepción Preliminar, Fondo, Reparaciones y Costas, 22 November 2016, Serie C No. 325.

Chapter 5
Justice without Time Limits—The Impact of International Law on Chilean Case Law on Reparation in Relation to Crimes Committed during the Dictatorship

Pietro Sferrazza Taibi and Francisco Félix Bustos

> No puedes volver atrás,
> no tienes más que seguir,
> que no te aturda el engaño,
> sigue, sigue hasta el final.
> La herida que va contigo,
> ¿Quién la puede mejorar?
> Es la sórdida pobreza,
> que se pretende ignorar,
> es un mar amargo
> y negro que se tiene que aclarar
>
> Víctor Jara, *No puedes volver atrás*

Contents

Both authors contributed equally.

P. Sferrazza Taibi (✉)
Centro de Derechos Humanos, Facultad de Derecho, Universidad de Chile, Santiago, Chile
e-mail: psferrazza@derecho.uchile.cl

F. F. Bustos
Profesor Asistente, Dpto. de Enseñanza Clínica del Derecho, Facultad de Derecho, Universidad de Chile, Santiago, Chile

Doktorand, Institut für Kriminalwissenschaften, Rechtswissenschaftliche Fakultät, Universität Münster, Münster, Germany
e-mail: fbustos@derecho.uchile.cl

O. Spijkers et al. (eds.), *Netherlands Yearbook of International Law 2022*, Netherlands Yearbook of International Law 53, https://doi.org/10.1007/978-94-6265-627-7_5

Abstract The purpose of this chapter is to examine the role of international human rights law in Chilean case law concerning civil claims for crimes committed during the Augusto Pinochet dictatorship (1973–1990). Due to the inadequacy of reparations granted by the Chilean governments and legislation, victims have taken their struggle to the courts demanding compensation. The case law on this problem has gone through various stages. One of the significant obstacles overcome was the application of the statute of limitations. Indeed, international human rights law provided the main arguments for national courts to conclude that all claims derived from crimes against humanity are not subject to the statute of limitations, regardless of their nature. The fight for the satisfaction of the right to reparation continues, with recent judgments from the Inter-American Court of Human Rights having important implications for Chilean case law. The chapter analyses a local experience in which the application of international human rights law has made progress toward achieving justice, truth, reparation, and guarantees of non-repetition. This experience can offer benefits for implementing similar strategies in transitional contexts that share characteristics with Chile's transitional process.

Keywords Crimes against humanity · Statute of limitations · Chilean dictatorship · Civil claims—right to reparation · Inter-American Court of Human Rights · International law enforcement · Conventionality control · International law of human rights · International criminal law · Transitional justice · *Res judicata*

5.1 Introduction

During the Chilean transitional period, the victims who suffered serious human rights violations under the Augusto Pinochet dictatorship (1973–1990) have dedicated themselves to an exhaustive and unwavering pursuit of truth, justice, reparation, and guarantees of non-repetition. This chapter aims to examine the evolution of national case law regarding the realization of the right to reparation.

Confronted with the impossibility to bring perpetrators to justice during the first years of the democratic transition and the inadequacy of public reparation policies implemented by the Chilean State, victims and their families resorted to the courts of justice, seeking compensation from the Treasury for the damages suffered and to establish judicial truth. However, achieving fulfilment of the right to reparation required overcoming various regulatory obstacles. Specifically, this chapter centres around the inadmissibility of the statute of limitations in civil suits brought by victims seeking accountability from the State through compensation claims.

To convince Chilean courts that civil claims arising from the commission of crimes against humanity remain valid regardless of the passage of time, human rights defenders had to invoke the application of international human rights law. This chapter thus contributes to the theoretical discourse on transitional justice by analysing the Chilean context as a model wherein the application of international human rights law played a pivotal role. In this sense, the courts have been understanding that reparation is not only a right of the victims that can be claimed judicially, but also an obligation rooted in international law.

The Chilean Constitution regulates a procedure for the reception of international treaties. The National Congress must approve the treaty through a process akin to that used for approving legislation. Upon completion of this procedure, the President of the Republic is vested with the authority to express the will of the Chilean State to be bound by the treaty.[1] Pertaining to the incorporation of sources of international human rights law, both in academic analysis and case law, extensive debate has revolved around the accurate interpretation to be applied to the singular provision addressing this matter: Article 5 of the Constitution. In essence, the discussion has arisen as a matter of normative hierarchy. Within the realm of judicial decisions, particularly within the Supreme Court, a prevailing stance maintains that treaties and international customs concerning human rights possess a constitutional normative standing.[2]

The position adopted by Chilean courts on this subject has been of paramount importance in overcoming impunity related to crimes committed during the dictatorship. Through the collaborative efforts of human rights defenders who have supported victim families during legal proceedings for decades, national case law has incorporated arguments from international law into its judgments to uphold, for instance, the prohibition of amnesty and the statute of limitations for such crimes.[3]

Moreover, international human rights law has played a pivotal role in shaping this legal precedent, providing essential benchmarks to convince national courts that civil procedural claims stemming from crimes against humanity must not be subject to statute of limitations. Consequently, the mere passage of time must not render the exercise of the right to an effective remedy impossible. In the context of civil claims, this right aims to demand reparation when the state's public policies on the matter, implemented at the administrative level, have proved insufficient.

---

[1] Sferrazza Taibi et al. 2021, pp. 295–298.

[2] Ibid., pp. 278–287.

[3] Fernández Neira 2010, pp. 469–487; Guzmán Dalbora 2008, pp. 134–154.

Chilean case law has invoked various arguments of general international law, such as the principle of good faith, the principle that the State cannot use internal regulations as a pretext to evade its international obligations, and the principle that all harm must be redressed. For its part, international criminal law has served as the basis for concluding that the crimes committed during the dictatorship meet the requirements of crimes against humanity,[4] which are not subject to the statute of limitations, amnesty, or other grounds for impunity.[5] If these crimes against humanity consequences apply to criminal liability, based on the principle of coherence, they must also extend to civil liability.

The traditional arguments employed to rationalize the statute of limitations, such as legal certainty, become entirely meaningless when dealing with the perpetration of crimes that transgress fundamental human values.[6] If the offences committed involve crimes against humanity of torture, extrajudicial executions, or enforced disappearances, the passage of time cannot bring about legal certainty. Despite the years that have elapsed, the pain of the victims endures. In such contexts, the only way to strengthen the rule of law and legal certainty is by establishing truth and justice, eradicating impunity, providing redress for victims, and implementing effective guarantees of non-repetition.

We contend that the pursuit of these essential objectives has not been a straightforward or unbroken process, and it remains an ongoing undertaking. This chapter examines the recent impact of the Inter-American Court of Human Rights' ruling in the case of *Órdenes Guerra vs. Chile* on the national legal framework and state practice. This precedent has not only clarified that civil claims for crimes against humanity are exempt from the statute of limitations but has also affirmed that the compensatory measures awarded by the judiciary are compatible with administrative reparations, confirming the conclusions that had been developed in Chilean case law.

A judicial model for obtaining reparations also accounts for some dilemmas typical of a transitional context. Teitel argues that reparations present a tension between the State's need to take charge of a past of serious human rights violations and the need to project its public policies towards the future.[7] In this sense, it is worth asking whether obtaining reparation through the courts is the most suitable mechanism to reconcile this tension. The judicial reparation model confirms a transactional relationship between the State and the victim,[8] makes the collective context of crimes against humanity invisible,[9] and inevitably implies a relationship

[4] On crimes against humanity, see Werle and Jessberger 2020, pp. 373–379.

[5] Inter–American Court of Human Rights ('IACtHR'), *Almonacid Arellano et al. v. Chile*, Preliminary Objections, Merits, Reparations and Costs, Judgment, 26 September 2006, paras. Series C No. 154, paras 93–104.

[6] There are other arguments that are traditionally invoked to justify the existence of the statute of limitations which we cannot address here. For an analysis of the arguments for and against the statute of limitations for international crimes, see Kok 2001, pp. 239–287.

[7] Teitel 2000, p. 119.

[8] Collins 2017, p. 245.

[9] García–Godos 2017, p. 191.

of conflict between the State and the victim who is not necessarily overcome by what a court ruling provides.

Therefore, this chapter outlines the path taken by the victims from the initial dismissals of civil claims for crimes committed during the dictatorship by Chilean courts to the current situation, where such actions are recognized based on international human rights standards. To explicate this journey, the chapter is divided into three section. The first section (Sect. 5.2) provides the contextual background of the reparation and truth measures that were instituted in the early years of the Chilean transition. The second section (Sect. 5.3) discusses the evolution of Chilean case law on civil claims for crimes against humanity, emphasizing the impact of international law. Finally, the third section (Sect. 5.4) analyses the key findings of the *Órdenes Guerra* ruling, highlighting its significant influence on subsequent Chilean case law, and offering some potential future projections.

5.2 Context: The Difficult Paths to Truth and Justice

The Chilean dictatorship lasted from 1973 to 1990 and relinquished power within the framework of an agreed transition, under the shadow of the Constitution imposed by the *de facto* regime.[10] This Constitution included the provision for General Pinochet to remain as Commander in Chief of the Army, and many other clauses giving great veto power to the Chilean right-wing defenders of Pinochet's political project.[11] As a result, the first democratic government had limited room for manoeuvre.[12] In terms of transitional justice, prosecution did not seem possible as the judiciary had been completely designated by the dictatorship.[13] Additionally, the military justice system, which still hierarchically depended on Pinochet (as Commander in Chief), had a very broad jurisdiction. Furthermore, the criminal statute of limitations[14] and the amnesty Decree Law[15] created additional obstacles that seemed insurmountable.[16]

[10] See Lovera Parmo 2022, pp. 79–100.

[11] Accatino 2020, pp. 409–413.

[12] Collins and Hau 2016, pp. 208–212.

[13] Matus Acuña 2016, pp. 218–220.

[14] See Código Penal [Chilean Penal Code], entered into force 12 November 1874, Diario Oficial (Chile), which includes provisions on statute of limitations in art 93 n° 6 and 94. The statute of limitations for the most serious crimes was reduced to 15 years by Ley 11.183, Introduce las modificaciones que indica en el Código de Procedimiento Civil, 18 May 1953, Diario Oficial (Chile), art 4 n° 5.

[15] Decreto Ley 2.191, Concede Amnistía a las personas que indica por los delitos que señala, 19 April 1978, Diario Oficial (Chile). The assassination of Orlando Letelier and Ronni Moffitt in Washington D.C. (on September 21, 1976, in the context of *Operation Cóndor*) was expressly exempted from the amnesty, due to pressures from the government of the United States. See Veloso 2008, pp. 7–12.

[16] Nino 1996, pp. 36–38; Collins 2013, pp. 98–99.

Nevertheless, President Patricio Aylwin (1990–1994), within weeks of taking office, was able to create through administrative channels the National Truth and Reconciliation Commission (*Comisión Nacional sobre Verdad y Reconciliación*), also known as the "Rettig Commission" (after its president).[17] Its purpose was to investigate the truth behind disappeared detainees, extrajudicial executions, and victims of tortures leading to death.[18] The Commission's report[19] was publicly presented by the President, marking a significant milestone in the state's recognition of its policy of committing massive and systematic crimes. The President also asked for forgiveness on behalf of the entire nation: "That is why I dare, in my capacity as President of the Republic, to assume the representation of the entire Nation to, in its name, ask forgiveness from the victims' families".[20]

The government presented a bill that would later become Law 19.123, creating the National Commission for Reparation and Reconciliation (*Comisión Nacional de Reparación y Reconciliación*).[21] The purpose of this organization was to promote the reparation of moral damages to the victims and to provide social and legal assistance to their relatives.[22] The law proposed a single reparation pension for direct relatives of the victims in addition to some forms of guaranteed medical assistance.[23] It was, however, a limited form of addressing the state's duty to make reparations, by means of assistance pensions.

Although the democratic government addressed truth and reparation, the lack of justice was deeply felt.[24] Relatives of the victims and human rights lawyers persisted in their endeavours to hold the perpetrators accountable for a range of crimes, including forced disappearances, extrajudicial executions, tortures, and other atrocities. During the early years, only a few criminal prosecutions were developed, in mainly isolated cases,[25] which contrasts with the current situation.

---

[17] Cavallo 2012, pp. 25–36. Raúl Rettig served as an ambassador under the Salvador Allende government.

[18] Decreto Supremo 355, Crea Comisión de la Verdad y Reconciliación, 25 April 1990, Diario Oficial (Chile), art 1.

[19] An English translation of the 'Report of the Chilean National Commission on Truth and Reparation' including an introduction by Professor José Zalaquett (1942–2020), a renowned human rights defender and co–author of the Commission's report is available through the University of Notre Dame Press. The translation can be accessed via the United States Institute of Peace. See Chilean National Commission on Truth and Reconciliation 1993.

[20] Comisión Nacional de Verdad y Reconciliación 1991, Mensaje a la Nación del Presidente Patricio Aylwin al dar a conocer el Informe de la Comisión de Verdad y Reconciliación 4 de marzo de 1991 [Message to the nation by President Patricio Aylwin at the release of the Report of the Truth and Reconciliation Commission, 4 March 1991], p. 1314. The original is in Spanish. Translation by us.

[21] Ley 19.123, Crea Corporación Nacional de Reparación y Reconciliación, establece pensión de reparación y otorga otros beneficios en favor de personas que señala, 8 February 1992, Diario Oficial (Chile).

[22] Ibid., art 2.

[23] Lira 2006, p. 56.

[24] Collins et al. 2021, pp. 33–35.

[25] Collins and Hau 2016, p. 225.

Thanks to the tenacity of human rights lawyers, family members, and survivors, almost 500 criminal proceedings for crimes against humanity perpetrated during the dictatorship have been concluded in Chile to date,[26] with hundreds of criminal trials still pending. Some of the *milestones* that explain this process are the transfer of jurisdiction from military tribunals to the civil courts to hear these crimes; the renewal of the judiciary; the specialization of the chambers of the Supreme Court, giving the Second Chamber (Criminal) the exclusive powers to hear these cases;[27] the arrest of Augusto Pinochet in London, which marked the beginning of his political demise;[28] the progressive recognition of international law by the Criminal Chamber; and the judgment of the Inter-American Court of Human Rights in the case of *Almonacid Arellano et al. v. Chile*,[29] which had a decisive influence on the domestic jurisdiction. After that ruling, the Chilean Supreme Court followed the findings of the Inter-American Court of Human Rights. Thus, in the landmark *Molco* case,[30] the Chilean court sentenced the defendants for the crime of murder under the Chilean Criminal Code (of 1874) and acknowledged that—at the same time[31]—the crimes committed during the dictatorship are considered crimes against humanity under international law and, consequently, any form of amnesty or statute of limitations is strictly prohibited.[32]

Before delving into the legal developments regarding the right to reparations at the Supreme Court[33] through the increasing influence of international law,[34] it is important to first review the administrative measures and welfare pensions available to victims of the dictatorship. Indeed, one of the main reasons that explains the filing of reparation claims is the unsatisfactory nature of those measures.

The National Truth and Reconciliation Commission's Report includes various proposals for reparation and guarantees of non-repetition related to public reparation for the dignity of the victims.[35] These suggestions include symbolic vindication and reparation, along with the solemn reestablishment of the good name of victims who were accused of crimes never proven and for which they were never able to defend themselves. Additionally, the report contains recommendations regarding the legal status of victims of enforced disappearance who, for all intents and purposes, are still listed as *alive* in public records (as there are no death certificates), causing great

[26] Bustos 2022, pp. 192–193.

[27] Collins et al. 2023, p. 4.

[28] Roht-Arriaza 2006, pp. 170–181.

[29] IACtHR, *Almonacid Arellano et al. v. Chile*, Preliminary Objections, Merits, Reparations and Costs, Judgment, 26 September 2006, Series C No. 154, paras. 93–114. In this respect, *see* González Morales 2013, pp. 276–289.

[30] Corte Suprema de Chile [Supreme Court], *Mario Superby Jeldres y Hugo Vásquez Martínez ('Caso Molco')*, 13 December 2006, Rol 559–2004, Cassation Judgment, paras 12–26.

[31] On this "dual subsumption", see Cárdenas 2022, pp. 25–37.

[32] See Collins et al. 2023, p. 11; Bustos 2023, pp. 91–94.

[33] Gattini et al. 2019, pp. 181–183.

[34] Cárdenas 2013, p. 123.

[35] Comisión Nacional de Verdad y Reconciliación 1991, pp. 1253–1267.

complexities and grief to their families.[36] In terms of social welfare, the recommendations "aim to propose ways to repair the moral and patrimonial damage that affects the direct relatives of the victims. These individuals have experienced profound alterations in their life projects because of the violations that this Commission has learned of".[37]

The Report's conclusions also state:

> "It is certainly not possible to establish a correlation between the pain, helplessness and hopes of the victims' families and the measures suggested below. The disappearance or death of a loved one is an irreparable loss. However, moral and material reparation appears as absolutely necessary task for the transition to a fuller democracy".[38]

In the area of social welfare recommendations, suggestions were made including a proposal for a single reparation pension, specialized healthcare measures, and others related to education and housing. In response to these recommendations, Law 19.123 was enacted, which established a life pension of $140,000 Chilean pesos (approximately 150 euros) for certain relatives of the victims,[39] including the surviving spouse, the victim's mother (or father when the mother is absent), the mother or father of the victim's children of non-marital filiation, children under 25 years of age, or disabled individuals of any age.[40]

Law 19.123 also established that National Reparation and Reconciliation Corporation would be the successor public body to the Rettig Commission, with the power to review individual cases in which its predecessor had not been able to decide on the status of victim of human rights violations, and for which the Commission did not have timely knowledge or sufficient background information to make a pronouncement.[41] This allowed for the identification and qualification of additional cases of victims of summary executions and forced disappearances,[42] who were eligible for the assistance benefits. However, it was not a permanent commission. The background information had to be submitted within a limited period.[43]

---

36 This only finally started to be resolved with the Ley 20.377, Sobre declaración de ausencia por desaparición forzada de personas, 25 August 2009, Diario Oficial (Chile).

37 Comisión Nacional de Verdad y Reconciliación 1991, p. 1258. The original is in Spanish. Translation by us.

38 Comisión Nacional de Verdad y Reconciliación 1991, p. 1253. Translation by us. *See* Hidalgo and Toro 2017, pp. 89–103.

39 Ley 19.123, Crea Corporación Nacional de Reparación y Reconciliación, establece pensión de reparación y otorga otros beneficios en favor de personas que señala, 8 February 1992, Diario Oficial (Chile), arts 17–18.

40 Ibid., art 20. This regulation has been improved and its coverage extended by Ley 19.980, Modifica la Ley 19.123, Ley de reparación, ampliando o estableciendo beneficios en favor de las personas que indica, 29 October 2004, Diario Oficial (Chile) and Ley 20.405, Del Instituto Nacional de Derechos Humanos, 24 November 2009, Diario Oficial (Chile).

41 Ley 19.123, Crea Corporación Nacional de Reparación y Reconciliación, establece pensión de reparación y otorga otros beneficios en favor de personas que señala, 8 February 1992, Diario Oficial (Chile), arts. 1–2. See Collins et al. 2013b, p. 99.

42 Corporación Nacional de Reparación y Reconciliación 1996, p. 28.

43 Subsequently, the Corporation was succeeded by the Programa Continuación Ley 19.123 [Continuation Program Law 19.123], currently the Unidad Programa de Derechos Humanos [Human Rights

During the dictatorship, victims, surviving relatives, and human rights defenders had the right to access health and psychological care through the Program for Reparation and Comprehensive Health Care (*Programa de Reparación y Atención Integral en Salud y Derechos Humanos*) also called PRAIS, established by the Presidency of the Republic.[44] The National Office of Return (*Oficina Nacional de Retorno*) was also created to facilitate the reintegration of exiles.[45] Symbolic measures were also implemented such as the construction of a memorial at General Cemetery in Santiago in 1993, called Memorial of the Detained-Disappeared and the Politically Executed (*Memorial del Detenido Desaparecido y del Ejecutado Político*)[46] and the establishment of the National Day of the Disappeared (*Día Nacional del Detenido Desaparecido*)[47], and of the National Day of the Politically Executed (*Día Nacional del Ejecutado Político*),[48] among others.

Finally, thirty years after the coup d'état, during the government of President Ricardo Lagos, the National Commission on Political Prisoners and Torture (*Comisión Nacional de Prisión Política y Tortura*), also known as Valech Commission (*Comisión Valech*), was established.[49] Its purpose was to acknowledge victims of the massive and systematic practice of torture and to prepare and submit a report with recommendations.[50] This initiative aimed to fulfil an obligation for the benefit of survivors and human rights organizations. It was one of the duties of the Commission, to propose the conditions, forms, and modes of "austere and symbolic" reparation measures that may be granted to recognized persons who have not received to date any other benefit of a reparatory nature derived from such status.[51]

Afterwards, a new reparation bill was passed,[52] which established a modest pension for the victims as a form of compensation, some health, and educational

Program Unit]. See Ley 20.885, Crea la Subsecretaría de Derechos Humanos y adecúa la Ley Orgánica del Ministerio de Justicia, 5 January 2016, Diario Oficial (Chile). Since 2009 this body has been expressly empowered to file lawsuits in cases of victims of the dictatorship who were executed or disappeared and recognized by the State of Chile. See Ley 20.405, Del Instituto Nacional de Derechos Humanos, 10 December 2009, Diario Oficial (Chile).

44 Collins 2013a, p. 92.

45 Ley 18.994, Crea Oficina Nacional de Retorno, 14 August 1990, Diario Oficial (Chile). See Collins 2013a, p. 92.

46 Collins 2013a, p. 92.

47 Decreto 121, Establece Día Nacional del Detenido Desaparecido, 10 October 2006, Diario Oficial (Chile).

48 Decreto 119, Establece Día Nacional del Ejecutado Político, 5 January 2010, Diario Oficial (Chile).

49 Decreto Supremo N° 1040, Crea la Comisión Nacional sobre Prisión Política y Tortura, para el esclarecimiento de la verdad acerca de las violaciones de Derechos Humanos en Chile, 26 September 2003, Diario Oficial (Chile). Monsignor Sergio Valech presided over the Commission.

50 Comisión Nacional sobre Prisión Política y Tortura 2004, pp. 21–22, 515–520.

51 Decreto Supremo N° 1040, Crea la Comisión Nacional sobre Prisión Política y Tortura, para el esclarecimiento de la verdad acerca de las violaciones de Derechos Humanos en Chile, 26 September 2003, Diario Oficial (Chile), art 2.

52 Ley 19.992, Establece pensión de reparación y otorga otros beneficios a favor de las personas que indica, 17 December 2004, Diario Oficial (Chile).

benefits. Critics of this regulation point to several issues, including the meagre pension offered to survivors, which starkly contrasts with the obligation to provide reparations.[53] Additionally, survivors lack adequate social and legal support, unlike the relatives of executed or disappeared victims; and the background information provided became secret even for the justice system.[54] These shortcomings have been cited as major concerns with the regulation.

In the mid-1990s, due to the obstacles preventing the achievement of criminal justice, some lawyers suggested to the relatives of the disappeared and executed victims to file compensation claims against the State based on the information contained in the Rettig Report. The aim was to establish judicial responsibility and uncover part of the truth about the events.[55] However, as will be explained, these claims were rejected, leading to a long road towards reparations.[56]

5.3 The Inapplicability of the Statute of Limitations to Civil Claims

This section aims to elucidate the development of Chilean case law concerning civil actions for crimes against humanity committed during the dictatorship. The initial part will detail how the identification of the appropriate regulation for these cases was resolved. Subsequently, the second part will delve into the role played by international human rights law in resolving such cases.

5.3.1 Untangling the Legal Knot: The Complexities of the Applicable Legal Regime

One of the problems concerning the civil responsibility of the State for crimes committed by state agents during the dictatorship has been identification of the applicable legal framework. This issue has been arduously discussed within national administrative law and has given rise to two phases in legal precedents. A potential third stage could involve courts recognizing the prohibition of the statute of limitations for civil claims arising from crimes against humanity.

In the first stage, the thesis prevailed according to which the responsibility of the State is "objective", normatively based on the norms of the Constitution. It was

[53] Sferrazza Taibi and Bustos 2019, p. 153.

[54] Ibid.

[55] Gattini and Bustos 2022, p. 236.

[56] Please note that we will not be discussing other forms of reparation requested by survivors and family members, such as the prevention of homage to perpetrators of dictatorship–era atrocities. See Sferrazza Taibi and Bustos 2021, pp. 347–351.

considered that the responsibility of the State was of public law and that it was regulated in Article 38, second paragraph of the Constitution, a norm that enshrines the principle of reparation for any damage caused by the Administration. Consequently, it was argued that establishing a causal relationship between the action of the administrative entity and the resulting damage was necessary. This perspective held sway from the 1970s until the late 1990s.[57] In this period, reparations were occasionally granted through settlements.[58]

In the second phase, the Chilean case law was more inclined towards accepting the thesis of the "subjective" responsibility of the State. In accordance with this second version, the basis of the State's responsibility did not rest upon the Constitution, but rather on the law, specifically, Articles 4 and 44 of Law 18.575 on General Bases of the State Administration,[59] which establishes the responsibility for "lack of service" of the administrative body.[60] In Chilean legal practice, "lack of service" has a broad definition, referring to the failure or negligence of the government's administration to perform their public functions or services. This could include abnormal performance or irregular actions. There are three circumstances that could result in a "lack of service": (1) when the State fails to take necessary action; (2) when the State acts too late; and (3) when the State acts in a manner that contradicts the legal system.[61] Since the appointment of Pedro Pierry to the Supreme Court in 2006,[62] the court has expanded on this concept of lack of service to define the State's liability.[63]

The Supreme Court has determined that in these specific legal proceedings, the rules of tort liability from the Civil Code can be applied as a subsidiary measure. This includes the four years provision related to the statute of limitations for civil claims.[64] This trend was imposed at the beginning of the year 2000, because of the appointment of Urbano Marín as judge of the Supreme Court.[65] For example, said

[57] Cordero Vega 2015, pp. 679–687.

[58] In the Letelier and Moffitt case, the agreement was reached in 1991 via dispute settlement with the United States. See Chile–United States: Agreement to Settle dispute concerning compensation for the deaths of Letelier and Moffitt 1991. International Legal Materials 30(2): 421–424. In the *Quemados* case, one of the victims reached a settlement in the context of a civil claim Court of Appeals of Santiago, *Quintana con Fisco*, judicial settlement, 29 November 2000, Rol 5507–1997.

[59] Ley 18.575, Orgánica Constitucional de Bases Generales de la Administración del Estado, 17 November 2001, Diario Oficial (Chile).

[60] Cordero Vega 2015, pp. 687–690; Bermúdez Soto 2011, pp. 505–507.

[61] Bermúdez Soto 2011, pp. 619–620.

[62] Professor Pierry teaches administrative law, and had advocated since the 1970s, that the state liability was governed by the rules of the Civil Code. From the 1990s until 2006 he was a *Consejero* [Counselor] at the Consejo de Defensa del Estado [State Defense Council], the institution in charge of defending the Treasury. See Gattini et al 2019, p. 181.

[63] Cordero Vega 2015, p. 704.

[64] DFL 1, Código Civil [Civil Code], 30 May 2000, Diario Oficial (Chile), art 2332. See Cordero Vega 2015, pp. 690–694; Castillo 2022, pp. 29–37.

[65] Cordero Vega 2015, pp. 687–689.

Court adopted this position in the *Domic Bezic* case, regarding the murder of Jorge Jordán Domic Bezic in a military compound in La Serena.[66]

In a third phase, which is currently in force, the courts recognize the prohibition of statute of limitations of civil claims, applying international human rights law standards,[67] as will be reviewed next.

5.3.2 *Analysing the Landmark Case Law on Crimes Committed during the Dictatorship*

With respect to crimes committed during the dictatorship, in Chilean procedural practice, civil claims for compensation are usually filed within the framework of criminal proceedings in accordance with what is regulated in the old Code of Criminal Procedure.[68] Generally, a civil claim is filed against the State or the perpetrators of the crimes, or both jointly, and its purpose is to accomplish the payment of compensation for damages.

It is also possible to file a civil claim without criminal proceedings in progress, directing it against the Treasury, in accordance with the rules of the special civil procedure on "Treasury Trial".[69] Whatever the case, it is quite common for both the defence of the accused and the Treasury, the latter represented by the State Defence Council (*Consejo de Defensa del Estado*), to oppose the statute of limitations as a defence.

It is possible to differentiate three stages in the case law on civil claims regarding the crimes against humanity committed during Pinochet's dictatorship. In the first stage, spanning from the late 1990s to around 2008, domestic courts determined that the statute of limitations applied to civil suits involving crimes against humanity perpetrated under the dictatorship. This conclusion was reached by interpreting the Civil Code's rules.[70]

In the second stage, spanning from 2008 to around 2014, the Criminal Chamber of the Supreme Court accepted the first claims filed in criminal proceedings,[71] because

---

[66] Corte Suprema de Chile [Supreme Court], *Domic Bezic con Fisco*, 15 May 2002, Rol 4753–2001, Cassation Judgment, paras 4–9, 15. The preeminence of this interpretation was reinforced by judge Pierry.

[67] Sferrazza Taibi and Bustos 2020, pp. 394–398.

[68] Código de Procedimiento Penal [Code of Criminal Procedure], 19 February 1901, art 40.

[69] Código de Procedimiento Civil [Code of Civil Procedure], 30 August 1902, arts 748–752.

[70] The details of some of these cases are explained in IACtHR, *Órdenes Guerra et al. v. Chile*, Merits, Reparations and Costs, Judgment, 29 November 2018, Series C No. 372, paras 43–75.

[71] Corte Suprema de Chile [Supreme Court], *Episodio Fernando Vergara Vargas*, 8 September 2008, Rol 6308–2007, Replacement Judgment, para. 21. See also Gattini and Bustos 2022, p. 237, Werle and Vormbaum 2022, p. 97.

these actions derive from crimes against humanity, and therefore the statute of limitations could not be applied.[72] On the other hand, the compensation claims that were known by the Constitutional Chamber of said Court, were rejected based on the application of the statute of limitations.[73]

A third phase began in 2014, when the Supreme Court decided to adjust its internal distribution of cases to its specialized benches. As a result of this reorganization, all criminal and civil matters pertaining to cases requiring processing under the old criminal procedure would be dealt with the Criminal Bench of the Supreme Court.[74] After this modification, all judicial processes for crimes of the dictatorship, whether criminal or civil, began to be heard by the Criminal Chamber, which has argued against the statute of limitations on civil claims.[75] The main arguments in favour of this position will be explained below.

In previous case law, the argument was made that a specific provision was required to exclude the applicability of the statute of limitations. In its absence, the general civil law rules should be applied. Along these lines, it was argued that international law did not contain this kind of specific rule.[76] For its part, the current case law in favour of the prohibition of statute of limitations has relied on international law to establish its legal foundation. In substantiation of this stance, domestic courts invoked the second paragraph of Article 5 within the Constitution, which pertains to the incorporation of international human rights law.[77] Consequently, the implementation of international

---

[72] Gattini et al. 2019, p. 187; Gattini and Bustos 2022, p. 237. Judges Hugo Dolmestch (a career judge and former Special Investigative Magistrate for human rights violations) and Carlos Künsemüller (a professor of Criminal Law at the University of Chile) of the Criminal Chamber were among the first magistrates to align their viewpoint with international human rights law.

[73] Corte Suprema de Chile [Supreme Court], *Jimeno Chadwick con Fisco*, 13 January 2009, Rol 2797–2007, Cassation Judgment, para 6; Corte Suprema de Chile [Supreme Court], *Retamales con Fisco*, 27 August 2009, Rol 5600–2007, Cassation Judgment, paras. 5–9. Exceptionally, an occasional verdict from the criminal bench would accept the inapplicability of statute of limitations. See Corte Suprema de Chile [Supreme Court], *Episodio Liquiñe*, 25 September 2008, Rol 4662–2007, Replacement Judgment, para 48.

[74] Corte Suprema de Chile [Supreme Court], *Auto acordado que distribuye las materias de que conocen las salas especializadas de la Corte Suprema durante el funcionamiento ordinario y extraordinario*, 26 December 2014, para 1.B.1.

[75] Gattini et al. 2019, p. 187. See Corte Suprema de Chile [Supreme Court], *Villa Grimaldi, episodio Iván Olivares Coronel, Pedro Labra Saure, Jaime Ossa Galdames y Gustavo Ramírez Calderón*, 31 August 2016, Rol 20506–2016 Cassation Judgment, para 7; Corte Suprema de Chile [Supreme Court], *Villa Grimaldi, episodio Vicente Atencio Cortez*, 6 October 2016, Rol 28637–2016, Cassation Judgment, paras 19–23.

[76] Corte de Apelaciones de Santiago [Court of Appeals of Santiago], *Episodio Jécar Nehgme*, 20 June 2007, Rol 12811–2006, Judgment, para 12.

[77] Corte Suprema de Chile [Supreme Court], *Morales Saavedra con Fisco*, 29 January 2019, Rol 12636–2018, Replacement Judgment, paras 2, 4–5; Corte Suprema de Chile [Supreme Court], *González con Fisco*, 13 June 2018, Rol 8105–2018, Cassation Judgment, paras 5–6; Corte Suprema de Chile [Supreme Court], *Caso Caravana, episodio San Javier*, 15 October 2008, Rol 4723–2007, Replacement Judgment, paras 10–12; Corte Suprema de Chile [Supreme Court], 8–9; Corte Suprema de Chile [Supreme Court], *Episodio Fernando Vergara Vargas*, 8 September 2008, Rol 6308–2007, Replacement Judgment, para. 21.

human rights law has rendered the domestic regulations concerning the statute of limitations for civil claims infeasible, implying that international law assumes a superior position within the normative hierarchy.[78] Indeed, the crimes committed during the dictatorship qualify as crimes against humanity and due to this nature, the statute of limitations cannot be applied.[79]

Based on this, case law has invoked several fundamental principles of international law to assert that the Chilean State has a duty to provide reparation. These principles include the obligation to act in good faith when complying with international treaties, the prohibition against invoking domestic laws to justify exemption from fulfilling international obligations, and the recognition of the right to reparation as a customary and *jus cogens* rule.[80]

An important argument in favour of the prohibition of the statute of limitations of civil claims is based on the principle of coherence. This principle involves applying the same normative criteria to similar situations. Given the presence of compelling arguments advocating that international law forbids the imposition of a statute of limitations on criminal claims concerning core international crimes—such as war crimes and crimes against humanity[81]—the principle of coherence posits that it would make no sense to abolish the statute of limitations for criminal procedure, while preserving it for civil reparation proceedings.[82] The coherence thesis has been confirmed by two

[78] Corte Suprema de Chile [Supreme Court], *Morales Saavedra con Fisco*, 29 January 2019, Rol 12636–2018, Replacement Judgment, para 2; Corte Suprema de Chile [Supreme Court], *González con Fisco*, 13 June 2018, Rol 8105–2018, Cassation Judgment, para 4; Corte Suprema de Chile [Supreme Court], *Caso Caravana, episodio San Javier*, 15 October 2008, Rol 4723–2007, Replacement Judgment, paras 12–13; Corte Suprema de Chile [Supreme Court], *Ortega con Fisco*, 8 April 2010, Rol 2080–2008, Cassation Judgment, paras. 10–11, 13.

[79] Corte Suprema de Chile [Supreme Court], *Ortega con Fisco*, 8 April 2010, Rol 2080–2008, Cassation Judgment, para 7; Corte Suprema de Chile [Supreme Court], *Episodio Fernando Vergara Vargas*, 8 September 2008, Rol 6308–2007, Replacement Judgment, para. 21.

[80] Corte Suprema de Chile [Supreme Court], *Morales Saavedra con Fisco*, 29 January 2019, Rol 12636–2018, Replacement Judgment, paras 2, 4, 5; Corte Suprema de Chile [Supreme Court], *González con Fisco*, 13 June 2018, Rol 8105–2018, Cassation Judgment, paras 4–6; Corte Suprema de Chile [Supreme Court], *Ortega con Fisco*, 8 April 2010, Rol 2080–2008, Cassation Judgment, paras. 10–12; Corte Suprema de Chile [Supreme Court], *Episodio Fernando Vergara Vargas*, 8 September 2008, Rol 6308–2007, Replacement Judgment, para. 21.

[81] Regarding this issue, see Ambos 2013, pp. 428–430, who posit the existence of an emerging customary rule; Cassese 2003, pp. 317–319, for whom there are specific customary rules that render statute of limitations inapplicable with regard to some crimes: genocide, crimes against humanity, torture; Pinzauti 2018, p. 256, defending a similar conclusion; Kok 2001, pp. 380–381, asserting that there is sufficient practice and *opinio iuris* to conclude the existence of a customary rule prohibiting statute of limitations on core international crimes.

[82] Aguilar Cavallo 2008, p. 182; Campos Poblete 2011, p. 157; Céspedes Muñoz 2011, p. 144; Guzmán Dalbora 2008, p. 154; Bustos 2018, pp. 458–460; Sommer 2018, p. 291. See the following case law: Corte Suprema de Chile [Supreme Court], *Morales Saavedra con Fisco*, 29 January 2019, Rol 12636–2018, Replacement Judgment, para 2; Corte Suprema de Chile [Supreme Court], *González con Fisco*, 13 June 2018, Rol 8105–2018, Cassation Judgment, para 5; Corte Suprema de Chile [Supreme Court], *Villa Grimaldi, episodio Vicente Atencio Cortez*, 6 October 2016, Rol 28637–2016, Cassation Judgment, paras 20–23; Corte Suprema de Chile [Supreme Court], *Villa Grimaldi, Episodio Iván Olivares Coronel, Pedro Labra Saure, Jaime Ossa Galdames y Gustavo*

important international *soft law* instruments: the *Set of Principles for the Protection and Promotion of Human Rights through Action to Combat Impunity*[83] and the *Basic Principles and Guidelines on the Right to a Remedy and Reparation for Victims of Gross Violations of International Human Rights Law and Serious Violations of International Humanitarian Law*.[84]

Turning to another argument, it has traditionally been argued that legal certainty is a cornerstone of the statute of limitations. However, this argument fails to justify exemptions for international crimes, which pose a threat to humanity. In such cases, legal certainty can only be maintained if the legal system does not hinder the prosecution of perpetrators and the imposition of civil liability.[85] Atrocious crimes involve state perpetrators who participated in their commission and victims who suffered their consequences. Given the gravity of these crimes, the harm caused cannot be remedied by the mere passage of time. Instead, if the victims do not receive reparation, the passage of time can intensify their suffering.[86] Moreover, if the State itself was involved in the commission of the crimes, it cannot be justified that the passage of time promotes impunity, as statute of limitations is an institution conceived to be applied during periods of peace and normalcy. Therefore, it is the value of justice that must prevail over the predictability of legal relationships. According to Zaffaroni, applying the civil statute of limitations to crimes against humanity is a "legal scandal", as it implies that the commission of this type of crimes would constitute a legitimate title founded on the mere passage of time and opposable to the right of the victims.[87]

Another issue concerns the legal nature of civil claims. The national case law that has supported the application of statute of limitations has deemed civil claims seeking compensation to possess a private legal nature.[88] Consequently, it has been argued that the four-year statute of limitations laid down by the Civil Code for tort liability should be applied (Articles 2497 and 2332).[89] However, case law that finds statute of limitations to be inapplicable has clarified that civil claims arising from international crimes do not have a merely patrimonial character. Rather, they have a humanitarian and reparatory purpose and should be regulated according to international human rights law.[90]

Ramírez Calderón, 31 August 2016, Rol 20506–2016, Cassation Judgment, para 7; Corte de Apelaciones de Santiago [Court of Appeals of Santiago], *Muñoz con Fisco*, 1 June 2009, Rol 270–2006, Judgment, para 7; Corte Suprema de Chile [Supreme Court], *Ortega con Fisco*, 8 April 2010, Rol 2080–2008, Cassation Judgment, para 12.

[83] Commission on Human Rights 2005, principles 23 and 32.

[84] UNGA 2005, paras 6–7.

[85] Aguilar Cavallo 2008, p. 179; Filippini 2012, p. 144; Pinzauti 2018, p. 352.

[86] Van Boven 1993, para 135.

[87] Zaffaroni 2005, pp. 263–264.

[88] Corte Suprema de Chile [Supreme Court], *Carrasco con Fisco*, 10 June 2009, Rol 4771–2007, Replacement Judgment, para 2.

[89] Ibid., paras 3–5.

[90] Aguilar Cavallo 2008, pp. 178, 183, 184, 189; Céspedes Muñoz 2011, p. 146.

5.4 Unpacking the Significance of the Landmark Inter-American Court of Human Rights' *Órdenes Guerra and Others vs. Chile* Judgment

According to Article 68(1) of the *American Convention of Human Rights*, "The States Parties to the Convention undertake to comply with the judgment of the Court in any case to which they are parties".[91] The Court has interpreted its monitoring powers enshrined in the *American Convention* and has created a procedure for monitoring compliance with its judgments and other decisions.[92] On the other hand, based on a broad interpretation of Article 63, the Court has developed the content of a variety of reparation measures whose compliance it imposes on States that have infringed human rights in a case brought before it. Among the measures that are usually decreed are restitution; monetary compensation; measures of satisfaction; rehabilitation; guarantees of non-repetition (among which it can order legislative modifications); and investigation, prosecution, and punishment of all those responsible for the commission of serious crimes.[93]

The Inter-American Court of Human Rights rendered a ruling on the issue of prohibiting statute of limitations for civil claims in the case of *Órdenes Guerra and Others vs. Chile*. The case revolved around the application of statute of limitations by national courts between 1997 and 2001, to dismiss civil lawsuits filed by relatives of victims of forced disappearances and extrajudicial executions that occurred during the dictatorship era.[94]

The Inter-American Court found that applying statute of limitations to civil claims constituted a violation of the rights of access to justice and to due process of law enshrined in Articles 8 and 25 of the *American Convention on Human Rights*.[95] To support its decision, the Court drew upon examples of international practice from the universal system of human rights,[96] as well as case law from the national courts in Colombia, Argentina and Chile.[97] Notably, at the time of the Inter-American Court's ruling, the Chilean Supreme Court had already issued several judgments rejecting the admissibility of the civil statute of limitations concerning crimes against humanity.[98]

---

[91] See American Convention on Human Rights, opened for signature 22 November 1969, 1144 UNTS 123, entered into force 18 July 1978.

[92] Urueña 2021, p. 231.

[93] Pérez–León Acevedo 2019, pp. 319–325; Grossman et al. 2018, pp. 119–481, with copious citations from judgments.

[94] IACtHR, *Órdenes Guerra et al. v. Chile*, Merits, Reparations and Costs, Judgment, 29 November 2018, Series C No. 372, paras 40–75.

[95] Ibid., para 102.

[96] The sources cited by the Court are as follows: Commission on Human Rights 1993; Working Group on Enforced or Involuntary Disappearances 1998; Commission on Human Rights 2005; UNGA 2005.

[97] IACtHR, *Órdenes Guerra et al. v. Chile*, Merits, Reparations and Costs, Judgment, 29 November 2018, Series C No. 372, paras 79–82.

[98] Ibid., paras 83–85, 94.

The Inter-American Court emphasized that the prohibition of statute of limitations in relation to these claims is rooted in the State's obligation to provide reparation to the victims.[99]

The purpose of this section is to provide a detailed analysis of this judgment, including the standards it establishes and the impact it has had on Chilean case law. In pursuit of this aim, we will scrutinize whether the Inter-American Court deems reparations bestowed via an administrative public policy to be compatible with those sought by plaintiffs within legal tribunals. Additionally, we will explore whether a change in jurisprudential trends in domestic courts can constitute a guarantee of non-repetition in accordance with Inter-American case law. We will also discuss some of the obstacles that hinder the proper implementation of this judgment in light of conventionality control. To grasp this section accurately, it is crucial to recall that the doctrine of control of conventionality mandates an international obligation on public authorities in all state parties to the *American Convention on Human Rights*. This obligation entails interpreting any domestic legal norm in alignment with the interpretation of that treaty as established by the case law of the Inter-American Court of Human Rights.[100]

Furthermore, we will examine the internal repercussions of this judgment, particularly considering the Chilean Supreme Court's decision in the *Paine* case. We will evaluate whether the highest national court complied with the *Órdenes Guerra*'s judgment or applied conventionality control. Finally, we will address whether there are new exceptions to *res judicata* that can be established based on the victims' right to reparations.

5.4.1 Balancing the Complementarity of Administrative and Judicial Reparations

This judgment holds notable significance as it establishes the compatibility of compensatory awards provided through administrative entities within the framework of state public policies with the compensations granted by courts of law based on claims initiated by victims. According to the Chilean Supreme Court and the Inter-American Court, these categories of reparations are complementary and non-exclusive.[101] To adopt a contrary stance would contravene the right of serious human rights violations to have access to justice and to request a judicial declaration of State responsibility, a principle previously affirmed by the Inter-American Court in the

[99] Ibid., para 95.

[100] Burgorgue–Larsen 2018; Nageshi 2022, pp. 21–22; González–Dominguez 2018, pp. 65–68.

[101] Corte Suprema de Chile [Supreme Court], *Villa Grimaldi, Episodio "Ocho de Valparaíso"*, 13 April 2015, Rol 20288–2014, Cassation Judgment, paras 10–14; IACtHR, *Órdenes Guerra et al. v. Chile*, Merits, Reparations and Costs, Judgment, 29 November 2018, Series C No. 372, paras 97–101, 123.

matter of *García Lucero et al. vs. Chile.*[102] In fact, this fundamental right empowers victims to pursue compensation as a form of reparation within domestic courts. While we maintain that this criterion is appropriate, we deem it essential to recognize that certain impediments hinder the access of some victims to the judicial system. Certain obstacles encompass the financial implications linked with the entrance into legal proceedings or an absence of comprehension regarding the complexities of the judicial system.[103]

5.4.2 Jurisprudential Changes and Guarantees of Non-Repetition

Órdenes Guerra's judgment presents another noteworthy aspect concerning the guarantees of non-repetition. The Inter-American Court declared that the issue surrounding the prohibition of the statute of limitations on civil claims did not arise from the absence of national regulations, but rather from the incorrect interpretation of national rules considering international human rights law by national courts. According to the Inter-American Court's judgement, this issue can be resolved if domestic courts appropriately apply conventionality control in similar cases.

The affirmation made in the judgment considered two factors: first, the Supreme Court had already established its stance on the prohibition of the statute of limitations on civil claims at the time of the ruling; and second, during the process before the Court, the Chilean State acknowledged that changing this interpretation would violate the fundamental rights outlined in the *American Convention on Human Rights*. Based on these arguments, the Inter-American Court did not mandate a change to Chilean legislation as a non-repetition guarantee.[104]

To date, even the Third Bench (Constitutional) of the Supreme Court recognizes the non-applicability of statute of limitations to reparatory claims for crimes against humanity, based on international law.[105] It is also interesting to note that the Chilean state has officially assumed this position originated in the Criminal Bench of the Supreme Court, presenting it to the United Nations treaty bodies as a form of complying with its international obligations.[106]

---

[102] IACtHR, *Órdenes Guerra et al. v. Chile*, Merits, Reparations and Costs, Judgment, 29 November 2018, Series C No. 372, paras 99–100; IACtHR, *García Lucero et al. v. Chile,* Preliminary Objections, Merits and Reparations, 28 August 2013, Series C No. 267, para 190.

[103] Collins et al. 2019, pp. 116–117.

[104] IACtHR, *Órdenes Guerra et al. v. Chile*, Merits, Reparations and Costs, Judgment, 29 November 2018, Series C No. 372, paras 128–134.

[105] Corte Suprema de Chile [Supreme Court], *Torres con Fisco*, 4 April 2023, Rol 9797–2022, Cassation Judgment, paras 14–16.

[106] Committee on Enforced Disappearances 2019, para 25. The Committee also encourages the State party to reflect in its legislation the position adopted by the Supreme Court with respect to the non–applicability of statutory limitations to civil claims for damages arising from enforced disappearance.

However, the Inter-American Court acknowledged that in Chile, judicial decisions only have a relative effect limited to the specific case. Given this, the Inter-American Court recognized that the jurisprudential correction implemented by the Supreme Court could be subject to modification.[107] *Órdenes Guerra*'s judgment took great care to emphasize that Chilean state bodies, particularly the courts of justice, must exercise conventionality control while considering the international criteria for the prohibition of statute of limitations.[108] The Inter-American Court even addressed the situation of individuals who would be in the same position as the victims in the case, namely, victims whose civil claims were rejected due to statute of limitations.[109] With regards to such victims, the Inter-American Court explicitly urged the Chilean State to promptly find a solution to enable them to access the appropriate compensation.[110] The Court also cautioned that it could not rule out the possibility of resolving similar cases in the future.[111] Therefore, although *Órdenes Guerra* did not impose a specific measure for ensuring non-repetition, it did send a clear message to the Chilean State. With a great level of precision, it outlined the correct interpretation that Chilean courts should follow when applying conventionality control in relation to the prohibition of civil statute of limitations.

5.4.3 Control of Conventionality and Practice of State Bodies

Despite the issuance of *Órdenes Guerra*, some obstacles persist. The State Defence Council (*Consejo de Defensa del Estado*), representing the Treasury and acting as a party in civil lawsuits for crimes of the dictatorship, continues to oppose in the first instance the statute of limitations of civil claims as a defence.[112] Even when the sentence passed by the court of first instance rejects this defence, the Council files appeals or cassation appeals, leading to significantly extended trial durations that harm victims, who are forced to wait for a long time before their right to effective reparation can be satisfied.[113]

We contend that the position of this body is incomprehensible considering the conventionality control. It should be remembered that not only the courts are obliged to carry out this control, but also all State bodies, regardless of the function they

[107] IACtHR, *Órdenes Guerra et al. v. Chile*, Merits, Reparations and Costs, Judgment, 29 November 2018, Series C No. 372, para 132.

[108] Ibid., para 135.

[109] Ibid., para 137.

[110] Ibid.

[111] Ibid., para 134.

[112] They also claim that the victims have already received a reparation through pensions, voluntarily established by the State, but the Criminal Chamber of the Supreme Court and the rest of the judiciary have dismissed this argument. They point out that these pensions do not cover all the damages suffered and are not incompatible with the right to reparation. See IACtHR, *Órdenes Guerra et al. v. Chile*, Merits, Reparations and Costs, Judgment, 29 November 2018, Series C No. 372, para 97.

[113] Collins et al. 2019, pp. 118–119; Gattini et al. 2019, pp. 186–188.

perform.[114] Conventionality control serves not only to scrutinize internal regulations but also the practices of state bodies.[115] Therefore, when the State Defence Council opposes the statute of limitations as a defence, it engages in an unconventional practice that contradicts the international instruments of the Inter-American system and the Inter-American Court's case law. Furthermore, by impeding compliance with the ruling in *Órdenes Guerra*, the State Defence Council violates the principle of international *res judicata*, which requires the convicted state to effectively implement the Court's judgments.[116]

5.4.4 Enforcing International Judgments: Analysing Compliance and Conventionality Control

Despite this hurdle, *Órdenes Guerra vs. Chile* judgment has spurred the evolution of novel legal arguments within Chilean case law pertaining to crimes committed during the dictatorship in relation to the right to reparation. To fully grasp the significance of this development, a brief allusion to a case known as Paine Main Episode (*Paine Episodio Principal*) is necessary. Paine references the rural town where the events unfolded. The case involves extrajudicial executions and enforced disappearances perpetrated in reprisal by State agents, aided by civilians, against peasant victims residing on land expropriated within the context of the Agrarian Reform during President Salvador Allende's administration. *Paine Episodio Principal* is one of the legal proceedings linked to the case and is confined to 38 individuals out of a total of 70 victims.[117]

The facts refer to two contexts of widespread extrajudicial executions, the first occurring between September 24 and October 3, 1973, and the second taking place from October 8 to October 16 of the same year. Thirty-four relatives of the victims filed lawsuits against the Chilean Treasury seeking compensation for non-material damages. While most of the claims were granted, the compensation requests of four victims were denied based on the defence of *res judicata* raised by the Treasury. This argument was posited by the court of first instance and uphold by the Appeals Court of San Miguel.[118]

---

[114] IACtHR, *Myrna Mack Chang v. Guatemala*, Merits, Reparations and Costs, Judgment, 25 November 2003, Series C No. 101, Reasoned Concurring Opinion of Judge Sergio García Ramírez, para 27.

[115] IACtHR, *Radilla Pacheco Vs. México*, Preliminary Objections, Merits, Reparations, and Costs, Judgment, 23 November 2009, Series C No. 209, para 338; IACtHR, *Fernández Ortega et al. v. Mexico*, Preliminary Objection, Merits, Reparations, and Costs, Judgment, 30 August 2010, Series C No. 215, para 235.

[116] García Ramírez 2006, pp. 158–159; Pizzolo 2007, pp. 307–309.

[117] Carrasco Leichtle 2017, pp. 43–54; Gattini et al. 2019, pp. 168–169; Sferrazza Taibi and Bustos 2022, pp. 341–345; Gattini and Bustos 2022, pp. 242–243.

[118] Court of Appeals of San Miguel, *Caso Paine, Episodio Principal*, 10 November 2020, Rol 3221–2019, Judgment.

The issue had arisen due to one of the victims initiating a civil claim in a prior judicial proceeding, which was rejected due to the application of the statute of limitations.[119] The same scenario unfolded in another judicial proceeding initiated by the other three victims.[120] Therefore, there were previous final judgments that had dismissed the civil lawsuits of these four victims.

However, unlike the cases mentioned earlier,[121] during the cassation appeal hearing in *Paine Episodio Principal* case, the Criminal Chamber of the Supreme Court chose to annul the judgment of the Court of Appeals of San Miguel and issue a new judgment rejecting the defence of *res judicata* and granting the civil claim for compensation of damages.[122] The arguments presented in this ruling are significant, especially considering that it was issued after the *Órdenes Guerra*'s judgment.

Although this judgment of the Inter-American Court was not explicitly cited by the Supreme Court, the latter determined that the annulled judgment of the Court of Appeals had not properly applied international human rights law, resulting in an error in accepting the defence of *res judicata*.[123] The main argument was that the victims' right to comprehensive reparation cannot be denied based on *res judicata*, particularly in cases where the State is accountable for crimes against humanity.[124] The Supreme Court applied the conventionality control and interpreted national regulations concerning *res judicata*, specifically Article 173 of the Code of Civil Procedure, in harmony with international standards. Consequently, in the opinion of the Supreme Court, the *res judicata* defence must be set aside to ensure the State's fulfilment of its obligation to provide full reparation for harm caused by crimes against humanity.[125]

The Supreme Court clarified that previous judgments that had applied the civil statute of limitations were not null and void. Instead, the control of conventionality resulted in the non-application of *res judicata* in the new legal procedure. This last argument is somewhat perplexing because, on one hand, the judgment of the Supreme Court rejected the defence of *res judicata*, and on the other hand, it affirmed that the previous judgments accepting the statute of limitations maintain a binding effect. This argument is not very accurate. Consequently, several questions arise: What did the Supreme Court want to argue? What is the relationship between this Supreme

[119] Corte Suprema de Chile [Supreme Court], *Tamayo con Fisco*, 14 April 2011, Rol 123–2009, Cassation Judgment, paras 3–13.

[120] Corte Suprema de Chile [Supreme Court], *Gaete con Fisco*, 30 November 2012, Rol 2724–2010, Cassation Judgment, paras 2–15.

[121] The Supreme Court had the opportunity to discuss this issue a couple of times before due to new claims in cases where the civil statute of limitations had been applied, which were rejected, either in divided or unanimous votes. See Corte Suprema de Chile [Supreme Court], *Caso Paine, Francisco Godoy Román*, 14 November 2019, Rol 20.520–2018, Cassation Judgment, paras 6–10; Collins et al. 2020, p. 30.

[122] Gattini and Bustos 2022, pp. 246–248. Corte Suprema de Chile [Supreme Court], *Caso Paine, episodio principal*, 14 June 2022, Rol 149.250–2020, Cassation Judgment, paras 41–47.

[123] Corte Suprema de Chile [Supreme Court], *Caso Paine, episodio principal*, 14 June 2022, Rol 149.250–2020, Cassation Judgment, para 39.

[124] Ibid., para 40.

[125] Ibid., paras 43–47.

Court ruling and the case law of the Inter-American Court, especially in the context of the *Órdenes Guerra* case? Did the Supreme Court in the Paine Main Episode comply with the *Órdenes Guerra* ruling or did it generally apply conventionality control?

At this point, it is advisable to pause for a moment to elucidate two effects of the Inter-American Court's judgments. According to Ferrer Mac-Gregor, first, the judgments rendered by the Inter-American Court carry a binding effect for the parties involved in the judicial proceedings, giving rise to the authority of "international *res judicata*".[126] For that reason, all branches of the State that have been condemned by the Court's verdict must adhere to the judgment.[127]

Furthermore, judgments of the Inter-American Court also possess an *erga omnes* effect on all States parties to the *American Convention on Human Rights*. Consequently, all authorities within these states are obligated to ensure compliance with the Convention's norms and to undertake conventionality control, by interpreting and applying the treaty provisions of the Inter-American system according to the Court's interpretation in its rulings (*res interpretata*).[128]

A potential explanation for the question at hand regarding the *Paine* case could be that the Chilean Supreme Court complied with the *Órdenes Guerra* verdict (international *res judicata*).[129] However, to arrive at this conclusion, one must consider, as Ferrer Mac-Gregor suggests, that not only the operative part but also the considerations and reasoning of the Inter-American Court rulings carry the authority of *res judicata*. In fact, the grounds of the sentence constitute the factual and legal basis for the judicial decision.[130]

Another possible answer, which in our view is more accurate, suggests that the Supreme Court exercised conventionality control in alignment with the Inter-American Court's recommendation to apply a specific judicial interpretation. In fact, in its arguments on this matter, the Supreme Court does not refer to *Órdenes Guerra*. Instead, it explicitly states that its decision stems from the application of conventionality control.[131]

In conclusion, the *Órdenes Guerra* judgment is highly significant as it establishes a standard on the prohibition of the statute of limitations on civil claims, which is mandatory not only for Chile but also for all other member states of the *American Convention on Human Rights* through conventionality control.[132]

---

126 Ferrer Mac-Gregor 2013, p. 655.

127 Ibid., pp. 655–656.

128 Ibid., pp. 656–657.

129 Gattini and Bustos 2022, pp. 239–240.

130 Ferrer Mac-Gregor 2013, p. 657.

131 Corte Suprema de Chile [Supreme Court], *Caso Paine, episodio principal*, 14 June 2022, Rol 149.250–2020, Cassation Judgment, paras 43 and 45.

132 Da Rin 2019–2020, pp. 556–557.

5.4.5 *Rethinking* Res Judicata*: Exploring the Possibility of a New Exception*

There is one last interesting question that needs to be addressed: Did the *Paine* argumentation create a new exception to the force of *res judicata* in relation to the commission of crimes against humanity or did it apply the "apparent" or "fraudulent" *res judicata* theory? In attempting to answer this question, it is necessary to explain the concept of "apparent" or "fraudulent" *res judicata.*

As outlined by Mañalich, the expression "fraudulent *res judicata*" designates a criterion for disregarding the binding effect of a judgment pronounced after a legal proceeding characterized by irregularities in its progression or conclusion, to the extent that the force of *res judicata* must be considered apparent.[133] In other words, it is a case of *res judicata* obtained by fraud, and for that reason, it should not even be considered.

The concept of fraudulent *res judicata* has been developed by the Inter-American Court as an exception to the *ne bis in idem* principle. This principle, enshrined in Article 8.4 of the *American Convention on Human Rights*, safeguards the right to due criminal process. The Court has identified three scenarios where the application of the *ne bis in idem principle* is not applicable: firstly, when a court acquits an individual of a human rights violation with the intention of absolving them of criminal responsibility; secondly, when the judicial process lacks impartiality and independence, thereby contravening the due process of law; and thirdly, when there is no genuine effort to prosecute the perpetrator.[134] In any of these situations there would be fraudulent *res judicata.*

In relation to a crime committed during the dictatorship, there was a prior case in which the Inter-American Court invoked the doctrine of fraudulent *res judicata*: *Almonacid Arellano et al. v. Chile.* In this judgment, the Court ordered the nullification of a judgment by national military courts that had acquitted the perpetrator responsible for the extrajudicial execution of the communist leader Luis Alfredo Almonacid Arellano. In this case, two of these conditions were met. Firstly, the case was heard by courts that did not uphold the guarantees of independence and impartiality. Secondly, the application of Decree Law 2.191, which establishes an amnesty regarding crimes committed during the dictatorship, prevented those allegedly responsible from being brought before the courts and favoured impunity.[135]

---

[133] Mañalich 2021, p. 466. In the same terms, see Rome Statute of International Criminal Court, opened for signature 17 July 1998, 2187 UNTS 39, entered into force 1 July 2002, art 20(3).

[134] See IACtHR, *Carpio Nicolle et al. v. Guatemala*, Merits, Reparations and Costs, Judgment, 22 November 2004, Series C No. 117, paras 131–133; IACtHR, *Gutiérrez Soler v. Colombia*, Merits, Reparations and Costs, Judgment, 12 September 2005, Series C No. 132, para 98; IACtHR, *Almonacid Arellano et al. v. Chile*, Preliminary Objections, Merits, Reparations and Costs, Judgment, 26 September 2006, Series C No. 154, para 154; IACtHR, *Nadege Dorzema et al. v. Dominican Republic*, Merits, Reparations and Costs, Judgment, 24 October 2012, Series C No. 251, paras 195–196.

[135] IACtHR, *Almonacid Arellano et al. v. Chile*, Preliminary Objections, Merits, Reparations and Costs, Judgment, 26 September 2006, Series C No. 154, paras 154–155.

In the *Paine* case, the Supreme Court did not appear to apply the theory of fraudulent *res judicata*, as there was no explicit reference to this concept in the decision.[136] On the contrary, the Court expressly affirmed the validity of the previous judicial proceedings. Therefore, in *Paine* the Supreme Court seems to have drawn up a new exception to *res judicata* in the civil process, justified by the need to comply with the control of conventionality and satisfy the right to comprehensive reparation[137] which was denied without complying with international human rights law. In any case, it is worth wondering if in future cases, the Inter-American Court might develop an argument to extend some limits to the application of *res judicata* to judgments of a civil nature.

We argue that the Supreme Court's argument is overly general. It is to be expected that in future judgments the Supreme Court will provide more comprehensive reasoning addressing all the issues that have been raised throughout this section.

5.5 Conclusions

We have examined how the Chilean State has applied international human rights law to address the right to reparation, tracing its evolution over the past few decades. In the initial phase, following a highly negotiated transition in which criminal prosecution was deemed impossible, truth and reparation were the sole or apparent means through which the fledgling democracy could confront the aftermath of the dictatorship. During this period, reparation efforts were inadequate, involving the provision of pensions and assistance measures.

Initially, pensions were provided solely to the relatives of executed and disappeared victims. It was not until the 2000s that similar measures were implemented for those who had suffered from political imprisonment and torture. However, these measures fell short of providing full reparation. Consequently, many victims filed compensation claims in court, only to have them mostly rejected based on the statute of limitations of four years established in the Civil Code, grounded on the legal principle of certainty over time and in the developments of the Third Chamber (Constitutional) of the Supreme Court, inspired by doctrines of administrative law.

Fortunately, the Inter-American system of protection and international law proved essential in bringing justice to victims. Specifically, the Criminal Chamber of the Supreme Court recognized that the dictatorship committed crimes against humanity, since the *Molco Case* (2006) and therefore stated that the statute of limitations was inapplicable following the Inter-American judgment of *Almonacid Arellano* (2006). Additionally, this same principle of prohibition of the statute of limitations was extended to civil claims based on international law arguments, as the principle of good faith, the principle that the State cannot use internal regulations as a pretext to evade its international obligations, and the principle that all harm must be redressed as

[136] Gattini and Bustos 2022, p. 242.

[137] Gattini and Bustos 2022, pp. 248–249.

a norm of *jus cogens*, especially with regard to crimes against humanity, as understood by the Inter-American Court of Human Rights and the Chilean Supreme Court.

The situation has resulted in a coherence problem at the level of the Supreme Court of Justice concerning the success of lawsuits against the State. The Criminal Chamber started compensating the victims of cases that arose within the framework of a criminal trial. On the other hand, the Constitutional Chamber maintained the old case law, rejecting lawsuits brought by victims based on the statute of limitations of the Chilean Civil Code. This situation resulted in unacceptable discrimination and inequality before the law, for victims of atrocities that the State had acknowledged in its truth reports.

Administrative corrections were made to ensure that the Criminal Chamber of the Supreme Court could handle all matters related to crimes committed during the dictatorship, to standardize criteria. By the time the first complaints about rejected lawsuits in the 1990s and 2000s reached the Inter-American Court of Human Rights, this internal change enabled the Chilean state to adopt a new approach, acknowledging its responsibility for the lack of redress.

The Inter-American Court found in *Órdenes Guerra and Others vs. Chile* that applying the statute of limitations to civil claims violated the rights of access to justice, judicial guarantees, and judicial protection enshrined by Articles 8 and 25 of the *American Convention on Human Rights*. To support its decision, the Court cited examples from international practice in the universal system, as well as case law from national courts. The Court emphasized that the prohibition of the statute of limitations in relation to these claims is rooted in the State's obligation to provide reparation to the victims.

Órdenes Guerra's case sets out the state's duty to care for victims in similar situations. This judgment has led to an important development, as the *res judicata* exception has been defeated in cases of victims of international crimes whose claims were previously dismissed due to civil statute of limitations. In the Paine Main Episode case, the Criminal Chamber of the Supreme Court confirmed that the right to reparation takes precedence based on the obligation to fulfil good faith commitments, make reparations, and provide reparations. This obligation to make reparations and the conventionality control application allows for historical injustices to be repaired.

These interpretations have been extended to new cases, raising questions about the limits of the *res judicata* exception and the possibility of this doctrine being applied in the Inter-American Court. They also demonstrate that in Chile, international law continues to emphasize that the passage of time cannot be a barrier to justice for core international crimes.

References

Accatino D (2020) Justicia de transición y nueva constitución. In: Muñoz F, Ponce de León V (eds) Conceptos para una nueva Constitución. DER Ediciones, Santiago, pp 409–419.

Aguilar Cavallo G (2008) Crímenes internacionales y la imprescriptibilidad de la acción penal y civil: referencia al caso chileno. Ius et Praxis 14(2): 147–207.

Ambos K (2013) Treatise on International Criminal Law. Volume I: Foundations and General Part. Oxford University Press, Oxford.

Barros Bourie E (2006) Tratado de Responsabilidad Extracontractual. Editorial Jurídica de Chile, Santiago.

Bermúdez Soto J (2011) Derecho administrativo general. Thomson Reuters, Santiago.

Burgorgue-Larsen L (2018) Conventionality Control: Inter-American Court of Human Rights (IACtHR). https://doi.org/10.1093/law-mpeipro/e3634.013.3634/law-mpeipro-e3634. Accessed 20 August 2023.

Bustos F (2018) Improcedencia de aplicar la prescripción gradual a crímenes de lesa humanidad, e imprescriptibilidad de la acción civil reparatoria. Revista de Ciencias Penales XLV: 456–460.

Bustos F (2022) La obediencia jerárquica en el derecho penal internacional: Un examen a la jurisprudencia chilena por crímenes de lesa humanidad (1995-2020). In: Guerrero C (ed) El derecho penal internacional en Chile y ante la Corte Penal Internacional. Ius Civile, Santiago, pp 189–213.

Bustos F (2023) La circunstancia agravante del artículo 12 Nº 8 del Código Penal y su (in)aplicación en causas sobre crímenes de lesa humanidad. Un análisis jurisprudencial (1993–2020). Ius Civile, Santiago.

Campos Poblete M (2011) La prescripción de las acciones reparatorias civiles emanadas de los crímenes de lesa humanidad. Derecho y humanidades 18: 145–162.

Cárdenas C (2013) La aplicabilidad del Derecho Internacional por tribunales chilenos para interpretar la ley N° 20.357. Revista de Derecho (Coquimbo) 20(2): 121–145.

Cárdenas C (2022) Labeling Crimes against Humanity in Domestic Jurisdictions: Does *nomen iuris* Matter? The Case of Crimes in Colonia Dignidad. In: Jessberger F, Vormbaum M, Burghardt B (eds) Strafrecht und Systemunrecht. Festschrift für Gerhard Werle zum 70. Geburtstag. Mohr Siebeck, Tübingen, pp 25–37.

Carrasco Leichtle T (2017) Cambio generacional y radicalización campesina. Evolución del proceso de Reforma Agraria en Paine (1967-1973). Polis, Revista Latinoamericana 47: 43–54.

Cassese A (2003) International Criminal Law. Oxford University Press, Oxford.

Castillo R (2022) Responsabilidad patrimonial del Estado por violaciones a los derechos humanos. M.A. thesis. Universidad de Concepción, Concepción.

Cavallo A (2012) La historia oculta de la transición. Memoria de una época 1990–1998. Uqbar, Santiago.

Céspedes Muñoz C (2011) Imprescriptibilidad de la acción civil derivada de la comisión de crímenes de lesa humanidad. Sentencia Excma. CS de 08 de abril de 2010. Revista de Derecho y Ciencias Penales 16: 131–150.

Chilean National Commission on Truth and Reconciliation (1993) Report of the Chilean National Commission on Truth and Reconciliation. https://www.usip.org/sites/default/files/resources/collections/truth_commissions/Chile90-Report/Chile90-Report_PartI.pdf Accessed 25 August 2023.

Collins C (2013a) Chile a más de dos décadas de justicia de transición. Política. Revista de Ciencia Política 51(2): 79–113.

Collins C (2013b) La política de la justicia: Chile más allá del caso Pinochet. In: Collins C et al. (eds) Las políticas de la memoria en Chile: desde Pinochet a Bachelet. Universidad Diego Portales, Santiago, pp 85–115.

Collins C (2017) ¿El fin de la impunidad? Justicia tardía y acciones judiciales postransicionales en América Latina. In: Jimeno Aranguren R (ed) Justicia transicional: historia y actualidad. Aranzadi, Navarra, pp 241–276.

Collins C, Hau B (2016) Chile: Incremental Truth, Late Justice. In: Skaar et al. (eds) Transitional Justice in Latin America. The Uneven Road from Impunity Towards Accountability. Routledge, New York, pp 126–150.
Collins C et al. (2019) La memoria en los tiempos del cólera: verdad, justicia, reparaciones, y garantías de no repetición por los crímenes de la dictadura chilena. In: Vargas Rivas F (ed) Informe Anual sobre Derechos Humanos en Chile. Universidad Diego Portales, Santiago, pp 23–132.
Collins C et al. (2021) Conversar con el pasado, transformar este presente: Justicia transicional como justicia constituyente. In: Vargas Rivas F (ed) Informe Anual sobre Derechos Humanos en Chile. Universidad Diego Portales, Santiago, pp 29–101.
Collins C et al. (2023) Jurisprudential Milestones in Human Rights Cases: Chile 1990–2023. Universidad Diego Portales, Santiago.
Comisión Nacional de Verdad y Reconciliación (1991) Informe de la Comisión Nacional de Verdad y Reconciliación. Santiago.
Comisión Nacional sobre Prisión Política y Tortura (2004) Informe de la Comisión Nacional sobre Prisión Política y Tortura. Ministerio del Interior, Santiago.
Commission on Human Rights (1993) Study Concerning the Right to Restitution, Compensation and Rehabilitation for Victims of Gross Violations of Human Rights and Fundamental Freedoms. Final Report Submitted by Mr. Theo van Boven, Special Rapporteur, E/CN.4/Sub.2/1993/8, 2 July 1993.
Commission on Human Rights (2005) Promotion and Protection of Human Rights. Impunity. Report of the Independent Expert to Update the Set of Principles to Combat Impunity, Diane Orentlicher. Addendum. Updated Set of Principles for the Protection and Promotion of Human Rights through Action to Combat Impunity, E/CN.4/2005/102/Add.1, 8 February 2005.
Committee on Enforced Disappearances (2019) Concluding Observations on the Report Submitted by Chile under Article 29 (1) of the Convention, CED/C/CHL/CO/1, 8 May 2019.
Cordero Vega L (2015) Lecciones de Derecho Administrativo, 2nd edn. Thomson Reuters, Santiago.
Corporación Nacional de Reparación y Reconciliación (1996) Informe sobre calificación de víctimas de violaciones de derechos humanos y de la violencia política, 11th edn. Andros, Santiago.
Correa C (2019) Artículo 63. In: Steiner C, Fuchs MC (eds) Convención Americana sobre Derechos Humanos: Comentario, 2nd edn. Konrad Adenauer Stiftung, Bogotá, pp 1019–1099.
Da Rin N (2019–2020) La imprescriptibilidad del derecho a obtener reparación integral de las víctimas de delitos de lesa humanidad. Derechos en Acción 5(14): 547–557.
Díaz Martínez G A (2017) La imprescriptibilidad de las acciones civiles por daños y perjuicios emanadas de delitos de lesa humanidad (Una mirada crítica sobre el fallo "Villamil" de la C.S.J.N.). Redea. Derechos en Acción 2(4): 140–158.
Feddersen M (2010) La prescripción de las acciones reparatorias en la jurisprudencia de la Corte Suprema. Observatorio de Derechos Humanos, Santiago.
Fernández Neira K (2010) Breve análisis de la jurisprudencia chilena, en relación a las graves violaciones a los derechos humanos cometidos durante la dictadura militar. Estudios Constitucionales 8(1): 467–488.
Ferrer Mac-Gregor E (2013) Eficacia de la sentencia interamericana y la cosa juzgada internacional: vinculación directa hacia las partes (res judicata) e indirecta hacia los Estados Parte de la Convención Americana (res interpretata) (Sobre el cumplimiento del Caso Gelman Vs. Uruguay). Estudios Constitucionales 11(2): 641–694.
Filippini L et al. (2012) Prescripción de acciones civiles por complicidad con el terrorismo de estado. Revista Argentina de Teoría Jurídica 13: 137–149.
García Ramírez S (2006) La jurisdicción interamericana de derechos humanos (Estudios). Comisión de Derechos Humanos-Corte Interamericana de Derechos Humanos, México D.F.
García-Godos J (2017) Reparations. In: Simić O (ed) An Introduction to Transitional Justice. Routledge, New York.
Gattini Zenteno A, Bustos F (2022) El caso Paine, episodio principal, contra Nelson Iván Bravo Espinoza y otros: Imprescriptibilidad de la acción civil e ineficacia de la excepción de cosa

juzgada en casos de crímenes de lesa humanidad. Anuario de Derechos Humanos 18(2): 231–252.
Gattini Zenteno A et al. (2019) Crímenes contra la humanidad. Imprescriptibilidad acción civil. Corte IDH. Caso Órdenes Guerra y otros vs. Chile. Fondo, Reparaciones y Costas. Sentencia de 29 de noviembre de 2018. Serie C No. 372. Debates sobre derechos humanos 3: 181–189.
González Morales F (2013) Sistema Interamericano de Derechos Humanos. Tirant lo Blanch, Valencia.
González-Dominguez P (2018) The Doctrine of Conventionality Control. Intersentia, Cambridge.
Grossman C et al. (2018) International Law and Reparations. The Inter-American System. Clarity Press, Atlanta.
Guzmán Dalbora J L (2008) Chile. In: Ambos K, Malarino E (eds) Jurisprudencia latinoamericana sobre Derecho penal internacional. Konrad Adenauer Stiftung, Montevideo, pp 131–158.
Hidalgo P, Toro C (eds) (2017) Idealista sin ilusiones. Conversaciones con José Zalaquett. Lolita, Santiago.
Kok R A (2001) Statutory Limitations in International Law. TMC Asser Press, The Hague.
Lira E (2006) The Reparations Policy for Human Rights Violations in Chile. In: De Greiff P (ed) The Handbook of Reparations. Oxford University Press, pp 55–101.
Lovera Parmo D (2022) Chile. In: Hübner Mendes C et al. (eds) The Oxford Handbook of Constitutional Law in Latin America. Oxford University Press, Oxford, pp 97–110.
Mañalich R JP (2021) Cosa juzgada fraudulenta en el caso "quemados". Política criminal 16(31): 456–491.
Matus Acuña A (2016) El Libro Negro de la Justicia chilena, rev. edn. Ediciones B, Santiago.
Nageshi Y (2022) Conventionality Control of Domestic Law. Nomos, Baden-Baden.
Nash Rojas C (2009) Las Reparaciones ante la Corte Interamericana de Derechos Humanos, 2nd edn. Universidad de Chile, Santiago.
Nino C (1996) Radical Evil on Trial. Yale University Press, New Haven.
Núñez Donald C (2015) Control de Convencionalidad: Teoría y Aplicación en Chile. Tribunal Constitucional, Santiago.
Payne L A et al. (2020) Transitional Justice and Corporate Accountability from Below. Deploying Archimedes' Lever. Cambridge University Press, Cambridge.
Pérez-León Acevedo J P (2019) Reparations for victims of mass atrocities. Actual and Potential Contributions of the Inter-American Court of Human Rights to the International Criminal Court. Global Community Yearbook of International Law and Jurisprudence 18(1): 305–335.
Pinzauti G (2018) Principle 23. Restrictions on Prescriptions. In: Haldemann F, Unger T (eds) The United Nations Principles to Combat Impunity. Oxford University Press, Oxford, pp 250–257.
Pizzolo C (2007) Sistema Interamericano. Ediar Jurídicas-UNAM, Buenos Aires.
Roht-Arriaza N (2006) The Pinochet Effect. Transnational Justice in the Age of Human Rights. University of Pennsylvania Press, Philadelphia.
Sferrazza Taibi P, Bustos F (2019) La constitucionalización del derecho a no ser sometido a tortura ni a tratos crueles, inhumanos o degradantes. In: Aguilar G (ed) Nuevos derechos para una Nueva Constitución. Tirant lo Blanch, Santiago, pp 139–158.
Sferrazza Taibi P, Bustos F (2020) Economic complicity under Chilean Law. In: Bohoslavsky J P, Fernández K, Smart S (eds) Pinochet's Economic Accomplices. An Unequal Country by Force. Lexington Books, New York, pp 389–405.
Sferrazza Taibi P, Bustos F (2021) La protección judicial del derecho a la memoria: la remoción de las imágenes de un genocida. Revista de Derecho (Valdivia) 34(1): 341–352.
Sferrazza Taibi P, Bustos F (2022) Persecución judicial de la complicidad económica y de civiles por la comisión de crímenes de lesa humanidad durante la dictadura en Chile. In: Galain P (ed) Responsabilidad empresarial, derechos humanos y la agenda del Derecho penal corporativo. Tirant lo Blanch, Santiago, pp 331–374.
Sferrazza Taibi P et al. (2021) La aplicación del Derecho internacional de los derechos humanos en Chile: diagnósticos y propuestas para una Nueva Constitución transformadora. Revista Brasileira de Políticas Públicas 11(2): 275–312.

Sommer CG (2018) La imprescriptibilidad de la acción reparatoria por crímenes de lesa humanidad y la responsabilidad del Estado. Comentarios sobre la jurisprudencia y la legislación argentinas. Revista Derecho del Estado 41: 285–315.

Teitel R (2000) Transitional Justice. Oxford University Press, New York.

UNGA (2005) Res. 60/147, Annex. Basic Principles and Guidelines on the Right to a Remedy and Reparation for Victims of Gross Violations of International Human Rights Law and Serious Violations of International Humanitarian Law, 16 December 2005.

Urueña R (2021) Compliance as transformation: the Inter-American system of human rights and its impact(s). In: Grote R et al. (eds) Research Handbook on Compliance in International Human Rights Law. Edward Elgar, Cheltenham/Northampton, pp 225–247.

Veloso P (2008) Introducción. In: Veloso P (ed) Justicia, derechos humanos y el Decreto Ley de Amnistía. PNUD, Santiago, pp 7-12.

Werle G, Jessberger F (2020) Principles of International Criminal Law, 4th edn. Oxford University Press, Oxford.

Werle G, Vormbaum M (2022) Transitional Justice. The Legal Framework. Springer, Berlin.

Working Group on Enforced or Involuntary Disappearances (1998) General Comments on Article 19 of the Declaration, E/CN.4/1998/43, 12 January 1998.

Zaffaroni E R (2005) En torno a la cuestión penal. B de F, Montevideo/Buenos Aires.

Pietro Sferrazza Taibi Academic of the Centro de Derechos Humanos, Facultad de Derecho, Universidad de Chile, Chile.

Francisco Félix Bustos Profesor Asistente, Dpto. de Enseñanza Clínica del Derecho, Facultad de Derecho, Universidad de Chile, Chile; doctoral student (ANID-DAAD scholarship holder), Doktorand, Institut für Kriminalwissenschaften, Rechtswissenschaftliche Fakultät, Universität Münster, Germany.

Part II
The Role of International Criminal Law in the Development of Reparations

Chapter 6
Satisfaction and State Responsibility at the International Criminal Court: The Curious Crime of Aggression

Meagan Wong

Contents

Abstract In the event of a case of a crime of aggression at the International Criminal Court (ICC), the Court will have to determine the existence of State conduct of an act of aggression pursuant to the definition of the crime in Article 8 *bis* the Rome Statute of the ICC (Rome Statute). The uniqueness of this international crime is that an act of aggression, as an internationally wrongful act is a *conditio sine qua non* for the crime of aggression. As the ICC is not an inter-State court, a curious dimension arises as the Court will have to engage with State responsibility for aggression in addition to individual criminal responsibility for the crime of aggression. In accordance with the law of State responsibility, every internationally wrongful act entails an obligation on the wrongdoing State to make full reparation for injury caused by the wrongful act. As the ICC has jurisdiction over State conduct in relation to an act of aggression, this chapter enquires whether the Court may award reparation for the aforementioned internationally wrongful act. Whilst States Parties to the Rome Statute have conferred powers to the ICC to determine an act of aggression, the Court cannot award restitution or compensation at the inter-State level as this is not provided in the Rome Statute. That said, the Rome Statute does provide possible modalities of satisfaction as a reparation for an act of aggression.

M. Wong (✉)
University of Essex, Colchester, United Kingdom
e-mail: meagan.wong@essex.ac.uk

O. Spijkers et al. (eds.), *Netherlands Yearbook of International Law 2022*, Netherlands Yearbook of International Law 53, https://doi.org/10.1007/978-94-6265-627-7_6

Keywords Aggression · Crime of aggression · State responsibility · International Criminal Court · Reparation · Satisfaction · Content of State responsibility

6.1 Introduction

The International Criminal Court (ICC) is, at present, the only international court that has jurisdiction over the crime of aggression.[1] In the event of future proceedings on a case of the crime of aggression, the ICC will have to determine an act of aggression as a substantive element within the definition of the crime in the Rome Statute of the International Criminal Court (Rome Statute).[2] An unusual dynamic at the ICC arises, as the Court will need to decide on State conduct of aggression in the course of determining individual criminal responsibility for the crime of aggression.[3] As the ICC is not a forum for inter-State dispute settlement, it may appear rather curious for this Court to determine a breach of an international obligation by a State (an act of aggression),[4] and even more curious that the ICC may also engage with State responsibility.[5] The crux of this chapter delves into the content of State responsibility, which is the new legal relationship that arises from the breach of the international obligation,[6] i.e., the act of aggression; of which, legal consequences are entailed for the aggressor State,[7] including the obligation to make full reparation for damage caused by the wrongful act.[8]

In the *Factory at Chorzów* case, the PCIJ held:

> The decision whether there has been a breach of an engagement involves no doubt a more important jurisdiction than a decision as to the nature or extent of reparation due for a breach of an international engagement the existence of which is already established.[9]

Crawford has observed this to mean that it is 'axiomatic that jurisdiction to determine breach of an obligation implies jurisdiction to award reparation for any breach found.'[10] As the ICC has jurisdiction to determine State conduct in relation to an act of aggression, the question that arises is whether the Court is able to award reparation for injury caused by the aforesaid act of aggression.

---

[1] Resolution ICC-ASP/16/Res.5 (Activation of the jurisdiction of the Court over the crime of aggression), adopted on 14 December 2017.

[2] Rome Statute of the International Criminal Court (Rome Statute), Article 8 *bis*.

[3] Ibid.

[4] Pellet 2015, p. 562.

[5] See Wong 2021.

[6] International Law Commission, 'Draft Articles on Responsibility of States for Internationally Wrongful Acts', Yearbook of the International Law Commission 2001 (United Nations 2001) vol II (2) 26 (2001 ILC Articles), Part Two; see Higgins 2010; Stern 2010, p. 563.

[7] 2001 ILC Articles., Article 28.

[8] Ibid., Article 34.

[9] *Factory at Chorzów*, Jurisdiction, (1927) PCIJ Ser A No 9, 23.

[10] Crawford 2016, p. 690.

Consequently, there are conceptual implications for the analytical framework of State responsibility, but also real implications for the interests of the aggressor State and victim State, whose interests would thereby be engaged at the ICC in the case of a crime of aggression. Furthermore, the role of the ICC, if able to award reparation for aggression, bears relevance and practical significance because the Court may be a forum whereby the aggressor State may perform its obligation to make full reparation to the victim (injured) State for an act of aggression.

The present chapter is structured into three sections. First, the definition of the crime of aggression in Article 8 *bis* of the Rome Statute is set out, with particular attention to the State conduct element of the crime: an act of aggression, which by its character, gravity, and scale, constitutes a manifest violation of the Charter of the United Nations.[11] This is followed by establishing the jurisdictional regime in respect of the crime of aggression. The underlying premise is to ascertain the powers conferred by States Parties to the ICC to determine State conduct of aggression.

Secondly, as an act of aggression entails the international responsibility of the aggressor State, the forms of reparation relevant in the case of a crime of aggression at the ICC will be considered. The present chapter engages with the analytical framework of the International Law Commission's 2001 Articles on the Responsibility of States for Internationally Wrongful Acts (2001 ILC Articles)[12] on State responsibility. Accordingly, the forms of reparation for the purposes of Article 34 of the 2001 ILC Articles are restitution, constitution, compensation, and satisfaction. As the ICC is not an inter-State forum, and the aggressor and victim State are not parties to the proceedings in the case of a crime of aggression, it is difficult to see how the Court may award restitution or compensation to the victim State. Moreover, States Parties to the Rome Statute have not conferred powers to the ICC to award restitution or compensation when determining an act of aggression. The inquiry then shifts towards examining whether the ICC may award satisfaction as reparation for two reasons: (i) moral damage to a State for an act of aggression,[13] i.e., violation of sovereignty or territorial integrity is not financially assessable damage, and thus, satisfaction is the more appropriate remedy;[14] (ii) the ICC may not award restitution or compensation for an act of aggression, and thus satisfaction would then be the form of reparation for the victim State.[15]

Consequently, and thirdly, the focus is on satisfaction as a form of reparation for an act of aggression at the ICC. Drawing upon the institutional framework pursuant to the Rome Statute,[16] there are three possible modalities of satisfaction for an act of aggression: (i) initiation of an investigation in respect of a crime of aggression, which is indicative of the process of penal action against an individual whose conduct caused the act of aggression; (ii) determination by the ICC of an act of aggression

---

[11] Rome Statute, Article 8 *bis* (1).

[12] Ibid.

[13] 2001 ILC Articles, Article 31, Commentary 5.

[14] Ibid., Article 37, Commentary 3.

[15] Ibid., Article 37.

[16] Rome Statute, Articles 8 *bis*, 15 *bis* and 15 *ter*.

pursuant to Article 8 *bis* of the Rome Statute, which is akin to a declaration of wrongfulness; (iii) compensation pursuant to Article 75 of the Rome Statute, which may be a form of satisfaction.

Whilst it is generally accepted that State responsibility for aggression is the underlying premise for individual criminal responsibility for the crime of aggression,[17] the former has been largely neglected in scholarly contributions thus far.[18] Indeed, the mainstream view tends to acknowledge an act of aggression as the State conduct element of the crime,[19] but State responsibility, and the implications thereof, is rarely engaged with—or is dismissed as being outside of the mandate of the ICC.[20] Therefore, this chapter goes against the mainstream view and adopts a generalist international law analytical framework to argue that the ICC does have competence to determine State conduct of an act of aggression;[21] and that furthermore, the content of State responsibility is applicable at the Court in the case of a crime of aggression.[22]

This chapter contributes to a number of streams of scholarship. First, on the crime of aggression, this contribution builds upon and further develops scholarly views challenging the mainstream position that the ICC is not a competent forum to engage with State responsibility for aggression.[23] This contribution adds to this new stream of scholarship on the crime of aggression, by focusing on the content of international responsibility,[24] particularly on the potential forms of satisfaction available at the ICC for an act of aggression. This of course has practical implications for both aggressor State and victim State during the initiation of an investigation in respect of a crime of aggression.[25] Secondly, this chapter also contributes to scholarship on the content of international responsibility and reparation,[26] particularly as satisfaction is not considered in as much detail as compensation or restitution.[27] Further, this chapter also contributes to the discussion on reparation for the use of force—or act

---

[17] International Law Commission, 'Draft Code of Crimes against the Peace and Security of Mankind with commentaries', Yearbook of the International Law Commission, 1996, vol. II (Part Two), Article 9, Commentary 14: "The aggression attributed to a State is a *sine qua non* for the responsibility of an individual for his participation in the crime of aggression. An individual cannot incur responsibility for this crime in the absence of aggression committed by a State".

[18] On the amendments to the Rome Statute on the crime of aggression, see Fernández de Gurmendi 2002; Blokker 2007; Clark 2009; Kress and von Holtzendorff 2010; Blokker and Kress 2010; Zimmermann 2012; Barriga and Grover 2011; Barriga and Blokker 2016a; Blokker and Barriga 2016; Barriga and Blokker 2016a, b; Zimmermann 2018; Kress 2018.

[19] Kress 2016.

[20] Reisinger Coracini and Wrange 2016, p. 316.

[21] Wong 2021, pp. 968–972.

[22] Ibid., pp. 978–982.

[23] Wong 2021.

[24] 2001 ILC Articles, Part Two.

[25] Ibid., Article 43.

[26] Shelton 2002; Higgins 2010; Stern 2010; Gray et al. 2010; Barker 2010; Wyler and Papaux 2010; Wittich 2010.

[27] Satisfaction has received considerably less attention in scholarship on reparation, e.g. Gray 1999; Ibid., Shelton 2002; Gray 2013; more recently, Paparinskis 2020.

of aggression.[28] Thirdly, international law, and the law of State responsibility, are decentralized. The content of international responsibility flows from the breach of the international obligation,[29] i.e., the act of aggression, itself, regardless of any formal setting. Notably, and as will be pointed out in this chapter, the ICC, which already has jurisdiction over an act of aggression,[30] also has features in place within its international institutional framework, that may be characterized as modalities of satisfaction for the act of aggression. As such, there is a potential forum whereby aggressor State and victim State have consented to jurisdiction in regard of a crime of aggression, thereby enabling the former to (partially) discharge its obligation to make full reparation towards the latter.[31] The role of the Court in the case of the crime of aggression therefore shifts beyond the mainstream understanding of an international criminal court.[32]

6.2 The Crime of Aggression and the Rome Statute

It may appear curious that the ICC may determine the conduct of a State when prosecuting an individual for the crime of aggression. Yet, the ICC is an international organization, which means States Parties to the Rome State may confer powers on the Court through its constituent instrument, i.e., the Rome Statute. The present analysis commences by briefly touching upon the definition of the crime of aggression in the Rome Statute with particular reference to the competence of the Court to determine inter-State conduct in relation to an act of aggression.[33] The analysis then continues to consider how State consent to the exercise of jurisdiction is upheld in a case of the crime of aggression at the ICC.

6.2.1 *Article 8* **bis** *of the Rome Statute*

The crime of aggression in the Rome Statute is inherently unique and different from the other crimes within the jurisdiction of the Court, as the definition of the crime comprises State conduct (an act of aggression) as an element of the crime.[34] It may be questioned whether the ICC, as an international criminal court, has the competence to determine inter-State conduct in relation to an act of aggression.[35]

---

[28] E.g. Gattini 2002; Gray 2006; Murphy et al. 2013; Feighery et al. 2015; Lee 2023.

[29] 2001 ILC Articles, Part Two, Chapter I, Commentary 1-2.

[30] Rome Statute, Articles 15 *bis* and 15 *ter.*

[31] 2001 ILC Articles, Article 34.

[32] See Schabas 2013; Murphy 2013.

[33] Rome Statute, Article 8 *bis*

[34] Ibid.

[35] Reisinger Coracini and Wrange 2016, p. 316; see also Pellet 2015, p. 562.

From an international institutional law analytical framework, the answer is yes, as States Parties to the Rome Statute have expressly conferred powers to the ICC to determine an act of aggression in Article 8 *bis*.[36]

Article 8 *bis* (1) reads:

> For the purpose of this Statute, "crime of aggression" means the planning, preparation, initiation or execution, by a person in a position effectively to exercise control over or to direct the political or military action of a State, of an act of aggression which, by its character, gravity and scale, constitutes a manifest violation of the Charter of the United Nations.[37]

A crime of aggression for the purposes of Article 8 *bis*(1) Rome Statute arises from an act of aggression which, by its character, gravity and scale, constitutes a manifest violation of the Charter of the United Nations. Notably the language expressly stipulates that an '"act of aggression" means the use of armed force by a State against the sovereignty, territorial integrity or political independence of another State',[38] followed by specific acts of aggression in paragraphs (a) to (g), which explicitly encompass various forms of inter-State conduct.[39] Therefore, inter-State conduct in relation to aggression is very much a substantive element within the definition of the crime of aggression in Article 8 *bis* (1) of the Rome Statute. Consequently, the ICC has subject-matter jurisdiction over all substantive elements of the crime, which would include State conduct of an act of aggression.

Pursuant to Article 8 *bis* of the Rome Statute, there is no crime of aggression without State conduct of an act of aggression; accordingly, an individual cannot act within one or any of the modes of perpetration,[40] such as planning, preparing, initiating or executing—without the underlying State conduct of aggression.[41] Therefore, individual criminal responsibility for the crime of aggression is predicated upon State responsibility for aggression. In other words, the crime of aggression can only arise from an act of aggression, which is an internationally wrongful act of the aggressor State. As mentioned above, this is unique and different from the other crimes in the Rome Statute, as the other crimes can be perpetrated by an individual irrespective of State conduct.[42]

As an act of aggression pursuant to Article 8 *bis*(2) for the purposes of Article 8 *bis*(1) is a substantive element of the crime of aggression, it would follow that inter-State conduct of aggression falls within the jurisdiction *ratione materiae* of the Court and cannot be merely a preliminary or incidental finding.[43] In a similar vein,

---

[36] Rome Statute, former Article 5(2); Wong 2021, pp. 969–972.

[37] Ibid., Article 8 *bis*(1).

[38] Kress 2016, pp. 422–435.

[39] Ibid., pp. 434–450.

[40] Clark 2016a.

[41] See approach of International Military Tribunal in Nuremberg in relation to crimes against peace, 'Judgment of the International Military Tribunal for the Trial of German Major War Criminals, Nuremberg, 30 September and 1 October 1946 (Reproduced), Judgment' 1947, pp. 186–221; see also Wong 2021, pp. 965–968.

[42] Wong 2021, p. 968.

[43] But see Reisinger Coracini and Wrange 2016, p. 316.

as State conduct is a substantive element of the crime, a determination of an act of aggression is a legal finding and not a factual finding.[44]

6.2.2 *State Consent and the Exercise of Jurisdiction over the Crime of Aggression*

The jurisdictional regime over the crime of aggression at the ICC is *sui generis* in nature.[45] A distinct jurisdictional regime for the crime of aggression exists as compared to the other crimes within Article 5(1) of the Rome Statute.[46] First, from a procedural standpoint, the exercise of the Court's jurisdiction over the crime of aggression depends on how the jurisdiction was 'triggered'.[47] Pursuant to Article 13 of the Rome Statute, the Court's jurisdiction with respect to a crime of aggression may be 'triggered' by a State referral (Article 13(a)), a referral by the Security Council acting under Chapter VII of the UN Charter (Article 13(b)), or a *proprio motu* investigation by the Prosecutor (Article 13(c)). However, according to Articles 15 *bis* and 15 *ter* respectively, there is a different subject-matter jurisdictional regime based on whether the crime was referred to the Court by a State referral and *proprio motu* investigation (15 *bis*)—or a Security Council referral (15 *ter*).[48]

In the absence of a Security Council referral, i.e., a *proprio motu* investigation or State referral,[49] there is an additional institutional step, whereby an external determination of an act of aggression is required as a pre-condition for jurisdiction over the crime of aggression.[50] When the Prosecutor concludes that there is a reasonable basis to proceed with an investigation in respect of a crime of aggression, the Prosecutor shall first 'ascertain whether the Security Council has made a determination of an act of aggression by the State concerned.'[51] In the event that the Security Council has made a determination of an act of aggression, the Prosecutor may proceed with

---

[44] Wong 2021, pp. 969-971.

[45] Rome Statute, Articles 15 *bis* and 15 *ter;* see Barriga and Blokker 2016a

[46] Cf. Rome Statute, Article 12.

[47] O'Keefe 2015, p. 535.

[48] Cf. Rome Statute, Article 13; Wenaweser 2010, pp. 884-886; Barriga and Grover 2011, pp. 528-531; Blokker and Barriga 2016; Barriga and Blokker 2016b.

[49] Rome Statute, Article 15 *bis*.

[50] During the course of negotiations, this has been referred to as 'jurisdictional filter', see Blokker 2007; Kress and von Holtzendorff 2010, p. 1212; Wenaweser 2010, pp. 884–886. On background and negotiation history, see Fernández de Gurmendi 2002, pp. 601–603; Clark 2009, pp. 1113–1114; Kress and von Holtzendorff 2010, pp. 1183–1186. For an insight into the Review Conference, see Wenaweser 2010, pp. 885–886. See also see Report of the International Law Commission on the Work of its Forty-sixth Session, Draft Statute for an International Criminal Court, U.N. GAOR, 49th Sess., Supp. No. 10, at 70, art. 20(b), U.N. Doc. A/49/10 (1994) (hereinafter "Draft ILC Statute"), Article 23.

[51] The Prosecutor shall also notify the Secretary-General of the UN of the situation before the Court, including any relevant information and documents, Rome Statute, Article 15 *bis* (6).

the investigation in respect of a crime of aggression.[52] If the Security Council has not made a determination of aggression within six months after the date of notification, the Pre-Trial Division may authorize the commencement of the investigation in respect of a crime of aggression, and the Prosecutor may proceed with the investigation in respect of a crime of aggression.[53]

In contrast, in the event of a Security Council referral,[54] the Council would refer a situation in which one or more of the crimes within the Rome Statute (including the crime of aggression) appears to have been committed. There is no need for the Security Council to make a determination of an act of aggression;[55] the Council only needs to make a referral of a situation in which one (or more) crimes within the Rome Statute appear to have been committed.[56] It is clear that an external determination of an act of aggression, i.e., a determination by the Security Council prior to an initiation of investigation in respect of the crime of aggression is only required in the absence of a Security Council referral.[57] The underlying premise is for the Security Council to play a role with respect to the initiation of an investigation in respect to the crime of aggression at the ICC—either by referring a situation to the Court or by determining an act of aggression.[58]

The Rome Statute stipulates:

> A determination of an act of aggression by an organ outside the Court shall be without prejudice to the Court's own findings under this Statute.[59]

Accordingly, States Parties conferred the power to the ICC to make a substantive finding of an act of aggression.[60] Therefore, the Court has the competence to make its own determination of an act of aggression.

Secondly, Articles 15 *bis* and 15 *ter* respectively, give rise to different subject-matter jurisdiction over the crime of aggression.[61] The latter is relatively straightforward, in the event of a Security Council referral, the ICC may exercise jurisdiction over an act of aggression committed by any State—regardless of whether the alleged aggressor is a member of the Rome Statute.[62] The former, however, merits further

---

[52] Ibid., Article 15 *bis*(7).

[53] Ibid., Article 15 *bis*(8).

[54] Ibid., Article 15 *ter.*

[55] Kress and von Holtzendorff 2010, p. 1211; Blokker and Barriga 2016, pp. 647–648.

[56] Ibid., Blokker and Barriga 2016, pp. 647-648.

[57] Blokker 2007, pp. 876–878.

[58] The intention of the drafters was to safeguard the 'primary' role of the Security Council in relation to the maintenance of international peace and security in order to ensure that amendments to the Rome Statute is consistent with the UN Charter, see ibid., pp. 878–880; Barriga and Grover 2011, pp. 526–528.; see former Article 5(2) Rome Statute; Articles 24 and 39 of the UN Charter; Blokker 2007, pp. 876–878. On the reaction of the five permanent members of the Security Council after the consensus decision had been reached, see Blokker and Kress 2010, p. 894.

[59] Rome Statute, Article 15 *bis* (9) and 15 *ter*.

[60] Barriga and Blokker 2016a, pp. 638–640. Cf. Draft ILC Statute, Article 23.

[61] Wong 2016, pp. 198-204; Blokker and Kress 2010, p. 893.

[62] Rome Statute, Article 13(b); Blokker and Barriga 2016, pp. 648–650.

consideration as there is a narrower scope for the exercise of jurisdiction in the absence of a Security Council referral.[63] First, the Court shall not exercise jurisdiction over the crime of aggression when the act of aggression is committed by a national of a non-State Party or on the territory of a non-State Party.[64] Both alleged aggressor State and supposed victim States must be parties to the Rome Statute.

Article 12(1) of the Rome Statute stipulates, '[a] State which becomes a Party to this Statute thereby accepts the jurisdiction of the Court with respect to the crimes referred to in article 5'. It would appear accordingly that all States Parties accept the jurisdiction of the Court over the crime of aggression. This is reflected in Article 15 *bis(*4):

> The Court may, in accordance with article 12, exercise jurisdiction over a crime of aggression, arising from an act of aggression committed by a State Party, unless that State Party has previously declared that it does not accept such jurisdiction by lodging a declaration with the Registrar [...].[65]

It would appear accordingly that the ICC may exercise jurisdiction over an alleged act of aggression committed by a State Party unless it has declared that it does not accept the Court's jurisdiction over this crime. However, when the amendments to the Rome Statute on the crime of aggression ("Crime of aggression amendments") were adopted,[66] paragraph 1 stipulated that the Assembly of States Parties to the Rome Statute ("ASP"):

> Decides to adopt [...] the amendments to the Statute [...], which are subject to ratification or acceptance and shall enter into force in accordance with article 121, paragraph 5; and notes that any State Party may lodge a declaration referred to in article 15 *bis* prior to ratification or acceptance.[67]

The entry-into-force mechanism pursuant to Article 121(5) stipulates:

> Any amendment to articles 5, 6, 7 and 8 of this Statute shall enter into force for those States Parties which have accepted the amendment one year after the deposit of their instruments of ratification or acceptance. In respect of a State Party which has not accepted the amendment, the Court shall not exercise its jurisdiction regarding a crime covered by the amendment when committed by that State Party's nationals or on its territory.[68]

Notably, the second sentence of Article 121(5) appears at odds with Article 12(1).[69] Consequently, the subject-matter jurisdiction of the ICC over the crime of aggression becomes an issue of treaty interpretation of how Articles 12 and 121(5)

---

[63] On the background, see Wenaweser 2010, p. 884.

[64] Rome Statute, Article 15 *bis* (5); Zimmermann 2012, pp. 221-223; cf. Rome Statute, Article 12(2).

[65] Ibid., Article 14 *bis*(4).

[66] Resolution RC/Res.6 (The Crime of Aggression), adopted at the 13th plenary meeting, on 11 June 2010.

[67] On the background, see Clark 2009, p. 1113; Kress and von Holtzendorff 2010, pp. 1194–1999.

[68] On entry-into-force mechanisms at the Review Conference, see Wenaweser 2010, pp. 884–885; Barriga and Grover 2011, pp. 523–526; Barriga and Blokker 2016a, pp. 662–627.

[69] Wong 2016, pp. 203–205; Barriga and Blokker 2016a, pp. 627–634.

should be read together.[70] The two prevailing views can be surmised as whether all States Parties to the Rome Statute accept the jurisdiction of the Court over the crime of aggression (Article 15 *bis* (4) prevailing) unless they expressly opt-out;[71] or whether States Parties need to expressly ratify or accept the amendments to the Rome Statute on the crime of aggression (Article 121(5) prevailing).[72] Notably, both interpretations uphold State consent, but differ with regard to how consent should be expressed.

In 2017, the ASP adopted in New York, by consensus, Resolution ICC-ASP/16 Res.5 on the 'Activation of the jurisdiction of the Court over the crime of aggression' ("Activation Decision");[73] which confirmed 'in the case of a State referral or *proprio motu* investigation the Court shall not exercise its jurisdiction regarding a crime of aggression when committed by a national or on the territory of a State Party that has not ratified or accepted these amendments.'[74] According to the Activation Decision, the ICC can only exercise jurisdiction over the crime of aggression if both the alleged aggressor State and supposed victim State have ratified or accepted the amendments to the Rome Statute on the crime of aggression. That said, the jurisdiction of the Court over the crime of aggression pursuant to Article 15 *bis* of the Rome Statute is by no means entirely settled or established. The interpreter, i.e. the Court, will have to read Article 15 *bis*(4) together with Articles 12 and 121(5) of the Rome Statute, and decide what interpretive weight to accord to para.2 of the Activation Decision.[75] Regardless, State consent is upheld (whether expressly or impliedly) whichever interpretation is conducted by the interpreter.[76] Be that as it may, it is likely that the interpreter would follow the interpretation put forward in the Activation Decision.[77]

In light of the above, it is clear that States Parties to the ICC were aware of the inter-State nature of the crime of aggression in Article 8 *bis* of the Rome Statute and the need for State consent with respect to the exercise of jurisdiction over the crime as reflected in Articles 15 *bis* and 15 *ter* of the Rome Statute.

---

70 Zimmermann 2012; Wong 2016; Blokker and Barriga 2016, pp. 664–668.

71 Wong 2016, pp. 206–208. For criticism of the 'opt-out' mechanism see Zimmermann 2012, 223–224.

72 Wong 2016, pp. 204–210; on the prevalence of the second sentence of Article 121(5), see Table 6.1 at ibid., 205.; on the prevalence of Article 15 *bis*(4), see Table 6.2, at ibid., 208.

73 Resolution ICC-ASP/16 Res.5 (n 1); See also Kress 2018; on the background, see Barriga and Blokker 2016a, pp. 633–637.

74 Resolution ICC-ASP/16/Res.5, para.2.; see Zimmermann 2018, pp. 22–27.

75 Wong 2020, pp. 214–223.

76 Wong 2021, pp. 972–977.

77 The better argument is the Activation Decision is a Rule of the International Organization; and accordingly, may prevail over Articles 31 and 32 of the Vienna Convention on the Law of Treaties with regard to the interpretation of the Rome Statute when interpreted by one of its organs, Wong 2020, pp. 223–226.

6.3 The Content of the International Responsibility of a State and an Act of Aggression at the International Criminal Court

It is axiomatic that 'every internationally wrongful act of a State entails the international responsibility of that State.'[78] Recall the commentary of the ILC:

> the general obligation of reparation is formulated in article 31 as the immediate corollary of a State's responsibility, i.e. as an obligation of the responsible State resulting from the breach, rather than as a right of an injured State or States [...] the general obligation of reparation arises automatically upon commission of an internationally wrongful act and is not, as such, contingent upon a demand or protest by any State, even if the form which reparation should take in the circumstances may depend on the response of the injured State or States.[79]

The content of international responsibility flows by operation of law from the breach of the international obligation,[80] irrespectively and independently of, any formal finding of State responsibility in any judicial setting.[81] Hence, there are legal consequences for the aggressor State, who as the wrongdoing State has an obligation to cease that act, if it is continuing, or to offer appropriate assurances and guarantees of non-repetition, if circumstances so require.[82] Further, the aggressor State is also under an obligation to make full reparation for the injury caused by the internationally wrongful act, i.e. the act of aggression; such injury includes any damage, whether material or moral, caused by the act of aggression.[83] Material damage is understood to encompass damage to property or other interests of the State and its nationals which is assessable in financial terms.[84] Moral damage may take place in two forms: moral damage to a State; and moral damage to a State's nationals.[85] The former would include injury which is not financially assessable but would be considered to be an affront to the State, e.g., a violation of sovereignty or territorial integrity,[86] whilst the latter would refer to 'individual pain and suffering, loss of loved ones or the personal affront associated with an intrusion into one's home or private life.'[87]

As argued above, in the case of a crime of aggression at the ICC, Article 8 *bis*(1) of the Rome Statute requires a finding of an act of aggression as a substantive element of the crime. The Court, therefore, would make a formal finding—or determination—of an internationally wrongful act of a State pursuant to Article 8 *bis* of the Rome Statute even if it does not refer to the legal technical nomenclature of State responsibility. I

---

78 2001 ILC Articles, Article 1.

79 Ibid., Article 31, Commentary 4.

80 Ibid., Part Two, Commentary 1.

81 Ibid., Article 31, Commentary 4.

82 Rome Statute, Article 30.

83 Ibid., Article 31; see Stern 2010, p. 563 and see also p. 569.

84 2001 ILC Articles, Article 31, Commentary 5.

85 Ibid., Article 31, Commentary 5 and 16.

86 Crawford 2013, p. 487.

87 Ibid., pp. 486–487.

have made the point earlier,[88] that the determination of an act of aggression pursuant to Article 8 *bis* cannot be a 'preliminary' or 'incidental' matter during the proceedings on the crime of aggression because the act of aggression is a necessary condition, i.e., an element of the crime, for determining individual criminal responsibility of the defendant for the crime of aggression.[89] Therefore, an act of aggression pursuant to Article 8 *bis* of the Rome Statute is very much within the subject-matter jurisdiction of the ICC on the crime of aggression, and not one which is preliminary or incidental. The question that arises is whether the ICC has jurisdiction to award reparation for an act of aggression upon determining its existence pursuant to Article 8 *bis.* If so, the ICC may provide a setting to give effect to the aggressor State's obligation to make full reparation for injury caused by the act of aggression.

It should be clarified from the outset, that the ICC does have powers to make reparations to victims under Article 75 of the Rome Statute:

> The Court shall establish principles relating to reparations to, or in respect of, victims, including restitution, compensation and rehabilitation. On this basis, in its decision the Court may, either upon request or on its own motion in exceptional circumstances, determine the scope and extent of any damage, loss and injury to, or in respect of, victims and will state the principles on which it is acting.[90]

As will be elaborated further below, the reparations regime in Article 75 of the Rome Statute is different from reparation under the law of State responsibility and is specific only to the ICC. This is because reparations pursuant to Article 75 apply to victims of crimes within the jurisdiction of the Court (including the crime of aggression) —and not to the victim State which is injured by the act of aggression. By contrast, reparation under the law of State responsibility is premised on the obligation of the wrongdoing State to make full reparation to the injured State for injury caused by the internationally wrongful act. Thus, whilst the nomenclature is identical, restitution and compensation pursuant to Article 75 of the Rome Statute is different from restitution and compensation for the purposes of Article 34 of the 2001 ILC Articles. The former would not enable the aggressor State to discharge its duty to make full reparation for the injury caused to the victim State by the act of aggression.

6.3.1 Reparation and the Law of State Responsibility at the ICC

Article 34 of the 2001 ILC Articles stipulates:

---

[88] See also Wong 2021, p. 969.

[89] Ibid., 969–970. See also 'Judgment of the International Military Tribunal for the Trial of German Major War Criminals, Nuremberg, 30 September and 1 October 1946 (Reproduced), Judgment', 1946, paras 186–221.

[90] Ibid., Article 75(1); McCarthy 2012, pp. 76–84.

> Full reparation for the injury caused by the internationally wrongful act shall take the form of restitution, compensation and satisfaction, either singly or in combination, in accordance with the provisions of this chapter.[91]

Restitution, according to Article 35 of the 2001 ILC Articles, stipulates that the wrongdoing State, i.e., the aggressor State is under an 'obligation to make restitution, that is, to re-establish the situation which existed before the wrongful act was committed […]'.[92] The ILC commentary suggests this may take the form of 'material restoration or return of territory, persons or property, or the reversal of some juridical act, or some combination of them.'[93] It would follow that it is for the aggressor State to perform this obligation to make restitution. This is however at odds with a case of the crime of aggression at the ICC as the Court does not have the power to make an order for restitution against the aggressor State. When restitution is not available, compensation is the reparation that is intended to 'fill in any gaps so as to ensure full reparation for damage suffered.'[94]

Compensation pursuant to Article 36 of the 2001 ILC Articles applies when '[t]he State responsible for an internationally wrongful act is under an obligation to compensate for the damage caused thereby, insofar as such damage is not made good by restitution.[95] As compensation refers to financially assessable damage, this would include: i) pecuniary and non-pecuniary injury caused to individuals;[96] ii) pecuniary injury caused directly to the State.[97] Non-pecuniary injury—or moral damage, caused to a State would not be characterized as financially assessable damage.[98] Notably, the beneficiary of compensation for financially assessable damage in relation to an act of aggression is the victim State.[99] This was the approach followed by the ICJ in the *Congo v. Uganda* case.[100] That said, a notable contrast is between the use of force where the beneficiary of the obligation is the State, and possible other breaches associated with the use of force, such as international humanitarian law, international human rights law, that have harmed individuals and property, where it

---

[91] 2001 ILC Articles (n 6) Article 34; Recall as well, the well-known dicta from Chorzów Factory, whereby, '[r]eparation must, as far as possible, wipe out all the consequences of the illegal act and re-establish the situation which would, in all probability, have existed if that act had not been committed.' Factory at Chorzów, p. 47.

[92] 2001 ILC Articles, Article 35; Tanzi 2021; Crawford 2013, p. 510.

[93] Ibid., Article 35, Commentary 5.

[94] Ibid., Article 36, Commentary 3; *Lusitania Case,* UNRIAA, vol. VII (Sales No. 1956.V.5), p. 32, at p. 39 (1923); *Factory at Chorzów*, p. 47.

[95] Ibid., Article 36, Commentary 1.

[96] Ibid., Article 36, Commentary 5.

[97] Ibid.

[98] Ibid., Article 36, Commentary 1 "The qualification "financially assessable" is intended to exclude compensation for what is sometimes referred to as "moral damage" to a State, i.e. the affront or injury caused by a violation of rights not associated with actual damage to property or persons: this is the subject matter of satisfaction, dealt with in article 37."

[99] Cf. Rome Statute, Article 75.

[100] ICJ, *Case Concerning Armed Activities on the Territory of the Congo* (Democratic Republic of the Congo v. Uganda), ICJ, Judgement, February 9, 2022, at 408;

is an open question whether the State is under an obligation to (or at the very least should) distribute compensation to individuals and afflicted communities.[101]

The ICJ has declared '[i]t is a well-established rule of international law that an injured State is entitled to obtain compensation from the State which has committed an internationally wrongful act for the damage caused by it.'[102] Thus, the victim State is entitled to obtain compensation from the aggressor State. The ILC in its Commentary to Article 36 noted that 'it is equally well established that an international court or tribunal which has jurisdiction with respect to a claim of State responsibility has, as an aspect of that jurisdiction, the power to award compensation for damage suffered.'[103] This reflects the dictum of the Factory at Chorzów case, as quoted above, whereby jurisdiction to determine wrongful State conduct implies jurisdiction to award reparation for the injury caused by the wrongful act. As the ICC has jurisdiction with respect to an act of aggression pursuant to Article 8 *bis* of the Rome Statute, the concomitant question is whether the Court has the power to award compensation to the victim State for injury caused by the act of aggression.

The answer is that the drafters of to the Rome Statute (and the amendments thereof), i.e., the ASP, ultimately have discretion on how to confer powers on the ICC. As the Rome Statute (including its amendments on the crime of aggression) does not provide a mechanism that enables compensation to be awarded to the victim State for the act of aggression,[104] Article 8 *bis* can be read as conferring to the Court only the power to determine aggression—without awarding compensation for injury caused by the wrongful conduct.

As mentioned above, the ICC does have the power to award compensation pursuant to Article 75 of the Rome Statute. However, as also already mentioned, compensation awarded by the ICC pursuant to Article 75(1) of the Rome Statute is a different matter from compensation under Art 36 of the 2001 ILC Articles.[105] Three further points will be made.

First, compensation pursuant to Article 75 of the Rome Statute, is for the crime of aggression and not an act of aggression. Here, compensation is ordered upon a finding of individual criminal responsibility,[106] which is, and of course, an entirely separate regime than State responsibility.[107] Compensation pursuant to the former has been acknowledged as being 'as much about the restoration of dignity and the acknowledgement of the harm suffered, as it is about monetary compensation or

[101] See Democratic Republic of the Congo v. Uganda ibid.; and also Ahmadou Sadio Diallo (Republic of Guinea v. Democratic Republic of the Congo), Compensation, Judgment, I.C.J. Reports 2012, p. 324, para. 57.

[102] Gabčikovo-Nagymaros Project (Hungary/Slovakia) Judgment ICJ Reports 1997, p. 7, para. 152.

[103] 2001 ILC Articles, Article 36, Commentary 4; Factory at Chorzów; Fisheries Jurisdiction (Federal Republic of Germany v. Zeeland), Merits, Judgment, ICJ Reports 1974, p. 175, pp. 203-205, paras. 71-76; Military and Paramilitary Activities in and against Nicaragua (Nicaragua v. United States of America). Merits, Judgment. ICJ Reports 1986, p. 14, p. 142.

[104] Cf. Rome Statute, Articles 75 and 79.

[105] McCarthy 2012, pp. 129–130.

[106] Rome Statute, Article 75(2).

[107] Zegveld 2010, p. 79; McCarthy 2012, pp. 34–74; Ferstman 2020.

restitution';[108] whilst compensation with regard to the latter is purely functional to address actual losses that correspond with financially assessable damage.[109] Moreover, compensation, under the law of State responsibility, does not stem from the right or entitlement of the victim State to make a claim,[110] but rather from the new legal relationship that arises from the internationally wrongful act (aggression).[111]

Secondly, although compensation for the crime of aggression relates to injury caused by the underlying act of aggression, an order for an award of compensation pursuant to Article 75(2) of the Rome Statute is directed against a convicted person—and not the aggressor State.[112] Therefore, the obligation of the aggressor State to make full reparation for injury caused by the act of aggression is not fulfilled. Article 75(2) of the Rome Statute also enables the Court, where appropriate, to order that the award for reparations be made through the Trust Fund pursuant to Article 79 of the Rome Statute ("Victims Trust Fund").[113] As set out above, the content of international responsibility gives rise to an obligation on the aggressor State to make full reparation for injury caused by the act of aggression. An order for an award for compensation directly against a convicted person, or to be made through the Trust Fund, is entirely distinct from compensation or monetary payment from the aggressor State.

Thirdly, 'victims' of the crime of aggression who may benefit from compensation pursuant to Articles 75 and 79 of the Rome Statute, are natural persons, i.e., individuals—and not the victim (injured) State.[114] This appears to depart from general

---

[108] Ferstman 2002, p. 668.

[109] Notably, in the Commentary to Article 36, the ILC makes it clear that compensation 'is not concerned to punish the responsible State, nor does compensation have an expressive or exemplary character.', 2001 ILC Articles, Article 36, Commentary 4; Wittich 2010, p. 667; Crawford 2013, pp. 523–526.; See also Jorgensen 1997. Decisions of international courts and tribunals support the view that punitive damages are not awarded under international law: Corfu Channel case (United Kingdom v Albania), Merits, ICJ Reports 1949, pp. 4, 23; Velásquez Rodríguez (Reparations and Costs), Inter-Am Ct HR, Series C, No 7 (1989), para 38; Armed Activities on the Territory of the Congo (Democratic Republic of the Congo v Uganda), ICJ Reports 2005, pp. 168, 227, para 165; M/V 'Saiga' (No 2) (1999) 38 ILM 1323, para 159; Eritrea-Ethiopia Claims Commission, Final Award, Ethiopia's Damages Claims, 17 August 2009.

[110] 2001 ILC Articles, Article 31 Commentary 4.

[111] Ibid., Part Two, Commentary 1.

[112] Rules of Procedure and Evidence at the ICC, reproduced from the Official Records of the Assembly of States Parties to the Rome Statute of the International Criminal Court, First session, New York, 3-10 September 2002 (ICC-ASP/1/3 and Corr.1), part II.A ("ICC Rules of Procedure and Evidence"), Rule 98(1).

[113] Rome Statute, Article 79; Resolution ICC-ASP/1/Res.6 (Establishment of a fund for the benefit of victims of crimes within the jurisdiction of the Court, and of the families of such victims) ("Victims Trust Fund establishment resolution"), para.1.

[114] ICC Rules of Procedure and Evidence, Rule 85: (a)"Victims" means natural persons who have suffered harm as a result of the commission of any crime within the jurisdiction of the Court; (b) Victims may include organizations or institutions that have sustained direct harm to any of their property which is dedicated to religion, education, art or science or charitable purposes, and to their historic monuments, hospitals and other places and objects for humanitarian purposes.

international law,[115] whereby the rightful claimant of compensation is the victim of an act of aggression, i.e. the injured State. As mentioned above, pecuniary injury and non-pecuniary injury caused to individuals from the act of aggression, under general international law, would be considered as financially assessable damage for the victim State to claim. Thus, compensation towards natural persons for the crime of aggression appears to be a different beneficiary than the victim State. Indeed, States Parties to the Rome Statute may create rights for individuals within the institutional setting of the ICC pursuant to Articles 75 and 79 of the Rome Statute to be beneficiaries for compensation (reparations) in the case of a crime of aggression. The rights afforded to individuals to be beneficiaries for compensation (reparations) stem from the Rome Statute and apply only within the setting of the ICC –not general international law.[116]

Compensation pursuant to Article 75 of the Rome Statute, therefore, should not be confused with compensation under the law of State responsibility. For the purposes of the law of State responsibility, the ICC is not a competent forum to award inter-State compensation. Returning to the earlier inquiry on whether the ICC can provide a setting to give effect to the aggressor State's obligation to make full reparation for injury caused by the act of aggression, the relationship between compensation and satisfaction merits further discussion. The function of compensation is compensatory for financially assessable damage suffered by the injured State; and as such, is 'intended to offset, as far as may be, the damage suffered by the injured State as a result of the breach.'[117] Satisfaction, is concerned with non-pecuniary injury, particularly to the State, 'on which a monetary value can be put only in a highly approximate and notional way'.[118]As the ILC Commentary reads:

> Satisfaction [...] is the remedy for those injuries, not financially assessable, which amount to an affront to the State. These injuries are frequently of a symbolic character, arising from the very fact of the breach of the obligation, irrespective of its material consequences for the State concerned.[119]

Additionally, recall that full reparation requires satisfaction as a remedy when restitution and compensation are not adequate.[120] As already pointed out, the ICC is not a forum that can order an award for restitution or compensation at the inter-State level. It would appear therefore that satisfaction is the relevant form of reparation at the ICC for an act of aggression (from which, a crime of aggression arises). This is in line with bringing into effect the aggressor State's obligation to 'give satisfaction for the injury caused by that act insofar as it cannot be made good by restitution or compensation.'[121]

---

[115] Zegveld 2010, pp. 82–83.

[116] Rome Statute, Article 75(6).

[117] 2001 ILC Articles, Article 36, Commentary 4.

[118] Ibid.

[119] Ibid., Article 36, Commentary 3.; Gray et al. 2010, p. 580.

[120] Ibid., Article 34.

[121] Ibid., Article 37(1).

6.3.2 *Satisfaction and the Crime of Aggression at the International Criminal Court*

Satisfaction is generally understood as 'any measure which a responsible State is bound to take apart from restitution or compensation.'[122] Satisfaction is not a standard form of reparation, and its 'rather exceptional character' is that it is only required when restitution and/or compensation have not been able to provide full reparation.[123] Satisfaction, as an exceptional remedy, is flexible in nature.

The inquiry shifts to how satisfaction for the victim State of aggression may be relevant in the case of a crime of aggression. As the ICC is not an inter-State forum, the answer lies in whether the Rome Statute confers powers on the Court in this respect. Bearing in mind that the 2001 ILC Articles are not prescriptive, and satisfaction is a particularly flexible reparation, it can be argued that the Rome Statute provides three ways in which satisfaction for the victim State can be found.

First, and notably, the ICC itself, provides a forum for the prosecution of the crime of aggression.[124] Indeed, one of the known forms of satisfaction is 'disciplinary or penal action against the individuals whose conduct caused the internationally wrongful act.'[125] This is in line with the definition of the crime of aggression in Article 8 *bis* of the Rome Statute, whereby a person in a position effectively to exercise control over or to direct the political or military action of a State, has planned, prepared, initiated, or executed—the act of aggression (which by its character, gravity, and scale, constitutes a manifest violation of the UN Charter) could face criminal prosecution, i.e. penal action.[126] Accordingly, prosecution at the ICC would amount to penal action against the individual whose conduct caused the act of aggression.

It may be tempting to point out that satisfaction in relation to disciplinary or penal action against the individual(s) whose conduct caused the internationally wrongful act is generally understood to take place within the domestic setting of the wrong-doing State, i.e., under the nationality principle of jurisdiction. Accordingly, it would be for the aggressor State to conduct domestic prosecution of its nationals (State leaders) for the crime of aggression. That said, from an international institutional law standpoint, States Parties to the Rome Statute, including the aggressor State, have delegated their criminal jurisdiction to the ICC. Furthermore, as the jurisdictional regime for the crime of aggression at the ICC upholds State consent, the aggressor State has consented to penal action against its national whose conduct comprised planning, preparing, initiating, or executing the act of aggression. Prosecution at the ICC for the crime of aggression can be seen as a delegation of the competence of the aggressor State with respect to domestic prosecution for the crime of aggression, and consent to the exercise of the Court's jurisdiction over its national. Thus, it can be

---

122 Crawford 2013, p. 528.

123 Ibid., Article 37, Commentary 1.

124 Rome Statute (n 2) Articles 8 *bis*, 15 *bis* and 15 *ter*.

125 2001 ILC Articles (n 6) Article 37, Commentary 5.

126 Ibid.

argued that prosecution at the ICC for the crime of aggression may be characterized as a form of satisfaction for the victim State with regard to an act of aggression.

The question that arises is whether the defendant must be successfully convicted for the crime of aggression in order for the proceedings to be considered satisfaction or if the process itself of the initiation of proceedings at the ICC will suffice. As already mentioned, satisfaction as a reparation is flexible and the 2001 ILC Articles are not intended to be prescriptive.[127] Upon reflection, the better answer is the initiation of proceedings at the ICC, because the actual criminal trial is an entirely separate legal matter from the initiation of an investigation or act of prosecution itself.[128]

Which stage of the proceedings at the ICC in respect of the crime of aggression may potentially be characterized as satisfaction for the act of aggression? Pursuant to the Rome Statute, the initiation of an investigation in respect of a crime of aggression,[129] marks the beginning of the process for a trial in respect of the crime of aggression at the ICC. Thus, the initiation of an investigation in respect of a crime of aggression, can be characterized as a form of satisfaction for the victim State with regard to an act of aggression.[130] It goes without saying that the initiation of an investigation at the ICC in respect of the crime of aggression does not preclude the victim State from claiming satisfaction or any of the other forms of reparation in respect of the same act of aggression before another competent international court or tribunal.

Secondly, Article 8 *bis* itself requires the Court to make a determination of an internationally wrongful act. Recall the first paragraph of Article 8 *bis* which stipulates the State conduct element of the crime of aggression as an 'act of aggression, which by its character, gravity and scale, constitutes a manifest violation of the Charter of the United Nations.'[131] Recall also the second paragraph of Article 8 *bis,* which comprises particular instances of inter-State conduct that may qualify as acts of aggression for the purposes of the preceding paragraph. Both paragraphs of Article 8 *bis* expressly stipulate State conduct in relation to an act of aggression as a substantive element of the definition of the crime of aggression, thereby conferring jurisdiction on the Court to determine the legality of an act of a State when considering individual criminal responsibility. Consequently, the Court would be deciding upon the wrongfulness of State conduct.

---

[127] 2001 ILC Articles, Article 37, Commentary 5 ("The appropriate form of satisfaction will depend on the circumstances and cannot be prescribed in advance.").

[128] Rome Statute, Article 22 (*Nullum crimen sine lege*); Article 23 (*nulla poena sine lege*); Article 24 (non-retroactivity ratione personae); Article 25 (Individual criminal responsibility); Article 26 (Exclusion of jurisdiction over persons under eighteen); Article 27 (Irrelevance of official capacity); Article 28 (Responsibility of commanders and other superiors); Article 29 (Non-applicability of statute of limitations); Article 30 (Mental element); Article 31 (Grounds for excluding criminal responsibility); Article 32 (mistake of fact or mistake of law); Article 33 (superior orders and prescription of law). See also Clark 2016b.

[129] Ibid., Articles 15 *bis* and 15 *ter;* see also Article 53 (Initiation of an investigation); Article 54 (Duties and powers of the Prosecutor with respect to investigations).

[130] 2001 ILC Articles, Article 37, Commentary 5.

[131] Rome Statute, Article 8 *bis*.

Although declarations of wrongfulness are not formally listed in Article 37 of the 2001 ILC Articles,[132] the ILC has observed, 'one of the most common modalities of satisfaction provided in the case of moral or non-material injury to the State is a declaration of the wrongfulness of the act by a competent court or tribunal.[133] As I have also argued elsewhere, when the ICC has determined an act of aggression pursuant to Article 8 *bis,* this is akin to a declaration of wrongfulness, which may be considered as a form of satisfaction.[134] To clarify, the ICC does not need to formally pronounce that it is making a declaration of wrongfulness for this finding to take effect as a form of satisfaction.[135] Satisfaction as a remedy, is flexible. Recall the commentary on satisfaction by the ILC:

> while the making of a declaration by a competent court or tribunal may be treated as a form of satisfaction in a given case, such declarations are not intrinsically associated with the remedy of satisfaction. Any court or tribunal which has jurisdiction over a dispute has the authority to determine the lawfulness of the conduct in question and to make a declaration of its findings, as a necessary part of the process of determining the case.[136]

Thirdly, compensation under Article 75 of the Rome Statute, whilst not compensation for the purposes of the 2001 ILC Articles, may nevertheless be characterized as satisfaction. Article 37(2) of the 2001 ILC Articles stipulates 'satisfaction may consist in an acknowledgement of the breach, an expression of regret, a formal apology or another appropriate modality.'[137] Accordingly, compensation, for the purposes of the Rome Statute,[138] could fall within the ambit of 'appropriate modality' of satisfaction pursuant to Article 37(2) of the 2001 ILC Articles.[139] Indeed, the modalities

[132] 2001 ILC Article, Article 37, Commentary 6 ("a judicial declaration is not listed in paragraph 2 only because it must emanate from a competent third party with jurisdiction over a dispute, and the articles are not concerned to specify such a part or to deal with issues of judicial jurisdiction. Instead, article 37 specifies the acknowledgement of the breach by the responsible state as a modality of satisfaction;" See also Crawford 2013, p. 529.

[133] 2001 ILC Articles, Article 37, Commentary 6. *Corfu Channel case, Judgement of April 9th 1949* (n 117) pp. 35 and 36; See also Affaire du "Carthage" (UNRIAA (1913), vol. XI, pp. 460 ("in the event that a Power has failed to fulfill its obligations, whether general or special, vis-à-vis another Power, the recognition of this fact, especially in an arbitral award, already constitutes a serious sanction"); and *Affaire du "Manouba*", ibid., p. 475. This position has been followed in many subsequent cases, including the *Rainbow Warrior* arbitration (*Case concerning the difference between New Zealand and France concerning the interpretation or application of two agreements, concluded on 9 July 1986 between the two States and which related to the problems arising from the* Rainbow Warrior Affair, 30 April 1990, UNRIAA Vol. XX, pp. 215-284), to such an extent that declaratory relief can be said to have become the normal, and certainly the first, form of satisfaction in the case of non-material injury to a State.

[134] Wong 2021, pp. 980–982.

[135] Ibid., p. 981.

[136] 2001 ILC Articles, Article 37, Commentary 6.

[137] Ibid., Article 37(2).

[138] Rome Statute, Articles 75 and 79.

[139] 2001 ILC Articles, Article 37, Commentary 5 ("appropriate modalities of satisfaction may include 'a trust fund to manage compensation payments in the interests of the beneficiaries'); see also Article 36, Commentary, 4. See also Rainbow Warrior, p. 267, para 110 and p. 275, paras. 126-128.

of satisfaction expressed in Article 37(2) of the 2001 ILC Articles are not intended to be prescriptive, and as such there is flexibility to regard an order specifying compensation directly against a convicted person in respect of victim(s) of the crime of aggression or an award for reparations, including compensation, to be made through the Victims Trust Fund.[140] The latter,[141] in particular, merits further consideration, as the Commentary to Article 37(2) specifically refers to a 'trust fund to manage compensation payments in the interests of the beneficiaries.'[142]

The ASP has discretion to determine the criteria on how the Victims Trust Fund shall be managed.[143] It is not possible to envisage whether the alleged aggressor State would have made voluntary contributions to the Trust Fund. That said, this is not relevant as the Victims Trust Fund at the ICC was established by States Parties;[144] and as such, is a feature within the Court,[145] which can be managed in relation to compensation payments in the interests of beneficiaries with regard to the crime of aggression.[146] Clearly, States Parties to the Rome Statute of the ICC have consented to the Court's power to make an order for compensation directly against a convicted person or through a Trust Fund for the benefit of victims, and the families of such victims, of crimes within the jurisdiction of the Court.[147] Thus, in the case of a crime of aggression at the ICC, both aggressor State and victim State would have consented to individuals having the status of beneficiaries to receive compensation for this crime.

In light of the foregoing, an argument can be made that compensation for the crime of aggression pursuant to Articles 75 of the Rome Statute is a form of satisfaction for the victim State with regard to an act of aggression. Notably, this form of satisfaction may only materialise upon the conviction of an individual for the crime of aggression and is ultimately for the discretion of the Court.[148]

One may question the relevance of characterizing satisfaction as a reparation at the ICC for aggression, particularly as the ICC is not an inter-State forum. Indeed, one may tilt one's head at the idea of the ICC having the competence to award reparation for an internationally wrongful act by a State. Yet, the foregoing analysis has demonstrated how potential forms of satisfaction for the victim State with regard to an act of

---

[140] Rome Statute, Article 75(2).

[141] The ILC has identified "a trust fund to manage compensation payments in the interests of the beneficiaries" as one of the possible modalities of satisfaction, see 2001 ILC Articles, Article 37, Commentary 5.

[142] 2001 ILC Articles, Article 37, Commentary 5.

[143] Rome Statute, Article 79(3). On how the ASP have decided that the Trust Fund shall be funded, see Victims Trust Fund establishment resolution, para. 2. On organisation and management of the Trust Fund, see also McCarthy 2012, pp. 226–230.

[144] Ibid., Article 79.

[145] Victims Trust Fund establishment resolution (n 123); ICC-ASP/3/Res.7 (Establishment of the Secretariat of the Trust Fund for Victims); ICC-ASP/4/Res.6 (Regulations of the Trust Fund for Victims).

[146] McCarthy 2012, pp. 225–296.

[147] Rome Statute, Articles 75 and 79.

[148] Ibid., Article 75(2).

aggression are found within the powers already conferred on the Court in the Rome Statute. Indeed, States Parties have conferred the following powers and functions to the ICC: to exercise jurisdiction over the crime of aggression;[149] to determine an act of aggression;[150] to make an order directly against a convicted person specifying appropriate reparations to, or in respect of, victims, including compensation.[151] The relevance of characterizing features already within the Rome Statute as potential forms of satisfaction provide a better understanding of the remedies available at the ICC that give effect to the aggressor State's obligation to make full reparation for injury caused by an act of aggression. This also has implications for practice, as the supposed victim State would have to provide some form of notification to the alleged aggressor State pursuant to the initiation of an investigation in respect of the crime of aggression at the ICC.[152]

Notably, satisfaction can only give rise to partial reparation, and as such, cannot fully discharge the aggressor State from its obligation to make full reparation for damage caused by the act of aggression.[153] Therefore, the victim State, in principle, can claim reparation in respect of the same act of aggression before another competent international court or tribunal. Be that as it may, in the absence of any other competent inter-state dispute mechanism, it is of both relevance and significance, that the ICC does provide a setting for the aggressor State to partially discharge its obligation to make full reparation.[154] As pointed out by Oyarzábal, 'States have accepted international law and submitted to the authority of international institutions in the exercise of their "sovereignty" even if by doing this they become conditioned by their decisions or findings which although may not always be binding often carry great moral or political weight.'[155]

It should be clarified that this contribution does not suggest that the ICC is a 'surrogate' or alternative inter-State forum for aggression,[156] but rather, has considered the powers already conferred on the Court in the case of a crime of aggression.[157] Furthermore, the interests of the wrongdoing and injured State are already represented as both aggressor State and victim State have consented to jurisdiction in respect of a crime of aggression.[158] Notably, as the ICC is not a forum for inter-State dispute settlement, the supposed victim State cannot elect a form of reparation for aggression in a case of the crime of aggression;[159] but if satisfaction as a form of reparation is

[149] Ibid., Articles 5, 12, 8 *bis*, 15 *bis* and 15 *ter*.

[150] Ibid., Article 8 *bis*.

[151] Ibid., Article 75.

[152] 2001 ILC Articles, Article 43 (Notice of a claim by an injured State); Commentary, para. 2 and para. 3.

[153] Ibid., Article 37, Commentary 1.

[154] Wong 2021, pp. 988–989.

[155] Oyarzábal 2023, p. 229.

[156] Stahn 2010, p. 881.

[157] Rome Statute, Articles 8 *bis*, 15 *bis* and 15 *ter*.

[158] Oyarzábal 2023, p. 229.

[159] On Element of choice, see 2001 ILC Articles, Article 43.

already present within the institutional setting of the Rome Statute, the supposed victim State would have to serve notice of a claim to the alleged aggressor State by way of a modality of its discretion.[160] In a similar vein, a State other than the injured State,[161] who may refer a situation to the Prosecutor in which the crime of aggression appears to have been committed, would also have to serve notice of a claim to the alleged aggressor State.[162]

6.4 Concluding Remarks

This foregoing analysis has engaged with a rather curious international crime, in which State responsibility for aggression is a condition *sine qua non* for individual criminal responsibility for the crime of aggression. Against the grain of mainstream scholarship, this contribution has argued that the ICC, an international criminal court, in a case of the crime of aggression, may not only determine a breach of an international obligation by the aggressor State, but also engage with the content of State responsibility for aggression. Consequently, the ICC may be a forum whereby the aggressor State may partially discharge its obligation to make full reparation for injury caused by the act of aggression because satisfaction, as a reparation in itself, is not able to amount to full reparation for the purposes of Article 34 of the 2001 ILC Articles. The victim State, in principle, may elect other forms of reparation (including satisfaction) in other international courts and tribunals that may have jurisdiction over the same act of aggression.

The present contribution has also demonstrated that the specialist sub-field of international criminal law does not provide adequate nomenclature to engage fully with the relationship between State responsibility and individual criminal responsibility for aggression. A generalist international law analytical framework, drawing upon international institutional law, and the law of State responsibility, situates the crime of aggression at the ICC within an inter-State judicial setting in the international legal order. Indeed, it is important for the aggressor State and victim State to understand how their interests are fully affected in a case of the crime of aggression at the ICC. It is also important to appreciate, in practice, and in scholarship, that the ICC, despite being an international criminal court, may engage with State responsibility for aggression. This is not only an important reflection on satisfaction, and reparation for aggression, within a particular institutional setting, but also representative of the accruing paradigmatic shift towards multilateralism in our international legal order whereby a permanent international judicial institution, i.e., the ICC may engage with both State responsibility and individual criminal responsibility for aggression.

---

[160] Ibid.

[161] Ibid., Article 48; Rome Statute, Article 15 *bis*.

[162] 2001 ILC Articles, Article 48(3).

References

Barker J (2010) The Different Forms of Reparation: Compensation. In: Crawford J, Pellet A, Olleson S (eds) The Law of International Responsibility. Oxford University Press

Barriga S, Blokker N (2016a) Entry into Force and Conditions for the Exercise of Jurisdiction: Cross-Cutting Issues. In: Kress C, Barriga S (eds) Crime of Aggression: A Commentary, vol 1. Cambridge University Press

Barriga S, Blokker N (2016b) Conditions for the Exercise of Jurisdiction Based on State Referrals and Proprio Motu Investigations. In: Kress C, Barriga S (eds) Crime of Aggression: A Commentary, vol 1. Cambridge University Press

Barriga S, Grover L (2011) A Historic Breakthrough on the Crime of Aggression. 3 American Journal of International Law 517

Blokker N (2007) The Crime of Aggression and the United Nations Security Council. 20 Leiden Journal of International Law 867

Blokker N, Barriga S (2016) Conditions for the Exercise of Jurisdiction Based on Security Council Referrals. In: Kress C, Barriga S (eds) Crime of Aggression: A Commentary, vol 1. Cambridge University Press

Blokker N, Kress C (2010) A Consensus Agreement on the Crime of Aggression: Impressions from Kampala. 23 Leiden Journal of International Law 889

Clark R (2009) Negotiating Provisions Defining the Crime of Aggression, Its Elements and the Conditions for ICC Exercise of Jurisdiction Over It. 20 European Journal of International Law 1103

Clark R (2016a) Individual Conduct. In: Kress C, Barriga S (eds) Crime of Aggression: A Commentary, vol 1. Cambridge University Press

Clark R (2016b) General Principles of International Criminal Law. In: Kress C, Barriga S (eds) Crime of Aggression: A Commentary, vol 1. Cambridge University Press

Crawford J (2013) State Responsibility: The General Part. Cambridge University Press, Cambridge

Crawford J (2016) Flexibility in the Award of Reparation: The Role of the Parties and the Tribunal. In: Wolfrum R, Seršić M, Šošić T (eds) Contemporary Developments in International Law: Essays in Honour of Budislav Vukas. Brill

Feighery TJ, Gibson CS, Rajah TM (eds) (2015) War Reparations and the UN Compensation Commission: Designing Compensation After Conflict. Oxford University Press

Fernández de Gurmendi S (2002) The Working Group on Aggression at the Preparatory Commission for the International Criminal Court. 25 Fordham International Law Journal 589

Ferstman C (2002) The Reparation Regime of the International Criminal Court: Practical Considerations. 15 Leiden Journal of International Law 667

Ferstman C (2020) Reparations at the ICC: The Need for a Human Rights Based Approach to Effectiveness. In Ferstman C, Goetz M (eds) Reparations for Victims of Genocide, War Crimes and Crimes against Humanity. Brill

Gattini A (2002) The UN Compensation Commission: Old Rules, New Procedures on War Reparations. 13 European Journal of International Law 161

Gray C (1999) The Choice between Restitution and Compensation. 10 European Journal of International Law 413

Gray C (2006) The Eritrea/Ethiopia Claims Commission Oversteps Its Boundaries: A Partial Award? 17 European Journal of International Law 699

Gray C (2013) Remedies. In: Romano CPR, Alter KJ, Shany Y (eds) The Oxford Handbook of International Adjudication. Oxford University Press

Gray C, Barker J, Lauterpacht E, Wyler E, Papaux A (2010) The Different Forms of Reparation: Restitution. In: Crawford J, Pellet A, Olleson S (eds) The Law of International Responsibility. Oxford University Press

Higgins R (2010) Overview of Part Two of the Articles on State Responsibility. In: Crawford J, Pellet A, Olleson S (eds) The Law of International Responsibility. Oxford University Press

Jorgensen N (1997) A Reappraisal of Punitive Damages in International Law. 68 British Yearbook of International Law 247

Judgment of the International Military Tribunal for the Trial of German Major War Criminals, Nuremberg, 30 September and 1 October 1946 (Reproduced), Judgment. (1947) American Journal of International Law 172

Kress C, von Holtzendorff L (2010) The Kampala Compromise on the Crime of Aggression. 8 Journal of International Criminal Justice 1179

Kress C (2016) The State Conduct Element. In: Kress C, Barriga S (eds) Crime of Aggression: A Commentary, vol 1. Cambridge University Press

Kress C (2018) On the Activation of ICC Jurisdiction over the Crime of Aggression. 16 Journal of International Criminal Justice 1

Lee J (2023) Armed Activities on the Territory of the Congo (Democratic Republic of the Congo v. Uganda). 117 American Journal of International Law 113

McCarthy C (2012) Reparations and Victim Support in the International Criminal Court. Cambridge University Press, Cambridge

Murphy S (2013) International Judicial Bodies for Resolving Disputes Between States. In: Romano CPR, Alter KJ, Shany Y (eds) The Oxford Handbook of International Adjudication. Oxford University Press

Murphy S, Kidane W, Snider TR (eds) (2013) Litigating War: Mass Civil Injury and the Eritrea-Ethiopia Claims Commission. Oxford University Press

O'Keefe R (2015) International Criminal Law. Oxford University Press

Oyarzábal M (2023) The Influence of Public International Law upon Private International Law in History and Theory and in the Formation and Application of the Law (Volume 428). Brill

Paparinskis M (2020) A Case Against Crippling Compensation in International Law of State Responsibility. 83 Modern Law Review 1246

Pellet A (2015) Response to Koh and Buchwald's Article: Don Quixote and Sancho Panza Tilt at Windmills. (2015) 109 American Journal of International Law 557

Reisinger Coracini A, Wrange P (2016) The Specificity of the Crime of Aggression. In: Kress C, Barriga S (eds) Crime of Aggression: A Commentary, vol 1. Cambridge University Press

Schabas W (2013) International Criminal Court. In: Romano CPR, Alter K.J, Shany Y (eds) The Oxford Handbook of International Adjudication. Oxford University Press

Shelton D (2002) Righting Wrongs: Reparations in the Articles on State Responsibility. 96 American Journal of International Law 833

Stahn C (2010) The "End", the "Beginning of the End" or the "End of the Beginning"? Introducing Debates and Voices on the Definition of "Aggression"'. 23 Leiden Journal of International Law 875

Stern B (2010) The Obligation to Make Reparation. In: Crawford J, Pellet A, Olleson S (eds) The Law of International Responsibility. Oxford University Press

Tanzi A (2021) Restitution. Max Planck Encyclopedia of Public International Law

Wenaweser C (2010) Reaching the Kampala Compromise on Aggression: The Chair's Perspective. 23 Leiden Journal of International Law 883

Wittich S (2010) Punitive Damages. In: Crawford J, Pellet A, Olleson S (eds) The Law of International Responsibility. Oxford University Press

Wong MS (2016) Ratifying the Amendments to the Rome Statute of the International Criminal Court on the Crime of Aggression. 19 Max Planck Yearbook of United Nations Law Online 176

Wong MS (2020) The Activation of the International Criminal Court's Jurisdiction over the Crime of Aggression: International Institutional Law and Dispute Settlement Perspectives. 22 International Community Law Review 197

Wong MS (2021) Aggression and State Responsibility at the International Criminal Court. 70 International and Comparative Law Quarterly 961

Wyler E, Papaux A (2010) The Different Forms of Reparation: Satisfaction. In: Crawford J, Pellet A, Olleson S (eds) The Law of International Responsibility. Oxford University Press

Zegveld L (2010) Victims' Reparations Claims and International Courts: Incompatible Values? 8 Journal of International Criminal Justice 79

Zimmermann A (2012) Amending the Amendment Provisions of the Rome Statute: The Kampala Compromise on the Crime of Aggression and the Law of Treaties 10 Journal of International Criminal Justice 209

Zimmermann A (2018) A Victory for International Rule of Law? Or: All's Well That Ends Well? The 2017 ASP Decision to Amend the Kampala Amendment on the Crime of Aggression. 16 Journal of International Criminal Justice 19

Meagan Wong Lecturer in Law, University of Essex. The author is grateful to Emmanuel Giakoumakis and the anonymous reviewers for comments on an earlier version of this chapter.

Chapter 7
Satisfaction as a Remedy for Internationally Wrongful Acts: A Reassessment in Light of Inter-State Judicial Practice

Alice Ollino

Contents

Abstract This chapter reappraises the role of satisfaction twenty years after the adoption of the 2001 ILC Articles on Responsibility of States for Internationally Wrongful Acts and in light of inter-State judicial practice. The chapter demonstrates that inter-State courts and tribunals award satisfaction as a form of reparation for internationally wrongful acts, but they do so in a way that does not necessarily reflects ARSIWA and may occasionally appear controversial. There are three main emerging trends that seem to crop up from the analysis of jurisprudence. First, courts and tribunals often award satisfaction without referring specifically to non-material injury caused to the State, and use satisfaction as an alternative, rather than residual, remedy to restitution and compensation. Second, satisfaction seems to be strictly linked to certain typologies of internationally wrongful acts. Third, while applicant States appear to recognise different forms of satisfaction and request them depending on the circumstances of the case, judicial bodies almost exclusively resort to declarations of wrongfulness.

A. Ollino (✉)
University of Milano-Bicocca, Milan, Italy
e-mail: alice.ollino@unimib.it

O. Spijkers et al. (eds.), *Netherlands Yearbook of International Law 2022*, Netherlands Yearbook of International Law 53, https://doi.org/10.1007/978-94-6265-627-7_7

Keywords Satisfaction · Reparation · State responsibility · Non-material damage · Moral injury · Declaration of wrongfulness · International Court of Justice

7.1 Introduction

In 1986, Christine Gray noted that 'State practice on the award of satisfaction shows lack of objective standard in this area'. She argued that this casted 'considerable doubts on [the] (...) status [of satisfaction] as a legal remedy for breaches of international law'.[1] In the *Factory at Chorzów* case[2]—whose dictum on the principles of reparation reflects customary international law and is consistently cross-referenced by international courts and tribunals[3]—there is no mention of satisfaction as one of the potential forms of reparation.

Much has changed over the past thirty years. At the macro level, the completion of the 2001 ILC Articles on Responsibility of States for Internationally Wrongful Acts (ARSIWA)[4] has dramatically impacted the international rules on State responsibility, providing unity to the concept of remedies and bringing more clarity to principles of reparation that were previously uncertain. Although the ARSIWA still maintain the character of a non-binding instrument, they have been described as one of the founding pillars of international law,[5] and several articles contained therein are deemed to reflect customary international law. At a micro level, the ARSIWA have also affected the status of satisfaction by framing its contours more precisely and giving it an autonomous role among the consequences listed for an internationally wrongful act. Article 34 of ARSIWA stipulates that '[f]ull reparation for the injury caused by the internationally wrongful act shall take the form of restitution, compensation and satisfaction, either singly or in combination'. Article 37 describes the scope of satisfaction, determines its content, and lays out the relationship between satisfaction and other remedies, primarily *restitutio in integrum* and compensation. The content of Article 37 is reproduced without modification in the 2011 Draft Articles on the Responsibility of International Organizations,[6] to testify that the ILC considers satisfaction an '*acquis*' of international responsibility.

This chapter revisits the role of satisfaction more than twenty years after the adoption of the ARSIWA and in light of inter-State judicial practice. While the

[1] Gray 1986, p. 42.

[2] PCIJ, *Case Concerning the Factory at Chorzów (Germany v Poland)*, Merits, 13 September 1928, PCIJ Rep Series A No 17, p. 47.

[3] Gray 1986, pp. 12–13.

[4] ILC 2001, pp. 31 ff.

[5] See the statements made by representatives of States: UNGA, Sixth Committee 2004; UNGA, Sixth Committee 2007; UNGA, Sixth Committee 2019b.

[6] ILC 2011, pp. 46 ff.

contribution of the ARSIWA in shaping satisfaction as a remedy with its own identity is indisputable, some questions remain, making it timely to revisit its status.

Most of all, a reassessment of the scope and function of satisfaction appears appropriate given the genesis of Article 37. When the ILC conceptualised satisfaction as an autonomous form of reparation functional to covering moral and non-material damages caused directly to the injured State, it did so mainly by drawing on diplomatic practice.[7] Although more than 200 years of arbitral practice were available to the Commission, judicial cases referring to satisfaction and, more broadly, reparation for moral damages caused to the State, were relatively scant and tended to reject requests for this type of remedy. However, after the adoption of ARSIWA, judicial bodies have consistently referred to the rules in the articles,[8] including occasional references to Article 37.[9] Thus, it is appropriate to assess how and to what extent international courts and tribunals have used satisfaction and, to test the validity of the rule enunciated in ARSIWA concerning satisfaction against inter-State judicial practice.

Methodologically, the analysis is limited to inter-State judicial practice and does not encompass the practice of international courts and tribunals established to settle disputes between States and individuals or States and entities like multinational corporations. In this regard, Article 33 of the ARSIWA specifies that the obligations set out by the articles concerning the content of responsibility are only those owed by the wrongdoing State to another State, several States or the international community as a whole. Furthermore, satisfaction is described in ARSIWA as a remedy residual to restitution and compensation and typically requested for 'injuries, not financially assessable, which amount to *an affront to the State*'.[10] Consequently, the aim of this chapter is to examine primarily the practice of the International Court of Justice (ICJ), along with practice of inter-State arbitration tribunals, the International Tribunal on the Law of the Sea (ITLOS) and the United Nations Compensation Commission (UNCCC). That said, the following analysis does not discount the valuable role played by the remedy of satisfaction in the practice of other courts and tribunals.[11] On the contrary, not only have institutions such as the European Court of Human Rights, the Inter-American Court of Human Rights, or ICSID tribunals referred to the ARSIWA when applying its rules on reparation, including satisfaction;[12] some of these bodies are also well-known for having made use to satisfactory measures in alternative and more creative forms.[13]

---

[7] See *infra*, Sect. 7.2.

[8] See the UNGA, Reports of the Secretary-General 2007a, 2007b, 2010, 2013, 2016, 2019a, 2022.

[9] UNGA, Reports of the Secretary-General 2013, pp. 33, 2016, p. 37, 2019a, p. 37, 2022, p. 32.

[10] ILC 2001, pp. 105–106 (emphasis added).

[11] See Article 33(2): 'This Part is without prejudice to any right, arising from the international responsibility of a State, which may accrue directly to any person or entity other than a State'; see also ILC 2001, p. 95 para. 4.

[12] UNGA 2010, pp. 15–17; 2013, pp. 30–33; 2016, pp. 33–37; 2019a, pp. 34–37; 2022, pp. 30–32.

[13] This is true especially for the practice of the Inter-American Court of Human Rights, see Novak 2018, pp. 99–122. *Infra*, Sect. 7.3.3.

The chapter is structured as follows. Section 7.2 reappraises the definition and function of satisfaction as per Article 37 of ARSIWA. Section 7.3 tests the content of Article 37 against inter-State judicial practice. This section shows that courts and tribunals award satisfaction as a form of reparation for internationally wrongful acts, but they do so in a way that may deviate from the content of ARSIWA and occasionally appear controversial. In particular, there are some trends that emerge from judicial practice and deserve more scrutiny. These include the appreciation of satisfaction as a form of reparation not necessarily associated with non-material injury caused to the State, the link between satisfaction and specific typologies of internationally wrongful acts, and the almost exclusive use of declaration of wrongfulness as a viable form of satisfaction.

Overall, the following analysis provides an opportunity to reflect upon these developing practices and make broader considerations on the current status of rules on reparation in international law.

7.2 Article 37 of ARSIWA: Definition, Function and Uncertain Elements

The ARSIWA conceptualise satisfaction as a remedy of a subsidiary or subordinate nature.[14] Article 37 does not provide a stand-alone definition of satisfaction, but describes it in relation to other forms of reparation, i.e. restitution and compensation. The article indeed states that satisfaction is required by the responsible State only 'insofar as [the injury] cannot be made good by restitution or compensation',[15] and the commentary clarifies that this is a remedy of 'exceptional character' given 'only in those cases where those two forms [restitution and compensation] have not provided full reparation'.[16]

The residual and subsidiary nature of satisfaction must be read in light of the history that led the Commission to its codification. Originally, satisfaction was not conceived as an autonomous form of remedy. Garcia Amador, for instance, the first Special Rapporteur appointed by the Commission on the subject, acknowledged that the duty to make reparation comprised 'reparation proper (restitution, damage, or both) of the injury caused' and 'measures of "satisfaction" which have frequently accompanied those of reparation *strictu sensu*'.[17] According to him, satisfaction covered reparation for 'political and moral injury' caused to the State; however, different forms of reparation were frequently employed together with respect to the same injury, and it was difficult in some cases to determine the extent to which

[14] See also, on doctrine, Wyler and Papaux 2010, p. 624; Hoss 2011, paras. 5-7.

[15] ILC 2001, p. 105.

[16] Ibid.

[17] Garcia Amador 1961, para. 5. This position was also reflected in doctrine, see Reitzer 1938, pp. 125–6; Anzilotti 1964, p. 425.

reparation constituted compensation or satisfaction.[18] Special Rapporteur Riphagen held similar views. In his draft article 6 on reparation submitted to the Commission in 1985, satisfaction was not a self-standing type of reparation. Moral and non-material damages caused directly to the State were covered either by compensation or, when granted as apologies by the wrongdoing State, as guarantees of non-repetition.[19]

It was only with Special Rapporteur Arangio-Ruiz that satisfaction acquired a unique identity in the range of remedies to be provided by the responsible State. In his Second Report to the ILC, Arangio-Ruiz classified satisfaction as the specific kind of remedy devoted to the reparation of 'moral damage to the State', the latter comprising 'on the one hand, (…) the infringement of the State's right *per se* and, on the other, (…) the injury to the State's dignity, honour and prestige'.[20] While the Special Rapporteur conceded that, in practice, compensation and monetary satisfaction could easily be confounded, on the other hand, moral damage to the State was *exclusively typical* of international relations and required a separate type of remedy.[21] It should be noted, in any case, that the construction of satisfaction as an autonomous institution drew mostly on diplomatic practice. This area offered the most abundant material for analysis, which consisted mainly of apologies, excuses and honours to the flag provided to the injured State as a result of a number of typical breaches of international law.[22] International arbitral claims made by States for injury to their nationals—which instead constituted the large bulk of legal sources used to construe restitution and compensation—only occasionally referred to measures of satisfaction requested by or granted to the injured State.

From the perspective of ARSIWA, satisfaction qualifies as a form of reparation. This is gathered from the reading of Article 34 ('full reparation (…) shall take the form of restitution, compensation and satisfaction') and Article 37, according to which the responsible State, just like restitution and compensation, is 'under the obligation' to provide satisfaction. In this respect, there should be no distinction between these three types of remedies.[23] However, this may not necessarily be so. While restitution and compensation serve precisely to 'wipe out all the consequences of the internationally wrongful act'[24] and restore the situation before the breach, satisfaction may assume dimensions that oscillate between an afflictive aspect and the reconfirmation of the primary rule.

In fact, when Article 37 describes satisfaction as a form of reparation, it only tells half of the story. In the debates within the ILC, members of the Commission disagreed on the function performed by this remedy. For some, including Special

---

[18] Ibid., para. 54. Even more radically, Dominicé argues that a review of the international practice of the late 19th and first part of the 20th century points to the impossibility of distinguishing between compensation and satisfaction, Dominicé 1984, pp. 112–118.

[19] Riphagen 1985, pp. 8–10, and Riphagen 1981, p. 101.

[20] Arangio-Ruiz 1989, p. 6.

[21] Ibid., p. 7.

[22] Ibid., pp. 35–40.

[23] See Stoica 2021, p. 148.

[24] *Case Concerning the Factory at Chorzów*, p. 47.

Rapporteur Arangio-Ruiz, satisfaction held primarily an afflictive character, mainly when it consisted of an apology by the wrongdoing State or took the form of monetary satisfaction.[25] For others, including Special Rapporteur Riphagen, satisfaction concerned the *ex-ante* aspect of reparation since, by acknowledging the breach, the wrongdoing State re-confirms the credibility of the primary rule and re-establishes the legal order between the parties.[26] Although there is no reference to these distinct dimensions in the commentary on satisfaction, traces of the multifaceted nature of this remedy can be found in the commentary to Article 30, devoted to guarantees of non-repetition. Here the Commission states that assurance and guarantees of non-repetition may be sought by way of satisfaction and that there may be an overlap between the two. These are indeed future-looking measures, since 'the question is essentially the reinforcement of a continuing legal relationship' between the parties.[27]

Regarding the type of injury covered by satisfaction, one needs to look at the commentary since Article 37 only defines satisfaction as residual to restitution and compensation. The commentary states that satisfaction 'is the remedy for those injuries, not financially assessable, which amount to *an affront to the State*' and then notes that '[t]hese injuries are frequently of a symbolic character, arising from the very fact of the breach of the obligation, irrespective of its material consequences for the State concerned'.[28] In the prevalent conception of satisfaction, this remedy addresses reparation for moral damage and legal injury.[29] These concepts have different meanings and cannot be considered synonyms.[30]

The appreciation of moral damage to the State depends on either objective or subjective elements.[31] An objective approach to moral damage identifies the latter depending on the content of the primary rule violated. Accordingly, moral damage will ensue following breaches of primary rules that protect interests linked to the State as a *sovereign* entity,[32] like rules on territorial integrity or diplomatic relations. Instead, a subjective approach to moral damage identifies the latter based on the psychological attitude of the responsible State vis-à-vis the violation of a primary rule. This may occur when, for instance, the breach 'is made *defiantly* or

---

[25] Arangio-Ruiz 1989, para. 136; ILC 1990, para. 390.

[26] Riphagen 1981, para. 86; ILC 1981, para. 22; ILC 1990, para. 395–396, 402; ILC 2000b, para. 199.

[27] ILC 2001, p. 90 para. 11.

[28] Ibid., p. 106 (emphasis added).

[29] *Case concerning the difference between New Zealand and France concerning the interpretation or application of two agreements, concluded on 9 July 1986 between the two States and which relates to the problems arising from the Rainbow Warrior Affair*, Judgment, 30 April 1990, UN RIAA, vol. XX, pp. 272–273. Wyler and Papaux 2010, p. 626; Hoss 2011, para. 8–11.

[30] According to Brownlie, 'the term "breach of the duty" [injury] denotes an illegal act or omission, an "injury in the broad sense". "Damage" denotes loss, *damnum*, whether this is a financial quantification or physical injury or damage, or of other consequences of a breach of duty', Brownlie 2008, p. 459.

[31] Wyler and Papaux 2010, p. 626; Hoss 2011, para. 8–11.

[32] Wittich 2004, pp. 344–345.

with the *intention* to humiliate (...) [the] State'.[33] The ARSIWA reflects the objective approach by stating that non-material damage arises from the breach of an international obligation typically taking the form of violations of sovereignty or territorial integrity, attacks on ships or aircraft, ill-treatment of or deliberate attacks on heads of States, Governments, diplomatic or consular representatives, and violations of the premises of embassies or consulates.[34] There is no reference to the subjective attitude that a State may assume towards a given violation, probably because of the difficulty of the ILC to accommodate issues of State's fault, intention or other physiological attitudes in the ARSIWA.[35]

The question of legal injury is more problematic. Generally speaking, a legal injury is an injury arising from the sole infringement of an (international) obligation. The commentary of Article 37 does not dwell on the concept, yet some indications point to its inclusion. First, Article 31, paragraph 2, states that injury subject to reparation by the responsible State '*includes* any damage, whether material or moral' caused by the internationally wrongful act. The term 'includes' suggests, along with moral or material damage, other possible types of injury, including legal ones. Second, the fact that the commentary to Article 37 speaks of 'non-material injury' and specifies that injury may arise 'from the very fact of the breach of the obligation'[36] supports this conclusion. Third, the commentary to Article 45 of the 1996 draft articles provisionally adopted by the ILC on the first reading expressly stated that moral damage covered by satisfaction included 'legal' or 'juridical damage'.[37]

On the other hand, at least two issues ensue from acknowledging legal injury as part of damages covered by reparation. The first is the logical leap[38] that comes up as soon as the inclusion of legal injury is read against other provisions of the ARSIWA, most notably Article 48, regulating the implementation of responsibility by States other than the injured one. One would expect that States having 'a legal interest'[39] toward the respect of the obligation *erga omnes* or *erga omnes partes* and acting as members of the international community as a whole, or members of the group of States to which the obligation is owed, have the capacity to invoke the wrongdoing

---

[33] Barboza 2005, pp. 17–18 (emphasis added).

[34] ILC 2001, p. 106.

[35] On the removal of fault from the ARSIWA, Gattini 1999, pp. 397–404.

[36] The term was chosen by Special Rapporteur Crawford as a substitute to the notion or 'moral damage', see Crawford 2000, pp. 52–56.

[37] See ILC 1996, para. 5 p. 297. See also the observations made by Gaja, as chair of the drafting committee charged with the revision of the draft articles in 2000. In relation to Article 31, Gaja noted: '[t]he Committee had finally decided to define injury as consisting of any damage. The reference to 'moral' damage in addition to 'material' damage was meant to allow a broad interpretation of the word 'injury'. 'Moral' damage could be taken to include not only pain and suffering, but also the broader notion of injury, which some might call 'legal injury' and had been done to States', ILC 2000a, para. 16, p. 388. As to the introduction of legal injury and in the work on State Responsibility, Ago 1971, para. 74; ILC 1973, para. 12 p. 183.

[38] Stern 2010, pp. 563 ff.

[39] ICJ, *Barcelona Traction, Light and Power Company, Limited (Belgium v Spain)*, Judgment, 5 February 1970, ICJ Reports 1970 p. 3, p. 32, para. 33; ILC 2001, para. 1, p. 126.

State's responsibility *precisely* because they have suffered, at least, a legal injury.[40] Yet, the classification of States under Article 48 as '*other than the injured State*' prevents this conclusion. Instead, it construes international responsibility as a 'bundle of rights and obligations'[41] whose content is differentiated depending on the category of States invoking it.[42]

The other issue is whether distinguishing between moral damage and legal injury implies a distinction in how satisfaction may be awarded. Article 37 does not provide any indication and, besides listing examples of satisfactory measures, only points out that its appropriate form depends on the circumstances of the case.[43] According to some authors, moral and legal damage cannot give rise to the same satisfactory measures, being conceptually distinct.[44] Thus, moral damage to a State would be more appropriately addressed by issuing apologies, expressing regrets, or awarding symbolic damages. On the contrary, legal injury should be better repaired by acknowledging a breach, a declaration of wrongfulness by a competent court or tribunal, or providing guarantees of non-repetition. However, other scholars have branded the distinction as 'artificial'[45] and 'fictitious',[46] stressing the difficulty of identifying clear evidence in international practice and pointing to the conceptual shortcomings of the notion of legal injury.[47]

Turning finally to the question of mechanisms of satisfaction, the list of measures described in Article 37 is, indeed, non-exhaustive. Among the possible forms of satisfaction mentioned by the ARSIWA, a declaration of wrongfulness by a competent judicial authority and pecuniary satisfaction merit discussion. As to the declaration of wrongfulness issued by a competent court or tribunal, paragraph 2 of Article 37 does not list it, yet the commentary defines declaratory judgments as '[o]ne of the most common modalities of satisfaction'.[48] The reason for the non-inclusion is that the ARSIWA are not concerned with questions of judicial jurisdiction, which are preliminary and indispensable for a declaration of wrongfulness to display authority and legitimacy. Furthermore, while satisfaction may take the form of a declaration of wrongfulness, not all declarations of wrongfulness issued by a competent adjudicative body qualify as satisfaction.[49]

---

40 ILC 2001, p. 106 para. 6 and p. 127, para. 12.

41 Stern 2005, p. 97.

42 Notably, the State is injured – as such entitled to invoke reparation in the forms provided by Articles 31-39 – or it is a State 'other than the injured one' – as such only entitled to invoke cessation of the wrongful act, guarantees of non-repetition, and performance of the obligation of reparation in the interest of the injured States or the beneficiaries of the obligation.

43 ILC 2001, p. 106, para. 5.

44 Tanzi 1987, pp. 10, 21.

45 Wittich 2004, p. 350.

46 Iovane 1990, p. 164-166.

47 Pellet 1996, pp. 6–7.

48 ILC 2001, pp. 106–107.

49 ILC 2001, p. 106.

As to monetary satisfaction, the extent to which this form of reparation is recognised by contemporary international law is contentious.[50] The ARSIWA seemingly accept this type of remedy,[51] however, they pose two sets of different issues. First, it may be difficult to distinguish between monetary satisfaction and reparation granted as compensation, and the two may easily be confounded. Second, monetary satisfaction implies the idea of punishment, which is at odds with the conceptual tenets of reparation for an internationally wrongful act.[52] As explained in the following section, States have not refrained from demanding international courts and tribunals pecuniary satisfaction, especially when the breach consists in certain violations of international law. Yet, judicial authorities are much less inclined to recognise this form of reparation for non-material injury.

7.3 Satisfaction in Inter-State Judicial Practice

The following three paragraphs illustrate how international courts and tribunals have awarded satisfaction as a remedy for internationally wrongful acts in disputes between States. Overall, practice shows that applicant States request satisfaction when they seek reparation before a judicial authority for moral or non-material injury to the State. Likewise, international courts and tribunals make use of this remedy, which, at least in the practice of the ICJ, is the most awarded in the history of the Court, more than compensation and restitution.[53]

Cases analysed in the following paragraphs come from the caseload of the ICJ, inter-state arbitration tribunals, the ITLOS and the United Nations Compensation Commission. They have been selected because of their peculiar use of satisfaction as a form of remedy for internationally wrongful acts. While the analysis will show that courts and tribunals regularly award satisfaction, they often do it in a way that does not necessarily reflect Article 37 of ARSIWA and its commentary.

In this regard, at least three emerging ‘trends’ seem to crop up from the jurisprudence of international courts and tribunals. First, courts and tribunals often award satisfaction without referring specifically to non-material injury caused to the State. Instead of being regarded as a form of reparation residual to restitution and compensation, satisfaction is, in some cases, used simply as an alternative remedy to restitution and compensation if deemed more appropriate by a court. Second, satisfaction seems strictly linked to specific typologies of internationally wrongful acts. Again, it is not the acknowledgement of moral damage to the State that prompts a court to award satisfaction, but rather the recognition that there has been a breach of an obligation of ‘minor’ or more procedural character. Finally, while applicant States appear to

[50] Wyler and Papaux 2010, p. 630; Hoss 2011, para. 20–22; Barthe 2003, pp. 115–118.

[51] ILC 2001, p. 106, para. 5.

[52] Crawford 2013, pp. 481–483.

[53] Stoica 2021, p. 146; Gray 2013, p. 876.

recognise different forms of satisfaction and request them depending on the circumstances of the case, courts and tribunals almost exclusively resort to declarations of wrongfulness.

7.3.1 Satisfaction as an Alternative Rather than Subsidiary Form of Reparation

As illustrated above, Article 37 of ARSIWA provides that satisfaction is required in subordination to restitution and compensation, mainly when the injury is moral or non-material nature. However, some examples from inter-State judicial practice indicate that, rather than a form of reparation for non-material damage that 'cannot be made good by restitution or compensation', satisfaction is often used as a non-pecuniary form of reparation *alternative* to restitution or compensation.[54]

A first illustrative example is *Pulp Mills*. The dispute in *Pulp Mills* concerned Uruguay's commissioning and construction of two pulp mills on the River of Uruguay. Argentina argued that the authorisation and operation of the mills violated certain obligations incumbent upon Uruguay under the Statute of the River Uruguay, to which both States were parties. These included the procedural obligations to inform, notify and negotiate when issuing authorisation and concession for the construction of the mills;[55] and the substantive obligations to contribute to the rational utilisation of the river, to ensure the protection of its soil, woodland and quality of the water, and to protect and preserve the aquatic environment.[56]

In its submission before the ICJ, Argentina asked the Court to order the cessation of breaches of Uruguay's obligations with a continuing character (specifically, the obligation to take appropriate measures to protect and preserve the aquatic environment and prevent pollution);[57] full reparation in the form of restitution and compensation for damage caused following the authorisation and construction of the mills;[58] and appropriate guarantees and assurances of non-repetition.[59] Argentina excluded that satisfaction in the form of a declaratory judgment could constitute adequate reparation. Although the State did not reject the possibility of being *also* awarded this type of remedy, it explicitly affirmed that satisfaction *alone* would not fully compensate for the damage caused by Uruguay.[60]

---

[54] ILC 2001, Article 37(1).

[55] ICJ, *Case concerning Pulp Mills on the River Uruguay (Argentina v Uruguay)*, Judgment, 20 April 2010, ICJ Reports p.14, pp. 73–75.

[56] Ibid. p. 47.

[57] ICJ, *Case concerning Pulp Mills on the River Uruguay (Argentina v Uruguay)*, Memorial of Argentina, 16 January 2007, pp. 199–201.

[58] Ibid., pp. 201–205.

[59] Ibid., pp. 205–207.

[60] Ibid., p. 197, para. 8.2.

The Court however reached a different conclusion. Noting that Uruguay's responsibility concerned only violations of procedural obligations and not substantive ones, it ruled that a 'finding of wrongful conduct by Uruguay in respect of its procedural obligations per se constitutes a measure of satisfaction for Argentina'.[61] More specifically, the Court did not frame the injury suffered by Argentina as moral or non-material, but merely observed the other forms of reparation requested—restitution or compensation—would be out of proportion to the benefit deriving from them. Therefore, although the Court noted that Argentina considered satisfaction inadequate even if breaches were only procedural,[62] it constructed this remedy as sufficient for reparation.

Pulp Mills was not the first case where the Court used satisfaction to remedy injury that was not exclusively 'non-material'. A few years earlier, in the *Land and Maritime Boundary between Cameroon and Nigeria*, the ICJ had to decide on a land and maritime sovereignty dispute over the Bakassi Peninsula, a geographical area between Cameroon and Nigeria. The internationally wrongful acts listed by Cameroon in its submission to the Court included the violation of Cameroonian sovereignty over the Bakassi Peninsula, breaches of Nigeria's conventional and customary obligations regarding the use of force, and the military occupation by Nigeria of the Bakassi Peninsula. Cameroon argued to have suffered material and non-material damages. Material damages to the State of Cameroon and its people had ensued from the military occupation of the Bakassi peninsula, consisting mainly of repeated incursions, invasion of Cameroonian territory by the Nigerian army, and repeated attacks on the Bakassi peninsula. Cameroon requested the Court to award restitution and compensation in relation to this type of damage.[63] Furthermore, Cameroon contended to have suffered legal and moral injury following the violation of sovereignty and the prohibition of the use of force in international relations.[64]

Steering clear of the distinction between material and non-material injury, the Court only awarded satisfaction, asserting that a declaration of wrongfulness would adequately address the injury suffered by Cameroon following violations of sovereignty and the use of force, as well as the military occupation by Nigeria.[65] In particular, the Court neither suggested that material damages caused to Cameroon were insufficiently proven nor that injury suffered by this State was exclusively moral or non-material. The ICJ judges merely observed that, in light of a declaration of wrongfulness, they would not 'seek to ascertain whether and to what extent Nigeria's responsibility to Cameroon has been engaged as a result of that occupation'.[66]

[61] *Pulp Mills*, Judgment, p. 102, para. 269.

[62] Ibid., p. 102, para. 270.

[63] ICJ, *Case concerning the land and maritime boundary between Cameroon and Nigeria (Cameroon v Nigeria)*, Memorial of Cameroon, 16 March 1995, p. 637, para. 7.25 and p. 644 para. 7.46.

[64] Ibid., p. 645, para. 7.48 and 7.49.

[65] ICJ, *Case concerning the land and maritime boundary between Cameroon and Nigeria (Cameroon v Nigeria: Equatorial Guinea intervening)*, Judgment, 10 October 2022, ICJ Reports 303, p. 452, para. 319.

[66] Ibid.

It is a truism that political considerations likely drove the Court's decision to overlook restitution and compensation. Although Nigeria was indeed held responsible for certain violations of international law in territories falling within Cameroon's sovereignty, the judgment also found that Cameroon had unlawfully established its police and military presence in areas falling within Nigeria's sovereignty.[67] Hence, to ensure balance in the decision and given the difficulty in determining precisely the consequences of responsibility for both States, the Court dismissed Cameroon's request for restitution and compensation.[68] At the same time, the decision construes satisfaction not as a remedy for non-material damage but as a non-monetary form of reparation alternative to restitution or compensation in specific circumstances. By declaring that it would not ascertain *the extent to which* Nigeria's responsibility to Cameroon was engaged, the Court did not exclude that Nigeria's violations caused material injury to Cameroon. It simply preferred to overlook the precise scope of that material injury.

Interestingly, the Court's reasoning in the *Land and Maritime Boundary between Cameroon and Nigeria* also inspired an arbitral award in a dispute concerning over the delimitation of a maritime territory between Guyana and Suriname. Quoting the passage of the *Land and Maritime Boundary* case in which the ICJ refused to assess the extent of Nigeria's responsibility toward Cameroon, the tribunal rejected the claim of compensation requested by Guyana, asserting that a declaratory judgment would suffice to address the claim for reparation advanced by Guyana.[69]

Perhaps the judgment of the ICJ that best illustrates how satisfaction may be used as an alternative form of reparation is the 2007 *Bosnian Genocide* case. Notably, in this case, the Court found that Serbia was responsible for breaching its obligation arising from the Genocide Convention to prevent genocide in Srebrenica and punish individuals responsible for it.[70]

In its request for reparation, Bosnia and Herzegovina had asked for symbolic compensation for the injury caused by Serbia in an amount to be determined by the Court. However, the latter only awarded satisfaction in the form of acknowledgement of the breach. The ICJ contended that Bosnia would be entitled to compensation inasmuch as it could establish that a 'sufficiently direct and certain causal nexus' existed between genocide and Serbia's failure to prevent genocide; in other words, compensation would have been available had it been established 'with a sufficient degree of certainty that the genocide at Srebrenica would (…) have been averted if the Respondent had acted in compliance with its legal obligations'. Having found

[67] Ibid., pp. 450–452.

[68] See the Separate opinion of Judge Mbaye, ibid., pp. 536–537, and the Dissenting opinion of Judge Ajibola, pp. 593–601.

[69] *In the matter of an arbitration between Guyana and Suriname (Guyana v Suriname)*, Final Award, 17 September 2007, Arbitral Tribunal Constituted Pursuant to Article 287, and in Accordance with Annex VII, of the United Convention on the Law of the Sea, pp. 149–150, para. 450–453.

[70] ICJ, *Case concerning application of the Convention on the prevention and punishment of the crime of genocide (Bosnia and Herzegovina v Serbia and Montenegro)*, Judgment, 26 February 2007, ICJ Reports 43, pp. 219–226.

that this was not the case, the Court concluded that satisfaction in the form of a declaratory judgment would be 'the most appropriate' form of reparation.

Once again, it is unlikely that the Court resorted to satisfaction because it deemed Bosnia's injury exclusively non-material. One may argue, in fact, that at the merits stage the Court had, albeit implicitly, established that by failing to use due diligence to prevent genocide, Serbia had at least *contributed* to its occurrence in Srebrenica.[71] The Court had first clarified that a breach of an obligation to prevent genocide occurs when it is proved that a State 'manifestly failed to take all measures to prevent genocide *which were within its power, and which might have contributed to preventing* the genocide'[72]. Second, the Court found that Serbia had the capacity to influence the situation in Srebrenica as well as the means at disposal to act to prevent genocide.[73] Hence, while excluding that Serbia's omission was *the* cause of genocide,[74] the Court did not rule out that, by having power and capacity to influence and by refusing to act, Serbia's omission had *at least* contributed to material harm.[75]

Therefore, the Court's resort to satisfaction and refusal to award compensation may be read as the result of the application of a different test of causality at the reparation stage.[76] Here, the ICJ opted for a more stringent test—the but-for-test—in order to assess Serbia's wrongful conduct and decide on compensation. Yet, saying that it could not be proved with certainty that, without Serbia's omission, genocide would have been averted, does not exclude that Serbia's wrongful conduct influenced or contributed to its occurrence.

7.3.2 *Satisfaction as a Form of Reparation Awarded for Certain Typologies of Internationally Wrongful Acts*

The *Bosnian Genocide* case is illustrative of another trend slowly emerging in the practice of the ICJ. Specifically, the Court appears to resort to satisfaction as a remedy to repair injury caused by distinct typologies of internationally wrongful acts. In other words, satisfaction is not exclusively—nor necessarily—used to address cases in which the violation of the primary rules does not typically cause material damage, but touches directly upon States' sovereignty—for example because the internationally wrongful act consists in violations of rules on diplomatic immunities or territorial integrity.[77] The impression is that the Court uses it also when it wishes to emphasize

[71] Ibid., para. 430.

[72] Ibid. (emphasis added).

[73] Ibid., para. 434–435, 438.

[74] Ibid., para. 438.

[75] On this point, see also Gattini 2007, pp. 706–712.

[76] On the confusion between factual and legal causality and how such confusion affects the Court's reasoning, see Ollino 2022, pp. 20–22.

[77] Although this continues to be *also* the way in which the Court uses satisfaction, for instance when internationally wrongful acts concern violations of rules on diplomatic immunities or sovereignty

that the *typology* of primary rules underlying the international wrongful act requires a diverse, and possibly less severe, form of reparation.

This phenomenon is not novel and must be appraised against a broader international practice—starting with the jurisprudence of international human rights courts—that has progressively diversified the content of responsibility depending on the type of wrongful act.[78] The most relevant example is the Inter-American Court of Human Rights. This court has frequently awarded measures of satisfaction in innovative forms and in relation to specific violations of human rights obligations characterised by their gravity or their systematic and collective dimension.[79]

From a theoretical standpoint, the idea of diversifying the forms of reparation depending on the formal type of international wrongful acts is a reminder of the debates undertaken by the ILC during the work on ARSIWA. When Special Rapporteur Riphagen was appointed with the task of examining the content of international responsibility, it became immediately apparent that the determination of the legal consequences of a breach could not escape the categorisation of primary rules.[80] That issue, after all, had already emerged in the drafting of the first part of the project, with Ago classifying internationally wrongful acts depending on the underlying primary rule.[81] Ago's idea was that classifying primary rules based on their (formal) typology was essential for carving out secondary rules of responsibility, as different categories of obligations corresponded to different rules concerning their breach and, possibly, the kind of reparation.[82] Along this line, the Special Rapporteur had introduced the distinction, initially accepted by the Commission in the articles adopted on first reading, between international crimes and international delicts, between international wrongful act stemming from obligations of conduct, international wrongful acts stemming from obligations of result and international wrongful acts stemming from obligations to prevent, and between internationally wrongful acts instantaneous and continuous.[83]

Eventually, the ILC reduced these categorisations to a minimum under the aegis of Crawford, with the view of maintaining the high level of generality underlying

---

and territorial integrity: see ICJ, *Arrest Warrant of 11 April 2000 (Democratic Republic of the Congo v Belgium)*, Judgment, 14 February 2002, ICJ Reports p. 3, para. 75; ICJ, *Alleged violation of sovereign rights and maritime spaces in the Caribbean Sea (Nicaragua v Colombia)*, Judgment, 21 April 2022, ICJ, available at https://www.icj-cij.org/case/155 (last accessed 09 March 2023), p. 69 para. 197: 'Considering the *nature* of Colombia's internationally wrongful acts [violation of sovereignty rights], the Court considers that the remedies stated above [a declaration of wrongfulness] suffice to redress the injury that Colombia's internationally wrongful acts have inflicted on Nicaragua' [violation of sovereign right] (emphasis added).

[78] On this emerging trend, analysed against the recent ICJ decision on reparation in the *Armed Activities on the Territory of the Congo* case, see also Bonafè 2022, pp. 790–792.

[79] For instance, IACtHR, *Case of the "Mapiripán Massacre" v Colombia*, Merits, Reparation and Costs, 5 July 2004, Series C no 134, para. 315. See in general, Novak 2018, pp. 99–122.

[80] Riphagen 1980, para. 13, paras. 32-33; Riphagen 1982, para. 37.

[81] Ago 1977, pp. 4–20; Ago 1978, pp. 32–52.

[82] See, generally, Ago 1939, pp. 447–450.

[83] ILC 1996 draft articles 19 to 26.

the articles and emphasising the separation between secondary rules and primary obligations. However, questions on how the content and nature of primary obligations affect the application of secondary rules on responsibility are still lurking, and they resurface regularly in international practice,including recent practice by the ICJ.[84]

Within the context of reparation, it is worth querying whether the diversified formal categories of internationally wrongful acts may drive courts and tribunals to opt for certain measures of reparation instead of others. In the practice of the ICJ, specifically, measures of satisfaction in the form of declaratory judgements are deemed an adequate type of remedy when the breach concerns (i) either 'technical' and procedural obligations or (ii) primary rules of preventive or conduct-type nature.

7.3.2.1 Satisfaction in Case of Breach of 'Procedural' Primary Obligations

A first example of satisfaction used as a remedy to address a specific type of internationally wrongful act was given in *Pulp Mills*. As noted above, for the first time, the Court classified the obligations arising out of an environmental treaty as procedural or substantive,[85] eventually finding Uruguay only responsible for the breach of the former. The Court's reasoning on reparation made it clear that this distinction impacted the type of remedy awarded. The Court argued that because 'the operation of the (…) [mill] has not resulted in the breach of substantive obligations',[86] upholding Argentina's claim for compensation or ordering the mill's dismantling would not have been appropriate.[87]

A similar rationale underlined the more recent judgment *Construction of a Road in Costa Rica along the San Juan River*.[88] In relation to the claims submitted by Nicaragua and regarding environmental concerns, this case did not deal exclusively with the violation of procedural and substantive treaty obligations but also with the breach of the customary obligation to prevent transboundary environmental harm. Yet, the Court drew a distinction between procedure and substance to appraise the conduct of Costa Rica *vis-à-vis* the general obligation of preventing transboundary harm. It concluded that Costa Rica had violated the procedural obligation to conduct an environmental impact assessment (EIA). Instead, a violation of the substantive obligation to prevent significant transboundary harm was not sufficiently proven.[89]

---

[84] For an overview see, *ex multis*, Wolfrum 2011, pp. 363–383; Marchesi 2005, pp. 1–174.

[85] Critical on the distinction between substantive and procedural obligations and the consequences that such distinction may entail in relation to the breach of primary rules see ICJ, *Construction of a Road in Costa Rica along the San Juan River (Nicaragua v Costa Rica)*, Separate opinion of Judge Donoghue, especially para. 9.

[86] *Pulp Mills*, p. 104 para. 275.

[87] Ibid., para. 276.

[88] ICJ, *Construction of a Road in Costa Rica along the San Juan River (Nicaragua v Costa Rica)*, 16 December 2015, ICJ Reports 2015, pp. 665.

[89] Ibid., para. 217.

With respect to reparation, Nicaragua had asked the Court to order Costa Rica to restore to the extent possible the situation that existed before the road was constructed and provide compensation for the damage caused. The Court however only awarded Nicaragua satisfaction for violating the procedural obligation to conduct an EIA. The ICJ found that, although Costa Rica did not comply with the duty to conduct an EIA, it was not established that the construction of the road 'caused significant harm to Nicaragua *or was in breach of other substantive obligations under international law*. As such, restoring the original condition of the area where the road is located would not constitute an appropriate remedy for Costa Rica's breach of its obligation to carry out an environmental impact assessment'.[90] The formulation of the Court may suggest that it was not only the lack of a causal link between failure to conduct and EIA and material harm to justify satisfaction instead of restitution/compensation, but also the fact that Costa Rica's conduct merely involved a violation of procedural rather than substantive obligations.

While in *Pulp Mills* and *Construction of a Road* the Court emphasised the distinction between procedural and substantive obligations to diversify the content of reparation, there are other examples in which the Court appears to have opted for satisfaction when the breach involved primary rules of 'minor' or more 'technical' character. Already in the *Interim Accord* case, the Court deemed satisfaction an appropriate remedy following Greece's violation vis-à-vis FYROM (now North Macedonia) of the obligation 'not to object to the application by or the membership of the applicant in NATO'.[91] Here the Applicant itself had requested the Court to award a declaration of wrongfulness, since Greece's wrongful conduct had only given rise to legal injury and Greece's non-objection could not have assured FYROM's membership into NATO. In *Certain Questions of Mutual Assistance*, the ICJ had instead to decide on the refusal of the French government to execute an international letter rogatory issued by Djibouti and pursuant to Article 17 of the 1986 bilateral Convention on Mutual Assistance. Djibouti had asked for full reparation of damage in the form of restitution, compensation and satisfaction. Yet, the Court held that the violation only amounted to the breach of the obligation to notify Djibouti of refusing mutual assistance, and deemed satisfaction constituted an adequate remedy.[92]

7.3.2.2 Satisfaction in Case of Breach of Primary Obligation of Conduct

As noted in the previous section, in the *Bosnian Genocide* judgment, the ICJ found that Serbia was responsible for failing to prevent genocide and not for actively committing it. It may be argued that, by opting for satisfaction instead of compensation, the Court might have wished to transpose also at the reparation stage the

[90] Ibid., p. 739 para. 226.

[91] ICJ, *Application of the Interim Accord of 13 September 1995 (The Former Yugoslav Republic of Macedonia v Greece)*, Judgment, 5 December 2011, ICJ Reports 644, pp. 692–693, para. 167–168.

[92] ICJ, *Certain Questions of Mutual Assistance in Criminal Matters (Djibouti v. France)*, Judgment, 4 June 2008, ICJ Reports 2008, p. 177, p. 231 para. 152.

distinction between *commissive conduct causing genocide* and *omissive conduct occasioning it*. In other words, being the obligation violated one of 'conduct-type' nature and not 'of result', the judges might have wished to emphasise the distinction between assessing a State's contribution to (material) injury when damage ensues from the action of the State, and assessing it when damage stems from the action of private parties facilitated or supported by the State's wrongful omission.

In this regard, as showed above, there is room to contend that the Court's *choice* for the but-for-test for awarding compensation was a matter of policy, rather than a simple assessment of facts. Indeed, by establishing at the merits stage Serbia's power and means to act to prevent genocide and its failure to do so, the ICJ did not rule out a link of causality between Serbia's omission and material harm—i.e., genocide in Srebrenica. Yet, as proved by other judgments of the Court,[93] it is often hard to assess the causal link between harm and wrongful conduct when omissions are involved. Furthermore, as the Court had occasion to state elsewhere, the typology of the primary rule violated (whether of conduct-preventive nature or of result) may affect the scope of reparation owed by a State and a distinction should be made between commissive and omissive conduct.[94] Therefore, by dismissing compensation and opting for satisfaction in the *Bosnian Genocide*, the Court might have achieved two objectives. First, to be relieved from complicated assessments on causation between State's omission and wrongful conduct; second, to emphasise the juxtaposition between commission of genocide (which would entail compensation) and failure to prevent it.

Overall, it should be noted that these considerations are rather speculative as the Court has never clearly drawn a link between satisfaction and distinct typologies of internationally wrongful acts. Similarly, the cases in which a comparison between typologies of obligations emerged at the reparation stage are limited in number and lack theoretical explanation. Hence, asserting that the practice of the ICJ is moving toward diversifying forms of reparation depending on the underlying wrongful act is probably too far-fetched. At the same time, the monitoring of future cases by the Court may confirm whether the ICJ is moving toward this direction.

7.3.3 Declaratory Judgments as the (Almost) Exclusive Type of Satisfaction Recognised in Judicial Practice

The practice of the ICJ points to satisfaction as an alternative remedy for certain typologies of wrongful acts. At the same time, the declaratory judgement appears to be the prevalent and almost exclusive form in which courts and tribunals grant this type of remedy.

---

[93] ICJ, *The Corfu Channel Case (United Kingdom v Albania)*, Judgment, 15 December 1949, ICJ Reports 1949, p. 244, pp. 245–251; D'Argent 2014, pp. 224–232.

[94] ICJ, *Case Concerning Armed Activities in the Territory of the Congo (Democratic Republic of the Congo v Uganda)*, Merits, Judgment, 19 December 2005, ICJ Rep 168, paras. 342, 396.

It should not be surprising that declarations of wrongfulness by a competent court or tribunals are the most common modality of satisfaction.[95] They offer a quick and inexpensive solution to courts and tribunals for recognising that an internationally wrongful act was committed and suffered by the injured State. In the jurisprudence of the ICJ, a declaratory judgment is indeed the remedy most often awarded for breaches of international law,[96] and it has been regularly used also by other international courts and tribunals, including ITLOS, and other *ad hoc* arbitral tribunals.[97] Hence, while its function may not be exclusively reparatory,[98] declaratory judgments are a central and well-established remedy for internationally wrongful acts.

What deserves more scrutiny is the appreciation that declaratory judgments are practically the only form of satisfaction awarded by courts and tribunals, irrespective of the nature of the primary rule violated and the requests made by the injured party. Requests by applicants to obtain diversified forms of satisfaction depending on the underlying wrongful acts are not exceptional. For instance, in the *Land and Maritime Boundary* case, Cameroon requested the ICJ to grant a declaration of wrongfulness for violating certain international legal rules and to order Nigeria to apologise for its internationally wrongful acts linked directly to the honour, dignity and prestige of Cameroon.[99] In the *M/V "Saiga"*, Saint Vincent and the Grenadines requested ITLOS to award monetary satisfaction for moral damage caused to the State following violations of rules related to sovereignty and jurisdiction over the exclusive economic zone.[100] In the *Arctic Sunrise*, the Netherlands requested, in respect of the injury suffered directly by the State, both a declaratory judgment of Russia's wrongful conduct and the issuance of formal apologies by the wrongdoing State.[101] Similarly, in the *Duzgit Integrity Arbitration*, the requests submitted by Malta for the unlawful seizure and confiscation of a Maltese-flagged vessel included a declaration of wrongfulness and an apology from São Tomé and Príncipe.[102]

Requests for diversified forms of satisfaction may be motivated by the party's intention to distinguish between moral and legal damage. Therefore, when the underlying wrongful act impinges directly upon the injured State's sovereignty (for instance, in cases of violation of territorial integrity or interferences in areas under the

95 See ILC 2001, p. 106.

96 ICJ, *Corfu Channel (United Kingdom v Albania)*, Judgment, 9 April 1949, ICJ Reports 1949, pp. 4, 36.

97 See fn. 115, 116, 117, 119, 120.

98 On the different functions that declaratory judgments may serve, see McIntyre 2016, p. 177.

99 ICJ, *Case concerning the land and maritime boundary between Cameroon and Nigeria*, Memorial of Cameroon, 16 March 1995, pp. 645–646.

100 ITLOS, *The M/V "Saiga" (No. 2) Case (Saint Vincent and The Grenadines v. Guinea)*, Judgment, 1 July 1999, ITLOS Reports 1999, p. 10, Memorial of Saint Vincent and the Grenadines, pp. 328–333.

101 PCA, *In the Matter of the Artic Sunrise Arbitration (Kingdom of the Netherlands v. Russian Federation)*, Award, 14 August 2015, PCA Case 2014-02, Memorial of the Kingdom of the Netherlands, pp. 125–126.

102 PCA, *In the Matter of the Duzgit Integrity Arbitration (Malta v São Tomé and Príncipe)*, Award, 5 September 2013, PCA Case No 2014-07, para. 315.

State's sovereignty or functional jurisdiction) but it does not cause material damage, a declaration of wrongfulness as a form of satisfaction may be considered sufficient.[103] Conversely, when the underlying international wrongful act is particularly serious or the injured State believes that it directly affects its honour and dignity, other forms of satisfaction, such as apologies or monetary damages may be invoked.[104] Overall, these requests reflect the classic and traditional use of satisfaction as conceptualised in the ARSIWA.

However, courts and tribunals regularly deny requests beyond a declaration of wrongfulness, usually deeming declaratory judgments the only appropriate form of satisfaction.[105] In other words, there is no appreciation through satisfaction of the different nuances of moral damage, nor of the different degree of gravity and severity of internationally wrongful act suffered by the injured State.

This is particularly striking when satisfaction is requested by the injured party as part of damages resulting from international crimes, such as in situations of war reparations. The recent judgement of the ICJ on war reparations in the *Armed Activities on the Territory of the Congo* provides a good illustration of this point. The case concerned the determination of the amount of reparation owed by Uganda to the Democratic Republic of the Congo for several international wrongful acts committed between 1998 and 2003 and consisting of violations of the *ius ad bellum*, *ius in bello*, mass violations of human rights, and violations of international environmental rules. Aside from compensation claims, the DRC also asked the Court to award satisfaction in two forms. First, it requested Uganda to conduct a criminal investigation and prosecute officers and soldiers of the Uganda's military forces responsible for the mass human rights and humanitarian violations. Second, it asked the Court to adjudge pecuniary satisfaction for moral damages caused directly to the DRC by the use of force and for promoting acts of reconciliation between Congolese ethnic groups involved in the conflict through a reconciliation fund.[106]

The Court rejected both requests. As for the demand for investigation and prosecution, it affirmed that there was no need for these measures of satisfaction since Uganda was required to investigate and prosecute by virtue of its primary obligations arising from the first Geneva Convention and its two additional Protocols.[107] As for the request for monetary satisfaction, the Court's refusal was motivated by the

---

[103] *Alleged violation of sovereign rights and maritime spaces in the Caribbean*, p. 69.

[104] *Certain Questions of Mutual Assistance*, Memorial of Djibouti, paras. 178-180; *Ethiopia's Damage Claims (The Federal Democratic Republic of Ethiopia v. the State of Eritrea)*, Final Award, 17 August 2009, Eritrea Ethiopia Claims Commission, pp. 618–619; *Eritrea's Damage Claims (the State of Eritrea v. The Federal Democratic Republic of Ethiopia)*, Final Award, 17 August 2009, Eritrea Ethiopia Claims Commission, para. 278.

[105] *Case concerning the land and maritime boundary between Cameroon and Nigeria*, p. 452 para. 319; *In the Matter of the Artic Sunrise Arbitration*, p. 377; *In the Matter of the Duzgit Integrity Arbitration* para. 332; *The M/V "Saiga"*, para. 176.

[106] *Armed Activities on the Territory of the Congo (Democratic Republic of the Congo v. Uganda)*, Judgment, 9 February 2022, available at https://www.icj-cij.org/sites/default/files/case-related/116/116-20220209-JUD-01-00-EN.pdf (last accessed 26 March 2023), para. 385.

[107] Ibid., para. 390.

understanding that the global sum awarded by the Court as compensation already took into account all injuries suffered by the DRC. The Court also noted no basis in international practice for awarding pecuniary satisfaction for non-material harm caused to the State. In this regard, the ICJ judges quoted the final award by Eritrea-Ethiopia Claims Commission in the 2009 *Ethiopia's Damage Claim*, in which the Commission, on the same grounds, rejected Ethiopia's submission for moral damage caused to the State as a result of the use of force.[108]

Awarding pecuniary satisfaction would have enabled the Court to consider the extent and the gravity of the underlying international wrongful acts committed by Uganda and the importance of the substantive primary rules at stake.[109] Instead, the Court's approach demonstrates reticence not only toward diversifying the possible forms of satisfaction, but also toward using this remedy to address the exceptional character of certain violations of international law.[110]

Finally, recognising declaratory judgments as the prevailing form of satisfaction prompts a further remark. By considering declarations of wrongfulness adequate forms of satisfaction, international courts and tribunals underline the 'public' dimension of the violation at the expense of the 'private' character of the dispute. In other words, parties' requests as to other forms of satisfaction are often dismissed by courts and tribunals, which seems at odds with the idea that it should be the prerogative of the injured State to choose the mode of reparation deemed satisfactory.[111] Conversely, emphasis is put by judicial authorities on the recognition that an internationally wrongful act has occurred and that the underlying primary rule(s) violated must be reconfirmed. From this perspective, the prevalent dimension assumed by satisfaction is neither afflictive nor properly compensatory but is rather future-looking and aimed at re-establishing the international legal order previously wronged.

---

[108] Ibid., para. 392.

[109] Bonafè 2022, pp. 789–790.

[110] Admittedly, in the practice of courts and tribunals, awards of pecuniary satisfaction are sparse and seldomly recognised. Furthermore, the ILC work on State responsibility notably dismissed any punitive dimension of reparation, and stress that reparation should simply re-established the situation that existed before the breach. The Court emphasised this point also in the reparation judgment on the Armed Activities case, see *Armed Activities on the Territory of the Congo*, Judgment, 9 February 2022, para. 102. However, one may contend that, in that judgment, the amount of compensation finally awarded by the Court was noticeably much smaller than what requested by the claimant, even though reparation concerned grave breaches of fundamental rules of the international legal order, whose humanitarian, environmental and economic consequences unfolded over a long period of time and were the result of a multiplicity of causes. The Court could have acknowledged this issue without necessarily depicting a global sum as punitive.

[111] ILC 2001 p. 96 para. 4.

7.4 Conclusion

The foregoing remarks suggest that international courts and tribunals tend to award satisfaction in a way that does not reflect the content of Article 37 of ARSIWA. The first general evidence that can be gathered from this practice is that judicial authority does not necessarily enforce the concept of satisfaction as a residual remedy targeting primarily moral injuries constituting 'an affront to the State'. On the contrary, satisfaction is often awarded instead of restitution or compensation when the injury may also be material, yet determining its precise extent and scope would require either too complex causal inquiries or is deemed inappropriate by the competent court. The *Land and Maritime Boundary between Cameroon and Nigeria* and the 2007 *Bosnian Genocide* case offered two excellent examples of this tendency. The internationally wrongful acts established by the ICJ in both cases did cause some material damages to the injured States. Yet, the Court opted for avoiding complex elaborations on the exact extent such damages would require (monetary) reparation, perhaps owing to the difficult causal inquiries related to this operation and the sensitive political implications underpinning the dispute between the States. Instead, by way of satisfaction, the Court was able to address and establish severe violations of international law without engaging too much with their consequences. Such use of satisfaction appears therefore neither subsidiary to restitution and compensation—as the commentary to Article 37 suggests—nor inspired by the idea that this remedy should primarily target moral damages to the State.

Against this framework, one can also appraise the emerging tendency of the ICJ to opt for satisfaction to remedy certain typologies of wrongful acts. Section 3.1. illustrated that satisfaction is often the preferred type of remedy when the breach is procedural or the Court wishes to emphasise that the underlying wrongful acts is less serious and its minor gravity bears consequences at the reparation stage. It is perhaps no coincidence that the ICJ considered satisfaction a good alternative to compensation and restitution when the Court was confronted with the relationship between formal categories of obligations—procedural vs substantive obligations; obligations of result vs obligations of conduct—and reparation was required for one or the other.

In the future, one may expect the ICJ—and possible other judicial bodies—to resort more frequently to satisfaction to address certain types of internationally wrongful acts. In this regard, there seem to be some indications that the Court is not only increasingly making use of distinctions between categories of obligations in its judgments,[112] but also that such distinctions impinge on the way in which the Court should award reparation.[113] While these indications are still scant and lack

[112] See Ollino 2022, pp. 90–97.

[113] See ICJ, *Armed Activities on the Territory of the Congo (Democratic Republic of the Congo v. Uganda)*, Judgment, 19 December 2005, ICJ Reports p. 168, para. 77; ICJ, *Armed Activities on the Territory of the Congo (Democratic Republic of the Congo v. Uganda)*, Judgment, 9 February 2022, paras. 83, 95, 97.

theoretical elaboration, they support the findings that satisfaction may find alternative uses beyond redress for non-material and moral injuries.

Finally, that inter-State judicial practice seems to place less importance on the notion of moral injury to the State can be derived also by another indication. It is not unusual for applicant States to submit requests for reparation that address moral or non-material injury to the State and identify satisfaction as an adequate remedy. It is also common for States to diversify the forms of satisfaction requested in light of the severity of the underlying wrongful act or the substance of the allegedly violated primary rule. These requests often include a distinction between moral and legal injury, supporting the conclusions of ARSIWA.

However, courts and tribunals do not appear to back such distinctions nor grant forms of satisfaction beyond a declaration of wrongfulness. Essentially, if non-material damage is awarded by courts through satisfaction, there is no differentiation in its various forms ('moral' or merely 'legal') nor diversification of the types of satisfaction to be awarded. On the one hand, this may read a bit like a contradiction to what the Court is doing when using satisfaction as the preferred form of remedy for certain typologies of obligations. In other words, the Court acknowledges that the 'minor' character of some obligations and their lesser gravity when compared to others may entail opting for satisfaction rather than restitution or compensation. However, when asked to recognise the different nuances of non-material or moral damage that a State may suffer, the Court seems to be more reluctant, eventually opting for a declaration of wrongfulness as the only form of satisfaction awarded.

On the other hand, the Court's approach looks more coherent if seen through a different perspective. In fact, the emphasis on the *typology* of internationally wrongful acts violated, the use of declarations of wrongfulness as the almost exclusive form of satisfaction and the reticence toward recognising different forms of moral damage draw a picture in which reparation tends less toward the satisfaction (*sic*!) of the injured State, and more toward the re-establishment of an international legal order which was wronged by the violation of some of its primary rules.

It is well-known that the codification of State responsibility entailed a 'conceptual revolution'[114] in the way in which international responsibility was conceived. Prior to the ILC work on ARSIWA, international responsibility was mostly conceptualised in its 'private' and bilateral inter-State dimension, consisting mainly of the obligation to provide reparation for damage caused to the injured State.[115] This conceptual framework underwent a major change starting with Special Rapporteur Ago, who introduced the notion of international responsibility as 'a set of new legal relationships to which an internationally wrongful act by a State may give rise in the various possible cases'[116] along with the notion of international crimes.

In its current form, the ARSIWA oscillates between these two dimensions. The articles still heavily rely on a concept of international responsibility that is inter-subjective and is concerned mainly with the duty of the responsible State to repair

[114] Pellet 1996, p. 10.

[115] See Stern 1973.

[116] Ago 1971, p. 203, para. 9.

damage caused to the injured State and the faculty of the injured State to see its rights restored. At the same time, to this mostly private dimension of international responsibility the ARSIWA juxtapose a more 'public' element,[117] in which emphasis is on an 'objective order of legality' and the recognition that an international wrongful act offends not only the injured State but also an international legal order that must be restored.

The reluctance of courts to recognise through satisfaction different degrees of moral damages and the almost exclusive use of declarations of wrongfulness as the only adequate form of satisfaction may be read against this framework. By not distinguishing between forms of satisfaction depending on the degree of injury caused to the honour or dignity of the injured State, courts are minimizing the afflictive element of satisfaction and the 'private' character of the dispute. On the other hand, declarations of wrongfulness enable courts to provide a more 'public' dimension to the dispute between two States, by recognising the existence of a violation of the international legal order and by addressing it.

References

Ago R (1939) Le délit international. Collected Courses of the Hague Academy of International Law. Brill, Leiden.

Ago R (1971) Yearbook of the International Law Commission, vol II(1), Third Report on State Responsibility, UN Doc. A/CN.4/246 and Add.1-3

Ago R (1977) Yearbook of the International Law Commission, vol II(1), Sixth Report on State Responsibility, UN Doc. A/CN.4/302 and Add.1, 2, 3.

Ago R (1978) Yearbook of the International Law Commission, vol I(1), Seventh Report on State Responsibility, UN Doc. A/CN.4/307 and Add.1, 2.

Anzilotti D (1964) Corso di diritto internazionale. Cedam, Padova.

Arangio-Ruiz G (1989) Yearbook of the International Law Commission, vol. II, Second Report on State Responsibility, UN Doc. A/CN.4/425 & Corr.1 and Add.1 & Corr.1.

Barboza J (2005) Legal Injury: The Tip of the Iceberg in the Law of State Responsibility? In: Ragazzi M (ed) International Responsibility Today: Essays in Memory of Oscar Schacter. Brill Nijhoff, Leiden.

Barthe C (2003) Réflexions sur la satisfaction en droit international. Annuaire français de droit international, vol. 49, pp. 105–128.

Bisonnette P A (1952) La satisfaction comme mode de réparation en droit international. Imprimerie Granchamp, Annemasse.

Bonafè B (2022) Assessing Reparation for International Crimes: the Case of the Armed Activities on the Territory of the Congo. Rivista di diritto internazionale, vol 3, pp. 761–794.

Brownlie I (2008) Principles of Public International Law, 7th edn. Oxford University Press, Oxford.

Crawford J (2000) Yearbook of the International Law Commission, vol. I, Third Report on State Responsibility, UN Doc. A/55/10.

Crawford J (2013) State Responsibility: The General Part. Cambridge University Press, Cambridge.

[117] Notably, this public dimension emerges not only with the definition of an internationally wrongful act as provided by Article 2 of ARSIWA, but also with the concepts of *erga omnes* obligations and obligations *erga omnes partes*, and the rights granted to States other than the injured one to address violations of these obligations.

D'Argent P (2014) Reparation, Cessation, Assurances and Guarantees of Non-Repetition. In: Nollkaemper A, Plakokefalos I (eds) Principles of Shared Responsibility in International Law. Cambridge University Press, Cambridge.
Dominicé C (1984) La satisfaction en droit des gens. In: Mélanges G. Perrin, Lausanne.
Fasoli E (2012) La riparazione dei danni immateriali nei rapporti tra Stati. Editoriale Scientifica, Milan.
Garcia Amador (1961) Yearbook of the International Law Commission, vol. II, Sixth Report on State Responsibility, UN Doc. A/CN.4/134 and Add. 1.
Gattini A (1999) Smoking/No Smoking: Some Remarks on the Current Place of Fault in the ILC Draft Articles on State Responsibility. European Journal of International Law, vol. 10 no 2, pp. 397–404.
Gattini A (2007) Breach of the Obligation to Prevent and Reparation Thereof in the ICJ's Genocide Judgment. European Journal of International Law, vol. 18 no. 4, pp. 695–713.
Gray C (1986) Judicial Remedies in International Law. Oxford University Press, Oxford.
Gray C (2013) Remedies. In: Romano C, Alter K, Shany Y (eds) The Oxford Handbook of International Adjudication. Oxford University Press, Oxford.
Hoss C (2011) Satisfaction. Max Planck Encyclopedias of International Law. Oxford Public International Law.
ILC (1973) Yearbook of the International Law Commission, vol II, UN Doc. A/CN.4/SER.A/1973/Add.1.
ILC (1981) Yearbook of International Law Commission, vol. II/2, UN Doc. A.CN.4/SER.A/1981/Add.1.
ILC (1990) Yearbook of International Law Commission, vol. II/2, UN Doc. A/CN.4/SER.A/1990/Add.1.
ILC (1996) Draft Articles on State Responsibility with Commentary Thereto adopted by the International Law Commission on First Reading, UN Doc. A/51/10.
ILC (2000a) Yearbook of International Law Commission, UN Doc. A/CN.4/SER.A/2000/Add.1.
ILC (2000b) Yearbook of the International Law Commission, vol I, UN Doc. A/CN.4/SER.A/2000.
ILC (2001) Yearbook of the International Law Commission, vol II/2, UN Doc. A/56/10.
ILC (2011) Yearbook of the International Law Commission, vol II/2, UN Doc. A/66/10.
Iovane M (1990) La riparazione nella teoria e nella prassi dell'illecito internazionale. Giuffré, Milan.
Marchesi A (2005) Obblighi di condotta e obblighi di risultato. Contributo allo studio degli obblighi internazionali. Giuffré, Milan.
McIntyre J (2016) The Declaratory Judgment in Recent Jurisprudence of the ICK: Conflicting Approaches to State Responsibility? Leiden Journal of International Law, vol. 29, pp. 177–195.
Novak F (2018) The System of Reparation in the Jurisprudence of the Inter-American Court of Human Rights. Collected Courses of the Hague Academy of International Law, vol. 392. Brill, The Hague.
Ollino A (2022) Causality in the Law of State Responsibility: Considerations on the Congo v Uganda case. QIL-Questions of International Law, vol. 95, pp. 5–23.
Pellet A (1996) Remarques sur un revolution inachevé. Le projet d'articles de la CDI sur la responsabilité des Etats. Annuaire français de droit international.
Reitzer L (1938) La réparation comme Conséquence de l'Acte illicite en Droit International. Recueil Sirey, Paris.
Riphagen W (1980) Yearbook of the International Law Commission, vol. II(1), First Report on State Responsibility, UN Doc. A/CN.4/330 and Corr.1, 2, 3.
Riphagen W (1981) Yearbook of the International Law Commission, vol. II(1), Second Report on State Responsibility, UN Doc. A/CN.4/389 and Corr.1 & Corr.2. UN Doc. A/CN.4/344 and Corr.1 & Corr.2.
Riphagen W (1982) Yearbook of the International Law Commission, vol. II(1), Third Report on State Responsibility, UN Doc. A/CN.4/354 and Corr.1 and Add.1&2.
Riphagen W (1985) Yearbook of the International Law Commission, vol. II(1), Sixth Report on State Responsibility, UN Doc. A/CN.4/389 and Corr.1 & Corr.2.

Stern B (1973) La réparation et la théorie de la responsabilité internationale. Pedone, Paris.
Stern B (2005) A Plea for 'Reconstruction' of International Responsibility Based on the Notion of Legal Injury. In: Ragazzi M (ed) International Responsibility Today: Essays in Memory of Oscar Schachter. Martinus Nijhoff Publishers, Leiden/Boston.
Stern B (2010) The Obligation to Make Reparation. In: Crawford J, Pellet A, Olleson S, Parlett K (eds) The Law of International Responsibility. Oxford University Press, Oxford.
Stoica V (2021) Remedies before the International Court of Justice. Cambridge University Press, Cambridge.
Tanzi A (1987) Is Damage a Distinct Condition for the Existence of an Internationally Wrongful Act? In: Spinedi M, Simma B (eds) United Nations Codification of State Responsibility. Dobbs Ferry, New York.
UNGA (2007a) Responsibility of States for internationally wrongful acts: Compilation of decisions of international courts, tribunals and other bodies. Report of the Secretary-General, 1 February 2007, UN Doc. A/62/62.
UNGA (2007b) Responsibility of States for internationally wrongful acts: Compilation of decisions of international courts, tribunals and other bodies. Report of the Secretary-General, Add. 1, 17 April 2007, UN Doc. A/62/62.
UNGA (2010) Responsibility of States for internationally wrongful acts: Compilation of decisions of international courts, tribunals and other bodies. Report of the Secretary-General, 30 April 2010, UN Doc. A/65/76.
UNGA (2013) Responsibility of States for internationally wrongful acts: Compilation of decisions of international courts, tribunals and other bodies. Report of the Secretary-General, 30 April 2013, UN Doc. A/68/72.
UNGA (2016) Responsibility of States for internationally wrongful acts: Compilation of decisions of international courts, tribunals and other bodies. Report of the Secretary-General, 21 April 2016, UN Doc. A/71/80.
UNGA (2019a) Responsibility of States for internationally wrongful acts: Compilation of decisions of international courts, tribunals and other bodies. Report of the Secretary-General, 23 April 2019, UN Doc. A/74/83.
UNGA (2019b) Sixth Committee (2019) Summary Record of the 13th meeting, 15 October 2019, UN Doc A/C.6/74/SR.13.
UNGA (2022) Responsibility of States for internationally wrongful acts: Compilation of decisions of international courts, tribunals and other bodies. Report of the Secretary-General, 7 December 2022, UN Doc. A/77/74.
UNGA, Sixth Committee (2004) Summary Record of the 15th meeting, 28 October 2004, UN Doc A/C.6/59/SR.15.
UNGA, Sixth Committee (2007) Summary Record of the 28th meeting' 12 November 2007, UN Doc A/C.6/62/SR.13.
Wittich S (2004) Non-Material Damage and Monetary Reparation in International Law. Finnish Yearbook of International Law, pp. 321-368.
Wolfrum R (2011) Obligation of Result Versus Obligation of Conduct: Some Thoughts About the Implementation of International Obligations. In: Arsanjani MH, Cogan J, Sloane R, Wiessner S (eds) Looking to the Future: Essays on International Law in Honor of W. Michael Reisman. Brill, Leiden.
Wyler E, Papaux A (2010) Satisfaction. In: Crawford J, Pellet A, Olleson S, Parlett K (eds) The Law of International Responsibility. Oxford University Press, Oxford.

Chapter 8
Extraordinary Experiments in Reparations: The Pursuit of Reparations at the Extraordinary Chambers in the Courts of Cambodia and the Extraordinary African Chambers

Christoph Sperfeldt

Contents

Abstract This chapter examines and compares the practice of reparations at two hybrid criminal courts, namely the Extraordinary Chambers in the Courts of Cambodia (ECCC) and the Extraordinary African Chambers (EAC). At both courts reparations were introduced through the participation of thousands of victims as civil parties in the proceedings. They both had a to grapple with numerous issues and challenges when operationalising generally worded reparations mandates, including in relation to the modalities, mechanisms, and resources for their realisation. Confronted with their time-limited existence, these courts had to make pragmatic choices—and yet they have chosen rather different pathways to discharge the responsibilities associated with their reparations mandates.

C. Sperfeldt (✉)
Macquarie Law School, Macquarie University, Macquarie Park, NSW 2109, Australia
e-mail: christoph.sperfeldt@mq.edu.au

Center for Human Rights and International Justice, Stanford University, California, USA

Center for the Study of Humanitarian Law, Royal University of Law and Economics, Phnom Penh, Cambodia

O. Spijkers et al. (eds.), *Netherlands Yearbook of International Law 2022*, Netherlands Yearbook of International Law 53, https://doi.org/10.1007/978-94-6265-627-7_8

Keywords Reparations · Extraordinary Chambers in the Courts of Cambodia · Extraordinary African Chambers · Hissène Habré · Civil parties · Trust fund

8.1 Introduction

Reparations have emerged as a central aspect in a more victim-oriented approach to justice in the wake of mass atrocities.[1] Yet, how to consider and deliver adequate, effective, and prompt reparations under circumstances frequently characterised by large-scale victimisation, severe economic obstacles, and difficult transitional contexts has challenged traditional notions of reparations, such as the 'full reparation' standard outlined in the *Chorzów Factory* case.[2] Some scholars have argued that mass atrocity contexts are 'extraordinary' in nature, and that justice responses developed primarily to deal with the more 'ordinary' crimes in peaceful societies may not adequately address the needs of societies affected by mass atrocity crimes.[3] Conscious of the difficulties associated with importing concepts and practices designed primarily in the context of stable situations into the complex environment of societies in the aftermath of mass atrocities, a dynamic and adaptable practice has emerged from institutions involved in such situations, ranging from administrative reparations programmes to international tribunals.

One of the more novel arenas where such reparations are practiced is international criminal justice. Created in 2002, the International Criminal Court (ICC) was the first international criminal tribunal to which victims can submit claims for reparations. However, there remains uncertainty as to the role reparations should occupy in international criminal justice.[4] Debates among scholars and practitioners on this subject have a normative undertone and reveal longstanding ideological fault lines, but often have limited empirical grounding.[5] The ICC and its associated Trust Fund for Victims (TFV) have remained at the centre of scholarly and public attention,[6] while other international(-ised) criminal courts or hybrid courts[7] have received less attention. Yet, the periphery of international criminal justice has often been more experimental with reparations, accumulating rich and diverse experiences.

The Extraordinary Chambers in the Courts of Cambodia (ECCC) issued their first reparations order almost two years before the ICC rendered its first reparations decision in the Lubanga case. Meanwhile, the Extraordinary African Chambers

[1] See Ferstman and Goetz 2020.

[2] PCIJ, *The Factory at Chorzow (Germany v. Poland)*, Merits, 13 September 1928, p. 47.

[3] See Aukerman 2002, pp. 39–97; Drumbl 2005, pp. 539–610.

[4] See Zegveld 2010, pp. 79–111.

[5] See McCarthy 2012; Cohen 2020.

[6] See Dwertmann 2009; Moffett 2014.

[7] The terms 'hybrid court' and 'internationalised criminal court' are used interchangeably in this chapter, both referring to courts with some mix of national and international elements, such as their framework and composition.

(EAC) have ordered Hissène Habré to pay almost US$140 million to the participating victims—the largest amount of compensation to date ordered by any international(-ised) criminal court, dwarfing the amounts ordered by ICC judges.[8] By shifting the focus beyond the courtrooms in The Hague to other internationalised criminal courts with reparations mandates, namely the ECCC and the EAC, this chapter distils some of the key issues in reparations through a comparative analysis of their practice.[9] The goal is to examine their experimental practice and contextualise it within broader challenges and developments surrounding reparations in international criminal justice.

In pursuing this endeavour, this chapter builds on my long-term engagement with the ECCC in Cambodia, since 2007, as well as fieldwork I conducted during my doctoral studies at and around the ECCC and the EAC. My approach has been socio-legal, bringing different strands of research and theories on law and society into conversation. Beyond documentary analysis, an ethnographically informed research approach was used to study the practice of reparations at both institutions. My fieldwork—mainly carried out between 2014 and 2019 including in Phnom Penh and Dakar—involved more than 60 interviews with individuals from a diverse set of actors, including from the courts, NGOs and victim associations, external observers or experts, government officials, and donors. While the ICC was also an important site for this research, we will not prominently discuss those findings in this chapter, which focuses on the experience of the ECCC and the EAC.[10]

After a brief comparative overview of both courts and the origin of their reparations mandates (Sects. 8.2 and 8.3), we will examine one key feature that both courts had in common and that provided the *raison d'être* for their reparations mandates: the participation of survivors as *parties civiles* or civil parties in the courts' proceedings (Sect. 8.4). I discuss how this modality of participation functioned in a context where courts had to deal with mass atrocity crimes and how its particularities influenced reparations processes and outcomes. We will then identify some key themes in reparations that have emerged from the courts' practice, namely how they adjudicated reparations (Sect. 8.5); how they dealt with the tricky question of whether reparations should be delivered in more individual or collective forms (Sect. 8.5.1); who should bear the responsibility for reparations (Sect. 8.5.2); and how reparations should be financed and administered (Sect. 8.6). I also consider the state of implementation of reparations to date, where possible, and their preliminary effects (Sect. 8.7). I conclude with some reflections on the role of hybrid courts in reparations after mass atrocities.

---

[8] The EAC judges ordered Habré to pay over CFA 82 billion to the civil parties. By comparison, the ICC's largest reparations order to date in the Ongwen case (February 2024) granted EUR 52 million to the victims.

[9] Thereby also decentring dominant euro-centric views of international criminal justice; see Gathii 2021, pp. 377–477.

[10] For my research comparing the ICC and ECCC practice, see Sperfeldt 2022.

8.2 Comparative Backgrounds of the ECCC and the EAC

Both courts had to deal with mass atrocities committed decades before the courts came into existence. While the ECCC had a mandate to try the 'senior leaders' and 'those who were most responsible' for crimes committed during the Khmer Rouge regime in between 1975 and 1979, the EAC's mandate was to prosecute those responsible for international crimes committed under the regime of Hissène Habré in Chad between 1982 and 1990. That is, both courts had to deal with a significant time lapse between the commission of crimes and their justice efforts, posing a range of challenges for the investigations and involvement of survivors. While the scale of atrocities committed by the Khmer Rouge in Cambodia was larger in scope—with an estimated number of those who died between 1.4 million to 2.2 million, almost a quarter of the population at that time[11]—a commission of inquiry estimated that around 40,000 individuals died as a result of the mass violence and widespread torture committed by the Habré regime.[12] Both situations concern low-income developing countries struggling with various socio-economic challenges, posing additional challenges for reparations.

In both instances, the states hosting these courts—Cambodia and Senegal—sought international involvement in the accountability process, frequently oscillating between hesitancy toward and embrace of international legitimating authority, expertise, and funding. Both states were early supporters of international justice, depositing their ICC Rome Statute ratification instruments in 2002 and 1999 respectively. Both situations involved arduous and drawn-out transnational advocacy and negotiation processes to bring about the respective hybrid courts.[13] With different political dynamics at play—i.e. in the case of the EAC mainly the question of whether and under what conditions Senegal would host the trial, and in the case of the ECCC the degree of political control over the process—the negotiations eventually resulted in the creation of two unique hybrid institutions. In the case of Cambodia, the Prime Ministers at the time sought assistance from the United Nations with an agreement concluded in 2003, while Senegal agreed with the African Union (AU) in 2012 to set up a specialised court. The resulting two extraordinary chambers—funded predominately through voluntary contributions made by international donors—not only shared similar names but also experiences in the way they brought together national and international features.[14]

The hybrid character of the ECCC, manifested in a mixed representation of the judicial and administrative leadership, is more pronounced than that of the EAC. The EAC resembles more a Senegalese court with a distinct mix of universal jurisdiction and internationalised features.[15] Due to French colonial rule, Cambodia and Senegal both have domestic legal systems that follow the civil law tradition. Yet,

[11] Tableau 2009.

[12] Chadian Ministry for Justice 1993.

[13] See Sperfeldt 2017a, pp. 1243–1260.

[14] See Ciorciari and Heindel 2014; Weill et al. 2020.

[15] See Williams 2013, pp. 1139–1160.

in both cases, unique blends of domestic and international law resulted from the negotiations that established these courts. The legal basis for the EAC's operation came in form of a Statute, which set out some general parameters for the trial, but otherwise consisted primarily of Senegalese criminal and criminal procedure law.[16] The ECCC's mix of Cambodian and international law was more noticeable, in that the ECCC agreement and corresponding law combined with judges-made Internal Rules significantly amended the law otherwise applied in Cambodia. I discuss these hybrid features specifically in relation to reparations more in the next section.

Both courts had a time-limited existence, which ended after they had completed their trials. The EAC's comparatively swift proceedings in its only trial resulted, in 2016, in the conviction of Hissène Habré with a sentence to life imprisonment.[17] Habré died a few years later in 2021. The ECCC on the other hand, took years and lengthy trials to complete two cases—simply known as *Case 001* and *Case 002*—with the latter being severed into two sub-trials, *Case 002/01* and *Case 002/02*. Other cases did not move to the trial stage. Judgments rendered between 2010 and 2022 in *Case 001* against Kaing Guek Eav, alias Duch, and in the sub-trials of *Case 002* against Nuon Chea and Khieu Samphan eventually ended in convictions and sentences to life imprisonment.[18] Reparations orders were made in the same judgments.

One significant difference between the two courts was their location. While the ECCC was located in Phnom Penh, in the country where the atrocities were committed and most survivors lived, the EAC was located in Dakar, Senegal, more than 3,500 km away from Chad. This provided different opportunities for engagement between the courts and the populations affected by the crimes before them. The combined outreach programs of the court and civil society in Cambodia achieved an unprecedented level of engagement with society, compared with other international(-ised) tribunals. The EAC on the other hand had to reach across borders to engage with local populations in Chad.[19] Ultimately, both courts relied to a significant extent on civil society to communicate and engage with survivors.[20] While in Cambodia more than a dozen local NGOs engaged with the ECCC across a range of different areas, the prominent and long-standing role of Chadian victims associations and their

---

[16] Statut des Chambres africaines extraordinaires au sein des juridictions sénégalaises pour la poursuite des crimes internationaux commis au Tchad durant la période du 7 juin 1982 au 1er décembre 1990, 22 August 2012 ('EAC Statute').

[17] A sentence upheld in an appeal judgment in 2017; see Chambre Africaine Extraordinaire d'Assisses d'Appel, *Le Procureur Général c. Hissein Habré*, Judgment, Appeal Chamber, 27 April 2017.

[18] ECCC, *Case 001,* Judgment, Trial Chamber, 26 July 2010 ('Case 001 Trial Judgment'). The sentence to life imprisonment against Duch was rendered on appeal; see ECCC, *Case 001,* Judgment, Supreme Court Chamber, 3 February 2012 ('Case 001 Appeal Judgment'). Two additional accused persons in *Case 002* died before a verdict was reached; see ECCC, *Case 002/01,* Judgment, Trial Chamber, 7 August 2014 ('Case 002/01 Trial Judgment'); ECCC, *Case 002/02,* Judgment, Trial Chamber, 16 November 2018 ('Case 002/02 Trial Judgment').

[19] See Petit 2022a, pp. 186–193.

[20] Sperfeldt 2012a, pp. 149–160.

partnership with Human Rights Watch stood out at the EAC.[21] These conditions also had an impact on the role survivors played in the proceedings at both courts and reparations.

8.3 Crafting Reparations Mandates

The (political) negotiations of a court's reparations mandate set many of the parameters for reparations outcomes and processes. They are therefore an important aspect in reparations. Here, hybrid courts are by their very nature experimental institutions, as they frequently merge various international and national elements, swinging between principled and practical concerns surrounding reparations in the context of mass atrocity trials.[22] As discussed further in the next section, the existence of a *partie civile* participation mechanism under the domestic laws of Cambodia and Senegal, which allows for reparations claims to be made in the framework of the criminal trial, was one key factor for the inclusion of reparations in the legal frameworks at the ECCC and the EAC.

Given the more universal jurisdiction-like nature of the Habré trial, which built upon the system of Senegalese criminal procedural law, the EAC Statute provided for the participation of direct and indirect victims of crime as *parties civiles*.[23] However, Article 27(1) of the Statute adapted these domestic provisions by stipulating that reparations measures 'shall include restitution, compensation and rehabilitation'—language similar to the ICC Rome Statute.[24] Other provisions under Article 27 also seem to be taken directly from the Rome Statute with little change,[25] as was the creation of a trust fund for the benefit of victims.[26] Thus, the EAC statutory reparations provisions blend the Senegalese civil party system with selective borrowing from the ICC's reparations mandate. More importantly, the incorporation of a victim participation and reparations function into the EAC never caused much debate during the establishment of the court, indicating a certain alignment with the ICC precedent.[27]

The journey was less smooth in Cambodia. Whilst a 1999 UN Group of Experts had recommended 'that any tribunal provide for the possibility of reparations by the defendant to his [sic] victims',[28] these recommendations were not taken up during

---

[21] Brody 2022.

[22] See also Balta et al 2019, pp. 15–38.

[23] EAC Statute, above n. 16, art. 14.

[24] Rome Statute of the International Criminal Court, 17 July 1998, art. 75(2).

[25] Art. 27(3) on the possibility of observations by convicted person, victims, and other interested persons or States is similar to Art. 75(3) in the Rome Statute; and Art. 27(4) on the preservation of victims' rights under national and international law is identical to Art. 75(6) in the Rome Statute.

[26] EAC Statute, above n. 16, arts. 28(1)-(2).

[27] See Sperfeldt 2020b, pp. 342–352.

[28] UNGA 1999, para 212.

the political negotiations that established the ECCC. Neither the 2003 agreement for the establishment of a hybrid court, nor the corresponding law on the establishment of the ECCC make any reference to reparations.[29] Despite the fact that Cambodia was a member of the ICC, its precedent on reparations played no role in the negotiations that determined the parameters for Cambodia's own domestic accountability process. Instead, reparations made their way into the ECCC's legal framework through the procedural rules (referred to as 'Internal Rules') adopted in 2007, by the court's own judges. This was done by reference to Cambodia's domestic laws which provide for the participation of civil parties and claims for reparations in criminal proceedings. I have detailed elsewhere the history of how the ECCC's judges essentially formed a reparations mandate for the court.[30] However, the ECCC judges were acutely aware of the scope of the alleged crimes and the unique challenges in Cambodia. They therefore limited reparations to 'collective and moral' measures, presumably excluding individual monetary compensation from the permissible forms of reparations that civil parties could seek.[31] Yet, the judges felt they had no mandate to establish a trust fund through the procedural rules, leaving important questions regarding the funding and implementation of collective reparations unanswered. Eventually, this led to additional reforms of the reparations framework half-way through the ECCC's proceedings, which empowered the court's own Victim Support Section to implement externally-funded projects that would give effect to the awards sought by civil parties. We will further discuss this unique solution in the next section.

Ultimately, the reparations mandates at both courts were not part of a grand design for an effective reparations framework, but rather the product of political or judicial negotiations, in which reparations did not feature high on the agenda. In fact, little time was spent to consider how these frameworks would work in practice. Eventually, both courts crafted legal frameworks for their reparations mandates by negotiating adjustments to their own domestic procedures, rather than wholesale importing international rules and precedent. In the case of the EAC, this led to an expansion of the opportunities for reparations, including new forms of reparations and a trust fund to finance reparations that did not exist under domestic law. At the ECCC, the court's more cautious judges restricted the forms of permissible reparations, mainly by limiting these to collective and symbolic awards. Importantly, the reparations frameworks at both courts built primarily on the host states' civil law tradition, which allowed victims to participate as civil parties in the proceedings and present claims for reparations.

[29] Agreement between the United Nations and the Royal Government of Cambodia Concerning the Prosecution under Cambodian Law of Crimes Committed during the Period of Democratic Kampuchea, United Nations and Cambodia, 6 June 2003 ('ECCC Agreement'); and Law on the Establishment of the Extraordinary Chambers in the Courts of Cambodia, with inclusion of amendments as promulgated on 27 October 2004, NS/RKM/1004/006 ('ECCC Law').

[30] Sperfeldt 2022, pp. 66–75.

[31] ECCC Internal Rules, 19 June 2007, Rule 23(11).

8.4 The Internationalisation of the *Partie Civile* and the Involvement of Survivors

The involvement of survivors in reparations is an important part of the reparations process. Such involvement is frequently carried out by courts by way of participation in the proceedings and consultations.[32] In accordance with the civil law tradition in Cambodia and Senegal, the central pathway for survivors to claim reparations before the ECCC and the EAC was by becoming a civil party.[33] This modality of participation is somewhat distinct from the role played by 'victim participants' at the ICC,[34] in that they are formally parties to the proceedings.[35] The ECCC, followed by the EAC, represented the first instance where victims participated as civil parties in the proceedings of an internationalised criminal court, effectively transposing a participation model usually used for domestic crimes to the specificities of a mass atrocity trial. Yet, there is no automatic link between a country's civil law system and the adoption of civil party participation in hybrid courts. The Special Tribunal for Lebanon, for instance, has only provisions for 'victim participants', and the court does not have powers to grant reparations. Instead, it defers reparation claims to the domestic courts of Lebanon.[36]

At the EAC, the civil party model was familiar not only to its Senegalese legal professionals but also to the survivors and their lawyers from Chad, another former French colony. The involvement of international lawyers and judges at the ECCC, however, led to substantial changes in the way the model would have otherwise operated under the Cambodian criminal procedure code. In particular, the ECCC judges were sceptical about how the civil party model would work in the specific context of its trials, including in relation to admissibility requirements and enforcement.[37] These concerns became more pronounced after the end of *Case 001*, triggering rules amendments in furtherance of trial management. This led to the introduction of collective participation—with all civil parties forming a single, consolidated group—combined with collective legal representation in form of two court-appointed Civil Party Lead Co-Lawyers.[38]

---

[32] Sperfeldt 2022, pp. 81–142.

[33] EAC Statute, above n.16, art. 14; ECCC Internal Rules (Revision 10), Rule 23 & 23*bis*. See Elander 2018; Killean 2018.

[34] Rules of Procedure and Evidence, International Criminal Court, 2019, rules 85–86.

[35] This also meant that there was no possibility at both hybrid courts for a separate reparations phase and additional reparations claims after the conclusion of the criminal trial, as exist at the ICC.

[36] See Zegveld 2019, pp. 321–345.

[37] Barriers cited in my interviews included statute of limitations for civil claims, unclear procedures under domestic law, uncertainties as to how a collective claim (moral and collective in nature) could have been carried out against a convicted person, high burden of proof (including medical examinations of harm, challenges by defence teams etc.), and uncertain enforcement through the domestic judiciaries: Sperfeldt 2022, p. 217. See also ECCC 2010.

[38] ECCC Internal Rules (Revision 5), 5 February 2010, Rules 23(4) and (5). See Sperfeldt 2022, pp. 105–110.

The cases at both courts were characterised by a comparatively large number of participating civil parties. This outcome was made possible by the efforts of civil society organisations in both situations that facilitated the participation of the vast majority of civil parties. Internationalised courts, as legal institutions, are often difficult to access for survivors without assistance, more so if they are located outside of the country where the crimes occurred. At the ECCC, intermediaries had to contend with a complex application form in a context where many elderly survivors, particularly those living in rural areas, were illiterate. Yet, 3,869 civil parties ultimately participated in *Case 002*[39]—with 82 per cent of all applications submitted through intermediary NGOs.[40] At the EAC, where intermediaries faced a less administratively burdensome process, the judges eventually recognised a total of 7,396 civil parties, both direct and indirect victims.[41] Most civil parties were associated with local victim associations, including the *Association des Victimes de Crimes du Régimes de Hissène Habré* (AVCRHH) and the *Association des Victimes de Crimes et Repressions Politiques* (AVCRP), and received additional support from local NGOs. Without the efforts of these intermediaries both courts would have seen only a fraction of participating survivors.

In addition to participation, consultations with survivors have become the most important modality through which courts seek the views of those who are meant to benefit from reparations. The nature and extent of consultations depend on the number of victims involved and the amount of resources available for this task. The temporary nature of hybrid courts has left their lawyers frequently underprepared for reparations. This is further compounded by the fact that reparations are usually the last issue addressed at trial. Here again the EAC and victim lawyers were able to rely on the well-organised victim associations in Chad, which, in conjunction with local and international NGOs, gathered and channelled civil parties' inputs into the court's process. Most of the consultations with Chadian civil parties took place between the Closing Hearings and the pronouncement of the trial judgment in 2016—apparently inspired by the way Cambodian NGOs had organised consultations with civil parties.[42] This network provided civil parties with a more coherent and authoritative representation of their reparations claims at trial. Eventually, the

---

[39] ECCC, *Case 002*, above n. 18: initially the Office of Co-Investigating Judges admitted 2,117 individuals as civil parties. An additional 1,752 individuals were admitted by the Pre-Trial Chamber following appeals against the admissibility decision. The more confined charges in *Case 001* led to around 90 civil parties participating at trial stage, with 76 declared admissible on appeal.

[40] ECCC, *Case 002*, 'Closing Order', Co-Investigating Judges, Case File 002/19-09-2007-ECCC-OCJI, D427, 15 September 2010, para 11.

[41] The judges declared inadmissible the claims of another 3,489 individual victims. Chambre Africaine Extraordinaire d'Assisses d'Appel, *Le Procureur Général c. Hissein Habré*, Appeal, 27 April 2017, para 226 ('Habré Appeals Reparations Judgment').

[42] The AVCRHH used a network of 23 civil party focal points for consultation, with Carayon and Sulzer noting that this model was inspired by the way the Cambodian Human Rights and Development Association (ADHOC) had facilitated consultations with ECCC civil parties: see Carayon and Sulzer 2020, p. 170.

EAC received two civil party reparations claims from these victim associations.[43] Both claims expressed a clear preference for individual financial compensation. Civil parties affiliated with the AVCRHH also asked for complementary collective reparations measures, including development projects in survivors' communities, monuments, inclusion of the Habré period into schools' teaching curriculum, a memorial day, and educational centres for the victims' children in their communities.[44]

Due to the longer proceedings and the specificities of the ECCC's reparations regime, there was more time for consultations. While the smaller number of civil parties in *Case 001* allowed for more regular and intensive consultations, the much larger number of civil parties in *Case 002*, spread out across the entire country, made meaningful consultations more challenging. Rules amendments enacted before the *Case 002* trial required civil parties to submit to the Trial Chamber 'initial specification' of their requests at the beginning of the trial.[45] This meant that at least some consultations with civil parties had to be organised prior to the start of the trial—a situation rather different from the EAC, where reparations were only addressed at the end of the trial. Similar was the crucial role played by NGO intermediaries in ECCC consultations, which enabled many, mostly pro bono lawyers to access their clients. Yet, the reliance on NGO funding meant that consultations were uneven, with civil parties whose participation was facilitated by more well-resourced NGOs having more opportunities for consultations than others. In their initial specification for *Case 002*, the Civil Party Lead Co-Lawyers requested collective reparations falling into four broad categories: (1) memorialisation/remembrance; (2) rehabilitation; (3) documentation/education; and (4) other awards.[46]

Overall, the EAC and ECCC experiences demonstrate both the feasibility and challenges associated with the civil party model when it is transposed to an internationalised mass atrocity trial with a potentially large number of participating civil parties. Both courts felt it necessary to make some adjustments to the domestic procedures of the countries in which they were based, especially in relation to reparations. While the EAC otherwise implemented rather swiftly a process largely in accordance with the civil party procedure, the ECCC judges changed course half-way through the trials introducing a new mode of collectivised participation, representation, and reparation, which more resembled the kind of strategies also adopted in some of the ICC cases.[47] These changes to the rights of parties represented, in effect, a departure from the civil party system as provided under Cambodian law in all but name.[48] Much

[43] Reparations Submission by Civil Parties Abaifouta et al., *Ministère Public c. Hissein Habré*, 10 June 2016 ('Reparations Submission Abaifouta et al'); Reparations Submission by Victim Groups AVCRP and RADHT, *Ministère Public c. Hissein Habré*, 10 June 2016 ('Reparations Submission AVCRP and RADHT').

[44] Reparations Submission Abaifouta et al, above n. 43, paras 147-152.

[45] ECCC Internal Rules (Revision 9), 16 January 2015, Rule 80*bis* (4).

[46] ECCC, *Case 002*, 'Initial Specifications for Reparations Requests in Case 002', presented at the Initial Hearing on 29 June 2011, Transcript E1/6.1/TR002/20110629 Final EN.

[47] Killean and Moffett 2017, pp. 713–740.

[48] See Werner and Rudy 2010, pp. 301–309.

of this was driven by trial management concerns rather than a desire to make participation more meaningful for civil parties—much of which is arguably determined outside the courtrooms.

Here both cases hold lessons for how comparatively strong, in-country-based civil society organisations can overcome some of the more practical participation barriers that exist at international(-ised) criminal courts, especially with regards to communication.[49] These intermediaries relied on creative communication strategies involving civil party focal points or representatives across different geographical areas of the country in Chad or Cambodia. Indeed, the experience at the ECCC and the EAC demonstrates the feasibility of rather large-scale survivor participation in reparations proceedings—at a level similar to or above the largest cases currently before the ICC.[50] However, it also highlights the importance of regular communication and engagement with survivors outside the court. Moreover, many details regarding reparations changed in the lead up to and even after a reparations order, highlighting the importance of ongoing consultations throughout adjudication and implementation processes.

8.5 Adjudicating Reparations

Transmitted to the courts for their consideration, victims' reparations requests continue to be transformed, mostly to make them fit into the constraints of courts' reparations mandates and with what legal practitioners consider feasible. These debates culminate during the adjudication of reparations, where lawyers and judges frequently balance competing legal and social imperatives.[51]

The two cases at the ECCC had to contend with rather different frameworks. The adjudication of *Case 001* was carried out under the original procedural framework conceived of by the judges, where reparations had to be borne exclusively by convicted persons, as would be the case under domestic criminal procedural law.[52] After the defendant in *Case 001* was found to be indigent, the judges rejected most of the civil parties' reparations requests as there were no funds to satisfy these claims. They only granted two symbolic reparations: the inclusion in the judgment of the names of civil parties and their relatives who had died, and the publication of statements of apology by the convicted person.[53] *Case 001* provides an example of how judges in the context of a mass atrocity trial dealt with a traditional civil party reparations claim, which solely relied on assets of convicted persons. As noted above,

[49] See Sperfeldt and Oeung 2019, pp. 85–105.

[50] In 2022, for instance, approximately 4,100 victims were participating in the Ongwen case and around 2,100 victims in the Ntaganda case. See https://www.icc-cpi.int/sites/default/files/2022-12/OngwenEng.pdf. Accessed 23 March 2023.

[51] Sperfeldt 2022, pp. 165–238.

[52] ECCC Internal Rules, 12 June 2007, rule 23(11). See Sperfeldt 2012b, pp. 457–489.

[53] ECCC, Case 001 Trial Judgment, above n. 18.

judges recognised these deficiencies and amended the Internal Rules prior to *Case 002*. With no trust fund or similar funding mechanism provided for under the ECCC agreement, the judges decided to broaden the mandate of the court's Victim Support Section to seek donor funding and engage in reparations projects in collaboration with external actors.[54] This new modality kickstarted a process of 'projectification' of ECCC reparations, with the judges ultimately recognising two dozen such reparation projects in two separate judgments in 2014 and 2018 relating to the two sub-trials of that case: 11 projects in *Case 002/01* and 13 projects in *Case 002/02*.[55] We have provided elsewhere an overview of these different reparations projects.[56]

At the EAC, where reparations were not limited to collective measures, the judges simply did what they knew best from their domestic practice: they assessed the harm of civil parties and calculated compensation amounts.[57] Habré was eventually ordered to pay over CFA 82 billion (almost US$140 million) to the civil parties—regardless of his ability to afford this sum.[58] The judges rejected all proposed collective measures. The outcome was a substantial reparations order against Hissène Habré that left open many questions regarding its implementation. These contrasting experiences between the ECCC and the EAC can be put down to very different views and approaches regarding the modality of reparations, such as whether they should be individual or collective in nature (Sect. 8.5.1), and the responsibility for reparations (Sect. 8.5.2), including who should pay for reparations—two issues that I will now discuss in more detail, as they expose different views of reparations held across both courts.

8.5.1 Individual vs. Collective Reparations

The 2005 UN Basic Principles and Guidelines on the right to reparation conceive of reparations as an umbrella concept that combines various forms of redress.[59] One longstanding debate surrounds the types of reparations that may be appropriate in situations characterised by mass atrocities and mass victimisation, and whether individual or collective measures are more suited to addressing the harm in these contexts. Contrary to the predominantly individualised approach to reparations in domestic settings dealing with ordinary crimes, programmes aiming to address the consequences of mass atrocities often consider collective forms of reparations. Many scholars and practitioners argue that the nature and gravity of such crimes, in which entire communities are targeted, may render inappropriate or even unfeasible

[54] ECCC Internal Rules (v6), 17 September 2010, Rule *23quinquies* (1)-(3). See Sperfeldt 2022, pp. 211–212.

[55] ECCC, Case 002/01 Trial Judgment, above n. 18, paras 1151-1160; ECCC, Case 002/02 Trial Judgment, above n. 18.

[56] Sperfeldt and Hughes 2020, pp. 545–565.

[57] Sperfeldt 2020b, pp. 342–352.

[58] Habré Appeals Reparations Judgment, above n. 41, paras 938-939.

[59] UNGA 2005, paras 19–23.

approaches that rely solely on individual reparations.[60] Collective reparations are frequently presented as an answer to this dilemma,[61] and they have also increasingly been regarded as a solution to the conundrum of how to meet expectations for redress and repair in mass atrocity trials.[62]

The EAC and the ECCC have dealt with this conundrum rather differently. ECCC judges from the outset worried about processing potentially thousands of individual civil party claims and the feasibility of monetary awards in Cambodia.[63] Moreover, there were concerns about the societal implications of providing compensation to a relatively small number of civil parties, without addressing the broader needs of victim constituencies, who did not have the opportunity to participate in the trials. From the judges' point of view, collective and symbolic reparations appeared to be the less problematic path. They therefore limited reparations to 'collective and moral' measures through their rule-making powers. The ECCC Supreme Court Chamber later clarified that one of the purposes of reparations was to contribute to 'national reconciliation' and, as such, the term 'collective' reparations should be interpreted as meaning 'to favour those measures that benefit as many victims as possible', and that therefore 'the most inclusive measures of reparation should be privileged'.[64] This approach softened the exclusive targeting of civil parties through court-ordered reparations and opened the door for collective measures that could benefit broader victims' collectives.[65]

Unlike their peers at the ECCC, the EAC judges declined to consider broader reparations measures and constituencies. Instead, they enacted the traditional civil party model with its focus on redress to the victims before the court. Noting the persistence of harm at the individual or family level and citing a general lack of confidence in state structures, Chadian civil parties themselves had expressed a strong preference for individual monetary compensation.[66] The EAC judges accepted this request. They identified civil parties' harm, calculated the defendant's liability and issued the largest compensation order to date by any international(-ised) criminal court for the benefit of the civil parties participating at trial.[67] This was fully in line with how a civil party claim would have ordinarily worked at the domestic level, with EAC judges clearly not sharing the concerns of their ECCC colleagues over monetary compensation. While one of the civil party groups had also asked to set aside 30 percent of the claimed amount to finance collective reparations measures, the EAC judges rejected all collective reparations requests, mainly on the grounds that they

---

[60] See Roht-Arriaza 2004, pp. 121–139.

[61] See International Center for Transitional Justice 2009.

[62] See Tapia Navarro 2018, pp. 67–96.

[63] Sperfeldt 2022, ch 7.

[64] ECCC, Case 001 Appeal Judgment, above n. 18, paras 655-659.

[65] See Sperfeldt 2020a, pp. 479–504.

[66] Reparations Submission Abaifouta et al, above n. 43, paras 30-31.

[67] For the purpose of calculating the compensation, civil party lawyers and trial judges borrowed from mass claims processes and categorized victims into groups on the basis of the nature of the harm they suffered. See Sperfeldt 2020b, p. 343.

lacked the requisite details which would have allowed the judges to assess their feasibility.[68] Moreover, the judges rejected all measures that required the involvement of the Chadian state, including those relating to school education and a public commemoration day. The EAC judges argued that as the Chadian state was not party to the proceedings, it was unable to impose obligations on the state.[69]

At the core of the diverging practices surrounding individual vs. collective reparations at the ECCC and EAC are contestations over the very purpose of court-ordered reparations. On the one hand are those sharing more accountability-based conceptions of reparations that have driven the EAC practice by focusing on the specific case at hand and promoting benefits for the individual victims before the court. This model aligned with the traditional civil party claim and what the EAC judges knew from their domestic practice and felt most comfortable with. More practically, this approach also avoided infringing on another state's territory and jurisdiction, namely Chad, where the EAC judges lacked authority. On the other hand are those holding broader transitional justice-oriented conceptions of reparations, who consider the complexities of the social contexts and seek to promote more symbolic benefits for larger victim collectives—a practice pursued by the ECCC and articulated throughout its judgments.[70] This translated into an aversion against individual monetary compensation and the delivery of dozens of collective projects with only tenuous links to the criminal trial. The ECCC was able to capitalise in this endeavour on its in-country location, support from development donors, and the implementation capacity of local civil society. Both of these conceptions of reparations have also permeated the ICC's jurisprudence, with ICC judges oscillating between competing legal and social imperatives when considering the specific circumstances of each case or situation.[71]

8.5.2 Responsibility for Reparations

A key issue in reparations is the question of who should bear the responsibility for reparations and who should pay for it. Central to prevalent accountability-based conceptions of reparations in international criminal justice is the responsibility and liability of individual convicted persons. This is also what Cambodia and Senegal knew from their domestic criminal procedures. Yet, when transposed to a mass atrocity trial the dilemma becomes apparent: Not only are convicted persons' assets never enough to afford relief for the harm caused by mass atrocities, but often these

[68] Chambre Africaine Extraordinaire d'Assises, *Ministère Public v. Hissein Habré*, Judgment, 30 May 2016, civil judgment rendered on 29 July 2016, published in conjunction with criminal judgment, paras 69-71 ('Habré Trial Reparations Judgment').

[69] The judges' reasoning for rejecting collective measures is strikingly similar to the way ECCC judges had dealt with such claims in *Case 001*. Sperfeldt 2020b, pp. 345–346.

[70] See also Leyh and Fraser 2019, pp. 39–59.

[71] Sperfeldt 2022, pp. 234–238.

assets are also out of reach. Again, major differences in approach emerged between the ECCC and EAC, and how they dealt with this dilemma.

In *Case 001* at the ECCC, the convicted person was the only legally permissible avenue for making a reparations order, which evaporated after Duch was declared indigent. Civil party lawyers in that case had argued that indigence of an accused should not affect the issuance of a reparations order.[72] Yet, the Supreme Court Chamber upheld the Trial Chamber's ruling not to make a reparations order against an indigent convicted person. The judges argued 'that an award that, in all probability, can never be enforced, i.e., is de facto fictitious, would belie the objective of effective reparation…'.[73] ECCC judges resisted issuing such 'fictitious awards' that, even if symbolically important, would have little prospect for implementation and be 'confusing and frustrating for the victims'.[74]

Yet, this is precisely what the EAC judges did. Civil party lawyers in the Habré trial had highlighted the importance of ordering compensation independently of the availability of funds, so as to give effect to reparations' function of recognising victims' harm and to account for any assets that might be located in future.[75] In ordering compensation purely on the basis of harm and above and beyond any known assets of the convicted person, the EAC judges arguably simply followed domestic practice. In setting a signal for accountability through a heavy reparations order, the EAC's approach diverts from the practice at the ECCC, which had more cautiously limited itself to what appeared feasible at the time of the reparations order.[76] The ICC arguably walked a middle path in the aftermath of the 2015 *Lubanga* appeals reparations judgment: ordering reparations against convicted persons regardless of indigence, but keeping the amounts reasonable enough so that they were still feasible to implement through the Trust Fund's fundraising efforts.[77]

More practically, how could courts get their hands on any assets held by defendants? At the ECCC, judges merely relied on self-declarations by accused persons when finding them indigent for reparations purposes. Even though it was widely assumed that Duch did not own much property, observers speculated that some

---

[72] ECCC, *Case 001*, 'Appeal against Judgment on Reparations by Co-Lawyers for Civil Parties Group 2', Civil Party Group 2, F13, 2 November 2010, para 26.

[73] ECCC Case 001 Appeal Judgment, above n. 18, paras 666-667. The SCC judges recognised that under domestic civil action, indigence of a convicted person would not preclude granting compensation, but the judges did not think that this was applicable to the *sui generis* regime at the ECCC.

[74] Ibid., para 668.

[75] Reparations Submission Abaifouta et al, above n. 43, paras 153-157.

[76] The Supreme Court Chamber noted in *Case 001* that 'in purely abstract terms it is imaginable that Kaing Guek Eav may enrich himself in the future ... Such possibilities are nevertheless so remote that they can practically be excluded, and, as such, cannot constitute a basis for ordering reparations.' ECCC Case 001 Appeal Judgment, above n. 18, para 688.

[77] ICC, *Prosecutor v Lubanga*, Judgment on the Appeals against the Decision Establishing the Principles and Procedures to Be Applied to Reparations of 7 August 2012, Appeals Chamber, ICC-01/04-01/06-3129, 3 March 2015. See Stahn 2015, pp. 801–813; Sperfeldt 2022, pp. 190–194.

of the accused in *Case 002* possessed assets.[78] After civil party lawyers had filed requests for full investigations into the properties owned by charged persons and measures to preserve any assets for reparations, the Pre-Trial Chamber found that these requests were outside the scope of investigations and that the ECCC's statutory framework lacked provisions permitting pre-trial freezing of such assets—indicating that the ECCC, as a specialised court, saw itself further removed from the domestic system than the EAC.[79] Overall, ECCC officials never seriously pursued the income or property of accused persons, based on a widespread belief that this would create unjustifiable burden and yield minimal benefits for civil parties.[80]

Such arguments were more difficult to make at the EAC, where it was widely believed that Hissène Habré had taken considerable public assets within him when he fled Chad.[81] Early in the proceedings, the EAC investigating judges had ordered the identification and preservations of Habré's assets.[82] The Trial Chamber later noted that Senegalese authorities had confiscated one property in Dakar and two bank accounts. In addition, it was believed that Habré might hold further assets in Europe, including under the names of family members.[83] The EAC investigating judges' action to preserve Habré's assets was swifter than that of its peers at the ECCC, also because it could rely on powers under Senegalese criminal procedural law that the ECCC claimed to lack. The bottom line is that despite all the rhetoric in international criminal justice surrounding the importance of convicted persons' liability for reparations, only limited capacities are devoted to investigating the assets of defendants. Similarly, almost all defendants in the first cases at the ICC have been declared indigent.[84] Against this background, the EAC's record of securing at least some assets for reparations purposes looks respectable. Still, the value of these assets (estimated at below US$ one million[85]) as well as any other assets potentially located in future are likely to fall drastically short of what is needed to satisfy the EAC's reparations order.

Considering that in both cases leading figures of the former regimes committed atrocities in the name of the state and by relying on state institutions, civil parties at both courts also raised notions of state responsibility for reparations in the proceedings, either directly or indirectly (such as through reparation requests for public education or health measures, national commemoration days etc.). In both cases, the courts were resolute in defending the distinct nature of criminal proceedings which

[78] Fawthrop 2013.

[79] ECCC, *Case 002*, Decision on Appeal of Co-Lawyers for Civil Parties Against Order on Civil Parties' Request for Investigative Actions Concerning All Properties Owned by the Charged Persons, Pre-Trial Chamber, D193/5/5, 4 August 2010, paras 23-25.

[80] Sperfeldt 2022, pp. 223–226.

[81] Grovestins 2016.

[82] Habré Trial Reparations Judgment, above n. 68, paras 65 and 73.

[83] See Birkett 2019, pp. 151–161.

[84] An exception is ICC, *The Prosecutor v Jean-Pierre Bemba Gombo*, Appeal ICC-01/05-01/08, 8 June 2018, where some assets were confiscated: Birkett 2021.

[85] Media reports and observers estimated the value of the property at around EUR 700.00: author's interview with international NGO staff, 29 May 2015.

deal with individual criminal and *not* state responsibility. Yet, both the courts and civil parties did attempt to find creative ways to involve or implicate the state in court-ordered reparations.

In Cambodia, there was some hope that the ECCC's in-country location and the government's participation in the creation and operation of the court could have a positive effect on state involvement in reparations. Yet, attempts during the trials to encourage more government participation proved futile. In response to certain reparations requests by civil parties, ECCC judges in *Case 001* stated that they would not infringe on areas of state responsibility. The Trial Chamber noted that '[it] has no jurisdiction over Cambodian or other national authorities or international bodies.'[86] Still, non-financial government support remained relevant for reparations projects in *Case 002*. The ECCC judges had noted that they would endorse reparations that infringe on government prerogatives 'where it is clear that such measures have been approved or implemented by the Royal Government of Cambodia', thus opening the door for government participation in reparations.[87] Such support was relevant for some reparations measures, including a national day of remembrance, the inclusion of judicial findings in the Cambodian school curriculum, and a public repository of ECCC archival records. The government's nominal support for these initiatives, some of which had already been externally funded, and the lack of more substantial government backing is widely viewed a missed opportunity to broaden reparations at the ECCC.

Civil parties at the EAC tried to push the envelope further, with one group requesting the court to declare the Chadian state responsible for reparations.[88] This was inspired by a precedent in an earlier ruling by a domestic court in Chad.[89] The Trial Chamber rejected the request on the basis that the Chadian state was not party to the proceedings, further noting that the EAC Statute limits its jurisdiction to natural persons.[90] As discussed above, requests for collective reparations that required state involvement met the same fate. The EAC Appeals Chamber had sought the views of the Chadian state and merely noted that 'the Chadian government did not respond favourably to the collective reparations solicited by the civil parties'.[91] Whilst the Chadian state had contributed to the operational costs of the EAC and even pledged to contribute to the trust fund, it has so far been hesitant to acknowledge its broader responsibility for reparations.[92] Curiously, in 2014, the Chadian government had

[86] ECCC Case 001 Trial Judgment, above n. 18, para 663.

[87] ECCC, *Case 002*, 'Initial Specification of the Substance of Reparations Awards Sought by the Civil Party Lead Co-Lawyers Pursuant to Internal Rule 23quinquies(3)', Trial Chamber, Memorandum, E125, 23 September 2011.

[88] Reparations Submission AVCRP and RADHT, above n. 43, p. 16.

[89] In 2015, a Chadian court convicted a number of former security agents of the Habré regime and ordered CFA 75 billion to around 7,000 civil parties, stipulating that 50 percent of the amount be carried by the Chadian state. To date, the Chadian authorities have failed to implement these measures: see Sperfeldt 2017a, pp. 1250–1251.

[90] Habré Trial Reparations Judgment, above n. 68, paras 75–76.

[91] Habré Appeals Reparations Judgment, above n. 41, para 843.

[92] Diab 2018, pp. 141–163.

asked the EAC to join the proceedings as a civil party on the grounds that the state had suffered harm when Habré pillaged the country.[93] The EAC judges refused to admit the application, as these crimes went beyond the court's jurisdiction.[94] Thus, rather than taking responsibility for the crimes committed by former agents of the state, the Chadian government portrayed itself as a victim of these crimes.

At both courts, the supposedly primary bearer of responsibility and source of reparations, namely the convicted person, was not seen to provide opportunities for adequate and effective reparations. This did not hinder the EAC from issuing a substantial reparations order against the convicted person. However, the ECCC judges' more feasibility-oriented practice led to rules changes that, in essence, separated the reparations award from the liability of the defendant. This new avenue was introduced in addition to the traditional civil party claim, which was maintained in the rules, but not further operationalised. The Rules amendments forced civil parties to make a choice: either direct a claim against the accused—and be subject to high standards of proof and in most likelihood get nothing—'or' propose an externally pre-financed reparations project under the new, less legalistic avenue.[95] With state responsibility for reparations out of reach for criminal courts and convicted persons' assets either unavailable or insufficient, both courts eventually turned their hopes to external funding for reparations.

8.6 Financing and Administrating Reparations

Questions surrounding the financing and effective administration of reparations have plagued the responsible institutions in international criminal justice and beyond. During the negotiations of the ICC Rome Statute, negotiators considered early on the limitations of a model where reparations for mass atrocities were borne (only) by individual convicted persons. The creation of a separate Trust Fund for Victims (TFV) able to receive voluntary contributions appeared as an acceptable compromise. Additionally, a trust fund was seen to be a suitable vehicle to administer collective awards.[96] Compared to direct individual awards, collective forms of reparations involve a more indirect form of delivery, often requiring court-affiliated entities and non-state actors to play an intermediary role in turning financial contributions into collective measures. The model of a court-associated trust fund has since gained prominence as a response to the funding problems outlined above.

One year after the adoption of the Rome Statute, the UN Group of Experts in Cambodia also recommended a special trust fund for reparations.[97] Yet, this recommendation was not taken up during the ECCC's negotiations. In contrast, inspired

93 Magnien 2014.

94 Habré Trial Reparations Judgment, above n. 68, para 81.

95 ECCC Internal Rules (Revision 6), 17 September 2010, Rules 23*quinquies* (3).

96 Sperfeldt 2017b, pp. 351–377.

97 UNGA 1999, para 212.

by the ICC/TFV precedent, the EAC Statute did provide for the establishment of a Trust Fund for the benefit of victims.[98] The language of Article 28 suggests that the drafters of the Statute were mindful of providing some flexibility when it comes to the funding and beneficiaries of reparations, visible in provisions enabling external voluntary contributions and the award of reparations to 'victims', whether or not they participated in the proceedings.[99] While it was optional for the EAC to use the Trust Fund as an intermediary for a reparations order,[100] the civil parties and victim advocates asked the judges to entrust the Fund with implementing the reparations order.[101] In following these arguments, the EAC Appeals Chamber tasked the Fund with carrying out the individual reparations order and further ruled that all frozen assets and relevant judicial records be turned over to it.[102] The Chamber also invited the Fund to collaborate with the civil parties, the Chadian government, and other interested organisations on the implementation of collective reparations that were not granted in the order. Thus, the entire implementation of the EAC's reparations order was handed to—and thus made dependent on—an institution that, at the time of the order, only existed on paper.

Without a mandate to establish a trust fund, the ECCC judges had to be more creative. Following the amendments of the ECCC's rules on reparations after *Case 001*, which provided for a more flexible, project-based path to reparations, the judges expanded the responsibilities of the court's own Victim Support Section (VSS) to engage in reparations, including by collaborating with external actors and seeking voluntary donor funding.[103] This significantly expanded the VSS' functions but did not provide it with the necessary resources and expertise to implement its new mandate. Because of these constraints, the VSS leveraged existing local NGO projects for the purposes of reparations. In 2013, the German government committed almost EUR 500,000 to fund several of the proposed reparations projects in *Case 002/01*, followed by the Swiss development agency and other donors.[104] Overall, external donors contributed more than USD 770,000 to reparations in *Case 002/01*.[105] Donor support further increased in *Case 002/02*, with the European Union alone committing more than EUR one million to collective reparation projects. Most of this funding was channelled through Cambodian NGOs, which emerged as central actors in conceiving

[98] Statute of the Extraordinary African Chambers, 22 August 2012, arts 28 (1)-(2), stipulating that 'the Trust Fund shall be financed by voluntary contributions', and providing further that 'reparations shall be open to all victims, individually or collectively, whether or not they participated in the proceedings before the Extraordinary African Chambers'.

[99] Ibid., arts 28(1)-(2).

[100] Ibid., art 27(2): 'The Extraordinary African Chambers *may* order that the award for reparation be made through the Trust Fund provided for in Article 28 below' (italic by the author).

[101] Reparations Submission Abaifouta et al., above n. 43, para 64; REDRESS 2017.

[102] Habré Appeals Reparations Judgment, above n. 41, paras 613-614.

[103] ECCC Internal Rules (Revision 6), 17 September 2010, rules 23*quinquies* (1)-(3).

[104] ECCC 2013, p. 8.

[105] ECCC 2014.

and implementing ECCC reparations projects. All of these projects were completed before the ECCC ended its judicial proceedings in 2022.[106]

The journey toward reparations has been more protracted at the EAC. After the final judgment in 2017, the creation of the Trust Fund was slowly set into motion, frequently slowed down by the internal politics in Chad. The Fund was formally established under the auspices of the African Union (AU), following a resolution in 2016 and the adoption of the Fund's statute in early 2018.[107] However, it took until 2019 before an agreement was concluded with Chad for the establishment of the Fund's headquarter in N'Djamena. A change of government in Chad in 2022 eventually brought some movement. The new president tentatively allocated EUR 15 million toward a contribution to the trust fund. This comes on top of USD 5 million reportedly allocated by the AU.[108] So far, no other donors have volunteered additional contributions. At the time of writing, civil parties and other victims of Habré are still waiting for reparations to materialise. Many of the elderly civil parties have already passed away before they were able to see the compensation owed to them.[109]

Following the establishment of the ICC/TFV, the model of a court-associated trust fund is frequently suggested as a solution to international(-ised) criminal court's woes with reparations. It provides a focal point for dedicated implementation expertise that is usually not available in courts and enables the administration of external funding toward reparations. Yet, the example of the ICC/TFV and the EAC show that voluntary contributions will not simply plug the gap in funding. Funding judicial reparations, even more so financial compensation, does not easily attract donors who are more inclined to fund humanitarian and development programmes.

Moreover, the ECCC experience shows that there are alternatives to the trust fund model. The ECCC's expanded reparations project mandate has drawn in new actors and mobilised new resources, mainly in form of international development funding. This has expanded the opportunities for reparations in the ECCC context and positively contributed to further localising the ECCC's justice process through an enhanced involvement of civil society. This practice has resulted in more symbolic collective measures to wider constituencies, but with often little tangible benefits for the participating civil parties. The ECCC has advanced this pragmatic approach with its focus on the swift delivery of reparation projects to a degree that the reparative value of the resulting projects is being questioned.[110] This is also because the practice of using third party funding for reparations blurs the boundaries between reparations and other forms of victim assistance or development support. The question of whether

---

106 Sperfeldt and Hughes 2020.

107 African Union, Assembly/AU/Dec.615 (XXVII), 'Décision sur l'affaire Hissein Habré', adopted at the AU summit in Kigali, 17-18 July 2016.

108 Petit 2022b. Ahead of presidential elections in 2024, the Chadian government announced the release of CFA 10 billion (USD 16.5 million) in state funds to relaunch the reparation process.

109 Sperfeldt 2021.

110 Killean and Moffett 2020, pp. 1–29.

or under what circumstances this actually matters can only be answered by the survivors themselves.

8.7 Impact of Reparations

Despite the fact that many pressing questions about reparations can only be answered by those who are to benefit from them, we still know relatively little about how reparations ordered by international(-ised) criminal courts and the final reparations outcomes are received by civil parties and victim participants. Empirical information is scarce, and evaluation practices at courts or their affiliated entities are uneven. This holds true for the ICC/TFV as well as for temporary hybrid courts like the EAC and ECCC with reparations mandates.[111] Since no reparations have as yet materialised from the EAC process and no comprehensive survey has been undertaken among EAC civil parties, we focus in this section on the ECCC experience, where implementation of *Case 002* reparations projects has been completed.[112]

Some common threads can be distilled from existing surveys among civil parties regarding their reparations experience. First, even years after the reparations order in *Case 002/01*, most civil parties were not aware or had little knowledge of the reparations projects granted by the ECCC.[113] This data reflects the gradual but continuous decrease in outreach after *Case 001*. It shows that one-off consultations, without continuous communication, are insufficient to realise reparative effects among civil parties. Notwithstanding the lack of knowledge among civil parties about the reparations outcomes, most civil parties still believed it was important to provide reparations to victims.[114] Even though a majority of respondents was supportive of collective reparations, a sizable proportion of civil parties also sought individual reparations, including monetary compensation—a measure that was beyond the ECCC's mandate.[115] Among the motivations cited by civil parties for reparations were: to alleviate suffering, to commemorate the dead, and to remind the next generations of the Khmer Rouge regime lest the atrocities be forgotten.[116] Many of these aims would align with ECCC's reparations projects, but without knowledge of or participation in these projects, reparative effects among civil parties remain in doubt.

Overall, the lack of empirical data and more thorough evaluations of reparations remains a significant shortcoming of courts' practices, as it has limited our insights into what makes reparations effective in the specific context of such tribunals.

[111] See Human Rights Center 2015. See also Chap. 9 by Balta, de Waardt and Vaes in this volume.

[112] Sperfeldt and Hughes 2022.

[113] This was true with 80 to 90 percent of civil parties interviewed in more recent surveys. Among the few who knew about the reparations, a majority was satisfied with the outcomes. Sperfeldt et al. 2016, p. 57; Williams et al. 2018, pp. 116–117.

[114] Sperfeldt et al. 2016, p. 59; Williams et al. 2018, pp. 109–113.

[115] See Kirchenbauer et al. 2013, pp. 19–20. See also Williams et al. 2018, p. 115.

[116] Sperfeldt et al. 2016, p. 59; Kirchenbauer et al. 2013, p. 40.

As a consequence, debates on reparations among legal professionals and scholars frequently remain in normative spheres that do not sufficiently consider survivors' views—arguably the true litmus test for reparations.

8.8 Conclusion

This examination of the reparations at the ECCC and the EAC has revealed some experiences and practices that hold lessons for the future development of reparations in international criminal justice, regarding both the limitations but also the opportunities that exist. Yet, despite the fact that only few such tribunals have a reparations mandate, there has been little cross-institutional learning. Although the ECCC and EAC's existence overlapped with the ICC's first reparations cases, little systematic exchange existed between these courts. It is true that the EAC looked to the ECCC, as the only other hybrid court with a civil party reparations regime. Yet, the better-resourced ICC and its TFV have often struggled to look outside the box in The Hague. Geographically removed from the situations they are dealing with and mindful of their nature as permanent institutions, they have moved cautiously from case to case while focusing on upholding the legality of their decisions. Against this background, I have argued in this chapter that there is much to learn by turning our gaze to the 'periphery' of international criminal justice, where cash-strapped hybrid courts are forced to innovate when implementing their reparations functions during a short-lived existence.[117]

There have been similarities and differences in how the ECCC and EAC approached their reparations functions. Both have shown how civil party participation can be adapted to the requirements of a mass atrocity trial. Pre-trial coordination and the organised representation of civil parties at the EAC meant that the court could implement a model it knew from its domestic practice. Concerns surrounding the efficacy of reparations, however, led the ECCC to introduce amendments that departed from the civil party model and eventually more closely resembled the victim participants before the ICC. Both courts have relied to a significant extent on the support of local civil society in their engagement with survivors. This partnership enabled the participation of thousands of civil parties in the proceedings, with most of this engagement being carried out outside the courts. It also created some level of ownership in the societies affected by the legacy of mass atrocities. Without such partnerships, courts would have to provide more funding to their outreach and participation functions than they currently afford. Otherwise reparations remain inaccessible to the survivors affected by the courts' proceedings.

Both courts have also demonstrated the limitations of recasting mass atrocity trials as a site for realising societal reparative justice ambitions, reflected in diverging

[117] See also Sperfeldt 2013, pp. 1111–1137.

approaches at the EAC and ECCC.[118] While the EAC followed the civil parties' preference for individual compensation, the ECCC remained suspicious about the feasibility and desirability of monetary awards. Its preference for collective reparations meant that a sophisticated process had to be created whereby various intermediaries and external donors became involved in the design and implementation of projects that were meant to give effect to civil parties' reparations requests. Both approaches have drawbacks, as there is no easy way out of the reparations conundrum. The ECCC's collective approach created a new space of connection with society and opportunities to engage with the past. The delivery of two dozen reparation projects was ultimately more than most observers had initially expected, although their impact on civil parties appeared to be more limited. The EAC on the other hand had to deal with the cross-border implications of its justice process, when it awarded reparations that have to be implemented in another state. The initial experience suggests that universal jurisdiction trials will struggle to deliver reparations to victims in far-away countries beyond their jurisdiction. Such trials will prove most effective on reparations, if they get hold of the accused, have access to some of the defendant's assets and can count on minimal cooperation by the state concerned.[119]

Overall, the experience at both courts shows how demands for reparations from survivor communities have transformed the traditional model of international criminal justice. The ECCC and EAC struggled with the effects of this transformation but also demonstrated capacity for adaptation and innovation. It is perhaps in the nature of hybrid courts in particular that they prove to be more responsive to their environment, more so in relation to their reparations mandates. A look at international criminal justice's periphery can therefore yield important insights to inform ongoing debates on the merits and challenges with reparations in international criminal justice. More fundamentally, the many contestations over the form and direction of reparations—visible not only at the EAC and ECCC but also the ICC and beyond—are not just about different visions of justice but also about the very purpose and role that reparations in international(-ised) criminal trials should occupy. Divergence in practice across these courts suggests that no consensus is to emerge soon. Rather these contestations have become constitutive of reparations in international criminal justice and play out differently in various contexts. The EAC and ECCC experience also underlines that international(-ised) criminal courts are no substitute for the primary responsibility of states for reparations for mass atrocity crimes. While these courts' role in reparations will always be a more modest and complementary one, my account also shows that effective and meaningful approaches to reparations will require new ways of thinking about recognition and repair in the aftermath of mass atrocities that push beyond criminal courts' comfort zones.

Acknowledgement My collaboration with Rachel Hughes inspired the choice of this chapter's title. Christoph Sperfeldt is the recipient of an Australian Research Council Discovery Early Career Researcher Award (project number DE240100636).

[118] See Kendall 2015, pp. 352–376.

[119] Sperfeldt 2020b, pp. 349–350.

References

Aukerman MJ (2002) Extraordinary Evil, Ordinary Crime: A Framework for Understanding Transitional Justice. Harvard Human Rights Journal 15: 39–97

Balta A, Bax M, Letschert R (2019) Between Idealism and Realism: A Comparative Analysis of the Reparations Regimes of the International Criminal Court and the Extraordinary Chambers in the Courts of Cambodia. International Journal of Comparative and Applied Criminal Justice 45(1): 15–38

Birkett D (2019) Victims' Justice? Reparations and Asset Forfeiture at the Extraordinary African Chambers. Journal of African Law 63(2): 151–161

Birkett D (2021) Asset Freezing at the International Criminal Court and the United Nations Security Council: A Legal Protection Perspective. PhD thesis, University of Amsterdam.

Brody R (2022) To Catch a Dictator: The Pursuit and Trial of Hissène Habré. Columbia University Press

Carayon G, Sulzer J (2020) The Real Fight Begins: Victims Struggle for an Effective Right to Reparation. In: Weill S, Seelinger KT, Carlson KR (eds) The President on Trial. Oxford University Press, Oxford, pp 167–178

Chadian Ministry of Justice (1993) Les Crimes et Détournements de l'ex-Président Habré et de ses Complices [The crimes and embezzlements of former President Habré and his accomplices: Report of the National Commission of Inquiry]: Rapport de la Commission d'Enquête Nationale du Ministère de la Justice. L'Harmattan, Paris

Ciorciari J, Heindel A (2014) Hybrid Justice: The Extraordinary Chambers in the Courts of Cambodia. University of Michigan Press, Ann Arbor

Cohen M (2020) Realizing Reparative Justice for International Crimes: From Theory to Practice. Cambridge University Press, Cambridge

Diab N (2018) Challenges in the Implementation of the Reparation Award Against Hissein Habré: Can the Spell of Unenforceable Awards across the Globe Be Broken? Journal of International Criminal Justice 16(1): 141–163

Drumbl M (2005) Collective Violence and Individual Punishment: The Criminality of Mass Atrocity. Northwestern University Law Review 99(2):539–610

Dwertmann E (2009) Reparation System of the International Criminal Court: Its Implementation, Possibilities and Limitations. Brill Academic Publishers

ECCC (2010) Eight ECCC Plenary Session Concludes, Press Release, 17 September 2010. https://www.eccc.gov.kh/sites/default/files/media/ECCC_PR_17Sep2010_%28Eng%29.pdf. Accessed 12 October 2023

ECCC (2013) The Court Report. Issue 63, August 2013. https://www.eccc.gov.kh/sites/default/files/publications/The%20Court%20Report%20August%202013_0.pdf. Accessed 12 October 2023

ECCC (2014) Information for Media: Case 002/01 Judgment 7 August 2014. Press Kit, 7 August 2014. https://www.eccc.gov.kh/sites/default/files/articles/Press%20kit%20Case%20002-01.pdf. Accessed 12 October 2023

Elander M (2018) Figuring Victims in International Criminal Justice: The Case of the Khmer Rouge Tribunal. Routledge, Abingdon

Fawthrop T (2013) Khmer Rouge Leader Ieng Sary Had US$20m in Hong Kong Account. South China Morning Post. 31 March 2013. https://www.scmp.com/news/asia/article/1203492/khmer-rouge-leader-ieng-sary-had-us20m-hong-kong-account. Accessed 12 October 2023

Ferstman C, Goetz M (2020) Reparations for Victims of Genocide, War Crimes and Crimes Against Humanity: Systems in Place and Systems in the Making, 2nd edn. Martinus Nijhoff Publishers

Gathii JT (2021) The Promise of International Law: A Third World View. American University International Law Review 36(3): 377–477

Grovestins A (2016) Victims' Lawyers Start Battle to Seize Habré's Millions. Justice Hub. 4 August 2016. https://justicehub.org/article/victims-lawyers-start-battle-to-seize-habres-millions/. Accessed 12 October 2023

Human Rights Center (2015) The Victims' Court? A Study of 622 Victim Participants at the International Criminal Court. UC Berkeley, Berkeley

International Center for Transitional Justice (2009) The Rabat Report: The Concept and Challenges of Collective Reparations. New York

International Criminal Court (2019) Rules of Procedure and Evidence. ICC, The Hague

Kendall S (2015) Beyond the Restorative Turn: The Limits of Legal Humanitarianism. In: De Vos C, Kendall S, Stahn C (eds) Contested Justice: The Politics and Practice of International Criminal Court Interventions. Cambridge University Press, Cambridge, pp 352–376

Killean R (2018) Victims, Atrocity and International Criminal Justice. Routledge, Abingdon

Killean R, Moffett L (2017) Victim Legal Representation before the ICC and the ECCC. Journal of International Criminal Justice 15(4): 713–740

Killean R, Moffett L (2020) What's in a Name? "Reparations" at the Extraordinary Chambers in the Courts of Cambodia. Melbourne Journal of International Law 21(1): 1–29

Kirchenbauer N et al (2013) Victim Participation before the Extraordinary Chambers in the Courts of Cambodia: Baseline Study of the Cambodian Human Rights and Development Association's Civil Party Scheme for Case 002. Phnom Penh: ADHOC

Leyh BM, Fraser J (2019) Transformative Reparations: Changing the Game or More of the Same? Cambridge International Law Journal 8(1): 39–59

Magnien N (2014) Chad Can't Be a Civil Party in Habre Case, Rules EAC. International Justice Tribune

McCarthy C (2012) Reparations and Victim Support in the International Criminal Court. Cambridge University Press, Cambridge

Moffett L (2014) Justice for Victims before the International Criminal Court. Routledge, Milton Park/New York

Petit F (2022a) Outreach for the EAC: An Extraordinary Experience. In: Weill S, Seelinger KT, Carlson KR (eds) The President on Trial. Oxford University Press, Oxford, pp 186–193

Petit F (2022b) Chad's President Promises to Compensate Habré Victims. Justice Info, 14 Oct 2022. https://www.justiceinfo.net/en/107774-chad-president-promises-compensate-habre-victims.html. Accessed 12 October 2023

REDRESS (2017) 'Demande d'autorisation de présenter une soumission d'amicus curiae concernant la question des réparations' [Request for leave to make an amicus curiae submission regarding the issue of reparations], submitted to EAC Appeals Chamber

Roht-Arriaza N (2004) Reparations in the Aftermath of Repression and Mass Violence. In: Stover E, Weinstein HM (eds) My Neighbor, My Enemy: Justice and Community in the Aftermath of Mass Atrocities. Cambridge University Press, Cambridge, pp 121–139

Sperfeldt C (2012a) 'Cambodian Civil Society and the Khmer Rouge Tribunal', 6(1) International Journal of Transitional Justice, 149–160

Sperfeldt C (2012b) Collective Reparations at the Extraordinary Chambers in the Courts of Cambodia. International Criminal Law Review 12: 457–489

Sperfeldt C (2013) From the Margins of Internationalised Criminal Justice: Lessons Learned at the Extraordinary Chambers in the Courts of Cambodia. Journal of International Criminal Justice 11(5): 1111–1137

Sperfeldt C (2017a) The Trial against Hissène Habré: Networked Justice and Reparations at the Extraordinary African Chambers. International Journal of Human Rights 21(9): 1243–1260

Sperfeldt C (2017b) Rome Legacy: Negotiating the Reparations Mandate of International Criminal Court. International Criminal Law Review 17(2): 351–377

Sperfeldt C (2020a) Reparations at the Extraordinary Chambers in the Courts of Cambodia. In: Ferstman C, Goetz M (eds) Reparations for Victims of Genocide, War Crimes and Crimes Against Humanity: Systems in Place and Systems in the Making, 2nd edn. Martinus Nijhoff Publishers, pp 479-504

Sperfeldt C (2020b) Reparations at the Habré Trial in Context. In: Weill S, Seelinger KT, Carlson KR (eds) The President on Trial. Oxford University Press, Oxford, pp 342–352

Sperfeldt C (2021) Victims of Habré's Rule Haven't Been Paid a Cent of the Compensation Due to Them. The Conversation, 29 September 2021. https://theconversation.com/victims-of-habres-rule-havent-been-paid-a-cent-of-the-compensation-due-to-them-168115. Accessed 12 October 2023

Sperfeldt C (2022) Practices of Reparations in International Criminal Justice. Cambridge University Press, Cambridge

Sperfeldt C, Hughes R (2020) The Projectification of Reparation. Journal of Human Rights Practice 12(3): 545-565

Sperfeldt C, Hughes R (2022) Extraordinary Experiments in Reparation. Opinio Juris, 1 November 2022. http://opiniojuris.org/2022/11/01/symposium-on-the-eccc-extraordinary-experiments-in-reparation/. Accessed 12 October 2023

Sperfeldt C, Hyde M, Balthazard M (2016) Voices for Reconciliation: Assessing Media Outreach and Survivor Engagement for Case 002 at the Khmer Rouge Trials. East-West Center and Handa Center for Human Rights and International Justice

Sperfeldt C, Oeung J (2019) The Evolution of Cambodian Civil Society's Involvement with Victim Participation at the Khmer Rouge Trials. In: Kent L, Wallis J, Cronin C (eds) Civil Society and Transitional Justice in Asia and the Pacific. ANU Press, Canberra, pp 85–105

Stahn C (2015) Reparative Justice after the Lubanga Appeal Judgment. Journal of International Criminal Justice 13: 801–813

Tableau E (2009) Khmer Rouge Victims in Cambodia, April 1975–January 1979: A Critical Assessment of Major Estimates. Democratic Expert Report, Doc No. ECCC D140/1/1

Tapia Navarro N (2018) Collective Reparations and the Limitations of International Criminal Justice to Respond to Mass Atrocity. International Criminal Law Review 18(1): 67–96

UNGA (1999) Report of the Group of Experts for Cambodia Established Pursuant to General Assembly resolution 52/135

UNGA (2005) Basic Principles and Guidelines on the Right to a Remedy and Reparation for Victims of Gross Violations of International Human Rights Law and Serious Violations of International Humanitarian Law, UN Doc A/RES/60/147

Weill S, Seelinger KT, Carlson KB (2020) The President on Trial: Prosecuting Hissène Habré. Oxford University Press; Oxford

Werner A, Rudy D (2010) Civil Party Representation at the ECCC: Sounding the Retreat in International Criminal Law? Northwestern Journal of International Human Rights 8(3): 301–309

Williams S (2013) The Extraordinary African Chambers in the Senegalese Courts: An African Solution to an African Problem? Journal of International Criminal Justice 11(5): 1139–1160

Williams T et al (2018) Justice and Reconciliation for the Victims of the Khmer Rouge? Victim Participation in Cambodia's Transitional Justice Process. Centre for Conflict Studies/Centre for the Study of Humanitarian Law, Marburg/Phnom Penh

Zegveld L (2010) Victims' Reparations Claims and International Criminal Courts. Journal of International Criminal Justice 8:79–111

Zegveld L (2019) Victims as a Third Party: Empowerment of Victims. International Criminal Law Review 19: 321-345

Table of Cases

ICC, *Prosecutor v Lubanga*, Appeal ICC-01/04-01/06-3129, 3 March 2015

ICC, *The Prosecutor v Jean-Pierre Bemba Gombo*, Appeal ICC-01/05-01/08, 8 June 2018

PCIJ, *The Factory at Chorzow (Germany v. Poland)*, Merits, 13 September 1928

ECCC, *Case 001*, 'Judgment', Trial Chamber, Case File 001/18-07-2007/ECCC/TC, E188, 26 July 2010

ECCC, *Case 001*, 'Appeal Judgment', Supreme Court Chamber, Case File 001/18-07-2007-ECCC/SC, F28, 3 February 2012

ECCC, *Case 001*, 'Appeal against Judgment on Reparations by Co-Lawyers for Civil Parties Group 2', Civil Party Group 2, F13, 2 November 2010

ECCC, *Case 002*, 'Closing Order', Co-Investigating Judges, Case File 002/19-09-2007-ECCC-OCJI, D427, 15 September 2010

ECCC, *Case 002*, 'Decision on Appeal of Co-Lawyers for Civil Parties Against Order on Civil Parties' Request for Investigative Actions Concerning All Properties Owned by the Charged Persons', Pre-Trial Chamber, D193/5/5, 4 August 2010

ECCC, *Case 002*, 'Initial Specifications for Reparations Requests in Case 002', presented at the Initial Hearing on 29 June 2011, Transcript E1/6.1/TR002/20110629 Final EN

ECCC, *Case 002*, 'Initial Specification of the Substance of Reparations Awards Sought by the Civil Party Lead Co-Lawyers Pursuant to Internal Rule 23quinquies(3)', Trial Chamber, Memorandum, E125, 23 September 2011

ECCC, *Case 002/01*, 'Judgment', Trial Chamber, Case File No 002/19-09-2007/ECCC/TC, E313, 7 August 2014

ECCC, *Case 002/02*, 'Case 002/02 Judgment', Trial Chamber, Case File No 002/19-09-2007/ECCC/TC, 16 November 2018

Chambre Africaine Extraordinaire d'Assises, *Ministère Public v. Hissein Habré*, Judgment, 30 May 2016

Chambre Africaine Extraordinaire d'Assisses d'Appel, *Le Procureur Général c. Hissein Habré*, Appeal, 27 April 2017

Reparations Submission by Civil Parties Abaifouta et al, *Ministère Public c. Hissein Habré*, 10 June 2016

Reparations Submission by Victim Groups AVCRP and RADHT, *Ministère Public c. Hissein Habré*, 10 June 2016

Table of Rules and Treaties

Agreement between the United Nations and the Royal Government of Cambodia Concerning the Prosecution under Cambodian Law of Crimes Committed during the Period of Democratic Kampuchea, 6 June 2003 ('ECCC Agreement')

Law on the Establishment of the Extraordinary Chambers in the Courts of Cambodia, with inclusion of amendments as promulgated on 27 October 2004, NS/RKM/1004/006 ('ECCC Law').

ECCC Internal Rules (v1, 2007) to (v10, 2022).

Statut des Chambres africaines extraordinaires au sein des juridictions sénégalaises pour la poursuite des crimes internationaux commis au Tchad durant la période du 7 juin 1982 au 1er décembre 1990', 22 August 2012 [Statute of the Extraordinary African Chambers]

Rome Statute of the International Criminal Court, 17 July 1998

Chapter 9
ECCC Reparations Inside and Out: Unpacking Rhetorics on Reparative Justice for Victims of Mass Crimes

Alina Balta, Mijke de Waardt and Marola Vaes

Contents

Abstract In a significant step for international criminal law, the Extraordinary Chambers in the Courts of Cambodia (ECCC or the Court) enabled victims to participate in proceedings as civil parties and claim reparations, which in practice materialised in several reparation measures. To explore whether and how these measures contributed to reparative justice for their beneficiaries, this chapter combines a top-down legal approach with a bottom-up empirical one. The premise of our exploration was that an understanding of reparative justice as both procedural and substantive justice is crucial to understanding the contribution of the ECCC's reparations towards

---

A. Balta
The Netherlands Institute for the Study of Crime and Law Enforcement (NSCR), Amsterdam, The Netherlands

M. de Waardt (✉)
The Netherlands Institute for the Study of Crime and Law Enforcement, Amsterdam, The Netherlands
e-mail: mdewaardt@nscr.nl

M. Vaes
Independent Scholar, Amsterdam, The Netherlands

M. de Waardt
Criminology, Vrije Universiteit Amsterdam, Amsterdam, The Netherlands

O. Spijkers et al. (eds.), *Netherlands Yearbook of International Law 2022*, Netherlands Yearbook of International Law 53, https://doi.org/10.1007/978-94-6265-627-7_9

reparative justice for victims. We took the Court, its legal framework, and case-law as our starting point. After the top-down legal analysis, we focused on findings resulting from our empirical study based on narratives from 55 victims about the actual changes in their lives due to the reparations. We noticed that reparative justice is influenced by three considerations. First, the legal framework of international courts, the rights pertaining to their reparations' regime, and the opportunities and limitations embedded therein. Second, the capacity of courts and the multitude of actors involved in materialising the victims' rights as well as the quality of their work. Third, what were thought to be clear tangible benefits for victims failed to be perceived as such, mainly because of their actual limited impact, while what were thought to be by-products of the reparations' projects brought about meaningful and tangible benefits to victims. We consider that our analysis and findings have important implications for international courts featuring reparations regimes that aim to provide reparative justice to victims.

Keywords Reparations · Extraordinary Chambers in the Courts of Cambodia · Mass crimes · Victims · Reparative justice · Narratives · Tangibility of reparations

9.1 Introduction

Granting victims of international crimes a role within international criminal law (ICL) institutions constitutes an important normative development in international law.[1] It refutes the previously held contention that victims are a forgotten party in their own trials,[2] demonstrated by the scarce attention paid to them by the former *ad-hoc* and military ICL tribunals that centred solely on the prosecution of the accused persons.[3] In the past decades, this normative development was formalised by the inclusion of a reparations regime within the mandate of international courts such as the International Criminal Court (ICC) and the Extraordinary Chambers in the Courts of Cambodia (ECCC). For the first time in the context of ICL-based courts, in addition to their focus on punishing the perpetrators, these courts recognised the victims' role as active participants within trials. Moreover, they bestowed upon victims the possibility to request reparations, in addition to other prerogatives, such as voicing their views and concerns as well as benefiting from the right to information, protection, and assistance.[4] The reparations would be awarded against and borne by individuals found criminally responsible for causing harm to victims.[5]

[1] E.g. McCarthy 2012, p. 359; Teitel 2014, pp. 63–64; Kendall 2015, p. 359.

[2] See Christie 1977, p. 1; Wemmers 2009b, p. 20; Pemberton et al. 2019, p. 404.

[3] Groenhuijsen and de Brouwer 2010, p. 273; Moffett 2015, p. 282.

[4] Rome Statute of International Criminal Court, opened for signature 17 July 1998, 2187 UNTS 39, entered into force 1 July 2002, ('Rome Statute'). Internal Rules of ECCC 2007, Rule 23.

[5] Rome Statute, art 75. Internal Rules of ECCC 2007, Rule 23(11).

Central to the inclusion of a reparations regime within the mandate of these courts is the idea that providing reparations might contribute towards repairing the harm caused and afford reparative justice to victims of international crimes.[6] This aspiration is laid out in the courts' legal bases and reiterated in their case law and other court documents.[7] According to the ICC and the ECCC's legal bases, reparations aim to address,[8] acknowledge, and provide benefits for the harm[9] suffered by victims.

This normative development and the aspirations of these courts fit within developments that have occurred in the general thinking about the intended objectives of reparations in both judicial and national administrative settings. Over the last 15 years, understandings of reparations have expanded from a focus on repairing individual victims and punishing individual perpetrators to goals that are supposed to prompt profound transformations within post-conflict societies. As transitional justice scholars and practitioners started to look beyond trials and truth commissions in the early 2000s to acknowledge the legacies of harm and to avert atrocities from re-occurring, justice aims and, therefore, the modalities of reparations increasingly expanded in relevant debates.[10] Besides addressing the harms of victims through material compensation, reparations needed to reform governments, strengthen reconciliation and democracy, and repair social, economic, political, and historical inequalities.[11]

With the amplification of the orientation and modalities of reparations, debates evolved around the actual effects of reparations within particular contexts. So far, studies on reparations have mainly focused on the normative assumptions of what reparations *should* do, instead of what they were *actually* doing. Scholars started to adopt contextualised approaches to reparations in order to delve into their possibilities and limitations in particular locations. To explore the possible effects of the respective reparative modalities, we therefore see over the last decade more studies recommending empirical research that probes victims' perceptions of and satisfaction with reparations,[12] and victims' participation in reparations efforts.[13] This means that normatively much is known about the conceivable effects of reparations based on

[6] As is known, the inclusion of reparations regimes within the mandates of international courts is not unique to ICL-based courts, as they are firmly anchored in the mandates of International Human Rights Law ('IHRL') institutions such as the European Court of Human Rights ('ECtHR') and the Inter-American Court of Human Rights ('IACtHR') which long predate the ICL-based courts.

[7] See, for instance, in relation to the International Criminal Court ('ICC'), *Lubanga case*, Appeals Chamber, Amended order for reparations, 3 March 2015, ICC-01/04-01/06-3129, para 71. ICC, *Katanga case*, Trial Chamber, Order for Reparations pursuant to Article 75 of the Statute, 24 March 2017, ICC-01/04-01/07-3728-tENG, paras 15, 267. see also, in relation to the Extraordinary Chambers in the Courts of Cambodia ('ECCC'), Case 001, Supreme Court Chamber: Appeals Judgment, 3 February 2012, 001/18-07-2007-ECCC/SC, paras 658, 699.

[8] Rome Statute, art 75.

[9] Internal Rules of ECCC, 2015, Rule 23(1).

[10] García-Godos 2013, pp. 241–255.

[11] Laplante 2015, p. 513; McGonigle Leyh and Fraser 2019, pp. 39–59.

[12] De Waardt 2013, pp. 830–834.

[13] Ottendoerfer 2018, pp. 905–31.

research studies, but nonetheless, not much is known yet empirically about the actual effects of the right to and materialisation of reparations in the lives of survivors.

Against this background, this chapter aims to contribute to the empirical exploration of the effects of reparations awarded by ICL-courts—specifically the ECCC—and their actual contribution to reparative justice. In a significant step for ICL, the ECCC enabled victims to participate in proceedings as civil parties and to avail themselves of a set of rights, including the right to claim reparations, which in practice materialised as several measures of reparations that the civil parties could benefit from. This chapter addresses the victims' engagement with the ECCC for the purpose of reparations, the actual form of these reparations in the case law, and the difference they subsequently made in the lives of survivors of the Khmer Rouge regime.[14] In essence, this chapter examines whether and how they contributed towards reparative justice for victims. In the ECCC context, reparations have been already awarded to civil parties and were widely implemented, providing a fertile ground to study the survivors' perceptions about the actual changes in their lives as result of the reparations. In addition, considering that the ECCC has been hailed for its victim-oriented approach,[15] it is paramount to inquire the survivors' lived experience of this approach.

Our method combines top-down legal and bottom-up empirical approaches. While we take the ECCC, its legal framework, and case-law as a starting point in this research, we then focus on findings resulting from our analysis of the victims' narratives. We argue that understanding reparative justice as both procedural and substantive justice is crucial to comprehending the ECCC's reparations regime's contribution to reparative justice for victims. We therefore introduce a taxonomy of reparative justice to articulate the potential implications of bestowing such rights on victims. We argue that the process whereby reparations are provided and the outcome of this process inform victims' perceptions of reparative justice. The second part of the chapter puts forward the ECCC's reparations regime and its subsequent case-law focused on how the reparations materialised in practice, similarly structured alongside the procedural and substantive dimensions. As we show, the rights statutorily bestowed upon victims correspond to and inform the elements of reparative justice theory. Next, we shift our focus to the results of our empirical research with 55 male and female victims of the Khmer Rouge regime, which elicit how civil parties perceived their experiences with the Court and the reparations measures awarded.

To conclude, we examine the ECCC's potential contribution to reparative justice for victims and the interplay between the findings of our study and the taxonomy on reparative justice. We highlight several positive aspects of the ECCC's reparations regime, but also reveal that what were thought to be clear tangible benefits for victims failed to be perceived as such, mainly because of their actual limited impact.

[14] In this chapter, the terms victims, survivors, and civil parties are used interchangeably, aware that from a legal point of view, not all victims or survivors may qualify as civil parties. Moreover, given that victims/survivors in many post-conflict societies use the words interchangeably, or avoid using one of the two words because of negative connotations, shows that it is difficult to use one term to identify those involved.

[15] See, for instance, McGonigle Leyh 2012, p. 375.

Conversely, what were thought to be by-products of the reparations projects brought about significant and meaningful benefits to victims.

9.2 Reparative Justice: A Proposed Taxonomy to Understand International Courts' Reparations Regimes and Victims' Experiences

In the aftermath of mass atrocities characterised by mass victimisation, reparations aim to repair the harm incurred by crimes and are assumed to be an essential means to provide reparative justice for the benefit of individual and collective victims.[16] Yet, attempting to understand what informs victims' perceptions of reparative justice in the aftermath of such victimisation is a complex endeavour. One reason is because the needs and wishes of victims vary significantly depending on a multitude of personal and contextual factors that also change across time.[17]

Previous normative and empirical studies are essential for understanding how reparations in the context of international(ised) courts may contribute to reparative justice for victims. These studies show how individuals participating in court proceedings experience the procedures they were involved in (i.e. procedural justice), and how the outcomes they receive (i.e. substantive justice) influence their perceptions of justice.[18] These notions were imported into victimological research in relation to victims of international crimes, and consistently show that how courts proceed and how they treat victims is important to victims' sense of justice.[19]

Consequently, since reparations provided by international courts through reparations regimes include both a process and an outcome,[20] we extrapolate that the process whereby reparations are provided and its outcome inform the victims' perceptions of reparative justice, which is made up of procedural justice and substantive justice. In this chapter, procedural justice is operationalised using four elements: voice, interaction, information, and length of proceedings. Substantive justice is operationalised in terms of tangible reparations that respond to victims' harm and preferences. Each of the elements[21] will be elaborated in turn.

Within procedural justice, voice refers to the opportunity for victims to express their views, concerns, and opinions in the context of reparations proceedings that

---

[16] Van Boven 2013, p. 25; Bass 2012, p. 176; Wemmers 2014, p. 222.

[17] For an elaboration on justice for victims in the context of international crimes, see Balta et al. 2019, pp. 221, 223.

[18] E.g. Wemmers 1996; Laxminarayan 2012; McGonigle Leyh 2011.

[19] Wemmers 1996; Wemmers 2009a, pp. 211–222; Killean 2016, p. 31; Laxminarayan 2012, p. 120; McGonigle Leyh 2011, p. 47; Moffett 2014; Wemmers 2014, p. 222.

[20] See van Boven 2009, p. 22; Shelton 2015, p. 16; Moffett 2014.

[21] The choice for these elements is primarily informed by a systematic review of the relevant literature, which indicates that these elements have been found to contribute to the victims' perception of both procedural and substantive justice.

concern them.[22] This may have positive implications, as international courts can constitute a forum that enables victims to recount their stories, attend to the intrinsic motivations of victims for expressing their voice, and provide acknowledgment of their suffering and harm. Interaction and its quality,[23]—whether victims are treated with respect, dignity, and sensitivity—are relevant throughout the proceedings, and can include encounters with the judges during oral testimonies and interaction with other court actors, for instance, the legal representatives.[24] Interacting with victims of mass atrocities is a sensitive matter, with many victims being at risk of suffering secondary victimisation in the context of court proceedings.[25] Information refers to a court's provision of information to victims regarding their rights, for instance to participate in a case to request reparations, to access available support or protection, the choices that are available, and the expectations they can have of the court.[26] It also refers to the information and the updates victims receive regarding the procedural and factual developments in their case.[27] A connected issue is outreach to raise awareness and to inform the victims about the court's existence, the opportunities to request and benefit from reparations, and the various ways in which they may participate in proceedings.[28]

Victims' evaluation of procedural justice in the process of obtaining reparations before international courts may also be informed by the length of proceedings. Delays can have several implications for victims, as they may negatively affect the victims, inducing frustration and disappointment. Extended trials may result in distrust in the proceedings and frustration,[29] especially when coupled with lack of interaction and information, which might result in victims withdrawing from proceedings.[30] The timely resolution of the proceedings appears to represent an important element in a victims' evaluation of both procedural and substantive justice.

Substantive justice in the context of reparations proceedings refers to the outcome of proceedings,[31] which may encompass different types of reparations that the victims might actually receive, i.e. tangible reparations. The potential tangible reparations that victims of mass atrocities might receive are best captured by the van Boven/Bassiouni Principles, which constitute the state of the art in regard to reparations[32] and aggregate decades of research on reparations for victims of gross violations

---

[22] Lind and Kanfer 1990, p. 952.

[23] See Bies and Moag 1986; Colquitt 2001, p. 386.

[24] See also Cody and Koenig 2018, p. 1.

[25] Victims may suffer secondary victimisation as a result of treatment by court officials, which can include inappropriate attitudes, denial of their rights, etc. See Orth 2002, p. 313; Groenhuijsen and Pemberton 2011.

[26] Assembly of States Parties 2009, p. 4.

[27] See e.g. Letschert and van Boven 2011, p. 157.

[28] See e.g. Assembly of States Parties 2009, p. 19.

[29] Letschert 2017, p. 26.

[30] Cody and Koenig 2018, p. 1; Cody et al. 2015, p. 44.

[31] E.g. Laxminarayan 2012, p. 37.

[32] Zwanenburg 2006, p. 641.

of international human rights law and serious violations of international humanitarian law.[33] Consequently, according to these Principles, victims of these crimes might receive individual and collective reparations, which could entail restitution, compensation, rehabilitation, satisfaction, and guarantees of non-repetition as modalities. Furthermore, since substantive justice is necessarily informed by how victims perceive the tangible reparations, this chapter posits that the tangible reparations that courts award can contribute to substantive justice for victims if they respond to the victims' preferences.[34] It is important to acknowledge that in situations of mass atrocities rife with large numbers of victims and massive harm, contributing to substantive justice for victims entails complex challenges that require difficult choices.[35]

9.3 Reparations at the ECCC: Legal Framework and Subsequent Practice

The ECCC was established as a reaction to the 1975–1979 conflict in Cambodia under the Khmer Rouge regime, which claimed the lives of approximately 1.7 million people or 21% of the population.[36] The Court came into existence in 2006, as a result of extensive negotiations between the Cambodian Government and the United Nations, and operates on the basis of its Internal Rules (IRs).[37] It aimed to conduct trials against those persons responsible for the genocide and crimes against humanity during the Khmer Rouge regime, while pursuing justice and national reconciliation, stability, peace, and security at the national level.[38] In giving effect to its mandate, the ECCC featured a reparations regime, which entails an extensive set of rights for the victims, including the right to participate in the trials as civil parties and receive reparations of moral and collective character. This section introduces the ECCC's reparations regime structured alongside procedural and substantive aspects pertaining to the process of obtaining reparations and the outcome of the process at the ECCC, and how they materialised in the ECCC's case law.

---

[33] As the Van Boven/Bassiouni Principles' provisions explain, 'the Principles do not entail new international or domestic legal obligations but identify mechanisms, modalities, procedures and methods for the implementation of existing legal obligations under international human rights law and international humanitarian law which are complementary though different as to their norms.' United Nations General Assembly ('UNGA'), 2005, preamble.

[34] Urban Walker 2015, p. 219; McCarthy 2009, pp. 250, 253; Wemmers 2014, p. 231.

[35] See, for instance, Letschert and van Boven 2011, p. 166.

[36] Chandler 2000.

[37] For more details as to the ECCC's legal basis and its coming into existence, see McGonigle 2009, pp. 128–135. UNGA 2003.

[38] ECCC Internal Rules 2015. See also UNGA 1997.

9.3.1 Procedural Aspects

According to the IRs, a victim is 'a natural person or legal entity that has suffered harm as a result of the commission of any crime within the jurisdiction of the ECCC'.[39] The notion of a civil party 'refers to a victim whose application to become a Civil Party has been accepted by the Co-Investigating Judges or the Trial Chamber in accordance with these IRs.'[40] In order for a civil party's action to be admissible before the ECCC, the applicant must be clearly identified and demonstrate that they suffered physical, material, or psychological injury upon which a claim for reparations may be based. The injury must be the direct consequence of at least one of the crimes alleged against the charged person.[41] As civil parties, victims acquire several procedural rights, including the right to come forward to testify before judges, to file submissions, to attend and testify during hearings, to be informed, and to claim reparations.[42] Most of these rights are usually exercised through the civil parties' lawyers. As such, pursuant to the IRs, the civil parties may participate in the ECCC proceedings as a consolidated group,[43] represented by Civil Party Lead Co-Lawyers.[44]

In the three cases before the ECCC,[45] several thousand victims were granted the status of civil party and were able to exercise their procedural rights; namely, 93 civil parties in case 001,[46] and a total of 3.869 in both segments of case 002.[47] The majority

---

[39] ECCC Internal Rules 2015, p. 85.

[40] Ibid., p. 83.

[41] Ibid., Rule 23bis.

[42] Ibid., Rules 12bis, 23 quinquies, 23(4), 91, 92, and 94. The reparations submissions must provide a description of the awards sought, reasoning as to how the reparations respond to the harm caused by the crimes, as well as the elaboration on the mode of implementation sought.

[43] According to the revised Internal Rules which took place after case 001, civil parties may participate as individuals only at the pre-trial stage, while at the trial stage and beyond they comprise a single, consolidated group. Pursuant to Internal Rules revision 5, 2 February 2010, and then revision 6, 17 September 2010. Before these revisions, in case 001, the civil parties were grouped into four groups.

[44] ECCC Internal Rules 2015, Rule 12ter.

[45] Namely, cases 001, 002/01, and 002/02. Following an initial hearing, case 002 has been severed into two separate cases – case 002/01 and case 002/02 - both concerning the same accused persons, but different crimes, as set forth in the Indictment. ECCC, *Case 002*, Office of the Co-Investigating Judges: Closing Order, 15 September 2010, 002/19-09-2007-ECCC-OCIJ. Case 001 concerns Duch, who was found guilty of crimes against humanity and war crimes, for his role as chairman of S-21 prison. See ECCC, *Case 001*, Trial Chamber: Judgment, 26 July 2010, 001/18-07-2007/ECCC/TC, para 141. Case 002 concerns Nuon Chea and Khieu Samphan. In case 002/01, the accused were found guilty of crimes against humanity and in case 002/02 of crimes against humanity, war crimes, and genocide. They committed their crimes in their roles of Chairman of the Democratic Kampuchea National Assembly and Deputy Secretary of the Communist Party of Kampuchea, and Head of State of Democratic Kampuchea. See ECCC, *Case 002/01*, Supreme Chamber Court: Appeal Judgement, 23 November 2016, 002/19-09-2007-ECCC/SC and ECCC, *Case 002/02*, Supreme Chamber Court: Appeal Judgement, 22 December 2022, 002/19-09-2007-ECCC/SC.

[46] ECCC, *Case 001*, above n. 45, para 637.

[47] ECCC, *Case 002/02*, Trial Chamber: *Case 002/02* Judgement, 16 November 2018, 002/19-09-2007/ECCC/TC, para 4407.

of civil parties could exercise their rights through their lawyers and only a handful of them could interact directly with the Court and testify during proceedings. Across the three trials, nearly 120 civil parties, both direct and indirect victims, testified: 22 civil parties in case 001; 31 in case 002/01; and 63 in case 002/02.[48] Of the limited number of civil parties who testified in the trial, some of them advanced requests relating to reparations,[49] but most expressed that they want to leave it up to their lawyers to make submissions on reparations,[50] hinting perhaps to the civil parties' scarce knowledge of reparations.[51]

The victims primarily engaged with the Court, including to submit their claims for reparations, through written submissions compiled and submitted by their lawyers, which consisted of information collected via application forms, meetings, and discussions.[52] However, due to the scarce funding, victims' lawyers mainly engaged with their clients at public forums of civil parties that were increasingly organised by the Court's Victims Support Section (VSS) in case 002 and the network of intermediary NGOs.[53] In case 001, due to the VSS's lack of capacity and resources, informing the Cambodian population about the ECCC and the possibility of participating in trials by filling out victim application forms was performed by the intermediary NGOs.[54]

---

[48] ECCC, *Case 001*, above n. 45, para 637. ECCC, Case *002/01*, Trial Chamber: Case 002/01 Judgment, 7 August 2014, 002/19-09-2007/ECCC/TC, para 32. ECCC, *Case 002/02*, above n 47, para 54.

[49] For instance, in case 002/01 the following proposals were put forward: a day/week of remembrance, library with records of Khmer Rouge regime, medical treatment, religious ceremony according to Cambodian tradition, construction of a road, and of a stupa, as a symbol for the people to recall what happened.

[50] These observations are drawn from analysing the transcripts of civil parties' testimonies. The typical dialogue between the Court and the civil parties would be: "The Court: In this case, you have applied as a civil party. Are you seeking reparations by yourself or you will waive these rights to your lawyer to act on your behalf? Civil Party: I will leave it to my lawyer to seek reparations." *see* During the testimony of Martine Lefeuvre, civil party in Case 001. ECCC, *Case 001,* Transcripts of Hearings, Trial Day 59, 17 August 2009, 001/18- 07-2007-ECCC/TC.

[51] Previous research on ECCC found out that the majority of the civil parties interviewed in the study had a very low understanding of their role in the ECCC proceedings, including of reparations. Hoven and Scheibel 2015, p. 172.

[52] ECCC, *Case 001*, Civil parties' Co-Lawyers' Joint Submission on Reparations, 14 September 2009, 001/18-07-2007-ECCC/TC. ECCC, Demande Definitive De Reparations Des Co-Avocats Principaux Pour Les Parties Civiles En Application De La Regle 80bis Du Reglement Interieur Et Annexes Confidentielles, 8 Octobre 2013, 002/19-09-2007-CETCICPI. ECCC, *Case 002/02,* Civil Party Lead Co-Lawyers' Final Claim for Reparation in Case 002/02 with confidential annexes, 30 May 2017, 002/19-09-2007-ECCC/TC.

[53] Sperfeldt 2018, p. 178; see also Sperfeldt 2022; Tibori-Szabó et al. 2017, p. 440.

[54] As reported by Helen Jarvis, former Chief of the VSS, in Jarvis 2014, p. 22.

9.3.2 Substantive Aspects

The ECCC's reparations regime equally entails prerogatives in relation to the outcome of reparations proceedings. According to the IRs, 'if an Accused is convicted, the Chambers may award only collective and moral reparations to Civil Parties.'[55] Although the IRs do not define the exact meaning of 'collective and moral reparations', they clarify that the reparations measures cannot entail monetary payments. They further specify that the reparations measures must acknowledge the harm suffered by civil parties as a result of the commission of the crimes for which an accused is convicted, and provide benefits to the civil parties to address this harm.[56]

In case 001, despite extensive requests for reparations by the civil parties,[57] the reparations award entailed: (i) the inclusion in the judgment of names of civil parties and their deceased relatives; and (ii) the compilation and publication of all statements of apology made by the accused throughout the trial.[58] Relying on its IRs, the Court explained that extensive reparations awards cannot be made against the accused as he was declared indigent.[59] Due to the limited character of reparations in case 001, the IRs were amended by the judges before case 002 commenced[60] in order to offer an alternative possibility to the civil parties to claim reparations.[61] Pursuant to the amendment, in addition to the Chamber's order that the costs of the reparations award shall be borne by the accused, the civil parties Lead Co-Lawyers may also request the Chamber to recognise that specific reparations measures (designed or identified in cooperation with the VSS) are appropriate for implementation using external funding.[62]

In case 002, this amendment enabled the VSS and the Lead Co-Lawyers to seek funding for reparations from donors and to develop these projects in collaboration with external governments and NGOs.[63] As such, in case 002, the Court endorsed the majority of reparations put forward by the Lead Co-Lawyers:[64] (i) in case 002/01, 11 of 13 reparations projects concerning commemoration, rehabilitation, and public

---

[55] ECCC Internal Rules 2015, Rule 23 (1) quinquies.

[56] Ibid., Rule 23 (1) quinquies.

[57] ECCC, *Case 001 Joint Submission*, above n. 52.

[58] ECCC, *Case 001 Judgment*, above n. 45, p. 238.

[59] This was a direct application of the key provision explained above, according to which reparations measures must be directed against and be borne by the accused. ECCC, *Case 002*, Trial day 215, 16 October 2013, 002/19-09-2007-ECCC/TC, p. 138. ECCC, *Case 001*, Judgment, above n. 45, p. 240. This principle was confirmed on appeals. *See* ECCC, *Case 001*, Supreme Court Chamber: Appeals Judgment, above n. 7, para 668.

[60] ECCC Internal Rules 2015, Rule 3.

[61] ECCC Internal Rules 2010, Rule 23 (3) quinquies.

[62] Ibid.

[63] ECCC, *Case 002/01*, Judgment, above n. 48, para 1113.

[64] ECCC, *Case 002*, Demande Definitive, above n. 52.

education;[65] and (ii) in case 002/02, 14 of 15 projects concerning remembrance of the victims and memorialisation of the suffering endured, therapy and psychological assistance to the victims, and documentation and education.[66] Interestingly, due to the change in the IRs, the civil parties could already benefit from these reparations measures in case 002, even before they were endorsed by the Court in its judgment.[67]

Having described the ECCC's reparations regime and its materialisation in practice, the following sections unpack and explore the actual impact of the procedural and substantive aspects of reparations on the civil parties based on empirical research. This next section will first introduce the methodology we utilised for performing this empirical research.

9.4 Method

The current study was part of a larger research project on four cases at four different international courts: the ECCC, the ICC, Inter-American and European Courts of Human Rights.[68] The aim of this chapter is understanding whether, and if so how, reparations awarded through international justice procedures contribute to a sense of justice among survivors. In order to unravel survivors' subjective experiences with the Court's reparations proceedings and outcomes as well as what kind of meanings survivors attach to them, qualitative research methods were chosen. Specifically, we carried out extensive in-depth life-history research combined with semi-structured interviewing with survivors, based on the insight that narrative-based inquiries enable exploring into how people give meaning to their lived experiences.[69] This in-depth life-history methodology enabled us to have insights into the ways survivors give meaning to the challenges they have faced throughout their lives, and to the experiences that could or have helped them in order to be able to confront these challenges, i.e. social or professional support, legal procedures, and measures that are especially designed to attend the interests of survivors, including reparations. To co-create a life history, respondents were invited to draw a life-line on which they indicated the most important events in their lives, from their childhood onward. [70] Afterwards, respondents were asked to choose and organise their experiences and explain their decisions, to obtain insights in their own interpretations.

---

[65] ECCC, *Case 002/01*, Judgment, above n. 48, pp. 617–620. Two projects were not endorsed as the relevant funding had not been secured.

[66] ECCC, *Case 002/02*, Judgment, above n. 47, pp. 2224–2229. One project was not endorsed as it did not meet the requirements of Internal Rule 23 quinquies(1).

[67] See Hughes, https://www.iias.asia/sites/iias/files/nwl_article/2019-05/IIAS_NL80_20.pdf. Accessed 28 September 2023.

[68] See, *inter alia,* Bax et al. 2023, pp. 383–398; de Waardt et al. 2021, pp. 169–189; Balta et al. 2019, above n. 17.

[69] Gough 2008, pp. 623–624.

[70] Nelson 2010; McAdams 2008.

The life histories-based inquiries were combined with semi-structured open-ended questions that addressed the victims' definitions, feelings, experiences, and perceptions regarding a variety of transitional justice topics, including their relationship with the ECCC and the reparations awarded. The data for this chapter was collected and translated into English with the support of the Transcultural Psychosocial Organisation (TPO) Cambodia. Life-history research and interviewing was conducted with 31 female and 24 male survivors of the Khmer Rouge regime in eight different provinces in Cambodia, of which 31 interviews took place in cities and 24 in villages and rural areas.[71] We have used purposeful sampling.[72] Data were analysed by identifying the relevant features of text fragments, and establishing inter-relationships among codes using the ATLAS.ti 8 for Windows. Codes were developed in an iterative manner. Firstly, codes emerged as a result of open, line by line, coding (e.g. significant experiences, references to the ECCC). Subsequently, all codes were checked for duplicates and combined when needed. Consequently, axial coding was conducted to explore whether there were overarching themes and to establish interrelationships amongst codes (e.g. meanings of reparations, external reactions to victimising experiences and support). Finally, selective coding was used based on a priory existing theories on reparations and the ECCC.[73]

Based on our qualitative research findings, the survivors' experiences with the Court are best understood from a timeline. This timeline is dissected in three relevant episodes that impacted the civil parties' perceptions of the procedures: (1) filing the civil party complaint; (2) engagement with the trials; and (3) engagement with the results of the trial (particularly reparations). The first two relate to procedural justice and are presented in Sect. 9.5.1, and the last in Sect. 9.5.2 about substantive justice.

When reading the empirical analysis, it is important to recall that a consequence of studying the meaning of processes through the eyes of the person for whom processes have been developed, people may talk about certain issues because they associate them with formal processes, not because they are formally part of the processes under study. In other words, victims may raise issues as reparations and deem them as very important or unimportant because they associate those issues with reparations, when in fact these issues are by-products and not part of the actual reparations decision-making. They may be the result of other developments that may have happen in the context of the ECCC. However, the aim of this study is to gain insights into what victims see as meaningful, regardless of whether this is technically part of the Court-awarded reparations, in order to increase our knowledge of the effects of reparations according to victims.

---

[71] As all data was anonymised, we used interview code numbers when referring to excerpts from interviews.

[72] This contains identifying and selecting individuals that are particularly knowledgeable about or experienced with a phenomenon of interest. A meaningful sample was chosen that fits the parameters of the research project. Tracy 2020.

[73] The study protocol was approved by the ethics review board of Tilburg Law School, Tilburg University, The Netherlands.

9.5 Survivors' Experiences with ECCC's Reparative Justice

9.5.1 Experiences with the ECCC: Procedural Justice

Regarding the civil parties' experiences with the ECCC's proceedings, our findings show that most interviewees believed that their participation was beneficial to them as victims because it helped release a part of their suffering through the effort of finding justice. However, as we show, most interviewees also expressed at least some form of criticism on aspects of their participation as civil parties. It is important to stress that engaging with the multitude of voices of survivors through participation schemes is a challenge for all transitional justice mechanisms, and perhaps even more so for reparations delivered through courts.[74]

In terms of the first phase of the timeline, i.e. filing the complaint, our interviewees recall that they met the opportunity to file a civil party complaint, decades after the Khmer Rouge crimes took place, with both suspicion and great expectations. For some, acquiring official civil party status represented a first step towards acknowledgment of victimhood. Others, however, expressed great disappointment in relation to the information and interaction because they never received feedback on their application.

Second, in relation to engagement with the trials and particularly voice, it is noteworthy that the victims' positive experiences of participation are not connected to what perhaps represents the most straightforward conception of participation: consultation. As explained above, consultations became the most important modality through which civil party lawyers solicited the victims' views on reparations throughout the trial process. In fact, in our sample, only four interviewees briefly mention being consulted on reparations.

The way interviewees spoke about interactions with the Court *other* than consultation gives much insight into their experience of being involved in the process as civil parties. Nearly two-thirds of our interviewees have paid at least one visit to the ECCC to witness a hearing, of which 11 mention having testified in court. Although not all have physically engaged with the Court, many interviewees experienced these interactions as positive. The main reason was that the ECCC collectively helps victims to find justice, and is seen as a vehicle for forcing those responsible to admit guilt, to learn and disseminate historical truths, and tell personal truths. Many interviewees therefore concluded that what the ECCC has been doing is good already and that they accept the way the Court dealt with those criminals.

However, in addition to these positive evaluations of the Court, the respondents also frequently raised questions, pointed out negative experiences, and critically asserted that "the law could never make everyone happy".[75] More specifically, disappointing experiences with the trial proceedings seem to have to do with the lack of

[74] See Sperfeldt 2018, above n. 53.

[75] Interview, Cam_Ben_024.

information and the length of proceedings. Some interviewees were greatly disappointed that they have not received any new information about their case, sometimes even for years. About 2/3 of the civil parties in our study were not completely up to date about the status of their trials. Second, the lack of awareness among respondents pertains mostly to not knowing the (exact) outcomes of case 002, i.e. knowledge of how the accused was sentenced and what types of reparations were granted to civil parties. This reveals the effect of deficiency of information by the legal representatives[76] and/or of outreach by the Court. The fact that many interviewees, like most Cambodians, live in rural areas with limited access to national media represents an additional challenge in this matter.[77] Or as one respondent puts it: 'I wished to hear it by my own ears; there is no device that I can use to listen to any news in my house.'[78] As a result, respondents requested that 'the ECCC should release the result of the trial to citizens and the reasons why it led to such terrible regime.'[79]

Finally, interviewees also expressed their discontent with the length of the Court's proceedings.[80] This is captured by the following statement: 'They killed many people in a very short time, but [only] 3, 4 of them were put in a long process of the trial'.[81] In other words, interviewees think that the Court takes too long—a salient issue because several civil parties, many of whom are of old age, have already died and thus have not received justice—and regret that it leaves the unit chiefs and cadres that directly harmed the victims unaddressed. Combined, these criticisms lead some interviewees to state that the ECCC is 'not effective, but [only] symbolic'.[82]

9.5.2 Survivors' Lived Experiences with the Reparation Projects: Substantive Justice

This section zooms in on the third episode in the participation timeline, i.e. experiences of substantive justice, hence, with the reparation projects as outcomes of the trials. Our findings first address the main projects or activities that those interviewed

---

76 When interviewees refer to their legal representatives (i.e. 35 persons) most of them explain that they have only been in contact once with their lawyer, namely when they filled in their complaint; others mention that legal representatives would call them if there was an information meeting about the ECCC; five persons mentioned that their lawyer would call them in case there was a development; two persons explained that they contacted their lawyers by themselves if they wanted to receive an update. Moreover, one third of the interviewees is not aware of the names of their lawyers.

77 Pham 2011.

78 Interview, Cam_BEN_061.

79 Interview, Cam_NonBEN_062.

80 For context, the crimes took place in 1975–1979 and the convictions became final in 2012, 2016, and 2022. Other research has similarly found out that victims are generally dissatisfied with regard to the lengthy procedures of ECCC. Pham et al. 2009, p. 40. This is a common downside of international criminal justice proceedings. See also Balta et al. 2019, above n. 17, p. 2.

81 Interview, Cam_BEN_015.

82 Interview, Cam_NonBEN_029.

spoke fondly about, and *why*, while the final part of this section pays attention to the main sources of disappointment among respondents. On the basis of the expressed lived experiences of civil parties, we look at how the tangible outcomes (both officially ordered reparations and issues survivors perceive as being part of the reparations ordered by the ECCC) are perceived (what is substantive justice) and how they respond to victims' preferences (what ought to be substantive justice).

9.5.2.1 "They Paid for my Trips": NGO Engagement

Our analysis of the survivors' lived experiences with the reparations projects revealed that the NGOs that provided reparations are considered an extension of the Court. This instills a sense of justice through the organisation of services and activities that civil parties are invited to take part in. Survivors' engagement with the reparations, which were ordered by the Court but implemented by NGOs, is therefore best understood as comprising of the respondents' experiences with the NGOs involved in outreach and implementation of particular projects.

Firstly, our data suggests that respondents appreciated the *tangible* 'benefit' associated with merely being involved in activities organised for civil parties. To illustrate, the ability to 'go on trips with NGOs' is often reported by respondents as a main benefit of their civil party status, and something that already helps 'repair the pain'. As one respondent recalls: '[A]fter I filed the complaint, the NGOs facilitated the process that made me happy; being involved in activity that I am provided with some allowance also helped me.'[83] Similarly, another respondent asserted that 'I am happy, as being a civil party, I get some support such as stuff and snacks for me and the kids.'[84] Importantly, the following quote illustrates how the travel allowance and food provided during such activities already instilled a sense of 'feeling compensated' as a civil party:

> I understand that so far I have been invited to the ECCC and met with other NGOs, and they paid for my trips. I thought being involved in such a case is a part of being compensated.[85]

Other concrete benefits associated with the 'trips' and 'meetings' that respondents collectively refer to involve the emotional support and comfort found in meeting other victims. Respondents express the emotional release through sharing their experiences with other victims during get-togethers: 'I was so happy riding the boat with them. I sang and danced on the boat. It was also nice to gather with other victims from the regime and share our experiences.'[86] Respondents also spoke fondly of projects involving personal engagement with the NGOs' staff and their services. This finding suggests that the interaction with the NGOs, although not a form of Court-ordered reparations, was appreciated by the victims.

---

83 Interview, Cam_BEN_015.

84 Interview, Cam_BEN_018.

85 Interview, Cam_BEN_001.

86 Interview, Cam_NonBEN_062.

9.5.2.2 "Victims Feel Relief": Benefits of Mental Health Support Combined with Buddhism

A main finding is that receiving mental health support from NGOs—which was a Court-ordered reparation—is greatly appreciated by respondents. Of the 55 admitted civil parties in our sample, 31 engaged in either Testimonial Therapy, Self-Help Groups, or both, which are interventions designed to address post-traumatic stress in Khmer Rouge survivors.[87] The positive impact of these reparation projects is attributed to their ability to reduce such distress, or in respondents' words: 'I have learned a lot [about my mental health]. It helped me to reduce the intense feeling in my heart'.[88] Another respondent referred to mental health support as 'the process that made it possible for victims to feel relief, to be able to reduce the pain.'[89]

It is important to note that the above mentioned mental health programmes involve 'ritualistic and religious practices in cooperation with local pagodas and Buddhist monks, reflecting the significance of traditional coping mechanisms in Cambodia's spirit-based culture.'[90] Theravada Buddhism has been Cambodia's state religion since the Thirteenth Century, and is still significant to many people's lives and their experience of community, despite the Khmer Rouge's extreme attempts to destroy it.[91] As children, Cambodians already learn and embody Buddhist modes of 'thinking, feeling, speaking, [and] moving'.[92] Buddhism and its central tenets, therefore 'resurged, and were re-imagined after the regime'.[93] Because of this, Bennet argues, Buddhism has been central to the way many Cambodians have come to deal with the Khmer Rouge.[94]

As our study showcases, respondents indeed experience that including Buddhist rituals in mental health interventions is beneficial for them:

> There are also organisations [...], which help us psychologically and educate us about daily life in order to feel release from trauma. There were testimonial programmes and healing with blessings by the monks, which also makes us feel better. In sum, these are the parts of taking care of us as the victims.[95]

---

[87] See TPO Cambodia, http://tpocambodia.org/justice-and-relief-for-survivors-of-the-khmer-rouge/, accessed 10 October, 2023

[88] Interview, Cam_BEN_013.

[89] Interview, Cam_BEN_008.

[90] See http://tpocambodia.org/justice-and-relief-for-survivors-of-the-khmer-rouge/, accessed 10 October, 2023.

[91] Harris 2008; see also Bennett 2018, p. 10. The Khmer Rouge, who saw Buddhism as a threat to their power, took extreme measures to destroy it, with only a handful of monks surviving the genocide.

[92] See Bennett 2018; Ledgerwood 2008, p. 47.

[93] Ibid.

[94] Ibid.

[95] Interview_CamBEN_003.

The next sections demonstrate, however, that the performance of such rituals also have other important functions beyond 'calming the mind'.[96]

9.5.2.3 "Doing Good Deeds": Remembrance in Private Lives

Further, we observed that projects aiming at 'taking care of' the dead—which are partly Court-ordered reparations—appeared important for the respondents. Those interviewed appreciated the idea of a 'stupa' or Buddhist shrine/memorial, which is or should be constructed close to their residence, as a peaceful destination for the souls and/or bodies of deceased loved ones.[97] The latter were often killed violently and then abandoned—hence not given an appropriate resting place. In addition, as worldviews of Cambodians include the 'social existence' of the dead—instead of disappearance—relationships with them have to be maintained.[98] A stupa erected in the name of the deceased relatives of civil parties represents a tangible place where survivors can spiritually locate the souls of deceased loved ones and keep in contact with them. As one interviewee said:

> We asked the court for a stupa in S21 prison and one in each province. During the inauguration of the stupa in Toul Sleng, I didn't see my sibling's name on the stupa so I asked my lawyer. He said they had not yet finish completing everyone name." […] I feel better for my sibling to be there.[99]

The significance of an allocated place of remembrance is connected by respondents to a need to cope with their experience of 'Kum Num', or lasting feelings of grief and/or anger. As one respondent said:

> If there are reparations for those who died during the Pol Pot regime, survivors can make a ceremony to dedicate to those who died. [Then survivors] will feel relieved and the Kum Num will disappear little by little. […] If there is no reparation, the Kum Num will increase inside of us.[100]

Importantly, this quote also points to the central role of *dedication* or bringing offerings to the souls of the deceased in this process. Meritorious acts, such as prayer and donations of food and flowers, enable the accumulation of Karma, adding force

---

[96] Agger 2015, pp. 543–560.

[97] A stupa, according to Rachel Hughes, is 'a sacred structure that contains the remains of the deceased—especially those of greatly revered individuals—in Buddhist cultures. The construction of stupa is a significant activity that produces merit for the living and encourages the remembrance of the dead.' As mentioned in Sion 2011, pp. 1–21.

[98] See Agger 2015.

[99] Interview, Cam_Ben_023. We note that the stupa our interviewee refers to was in fact constructed with financial support from the Cambodian Government and other donor countries and not as part of the reparations provided by the ECCC. See ECCC, The Court Report, Issue 84, April 2015, pp. 8–9. Nonetheless, in addition to the tangible reparative benefit that stupa can have for survivors, this fragment also shows the difficulty for many, including victims, to designate the responsible entity behind measures for victims.

[100] Interview, Cam_NonBEN-043.

to the transition to the next life.[101] For this reason, the accumulation of Karma is a central driving force of Buddhist action in Cambodia, a cosmological means of understanding and narrating the world.[102] Reincarnation and Karma became particularly salient due to the massive number of dead created by the Khmer Rouge regime. Performing funeral rites is believed to be essential for the transmigration of the soul, and this unfulfilled obligation left survivors with a sense of guilt.[103] Our observations underline this extreme salience of 'tvea bon', or 'doing good deeds" in the current lives of respondents.

Additionally, it is a wish of respondents to increase benevolent Karma in society at large, in order to prevent atrocities from happening again in the future. The latter is a main priority for respondents, which was revealed when asking them more broadly about their future wishes. 'I do not want our country to go back to the genocide time. I do not want the next generation to experience the pain like what I did.'[104] Or as other respondents claimed: '[we should] avoid mass killing and forced marriage like animals';[105] and '[w]hatever it takes, don't let the dark period of 3 years, 8 months, and 20 days [a metaphor for the Khmer Rouge regime] come back again.'[106] Preventing atrocities from happening again is thus a matter for which respondents take great responsibility. Merit-building by younger and future generations is therefore important: 'I won't lead my next generations to fall in that path again. I will lead them to do as many good deeds as possible.'[107]

9.5.2.4 "Young Generations Should Learn": Remembrance in Public Spaces

Respondents further stressed the importance of remembrance sites, not only for relating and making meritorious offers to the dead *in private*, but also for reminding the *public* of the atrocities. Various such projects were order by the Court. Many survivors made the connection with the need to inform younger or future generations about what happened in their lives during the Khmer Rouge period. In the responses, we observed a connection between the need to improve individual well-being and to make known to others in the public space what has happened. We noticed that although places for remembrance and education are built, many survivors talk about the promising advantages of such places for improving the current situation and, to a lesser degree, about visiting these sites themselves:

[101] See Bennett 2018.
[102] Ibid.
[103] Um 2021.
[104] Interview, Cam_BEN_014.
[105] Interview, Cam_BEN_014.
[106] Interview, Cam_NonBEN_039.
[107] Interview, Cam_BEN_015.

> I do [like them], but I have never seen it though. For me, I want young generations to learn from it; having farming tools used in the Khmer Rouge displayed in the stupa.[108]

Or as another interviewee claimed: 'They could see it [the stupa] as a model and never let such a regime to happen again. To let the next generations see and know'.[109] These accounts illustrate the potential strength of this reparative measure according to survivors, even if they have never seen the stupa.

This also seems to hold for other structures that respondents see as able to serve the important function of educating those who have not lived through the regime about the truth of its horrors: 'I want it to be a sacred place where people can pray. I also want it to be a library to place documents from the Khmer Rouge time, so younger generations can study and learn how deadly it was.'[110] Similarly, it applies to how respondents connect activities of sharing personal truths in the public space to preventing atrocities from happening again:

> For me personally I am quite satisfied that NGOs helped to publish my story, to share it with the young generation. It is a part of a mental compensation that my true story is revealed and shared with youths, to study it and understand what actually happened in the old time. Youths in the next generation are future leaders and it is their responsibility to not make it happen again, and it is a lesson for them to be good leaders; to avoid all of those bad conducts.[111]

The observation that there is a need for sharing information about the Khmer Rouge period in the *public* space corresponds to other literature about Cambodia where authors concluded that until the creation of the ECCC there was little room for publicly remembering Cambodia's recent past.[112]

9.5.2.5 "It Has Little Meaning": Disappointment with Reparations

By querying opinions on reparations granted by the Court, our observation is that respondents contrast 'what ought to be' with 'what is', or rather, 'what is *not*'. The first disappointment concerns the religious and commemorative structures and their limited impact. The interviewees indicated that the only two built to date to commemorate the victims of the Khmer Rouge stand in Phnom Penh, at Choeung Eck (or 'the killing fields') and at Tuol Sleng, the Khmer Rouge's notorious S21 torture center. We note that these stupas are not part of the ECCC-ordered reparations, which demonstrates that it is not always clear to victims where the various reparations come from, hinting at the scarce information victims actually possess about the ECCC reparations. Respondents reported that these memorials are simply too far away: '[The stupa] is to store documents for the next generations. Phnom Penh is too far if people want to learn about it locally.'[113]

---

[108] Interview, Cam_NonBEN_062.

[109] Interview, Cam_NonBEN_042.

[110] Interview, Cam-BEN_060.

[111] Interview, Cam_BEN_008.

[112] E.g. Manning 2012, pp. 165–181; Gray 2017.

[113] Interview, Cam_BEN_014.

The remoteness of existing stupas not only makes them *intangible* for survivors who are not able to travel to the capital, it undermines their promising value. Further, as the following quote in relation to a documentary centre illustrates, the location of the memorials complicates their purpose of educating and reminding others of what happened:

> The location is not an interesting place; it's near the Thailand border and is very remote. In our discussion, I agreed to have it there. But, I suggested making it more interesting because it's far from the town. If it's not attractive enough, no one would go and read such documents.[114]

If reparation structures built for the purposes of remembrance are not easily accessible, they cannot accommodate victims' needs for praying, merit-making, sharing experiences, and educating. This provokes questions about substantive justice as a result of the reparations for victims. In this regard, the same respondent concluded: 'The collective compensation was granted, but as a civil party and a representative; [I think] it has little meaning.'[115]

As a result, respondents who are disappointed with the reparations granted propose alternative measures that they deem more appropriate for repairing the harm done, for example a centre for retired survivors or free medical services. The alternative suggestions that respondents deem appropriate for reparations are not unidimensional, but when observing them together it appears that the respondents' second disappointment concerns the lack of individual financial compensation by the Court, as it is the most frequently proposed measure by the victims. It also signals a collective awareness that what the Court granted was not in line with what victims asked for:

> What victims asked to compensate was kinds of benefits to fix what they have lost; lives, properties, family segregation during the genocide. But, the lawyers said the court does not have such type of compensation while victims asked for it.[116]

Respondents also indicated that they were aware that the court could only provide collective reparations, but they still asked for individual compensation. The fact that the court did not grant this type of reparation in line with civil parties' requests is unsettling for respondents:

> The court announced that there will be no individual compensation, but only collective compensation. That upsets me. [...] The justice I want is the compensation to individuals; that will reduce the pain I have.[117]

When asked why financial compensation is important, respondents often express that money could instantly improve victims' living conditions, an efficiency they contrast with the slow pace of the legal process:

---

[114] Interview, Cam_NonBEN_040.

[115] Ibid.

[116] Interview, Cam_NonBEN_032.

[117] Interview, Cam_BEN_059.

> I could spend that money buying things to reduce my suffering, like buying a motorbike or car. A compensation we don't need to wait for is imprisoning them. Our parents and siblings have already died, they could rest in peace, but we live with suffering. Thinking about those incidents always brings back the anxiety to the living. That's it. Only that kind of [financial] compensation could already make them [victims] feel happy.[118]

These complaints are a reminder of the fact that the ECCC operates in an environment, where many citizens live in very poor conditions.[119] Indeed, in their 2011 population-based study the Berkeley Human Rights Center found that 83% of their respondents would rather focus on problems that Cambodians face in their daily lives rather than address crimes committed during the Khmer Rouge regime, while 63% would rather spend money on something other than the ECCC.[120] This resonates with our own observations, to the extent that respondents—who commonly rated their present living conditions between 'average' and 'poor'—frequently mentioned socio-economic improvements as their main future wishes.

In part, these responses were driven by needs for reducing poverty in the respondent's family and better support for their children and grandchildren. However, most often respondents also expressed they could use money to visit temples, perform religious ceremonies and do 'good deeds'. The following words of a respondent exemplify this by drawing a comparison to responses to a national tragedy in Cambodia. During the 2010 'Water Festival', Cambodia's biggest annual festival, 353 people lost their lives in a stampede on Phnom Penh's Koh Pich Bridge. In response to the tragedy, members of the public, national and international companies, charities, and government bodies pledged huge amounts of financial compensation to families of those who died or were injured.[121]

> I like the communal compensation, but I also [want] some in individual; so that I can use it to do good deeds or celebrate religious ceremonies. Being a civil party, it's my own expense to cover; for family [members] of those who died in the stampede in Koh Pich, they also got cash compensation.[122]

A final criticism refers to outcome-related aspects of the ECCC other than the tangible reparations projects. It refers to the repeated perception among respondents that perpetrators before the Court denied their role in the crimes committed. The following quote illustrates how this undermines victims' sense of recognition and justice in particular:

> The tragedy on me and the whole country from 1975 to 1979 [was] caused by the leaders of the country. […] They [the leaders] should be responsible for it. However, they denied. They have not admitted that they have killed people, starved people to death, and other crimes. This seemed like there is injustice in ECCC. The ECCC is viewed as a court to ensure justice for all victims in the genocide, and the most senior leaders are sentenced a life time in jail.

---

118 Interview, Cam_NonBen_027.

119 See Human Development Reports, http://hdr.undp.org/en/countries/profiles/KHM, accessed 10 October 2023.

120 See Pham et al. 2009.

121 Cambodian Center for Human Rights 2011.

122 Interview, Cam_NonBEN_039.

> [...] However, it is not a full image of justice we want as the convicted persons have not yet proved themselves guilty.[123]

The results presented in this section indicate that ECCC victims could not easily identify the Court-awarded reparations—indicating the scarcity of information that victims actually possess regarding the reparations that were allegedly designed for their benefit. Furthermore, despite the fact that dozens of reparations projects were endorsed by the Court and implemented by NGOs, the victims only raised and reflected upon the above-mentioned projects. This indicates that not all reparations were actually seen as tangible for the victims or indeed responded to their preferences for reparations.

9.6 Concluding Remarks

To extend beyond what normatively is known about the conceivable effects of reparations, this study combined a top-down legal approach with a bottom-up empirical one in order to explore the effects of reparations awarded by ICL-courts, specifically the ECCC. In a significant step for ICL, the ECCC enabled victims to participate in proceedings as civil parties and to avail themselves of a set of rights, including the right to claim reparations, which resulted in several measures of reparations for the benefit of civil parties. To explore whether and how the respective reparative modalities contributed towards reparative justice for victims, we took the Court, its legal framework and case-law as a starting point. In addition, considering that the ECCC has been hailed for its victim-oriented approach, it was paramount to inquire into survivors' lived experiences. Hence, after our top-down legal analysis, we focused on findings resulting from analysis of our empirical study based on victim's narratives about the actual changes in their lives from the reparations.

The rationale of our exploration was that an understanding of reparative justice as both procedural and substantive justice is crucial to comprehend the ECCC's reparations regime's contribution towards reparative justice for victims. Therefore, we introduced a taxonomy of reparative justice to help us understand how the process whereby reparations are provided and the outcome of this process inform victims' perceptions of reparative justice.

In terms of procedural justice, our study confirms that voice, interaction, information, and the length of proceedings are all elements that appear to inform the victims' evaluation of their engagement with the ECCC's proceedings. As victims indicated, engaging with the Court helped them to release a part of their suffering. Regarding their experiences at the trial stage, many respondents appeared to appreciate the overall process of a Court 'seeking justice for victims', which stirred high hopes from the beginning. In addition, several respondents reflected on and/or criticised the way their rights materialised in practice. The victims in our sample who went to the Court appeared to appreciate their *direct* involvement with the Court,

[123] Interview, Cam_BEN_008.

either by witnessing a hearing or by testifying, rather than the consultations with their lawyers. Furthermore, because of the unsatisfactory outreach activity, a large part of our respondents did not recently engage with the trial proceedings and were unaware of the outcomes of their case.[124] This lack of information and thus detachment from the justice process represents a main source of disappointment. Victims also deplored the length of proceedings, with many of them passing away before knowing the outcome of the trials. Procedural justice for victims is therefore not only about ensuring that victims benefit from a whole range of corresponding procedural rights but also about their quality, i.e. realising them in practice in a way that is meaningful for the victims.

In terms of substantive justice and tangible outcomes for victims, our findings confirm that the structural limitations embedded within the ECCC's legal framework—with reparations being of collective and moral character—limited from the outset the content of reparations and the ECCC's potential contribution to substantive justice.[125] We also noticed that the lack of individual reparations (i.e. compensation) disappointed the victims and failed to improve their daily living conditions or address the individual losses and economic hardship that they suffered. Sperfeldt et al. (2020) concluded that it appears that these reparations measures were 'driven by which projects NGOs were in a position to offer and/or what donors wanted to fund, rather than primarily by participating survivors' preferences and needs'.[126] Substantive justice in the context of the ECCC could therefore be described as funding driven, not civil party driven.

However, in our study, we also tried to go beyond the finding that there is a discrepancy between survivors' expectations and the contents of the awarded reparations. We also analysed the meanings survivors attached to what was provided, even though these reparations were not in line with what they had hoped. We therefore examined survivors' experiences with the reparations that are meaningful according to our respondents. Our findings indicate that victims could not easily delineate the Court-awarded reparations, although the Court endorsed dozens of reparations projects implemented by NGOs. Our study shows that only a small amount of the reparation projects were salient for the respondents, because they only mentioned a limited number of the projects on their own accord. This finding highlights the scarcity of information that victims possess as to the reparations and, at the same time, it is likely that not all reparations were actually seen as tangible for the victims.

Even though the reparations projects the survivors spoke about were limited, the experiences they shared as a result of engaging with the projects demonstrated positive aspects. Firstly, the 'fun' and reimbursement offered during NGO activities offered a sense of 'compensation'. Next, targeted mental health care helped beneficiaries release psychological 'tension' and find comfort in sharing painful experiences with other victims. Subsequently, for some, the construction of stupas enabled

[124] Similarly, see Hoven and Scheibel 2015.

[125] Similarly, see Williams et al. 2018, p. 12.

[126] Sperfeldt and Hughes 2020, p. 14.

locating and maintaining relationships with deceased relatives and offered a designated place for doing the 'good deeds' that are required to increase the likelihood that the survivors, the deceased, and subsequent generations will have a better future. Lastly, knowing about—rather than actually visiting and benefiting from them—the religious and commemorative structures built—i.e. stupas, libraries or other documentation centers—attends to a need for sharing and educating the wider public about 'the truth' of the Khmer Rouge regime. In terms of tangibility, one important finding of our research relates to the importance of religious and commemorative structures for redressing harm. Unless they are built in people's local environments, they undermine their promising value because they cannot serve the survivors' expressed needs for memorialisation and merit-making, which is equally important according to their Buddhist experience of what it means to 'repair' the harm suffered.

Noting the victims' responses to what is important to them in terms of reparations, our study confirms that compensation, rehabilitation, satisfaction, and guarantees of non- repetition, which have all been mentioned, are seen as being important to redress their harm. Moreover, the empirical finding that activities that are in fact by-products of the actual reparations projects are perceived as awarded reparations by the ECCC because they are tangible, illustrates that it is the victims who evaluate what is actually substantive justice for them.

Victims' conceptions of reparative justice are indeed dependent on both the process and outcome of international courts awarding reparations, which in turn inform their perceptions of procedural and substantive justice. However, as our research demonstrated, while reparative justice made out of procedural justice and substantive justice remains an important taxonomy to understand the impact of international courts' reparations regimes, we believe that the discussion on reparative justice and how victims perceive it is more complex and fluid. We noticed that reparative justice is influenced by three aspects. First is the legal framework of international courts, the rights pertaining to their reparations' regime, and the opportunities and limitations embedded therein. Second is the capacity of courts and the multitude of actors, including lawyers and NGOs, to materialise the said rights in a manner that is meaningful to victims. Third is the victims' own perceptions of what they view as reparative justice: while Court-ordered reparations failed to be perceived as meaningful by victims (mainly because of their actual limited impact), the by-products of reparations' projects brought significant and meaningful benefits to victims.

Therefore, we posit that courts with reparative justice mandates would benefit from understanding and acknowledging these matters, to better grasp the effects of the reparations they award and their actual contribution to reparative justice for victims. Having this knowledge would ultimately contribute to a more robust rhetoric on reparative justice and its actual realisation, to the extent possible.

Acknowledgement The authors express their gratitude to the many Cambodians who shared their time and experiences. We thank Sopheap Taing for her research assistance and all the useful conversations in which we exchanged knowledge. We are grateful to Rianne Letschert for sharing her wisdom and trust. We thank the guest editors of this special issue and the anonymous reviewers for their constructive feedback. The research for this chapter was supported by the Netherlands Organization for Scientific Research.

References

Agger I (2015) Calming the mind: Healing after mass atrocity in Cambodia. Transcultural psychiatry 4: 543–560

Balta A, Bax M, Letschert R (2019) Trial and (Potential) Error: Conflicting Visions on Reparations Within the ICC System. International Criminal Justice Review 29: 221–248

Bass G (2012) Reparations as a Noble Lie. In: Williams M, Nagy R, Elster J (eds) Transitional Justice, Nomos Li, Volume 34. De Gruyter, Berlin, pp 166–179

Bax M, de Waardt M, Letschert R (2023) Massavictimisatie [Mass victimisation]. In: van Doorn J (ed) Slachtoffers: Onderzoek, Beleid en Praktijk [Victims: Research, Policy, and Practice]. Wolters Kluwer, Deventer, pp 383-398

Bennett C (2018) Karma after Democratic Kampuchea: Justice Outside the Khmer Rouge Tribunal, Genocide Studies and Prevention: An International Journal 3: 68–82

Bies R, Moag JF (1986) Interactional Justice: Communication Criteria of Fairness. In: Lewicki RJ, Sheppard BH, Bazerman MH (eds) Research on Negotiations in Organizations. JAI Press

Cambodian Center for Human Rights (2011) The Koh Pick Tragedy: One year on, questions remain. https://cchrcambodia.org/storage/posts/1538/2011-11-20-reports-eng-the-koh-pich-tragedy-one-year-on-questions-remain.pdf

Chandler D (2000) Voices from S-21: Terror and History in Pol Pot's Secret Prison. University of California Press

Christie N (1977) Conflicts As Property. The British Journal of Criminology 17: 1–15

Cody S, Koenig A (2018) Procedural Justice in Transnational Contexts. Virginia Journal of International Law 58: 1–30

Cody S, Stover E, Balthazard M, Koenig A (2015) The Victims' Court? A Study of 622 Victim Participants at the International Criminal Court. Human Rights Center, University of California, Berkeley

Colquitt J (2001) On the Dimensionality of Organizational Justice: A Construct Validation of a Measure. Journal of Applied Psychology 86: 386–400

de Waardt M (2013) Are Peruvian Victims Being Mocked? Politicization of Victimhood and Victims' Motivations for Reparations. Human Rights Quarterly 35(4): 830–849

de Waardt M, Georgiou D, Celal E (2021) Attempts at Redress Through the Lens of Social Identity: Housing, Land and Property of the Displaced in Cyprus. International Journal of Transitional Justice, 15: 169–189

García-Godos J (2013) Victims' Rights and Distributive Justice: In Search of Actors. Human Rights Review 14(3): 241–255

Gough N (2008) Life Stories. In: Given LM (ed) The SAGE encyclopedia of qualitative research methods. SAGE Publications, Inc, Thousand Oaks, CA

Gray T (2017) No Justice without Narratives: Transition, Justice and the Khmer Rouge Trials. Transitional Justice Review 1: 63–96

Groenhuijsen M, de Brouwer A-M (2010) Participation of Victims: Commentary. In: Klip A, Sluiter G (eds) Annotated Leading Cases of International Criminal Tribunals: The International Criminal Court 2005-2007. Intersentia, pp 273–280

Groenhuijsen M, Pemberton A (2011) Genocide, Crimes against Humanity and War Crimes: A Victimological Perspective on International Criminal Justice. In: Letschert R, Haveman R, de Brouwer A, Pemberton A (eds) Victimological Approaches to International Crimes: Africa. Intersentia, pp 9–34

Harris I (2008) Cambodian Buddhism: History and Practice, Honolulu: University of Hawai'i Press

Hoven E, Scheibel S (2015) Justice for victims' in trials of mass crimes: Symbolism or substance? International Review of Victimology, 21(2): 161–185

Jarvis H (2014) Justice for the Deceased: Victims' Participation in the Extraordinary Chambers in the Courts of Cambodia. Genocide Studies and Prevention: An International Journal 8: 19–27

Kendall S (2015) Beyond the Restorative Turn: The limits of legal humanitarianism. In: de Vos C, Kendall S, Stahn C (eds) Contested Justice: The Politics and Practice of International Criminal Court Interventions. Cambridge University Press, pp 352–376
Killean R (2016) Procedural Justice in International Criminal Courts: Assessing Civil Parties' Perceptions of Justice at the Extraordinary Chambers in the Courts of Cambodia. International Criminal Law Review 16: 1–38
Laplante L (2015) Just Repair. Cornell International Law Journal 48(3): 513–578
Laxminarayan M (2012) The Heterogenity of Crime Victims: Variations in Procedural and Outcome Preferences. Wolf Legal Publishers
Ledgerwood J (2008) Buddhist Practice in Rural Kandal Province, 1960 and 2003. People of Virtue: Reconfiguring Religion, Power and Moral Order in Cambodia Today
Letschert R (2017) Expert Report on the Views and Concerns of the Victims Participating at the Special Tribunal for Lebanon, Maastricht University
Letschert R, van Boven T (2011) Providing Reparation in Situations of Mass Victimization Key Challenges Involved. In: Letschert R, Haveman R, de Brouwer A, Pemberton A (eds) Victimological Approaches to International Crimes: Africa. Intersentia, pp 155-186
Lind A, Kanfer R (1990) Voice, Control, and Procedural Justice: Instrumental and Noninstrumental Concerns in Fairness Judgments. Journal of Personality and Social Psychology 59: 952–959
Manning P (2012) Governing memory: Justice, reconciliation and outreach at the Extraordinary Chambers in the Courts of Cambodia. Memory Studies 5:165–181
McAdams D (2008), The life story interview. Northwestern University, Evanston, IL
McCarthy C (2009) Reparations under the Rome Statute of the International Criminal Court and Reparative Justice Theory. The International Journal of Transitional Justice 3: 250–271
McCarthy C (2012) Victim Redress and International Criminal Justice: Competing Paradigms, or Compatible Forms of Justice. Journal of International Criminal Justice 10: 351–372
McGonigle B (2009) Two for the Price of One: Attempts by the Extraordinary Chambers in the Courts of Cambodia to Combine Retributive and Restorative Justice Principles. Leiden Journal of International Law, 22: 128–135
McGonigle Leyh B (2011) Procedural Justice? Victim Participation in International Criminal Proceedings. Intersentia
McGonigle Leyh B (2012) Victim-Oriented Measures at International Criminal Institutions: Participation and its Pitfalls. International Criminal Law Review 12: 375–408
McGonigle Leyh B, Fraser J (2019) Transformative Reparations: Changing the Game or More of the Same? Cambridge International Law Journal 8(1): 39–59
Moffett L (2014) Justice for Victims at the International Criminal Court. Routledge Research in International Law
Moffett L (2015) Elaborating Justice for Victims at the International Criminal Court: Beyond Rhetoric and the Hague. Journal of International Criminal Justice 13: 281–311
Nelson I (2010) From quantitative to qualitative: Adapting the life history calendar method. Field Methods
Orth U (2002) Secondary Victimization of Crime Victims by Criminal Proceedings. Social Justice Research 15: 313–325
Ottendoerfer E (2018) Translating Victims' 'Right to Reparations' into Practice: A Framework for Assessing the Implementation of Reparations Programs from a Bottom-up Perspective. Human Rights Quarterly 40(4): 905–931
Pemberton A, Aarten P, Mulder E (2019) Stories as Property: Narrative Ownership as a Key Concept in Victims' Experiences with Criminal Justice. Criminology & Criminal Justice 19: 404–420
Pham P (2011) After the first trial: A population-based survey on knowledge and perception of justice and the Extraordinary Chambers in the Courts of Cambodia. Human Rights Center, University of California, Berkeley School of Law
Pham P, Vinck P, Balthazard M, Hean S, Stover E (2009) A Population-based Survey on Attitudes about Social Reconstruction and the Extraordinary Chambers in the Courts of Cambodia: So We Will Never Forget. Human Rights Center, University of California, Berkeley School of Law

Shelton D (2015) Remedies in International Human Rights Law. Oxford University Press
Sion B (2011) Conflicting sites of memory in post-genocide Cambodia. Humanity: An International Journal of Human Rights, Humanitarianism, and Development 2: 1–21
Sperfeldt C (2018) Practices of Reparations in International Criminal Justice. Unpublished dissertation, Australian National University
Sperfeldt C (2022) Practices of Reparations in International Criminal Justice. Cambridge University Press
Sperfeldt C, Hughes R (2020) The Projectification of Reparation. Journal of Human Rights Practice, 1–21
Teitel R (2014) Globalizing Transitional Justice: Contemporary Essays. Oxford Scholarship Online
Tibori-Szabó K, Bianchini B, Sehmi A, Studzinsky S (2017) Communication Between Victims' Lawyers and Their Clients. In: Tibori-Szabó K, Hirst M (eds) Victim Participation in International Criminal Justice: Practitioners' Guide. T.M.C. Asser Press, The Hague, pp 433-465
Tracy S (2020) Qualitative Research Methods. Wiley Blackwell, Hoboken
Um K (2021) Life After/Ward: Recovering Life After Social Death in Post-Genocide Cambodia, The UNESCO Slave Route Project: Healing the Wounds of Slavery. https://healingthewoundsofslavery.org/wp-content/uploads/2021/03/Um_Cambodia.pdf. Accessed 28 September 2023
Urban Walker M (2015) Making Reparations Possible: Theorizing Reparative Justice. In: Corradetti C, Eisikovits N, Rotond J (eds) Theorizing Transitional Justice. Ashgate, pp 211–222
van Boven T (2009) Victims' Rights to a Remedy and Reparation: the New United Nations Principles and Guidelines. In: Ferstman C, Goetz M, Stephens A (eds) Reparations for Victims of Genocide, War Crimes and Crimes against Humanity: Systems in Place and Systems in the Making. Martinus Nijhof Publishers
van Boven T (2013) Victim-oriented Perspectives: Rights and Realities. In: Bonacker T, Safferling C (eds) Victims of International Crimes: an Interdisciplinary Discourse, Springer, pp 17–27
Wemmers J (1996) Victims in the Criminal Justice System. Kugler Publications
Wemmers J (2009a) Victims and the International Criminal Court (ICC): Evaluating the Success of the ICC with Respect to Victims. International Review of Victimology 16: 211–222
Wemmers J (2009b) Where Do They Belong? Giving Victims a Place in the Criminal Justice Process. Criminal Law Forum 20: 395–416
Wemmers J (2014) The Healing Role of Reparation. In: Wemmers J (ed) Reparation for Victims of Crimes against Humanity: The Healing Role of Reparation. Routledge
Williams T, Bernath J, Tann B, Kum S (2018) Justice and Reconciliation for the Victims of the Khmer Rouge? Victim Participation in Cambodia's Transitional Justice Process. Centre for Conflict Studies, Marburg; Centre for the Study of Humanitarian Law, Phnom Penh; Swisspeace, Bern
Zwanenburg M (2006) The Van Boven/Bassiouni Principles: An Appraisal. Netherlands Quarterly of Human Rights 24: 641–668

Other Documents

Assembly of States Parties, Report of the Court on the strategy in relation to victims. ICC-ASP/8/45 (10 November 2009)
ECCC Internal Rules (2015), 9th revised version
ECCC, Case 001 (Supreme Court Chamber: Appeals Judgment) 001/18-07-2007-ECCC/SC (3 February 2012)
ECCC, Case 001 (Trial Chamber: Judgment) 001/18-07-2007/ECCC/TC (26 July 2010)
ECCC, Case 002/02 (Supreme Chamber Court: Appeal Judgement) 002/19-09-2007-ECCC/SC (22 December 2022)
ECCC, Case 002/02 (Trial Chamber: Case 002/02 Judgement) 002/19-09-2007/ECCC/TC (16 November 2018)

ECCC, Case 002 (Office of the Co-Investigating Judges: Closing Order) 002/19-09-2007-ECCC-OCIJ (15 September 2010)

ECCC, Case 002/01 (Trial Chamber: Case 002/01 Judgment), 002/19-09-2007/ECCC/TC (7 August 2014)

ECCC, Case 002/01 (Supreme Chamber Court: Appeal Judgement) 002/19-09-2007-ECCC/SC (23 November 2016)

ICC, Lubanga case (Appeals Chamber, Amended order for reparations) ICC-01/04-01/06-3129 (3 March 2015)

ICC, Katanga case (Trial Chamber, Order for Reparations pursuant to Article 75 of the Statute) ICC-01/04-01/07-3728-tENG (24 March 2017)

Rome Statute of the International Criminal Court (adopted 17 July 1998, entered into force 1 July 2002)

UNGA (1997) Identical letters dated 23 June 1997 from the Secretary-General addressed to the President of the General Assembly and to the President of the Security Council, A/51/930, S/1997/488

UNGA (2003) Khmer Rouge trials, A/RES/57/228

UNGA (2005) Basic Principles and Guidelines on the Right to a Remedy and Reparation for Victims of Gross Violations of International Human Rights Law and Serious Violations of International Humanitarian Law, Res 60/147

Alina Balta is an international criminal lawyer and researcher with specialised expertise in reparative justice and victimology.

Mijke de Waardt is a researcher at the Netherlands Institute Study of Crime and Law Enforcement (NSCR), and an assistant professor at the department of Criminology, Vrije Universiteit Amsterdam.

Marola Vaes is a slow-travelling documentarian and trained social scientist with a background in empirical peace research.

Part III
De-Colonialisation and the Law of Reparations

Chapter 10
A Century on from the *Chorzów Factory*: Reparations, National Wars of Liberation and the Limits of Wiping out the Consequences of Armed Conflicts

Luke Moffett

Contents

Abstract Reparations have been used, for nearly as long as war, to secure the peace. This chapter considers the place of reparations and the *Chorzów Factory* case in settling claims after armed conflict, in particular those emerging from colonialism and occupation, discussing the challenges of redressing the harm caused to civilians and other victims. In particular, it examines the limits of international law in the form of international humanitarian law and human rights law in providing a legal basis and often forum for victims' claims to be brought. From this survey it is apparent that in the past century, reparations for violations have been inadequate and in many cases absent. This has been particularly acute in wiping out the consequences in the majority of wars of national liberation that marked the mid-twentieth century and recent neo-colonial conflicts in the Middle East by Western powers. This raises fundamental questions about the extent of the obligation to wipe out the consequences of armed conflict in terms of whose harm is worth repairing and the flexibility with which the obligation is applied in practice.

Keywords Reparations · Colonialism · Armed conflict · National wars of liberation

---

L. Moffett (✉)
School of Law, Queen's University Belfast, Belfast, United Kingdom
e-mail: l.moffett@qub.ac.uk

O. Spijkers et al. (eds.), *Netherlands Yearbook of International Law 2022*, Netherlands Yearbook of International Law 53, https://doi.org/10.1007/978-94-6265-627-7_10

10.1 Introduction

The *Chorzów Factory* case is a foundational part of international law as the 'origin story' of the legal authority on the obligation to make reparations.[1] The case establishes that reparations must,

> as far as possible, wipe out all the consequences of the illegal act and re-establish the situation which would, in all probability, have existed if that act had not been committed.[2]

This dictum proclaims a legal utopia of redress for international wrongs. In practice, wiping out all the consequences of many violations, including those committed in armed conflict, is impossible. Yet such a legal narrative beguiles the vexed nature of remedying international violations. Reparations have come about in the aftermath of armed conflict not simply to comply with international law, but also to secure peace. Ironically, the *Chorzów Factory* case as the touchstone for understanding the secondary rules for repairing international wrongdoing, is a case where reparations were never ordered, as the parties settled.[3] This chapter points to three issues in appreciating the dictum in light of recent developments around reparations for armed conflict, namely: their absence for wars of national liberation; the flexibility of the standard's application when it comes to full reparations; and their contemporary blind-spots in times of war.

Nearly a century on from the judgment, the wisdom of the judges continues to reverberate through time. While the *Chorzów Factory* dictum is often invoked to legally base the authority of reparation decisions,[4] in practice the customary rules have fallen short of wiping out the consequences for all the violations committed in the commencement and duration of armed conflict. This does not make the dictum defunct, but rather requires a more nuanced appreciation of the flexibility of making reparations for the consequences of war. This chapter traces out some of the context and consequences of the *Chorzów Factory* dictum, before starkly contrasting it to the reparation practices that followed the WWII. The chapter emphasises that over the past century, States have waived away their citizens' claims for redress arising out of armed conflict, prioritising other foreign policy goals. A final consideration is how in the past seventy-five years we have constructed an international legal architecture for armed conflicts that both progresses and delimits victims' rights for reparations.

---

[1] Brown notes that key international legal texts extensively make reference to the case and the most frequent case cited from the Permanent Court of Justice. Brown 2017, pp. 61–88, 61.

[2] PCIJ, *Germany v Poland, The Factory at Chorzów* (Claim for Indemnity) (The Merits), Judgment No.13, 13 September 1928 ('Chorzów Factory' case), para. 125.

[3] Brown 2017, p. 63.

[4] ICJ, Armed Activities on the Territory of the Congo (*Democratic Republic of the Congo v Uganda*), Judgment on Reparations, 9 February 2022, (*Reparations Judgment* 2022), [2022] ICJ, Rep 13 para.100; IACtHR, *Case of Aloeboetoe et al. v. Suriname*, Judgment (Reparations and Costs) 10 September 1993 (*Aloeboetoe et al. v. Suriname 1993*), para. 43; ECtHR, *Case of Papamichalopoulos and Others v. Greece (Article 50)*, Court (Chamber), Judgment (Just Satisfaction), 31 October 1995, Application no. 14556/89 (*Papamichalopoulos and Others v. Greece 1995*), para. 36.

This has broader implications in how we see the consequences of armed conflict and remedy them.

This chapter begins by discussing the place of the *Chorzów Factory* case, in light of the practice of reparations in international law over the past century. In particular its place in the aftermath of the WWI and the role of international law in framing war reparations after the WWII. In this inception period, reparations for violations of going to war and those atrocities committed within have been elucidated and elided. The following section discusses the absence of reparations for wars of national liberation movements as empires collapsed, and new countries emerged. The final section reflects on the state of international law, in how it has both expanded the purview of reparations to individuals, but also continues to circumscribe the extent to which harms caused by military operations can be claimed. It is argued that despite the continued legal relevance and reliance on the *Chorzów Factory* dictum in international law, the obligation to make reparations for the consequences of war remains restrained.

10.2 The *Chorzów Factory* Case and Reparations for War

The *Chorzów Factory* case arose in the aftermath of the First World War, where there was energy for multilateral legalism and hope that international law would secure international peace. The 1919 Treaty of Versailles set out that Germany accepted responsibility for 'all the loss and damage' caused by the war,[5] with a reparation commission to arrive at a global sum of reparations to be paid to Allied nations. In addition Germany committed itself to being subject to mixed arbitrational tribunals that would adjudicate on individual claims of compensation for private losses as a result of the First World War.[6] The *Chorzów Factory* case was one of thousands of claims that arose in the aftermath of the Versailles Treaty that eventually ended up being before the Permanent Court of International Justice (PCIJ).

The elegant simplicity of the PCIJ judgments in the *Chorzów Factory* case in suggesting that wrongful acts should see their full consequences remedied, proved in practice that reparations were mercurial. At the same time, the failure to secure reparations from Germany that it could not pay in reality, fuelled Germans' sense of collective victimhood and the rise of nationalism, as well as reflecting bad economics, by creating trade deficits for Western allies.[7] Rather than settle the grievances of the war, reparations became a symbol of Allied vindictiveness in impoverishing Germany that fuelled discontent and conflict across Europe. This was apparent with France and Belgium's invasion of the German Ruhr valley to physically remove resources in response to Germany's default on reparations payments, leading one commentator to

[5] Treaty of Versailles 1919, Article 321.

[6] Treaty of Versailles 1919, Articles 297 and 304.

[7] Turgeon 1973, pp. 111–125, 123.

remark that they collected 'reparations at gunpoint'.[8] As such, the delayed payment became a way for France to continue 'the war by economic means'.[9] Despite the failure of reparations, Payk finds that this period and the use of reparations is marked as the beginning of the 'reign of law' in international relations, with victors no longer at the end of hostilities claiming reparations as 'spoils of war', but on a legal basis.[10] However in practice reparations remained a point of contention, reflecting an imposed peace, rather than Germany's ownership of their wrongdoing and the legal obligation to remedy the harm caused.

Despite the legal prowess of the *Chorzów Factory* dictum, in the aftermath of the Second World War inter-State reparations were a prickly subject to broach. The Allies were at cross-purposes around imposing reparations on the Axis nations, especially given the experience of the Versailles settlement. The United States was keen to ensure the recovery of Germany and Japan's economies and their contribution to the newly-emerging multilateral order.[11] The Soviets were adamant about securing reparations against Germany for their losses, including the large-scale theft of cultural property in eastern Europe. The Potsdam Agreement and the Treaty of San Francisco recognised the need to allow each country's people to have sufficient resources to subsist without external assistance, reflecting that reparation demands should be measured and feasible.[12] Many nations waived their right to claim reparations from Germany and Japan through a range of peace treaties and bilateral agreements.[13] By way of example, several former French colonial territories occupied by Japanese forces during the war, such as Laos and Cambodia, waived their right to reparations from the Japanese, in favour of normalising their relations as nation States.[14] This reflected strategic decisions to rebuild economic ties and secure allies for the growing Cold War, but this in turn marginalised victims as mere 'objects' of concern, rather than rights-holders.[15]

The post-Second World War period did not reaffirm in practice the dictum of the *Chorzów Factory*, and indeed a number of victims of atrocities have spent decades since seeking redress. Given the prevalence of the practice of settlement and waiving full reparations, the International Court of Justice in the *Jurisdictional Immunities*

[8] Henig 1995, p. 38.

[9] Such as invading Germany between 1921 and 1923 to expropriate by force what was owed in reparations. See Schuker 1976, p. 14.

[10] Payk 2018, p. 817.

[11] See Kuklick 1972.

[12] The Berlin (Potsdam) Conference, 17 July–2 August 1945, Chapter II(B)(19); and Treaty of San Francisco 1951, Article 14.

[13] West Germany signed bilateral treaties with European countries after the Second World War that did make reparations to the amount of DM 900 million, with recipient States responsible for allocating such money, with France receiving DM 400 million and Britain obtaining DM 11 million, prioritising ill-treated resistance fighters and prisoners of war. See Henry 2007, pp. 31–32. In Asia amounted to US$1,486 million to Burma, the Philippines, Indonesia, South Vietnam, Laos, Cambodia, Thailand, and South Korea, but in the end Japan only paid $606 million. Gunn 2011.

[14] Gunn 2011.

[15] See Buxbaum 2013.

case involving Nazi atrocities in Italy and Greece, upheld the discretion of States to reach a peace settlement, precluding a rule in international law for full reparations,

> against the background of a century of practice in which almost every peace treaty or post-war settlement has involved either a decision not to require the payment of reparations or the use of lump sum settlements and set-offs, it is difficult to see that international law contains a rule requiring the payment of full compensation to each and every individual victim as a rule accepted by the international community of States as a whole as one from which no derogation is permitted.[16]

As discussed in the final section, this finding of the Court grates against the upward trajectory of individual rights in international law, particularly with human rights, and the enthusiasm in which reparations are treated in some quarters. This decision reflects the pre-eminence of States in the international legal order, to forgo the rights of those within their jurisdiction, despite the long-term consequences victims of war are left to live with.

Despite the unwillingness of States to make reparations part of a global peace settlement of the Second World War, there were some domestic programmes and bilateral agreements that provided for reparations. Germany and Japan established domestic reparation programmes for their own citizens.[17] Germany also established a range of programmes for victims of Nazi persecution, in particular for the Holocaust.[18] In 1988, the United States established a reparation programme for its discriminatory internment of Japanese Americans during the war.[19] In the case of Guam, an unincorporated territory of the US, it only saw a reparations programme established in 2016 by the US government after it waived its claims to reparations from Japan.[20] This domestic provision of compensation for inter-State claims has been a common practice and more recently used to end protracted litigation that negatively impacts on each country's foreign relations and foreign assets, such as with Italian victims' claims for Nazi atrocities before the ICJ and South Korean victims of Japanese forced labour and sexual slavery.[21] Such practices are pragmatic responses to redress the past with pressure from victims, rather than strict adherence to the legal doctrine of reparation obligations in international law per the *Chorzów Factory* dictum. It could also suggest that victims' States waiving away their claim to reparations from

[16] ICJ, *Jurisdictional Immunities of the State (Germany v. Italy: Greece Intervening),* Judgment, 3 February 2012 *(Jurisdictional Immunities 2012)*, [2012] ICJ Rep 2012, para. 94.

[17] In Germany there were two programmes established, one for civilians victimised by the war and the other as part of the bilateral 1952 Luxembourg Agreement with Israel for victims of Nazi persecution. See Greenstein 2020. In Japan in 1952 the Act to Relieve the Wounded or Sick and the Bereaved Families of those Killed during the War was passed. See Koder 1988.

[18] See Bazyler 2003.

[19] Civil Liberties Act 1988.

[20] Guam World War II Loyalty Recognition Act.

[21] Caroli 2023; and Smith J, Choi S-H and Murakami S (2023) South Korea companies to pay to resolve forced labour dispute with Japan https://www.reuters.com/world/asia-pacific/south-korea-announce-plans-resolve-forced-labour-dispute-with-japan-2023-03-06/. Accessed 2 December 2024.

a wrongful State does not obliterate victims' right, but rather transfers the obligation to the claimant State to fulfil.

In the post-WWII period the place of reparations in resolving armed conflicts was diminished. With inter-State armed conflicts the practice of reparations was limited to a handful of examples. States often waived their claims for reparations[22] or ended hostilities without either addressing such claims or signing a peace agreement.[23] The majority of armed conflicts since 1945 have been non-international ones or wars of national liberation: the first few decades that followed the Second World War witnessed the emergence of numerous countries being recognised by the United Nations. Despite this shift, there remains a profound gap in the practice of reparations for wars related to the decolonialization period, where despite the scale of atrocities committed, attention to remedying the consequences of such wrongdoing has not been forthcoming.

10.3 National Wars of Liberation and the End of Empire

The past century witnessed dozens of countries emerge from colonialism, at a cost of millions of civilians killed and maimed. These struggles of national liberation have often been overlooked in discussions on reparations, and it is only in recent years that attention has moved to redressing their injurious consequences.[24] While many of these wars were non-international armed conflicts, they were framed in global power struggles as part of the Cold War, with little concern for the human cost on the ground. The Algerian war of independence against the French is a key example of this, where the 1962 Evian Accords make no mention of reparations or victims of the brutal eight-year war of independence that killed hundreds of thousands of civilians, and left millions displaced.[25] The war in Vietnam involved inter-State dimensions, but similarly ended with a peace agreement. The North Vietnamese were keen for reparations to be included in the final settlement, given the scale of destruction caused to the country, though the Americans framed it as $2.5 billion in economic aid for reconstruction.[26] Military advances by the Viet Cong quickly outpaced such negotiations, and the final peace agreement did not stipulate any reparations, but hailed a 'new era of reconciliation' with the United States contributing 'to healing the wounds of war and to post-war reconstruction'.[27] Subsequently there have been unsuccessful

[22] As with the Falklands War, conflict around the Suez Canal and inter-state conflicts in Latin America. See Joint Statement by the British and Argentine Delegations, Madrid, 19 October 1989, para. 3; El Salvador and Honduras– Article 42, General Peace Treaty Between the Republics of El Salvador and Honduras 1980; and Sullo and Wyatt 2014, para. 24.

[23] Such as after the Korean War.

[24] For instance, Seong-Hak Kim 2022; Sarkin 2009; and Herik 2012.

[25] See France-Algeria independence agreements, *International Legal Materials*, 1(2)(1962), 214-230.

[26] See Kennedy et al. 1998.

[27] Agreement on ending the war and restoring peace in Viet-Nam, 27 January 1973, Article 21.

claims by some victims for the use of herbicides against the US government and companies, despite affected US veterans succeeding in having a support programme established for them.[28] These experiences bring into sharp focus the extent of the obligation for 'full reparations' for wrongdoings during an armed conflict.

In other colonial contexts, the former colonial masters' attention was about maintaining their economic and foreign policy interests as well as their regional influence.[29] For any violations that did occur there was a lack of legal recognition on their part of any international wrongdoing, as they were dealing with rebellion and insurrection as an internal insecurity matter. In the case of Portugal, which fought against liberation movements in Angola, Guinea and Mozambique for 13 years until 1974, the UN Security Council ordered Portugal to make compensation for its armed attack against Guinea,[30] but Portugal also demanded reparations from the UN for sanctions on its Mozambique trade for violating embargoes on Rhodesia.[31] The 1974 Lusaka Accord for Mozambique, the 1974 Algiers Accord for Guinea, and the 1975 Alvor Agreement for Angola made no reference to reparations; instead, Portugal recognised their independence, transferred power to national liberation movements and secured the property rights of Portuguese citizens in those countries.[32]

These wars of independence were not like the inter-State armed conflicts of the World Wars, but lasted decades, subjugating peoples and vast territories by colonial powers by using more technologically advanced weaponry. The violence used to maintain such control reached the magnitude of what today could be described as crimes against humanity and genocide, given the systematic attempts to wipe out in whole or in part particular groups of people who resisted.[33] Indeed, colonial forces fighting against rebellions used counter-insurgency tactics that not only stripped away many legal protections for civilians and enemy combatants, but also dehumanised them as 'savages', which continues to create an 'implicitly sanitised account' of colonialism.[34] At the same time, colonial forces had legal requirements on the use of lethal force diluted down, 'creating a permissive environment for excessive killing' when suspected 'criminals' or 'bandits' were shot with impunity and without identification.[35] In the end, the recognition of independence on these former colonies was an act of benevolence of the former colonial masters, with no efforts to account

[28] See Palmer 2007; Agent Orange Act 1991.

[29] For instance the peace agreement between Portugal and Mozambique that detailed the importance of maintaining economic and diplomatic relations, as well as non-discrimination for those Portuguese who remained in Mozambique—Acordo de Lusaka 1974.

[30] UN Security Council (1970) Resolution 290 (1970), UN Doc. S/RES/290.

[31] Whitaker 1970, p. 31.

[32] In the aftermath of independence, all three countries saw tens of thousands killed in repression (Guinea) or war (Angola and Mozambique).

[33] Sarkin 2009, p. 16.

[34] Wagner 2018, p. 218.

[35] Bennett and Romijn 2022, p. 35.

for the grave and systemic nature of their violations, including the use of chemical weapons and Dum-Dum bullets.[36]

National liberation movement demands for reparations risked complicating peace negotiations and delaying the achievement of independence. For those who succeeded in gaining their independence, they did not want to financially burden the nascent public treasury with settling victims' claims.[37] For these liberation movements, their focus was on self-determination as a means to redress the past, demonstrating that they could govern themselves better than their former colonial masters. Atrocities committed by colonial forces were seen to deepen grievances and fuel the efforts of such liberation movements to remedy them through independence.[38] Violence committed by such movements was also left unredressed, with further atrocities committed in subsequent internal armed conflicts, with civilians suffering the price for freedom. In such circumstances, victims' suffering typified colonial subjects 'collective subordination' and became part of their 'sacrifice' to the new nation.[39] During this period human rights was embryonic and the right of reparations for individuals for violations was not firmly established. Only in subsequent years did redress claims come about as victims became organised and spoke out about their suffering, which played into national identity and narratives of the past that justified the new State's existence, rather than promoting redress for all victims.[40]

In the past decade there has been a handful of high-profile successful claims for violations committed during decolonialization. These claims took decades to ripen for a number of reasons, as they required the right circumstances—including a legal basis to make such historical claims, an appropriate legal forum, sufficient evidence to buttress the claim, and the direct victims still being alive. In the Netherlands there have been a number of claims against Dutch colonial forces in the Indonesian war of independence, that resulted in compensation for victims who were alive at the time of the atrocities, namely widows and children of those men extra-judicially executed.[41] Only in 2023 did the Indonesia government establish a reparations programme for the violence in the post-colonial period that resulted in over 500,000 fatalities.[42] In the United Kingdom, the British government in 2013 settled similar historic colonial claims for the torture and ill-treatment of interned civilians during the Mau-Mau

---

[36] See Wagner 2018.

[37] The Irish Free State settled its claims over the war of independence with Britain through the Shaw inter-state claims commission, and the resulting Irish civil war saw the Irish treasury being heavily burdened with the cost of compensation, which amounted to 6% of the annual budget. See Clark 2014, p. 28.

[38] Gross 2015, pp. 36–37.

[39] Humphrey 2020, p. 268.

[40] Seong-Hak Kim 2022, p. 488.

[41] Such as the Rawagede case, see Herik 2012; and Immler and Scagliola 2020.

[42] Teresia A (2003) Indonesia starts reparations programme for victims of its bloody past. https://www.reuters.com/world/asia-pacific/indonesia-starts-reparations-programme-victims-its-bloody-past-2023-06-27/. Accessed 08 December 2024

insurgency in Kenya in the 1950s,[43] as well as for torture of Greek Cypriot members of the guerrilla group Eoka.[44] In these British cases, settlements were made ex gratia, admitting no fault by the British government, despite claims of torture, it indicated a pattern of violence that continued into the British army's response to violence in Northern Ireland in the 1970s.[45] This would suggest that they were not isolated instances, but part of a systematic plan or policy in counter-insurgency operations, and that the use of settlements dilutes victims' rights to reparation, preventing a full accounting of such violations.[46]

In recent years we have seen a shift from inter-State claims to individual victims or groups of them bringing claims against former colonial powers, reflecting a lack of interest of their home State to convey, such claims on their behalf or to avoid complicating their foreign relations, such as Indonesian victims against the Dutch government. Claims more distant in time, where violations were committed over a hundred years ago, such as the massacres by German forces of the Herero and Nama in Namibia, have been met with efforts to provide a development fund, rather than individual compensation or on a legal basis.[47] This points to a profound gap in international law on what consequences should be remedied and the waivable nature of the obligation to redress. While some have pointed to successful cases as indicating that redress is possible for historical colonial crimes and consistent with the principles set down in the *Chorzów Factory* case,[48] in reality successful claims arising from Dutch and British colonialism represent a small percentage of the total victim population and the amount paid was a symbolic amount of compensation.[49] Efforts to make more comprehensive redress, such as Belgium's atrocities in the Belgian Congo, continue to face political resistance to recognise the violence used in empire

[43] Compensation was paid to 5,228 claimants amounting to £19.9 million. See William Hague Statement to Parliament on settlement of Mau Mau claims, 6 June 2013; and *Mutua & Ors v The Foreign and Commonwealth Office* [2012] EWHC 2678 (QB).

[44] For 33 claimants to the amount of £1 million, see Statement by Alan Duncan, Minister for Foreign and Commonwealth Affairs, on civil litigation brought by 33 Cypriot nationals against Her Majesty's Government in connection with the Emergency Period in Cyprus, 1955-1959, 23 January 2019. The Cyprus Act 1960 granting Cyprus independence made no reference to claims for violations during the emergency.

[45] For instance the Hooded men litigation, *Ireland v UK*, (1979-80) 2 EHRR 25, as well as more recently with a Northern Irish court awarding £350,000 in compensation to the victim of water-boarding as torture by the British army in 1972—*William (Liam) Holden v Ministry of Defence and Chief Constable of PSNI*, 24 March 2023.

[46] See Cobain 2013.

[47] This amounted to $1.1 billion over 30 years, where white settlers in Namibia continue to own the majority of the land in territories of those killed—see Cotterill J (2022) Battle for Namibia reparations: German deal 'was never about us'. https://www.ft.com/content/ab289014-0414-4514-a77e-a3f030505e0f. Accessed 08 December 2024.

[48] Menachery Paulose and Rogo 2018, pp. 377–378.

[49] A second set of Mau-Mau claims was dismissed due to the passage of time being inequitable on the defendant—*Kimathi & Others v The Foreign and Commonwealth Office* [2018] EWHC 2066. In Indonesia victims of Dutch colonial crimes rejected efforts to create an administrative scheme with an average payout of €5,000, which was lower than other Dutch court awards for similarly affected victims—see BBC Indonesia (2020) Refusing Dutch offer for damages.

building and colonialism in itself as an inherent wrong, instead preferring to maintain the status quo in that the means used in the past were part of the civilizing mission, legitimate state-building and the maintenance of order.[50] Despite some recognition of historical injustice, this predominant position signifies that the political culture which justified such violence continues to shape domestic and international law to the exclusion of victims' right to reparation.[51]

While such colonial powers were (and most continue to be) unwilling to recognise the wrongfulness of their colonial rule or the way in which the waged their counter-insurgency operations, they prioritised their own nationals to ensure redress for their losses. This is a clear racial hierarchy of victimhood, where white settlers are at the top benefiting from redress, then auxiliary colonial forces, with colonised civilians at the bottom. In Indonesia after the Second World War, restitution claims for colonial violations were seen as being only for Dutch victims, as they were just in the Dutch language and for the settler colonial class.[52] Similarly with regards to the Algerian war of independence against French colonialism, settler communities of European descent who had to leave Algeria after independence or lost property were the first to campaign and succeed in securing reparations from the French government in the 1970s.[53] However, 'native' communities were not eligible, despite them suffering the majority of violence including the tens of thousands who were killed, thousands who were tortured and numerous others exposed to nuclear weapons tests.[54] This has been challenged in recent years, with a law passed in 2021, to compensate those of Algerian descent who fought for the French in the war, but not for civilians who suffered.[55] Other violations, such as rape, were never redressed in Indonesia and Algeria, as there were 'no mechanisms and no leverage' for victims to seek a remedy, whereas rape was, only relatively recently, considered a crime against morality, rather than against a person.[56] Only a couple of cases in recent years for rape in Algeria and Indonesia have succeeded, due to domestic laws either amnestying the actions of the colonial powers or statutes of limitations prohibiting such claims.[57]

Compensation for colonialism, and in particular national wars of independence expose a clear power dynamic between States and victims, in terms of who is speaking for those harmed, the place of international law in ensuring the right to reparations for wrongdoing, and recognition of suffering of the past. It is apparent that in hind-sight counter-insurgency efforts to maintain the colony would now likely amount to

[50] See Rosoux 2022.

[51] See Stahn 2020; Gallen 2023.

[52] Keppy 2010, p. 256.

[53] Two laws were passed in 1970 and 1978. See Vince 2020, p. 171.

[54] See Slyomovics 2021.

[55] Kessous M (2022) France stalls on compensation for colonial troops who served in Algerian War, https://www.lemonde.fr/en/politics/article/2022/09/21/delicate-question-of-compensation-for-harkis-and-their-children_5997767_5.html. Accessed 08 December 2024.

[56] Scagliola and Vince 2022, p. 112.

[57] Ibid., pp. 114–115. Such as *Mohamed Garne v France* (2001) and *Tremimi v the State of the Netherlands* (2016), C/09/483032 / HA ZA 15-200.

international crimes; despite this, the law remains impotent in providing a forum for victims to claim redress. Reparations for colonialism have only arisen in such circumstances through victims organising themselves and putting legal, political and moral pressure on responsible States, which has resulted in piecemeal redress. As Lord Kerr notes in his separate opinion in the claims of 24 Malayan plantation workers shot dead by British colonial soldiers in 1948, their lack of legal basis to open up an investigation under the procedural obligations of the right to life exemplified that 'the law has proved itself unable to respond positively to the demand that there be redress for the historical wrong … [that] may reflect a deficiency in our system of law.'[58]

Despite efforts to end colonialism, there are still ongoing cases of colonialism and occupation nearly 80 years after the creation of the United Nations. In particular the Western Sahara, Chagos Islands and Palestine. All three of these cases have been before the International Court of Justice as advisory opinions. In the *Construction of a Wall in Palestine* the *Chorzów Factory* case was invoked for the 'obligation to make reparation for the damage caused to all the natural and legal persons concerned' including the return of land and property as well as compensation if restitution is 'materially impossible'.[59] The United Nations has established two Palestinian claim bodies for reparations. The first, the UN Conciliation Commission, was tasked with documenting and seeking reparations and return of hundreds of thousands of Palestinians refugees who suffered forced displacement as a result of the Nakba in 1948.[60] Israel initially indicated that it would pay compensation to some Palestinian refugees, but only those who had lost agricultural land, and would not include restitution. The efforts by the UN to secure reparations for Palestinian refugees at the Lausanne Conference in 1949 were met by Israeli counter-claims for war damages against Arab states, which were beyond the Commission's mandate, and in the face of such resistance the Commission documented in detail the refugees' losses in the hope that future reparations would be made.[61] The second body, a register of damage for the Israeli Wall Advisory Opinion case at the ICJ, has received tens of thousands of applications.[62] In both cases no reparations have been made, despite the respective bodies finding that most of the claims had merit and eligible for compensation.[63] It is likely that subsequent proceedings at the ICJ will only see more claims being made for the annihilation of Gaza with no effort to change the responsible State's

[58] *Keyu and others v Secretary of State for Foreign and Commonwealth Affairs and another*, UK Supreme Court, 25 November 2015, para. 285.

[59] ICJ, *Legal Consequences of the Construction of a Wall in The Occupied Palestinian Territory*, Advisory Opinion, 9 July 2004 (*Wall Adivisory Opinion 2004*), [2004] ICJ Rep. 2004, paras 152–153.

[60] UNGA 1948.

[61] Fischbach 2021.

[62] UNGA 2020.

[63] The UN Register of Damage has found over 37,000 eligible out of over 71,000 claims. A register of damage has been proposed by the UN General Assembly with regards to Russia's invasion of Ukraine as a contemporary imperial conquest, but without some sort of peace settlement, it is unlikely that reparations will be paid out through it alone. See UNGA 2022.

behaviour in its production of tens of thousands more victims waiting on redress. The most recent Advisory Opinion in July 2024 has reiterated that Israel's occupation of Palestine remains illegal and requires reparation. This continuing litigation indicates that the legal institutions of the UN have failed to end colonialism by the West's allies and remedy the harm suffered by generations of civilians, with efforts in recognising such victims' claims as token legalism.

The review of the post-Second World War practice in relation to the injury caused during the liberation movements against colonial subjugation, points to the limitations of the principle enunciated in Chorzów Factory as such violations were not explicitly violations of international law and in practice there have been little efforts to recognise systematic wrongdoing of colonial powers. Instead of wiping out the consequences of such wrongdoing, States have repudiated victims' claims and created an exclusionary legal framework that maintains the legitimacy and legality of their past actions. These blind-spots and biases continue to colour international law in how it recognises victims' claims for reparations for harm suffered during wars of national liberations and the limitations of international law for harmful consequences of armed conflict, to which we now turn.

10.4 The Contemporary International Legal Architecture in Armed Conflict

The century that followed the *Chorzów Factory* case, has witnessed the adoption of reparations for armed conflict across the world, with the majority of countries having implemented reparations in some shape or form.[64] This is not to suggest the ubiquity of reparations for war. Nor does it establish that post-*Chorzów* there was consensus on the obligation for States to make reparations for all wrongful acts. Indeed, in 1985 Gray stated that there was no international law on remedy, as such measures were often an 'afterthought' and they had 'a limited role in international relations' given their consistent breaches of obligations without judicial claims for redress.[65] Despite this, in the past three decades we have witnessed a solidifying of the norm through the International Law Commission's Articles on State Responsibility for Internationally Wrongful Acts, but at the same time reached a legal ceiling for the upward trajectory of victims' right to reparations.[66] This is apparent in the legal and procedural limitations imposed on those harmed by military operations and their ability to be recognised as right-holders.[67] It is suggested, that there are still lessons to be

[64] For some of these see the Reparations Database—https://reparations.qub.ac.uk/reparations-database/. Accessed 08 December 2024.

[65] Gray 1986, pp. 25, 29.

[66] The issue is a current focus of the International Law Commission, see ILC (2019) Report of the International Law Commission, A/74/10 Annex B (2019).

[67] See Van de Put 2023.

learned from the oft-cited dictum in the *Chorzów Factory*. To explore this proposition, this last section is split into two sub-sections. The first subsection addresses the qualification of the legal obligation to make reparation 'as far as possible'. The second sub-section discusses what amounts to wrongdoing in international law for atrocities committed in armed conflict, in particular the continuing blind-spot with counter-insurgency operations.

10.4.1 'As Far as Possible'

Chorzów Factory remains a touchstone for the customary obligation to make reparation for a breach of an international obligation. Reparations must be in adequate form, so as to wipe out, 'as far as possible', the consequences of such breach. When it comes to armed conflict, there are few examples where this notion of 'full' reparations has been applied in practice, given the scale of devastation and the destruction it involves. In 1991, the UN Security Council established that Iraq was fully liable for any direct losses sustained as a result of its invasion and occupation of Kuwait.[68] The resultant UN Claims Commission (UNCC) paid out $52.4 billion to over 1.5 million claimants, making it one of the most substantive reparation programmes after the German Second World War schemes. In contrast, the Eritrean-Ethiopian Claims Commission took a cautious approach as the State practice of the twentieth century did not provide clear guidance on whether full liability should be imposed on either of the parties, finding that it was 'heavily shaped by motives of policy and revenge unrelated to the principles of law' with reparations under the Treaty of Versailles having a 'brief and unsatisfactory history'.[69] Instead it distinguished the two parties as equally situated belligerents and found each of the parties responsible for violations giving a global sum to be paid by each side.[70] While these two examples were dealing with *jus ad bellum* as well, other adjudicatory bodies on violations during armed conflict have not imposed 'full' reparations, despite the *Chorzów Factory* case being often cited as the legal basis for the secondary rule or reparations for wrongdoing.[71]

The *Chorzów Factory* case takes a more subtle approach in its iteration of the secondary rule to remedy wrongdoings, by requiring the wrongdoer to, 'as far as possible' wipe out all the consequences. This phrasing is often overlooked in discussions on reparations, but it speaks to the malleability of the norm to circumstance. Lauterpacht remarked that the phrase 'as far as possible' contains words which have

[68] See UN Security Council (1991) Resolution 687, UN Doc. S/RES/687, para. 16. Wühler 2000, p. 17.

[69] EECC, Decision 7, Guidance Regarding Jus ad Bellum Liability, 27 July 2007, para. 22.

[70] Ibid., para. 32.

[71] *Aloeboetoe et al. v. Suriname* 1993, para. 43; *Papamichalopoulos and Others v Greece 1995,* para. 36.

a 'pronounced elasticity', with its interpretation a 'matter of degree'.[72] International legal obligations on secondary rules of reparations remain under-developed or at least aspirational or 'porous'.[73] Constructive ambiguity is seen by some as a benefit of reparations, allowing it to be 'both normatively thick (so it can be deployed critically) and empirically informed (so that it does not abstract from the peculiarities of transitional contexts)'.[74] This mediated application of the obligation to make reparations for wartime wrongdoing can be seen more recently in the *DRC v Uganda* case, involving Uganda's occupation and annexation of the north-eastern Congolese province of Ituri between 1998 and 2002, as well as damages sustained in other provinces of the DRC.[75] Here the Court did not strictly account for all losses, but arrived at a global sum for evidenced violations as the responsibility of Uganda.[76] This evinced the circumstances of the case, where nearly two decades on from the war, the passage of time made it difficult to sufficiently evidence of the loss and damage caused, many victims had subsequently died or been displaced, and there was a lack of sufficient documentary and testimonial evidence in remote areas of Ituri. Despite the appointment of experts,[77] they were mostly unable to shed further light on these issues, leaving the court to make reasoned estimated of the harm caused 'within the range of possibilities indicated by the evidence.'[78] As a result the Court drawing from the findings of the EECC in drawing from mass claims processes in easing the burden of proof with a proportionate reduction of compensation awarded. Accordingly the case indicates the difficulty of awarding reparations in 'full', but the leading international judges made a concerted effort to provide in the spirit of *Chorzów Factory* redress 'as far as possible'.

The phrasing of 'as far as possible' also suggests the need for proportionality in balancing competing interests in the discharge of the obligation to make reparations. This is apparent in the *Chorzów Factory* dictum, where it speaks of the recognising that wiping out the consequences may not be feasible in restitution terms, thus other forms of reparations may be needed.[79] The obligation to remedy the harm caused is mediated by the need for appropriate reparations, both in terms of that they are proportionate to the gravity of the harm caused and the capacity of the wrongdoer to fulfil it. In the particular context of war reparations, meaningful lessons can be drawn from the 2005 UN Basic Principles on the Right to Remedy and Reparations, which state that reparation 'should be proportional to the gravity of the violations

---

72 Lauterpacht 1977, p. 568.

73 de Greiff 2004, p. 342.

74 de Greiff 2006, p. 14.

75 ICJ, Armed Activities on the Territory of the Congo (*Democratic Republic of the Congo v. Uganda*), Judgment, 19 December 2005 (*DRC v Uganda 2005*), I.C.J. Reports 2005, para. 259; *Reparations Judgment 2022*, paras. 69, 100, and 106.

76 See Fikfak 2022. In this case the Congolese government claimed $11 billion USD in losses, but the Court awarded $325 million USD.

77 See Murphy and Parkhomenko 2023.

78 *Reparations Judgment 2022*, para. 106.

79 *DRC v Uganda 2005*, p. 47.

and the harm suffered'.[80] The 2005 UN Principles may be a soft-law instrument adopted by the UN General Assembly, but nonetheless reflects nearly two decades of discussion and negotiation on the content of the obligations and rights with respect to reparations in peace and war, taking into account the contemporary jurisprudence and domestic reparation laws.[81] The Principles set out five forms of reparations (restitution, compensation, rehabilitation, measures of satisfaction, and guarantees of non-repetition) as part of 'full and effective reparation', which should be 'appropriate and proportional to the gravity of the violation and the circumstances of each case'.[82]

The ILC's Articles on State Responsibility also sets out a number of forms of reparation in order for such measures to be appropriate by being proportionate to the gravity of the breach.[83] This is apparent with restitution, which according to the ILC is intended to,

> re-establish the situation which existed before the wrongful act was committed, provided and to the extent that restitution: (a) is not materially impossible; (b) does not involve a burden out of all proportion to the benefit deriving from restitution instead of compensation.[84]

Similarly, satisfaction should not 'be out of proportion to the injury and may not take a form humiliating to the responsible State.'[85] In both cases, the obligation to make 'full' reparations is moderated by considerations of proportionality. Proportionality in such cases balances the individual right against collective values, such as ensuring that the law is upheld, but does not undermine the political independence of a State or its economic collapse.[86] Similarly Additional Protocol I to the Geneva Conventions states that a responsible party for violations will be liable for compensation 'if the case demands', with the Commentaries outlining that such an obligation is to be 'proportional to the loss suffered'.[87]

Accordingly, reparations to wipe out the injurious consequences of armed conflict 'as far as possible' signifies a more conciliatory approach to remedying wrongdoing. Whilst the law governing reparations cannot be utilised as a means for revenge to bankrupt or destabilise a wrongdoer, it nonetheless requires a substantive engagement

---

[80] UN General Assembly (2005) Basic Principles and Guidelines on the Right to a Remedy and Reparation for Victims of Gross Violations of International Human Rights Law and Serious Violations of International Humanitarian Law, UN Doc. A/RES/60/147, Principle 15.

[81] Evans 2012, pp. 127–128.

[82] UN General Assembly (2005) Basic Principles and Guidelines on the Right to a Remedy and Reparation for Victims of Gross Violations of International Human Rights Law and Serious Violations of International Humanitarian Law, UN Doc. A/RES/60/157, Principle 18.

[83] UN General Assembly (2002) Responsibility of States for Internationally Wrongful Acts, UN Doc. A/RES/56/83, corrected by UN Doc. A/56/49(Vol.I)/corr.4 (ARSIWA) - Restitution, compensation and satisfaction (Articles 35-37), but also makes reference to non-repetition as a remedy (Article 30).

[84] ARSIWA, ibid., Article 35.

[85] Ibid., Article 37.

[86] See Moffett 2023, pp. 58–59; Paparinskis 2020.

[87] Commentaries para. 3652.op

to redress the harm caused. This can be seen from the EECC which was particularly attuned to crippling compensation awards on a responsible State.[88] It held that,

> Huge awards of compensation by their nature would require large diversions of national resources from the paying country—and its citizens needing health care, education and other public services—to the recipient country ... [it is] necessary to limit its compensation awards in some manner to ensure that the ultimate financial burden imposed on a Party would not be so excessive, given its economic condition and its capacity to pay, as to compromise its ability to meet its people's basic needs.[89]

In the case of *DRC v Uganda*, the responsible State highlighted this issue to the ICJ, which considered the EECC's findings, but found the total amount awarded and the five-year period of payment was within 'the capacity of Uganda to pay'.[90] This exhibits the countervailing position of reparations in balancing adequate and effective reparations for victims/injured state, so they are not impossible or humiliating for those responsible to fulfil. As Torres finds, full reparation is rarely applied, instead reparations are about finding a 'pragmatic solution' that is 'instrumental' for states' interests.[91] Such a position may reflect the hard lessons of reparations from the two world wars, but is pragmatic and exhibits the nature of reparations in balancing competing interests to find a legal peace.[92] That said, there remains a significant gap between civilians experiencing harm caused during armed conflict and the obligation to make reparations. This stems from States limiting international laws encroaching on their conduct of hostilities by delimiting what is considered wrongful and the obligation to make reparations.

10.4.2 Reparations for Violations During Armed Conflict

Since the Second World War, international law has both advanced and constrained reparations in relation to violations that occur during armed conflict. Advanced in the sense that the right to reparations has accrued for individuals and collective groups beyond States alongside a range of measures to respond to gross violations of human rights.[93] At the same time, reparations in armed conflict have been constrained, with international humanitarian law not recognising a general individual right to reparations,[94] whereas the limited jurisdiction of human rights bodies in such situations (in particular *vis-à-vis* extraterritorial military operations and collateral damage) being an additional limitation. These contradictions are somewhat captured and

---

88 ASRIWA, Articles 35(b) and 37(3).

89 Eritrea-Ethiopia Claims Commission—Final Award—Eritrea's Damages Claims, 17 August 2009. VOLUME XXVI pp. 505–630, paras. 21–22.

90 *Reparations Judgment 2022*, paras. 110 and 407.

91 Torres 2021, p. 215.

92 See Moffett 2023.

93 See Evans 2012; Ferstman and Goetz 2020.

94 Or collective right to reparation—see Rosenfeld 2010, p. 738.

glossed over in the 2005 UN Basic Principles. While it does set-out victims' rights, it overstates the obligation to make reparations in international humanitarian law and does not address lawful uses of force that cause civilian harm.[95] The International Committee of the Red Cross's IHL customary database suggests, that there is an 'increasing trend' to support the notion that victims of IHL violations have a right to reparations,[96] but this is not substantiated by State practice and *opinio juris.*[97] The practice of institutions such as the International Criminal Court (ICC) awarding reparations to victims of war crimes, and other international crimes committed during armed conflict supports this 'trend'; that is not however a general right to reparations for all victims, but only those who are eligible based on the convicted person and the charges of which they are convicted.[98]

While international humanitarian law governs the conduct of hostilities, it provides little ambit for reparations, with the right to compensation confined to States as rights holders.[99] This position is slowly changing with developments in domestic reparation programmes, as in Colombia, Peru and Philippines, and increasing recognition of the right to reparations for war crimes, such as before the ICC.[100] The most substantive development for reparations in times of armed conflict has come from the recognition of victims' right to remedy and reparations for violations of international human rights law during peace and during wartime. Reparations in human rights law are based on findings of a violation, but rather than remedying the consequences of the breach itself, they are focused on redressing the harm caused to the human.[101] Human rights laws as more *lex specialis* development of the right to remedy, can be complementary to international humanitarian law, especially when dealing not just with State violations, but also those by non-State armed groups.[102] As such, human rights law has moved beyond the *Chorzów Factory* paradigm of responsibility for reparations in two regards: the rights of individuals and groups; and the forms of reparations.

On the one hand, human rights law has shifted the standing to bring claims beyond the inter-State relationship to empower individuals and groups.[103] The PCIJ was reluctant to recognise individual rights under public international law at the time of the *Chorzów Factory* case, finding that reparations are a well-established principle of international law, but they do not 'create direct rights and obligations for private

[95] Germany was one of thirteen countries that abstained from the vote, explaining that it did not equate rights in human rights law to those in IHL, this was during a context of ongoing claims from Italian POWs for compensation that later went before the ICJ. See Echeverria 2017, p. 243.

[96] Rule 150.

[97] Marxsen 2018, p. 535.

[98] Moffett and Sandoval 2021.

[99] Protocol Additional to the Geneva Conventions of 12 August 1949, and relating to the Protection of Victims of International Armed Conflicts (Protocol I), adopted 8 June 1977, Article 91.

[100] See Salmón and Pérez-León-Acevedo 2022.

[101] Shelton 2015, p. 2.

[102] See *Wall Advisory Opinion 2004*, para. 106; and Fortin 2022.

[103] See Boven 2020, p. 17.

individuals' unless it is the 'very object of an international agreement' intended by the parties and can be enforced in national courts.[104] It could be said, that the *Chorzów* dictum that the harm suffered by individuals is a 'convenient scale' for measuring the harm sustained by the State. The evolution of international human rights law in the past 75 years has fundamentally changed this position, creating supranational bodies and a range of conventions that bind States that create such individuals rights.[105] In recent years, the ICJ has recognised individuals have a right to reparations where States violate their human rights obligations as an extension of the *Chorzów Factory* dictum,[106] which is broadly reflective of international norms codified in the 2005 UN Basic Principles. Moreover, the UNCC represented a shift away from the traditional State-centric approach by allowing international organizations, non-governmental organizations (NGOs), and corporations to be beneficiaries,[107] abandoning the 'State-to-State fiction' around an injured party.[108] However, it excluded Iraqi victims from being able to claim.[109]

Human rights law has also developed the form of restitution or compensation, to also include rehabilitation, measures of satisfaction (such as memorials, acknowledgment of responsibility, clarification of facts), and guarantees of non-repetition (institutional and organisational reforms).[110] For instance in the *Mapiripán massacre* case over 100 paramilitaries attacked the town of Mapiripán and detained, tortured, and executed at least 49 civilians, destroying their bodies, and throwing them into a river, displacing the surviving civilians. Finding numerous violations by the Colombian government in its failure to prevent private actors from committing such violence, the Court ordered the State to construct a memorial, provide rehabilitation to survivors and their families, identify, recover, and return the remains of victims to their next of kin, and guarantee the safe return of the survivors to Mapiripán, enabling them to reintegrate into the community and fostering the possibility of future reconciliation.[111] Unlike reparations in general international law, for gross violations of human rights, a combination of these five forms is often needed to adequately and effectively remedy the harm caused, such as torture, disappearance and sexual violence.[112] Indeed, Judge Yusuf in the *DRC v Uganda* case, found the majority's approach in awarding only compensation and the amounts reached was inadequate, taking a

---

[104] PCIJ (1928) *Jurisdiction of the Courts of Danzig (Pecuniary Claims of Danzig Railway Officials who have Passed into the Polish Service, against the Polish Railways Administration)*, Advisory Opinion 3 March 1928 (*Jurisdiction of the Courts of Danzig 1928*), Series B No.15, para. 27.

[105] Furuya 2020.

[106] ICJ, *Ahmadou Sadio Diallo (Republic of Guinea v. Democratic Republic of the Congo)*, Compensation, Judgment, 19 June 2012 (*Compensation Judgment 2012*), ICJ Rep. 2012, para. 17; and *Wall Advisory Opinion 2004*, paras. 152–153.

[107] Romano 1997, p. 362.

[108] Wassgren 1998, p. 488.

[109] Romano 1997, p. 372.

[110] Principles 19–23.

[111] IACtHR, *Case of the "Mapiripán Massacre" v. Colombia*, Judgment (Merits, Reparations, and Costs), 15 September 2005, paras. 305–315.

[112] Boven 2020, p. 37.

'narrow approach' to reparations that lacked consideration of the victims, given the collective dimensions of harm they had suffered the Court should have also awarded rehabilitation and measures of satisfaction.[113] With the majority of armed conflicts since the WWII being non-international armed conflicts, there is also increasing recognition that non-State armed groups have a legal obligation to make reparations and some do make efforts to remedy the harm they cause to civilians, or at least their supporters, through a range of measures, such as compensation, recovery of remains, restitution and apologies.[114]

While human rights law has heralded in a new age of reparations and vindication of victims' rights expanding the scope of remedies in international law, there remain blind-spots in the implementation of redress. This is particularly acute when it comes to over-sea military operations that have characterised many Western counter-insurgency operations in the past twenty-five years where airstrikes and special forces operations has been used to target suspected insurgents. Human rights law has been limited by its own rules on extraterritorial jurisdiction,[115] despite the effect such western militaries cause to civilians and the impunity they enjoy. While we are two decades on from 9/11, and the War on Terror, the 'forever wars' against suspected Islamic insurgents continue in the Middle East, the Sahel and Somalia. Although there have been numerous calls for reparations for Russia's invasion of Ukraine as a war of aggression within Western quarters, calls for redress for the violence carried out by coalition forces in the Middle East, Afghanistan and Africa that caused catastrophic harm to millions of civilians have been muted. The notion of the universality of rights, in particular the right to reparations, remains asymmetrical. In many ways, counter-insurgency operations in the War on Terror continue to be typified by a colonial mindset, wherein the victims of such violence are beyond recognition as legal subjects and worthy of redress. Civilian casualties are sanitised by making them more palpable by their invisibility and distance from countries responsible for such violence. This is apparent from the UK and Dutch's Royal Air Forces maintaining the myth of a 'clean war' that their use of airstrikes against ISIS resulted in little or no civilian casualties, despite their use of thousands of high explosive weapons in densely populated urban areas of Mosul and Raqqa.[116]

What has emerged, is the use of *ex-gratia* monetary awards, such as condolence payments, as no admission of liability settlements to those civilians affected by counter-insurgence operations to win 'hearts and minds' as a 'humanitarian

[113] *Reparations Judgment 2022*, Separate Opinion of Judge Yusuf, paras. 43–46.

[114] See Moffett 2020.

[115] Such as ECtHR, *Bankovíc and Others v. Belgium and others*, Grand Chamber Decision, 12 December 2001, Application no. 52207/99; and ECtHR, *Hanan v Germany*, Grand Chamber Judgment, 16 February 2021, Application no. 4871/16.

[116] PAX, Seeing Through the Rubble The civilian impact of the use of explosive weapons in the fight against ISIS, Airwars (2020); and Van Dort J (2021) Nederland probeert de mythe van de schone oorlog in stand te houden. https://www.trouw.nl/opinie/nederland-probeert-de-mythe-van-de-schone-oorlog-in-stand-te-houden~bc63e9e7/

gesture'.[117] For example, during the battle for Chora in Afghanistan in 2007, the Dutch air force bombed a civilian housing complex that resulted in the death of at least 18 civilians, for which it subsequently paid $10,000 ex-gratia. In 2023, the Dutch courts found that there had a been a failure to distinguish civilians from Taliban fighters, and despite the payments already made, compensation should be paid to the survivors.[118] Dickson suggests, that compensation practice in Europe during conflicts and counter-insurgency operations has been a means to 'buy off' victims, rather than to ensure non-repetition.[119] This practice of 'pay to violate' during an armed conflict, is inherently problematic for the broader goals of reparations in attempting to discourage similar violations recurring. In this way reparations can be gamed, where victims accept a pittance of money in exchange for forgoing future claims, reflecting the State's hegemony to offer victims something in exchange for them dropping any further claims or publicly speaking about such violations. This can be further exacerbated by the vulnerability and precarity of victims who may not be organized, have independent advice, or sufficient economic resources to challenge the State. State practice of 'condolence payments' in Afghanistan and Iraq has been criticized for unequal treatment of payments to victims, refusal to acknowledge responsibility, and a routine and impersonal process that undermines the effects of such measures.[120] Making amends can be seen as a means to 'control the narrative' and avoid individual responsibility.[121] In the United Kingdom there have been only fourteen prosecutions for violations committed during the wars in Iraq and Afghanistan, yet it has paid out £31.8 million in 6,633 cases across the two countries. The UK government's payments in Iraq average around £2,000 per death, despite the civil litigation amount in British courts being over £60,000.[122]

Such payments are often made *ex-gratia* with no legal responsibility attached, exhibiting an 'economic accounting' of harm, but not accountability, allowing a more bureaucratized way of paying for seriously harmed civilians, rather than an obligation to remedy the consequences.[123] This is further complicated in coalition force attacks that cause civilian deaths and losses, where it is difficult to ascertain who was responsible, who has to pay, and how to bring such a claim. The attacks in Yemen by different armed actors are a prime example of this.[124] There are more oblique effects of such payments in distinguishing who is deserving, which can impoverish families of non-State fighters who are killed, imprisoned, or left seriously injured in order to prevent resources being useful to the enemy. A prime example of the exclusion is

---

[117] Rosén 2016, p. 67.

[118] Van de Put S (2023) The Dutch Chora Judgment: Ex-Gratia Payments and Compensation. https://lieber.westpoint.edu/dutch-chora-judgment-ex-gratia-payments-compensation/.

[119] Dickson 2012, p. 300.

[120] Bonds 2019, pp. 369 and 372.

[121] Bijl et al. 2021, p. 284.

[122] Burke and Lattimer 2021, p. 3.

[123] Gilbert 2015, p. 404.

[124] *"Returned to Zero": The Case for Reparations to Civilians in Yemen*, Mwatana for Human Rights and the Allard K. Lowenstein International Human Rights Clinic (2022).

with the victims of the 2015 Hawija bombing, where civilians living near an ISIS bomb factory in northern Iraq were killed when Dutch jets bombed the site, with a secondary explosion devastating the area, killing civilians up to a kilometre away. At least eighty-five civilians were killed in the bombing, dozens more seriously injured, and over 6,000 houses, 1,200 shops, and essential civilian infrastructure destroyed or damaged.[125] While Western coalition forces dropped over 100,000 bombs against ISIS in Syria and Iraq, the Hawija bombing stands out as a case which was neglected for years— it was not reported or investigated until 2019, as those affected were seen as ISIS supporters. The devastation caused by the bombing also meant that civilians became more reliant on ISIS as only supporters of the group could access medical aid.[126] As the incident belatedly came to light in 2019, the Dutch government agreed to provide €4.4 million in community rehabilitation to Hawija through international organizations, but victims want an apology and individual compensation.[127]

Even where violations do occur, victims face a series of hurdles. Foreign sovereign immunity remains a substantive barrier to victims bringing claims in foreign courts. While the ICJ has settled this issue in the *Jurisdictional Immunities* case, it made no reference to the *Chorzów Factory* case, which was only referred to by dissenting Judge Cançado Trindade, who found it 'odd, if not surreal' that such immunity would obviate a State's duty to make reparations for internationally wrongful acts to waive the rights of individual victims that do not belong to the State.[128] Practices of waiving victims' rights away for harms caused in military operations is a common occurrence.[129] Victims who receive condolence payments, are often conditioned on them signing a waiver to any future claims, even if it later emerges that such harm amounts to war crimes.[130] Such practices demonstrate the inequality of bargaining position between civilians harmed by armed conflict and states responsible for their harm. Despite the advances made in realising the rights of victims to reparations, states frame the rules of war to limit their accountability and enforcement for the suffering they cause.

10.5 Conclusion

The *Chorzów Factory* case remains a significant contribution to international law through elucidating the obligation to make reparations for wrongdoing. In the near century since its dictum, reparations have evolved, but also been constrained. Over the past century we have seen a substantive shift from war being prohibited as a

---

[125] See PAX (2022) *After the Strike: Exposing the Civilian Harm Effects of the 2015 Dutch Airstrike on Hawija.* https://protectionofcivilians.org/report/after-the-strike/. Accessed 09 December 2024.

[126] Ibid., pp. 110–111.

[127] Ibid., p. 105.

[128] *Jurisdictional Immunities 2012*, Dissenting Opinion of Judge Cançado Trindade, paras 240–251.

[129] See Bufalini 2017.

[130] See n.124.

State's prerogative, to reparations no longer being considered the spoils of war, but an obligation owed for wrongdoing, to now individual and collective victims have a right to claim redress. However as the last section has underscored, there remains a way to go when it comes to armed conflict. Reparation continues to be a secondary rule, that has not yet been emancipated as a rule in its own right, instead caught on what amounts to wrongdoing in the form of a breach of international obligation or norm under international law. For victims, this means it allows States, often violators, to write the rules that exclude their actions amounting to wrongdoing. This is particularly acute for wars of national liberation, where colonial and successor States waived or failed to articulate victims' demands for redress. If we are serious about remedying harm caused by armed conflict, we need to confront our violent past and our continued illusion of reparations being for all kinds of wrongdoing. Using compensation to simply pay off victims affected by military operations fails to wipe out the consequences felt by civilians as it allows the recurrence of such harms, while at the same time devaluing the lives of those killed and maimed. Despite this, the *Chorzów* dictum provide legal principles to aspire to, which can shape negotiations around reparations to make them feasible so as to as far as possible redress the suffering caused by armed conflict.

Acknowledgement Thanks to the two reviewers and editors for the helpful comments on the initial draft of this chapter.

References

Bazyler M (2003) Holocaust Justice: The Battle for Restitution in America's Courts. New York University Press.

Bennett H, Romijn P (2022) Not an Afterthought: Accountability for Colonial Violence in the Dutch and British Metropoles. In: Brocades Zaalberg T, Luttikhuis B (eds) Empire's Violent End Book Subtitle: Comparing Dutch, British, and French Wars of Decolonization, 1945-1962. Cornell University Press, pp 25–48.

Bijl E, Wels W, Zeijden W (2021) On Civilian Harm: Examining the Complex Negative Effects of Violent Conflict on the Lives of Civilians. Pax.

Bonds E (2019) Callous Cruelty and Counterinsurgency: Civilian Victimization and Compensation in U.S.-Occupied Iraq. Social Currents 6(4): 361–376.

Boven T (2020) Victims' Rights to a Remedy and Reparation: The United Nations Principles and Guidelines. In: Ferstman C, Goetz M (eds) Reparations for Victims of Genocide, War Crimes and Crimes against Humanity Systems in Place and Systems in the Making, 2nd edn. Brill, 15–37.

Brown C (2017) Factory at Chorzów (Germany v Poland) (1927–1928). In: Bjorge E, Miles C (eds) Landmark Cases in Public International Law. Hart.

Bufalini A (2017) On the Power of a State to Waive Reparation Claims Arising from War Crimes and Crimes against Humanity. ZaöRV 77: 447–470.

Burke R, Lattimer M (2021) Reparations for Civilian Harm from Military Operations: Towards a UK Policy. Ceasefire: Centre for Civilian Rights.

Buxbaum R (2013) From Paris to London: The Legal History of European Reparation Claims: 1946–1953. Berkeley Journal of International Law 31(2): 323–347.

Caroli P (2023) German Crimes and Italian Money? Observations on the Sad Saga of Compensation to the Victims of Nazi Atrocities in Italy. Journal of International Criminal Justice 21(1): 211–231.
Clark G (2014) Everyday Violence in the Irish Civil War. Cambridge University Press.
Cobain I (2013) Cruel Britannia: A Secret History of Torture. Portobello.
Dickson B (2012) Counterinsurgency and Human Rights in Northern Ireland. In: Dixon P (ed) The British Approach to Counterinsurgency: From Malaya and Northern Ireland to Iraq and Afghanistan. Springer, pp 291–313.
Echeverria G (2017) The UN Principles and Guidelines on Reparation: Is There an Enforceable Right to Reparation for Victims of Human Rights and International Humanitarian Law Violations? PhD thesis, University of Essex.
Evans C (2012) The Right to Reparation in International Law for Victims of Armed Conflict. Cambridge University Press.
Ferstman C, Goetz M (2020) Reparations for Victims of Genocide, War Crimes and Crimes against Humanity Systems in Place and Systems in the Making, 2nd ed. Brill.
Fikfak V (2022) Establishing Damages for Mass Human Rights Violations. Cambridge Law Journal 81(2): 221–225.
Fischbach M (2021) Nakba Denial: Israeli Resistance to Palestinian Refugee Reparations. In: Bhabha J, Matache M, Elkin C (eds) Time for Reparations: A Global Perspective. University of Pennsylvania Press, pp 183–200.
Fortin K (2022) The Procedural Right to a Remedy When the State has Left the Building? A Reflection on Armed Groups, Courts and Domestic Law. Journal of Human Rights Practice 14(2): 387–414.
Furuya S (2020) The Right to Reparation for Victims of Armed Conflict. In: Correa C, Furuya S, Sandoval C (eds) Reparation for Victims of Armed Conflict. Cambridge University Press, pp 16–91.
Gallen J (2023) Transitional Justice and the Historical Abuses of Church and State. Cambridge University Press.
Gilbert E (2015) The Gift of War: Cash, Counterinsurgency, and 'Collateral Damage'. Security Dialogue 46(5): 403–421.
Gray C (1986) Is There an International Law of Remedies?. British Yearbook of International Law. 56(1): 25–47.
Greenstein C (2020) Patterned Payments: Explaining Victim Group Variation in West German Reparations Policy. International Journal of Transitional Justice 14(3): 381–400.
de Greiff P (2004) Reparation Efforts in International Perspective: What Compensation Contributes to the Achievement of Imperfect Justice. In: Doxtader E, Villa-Vicencio C (eds) Repairing the Irreparable: Reparations and Reconstruction in South Africa. David Phillips, pp 321–358.
de Greiff P (2006) Handbook of Reparations. Oxford University Press.
Gross M (2015) The Ethics of Insurgency: A Critical Guide to Just Guerrilla Warfare. Cambridge University Press.
Gunn G (2011) War Claims and Compensation: Franco-Vietnamese Contention over Japanese War Reparations and the Vietnam War. The Asia-Pacific Journal 9(49): 1–28.
Henig R (1995) Versailles and After: 1919–1933. Routledge.
Henry M (2007) Confronting the Perpetrators: A History of the Claims Conference. Vallentine Mitchell.
Herik L (2012) Addressing 'Colonial Crimes' through Reparations? Adjudicating Dutch Atrocities Committed in Indonesia. Journal of International Criminal Justice 10(3): 693–705.
Humphrey M (2020) Reentering Histories of Past Imperial Violence: Kenya, Indonesia, and the Reach of Transitional Justice. In: Moses AD, Duranti M, Burke R (eds) Decolonization, Self-Determination, and the Rise of Global Human Rights Politics. Cambridge University Press, pp 262–281.

Immler N, Scagliola S (2020) Seeking justice for the mass execution in Rawagede/Probing the concept of 'entangled history' in a postcolonial setting. Rethinking History: The Journal of Theory and Practice 24(1): 1–28.

Kennedy CS, Tucker NB, Lord W (Association for Diplomatic Studies and Training Foreign Affairs Oral History Project) (1998) Interview with Winston Lord (manuscript/mixed material). Retrieved from the Library of Congress, https://www.loc.gov/item/mfdipbib000710/.

Keppy P (2010) The Politics of Redress: War Damage Compensation and Restitution in Indonesia and the Philippines, 1940–1957. Brill.

Koder S (1988) Compensation to Civilian War Victims on Okinawa. Japanese Annual of International Law 31 (1): 58–81.

Kuklick B (1972) American Policy and the Division of Germany: The Clash with Russia over Reparations. Cornell University Press.

Lauterpacht H (1977) International Law: The Law of Peace, Vol.3. Cambridge University Press

Marxsen C (2018) Unpacking the International Law on Reparation for Victims of Armed Conflict. Zeitschrift für ausländisches öffentliches Recht und Völkerrecht 78: 521–540.

Menachery Paulose R, Rogo R (2018) Addressing Colonial Crimes Through Reparations: The Mau Mau, Herero and Nama. State Crime Journal 7(2): 369–388

Moffett L (2020) Violence and repair: The practice and challenges of non-State armed groups engaging in reparations. International Review of the Red Cross 102(915): 1057–1085.

Moffett L (2023) Reparations and War: Finding Balance in Repairing the Past. Oxford University Press.

Moffett L, Sandoval C (2021) Tilting at Windmills: Reparations and the International Criminal Court. Leiden Journal of International Law 34(3): 749–769.

Murphy S, Parkhomenko Y (2023) Now You See Them, Now You Don't: International Court-Appointed Experts, Wartime Reparations, and the DRC v. Uganda Case. Journal of International Humanitarian Legal Studies 14(1): 48–69.

Palmer M (2007) The case of Agent Orange. Contemporary Southeast Asia 29(1): 172–195

Paparinskis M (2020) A Case Against Crippling Compensation in International Law of State Responsibility. Modern Law Review 83(6): 1246–1286.

Payk M (2018) 'What We Seek Is the Reign of Law': The Legalism of the Paris Peace Settlement after the Great War. The European Journal of International Law 29(3): 809–824.

Romano C (1997) Woe to the Vanquished - A Comparison of the Reparations Process after World War I (1914–18) and the Gulf War (1990–91). Austrian Review of International and European Law 2: 361–390.

Rosén F (2016) Collateral Damage: A Candid History of a Peculiar Form of Death. Oxford University Press.

Rosenfeld F (2010) Collective Reparation for Victims of Armed Conflict. International Review of the Red Cross 92(879): 731–746.

Rosoux V (2022) Negotiating Post-Colonial Legacies: Conflicting Justice Notions in the Belgian Case. International Negotiation 28(3): 403–429.

Salmón E, Pérez-León-Acevedo J (2022) Reparation for victims of serious violations of international humanitarian law: New developments. International Review of the Red Cross, 104(919): 1315–1343.

Sarkin J (2009) Colonial Genocide and Reparations Claims in the 21st Century. Greenwood.

Scagliola S, Vince N (2022) The Places, Traces, and Politics of Rape in the Indonesian and the Algerian Wars of Independence. In: Brocades Zaalberg T, Luttikhuis B (eds) Empire's Violent End: Comparing Dutch, British, and French Wars of Decolonization 1945-1962. Cornell University Press, pp 96-199.

Schuker S (1976) The End of French Predominance in Europe: The Financial Crisis of 1924 and the Adoption of the Dawes Plan. University of North Carolina Press.

Seong-Hak Kim M (2022) History Is Not Destiny: Colonial Compensation Litigation and South Korea–Japan Relations. The Journal of Asian Studies 81: 475–491.

Shelton D (2015) Remedies in International Human Rights Law, 3rd edn. Oxford University Press.

Slyomovics S (2021) Repairing Colonial Symmetry: Algerian Archive Restitution as Reparation for Crimes of Colonialism? In: Bhabha J, Matache M, Elkin C (eds) Time for Reparations: A Global Perspective. University of Pennsylvania Press, 201–218.
Stahn C (2020) Reckoning with colonial injustice: International law as culprit and as remedy? Leiden Journal of International Law 33(4): 823–845.
Sullo P, Wyatt J (2014) War Reparations. Max Planck Encyclopedia of Public International Law. Oxford University Press.
Torres F (2021) Revisiting the Chorzów Factory Standard of Reparation—Its Relevance in Contemporary International Law and Practice. Nordic Journal of International Law 90(2): 190–227.
Turgeon L (1973) The Political Economy of Reparations. New German Critique 1.
UNGA (1948) Palestine - Progress Report of the United Nations Mediator, UN Doc. A/RES/194 (III).
UNGA (2020) Progress Report of the Board of the United Nations Register of Damage Caused by the Construction of the Wall in the Occupied Palestinian Territory, UN Doc. A/ES-10/839
UNGA (2022) Furtherance of remedy and reparation for aggression against Ukraine, UN Doc. A/ES-11/L.6.
Van de Put S (2023) Ex Gratia Payments and Reparations: A Missed Opportunity? Journal of International Humanitarian Legal Studies 14: 1–25.
Vince N (2020) The Algerian War, The Algerian Revolution. Springer.
Wagner K (2018) Savage Warfare: Violence and the Rule of Colonial Difference in Early British Counterinsurgency. History Workshop Journal 85: 217–237.
Wassgren H (1998) The UN Compensation Commission: Lessons of Legitimacy, State Responsibility, and War Reparations. Leiden Journal of International Law 11(3): 473–492.
Whitaker P (1970) The Revolutions of 'Portuguese' Africa. The Journal of Modern African Studies 8(1): 15–35.
Wühler N (2000) The United Nations Compensation Commission. In: Permanent Court of Arbitration (ed) Institutional and Procedural Aspects of Mass Claims Settlement Systems. Kluwer Law International.

Chapter 11
Racism as an Obstacle to Reparations for Colonial Crimes? The Doctrine of Intertemporal Law in the German-Namibian Context

Karina Theurer

Contents

Abstract Globally, demands for reparations for colonial crimes grow stronger. The German and Namibian governments were the first ones to negotiate and initial an interstate agreement to come to terms with their past. Unfortunately, they failed to respect, protect and fulfill minimum legal standards such as participation rights of affected communities. And they reproduced colonial patterns, eurocentrism, and racism. In January 2023, a lawsuit was filed against this agreement which could become a historic milestone in the decolonization of law with regard to reparations for colonial crimes. A key question in all of the legal struggles of Ovaherero and Nama for reparations has been which laws applied and were violated during German colonial rule. In this chapter, we will analyse to which extent the application of the doctrine of intertemporal law may be situated between the reproduction of colonial racism and the decolonization of our retrospective reconstruction of the laws at

K. Theurer (✉)
Universität zu Berlin, Unter den Linden 6, 10117 Berlin, Germany
e-mail: karina.theurer@gmail.com

O. Spijkers et al. (eds.), *Netherlands Yearbook of International Law 2022*, Netherlands Yearbook of International Law 53, https://doi.org/10.1007/978-94-6265-627-7_11

the time. It will also be analysed how a decolonized application of the doctrine of intertemporal law might look.

Keywords Reparations · Colonialism · Decolonization · Intertemporal law · Eurocentrism · Racism

11.1 Introduction

International law as we know it today evolved during European colonialism at the end of the 19th and during the 20th century. On the one hand, this newly emerging international law, in its hegemonic (European) interpretation, played a key role in formally legitimizing the systematic violence committed by colonial powers against non-European persons in "their" colonies. On the other hand, there have always been interpretations of the law that have worked to oppose this, but that might have turned out to be counterhegemonic at a certain period, and which now must be (re)discovered. This task is indispensable when we apply the doctrine of intertemporal law and ask ourselves, which laws "really" were in force one hundred years ago, when for instance German colonial troops committed serious colonial crimes in what is today Namibia. This endeavour of reconstructing the laws that "really" were in place 100 years ago, is also highly complex once we acknowledge the existence of a polycentric legal order before European international law was imposed by force and before it began to be recognized as universal. Decolonial and postcolonial scholars—such as Aníbal Quijano, Walter Mignolo, María Lugones, Silvia Rivera Cusicanqui, Oyèrónké Oyěwùmí or Gayatri Spivak—and legal scholars who identify themselves as representatives of Third World Approaches to International Law (TWAIL)—such as Antony Anghie, Makau Mutua, Sundhya Pahuja or James Thuo Gathii—describe the forceful imposition of European knowledge and of European laws at the time of colonialism. They describe what it meant (and means) in terms of power and identity. Their examples revolve around racialization, binary heteronormativity, gender relations, nuclear family, individualistic conceptions of ownership, commodification of goods, and capitalist modes of production, but they also consider an array of intersecting bodies of knowledge that were imposed. An essential feature of decolonial theory and TWAIL is to deconstruct colonial epistemic violence[1] and coloniality of power,[2] to practice epistemic disobedience,[3] to contribute to mitigating the transgenerational social, economic, political, and cultural exclusion of those formerly colonized (and their knowledge and laws), and to strive for substantive equality.[4]

Focusing on the example of the Ovaherero and Nama reparations claims, this chapter traces the extent to which the application of the doctrine of intertemporal law

[1] Spivak 1988.

[2] Quijano 2000; Lugones 2007; see as well Rivera Cusicanqui 1993.

[3] Mignolo 2009; see as well Rivera Cusicanqui 2010.

[4] Mutua 2019; Rivera Cusicanqui 1993; Gathii 2011.

may be situated between the reproduction of colonial racism and the decolonization of our retrospective perception of the laws at the time of German colonialism. It also analyses how a decolonized application of the doctrine of intertemporal law might look. With the exception of the introduction, the chapter consists of two sections: Sect. 11.2 describes the colonial crimes committed in what is today Namibia and outlines the interpretation of the laws in force at the time by German state authorities on the basis of the doctrine of intertemporal law. Section 11.3 analyses how retrospective Eurocentrism and the lack of historical research into the existence of legal pluralism or a polycentric legal order prior to the existence of European *(international) law* as universal *law*, leads to a reproduction of colonial racism. It also analyses how a non-Eurocentred application of the doctrine of intertemporal law in colonial contexts of historical injustice might look. The section considers judgements by the International Court of Justice (ICJ) which might suggest a dynamic interpretation of the second element of the doctrine of intertemporal law. In most legal texts and societal debates, reparations for colonial crimes are thought to be primarily about financial payments. This chapter concludes that reparations for colonial crimes first and foremost should consist of deconstructing colonial racism, refraining from reproducing it, and finding ways of overcoming it.

11.2 The Colonial Crimes in Namibia and the Application of the Doctrine of Intertemporal Law by German and Namibian State Authorities So Far

11.2.1 The Colonial Crimes Committed by Germany

When the first (outnumbered) German traders arrived in what is today Namibia, they signed treaties to purchase land and concluded trade agreements with the local Traditional Authorities, Chiefs and Capteins. At that time, Bismarck was still favouring the idea of chartered companies as a central feature of German colonialism. Ovaherero, Nama, Ovambo, Damara and San were racialized and racially despised, but nevertheless perceived as nations or tribes, that is, as political and social entities from whom land or cattle could be bought, or with whom alliances could be established in view of armed conflicts (so-called protection treaties).[5] Already during the 1890s, the German military committed massacres of the civilian population and there was already armed resistance against the colonial invasion and violence, both in the South of what is today Namibia, and in the Centre, for instance by Hendrik Witbooi or Kahimemua and Nikodemus.[6]

[5] See Zimmerer 2021, pp. 20–26; for a detailed analysis on the contradictory assessment of the legal nature of these contracts from a contemporary German perspective see: Hanschmann 2014.

[6] One example is the Hornkranz massacre in 1893 under Curt von François. For detailed information on the armed conflicts and early resistance fights, see Zimmerer 2021, pp. 22–26; Hillebrecht 2008, pp. 143–158.

By the end of the 19th century, nationalist rivalries between European empires intensified, and in 1884, Bismarck took the step of formal colonial rule in Namibia.[7] The increasing number of settlers and traders arriving led to more land grabbing, expropriation of livestock and other natural resources, flagrant racial discrimination and systematic sexual violence against women and girls. Impoverishment resulting from the systematic colonial transfer of wealth, violent racialized oppression, a rinderpest epidemic in 1897, and drought years between 1899 and 1902—led to the conflict intensifying.[8] In January 1904, Samuel Maharero headed an armed resistance by Ovaherero which threw back the colonial troops to a few garrisons in the centre of what is today Namibia. This was possible because most of the colonial troops were still in the south fighting an armed resistance by the Bondelswarts-Nama around Warmbad. Fearing a loss of prestige amongst European powers, the German government decided to send more troops and to hand over military command to Lothar von Trotha. He was well known for his racist convictions. In August 1904, he attacked the Ovaherero at Ohamakari, at the Waterberg. When his initial plan to enclose the Ovaherero did not turn out and the Ovaherero fled towards the Omaheke, he commanded the troops to seal off the desert. The water in the few fountains was systematically poisoned and fugitives that tried to escape were driven back into the desert. Thousands of people and cattle died of thirst or hunger, including women and children. In October 1904, Lothar von Trotha proclaimed a second extermination order against the Nama, who had taken up arms again in the south to fight German colonial rule. During that time, concentration camps were established, including one at Lüderitz, where people were forced to do forced labour until death to build the nearby railway tracks. Women and girls were systematically raped, and forced to scrape flesh from skulls, which were subsequently shipped to Germany for "research purposes".

A distinct body of laws was created that applied exclusively to "non-white" inhabitants of the German colony. This *apartheid* system enabled the inclusion of the indigenous inhabitants as German 'subjects,' but not as 'citizens'.[9] The colonial laws were not created by a legislative body but by the colonial administration itself. The same colonial administration had authority to execute these regulations and to act as judges. The system was openly racist, and it was practically impossible for non-white persons to have arbitrary decisions reviewed in local courts.[10] In sum, the apartheid regime was designed to convey a sense of lawlessness, inferiority and impotence to non-white persons and their representatives.

---

[7] Kössler 2015, pp. 49–58.

[8] Zimmerer 2021, pp. 17–35.

[9] Koskenniemi 2016, p. 275.

[10] In detail on this racist dual legal system: Fischer-Lescano 2022; Hanschmann 2014; on the hybrid character of these laws between international public law and domestic laws: Koskenniemi 2016, pp. 249–251 and 275–277.

11.2.2 The Doctrine of Intertemporal Law as Interpreted by German and Namibian State Authorities

The doctrine of intertemporal law is widely recognized today. It is used to determine what laws apply if the moment of legal adjudication is posterior to the relevant facts. Its aim is to ensure legal certainty in matters of international law. The doctrine as we know it today was developed in international jurisprudence at the beginning of the 20th century. It is closely linked to the doctrine of non-retroactivity of international treaties as enshrined in the Vienna Convention on the Law of Treaties. Most legal scholars and the International Court of Justice (ICJ) invoke two elements when they apply it. These two elements were originally defined in 1929, by Max Huber, who was a Judge of the Permanent Arbitration Court then. It is important to note that the matter he had to resolve was a dispute on territorial sovereignty that dated back to the 16th century but also depended on changes in laws since then until the 19th century. Max Huber in 1929 defined the first element as follows:

> "a juridical fact [is] appreciated in the light of the law contemporary with it, and not the law in force at the time when a dispute in regard to it arises."[11]

And the second element reads as follows:

> "As regards the question which of different legal systems prevailing at successive periods is to be applied in a particular case (the so-called intertemporal law), a distinction must be made between the creation of rights and the existence of rights. The same principle which subjects the act creative of a right to the law in force at the time the right arises, demands that the existence of the right, in other words its continued manifestation, shall follow the conditions required by the evolution of law."[12]

Amongst legal scholars, the second element of the doctrine of intertemporal law is highly controversial. Some argue that the second element only plays a role in disputes on territory.[13] Ulf Linderfalk refutes this position by outlining carefully that intertemporal law is about the applicability of international legal norms *ratione temporis*. He describes that, in essence, the dispute Max Huber had to resolve was about facts that can create rights and the application of laws that had changed over time, and which determine the ongoing existence of rights that originate in certain facts. He emphasizes that the second element is no exception to the first element.[14] In an article dated 2021, Steven Wheatley points to the epistemological challenges of intertemporal law. In particular, he shows how different conceptions of time lead to different conclusions.[15] He analyses the Advisory Opinion issued by the International Court of Justice on Chagos, that will be described in more detail in Sect. 11.3 and concludes convincingly that the ICJ has given pathway to a dynamic interpretation of

[11] PCA, *Island of Palmas (United States v. Netherlands)*, Decision, 4 April 1929, II RIAA, p. 845.

[12] Ibid.

[13] Higgins 1997.

[14] Linderfalk 2011.

[15] Wheatley 2021.

law via the second element of intertemporal law. About this dynamic interpretation of law, he writes:

> During the transition period from the old rule to the new, when there is some evidence that the law is changing, but not sufficient evidence to show that the law has changed, the old rule must be applied, because there is no guarantee that the law will change. Once the law has changed, however, we must apply the new rule from the moment of its crystallization. This will include the period between the moment of crystallization (identified with the benefit of hindsight) and the period when there is general agreement that the new rule is to be applied, even though, at the time, we would have applied the old rule. In other words, the second branch explains that our conclusions about the applicable law on a given day, during a period of transition in the law, can change, depending on when we examine the available evidence of state practice and *opinio juris*.[16]

As mentioned, the International Court of Justice and the Inter-American Court of Human Rights issued a few judgments, in which they had to determine the laws in force at the time within contexts of formal colonial rule. They will be elaborated further on in Sect. 11.3.

The German government has described its legal assessment of the laws in force at the time of German colonial rule in what is today Namibia in the most detailed manner in front of a District Court in the United States: Based on the Alien Torts Claims Act, which until recently made it possible for claims to be brought against foreign governments in specific cases of torts committed in violation of international law abroad, representatives of Ovaherero and Nama had filed an application against the German state in 2017.[17] The objectives of their lawsuit were: to force the German government to include them in the ongoing negotiations on reparations that the German and Namibian governments had initiated in 2015;[18] and to receive reparations for the genocide and further colonial crimes committed against them. In 2021, the Supreme Court decided to close the case due to lack of jurisdiction. Nevertheless, the public awareness that the lawsuit was able to rise, contributed to making the cause and the respective legal arguments more known worldwide.

In a nutshell, the German government concluded that no laws were violated when Ovaherero and Nama were deliberately and systematically killed during 1904 and 1908. The German government did not really mention the second element of the doctrine of intertemporal law but relied primarily on the first element of the doctrine. With regard to international laws of war and international humanitarian law, the German government argued that these rules were only applicable to international conflicts between states and only between those states that had ratified relevant

[16] Ibid.

[17] District Court, S.D. New York, *Vekuii Rukoro et al v Federal Republic of Germany*, Civ. No. 17-0062, filed on 5 January 2017. An amended complaint was filed on 14 February 2018 by the Plaintiffs.

[18] For more background information on those interstate negotiations and why they were unlawful in terms of international law: Theurer 2023c.

treaties.[19] The representatives of Ovaherero or Nama—according to the German government's interpretation of the laws at the time—were incapable of signing the treaties that might have granted international legal protection to their citizens because they had no legal subjectivity within international law.[20] When determining the legal subjectivity of Ovaherero and Nama, the German government relied on the differentiation between "civilized" and "uncivilized" nations. This categorization enabled the exclusion of "non-white" nations from the circle of legal subjects in newly emerging international law. As a result—according to the German government—international law did not apply and the Ovaherero and Nama were living under German jurisdiction, with German colonial law applying in what was today Namibia.[21] With regard to basic principles of humanity and rules on humanitarian protection in non-international armed conflicts, the German government argued that those only came to exist 40 years later, when they were first enshrined in Article 3 common to the Geneva Conventions of 12 August 1949.[22] With regard to genocide specifically, the German government argued, that this crime was only codified in the United Nations Convention in 1949, and as a result, did not exist as a crime before.

This legal argumentation based on the differentiation between "civilized" and "uncivilized" nations—in essence—was also brought forward by the Scientific Service of the German Federal Parliament (Bundestag) in 2016. The Scientific Service analysed whether the laws at the time had been violated by German state actors at the beginning of the 20th century in what is today Namibia. It argued that international treaties were not violated as the Ovaherero and Nama had no legal subjectivity and could not have become treaty members. When the Scientific Service analysed customary international humanitarian laws and basic principles of humanity, it argued that—first of all, the Hague Convention of 1899 codified the rules of the law of war that were part of customary law at that time.[23] It stated explicitly that, in particular, the so-called Martens clause in paragraph 7 of the preamble of the Hague Convention was interpreted such that the precepts of humanity and civilization prohibited genocide, regardless of the existence of a war between two states. Examples for a corresponding legal conviction are—according to the academic service of the German Bundestag—the condemnation of the Turkish massacre of the Armenians in the years 1894–1896 by France, the United Kingdom, and Russia as "crimes against humanity and civilization." Kaiser Wilhelm II had also distanced himself from the actions of the Ottomans.[24] Then the document reads as follows:

---

[19] *Vekuii Rukoro et al v Federal Republic of Germany*, Defendants Memorandum of Law in Support of Defendant's Motion to Dismiss, filed on 13 March 2018, 17 cv 00062 (LTS), p. 7.

[20] Ibid.

[21] *Vekuii Rukoro et al v Federal Republic of Germany* Defendants Memorandum of Law in Support of Defendant's Motion to Dismiss, filed on 12 January 2018, 17 cv 00062 (LTS), pp. 4–5.

[22] *Vekuii Rukoro et al v Federal Republic of Germany,* Defendants Memorandum of Law in Support of Defendant's Motion to Dismiss, filed on 13 March 2018, 17 cv 00062 (LTS), p. 7.

[23] Wissenschaftlicher Dienst des Bundestages 2016, p. 9.

[24] Ibid., p. 13.

> "However, this legal view was limited to members of the community of international law, which at the time consisted largely of European states. Indigenous peoples were, according to the prevailing view, "uncivilized" and thus excluded from the aforementioned principles [...] Only a minority considered indigenous peoples as subjects of international law of their own kind."[25]

As evidence for this prevailing opinion, the German academic service quotes only a scarce number of legal scholars who published at the beginning of the 20th century, and it quotes exclusively European sources. It is questionable whether the underlying data actually supports the conclusion drawn. The next section will get back to this point.

The German government confirmed this specific application of the doctrine of intertemporal law and its specific interpretation of the laws at the time in the Joint Declaration that both the German and the Namibian government initialled in May 2021. This text is the final result of their interstate negotiations on the reappraisal of the colonial crimes committed in what is today Namibia and that started in 2015. In clause 10, both governments state that the acts committed against the Ovaherero and Nama constituted genocide, but only from today's perspective. In clause 11, the German government only accepts a moral responsibility, and refuses any legal responsibility. In a nutshell, the Joint Declaration reproduces the legal argumentation by the German government denying that any laws were violated during 1904 to 1908. It thus also reproduces retrospectively the deeply racist differentiation between "civilized" and "uncivilized" nations that was at the core of excluding non-European nations from the "family of nations" within the newly emerging international (legal) order. As will be shown in detail in the following section, this specific determination of the laws in force at the time is profoundly problematic and unlawful. In the lawsuit Swartbooi *et al.,* which is still pending in front of the Namibian High Court, Patrick Kauta argues (*inter alia*) that by accepting this racist legal assessment, the Namibian cabinet might have violated its legal duty to refrain from reproducing colonial patterns.[26] In the lawsuit, Kauta asks the court to declare as unlawful and set aside the Joint Declaration.[27]

[25] Ibid., pp. 13–14.

[26] The lawsuit is still pending in front of the Namibian High Court. The founding affidavit and the supplementary affidavits were filed on 19 and 20 January 2023. All the documents can be accessed over the Namibian E-Justice-System inserting the case number: HC-MD-CIV-MOT-REV-2023/00023; see as well: Theurer 2023a.

[27] In detail: Theurer 2023c.

11.3 The Doctrine of Intertemporal Law as Bottleneck for Overcoming Colonial Racism

11.3.1 The Application of the Doctrine of Intertemporal Law by the ICJ and the Inter-American Court of Human Rights in Colonial Contexts

The difficulty of reconstructing a legal situation that existed a hundred years ago without reproducing European preconceptions and without being biased on the history of international law can be illustrated by a judgment the International Court of Justice took in 2002. The court had to resolve a dispute between Nigeria and Cameroon over the Bakassi Peninsula.[28] The relevant facts at least partly dated back to the end of the 19th century. On 10 September 1884, the Kings and Chiefs of Old Calabar signed a "Treaty of Protection" with Great Britain. The ICJ had to decide whether the Kings and Chiefs of Old Calabar had legal subjectivity under international law at the end of the 19th century. Ultimately, the question was whether transfer of title and sovereignty over the Bakassi Peninsula to Great Britain had occurred. The ICJ concluded that the Kings and Chiefs had no legal subjectivity because:

> Some treaties were entered into with entities which retained thereunder a previously existing sovereignty under international law. This was the case whether the protected party was henceforth termed 'protectorat' (as in the case of Morocco, Tunisia and Madagascar (1885; 1895) in their treaty relations with France) or "a protected State" (as in the case of Bahrain and Qatar in their treaty relations with Great-Britain). In sub-Saharan Africa, however, treaties termed "treaties of protection" were entered into not with States, but rather with important indigenous rulers exercising local rule over identifiable areas of territory. [...] In relation to a treaty of this kind in another part of the world, Max Huber, sitting as sole arbitrator in the Island of Palmas case, explained that such a treaty *'is not an agreement between equals; it is rather a form of internal organization of a colonial territory, on the basis of autonomy of the natives ... And thus suzerainty over the native states becomes the basis of territorial sovereignty as towards other members of the community of nations.'* (RIIA, Vol. II, pp. 858–859.)[29]

Edward Martin rightly (and a bit sarcastically) points out that "sub-Saharan (...) rulers" were quite likely to have had a different view on that matter. This comment goes right to the core of decolonial critical approaches to international law: Whose perspective are we to take when we determine and interpret the laws in force at the time? Whose perspective counts when in 2002 legal experts must determine the legal subjectivity of European and non-European entities in 1884 on the African continent? According to the particularly racist European perspective that was used to formally legitimize European colonialism, the African rulers were not able to represent their entities and they did not have any legal subjectivity within the newly emerging legal order. If we take the perspective of the African traditional leaders,

---

[28] ICJ, *Land and Maritime Boundary between Cameroon and Nigeria (Cameroon v. Nigeria; Equatorial Guinea Intervening)*, Judgment, 10 October 2002, ICJ Rep. 2002, p. 404.
[29] Ibid., para 205.

their legal subjectivity at the end of the 19th century would most probably be affirmed. Often, European legal scholars and state representatives during colonialism argued that African rulers did not exercise effective control over their territories. Edward Martin rightly refutes this assumption at least with regard to the political entities in the regions above mentioned and confirms that they—according to historical research—had exercised effective control over their territories and the inhabitants at the end of the 19th century.[30] Awn Shawkat Al-Khasawneh, who was a judge at the International Court of Justice in 2002, when the latter issued this judgment, condemned the findings of the court as Eurocentric and as a reproduction of colonial stereotypes. In his Separate Opinion to this judgment, he wrote:

> "[S]uch an approach is clearly rooted in a Eurocentric conception of international law based on notions of otherness, as evidenced by the fact that there were at the time in Europe protected principalities without anyone seriously entertaining the idea that they had lost their sovereignty to the protecting Power and could be disposed of at its will."[31]

The next section will elaborate further on this crucial question of perspective, and how the European bias and the retrospective imposition of European (racist) preconceptions could be mitigated.

Before we proceed to that, the importance of the second element of the doctrine of intertemporal law must be highlighted. As shown above, the German government and the German Scientific Service in 2016 did not even mention the second element. It seems that the second element might be of importance for the quest of decolonizing international law and for overcoming the colonial racist perspective interwoven into international law. In his Separate Opinion to the 2002 ICJ judgment, that I mentioned above, Judge Al-Khasawneh highlighted the importance of the second element of the doctrine of intertemporal law. He wrote:

> "At any rate, intertemporal law as formulated by Max Huber is not as static as some would like to think, for it should not be forgotten that its elusiveness is further increased by his immediately following statement that 'the existence of the right, in other words, its continued manifestation, shall follow the conditions required by the evolution of law'."[32]

In 1971, in the first progressive declaration on the legal status of Namibia by the ICJ, the Court had also put emphasis on the second element of the doctrine of intertemporal law. The International Court of Justice had to assess the United Nations General Assembly Resolution 2145 of 27 October 1966 and the notion of "sacred trust" that was contained within the Mandate given to Great Britain in 1920 and exercised by South Africa. In its advisory opinion, it had to determine the legal status of Namibia and whether the continuing presence of South Africa in Namibia was lawful. When interpreting the notion of "sacred trust", the South African government had based its argumentation on the colonial reality at the time the treaty was concluded, and thus strongly on the first element of the doctrine of intertemporal

[30] Martin 2021, pp. 27, 52–56.

[31] Al-Khasawneh 2002, p. 496.

[32] Ibid., p. 502.

law. The ICJ however, focused on the development towards the right of peoples to self-determination. It concluded that the notion of "sacred trust" in the League Convention was to be interpreted according to present day ideas about self-determination.[33] Clearly, the ICJ used the second element to overcome colonial conceptions and to pave way for the "new" principle of self-determination. As described above, Steven Wheatley also reads this advisory opinion as a proof of the ICJ using the second element for dynamic interpretation of international law.

In 2019, the ICJ issued a second advisory opinion in which it confirmed the dynamic interpretation of the laws in force at the time. In a sovereignty dispute between the United Kingdom and Mauritius over the Chagos Archipelago, which the British had detached from the territory of Mauritius in 1965 shortly before its independence, the ICJ had to determine to whom the Archipelago belonged. The British based their legal arguments strongly on the first element of the doctrine of intertemporal law, stating that at the time of detachment, the right to self-determination had not been recognized as customary international law. According to the ICJ however, the right to self-determination was in the process of being established during that time and subsequently held that the British could not rightfully argue that this right did not exist yet back then.[34]

In 1993, the Inter-American Court of Human Rights issued a decision that shows a dynamic interpretation of the law and the process of overcoming bodies of knowledge that were inscribed into law during colonialism but are considered to violate basic human rights today. It decided that—as an exception to the rule of prohibition of retroactive application of peremptory norms to treaties[35]—no treaty that contains provisions on slavery and thus today "contradicts the norms of *jus cogens superveniens* [...] may be invoked before an international human rights tribunal'.[36] This judgement can be read as being part of a process of constitutionalizing international law, with norms of *ius cogens* being at the top of a hierarchy of legal norms.

[33] ICJ, *Legal Consequences for States of the Continued Presence of South Africa in Namibia (South-West Africa) notwithstanding Security Council Resolution 276* (1970), Advisory Opinion, 21 June 1971, ICJ Rep. 1971, p. 16.

[34] ICJ, *Legal Consequences of the separation of the Chagos Archipelago from Mauritius in 1965*, Advisory Opinion, 25 February 2019, ICJ Rep. 2019, p. 95.

[35] International Law Commission 2001, p. 58: 'even when a new peremptory norm of general international law comes into existence, as contemplated by article 64 of the 1969 Vienna Convention, this does not entail any retrospective assumption'.

[36] IACtHR, *Aloeboetoe y otros vs. Surinam (Reparaciones y Costas)*, 10 September 1993, Serie C No. 15, para 57.

11.3.2 Decolonial Perspectives on the Laws in Force at the Time in Southern Africa as Part of the Legal Question of Reparations for Colonial Crimes in the German-Namibian Context

The difficulty of adjudicating historical injustice today and reconstructing laws that were in force 100 years ago is also reflected by the academic debate on that topic. Given that international law as we know it today was only beginning to emerge during the 19th century,[37] most legal scholars today agree that a kind of polycentric legal order, pluralist legal order or regionalism of international law existed before European international law became universal.[38]

Departing from that premise, several questions arise: If several legal orders existed, what do we know about the content of these legal orders regarding the region that is today Namibia? Which meta-rules or conflict of law rules might have governed cases with connections to more than one jurisdiction? What are the limits of retrospectively reconstructing legal norms that might have been part of a legal order different to the European one that became universal? Which legal debates and controversies existed during processes of European colonization that might have confronted racist notions such as the differentiation between "civilized" and "uncivilized" nations? How can we determine the laws in force at the time if we conclude that legal controversies were not yet resolved at the end of the 19th century? Do we then determine from todays' perspective as Steven Wheatley suggests when he defines the scope and content of the second element of intertemporal law? What might that mean for the question of legal subjectivity of non-European nations?

About transatlantic chattel slavery, Patrick Robinson, who serves as a judge at the International Court of Justice, wrote a highly interesting article: In it, he criticizes that international law literature is selective—and biased—when it examines state practice and the existence of customary laws prior to the 19th century. Regarding transatlantic chattel slavery, he quotes several acts of state practice that show that this practice was considered to be unlawful in Europe at least by some judges, lawyers and legal scholars. By exposing these contemporary controversies, he shows that the general ascertainment that slavery was not unlawful during the onset of European imperialism is simplistic, and ultimately wrong.[39] From a decolonial perspective, these reconstructions of controversies amongst European lawyers and legal scholars are essential in processes of adjudicating historical injustices. As shown above, governments that are confronted with demands for reparations for colonial crimes, as Germany, tend to argue that the crimes according to the prevailing opinion of lawyers and legal scholars were not unlawful at the time, and it is important to confront them with their lack of thorough research into the history of international law. Patrick Robinson

---

[37] With further references Koskenniemi 2011, pp. 153–155; Koskenniemi 2002.

[38] Kämmerer 2016; Hébié 2023, at 36:00.

[39] Robinson 2021.

goes further with his decolonial approach. He demands that non-European voices be included into the research on the laws in force at the time. In particular, he writes:

> A determination as to whether transatlantic chattel slavery was wrongful under customary international law at the time it was carried out is flawed if it is confined to an examination of European practice; there must also be an examination of the law, practice and customs of the place where the transaction of enslavement, that is, the capture and sale of West Africans, took place—West Africa; there must also be an examination of the law in other regions of the world.[40]

As described, neither the German government nor the Scientific Service of the Bundestag in 2016 did thorough research into the question when exactly the international polycentric legal order was substituted by the newly emerging European international law. They did not quote a single non-European legal scholar. They did not prove substantively whether "really" the racist differentiation between "civilized" and "uncivilized" nations was the "prevailing opinion" at the end of the 19th century. Instead, they simply assumed. They simply affirmed. And it seems that their assumptions might be more racist than the legal debate at the end of the 19th century actually was. In this vein, it is important to remember as well that sometimes powerful actors decide to act against existing laws, but their actions remain unlawful even if they manage to be victorious by force. It is very telling that Lothar von Trotha stated the following: "It goes without saying that war in Africa cannot be waged solely according to the Geneva Convention. […] A nation does not perish so quickly. My proclamation to the Herero nation had the purpose of making them aware of only one thought, namely that their rule was over."[41] If really Lothar von Trotha had thought that no humanitarian laws applied in the German colony, he would not have expressed himself the way he did. And the fact that he deliberately decided not to comply with those legal norms certainly does not prove he acted in a lawful way.

Matthias Goldmann, a German legal scholar who has been working on the topic of colonial crimes in Namibia for several years, contributed an expert affidavit to the lawsuit in front of the US Southern District Court in 2018. In this declaration, he describes the controversies and contradictions about the legal nature of protection treaties concluded by the German Empire with representatives of the Ovaherero and Nama, such as Samuel Maharero or several Nama captains.[42] He suggests that the contradictions indicate that the question of legal subjectivity was, at the very least, unresolved. And he concludes that these treaties could be defined as international treaties.[43] Felix Hanschmann also reconstructs the ambiguities and contradictions within German legal academic debate with regard to those treaties concluded with Ovaherero and Nama representatives.[44] Martti Koskenniemi in detail describes that the criteria of the differentiation between "civilized" and "uncivilized" nations were

---

[40] Ibid., p. 174.

[41] The quote was published in a newspaper article on 3 February 1909 in the Berliner Neueste Nachrichten, titled 'Politics and Warfare' (29th volume, No. 60, from page 1).

[42] Goldmann 2018.

[43] Ibid., pp. 15-20.

[44] Hanschmann 2014.

unclear at the end of the 19th century and that the Belgian Institute of International Law for that reason even abandoned an attempt to formulate a legal definition.[45] It is also not correct to conclude that not even a basic legal protection was granted to so-called "uncivilized" nations within the newly emerging international law, as the German government and the Scientific suggest. As Kenneth MacCallion argued in front of the lawsuit in the United States in 2017 already, Johann Caspar Bluntschli, a renowned theorist of the newly developing international law and a Professor at Heidelberg University wrote that:

> "Simply because certain peoples are considered [uncivilized], they should still be treated humanely, and one may not simply deprive them of human rights. They are perhaps difficult to subject to a legal order, and teaching them the ways of civilization may perhaps be a thankless task that requires great effort and potentially meager results. However, it is nonetheless the job and indeed the obligation of civilized nations, to try and promote civilized conduct in even the wildest of tribes, and help them achieve the heights of human dignity. Never again is it permitted for states or soldiers to hunt for wild peoples like foxes and wolves."[46]

It seems clear that any conclusion any judge, lawyer or legal scholar would want to draw on the matter of legal subjectivity of non-European representatives of polities and social entities before European international law clearly became universal would need to be based on thorough historical research. It does not suffice to depart from one's own personal stereotypes and unscientific preconceptions—as the German government and the German Scientific Service seem to have done in the above-mentioned legal assessments.

In an online dialogue entitled "International Law and Reparations for Colonial Harms: What Way Forward?" Mamadou Hébié criticizes the presumptuous entitlement to universality of European international law on the onset of European colonialism. In a slightly confrontational manner but right to the point on the matter he compares this presumptuous claim of universality with people living on the earth feeling entitled to determine laws by which people living on Mars or Venus are to be bound by.[47] He argues that it is indispensable to have a close look at precisely the moment in time when European colonialism started, and when undoubtedly the few people arriving on three ships in Haiti had in reality not brought universal law but were at the mercy of the people living there. Furthermore he argues that it is necessary to do more research into the legal norms that applied to the relations between colonial powers and local entities, particularly at the beginning of the processes of colonization, and into what he coins the regionalism of international law.[48] These remarks go right to the core of the application of the doctrine of intertemporal law in the German-Namibian context. As mentioned already, further historical research is necessary into when exactly European international law substituted former legal orders and became universal. Furthermore, it is necessary to know which legal regimes governed relations within Ovaherero, Nama, Damara or San polities or communities, which legal

[45] Koskenniemi 2002, pp. 127–143.

[46] Bluntschli 1868, at cmt. 2 to § 535, 299.

[47] Hébié 2023.

[48] Ibid., at 20:30 and 36:00; see as well: Hébié 2016; and Hébié 2015.

norms applied between these entities, and between them and the German colonial power, at the end of the 19th century, and during the relevant period, thus between 1904 and 1908.[49]

The Basel Archives (Namibia Resource Center) and the National Archives in Windhoek hold an immeasurable treasure of original documents. Amongst them are letters by Hendrik Witbooi and letters written by (Tjamuaha) Maharero and Samuel Maharero, in which they exchange views on laws of war and humanitarian laws.[50] In one of Hendrik Witbooi's letters to Hermanus van Wyk, dated 18 April 1893, he described the massacre of Hoornkrans committed by the German troops:

> And the Captain [von François] entered the camp and sacked it in so brutal a manner as I would never have thought a member of a White civilised nation capable of—nation which knows the rules and ways of war. But this man robbed me, and killed little children at their mother's breast, and older children, and women, and men. Corpses of people who had been shot he burned inside our grass huts, burning their bodies to ash. Sadly and terrifyingly, Captain went to work, in a shameful operation.[51]

This extract shows that Witbooi expected rules of war and humanitarian laws to be applied and to be respected. In particular, he criticizes the killing of children and the treatment of corpses. Whether he refers to precolonial rules or to the European international rules on war and humanitarian laws is unclear though. In a letter to Maharero dated January 5, 1890, Hendrik Witbooi reiterates the difference between soldiers and civilian population and affirms that women and children as non-combatants deserved protection in armed conflicts:

> While I was away you came and destroyed my settlement. You killed women and abducted children. Concerning the death of the men I will not say anything. [...] Now I ask you seriously: what moved you to kill my women and to carry my children away as prisoners? [...] Women and children are innocent of our conflict.[52]

Matthias Goldmann frames the approach to "reconstruct normative frameworks governing colonial encounters" and to "juxtapose colonial international law with autochthonous views of inter-polity law" as pluralistic approaches.[53] In his article he offers a very rich overview and analysis of letters by Ovaherero and Nama representatives that allows us to counter what he frames as conventional approaches, such as the position taken by the German government and the Scientific Service of the Bundestag described above.[54]

Of course, the attempt to reconstruct legal orders that existed prior to European international law becoming universal, or the attempt to reconstruct laws as they were in force in specific regions such as the southwestern part of Africa prior to German colonization, is difficult for several reasons. Firstly, because of the substitution and

---

[49] Theurer 2023c; Theurer and Kaleck 2020; Theurer 2019.

[50] See as well Lau 1995; Hillebrecht 2014.

[51] Lau 1995, p. 126.

[52] Lau 1995, p. 39.

[53] Goldmann 2023.

[54] Ibid., pp. 8–16.

partly erasure of indigenous knowledge, the sources are limited. Often, knowledge, was transmitted orally. Secondly, as Martti Koskenniemi rightly describes about legal concepts and histories of international law:

> But legal and political concepts are parts of the legal language of each period; their meaning cannot be grasped without a grasp of that language. [...] [H]istories of international law come to us through the historian's own conceptual prejudices [...][55]

He uses the notion of conceptual imperialism to describe the retrospective imposition of European concepts when legal scholars try to reconstruct "other" legal systems with probably best intentions in a decolonial vein. He rightly makes the point that:

> But as Onuma has pointed out, to the extent that [early postcolonial works by C.H. Alexandrowicz, R.P. Anand and T.O. Elias, for example] have been written in the vein of 'they, too, had an international law', they ended up, once again projecting European categories as universal.[56]

The decolonial scholar Silvia Rivera Cusicanqui points to yet another risk of retrospectively reconstructing not only "other" laws and legal orders, but also "other" concepts of gender, family, collective ownership, or whole cosmogonies: These knowledges and concepts have not stayed static since colonization but have partly merged into new hybrid concepts of law or gender or ownership. Focusing not on these new hybrid concepts but on the "original" laws or concepts when adjudicating legal claims or granting rights, such as in the context of territorial rights based on ancestral lands, bears the risk of anchoring indigenous communities in the past.[57]

In sum, it is indispensable to deconstruct Eurocentric perspectives and racist assumptions in our interpretations of histories of international law, and when we determine the laws that were in force at the time, but we also need to be aware that whenever we reconstruct, we do so from a very specific perspective and point in time. With respect to the retrospective reconstruction of ethical and legal principles and the distinction between them 100 years ago, Andreas von Arnauld rightly speaks of a "pluralist blurring of the lines between *lex lata* and *lex ferenda*, between legality and illegality".[58] For those and the other reasons previously described, as Edward Martin describes, it might not always be possible to determine with complete certainty which legal norms "really" were in force during a certain period. That might be the case during that period while a polycentric global legal order or, as Mamadou Hébié puts it, regionalism in international law, still existed, before European international law really became universal. As Mamadou Hébié emphasized, this process can only be considered as completed during the second half of the 20th century, certainly not on the onset of European colonialism.[59] As Matthias Goldmann rightly points to little knowledge legal historical research still has on meta-rules of the scope and order of

[55] Koskenniemi 2011, p. 166.

[56] Koskenniemi 2011, p. 168; Chakrabarty 2001, p. 28.

[57] Rivera Cusicanqui 1997; see as well Rivera Cusicanqui 2010; and Rivera Cusicanqui 1993.

[58] Von Arnauld 2021, p. 420.

[59] Hébié 2023.

precedence within the pluralism of inter-polity laws.[60] Departing from the example of the ICJ judgment on the territorial dispute between Cameroon and Nigeria, and referring specifically to contentious proceedings in front of courts, Edward Martin convincingly suggests the following: When the scarcity of historical documents and the limits of contemporary historiography cause serious challenges to a reconstruction of the social norms and legal standards in force at the time, there might be no conceivable way in a polycentric global legal order to set one legal order above the other—given we take it for granted that we do not want to reproduce the Eurocentric retrospective impositions described above. These constellations, according to Edward Martin, might constitute one of the rare examples of *non liquet* in contentious proceedings.[61] With respect to the challenging task of courts to determine the laws that were in force a long time ago and in a context of clashing legal views of European and non-European peoples, he writes in general terms:

> When two conflicting broader narratives of the historical context (and the therefore applicable law) collide—as is the case in contentious proceedings with an intertemporal dimension with a European and non-European legal point of view—it is of utmost importance that the process and method reaching a judgement does not *a priori* confirm the legal argument of one of the parties, while neglecting the others'. […] In more concrete terms, using the example of the Cameroon v. Nigeria judgment of the ICJ: if the methodology applied by the ICJ to establish the historic facts, and the historic rules governing the dispute already confirms the position of one of the historic signatories to the "Treaty of Protection", while negating the other, a situation of "différend" would have been created[62]

So which way forward is there, if really, we might have to face the conclusion that in certain historical contexts it might be impossible to determine the laws in force at the time with certainty?

The second element of the doctrine of intertemporal law might provide us with a solution, or rather, the second element in combination with an interpretation of international law based on human rights and *ius* cogens. As described in this chapter, the doctrine of intertemporal law is the bottleneck for overcoming colonial racism inscribed into (some of the) contemporary legal assessments of the laws that were in force at the time of European colonialism. Mamadou Hébié suggests interpreting the second element of the doctrine to determine from today's perspective the norms and values we as contemporary societies want to be guided by. He emphasizes that the doctrine in itself "does not tell us how to deal with the remnants of the past and its legacies." According to Hébié, the doctrine "says that situations which have been established in another system of law, for their continuing validity have to be assessed in the light of the contemporary rules."[63] His approach seems to be comparable to Makau Mutua. He points to the power of consent in agreeing on reparations for slavery within the international legal order and argues:

[60] Goldmann 2023, p. 8.

[61] Martin 2021, pp. 60, 78–85.

[62] Martin 2021, pp. 20–22. With reference to Jean-François Lyotard on p. 21, who used the term 'différend' for a situation in which accepting a method reaching settlements means accepting the position of one of the disputing sides while negating the other side's position.

[63] Hébié 2023, at 38:15.

> As the Nuremberg trial clearly showed, global powers can will accountability ex post facto for gross abuses even where no extant law prohibited such actions. Nuremberg is a great example of a constitutional moment in which society realizes that certain abuses, though not criminalized, are so inimical to morality and decency that leaving them unpunished sets an untenable precedent. In such a situation, dispensing with the general prohibition against retroactive laws is the more plausible option. The most exceptional circumstances may dictate an expedient waiver of this particular legal formality—or an aversion to retroactivity—as was the case in Nuremberg. Actions that shock the human conscience, such as slavery, should follow suit.[64]

What this section proposes is the following: If thorough and accurate historical research does not (yet) provide for a sufficient basis to determine the laws in force at the time, or even if the only available archival material seems to sustain racist differentiations already having been imposed, the second element of the doctrine of intertemporal law grants the leeway to renounce to continue reproducing colonial racism. A growing consensus seems to emerge globally about a legal obligation to reparations. But reparations in a very specific sense. Andreas von Arnauld suggests a state obligation to negotiate with the victims of historical injustice or their descendants as a form of satisfaction "in order to guarantee due acknowledgment of their human dignity and to address their demand to be heard".[65] And Benno Zabel, departing from the ethical need to narrate colonial dehumanization from the perspective of those affected, argues for a human right to collective political remembering of the victims and the descendants.[66] Even Axel Jörn Kämmerer, who in 2004 argued that law was not the adequate means to address historical injustice 100 years ago,[67] in 2016 affirmed that certain changes in international law might be necessary to mitigate the legacies of what he terms the "birth defect" of international law.[68]

Concretely about the German-Namibian context the following could be argued:

> First, the determination of the laws in force at the time as brought forward by the German government in front of the US District Court and by the German Scientific Service of the Bundestag in its Gutachten dated 2016, not only reproduce the most racist legal scholars by arguing that the prevailing opinion differentiated between "civilized" and "uncivilized" nations and that the latter were, again according to the prevailing opinion, not even granted basic minimum legal protection, as described in detail above, but it is a new act of racial discrimination in terms of Article 2 of the International Covenant on Civil and Political Rights (ICCPR) and the International Convention on the Elimination of Racial Discrimination (CERD). The reason is that both retrospectively construct a racist prevailing opinion without having done thorough historical research to prove such a prevailing opinion. Furthermore, they quoted not a single non-European scholar when they determined the laws in force at the time. And they did not do any research at all into the question when exactly the polycentric legal order was substituted by the newly emerging European international law.[69]

---

64 Mutua 2021, p. 24.

65 Von Arnauld 2021, p. 426.

66 Zabel 2023, pp. 131–161.

67 Kämmerer and Föh 2004.

68 Kämmerer 2016, p. 239.

69 Theurer 2023c; Theurer 2023b; partly already in Theurer and Kaleck 2020.

Second, even if historical research might sustain the findings that shortly before 1904, the differentiation between "civilized" and "uncivilized" nations had already been established as European state practice by force in what is today Namibia, one could ask from today's perspective and departing from the second element of the doctrine of intertemporal law whether this differentiation had lasted long enough in international law, to be rightfully invoked today, or whether it was quickly (and rightly) substituted by the right to self-determination and the principle of equality amongst all states. The prohibition of racist discrimination is one of the core principles of international law, forms part of *ius cogens*, and is one of the basic human rights enshrined in several human rights treaties. The Inter-American Court of Human Rights has rightly strengthened the realm of *ius cogens*. The second element of the doctrine of intertemporal law grants the leeway to renounce to continue reproducing colonial racism.

Third, in a case of *non liquet*, international law allows us to consent on a legal obligation to repair the harm inflicted during colonialism. Concretely, this should entail a legal obligation to stop reproducing colonial racism and to attempt to overcome social, economic, and cultural exclusion.

11.4 Conclusion

In this chapter we focused on the example of the Ovaherero and Nama reparations claims. About that specific context, it was described why the determination of the laws in force at the time by the German government and the German Scientific Service of the Bundestag is not only a reproduction of colonial racism but amounts to a new act of racism in terms of Article 2 ICCPR and CERD. It was shown that the application of the doctrine of intertemporal law, or rather the determination of the laws in force at the time according to its two elements and in view of contemporary *ius cogens*, is the bottleneck for overcoming colonial racism and eurocentrism.

I analysed how a decolonized application of the doctrine of intertemporal law in the German-Namibian context and regarding the quest for reparations might look. It is of essential importance to do further research on when the polycentric legal order was substituted by European (international) law and when the latter became universal. It is also of essential importance to do more research into legal norms and social standards amongst Ovaherero, Nama, Damara, and San prior to German colonization. Ambiguities and controversies amongst European legal scholars also are to be reconstructed. It might turn out to be impossible to reconstruct the laws in force at the time without reproducing pre-assumptions. In contentious court proceedings, this might mean that a court might find itself to be unable to decide a case in a legally binding manner but that it might have to declare a *non liquet*. I argue that the second element of the doctrine of intertemporal law allows for a dynamic interpretation of law and, for the affirmation that racist differentiations such as the one between "civilized" and "uncivilized" nations are not to be reproduced but overcome in a vein to decolonize law. That, in essence would amount to reparations. Reparations for colonial crimes are often thought to be primarily about financial payments. In my chapter, I conclude that reparations for colonial crimes first and foremost should consist of deconstructing colonial racism, refraining from reproducing it, and finding ways of overcoming it.

References

Al-Khasawneh AS (2002) Separate Opinion to the ICJs judgement on the case Land and Maritime Boundary between Cameroon and Nigeria, 492-505.

Anghie A (2005) Imperialism, Sovereignty and the Making of International Law. Cambridge University Press, Cambridge.

Bluntschli JC (1868) Das moderne Völkerrecht der civilisierten Staaten als Rechtsbuch dargestellt [The modern international law of civilised states presented as a law book], Beck, Nördlingen.

Chakrabarty D (2001) Provincializing Europe. Postcolonial Thought and Historical Difference. Princeton University Press, Princeton.

Fischer-Lescano A (2022) Deutschengrundrechte: Ein kolonialistischer Anachronismus [Basic German Rights: A Colonialist Anachronism]. In: Dann P, Feichtner I, von Bernstorff J (eds) (Post-)Koloniale Rechtswissenschaft. Geschichte und Gegenwarte des Kolonialismus in der deutschen Rechtswissenschaft. Mohr Siebeck, Tübingen, pp 339–367.

Gathii JT (2011) TWAIL: A brief history of its origins, its decentralized network, and a tentative bibliography. Trade Law and Development: 26-64.

Goldmann M (2018) Declaration to the proceedings of Vekuii Rukoro et al v. Federal Republic of Germany 17 cv 00062 (LTS), United States District Court Southern District of New York.

Goldmann M (2023) The Ambiguity of Colonial International Law: Three Approaches to the Namibian Genocide. Leiden Journal of International Law [forthcoming].

Hanschmann F (2014) The Suspension of Constitutionalism in the Heart of Darkness. In: Grotke K, Prutsch M (eds) Constitutionalism, Legitimacy, and Power: Nineteenth Century Experiences. Oxford University Press, Oxford, pp 243–261.

Hébié M (2015) Souveraineté territoriale par traité: une étude des accords entre puissances coloniales et entités politiques locales [Territorial sovereignty by treaty: a study of agreements between colonial powers and local political entities]. Presses Universitaires de France, Paris.

Hébié M (2016) The Role of the Agreements Concluded with Local Political Entities in the Course of French Colonial Expansion in West Africa. British Yearbook of International Law 85 (1): 21–89.

Hébié M (2023) Podcast: Centre for International Law Dialogues. National University of Singapore: International Law and Reparations for Colonial Harms: What Way Forward? https://cil.nus.edu.sg/event/cil-dialogues-international-law-and-reparations-for-colonial-harms-what-way-forward/. Accessed 1 October 2023.

Higgins R (1997) Time and the Law: International Perspectives on an Old Problem. International and Comparative Law Quarterly: 510-520.

Hillebrecht W (2008) The Nama and the War in the South. In: Zimmerer J, Zeller J (eds) Genocide in German South-West Africa: The Colonial War of 1904-1908 and its Aftermath. The Merlin Press, pp 143–158.

Hillebrecht W (2014) Hendrik Witbooi and Samuel Maharero: The Ambiguity of Heroes. In: Silvester J (ed) Re-viewing Resistance in Namibian History. University of Namibia Press, Windhoek.

Kämmerer JA, Föh J (2004) Das Völkerrecht als Instrument der Wiedergutmachung? Eine kritische Betrachtung am Beispiel des Herero-Aufstands [International Law as an Instrument of Reparation? A Critical Examination Using the Example of the Herero Uprising]. Archiv des Völkerrechts 42: 294–328.

Kämmerer JA (2016) Introduction. Imprints of Colonialism in Public International Law: On the Paradoxes of Transition. Journal of the History of International Law 18: 239–247.

Koskenniemi M (2002) The Gentle Civilizer of Nations. Cambridge University Press, Cambridge.

Koskenniemi M (2011) Histories of International law: Dealing with Eurocentrism. Rechtsgeschichte 19: 152–176.

Koskenniemi M (2016) Colonial Laws: Sources, Strategies and Lessons. Journal of the History of International Law 18: 248–277.

Kössler R (2015) Namibia and Germany. Negotiating the Past. University of Namibia Press, Windhoek.

Lau B (1995) The Hendrik Witbooi Papers. National Archives of Namibia, Windhoek.

Linderfalk U (2011) The application of international legal norms over time: The second branch of intertemporal law. Netherlands International Law Review: 147–172.

Lugones M (2007) Heterosexualism and the Colonial/Modern Gender System. Hypatia: A Journal of Feminist Philosophy 22 (1): 186-209.

Martin E (2021) The Application of the Doctrine of Intertemporality in Contentious Proceedings. Schriften zum Völkerrecht. Band 245. Duncker & Humblot.

Mignolo W (2009) Epistemic Disobedience, Independent Thought and De-Colonial Freedom. Theory, Culture & Society 26: 1–23.

Mutua M (2019) Podcast: The human rights movement—A truly universal system? Centre for Human Rights. University of Pretoria. https://www.chr.up.ac.za/art-season-1/art-episode-1-prof-makau-mutua. Accessed 1 October 2023.

Mutua M (2021) Reparations for Slavery: A Productive Strategy? In: Bhabha J, Matache M, Elkins C (eds) Time for Reparations. University of Pennsylvania Press, pp 19–34.

Quijano A (2000) Coloniality of Power, Eurocentrism, and Latin America. Nepantla: Views from South 1: 533–580.

Rivera Cusicanqui S (1993) Pachakuti: Los horizontes históricos del colonialismo interno [The historical horizons of internal colonialism]. In: Albó X, Barrios R (eds) Violencias encubiertas en Bolivia. CIPCA/ARUWIYIRI, La Paz, pp 33–54.

Rivera Cusicanqui S (1997) La noción de "derecho" o las paradojas de la modernidad postcolonial: indígenas y mujeres en Bolivia [The notion of "law" or the paradoxes of postcolonial modernity: indigenous people and women in Bolivia]. Temas Sociales, Revista de Sociología UMSA 19: 27–52.

Rivera Cusicanqui S (2010) Ch'ixinakax utxiwa. Una reflexión sobre practices y discursos descolonizantes [Ch'ixinakax utxiwa. A reflection on practices and decolonising discourses]. Tinta Limón Ediciones, La Paz.

Robinson P (2021) The Ascertainment of a Rule of International Law Condemning Transatlantic Chattel Slavery: Final Observations and Concluding Remarks. In: Stefanelli J, Lovall E (eds) Reparations Under International Law for Enslavement of African Persons in the Americas and the Caribbean. The American Society of International Law, pp 172–190.

Spivak GC (1988) Can the subaltern speak? In: Nelson C, Grossberg L (eds) Marxism and the interpretation of culture. University of Illinois Press, Illinois, pp 66–111.

Theurer K, Kaleck W (2020) Dekolonisierung des Rechts: Ambivalenzen und Potenzial. In: Theurer K, Kaleck W (eds) Dekoloniale Rechtskritik und Rechtspraxis. Nomos, Baden-Baden, pp 11–56.

Theurer K (2019) Racist repercussions and transgenerational exclusion. Legal means to deal with Germany's colonial legacy. Völkerrechtsblog, https://doi.org/10.17176/20191118-222635-0.

Theurer K (2023a) Litigating Reparations: Will Namibia Be Setting Standards? Völkerrechtsblog, https://doi.org/10.17176/20230125-095851-0. https://voelkerrechtsblog.org/de/litigating-reparations/. Accessed 1 October 2023.

Theurer K (2023b) Podcast: Centre for International Law Dialogues. National University of Singapore: International Law and Reparations for Colonial Harms: What Way Forward? https://cil.nus.edu.sg/event/cil-dialogues-international-law-and-reparations-for-colonial-harms-what-way-forward/. Accessed 1 October 2023.

Theurer K (2023c) Minimum Legal Standards in Reparation Processes for Colonial Crimes: The Case of Namibia and Germany. German Law Journal 24 (7): 1146-1168. https://doi.org/10.1017/glj.2023.81.

von Arnauld A (2021) How to Illegalize Past Injustice: Reinterpreting the Rules of Intertemporality. European Journal of International Law 32 (2): 401–432.

Wheatley S (2021) Revisiting the Doctrine of Intertemporal Law. Oxford Journal of Legal Studies: 484-509.

Wissenschaftlicher Dienst des Bundestages [Scientific Service of the German Parliament] (2016): WD 2 - 3000—112/16: Der Aufstand der Volksgruppen der Herero und Nama in Deutsch-Südwestafrika (1904-1908). Völkerrechtliche Implikationen und haftungsrechtliche Konsequenzen [The Uprising of the Herero and Nama Ethnic Groups in German South-West Africa (1904-1908). Implications under international law and consequences under liability law]. https://www.bundestag.de/resource/blob/478060/28786b58a9c7ae7c6ef358b19ee9f1f0/wd-2-112-16-pdf-data.pdf. Assessed 1 October 2023.

Zabel B (2023) Politisches Erinnern als Menschenrecht. [Political Remembrance as Human Right]. In: Gardei E, Soeffner H-G, Zabel B (eds) Vergangenheitskonstruktionen. Wallstein, Frankfurt am Main, pp 131–161.

Zimmerer J (2021) German Rule, African Subjects: state aspirations and the reality of power in colonial Namibia. Berghahn, New York.

Other Documents

International Law Commission, Yearbook of 2001.

Chapter 12
Repairing "Historical" Wrongs: The Church of Sweden's Approach to Redressing Colonial Abuses against the Sami

Ebba Lekvall

Contents

Abstract This chapter explores the process initiated by the Church of Sweden to repair colonial abuses against Sweden's indigenous people—the Sami. The Church, formerly the State church and a State institution, played an important role in the colonisation and oppression of the Sami, which led to loss of their traditional lands, language, religion, and culture—the effects of which are still felt today. Since the 1990s, the Church has worked to address its role in these abuses and to embark on a path towards reparation and reconciliation. This chapter first discusses Sweden's colonial context and the Church's involvement in abuses against the Sami. It then examines the legal obligation to provide adequate and effective reparation, before

The author would like to thank Carla Ferstman and Tara Van Ho for their feedback on earlier drafts of this chapter, as well as the two reviewers and editors for their comments.

E. Lekvall (✉)
Essex Law School and Human Rights Centre, University of Essex, Colchester, UK
e-mail: ebba.lekvall@essex.ac.uk

O. Spijkers et al. (eds.), *Netherlands Yearbook of International Law 2022*, Netherlands Yearbook of International Law 53, https://doi.org/10.1007/978-94-6265-627-7_12

investigating the reparation process initiated by the Church. This includes a critical analysis of the lack of participation by the Sami in the process and of the limits of the Church's approach to reparation. The chapter argues that while there have been some good faith efforts on the part of the Church, more is needed for the process and substance of reparation to be in line with international human rights law standards.

Keywords Indigenous rights · Sami · Reparation · Colonisation · Non-state actors · Reconciliation · Sweden

12.1 Introduction

In November 2021, and again in October 2022, the former Archbishop of the Church of Sweden (CoS), Antje Jackelén, issued a historic apology to the Sami[1] for colonial abuses. The Sami are an indigenous people whose traditional land, Sápmi, spans across parts of Norway, Sweden, Finland, and Russia. An estimated 20,000–40,000 Sami live in Sweden today.[2] In its apology, the Church acknowledged its role in the colonisation of Sápmi, and various abuses committed against the Sami.[3] The Church stated that its apology was only one step towards reconciliation and presented eight commitments for further work on reconciliation.[4] Since then, the Church has published an Action Plan to implement these commitments.[5] The Church's reconciliation process is part of a wider Swedish initiative to redress abuses committed against the Sami: in November 2021 the Swedish Government set up a truth commission (TC) with a mandate to "examine the policies pursued towards the Sami from a historical perspective and the consequences for the Sami people" ending 1 December 2025.[6] These Swedish processes are part of a broader regional context of reconciliation with the Sami. The Church of Norway started its reconciliation work before the CoS, and both Norway and Finland set up TCs prior to Sweden,[7] with the Norwegian TC releasing its report in June 2023.[8]

The aim of this chapter is to evaluate whether the CoS's reconciliation process can serve as both a catalyst for and a contribution to adequate reparation for its part

[1] Also spelled Saami or Sámi. I am using the English spelling as used by the Sami Parliament of Sweden.

[2] Krawchenko and McDonald 2023, p. 152.

[3] This is the Northern Sami word 'Sápmi'. Other versions include 'Sábme' (Lule Sami), 'Sábmie' (Ume Sami), and "Saepmi" (Southern Sami).

[4] Svenska kyrkan [Church of Sweden], Speech of Apology, https://www.svenskakyrkan.se/samiska/speech-of-apology. Accessed 1 December 2023.

[5] Svenska kyrkan [Church of Sweden] 2022.

[6] Regeringen [Government of Sweden] 2021, p. 1.

[7] Kuokkanen 2020, p. 293; West 2020, p. 3.

[8] Stortinget [Norwegian Parliament], Sannhets- og forsoningskommisjonen [The truth and reconciliation commission], https://www.stortinget.no/no/Stortinget-og-demokratiet/Organene/sannhets--og-forsoningskommisjonen/. Accessed 1 December 2023.

in the wrongs committed against the Sami. In doing so it investigates and critically analyses what international obligations the CoS arguably has to provide reparation to the Sami, and considers whether the mechanisms put in place by the Church meet the expectations of reparation as framed by international human rights law standards. My focus is on the Church alone, rather than Church and State processes together, for several reasons. First, the Church was a significant contributor to the abuses committed against the Sami and indeed, the civilising mission of the Church served as a crucial justification for the abuses. The Church committed these abuses as a former State actor, though the effect of these abuses continued to be felt after it became a separate institution in 2000, raising important questions concerning the Church's responsibility as both a former State entity and now as an entity separate from the State. Second, a thorough and focused analysis of the Church's process can influence the remainder of the Church's work and help to ensure that going forward the reparation provided is adequate and effective. Lastly, specifically considering the Church's process provides an opportunity for the TC (whose work is still at a nascent stage) to learn from the Church's approach when developing its own programmes of redress.

Despite these conciliatory initiatives in Scandinavia, redress for colonial abuses by churches against the Sami is an underexplored area of scholarship. Much of the existing literature on the Sami in Sweden focuses on aspects of history and colonisation,[9] self-determination and Sami political mobilisation,[10] and on current human rights abuses related to extractive industries, and rights to land and water.[11] Some scholars have researched reconciliation between State churches and the Sami and the CoS in particular, but from a theological perspective.[12] While some of the global literature on reparation engages with reconciliation processes with indigenous peoples,[13] the literature does not analyse the responsibility or role of churches in this process. Literature that does discuss the international rights and obligations of religious actors does not address obligations to redress colonial abuses against indigenous peoples.[14] In contrast, this chapter analyses the Church's obligation to provide reparation and the extent to which its reconciliation process serves as a basis for the adequate and effective reparation of abuses committed against the Sami.

Better understanding of the colonial abuses against the Sami and legal obligations to provide reparation are important considering Sweden's obligations under international law to respect human rights principles such as non-discrimination, self-determination, and cultural integrity,[15] and its commitment to implementing the UN

---

[9] E.g. Ahrén 2004; Lantto 2010.

[10] Mörkenstam 2005; Lantto and Mörkenstam 2008.

[11] E.g. Raitio et al. 2020; Allard and Brännström 2021; Össbo 2021.

[12] E.g. Nordbäck 2016; West 2020.

[13] E.g. Corntassel and Holder 2008; Morse 2008; Lightfoot 2015; Ka'ai 2020; Norman-Hill 2020.

[14] Cismas 2014.

[15] HRC 2016a, para 14. See also CERD 2018, para 16.

Declaration on the Rights of Indigenous Peoples (UNDRIP), which calls for reparation for indigenous peoples.[16] In analysing the Church's process, this chapter makes an important contribution to the literature regarding indigenous rights and redress for colonial abuses in Sweden, but also to the wider Nordic region, which is going through similar processes with the Sami. This research is also relevant for the broader context of reconciliation with indigenous peoples in settler colonial contexts and for the role of churches as non- or quasi-State actors. Looking specifically at the process undertaken by the CoS may inform other countries where churches had quasi-State functions and were involved in or even led abuses against indigenous peoples, as it maps out a way for churches to contribute to or lead processes of reconciliation and redress. This will be particularly relevant for reconciliation efforts between institutions, including churches, and indigenous peoples in established democracies with settler-colonial pasts, such as in Australia, Canada, and New Zealand.

This chapter begins by discussing Sweden as a settler colonial context and the colonisation of Sami traditional lands, before exploring the role of the Church in the colonisation of Sápmi and violations against the Sami. It then briefly explores issues of legal responsibility to provide reparation for violations against the Sami. The chapter then discusses the Church's approach to reparation, evaluating whether it meets reparation according to international human rights law (IHRL) standards. This begins with a critical analysis of the truth-seeking efforts and reparation provided to date—including the limited efforts to engage substantively with the Sami and the resulting lack of participation by them in the process—before evaluating the Church as well as the reparation envisioned through the Action Plan. The chapter concludes that while a good-faith and important effort, the Church's process does not comply with IHRL standards and that they should engage better with the mechanisms available in the field of transitional justice (TJ) to improve the chances of reconciliation.

12.2 Colonialism in the Swedish Context

The Sami describe the process by which the Swedish State took over traditionally Sami lands, exploited resources, and erased Sami culture and language as colonisation.[17] The Sami Parliament has highlighted how the situation of the Sami today is largely due to the effects of colonisation, including discrimination.[18] However, the term 'colonisation' has not gained traction in Sweden. For Össbo, this is partly due to a lingering perception that colonialism requires an ocean between the settler State

[16] UNGA 2007, art. 10–12, 28.

[17] E.g. Partapuoli 2015, p. 231.

[18] Sametinget [Swedish Sami Parliament], DO och Sametinget verkar för en samisk sanningskommission [The Discrimination Ombudsman and the Sami Parliament work for a Sami truth commission], https://www.sametinget.se/90491. Accessed 1 December 2023.

and its colony.[19] By this definition, Swedish expansion into Sápmi would not constitute colonialism. This is also the position taken by the Swedish government, which in a 1986 investigation into Sami rights found that "it is impossible to equate the Swedish influence over the traditional Sami settlement areas with what is commonly called colonialism."[20] Swedish governments have consistently refused to call the expansion into Sápmi colonisation.

The CoS, however, has openly acknowledged its role in what it sees to be the colonisation of the Sami.[21] Some Swedish scholars, like Gunlög Fur—currently a member of the TC and involved in the Church's truth-seeking project—also take a broader and more appropriate view of colonialism that is not limited to settlement of territories overseas. Fur defines it as "a process whereby a state power seizes the right to rule over an indigenous people's territory, culture and economy, under the pretext of having a superior social system."[22] According to Fur, colonialism also includes perceptions of racial/ethnic and cultural inequality between ruling and subordinate peoples, the pursuit of political dominance, and physical and economic exploitation of indigenous peoples.[23] Clearly, seeing colonialism as something only done by European powers to peoples in faraway places does not adequately capture the various contexts in which State powers have subjugated indigenous peoples and appropriated their lands. Colonialism undoubtedly encompasses all situations where a State imposes its rule on independent peoples based on notions of superiority. Swedish appropriation of Sami lands falls within this categorisation and this chapter will therefore refer to the Swedish State's expansion into Sápmi, and its treatment of the Sami, as colonisation.

12.3 The Colonisation of Sápmi

The colonisation of Sápmi began in earnest in the 15th century. At the time, Sami rights to their traditional lands were recognised and Sami customary law continued to govern Sami society and be applied by Swedish courts well into the 19th century.[24] For example, in 1751 a new border treaty was agreed between Norway and Sweden with an addendum, the so-called Lapp Codicil, which confirmed traditional Sami rights to land and water on both sides of the border.[25] Colonisation intensified in the 17thcentury, and until the mid-18th century the State pursued an active policy of colonisation to increase the Swedish population in the area.[26] Then, in the 19th

[19] Össbo 2020, pp. 420–421.

[20] Justitiedepartementet [Ministry of Justice] 1986, p. 164.

[21] E.g. Ekström and Schött 2006, p. 9.

[22] Fur 2016, p. 244.

[23] Ibid.

[24] Ahrén 2004, pp. 76–80.

[25] Lantto 2010, p. 545.

[26] Ahrén 2004, p. 74; Lantto 2010, p. 545; Fur 2016, pp. 246–248.

century the Sami were stripped of their rights to land. As theories of cultural hierarchy emerged, a view of the Sami as inferior coupled with a desire to take over Sami lands, water, and natural resources, led Swedish authorities to argue that the Sami nomadic way of life did not result in legal rights to land; only the permanent use of a specific area of land, e.g. agriculture, qualified for land title.[27] Accordingly, the 1886 Reindeer Grazing Act declared Sami traditional lands to be the property of the Swedish State. Furthermore, the Sami were not allowed to pursue other forms of livelihood than reindeer husbandry.[28] These colonial practices violated previously recognised rights to the land and discriminated against the Sami.

The current Reindeer Herding Act of 1971 states that only those who belong to a so-called 'sameby'—an administrative and economic association[29]—have the right to practice reindeer husbandry and to hunt and fish on traditional lands.[30] This presumes that nomadic land use does not give rise to legal rights to land. Therefore, while reindeer-herding Sami formally have rights to lands they have traditionally occupied, the land constitutes property of the State or private landowners and Sami rights are only usufruct rights.[31] However, non-reindeer herding Sami have no rights to use their traditional lands. Consequently, while the process of land colonisation in Sápmi appears to have happened without the violence and conflict seen in the colonisation of indigenous land in Canada or the United States, Sápmi is still colonised today.[32] Sweden has also not recognised Sami ownership or sovereignty over traditional lands, or negotiated land agreements, as done to an extent in Canada.[33] The consequences of this colonisation are still felt today; the Sami in Sweden continue to fight for their right to use their traditional lands against landowners and resource exploitation,[34] and Sweden has been criticised by various UN treaty bodies as well as the Special Rapporteur on the Rights of Indigenous Peoples for its lack of respect of Sami land and resource rights.[35]

---

[27] Ahrén 2004, pp. 81–82, 89.

[28] Ibid., pp. 89–90.

[29] Sametinget [Swedish Sami Parliament], Kontaktuppgifter till Sveriges samebyar [Contact information for Sami villages], https://www.sametinget.se/samebyar. Accessed 1 December 2023.

[30] Landsbygds- och infrastrukturdepartementet RSL [Ministry of Rural Affairs and Infrastructure] (1971) Rennäringslag (1971:437) [Reindeer Herding Act], 18 June 1971, paras 1, 25, Available at: https://lagen.nu/1971:437. Accessed 28 August 2023.

[31] Ahrén 2004, pp. 94–95; Össbo 2014, pp. 47–48.

[32] Partapuoli 2015, p. 231.

[33] E.g. Morse 2008.

[34] E.g. Swedish Supreme Court, 'Girjasdomen', Judgment, 23 January 2020, T 853–18; Human Rights Committee, *Kitok v. Sweden*, Views, 27 July 1988, Communication No. 197/1985; CERD, *Lars-Anders Ågren et al. v Sweden*, Views, 18 November 2020, Communication No. 54/2013.

[35] E.g. HRC 2011, para 50–51; Human Rights Committee 2016, para 38; CERD 2018, para 16.

12.4 The Church as an Actor of Colonial Violations

The CoS's presence in Sápmi was part of its mission to civilise the Sami through Christian evangelism and education.[36] The Church was from the mid-16th century the State church, completely subordinate to the State,[37] and until the mid-19th century priests largely functioned as government officials, exercising legal and educational duties, as well as running the population registration—a tool for the State to collect taxes.[38] As such, the Church was an important part of the State and played a major role in the abuses committed against the Sami. In the process of strengthening control over Sápmi and establishing functioning channels for exercising State power, Church and State affairs were constantly intertwined, making it sometimes difficult to separate the Church from State actions.[39] Nevertheless, some areas of abuse committed by the Church can clearly be identified and the Church's actions as part of the colonisation of Sami led to abuses that by today's standards would constitute serious violations of IHRL, including systematic discrimination and deprivation of indigenous lands and cultural heritage,[40] which require reparation.

A common argument against indigenous claims for reparation is that the abuses occurred when these acts were not illegal, and therefore fall under the principle of non-retroactivity.[41] However, although not recognised in international law until the mid-20th century, human rights were positive law in Europe and North America by the end of the 18th century,[42] meaning that at least some of the colonial abuses committed against indigenous peoples would have been illegal at the time. Furthermore, States have provided reparation, including apologies, restitution, and compensation for violations of indigenous peoples' right to land and self-determination occurring before modern-day IHRL existed.[43] Moreover, violating a sovereign nation has long since been considered illegal. It appears that at least until during the 14th century, Swedish kings recognised the Sami as a sovereign nation and that even after this, as seen above, the Crown recognised Sami rights to their lands and Sami customary law.[44] Consequently, the overall acts of colonisation would arguably have been unlawful at the time as they violated the sovereignty of the Sami nation.

Additionally, many abuses against indigenous peoples can be classified as so-called 'continuing violations', meaning that there is no issue of retroactivity.[45] A violation is continuing if it "has been commenced but has not been completed at the

[36] Anderzén 2016, pp. 373, 398; Elenius 2016, p. 481; Fur 2016, p. 242.

[37] Svenska kyrkan [Church of Sweden], Tidslinje [Timeline] https://www.svenskakyrkan.se/tidslinje. Accessed 1 December 2023.

[38] Pettersson 2000, pp. 18–19.

[39] Norlin and Sjögren 2016, p. 411.

[40] Francioni 2008, p. 27.

[41] Ibid., p. 42; Shelton 2008, p. 57.

[42] Shelton 2004, p. 273.

[43] Ibid., pp. 265–268.

[44] Ahrén 2004, p. 76.

[45] Francioni 2008, p. 43; Shelton 2008, p. 68.

relevant time."[46] For example, enforced disappearances are continuous violations until the victim is found.[47] Furthermore, acts that are not illegal when they first begin can become illegal as they continue and IHRL obligations enter into force.[48] There is also evidence that in IHRL the continuing effects may also constitute violations of human rights.[49] The UN Human Rights Committee has recognised that historical injustices leading to a failure to recognise indigenous rights to land constitutes as a continuous violation of the right to culture.[50]

12.4.1 Sami Traditional Lands

Through colonisation, the Church became an important owner of what used to be traditional Sami lands. When the Church presence in Sápmi increased in the 17th century,[51] priests received land to support themselves.[52] From the mid-18th century it became easier for the Church to acquire land as it was considered Crown property.[53] Today the Church manages 1.7% of the forests in Sweden, making it one of the largest forest managers in the country.[54] However, exactly how the Church acquired Sami lands remains largely unknown,[55] due to the failure of the Church to properly investigate land issues, as is discussed below.

Indigenous peoples have an important relationship to land and IHRL recognises their right to traditional lands and resources, including rights of ownership and development.[56] However, land is also intimately connected to culture. The UN treaty bodies for the International Covenant on Civil and Political Rights (ICCPR) and the International Convention on the Elimination of All Forms of Racial Discrimination (ICERD) have recognised that the right to culture includes ways of life associated with the use of land resources, especially for indigenous peoples, and have linked

---

[46] ILC 2001, commentary to art. 14(2), para 5.

[47] E.g. IACtHR, *Goiburú et al. v. Paraguay*, Judgment (Merits, Reparations and Costs), 22 September 2006, Series C No. 153, paras 80–83.

[48] E.g. ECtHR, *Papamichalopolous and Others v. Greece*, Judgment, 24 June 1993, Application no. 14556/89, para 40.

[49] E.g. Human Rights Committee, *Lovelace v. Canada*, Views, 30 July 1981, Communication No. 24/1977, paras 10–11.

[50] Human Rights Committee, *Chief Bernard Ominayak and Lubicon Lake Band v. Canada*, Views, 26 March 1990, Communication No. 167/1984, para 33.

[51] Fur 2016, p. 242.

[52] Norstedt 2016, p. 834.

[53] Ibid., pp. 837–848.

[54] Svenska kyrkan [Church of Sweden], Prästlönetillgångarna [Clergy salary assets], https://www.svenskakyrkan.se/prastlonetillgangarna. Accessed 1 December 2023.

[55] Norstedt 2016, p. 844.

[56] UNGA 2007, art. 26.

violations of non-discrimination with violations of rights to land and culture.[57] The Sami continue to stress the importance of land for their culture, including traditional lifestyles like reindeer herding, and spirituality.[58] That they still do not have rights to their own land is a continuing violation of this right, and also a violation of the right to culture and non-discrimination, which some scholars have likened to a form of 'cultural genocide.'[59]

12.4.2 Forced Christianisation

The Church's civilising mission constituted the most tangible threat to Sami culture and lifestyle.[60] The CoS in effect forcibly Christianised the Sami, which was an experience of physical and psychological abuse.[61] It was also a process of assimilation and destruction of religion, culture, and identity. The experience of Christianisation and assimilation is one the Sami share with indigenous peoples across the world.[62]

The Church's aim was to reform and discipline the Sami and their culture, which meant that Sami society had to be reshaped.[63] Its missionary work directly impacted on all of Sami society; the Sami were forced to baptise their children, get married in the Church, and have their dead buried by the Church rather than according to Sami traditions.[64] These requirements meant that the Sami had to completely change their world view.[65] Furthermore, expressions of Sami traditional religion were viewed as idolatry and sorcery.[66] Sami traditional drums and *yoik*—the traditional Sami way of singing and storytelling—were banned, and the possession and use of drums was punishable by death. At least one Sami was executed as a result, and most drums were destroyed.[67] Only in the 1990s was *yoik* beginning to be introduced into Church services in Sápmi. However, its use is contested among the Sami community; some see its use as a further act of colonisation and cultural appropriation by the Church, while others still consider it a heathen symbol with no place in the Church.[68]

---

[57] Human Rights Committee 1994, para 7; CERD 1997. See also e.g. ACtHPR *African Commission on Human and Peoples' Rights v. Republic of Kenya*, Judgment, 26 May 2017, Application No. 006/2012; IACtHR, *Indigenous Communities of the Lhaka Honhat (Our Land) Association v. Argentina*, Judgment (Merits, Reparations and Costs), 6 February 2020, Series C No. 400.

[58] Svenska kyrkan [Church of Sweden], Ságastallamat fredag 10.30 [Ságastallamat Friday 10.30], https://vimeo.com/showcase/9870404/video/762914497. Accessed 1 December 2023.

[59] E.g. Short 2010.

[60] Fur 2016, p. 290.

[61] Christoffersson 2016, p. 665.

[62] Ka'ai 2020; Norman-Hill 2020; Winder 2020, pp. 143–145.

[63] Fur 2016, p. 260.

[64] Ibid., pp. 260–263.

[65] Ibid., p. 262.

[66] Sundström 2016.

[67] Christoffersson 2016, pp. 659, 664–667.

[68] Stoor 2016, pp. 729–730.

Indigenous peoples have a right to practice their own culture and religion,[69] and a "right to not to be subjected to forced assimilation or destruction of their culture".[70] Since the Church's missionary work effectively destroyed Sami traditional religion and culture and assimilated the Sami into Christian subjects, its conduct regarding the Christianisation of the Sami violates Sami rights to religious practice, traditions, and culture. These violations are continuing; the traditional religion appears to have disappeared and the Sami continue to be Christianised.

12.4.3 Erasure of Sami Names

Through forced Christianisation of the Sami, the Church is also responsible for the erasure of Sami names—another way of assimilation and destruction of culture. From the 15th century until 1991, the Church controlled the national population registry,[71] giving priests great power over personal information, including names.[72] Because the Church did not accept traditional Sami names, most pre-Christian names were erased and Sami children were given Christian names when baptised.[73] The Church rarely accepted Sami versions of Christian names and often registered them in their Swedish forms.[74] Many priests also registered several Sami names as one single Swedish name.[75] The Church's practice has led to many Sami having a Swedish, primarily written, name and a Sami name, used primarily orally.[76] Some have told of the shock at hearing their official, Swedish name for the first time when starting school and the subsequent feeling of loss of identity.[77]

Names are important for a person's sense of identity and are also part of cultural heritage.[78] Sami names, as a unique cultural expression, have in many instances been wiped out. Additionally, the Sami were told their names were not good enough and since name and identity are intertwined, rejection of a name also means the rejection of the individual. This 'Swedishisation' of Sami names thus became part of the assimilation of the Sami and a violation of identity, with wounds that are

---

[69] International Covenant on Civil and Political Rights, 16 December 1966, UNTS Vol. 999, 23 March 1976, art. 27 [ICCPR]; UNGA 2007, art. 11.

[70] UNGA 2007, art. 26.

[71] Axelsson 2016, pp. 917–918.

[72] Frändén 2016, p. 800.

[73] Ibid.; Marainen 2016, p. 815.

[74] Frändén 2016, p. 803.

[75] E.g. Biera, Bera, Biete and Beahkka might be registered as the Swedish name Per. Ibid, p. 803; Marainen 2016, p. 815.

[76] Frändén 2016, p. 803.

[77] Marainen 2016, p. 812.

[78] Frändén 2016, pp. 798–799.

difficult to heal.[79] The Church's practice of erasing Sami names violates the rights to non-discrimination, culture, and the right not to be forcibly assimilated.[80]

12.4.4 Education

The Church was for a long time responsible for education in Sweden, including for the Sami. Education was used as part of the colonisation and civilising mission of the Church, with intensified efforts in the 18th century to further eradicate Sami religious and cultural expression.[81] By the mid-18th century, eight boarding schools had been established, each educating six students for a two-year period in reading and studies in Christianity. While the language of instruction was Sami, students spent all their time at the schools, including school holidays, and were not allowed to visit their families until they had been firmly anchored in their Christian faith.[82] During the 19th century, education of the Sami was provided through a mix of boarding schools, itinerant schools where teachers moved between communities to teach Sami children at home, and regular public schools.[83]

From the second half of the 19th century, local municipalities gradually took over responsibility for education in Sweden.[84] However, the Church remained partly in charge of Sami education through the creation of the residential school system in place between 1913 and 1962, which was established and run primarily by the Church. The 19th century cultural hierarchy theories, mentioned above, led to the emergence of a policy known as 'Lapp should remain Lapp'[85]—an expression coined by Vicar Vitalis Karnell in 1906[86]—and which included "large elements of social Darwinism and racism."[87] Senior Church officials, including Vicar Karnell, Bishop Olof Bergqvist, and the priest Georg Bergfors, were of the view that the nomadic, reindeer herding Sami were the 'real' Sami and that exposure to Swedish society, and a more civilised way of living, would lead to their extinction.[88] Proponents of this policy were also of the opinion that groups which gave up their traditional way of life would become degenerate and develop undesirable character traits. For example, Sami children who mixed with Swedish children would develop characteristics that

79 Ibid., p. 806.

80 ICCPR, above n. 69, art. 27; UNGA 2007, art. 2, 13.

81 Lindmark 2016, p. 350; Anderzén 2016, p. 373.

82 Lindmark 2016, pp. 352–353.

83 Anderzén 2016, p. 397.

84 Svenska kyrkan [Church of Sweden], Tidslinje [Timeline], https://www.svenskakyrkan.se/tidslinje. Accessed 1 December 2023.

85 Translation by the author. The term "lapp" is an old word for the Sami and is now considered derogatory.

86 Oscarsson 2015, p. 75.

87 Oscarsson 2016, p. 944. Translation by the author.

88 Norlin and Sjögren 2016, p. 417; Oscarsson 2016, pp. 944–951.

were not natural to them and would become suspicious, quarrelsome, and irritable.[89] Due to these views, the reindeer-herding Sami were barred from higher education and their children were not allowed in Swedish schools, but had to attend the so-called 'nomad schools', aimed at giving them the opportunity to continue their traditional way of life.[90] The point of these schools was therefore different to the residential schools in e.g. Australia, Canada, and the United States, or even Norway, where these schools were part of the States' assimilation policy of indigenous children.[91] The non-nomadic Sami, however, were not considered 'real' Sami—they were already lost as a race and were to be assimilated into the Swedish population.[92] Their children were consequently forcibly educated in Swedish public schools in the Swedish language.[93] This contributed to the division of the Sami as a community and the assimilation of non-nomadic Sami.[94]

Karnell, Bergqvist and Bergfors were highly involved in the creation, administration, and supervision of the 'nomad schools'.[95] Karnell took the initiative to create these schools and was hired as an expert when the question was being examined.[96] In 1916, Karnell became the first inspector of an inspectorate directly subordinate to the diocese in Luleå, where Bergvist was the bishop.[97] Influence over the schools was consequently concentrated in these two individuals, and the diocese supervised and controlled the practical implementation of the school charter through developing the curriculum and educating teachers.[98]

The education provided at the 'nomad schools' was of lower quality than in Swedish schools; the terms were shorter and the curriculum was based on the knowledge and skills the Sami were thought to need for a life of reindeer husbandry.[99] This shows the discriminatory nature of the policy as Sami children from reindeer-herding communities were denied education on par with that offered in public schools. The language of instruction was Swedish and, according to testimonies from former students, they were not allowed to speak Sami with each other[100]—leading to loss of their language.[101] These experiences led to a sense of double exclusion where the loss of language excluded individual Sami from their own communities, while at the same time being excluded from the majority Swedish community.[102] Other

89 Norlin and Sjögren 2016, p. 419.
90 Oscarsson 2016, p. 944.
91 E.g. Nergård 2020; Norman-Hill 2020; Winder 2020.
92 Oscarsson 2016, pp. 948-951,
93 Norlin and Sjögren 2016, p. 416.
94 Oscarsson 2016, p. 944.
95 Norlin and Sjögren 2016, pp. 417–432; Ibid., pp. 944–953.
96 Oscarsson 2016, p. 948.
97 Norlin and Sjögren 2016, p. 426; Ibid, pp. 943–944.
98 Norlin and Sjögren 2016, p. 431.
99 Ibid., pp. 419–420.
100 Blind and Huuva 2015, pp. 18, 37, 46.
101 Ibid., pp. 143, 163, 170–171; Svenska kyrkan [Church of Sweden] 2011, pp. 14–16.
102 Nordbäck 2016, p. 184.

testimonies explain how these schools also led to a loss of traditional knowledge and culture, as Sami history and culture was taught through the lens of the colonial power—in the colonial language.[103]

Furthermore, to prevent Sami children from getting used to the comforts of civilised society, after a suggestion from Karnell, many students in 'nomad schools' lived in huts modelled after traditional Sami dwellings with a Sami matron to make sure that students followed what was considered a 'real' Sami way of living, which included dressing in traditional Sami clothes and not eating with utensils.[104] Despite the schools being often plagued by disease outbreaks due to unsanitary conditions and overcrowding, the use of the huts for teaching and student accommodation was only changed in 1937.[105]

The 'nomad school' system is symbolically important as a negative experience in the collective memory of the Sami; it symbolises the division and unequal experiences within the Sami community, and unequal opportunities in life in relation to the majority population.[106] Furthermore, the consequences of the 'nomad school' system are not unlike those of other residential schools, which "permanently altered children by segregating them from their families, communities, and culture."[107] The 'nomad school' system led to violations of Sami rights to culture including language and was a system based on racial discrimination. These are serious violations the effects of which are still felt today, both by former students still alive and likely also through intergenerational trauma.

12.4.5 Racial Biology Research and Sami Remains

The Church also supported racial biological research, which legitimised discrimination, marginalisation, and the social and cultural oppression of the Sami.[108] While this is an area where the Church had a less direct role compared to the areas mentioned above, the Church contributed to the abuses. For example, during the 19th and early 20th century, Church officials sometimes assisted in collecting Sami remains in the name of research, and some priests participated in the looting of Sami graves.[109] These remains ended up in museums and institutes,[110] where many remain today. Indigenous peoples have a right to the repatriation of human remains,[111] and the

---

[103] Ibid., pp. 189–190.

[104] Oscarsson 2015, p. 97; Norlin and Sjögren 2016, p. 427.

[105] Oscarsson 2016, pp. 102–103.

[106] Norlin and Sjögren 2016, p. 432.

[107] Winder 2020, p. 145.

[108] Ojala 2016, p. 993.

[109] Ibid., pp. 998–1000.

[110] E.g. Mulk 2009, p. 208.

[111] UNGA 2007, art. 12(1).

Sami have for decades fought to have Sami remains identified and repatriated.[112] The fact that many remains have not been returned means the violation is ongoing.

Furthermore, Bishop Bergqvist actively supported the creation of the State Institute for Racial Biology in 1921, as well as the research of racial biologists, during his time as a member of Parliament.[113] The director of the Institute, Herman Lundborg, and other researchers were assisted in their research by Bergqvist and other Church representatives who introduced them to Sami communities in their parishes and local 'nomad schools'. Lundborg collected personal and physical information about the Sami, including height and various measurements of the head and face, and information provided by the local authorities about mental attributes. Lundborg also took photographs, and the photo collection from the Institute includes 38 albums of Sami photographs. Seven albums contain photos taken of children at various 'nomad schools', and some show children naked.[114] Thus, with the Church's facilitation, the Sami submitted their bodies to be measured from different angles and to be photographed in various states of undress.[115] In the Church's book about 'nomad schools', one Sami woman speaks about being photographed naked as a child while at school: "We had to undress, which didn't feel very good. ... It was not common for us to undress in front of each other. ... We were ashamed of being Lapps."[116] Forced undressing and nudity are humiliating acts, which constitute inhuman and degrading treatment under IHRL.[117]

12.5 The Obligation to Provide Reparation

Victims of human rights violations, including indigenous peoples, have a right to reparation, expressed in various human rights instruments.[118] These obligations are directly placed on States as primary addressees of IHRL. Indigenous scholars have warned that without reparation "for past harms and continuing injustices committed against our peoples, reconciliation would permanently enshrine colonial injustices

[112] Sametinget [Swedish Sami Parliament], Bakgrund: Repatriering av samiska kvarlevor [Background: repatriation of Sami remains], https://www.sametinget.se/samiska-kvarlevor. Accessed 1 December 2023.

[113] Oscarsson 2016, pp. 947–948; Hagerman 2016, pp. 974, 986.

[114] Hagerman 2016, pp. 971–986.

[115] Sjögren 2017, p. 81.

[116] Blind and Huuva 2015, pp. 131–132.

[117] E.g. ECtHR, *Aydın v. Turkey*, Judgment, 25 September 1997, Application No. 23178/94, para 84.

[118] E.g. ICCPR, above n. 69, art. 2(3); European Convention on Human Rights, 4 November 1950, ETS No. 005, 3 September 1953, art. 41 [ECHR]; American Convention on Human Rights, 22 November 1969, UNTS Vol. 1144, 18 July 1978, art. 63(1) [ACHR]; UNGA 2006; UNGA 2007.

and is itself a further injustice."[119] The question is who incurs international responsibility for the colonial abuses by the CoS against the Sami and thus is obliged to provide reparation.

The Swedish State has responsibility for the Church's conduct while it was the State Church, and therefore an overall responsibility to provide reparation. States are obliged to provide reparation for internationally wrongful acts that are attributed to them, including violations of IHRL.[120] The conduct of State organs, or entities exercising elements of governmental authority, are attributed to the State.[121] As it was subordinate to the State, the CoS was part of the State and acted on its behalf, making it a State organ,[122] or—as seen above—at least as an entity that exercised governmental authority. Its conduct at that time is thus attributable to the State, who therefore has a primary obligation to repair abuses against the Sami.

The separation of Church and State in 2000[123] raises complex issues around who owes reparation as a matter of international law, for which international law currently does not have clear answers. It could be argued that the State inherited the obligation from the Church, through State succession, which arises in different circumstances where a "once-recognised entity disappears in whole or in part to be succeeded by some other authority" and has implications for the transmission of obligations.[124] Nevertheless, as State succession is normally associated with changes in State territory, e.g. through cession of territory from one State to another, secession, and merger,[125] it may offer only limited assistance. Questions also arise regarding whether the Church can have limited international legal obligations as a non-State actor, similar to the development in related fields.[126]

These questions of international law are, however, not central to this chapter; instead an underpinning assumption is that since it played a role in the abuse of the Sami as a State actor, the Church shares an obligation with the State to provide reparation for the abuses until at least 2000. More importantly, as the Church has assumed responsibility to provide reparation or some sort of reconciliation process, it should do so in line with IHRL standards governing reparation to ensure that the reparation is effective and meaningful for the Sami communities in Sweden—regardless of whether an international legal obligation exists.

[119] Alfred 2005, p. 152.

[120] ILC 2001 art. 31; ICCPR, above n. 69, art. 2(3); ECHR, above n. 118 art. 41; ACHR, above n. 118, art. 63(1).

[121] ILC 2001 art. 4–5.

[122] Ibid., commentary to art. 4, para 1.

[123] Socialdepartementet [Ministry of Social Affairs] (1998) Lag (1998:1591) om Svenska kyrkan [Law on the Church of Sweden], 1 January 2000, para 3. Available at: https://lagen.nu/1998:1591. Accessed 1 December 2023.

[124] Shaw 2021, p. 835.

[125] Ibid., pp. 846–854.

[126] E.g. OHCHR 2011.

12.6 The Church's Approach to Reparation

According to a 2006 report, the CoS has worked on issues relating to the Sami since the early 1990s, including the repatriation of Sami remains, translation of Church books into Sami languages, Swedish ratification of the ILO-169 Convention, and reconciliation with the Church.[127] In 1996 the Sami Council of the CoS was created to advance Sami culture and rights in the Church and deliver opinions relating to Sami issues at national and diocesan levels.[128] Its 11 members currently include representatives from the Sami Parliament,[129] the Sami youth organisation Sáminuorra, as well as Church officials.[130] The 2006 report recommended that the Church initiate conversations about reconciliation with the Sami and indicated that reconciliation must, among other things, include the public acknowledgement of abuses and a desire to do better in the future.[131] Some have suggested that the Church's approach to reconciliation may be more secular than theological,[132] inspired by transitional justice—a "range of processes and mechanisms associated with a society's attempts to come to terms with a legacy of large-scale past abuses" and to achieve reconciliation.[133] The Church's Action Plan recognises that the reconciliation process requires *upprättelse*—which can be translated as 'reparation'—which the Church sees as meant to restore the victim and the relationship between victim and perpetrator, thereby laying the foundation for a joint future.[134]

The right to reparation in IHRL includes restitution, compensation, rehabilitation, satisfaction, and guarantees of non-repetition (GNR).[135] It is an important mechanism in TJ and for reconciliation.[136] Reparation should be adequate and effective and in proportion to the gravity of the violation and harm caused.[137] While the CoS does not identify them as such, two reparation measures—truth and apology—appear to have been provided by the Church. IHRL also recognises the right of those directly affected by decision-making to participate in and be consulted on the process.[138]

[127] Nordbäck 2016, p. 156: Ekström and Schött 2006, pp. 47–53.

[128] Ekström and Schött 2006, p. 105.

[129] Sametinget [Swedish Sami Parliament], Sametingets politiker [Politicians of the Sami Parliament], https://www.svenskakyrkan.se/samiska/samiska-radet. Accessed 1 December 2023.

[130] Svenska kyrkan [Church of Sweden], Samiska rådet i Svenska kyrkan [The Sami Council in the Church of Sweden], https://www.svenskakyrkan.se/samiska/samiska-radet. Accessed 1 December 2023.

[131] Ekström and Schött 2006, p. 105.

[132] Nordbäck 2016, pp. 155–157.

[133] UNSC 2004, para 8.

[134] Svenska kyrkan 2022, p. 33.

[135] E.g. UNGA 2006, para 18.

[136] UNGA 2014, paras 9, 11.

[137] Ibid.

[138] HRC 2016b, paras 31–35; UNGA 2021, para 89.

The UNDRIP specifically recognises the right of indigenous peoples to participate in decision-making on matters that affect their rights.[139]

Participation by affected communities is essential to the success and sustainability of processes to address colonial legacies and should occur in various stages of reconciliation efforts, including when designing and implementing truth-seeking and other forms of reparation.[140] Victim participation is important for the design of reparation as it can increase the fit between the reparation offered and expectations of victims,[141] and help ensure that reparation is adequate and effective. Particularly, "indigenous perspectives need to be incorporated at all stages, and indigenous peoples' full and effective participation is essential if the outcomes of such processes are to be successful and, indeed, legitimate."[142] The UN Special Rapporteur on the promotion of truth, justice, reparation and guarantees of non-recurrence has emphasised that it is impossible to remedy the past when affected communities do not feel included and are not part of the process, and that rendering these communities invisible is "tantamount to a new round of victimization."[143] The Sami Council has emphasised that a reconciliation process needs to include and make visible all Sami and that the goal of reconciliation is to overcome division.[144] Unfortunately, the Church's process has not included the level of participation by affected communities expected in such efforts.

The section below analyses the Church's approach to reparation and the measures provided to date. I query whether the Church's initiatives are capable of providing adequate and effective reparation due to the choice of mechanisms and measures, their implementation, and an overall lack of participation by Sami communities.

12.6.1 Truth

Truth is measure of satisfaction, one of the forms of reparation in IHRL,[145] as well as a freestanding human right[146] and one of the pillars of TJ.[147] Truth is also a prerequisite for reparation since, in order for reparation to be adequate and effective, it is necessary to know what happened and what needs to be redressed. Sami representatives have emphasised the importance of truth for reconciliation, saying that "we must know

---

139 UNGA 2007, art. 18.

140 Correa et al. 2009, pp. 397–412; HRC 2016b, para 38; UNGA 2021, para 50.

141 HRC 2016b, para 57.

142 HRC 2019, para 40.

143 UNGA 2021, para 92.

144 Ekström and Schött 2006, pp. 105–106.

145 E.g. UNGA 2006, para 22(b).

146 E.g. IACtHR, *Bámaca Velásquez v. Guatemala*, Judgment (Merits), 25 November 2020, Series C No. 70.

147 UNGA 2014, para 11.

what needs to be reconciled."[148] Victim participation is therefore important to ensure that it is not only the narrative of the oppressor that is considered and affirmed. The CoS has in several ways carried out what could be considered truth-seeking to understand and address its past and find a way toward reconciliation. However, the Church's truth-seeking appears to have provided no real opportunity for the voices of Sami communities across Sweden to be heard and therefore risks reinforcing colonial relationships rather than allowing the truth to come from the Sami so as to re-construct the relationship between the Church and Sami.

Truth-seeking is most commonly carried out through Truth Commissions[149] mandated to establish an accurate record of the past, clarify uncertain events, and "lift the lid of silence and denial from a contentious and painful period of history".[150] Truth-seeking mechanisms often hear testimonies in public hearings or collect written statements from witnesses, victims, and survivors and consider these when analysing past events.[151] Of course, truth-telling and truth-finding can be performed by actors other than TCs, e.g. victims and civil society organisations or national human rights bodies. For example, the Australian Human Rights Commission (AHRC) published a report in 1997 based on a National Inquiry into the forcible removal of indigenous children from their families—the so-called 'stolen generation'—and made several recommendations to the government.[152]

When considering violations from a colonial past, it is important to establish "a proper factual account of the violations committed, the resulting patterns of conduct and the power structures involved, and also the way in which colonial practices, standards and processes still have repercussions, or even continue, today".[153] Thus, to satisfactorily address colonial legacies, facts "that reveal connections between past violations with implications for present events" should be prioritised, which requires "serious and detailed studies" to be carried out.[154] TCs have been used to investigate colonial abuses against indigenous peoples in several contexts. For example, in Canada, the Indian Residential Schools Settlement Agreement established a Truth and Reconciliation Commission to promote education and awareness about the residential school system and to collect testimonies from survivors.[155] In May 2021, the Victorian Government established Australia's first formal truth-telling mechanism—the Yoorrook Justice Commission—to investigate "past and ongoing injustices experienced by First Peoples in Victoria" since colonisation through the

[148] Svenska kyrkan 2011, pp. 55–56.

[149] HRC 2013, para 27.

[150] Hayner 2011, p. 20.

[151] Ibid., pp. 20–22.

[152] AHRC 1997.

[153] UNGA 2021, para 45.

[154] Ibid., para 46.

[155] Corntassel and Holder 2008, p. 474.

collection of testimonies.[156] However, Corntassel and Holder have warned that strategies of modern TCs tend to be premised on colonial narratives and engage in what they call "politics of distraction", meaning shifting the discourse away from restitution of indigenous lands and resources and instead focusing on a process that ultimately rewards colonial injustices.[157] Separating TCs from an indigenous self-determination agenda and ignoring claims for restitution sets TCs up to fail for indigenous peoples, and limits the potential for decolonisation of relations and transforming "existing relationships that go beyond hollow, symbolic gestures."[158]

The Church's 2006 report recommended a hearing about Sami identity and experiences in the CoS. The Church's theological committee and the Sami Council subsequently organised a *Ságastallamat*—meaning conversation or dialogue in northern Sami.[159] The first two Ságastallamat took place in 2011 and 2022; two more are scheduled for 2026 and 2031.[160] However, the Ságastallamat is referred to by the Church not as a hearing, but as a conference,[161] and the Ságastallamat have so far mostly been a series of presentations by and discussions between Church leaders, members of the Sami Council and the Sami Parliament, and scholars involved in the reconciliation project.[162] In fact, so far the Ságastamallat has not provided a space for proper participation by the wider Sami community. During Ságastamallat 1 it appears that one representative from Sáminuorra—the only civil society organisation—was present,[163] and while the report from Ságastallamat 1 mentions some interviews were conducted to get an overview of the situation for the Sami and of important issues,[164] it is unclear how many interviews were conducted and with whom. Furthermore, while parts of Ságastallamat 1 were open to the public, the public could not participate, which was criticised by participants.[165] It therefore seems that the wider Sami community has had little space to speak about their personal experiences with Church abuses and their consequences. As was noted by some participants, the Sami must be allowed to verbalise loss and pain in a supportive space.[166] It is therefore questionable how much the Ságastallamat contribute to truth-finding.

As a consequence of Ságastallamat 1, the CoS produced two written pieces—both published in 2016—that could be seen as partly fulfilling a truth-seeking objective.

---

156 Yoorrook Justice Commission, About Yoorrook, https://yoorrookjusticecommission.org.au/overview/. Accessed 1 December 2023.

157 Corntassel and Holder 2008, p. 472.

158 Ibid., pp. 467, 479.

159 Ekström and Schött 2006, p. 18; Svenska kyrkan 2011, p. 3.

160 Svenska kyrkan [Church of Sweden], Ságastallamat, https://www.svenskakyrkan.se/samiska/sagastallamat. Accessed 1 December 2023.

161 Ibid.

162 Svenska kyrkan 2011, pp. 59–61; Svenska kyrkan [Church of Sweden], Ságastallamat 2 i Luleå [Ságastallamat 2 in Luleå], https://www.svenskakyrkan.se/sagastallamat/sagastallamat-2. Accessed 1 December 2023

163 Svenska kyrkan 2011, p. 61.

164 Ibid., p. 3.

165 Ibid., p. 55.

166 Ibid., p. 57.

First, it published a book about the Church run so-called 'nomad schools', which included testimonies from Sami who had attended these schools.[167] Archbishop Jackelén wrote in the foreword that the Church wants, and needs, to take responsibility for its past by documenting and making visible its part in Swedish colonial history.[168] This book is the only real space provided for individual Sami voices and testimonies to be heard in the Church's truth-seeking process. Of the 47 people involved in this project, everyone but one was Sami.[169] Ten of the 26 testimonies collected were included in the book. From Ságastamallat 2 it seems that some testimonies were not included due to the interviewee passing away or declining to give their consent for their interview to be included,[170] but it is not clear whether this is the case for all 16 testimonies not included in the book. This book is important and provides a certain measure of truth regarding a particular area of Church abuse against the Sami. It may therefore 'shine a light on Sami experiences and increase the knowledge about Sami history in Sweden.'[171] However, it is not on its own the kind of serious and detailed study required to find out the full truth about the Church's involvement in the creation and running of 'nomad schools'. It should therefore be seen in conjunction with the second truth-seeking mechanism, the White Paper Project (WPP).

The WPP led to the publication of a two-volume anthology containing 34 chapters written by almost 40 scholars discussing various aspects of the Church's past, such as missionary and education work, the Church's attitude towards Sami cultural expression, and the Church as a government authority, including its involvement in racial biology research.[172] The research was led by Umeå University and its steering group consisted of two representatives from the University, two representatives from the Church administration, two Sami representatives appointed by the Sami Council, as well as the president of the Sami Council.[173] While not made explicit, to my knowledge five of the nine members are Sami. The WPP steering group interpreted its mandate as being "to develop in-depth knowledge of the relations between the Church of Sweden and the Sami through history".[174] The scholars involved had academic freedom to choose the parameters of their research and all chapters were peer reviewed.[175] For some, this shows the autonomy of the project, visible in the distinction "between historical research and the ideological texts intended to inspire action".[176] However, while impressive in terms of research, the information in the anthology is presented in a scholarly way around academic research questions, rather

[167] Blind and Huuva 2015.

[168] Ibid., p. 8.

[169] Svenska kyrkan [Church of Sweden], Ságastallamat fredag 13.00 [Ságastallamat Friday 13.00], https://vimeo.com/showcase/9870404/video/762917620. Accessed 1 December 2023.

[170] Ibid.

[171] Blind and Huuva 2015, p. 8.

[172] Lindmark and Sundström 2016b.

[173] Lindmark and Sundström 2016a, p. 23.

[174] Ibid., p. 29.

[175] Ibid., p. 35; Norlin and Lindmark 2021, p. 140.

[176] Norlin and Lindmark 2021, p. 141.

than centring the discussion around findings of fact and allowing these to guide the account of the past and the truth. Thus, most of the findings do not lead to an adequate analysis of the harms suffered by the Sami. Few of the chapters provide more than superficial discussion of the harms caused by the Church and none of the discussions adequately connect this to human rights issues. The chapters of the WPP simply do not discuss the issues from a perspective of finding out how the Church's conduct impacted the Sami.

Moreover, the WPP failed—by the editors' own admission[177]—to address the Church's acquisition and use of Sami lands. One chapter in the WPP discusses the construction of churches on Sami lands from the 17th century,[178] but there is no discussion that links past events to present-day land issues and the WPP ignores the issue of restitution of indigenous lands and resources—a serious failing. According to some Sami scholars, this omission undermines the claim that the anthology is scholarly and even a veritable white paper, since land issues are the basis of most current conflicts between the State and the Sami and the trauma within Sami society.[179]

Additionally, the Church has said that the WPP is "the result of cooperation between the Church and academia",[180] which indicates that it was not conceived to be a place for wider Sami participation or for individual voices to be heard in the manner expected of truth-seeking mechanisms. Furthermore, it is difficult for anyone without previous knowledge of the anthology's authors, or of Sami names, to know who among the authors are Sami.[181] Moreover, while the steering group and some of the academics involved in the project are Sami, the WPP does not include any witness testimonies and is not based on such statements to include the experiences of the Sami, which means that Sami voices were largely absent from this production of the "truth".

Overall, the truth-seeking mechanisms implemented by the Church are not akin to a proper investigation into abuses connected to colonisation. While the mechanisms provide some information about power structures involved in past abuses, they do not provide a clear factual account of violations, patterns of conduct, and the effects, including harms to the victims, of colonial practices. This means that the truth-seeking done by the Church is not adequate or effective as a measure of reparation. Even if there was a desire to ensure the 'neutrality' of academic research, hearings and testimonies of individual Sami could have been combined with the anthology to produce a fuller account of the truth. At present there are overall ten testimonies or stories of individual Sami in the truth-seeking project of the Church. Given the extent of the abuses and their consequences, this is grossly inadequate.

---

[177] Lindmark and Sundström 2016a, p. 31.

[178] Norstedt 2016.

[179] Öhman 2016.

[180] Jackelén 2016, p. 12.

[181] Öhman 2016.

12.6.2 Apology

Apologies are another measure of satisfaction in IHRL,[182] and apologies that take a victim-centred approach emphasise the rights, agency, and perspective of victims.[183] Apologies have been made to indigenous peoples in other contexts by both States and churches. The United Church of Canada apologised for its role in colonisation of indigenous peoples in 1986 and for abuses at its residential schools in 1998,[184] and in 2008 the prime ministers of both Canada and Australia apologised for abuses against the indigenous peoples in their respective countries.[185] It has been said that "the power and importance of apology lie in its potential to offer to victims *a moral recognition or acknowledgement* of their human worth and dignity."[186] Indigenous scholars have further argued that to be meaningful, apologies must help reset the relationship between the State and indigenous peoples "away from hierarchical and colonial power relations and toward one grounded in mutual respect."[187] Of course, these points are just as relevant when the apologiser is an institution like the CoS.

The Church's apology at least partially fulfils the criteria for apologies.[188] It identified and acknowledged particular wrongs committed, admitted collective and organisational responsibility, and issued a statement of regret.[189] Nevertheless, due to the limited truth-seeking process and the lack of Sami participation, it is the Church's narrative that is being confirmed, rather than a narrative agreed between the Church and the wider Sami community, and thus is an imposition of a particular truth narrative. The Church apologised for the colonisation of Sápmi. However, as the issue of land has not been thoroughly investigated in the WPP, the Church cannot fully acknowledge the extent of this wrong. Furthermore, during the apology the Church presented eight commitments for the reconciliation process: to preach the gospel in Sami and in a culturally relevant way with respect for Sami spiritual and church traditions; to make Sami spirituality, theology, and church traditions visible within the Church; to contribute to the strengthening and revitalising of Sami languages in the activities of the Church; to increase knowledge and awareness of the Church's historical relations and abuses against the Sami and the consequences of this; to increase knowledge of and respect for the principles of indigenous rights within the

---

182 E.g. UNGA 2006, para 22(e).

183 UNGA 2019, para 6.

184 The United Church of Canada, The Apologies, https://united-church.ca/social-action/justice-initiatives/reconciliation-and-indigenous-justice/apologies. Accessed 1 December 2023.

185 Government of Canada, Statement of apology to former students of Indian Residential Schools, https://www.rcaanc-cirnac.gc.ca/eng/1100100015644/1571589171655; Parliament of Australia, Apology to Australia's Indigenous Peoples, https://www.aph.gov.au/Visit_Parliament/Art/Icons/Apology_to_Australias_Indigenous_Peoples. Both accessed 1 December 2023.

186 Govier and Verwoerd 2002, p. 140.

187 Lightfoot 2015, p. 17.

188 UNGA 2019, para 3. See also Smith 2014.

189 Svenska kyrkan [Church of Sweden], Speech of Apology, https://www.svenskakyrkan.se/samiska/speech-of-apology. Accessed 1 December 2023.

Church and in society; to increase Sami influence and participation in the Church; to strengthen Sami children and youth in their identity and spiritual development; and to promote cross-border Sami church life.[190] While these are forward-looking measures, there is no clear connection between these commitments and the wrongs identified—thus they do not serve the goals of guarantees of non-repetition, as required by an apology.[191]

When it comes to process requirements the apology appears to fulfil several aspects considered important to maximise the effectiveness of apologies.[192] First, the apology was offered by the Archbishop, the highest Church official, and thus the person with "the authority necessary to speak on behalf of the offender."[193] The apology also arguably took place in symbolically important locations; first in Uppsala Cathedral—the seat of the Archbishop of the Church of Sweden—in November 2021, then in Luleå Cathedral, which is located in Sápmi, in October 2022. Furthermore, the apology was carried out in what appeared as appropriately dignified ceremonies with important symbolism.

Both services gathered representatives from the Church, including the Sami Council, and the Sami community, e.g. from the Sami Parliament. They also included representatives of civil society, international witnesses from the Anglican Church of Canada, the Church of Norway, and the Lutheran Church of Finland, and the public.[194] The services included psalms and readings in both Swedish and various Sami languages, and in the second service in Luleå, *yoik* was also included.[195] Sami representatives read out testimonies relating to past abuses, which are available online in different languages.[196] Each service also included Sami artwork and the participants, including the Archbishop, sat at the altar in a symbolically important circle around a fire. Thus, at least some Sami were able to participate in the ceremony of

---

[190] Svenska kyrkan [Church of Sweden], Mål och handlingsplan för den fortsatta försoningsprocessen [Goals and action plan for the continued reconciliation process], https://www.svenskakyrkan.se/samiska/mal-och-handlingsplan#lasomatagandena. Accessed 1 December 2023. Translation by the author.

[191] UNGA 2019, para 3.

[192] Ibid., paras 30–39.

[193] Ibid., para 31.

[194] Svenska kyrkan [Church of Sweden], Svenska kyrkans ursäkt till det samiska folket [The Church of Sweden's apology to the Sami people], https://www.svenskakyrkan.se/samiska/ursakt-till-det-samiska-folket. Accessed 1 December 2023.

[195] Svenska kyrkan [Church of Sweden], Agenda för högtidsgudstjänsten i Uppsala domkyrka [Agenda for the service in Uppsala Cathedral], https://www.svenskakyrkan.se/samiska/ursakt-till-det-samiska-folket/agenda-gudstjanst; Svenska kyrkan [Church of Sweden], Agenda för högtidsgudstjänsten i Luleå domkyrka [Agenda for the service in Luleå Cathedral] https://www.svenskakyrkan.se/samiska/ursakt-till-det-samiska-folket/agenda-gudstjanst-lulea. Both accessed 1 December 2023.

[196] Svenska kyrkan [Church of Sweden], Samiska vittnesmål – på flera spark [Sami testimonies – in several languages], https://www.svenskakyrkan.se/samiska/samiska-vittnesmal. Accessed 1 December 2023.

the apology, even though it is unclear to what extent the Sami were involved in its planning.[197]

In order to maximise the effectiveness of apologies, there should also be prior consultation with the victims to ensure that the content and delivery of the apology is acceptable to them.[198] The apologies considered most effective have also allowed victims to participate in both the planning and in the ceremony of the apology.[199] As seen above, Sami representatives participated in the reconciliation service and ceremony where the apology was made. According to the Action Plan, the Church decided in June 2021 to deliver an official apology to the Sami after conversations within the Sami Council as well as between the Church and representatives of Sami civil society organisations and the Sami Parliament about the way forward.[200] Nevertheless, while there appears to have been some consultation in relation to the apology, it is not clear from the available material which, or how many, Sami civil society organisations the Church was in conversation with or the extent to which the Sami were consulted about the content and delivery. Further empirical research is needed to clarify this.

The apology, and the reconciliation process as a whole, seems to have been done in good faith. Nevertheless, they may perpetuate power imbalances, as warned against by indigenous scholars,[201] due to the lack of participation of the Sami, as discussed above, as well as the issue of whether the apology acknowledged the full truth. And while the apology was positively received by both the President of the Sami Parliament and representatives of the Sami Council,[202] it is unclear to what extent the apology resonated with the Sami in Sweden more broadly. Therefore, further empirical research is needed here too.

12.6.3 The Action Plan

The Church's Action Plan sets out how each of the eight commitments mentioned above will be implemented between 2022 and 2031.[203] However, the Action Plan only mentions 'reparation' once, and does not further discuss reparation or analyse which measures would "restore the victim and the relationship between victim and

---

197 Carranza et al. 2015, p. 17.

198 UNGA 2019, paras 30–35.

199 Carranza et al. 2015, p. 17.

200 Svenska kyrkan 2022, pp. 6–11.

201 Lightfoot 2015, pp. 17–19.

202 Svenska kyrkan [Church of Sweden], Svenska kyrkans ursäkt till det samiska folket [The Church of Sweden's apology to the Sami people], https://www.svenskakyrkan.se/samiska/ursakt-till-det-samiska-folket; Sametinget [Swedish Sami Parliament], Tal av Håkan Jonsson vid försoningsgudstjänst [Speech by Håkan Jonsson at reconciliation service], https://www.sametinget.se/162976. Both accessed 1 December 2023.

203 Svenska kyrkan 2022, p. 35.

perpetrator"[204] to achieve reconciliation. The apparent lack of understanding about reparation permeates the Action Plan and affects the ability of the commitments and suggested measures to provide adequate and effective reparation for the violations suffered by the Sami.

12.6.3.1 General Issues

First, Sami participation and consultation regarding the Action Plan and its measures appears inadequate. The Action Plan was developed by the Church Board "in close dialogue" with the Sami Council.[205] There appears to have been no consultation or participation of Sami civil society organisations, and no participation by the wider Sami community. This is significant as the Action Plan is the document that explicitly refers to reparation and that sets out the measures to be implemented to restore the victims and the relationship between the Church and the Sami.[206] Empirical research is needed to clarify the extent of Sami the participation in this process.

Second, as the commitments are not clearly linked to the findings from the Church's truth-seeking, it is difficult to understand which measures in the Plan are meant to redress which particular harm and how they could achieve this. Additionally, six of the eight commitments focus on improving the situation for the Sami within the Church, which is exclusionary. While the two commitments to educate both Church representatives and the public about past abuses and Sami indigenous rights could be directed at all Sami and are important GNR,[207] these measures are clearly inadequate to address the wide spectrum of violations caused to the wider Sami community by the Church's conduct.

Moreover, none of the measures of the Action Plan are aimed at Sami in their individual or personal capacity; the measures are all directed at the Sami as a community. Collective reparation is meant to undo collective harm caused to groups bound together by a common identity,[208] and has been recognised in IHRL as important for certain harms caused to indigenous groups.[209] Still, individual reparation is important to avoid minimising the particular harm done to individual victims.[210] It is therefore generally recognised that reparation mechanisms should ideally combine individual and collective reparation to adequately respond to the different types of harms.[211] Lastly, the Church's process does not provide for rehabilitation or compensation. In

[204] Svenska kyrkan 2022, 33.

[205] Ibid., p. 5.

[206] Ibid., p. 33.

[207] Ibid., pp. 26, 69-72; UNGA 2006, para 23.

[208] Rosenfeld 2010, p. 734.

[209] E.g. IACtHR, *Plan de Sánchez Massacre v. Guatemala*, Reparations, 19 November 2004, Series C No. 116, paras 109–111.

[210] Magarrell 2007, pp. 5–6.

[211] UNGA 2014, paras 31–33.

IHRL, compensation is provided for both physical and moral harm, and rehabilitation includes physical and psychological treatment.[212] Of course, which forms and modality of reparation will be adequate, depends on the views of victims and what they want. As noted above, it is unclear from the Action Plan to what extent there was, if any, discussion with the Sami community except perhaps members of the Sami Council. Proper discussion and consultation with the Sami, and further research into what reparation they want, is needed to ensure that the reparation provided is adequate and effective in repairing the harm.

12.6.3.2 Evaluation of Specific Measures in the Action Plan

The measures to promote Sami languages, spirituality, and culture in Church life could be considered measures of satisfaction as well as restitution of rights for the harms caused by Christianisation.[213] Nevertheless, only Sami involved in the Church, i.e. those who were successfully (forcibly) Christianised, may benefit from these measures. This is not only exclusionary; it uses a facet of Sami victimisation (forcible Christianisation) as a further, present-day justification for yet further exclusion. By comparison, the United Church of Canada established a Healing Fund in 1994 from which indigenous communities can apply for up to CAD 15,000 to create healing, culture, and/or language projects.[214] The Church should consult with the Sami and discuss whether similar projects could be helpful to help repair the harm caused by their loss of religion and culture.

The failure to repatriate human remains can lead to spiritual, psychological, and intellectual harm.[215] The Church has recently expressed a desire to contribute to repatriation,[216] and was involved in the reburial of Sami remains in 2019 and 2020.[217] Curiously, the issue of Sami remains is the only time the Action Plan links its measures to findings of abuses from the Church's truth-seeking. The Church explains how its advocacy work can assist in the repatriation of Sami remains. The Church is not presently in possession of the remains and is therefore not able on its own to organise repatriation and reburials. However, Archbishop Jackelén initiated discussions about obstacles to repatriation in 2017 and 2019 with the Sami Parliament, the Ministry of Culture, and several museums and institutions housing Sami remains.[218] The Action

---

[212] UNGA 2006, para 23.

[213] Svenska kyrkan 2022, pp. 25–26, 39–72; UNGA 2006, paras 19, 22.

[214] The United Church of Canada, Healing Fund, https://united-church.ca/community-and-faith/being-community/indigenous-ministries/healing-fund#downloads. Accessed 1 December 2023.

[215] HRC 2020, para 14.

[216] Svenska kyrkan [Church of Sweden], Svenska kyrkan vill bidra till repatriering av samiska kvarlevor [The Church of Sweden wants to contribute to the repatriation of Sami remains], https://www.svenskakyrkan.se/nyheter/svenska-kyrkan-vill-bidra-till-repatriering-av-samiska-kvarlevor. 17 November 2017, accessed 1 December 2023.

[217] Svenska kyrkan 2022, p. 72.

[218] Ibid., p. 71; Svenska kyrkan [Church of Sweden], Svenska kyrkan vill bidra till repatriering av samiska kvarlevor [The Church of Sweden wants to contribute to the repatriation of

Plan notes that the Sami have raised the issue of repatriation of other material from the former State Institute for Racial Biology. Assuming this means photographs of Sami held at current institutions, their repatriation could be an important form of restitution and satisfaction.[219] The Church could assist in the repatriation of photographs of Sami taken by racial biologists to, for example, Ájtte, the Sami museum in Jokkmokk or other institutions chosen by the Sami.

Nevertheless, the Action Plan fails to include measures to repair many of the other violations discussed above. First, while the apology has been offered as a measure of reparation for the loss of identity and culture that comes with the erasure of names, the Action Plan does not envision any additional reparation directly linked to this harm. Further consultation with the Sami about what measures would be adequate and effective reparation is necessary as what is currently offered is not proportionate.

Indigenous peoples have the right to restitution of their lands or, where this is impossible, compensation[220] as well as reparation for violations of the right to culture and for cultural destruction.[221] The WPP did not adequately investigate issues relating to Sami lands and since the Church still manages Sami traditional lands, colonisation persists and is an ongoing violation of Sami rights. According to the Action Plan, between 2022 and 2026, research on the Church's land holdings on traditional Sami lands will be carried out, as well as a survey of how the Church's land management and forestry affects reindeer herding and traditional Sami hunting, fishing, and crafts, with a view to developing long term, sustainable forms of Sami influence and to consider indigenous rights in the Church's land management and forestry.[222] This process seems to envision a deeper dialogue between the Church and Sami stakeholders than previously in the reconciliation process, which is encouraging and has the potential to be reparative. Nevertheless, it is important that dialogue and consultation is conducted with as many Sami stakeholders as possible.

Finally, and vital for the issue of reparation, the Action Plan is silent when it comes to reparation for the harm caused by the 'nomad schools'. Again, the Church needs to properly engage with the Sami about how to provide adequate and effective reparation for these harms. Truth, with Sami participation in creating the process and narrative, would be a start. Furthermore, reparation measures that are clearly linked to the abuses in the 'nomad schools' are needed. Any such reparation must be viewed by the Sami as an appropriate way to redress the harm and be developed through Sami participation and consultation. The CoS has not considered whether the Sami might wish to receive medical and psychological support.[223] Something similar to the Healing Fund in Canada, which supports "holistic and community-based healing to address the needs

Sami remains], https://www.svenskakyrkan.se/nyheter/svenska-kyrkan-vill-bidra-till-repatriering-av-samiska-kvarlevor. 17 November 2017, accessed 1 December 2023.

[219] UNGA 2007, art. 12(1).

[220] Ibid., art. 28.

[221] ICCPR, above n. 69, art. 27; ibid, art. 8.

[222] Svenska kyrkan 2022, pp. 61-67.

[223] UNGA 2006, para 21.

of individuals, families and communities",[224] might be considered. The Church has also not considered compensation payments to former students of the 'nomad school' system. Compensation payments were established for survivors of residential schools in Canada as part of the Indian Residential Schools Settlement Agreement, although the Agreement has been criticised for limiting eligibility to living survivors and for its low compensation amounts.[225] Any compensation provided to the Sami might therefore also consider compensation for the next of kin of survivors of 'nomad schools', given the likely intergenerational harms. The Church should consult the wider Sami communities in Sweden to discuss whether such measures would be meaningful to them as reparation.

12.7 Conclusion

This chapter investigated to what extent the Church of Sweden's reconciliation process is able to effectively meet the Church's obligation to provide reparation in accordance with IHRL. The range of abuses committed by the Church against the Sami led to loss of land, religion, language, and culture, as well as to the division of the Sami as a people. The consequences are still felt today and lived by many Sami who are fighting to reclaim their language and culture, and rights to traditional lands, water, and resources. While the CoS was a major actor in the colonisation of Sápmi and subsequent abuses against the Sami, as a State institution until 2000 its actions before then would be attributed to the State. Nevertheless, the Church also has responsibility to provide reparation for harms caused until then and should do so according to IHRL standards.

The CoS has made efforts to take responsibility for its role in the colonisation of Sápmi and to redress abuses against the Sami. Still, its approach suffers from defects that are likely to prevent adequate and effective reparation. First, the Church's process has not been victim-centred and has generally lacked participation of the Sami community in Sweden. Without hearing from the wider Sami communities in Sweden, it is questionable how the Church can provide adequate and effective reparation and how successful any reconciliation will be.

Second, while the truth-seeking undertaken by the CoS has to a certain extent established a record of the past and clarified some events, the lack of wider Sami participation means that the Church has not been able to establish a full understanding of the truth. Moreover, the WPP, did not adequately analyse the harms caused to the Sami by the Church's colonisation. Also, the issue of land remains inadequately explored and whether the Church's process will lead to reconciliation with the Sami

---

[224] Indian Residential Schools Settlement Agreement, Schedule M – Funding Agreement between the Aboriginal Healing Foundation and Canada, 8 May 2006, https://www.residentialschoolsettlement.ca/Schedule_M.pdf. Accessed 1 December 2023.

[225] Morse 2008, p. 283; Corntassel and Holder 2008, pp. 474–475.

might depend to a large degree on what happens with the investigation into this and the Church's subsequent actions as envisioned in its Action Plan.

Third, the lack of analysis of reparation in the Church's Action Plan makes it unclear whether the Church really understands its importance, and how to think about reparation. The Plan does not link the commitments to particular abuses recognised by the Church, which makes it unclear what the Church is trying to repair with a particular measure. Additionally, most of the measures will only benefit the Sami who are involved in the Church, which makes them inadequate as reparation for the Sami as a whole. Moreover, the lack of proper analysis and consultation with the Sami of what would be adequate reparation risks leading to inadequate and ineffective reparation and perpetuation of injustices.

Overall, the Church's process looks like a good faith effort and, while flawed, it is an important first step in the context of Sweden dealing with its colonial past and redressing the harm committed against the Sami. To increase the possibility of a successful reconciliation process, the Church should consider engaging more with principles developed by IHRL and transitional justice, particularly truth and reparation. The Church should also ensure proper participation by the Sami communities in Sweden affected by its abuses and the Church's reconciliation process must ultimately be guided by the wishes of the Sami.

Still, the Church's process is relevant for the Swedish TC. First, it can help clarify the extent of the responsibility of the Church and the State for reparation. Second, the work of the Church has the potential to positively impact the TC's work. The TC will hold public information meetings at various locations in Sweden, mostly in Sápmi, during 2023 and 2024, and at the time of writing 23 such meetings have occurred with four more scheduled in early 2024.[226] Individual Sami are also able to share their stories with the Commission.[227] This gives the TC the potential to hear from the broader Sami community and take their views into account, something the Church did not sufficiently do. The TC can draw valuable lessons from the Church's approach to reparation, including Sami participation, to ensure that its own recommendations of reparation are more in line with IHRL standards and provide adequate and effective reparation to the Sami.

References

AHRC (Australian Human Rights Commission) (1997) Bringing them Home: Report of the National Inquiry into the Separation of Aboriginal and Torres Strait Islander Children

[226] Sanningskommissionen för det samiska folket [The truth commission for the Sami people], Nyhetsbrev 2023-12-12 [Newsletter 2023-12-12], https://mailchi.mp/26061f8891b5/nyhetsbrev-sanningskommissionen-fr-det-samiska-folket-9386256?e=[UNIQID]. Accessed 19 December 2023.

[227] Sanningskommissionen för det samiska folket [The truth commission for the Sami people], Dela din historia [Share your story], https://sanningskommissionensamer.se/dela-din-historia/. Accessed 1 December 2023.

from Their Families. https://humanrights.gov.au/sites/default/files/content/pdf/social_justice/bringing_them_home_report.pdf. Accessed 28 August 2023
Ahrén M (2004) Indigenous people's culture, customs, and traditions and customary law – the Saami people's perspective. Arizona Journal of International & Comparative Law 21:63–112
Alfred T (2005) Wasáse: Indigenous pathways of action and freedom. Broadview Press
Allard C, Brännström M (2021) Girjas Reindeer Herding Community v. Sweden: Analysing the Merits of the Girjas Case. Arctic Review on Law and Politics 12:56–79
Anderzén S (2016) Kyrkans undervisning i Lappmarken under 1800-talet: En ständigt pågående process för att finna fungerande arbetsformer [The Church's education in Lapland during the 19th century: An ongoing process to find functioning working methods]. In: Lindmark D, Sundström O (eds) De historiska relationerna mellan Svenska kyrkan och samerna [Historical relations between the Church of Sweden and the Sami]. Artos & Norma, pp 371–402
Axelsson P (2016) Kyrkan, folkbokföringen och samerna [The Church, the population registry, and the Sami]. In: Lindmark D, Sundström O (eds) De historiska relationerna mellan Svenska kyrkan och samerna [Historical relations between the Church of Sweden and the Sami]. Artos & Norma, pp 915–942
Blind E, Huuva R-M (eds) (2015) "När jag var åtta år lämnade jag mitt hem och jag har ännu inte kommit tillbaka"—Minnesbilder från samernas skoltid ["When I was eight years old I left home and I have not yet returned"—Memories from Sami school days]. Verbum
Carranza R, Cristián C, Naughton E (2015) More Than Words: Apologies as a Form of Reparation. https://www.ictj.org/sites/default/files/ICTJ-Report-Apologies-2015.pdf. Accessed 28 August 2024
CERD (Committee on the Elimination of Racial Discrimination) (1997) General recommendation XXIII on the rights of indigenous peoples, UN Doc A/52/18, annex V
CERD (Committee on the Elimination of Racial Discrimination) (2018) Concluding observations on the combined twenty-second and twenty-third periodic reports of Sweden, UN Doc. CERD/C/SWE/CO/22-23
Christoffersson R (2016) Svenska kyrkan och samiska trummor [The Church of Sweden and Sami drums]. In: Lindmark D, Sundström O (eds) De historiska relationerna mellan Svenska kyrkan och samerna [Historical relations between the Church of Sweden and the Sami]. Artos & Norma, pp 657–680
Cismas I (2014) Religious Actors and International Law. Oxford University Press
Corntassel J, Holder C (2008) Who's Sorry Now? Government Apologies, Truth Commissions, and Indigenous Self-Determination in Australia, Canada, Guatemala, and Peru. Human Rights Review 9:465–489
Correa C, Guillerot J, Magarrell L (2009) Reparations and Victim Participation: A Look at the Truth Commission Experience. In: Ferstman C, Goetz M, Stephens A (eds) Reparations for Victims of Genocide, War Crimes and Crimes against Humanity: Systems in Place and Systems in the Making. Martinus Nijhoff Publishers, pp 385–414
Elenius L (2016) Stiftsledningen och Minoritetspolitiken. In: Lindmark D, Sundström O (eds) De historiska relationerna mellan Svenska kyrkan och samerna [Historical relations between the Church of Sweden and the Sami]. Artos & Norma, pp 469–518
Ekström S, Schött M (2006) Samiska frågor i Svenska kyrkan [Sami issues in the Church of Sweden], SKU 2006:1. https://www.svenskakyrkan.se/Sve/Bin%c3%a4rfiler/Filer/E2DC85BC-6AC7-487D-8A12-1BA37EE4AEEC.pdf. Accessed 28 August 2023
Francioni F (2008) Reparation for Indigenous Peoples: Is International Law Ready to Ensure Redress for Historical Injustice?. In: Lenzerini F (ed) Reparations for Indigenous Peoples: International and Comparative Perspectives. Oxford University Press, pp 27–45
Frändén M (2016) Svenska kyrkan och det samiska namnskicket: Övergripande perspektiv [The Church of Sweden and Sami names: Overall perspective]. In: Lindmark D, Sundström O (eds) De historiska relationerna mellan Svenska kyrkan och samerna [Historical relations between the Church of Sweden and the Sami]. Artos & Norma, pp 797–810

Fur G (2016) Kolonisation och kulturmöten under 1600- och 1700-talen [Colonisation and culture meetings during the 1600s and 1700s]. In: Lindmark D, Sundström O (eds) De historiska relationerna mellan Svenska kyrkan och samerna [Historical relations between the Church of Sweden and the Sami]. Artos & Norma, pp 241–281

Govier T, Verwoerd W (2002) Taking Wrongs Seriously: A Qualified Defence of Public Apologies. Saskatchewan Law Review 65:139-162

Hagerman M (2016) Svenska kyrkan och rasbiologin [The Church of Sweden and racial biology]. In: Lindmark D, Sundström O (eds) De historiska relationerna mellan Svenska kyrkan och samerna [Historical relations between the Church of Sweden and the Sami]. Artos & Norma, 961–992

Hayner P (2011) Unspeakable Truths: Transitional Justice and the Challenge of Truth Commissions, 2nd edn. Routledge

HRC (Human Rights Council) (2011) Report of the Special Rapporteur on the Rights of Indigenous Peoples, James Anaya, UN Doc. A/HRC/18/35/Add.2

HRC (Human Rights Council) (2013) Report of the Special Rapporteur on the promotion of truth, justice, reparation and guarantees of non-recurrence, Pablo de Greiff, UN Doc. A/HRC/24/42

HRC (Human Rights Council) (2016a) Report of the Special Rapporteur on the rights of indigenous peoples on the human rights situation of the Sami people in the Sápmi region of Norway, Sweden and Finland, UN Doc. A/HRC/33/42/Add.3

HRC (Human Rights Council) (2016b) Report of the Special Rapporteur on the promotion of truth, justice, reparation and guarantees of non-recurrence, UN Doc. A/HRC/34/62

HRC (Human Rights Council) (2019) Efforts to implement the United Nations Declaration on the Rights of Indigenous Peoples: recognition, reparation and reconciliation, Report of the Expert Mechanism on the Rights of Indigenous Peoples, UN Doc. A/HRC/EMRIP/2019/3/Rev.1

HRC (Human Rights Council) (2020) Repatriation of ceremonial objects, human remains and intangible cultural heritage under the United Nations Declaration on the Rights of Indigenous Peoples, Report of the Expert Mechanism on the Rights of Indigenous Peoples, UN Doc. A/HRC/45/35

Human Rights Committee (1994) General Comment No. 23: Article 27 (Rights of Minorities), UN Doc. CCPR/C/21/Rev.1/Add.5

Human Rights Committee (2016) Concluding observations on the seventh periodic report of Sweden, UN Doc. CCPR/C/SWE/CO/7

ILC (International Law Commission) (2001) Draft articles on Responsibility of States for Internationally Wrongful Acts, with commentaries, adopted at its fifty-third session

Jackelén A (2016) Förord [Foreword]. In: Lindmark D, Sundström O (eds) De historiska relationerna mellan Svenska kyrkan och samerna [Historical relations between the Church of Sweden and the Sami]. Artos & Norma, pp 11–18

Justitiedepartementet [Ministry of Justice] (1986) Samernas folkrättsliga ställning [The Status of the Sami in International Law], SOU: 1986:36. https://lagen.nu/sou/1986:36. Accessed 28 August 2023

Ka'ai T (2020) Aotearoa/New Zealand. In: Minton S J (ed) Residential Schools and Indigenous Peoples: From Genocide via Education to the Possibilities for Processes of Truth, Restitution, Reconciliation, and Reclamation. Routledge, pp 48–65

Krawchenko T, McDonald C (2023) Rendering the invisible visible: Sámi rights and data governance. In: Cambou D, Ravna Ø (eds) The Significance of Sámi Rights: Law, Justice, and Sustainability for the Indigenous Sámi in the Nordic Countries. Routledge, pp 152–165

Kuokkanen R (2020) Reconciliation as a Threat or Structural Change? The Truth and Reconciliation Process and Settler Colonial Policy Maing in Finland. Human Rights Review 21:293–312

Lantto P, Mörkenstam U (2008) Sami Rights and Sami Challenges: The modernization process and the Swedish Sami movement, 1886–2006. Scandinavian Journal of History 33:26–51

Lantto P (2010) Borders, citizenship and change: the case of the Sami people 1751–2008. Citizenship Studies 14:543–556

Lightfoot S (2015) Settler-State Apologies to Indigenous Peoples: A Normative Framework and Comparative Assessment. Native American and Indigenous Studies 2:15–39

Lindmark D (2016) Svenska undervisningsinsatser och samiska reaktioner på 1600- och 1700-talen [Swedish education efforts and Sami reactions during the 17th and 18th century]. In: Lindmark D, Sundström O (eds) De historiska relationerna mellan Svenska kyrkan och samerna [Historical relations between the Church of Sweden and the Sami]. Artos & Norma, pp 341–366

Lindmark D, Sundström O (2016a) Svenska kyrkan och samerna—ett vitboksprojekt: Presentation av projektet och antologin [The Church of Sweden and the Sami—a white paper project: Presentation of the project and the anthology]. In: Lindmark D and Sundström O (eds) De historiska relationerna mellan Svenska kyrkan och samerna [Historical relations between the Church of Sweden and the Sami]. Artos & Norma, pp 21–39

Lindmark D, Sundström O (eds) (2016b) De historiska relationerna mellan Svenska kyrkan och samerna [Historical relations between the Church of Sweden and the Sami]. Artos & Norma

Magarrell L (2007) Reparations in Theory and Practice. International Center for Transitional Justice. https://www.ictj.org/sites/default/files/ICTJ-Global-Reparations-Practice-2007-English.pdf. Accessed 28 August 2023

Marainen J (2016) Svenska kyrkan och det samiska namnskicket: Reflektioner kring några konkreta exempel [The Church of Sweden and Sami names: Reflections regarding specific examples]. In: Lindmark D, Sundström O (eds) De historiska relationerna mellan Svenska kyrkan och samerna [Historical relations between the Church of Sweden and the Sami]. Artos & Norma, pp 811–820

Mörkenstam U (2005) Indigenous Peoples and the Right to Self-Determination: The Case of the Swedish Sami People. The Canadian Journal of Native Studies 25:433–461

Morse B W (2008) Indigenous Peoples of Canada and Their Efforts to Achieve True Reparations. In: Lenzerini F (ed) Reparations for Indigenous Peoples: International and Comparative Perspectives. Oxford University Press, pp 271–316

Mulk I-M (2009) Conflict Over the Repatriation of Sami Cultural Heritage in Sweden. Acta Borealia 26:194–215

Nayar P K (2010) Postcolonialism: A guide for the perplexed. Continuum

Nergård J-I (2020) The colonisation of Sápmi. In: Minton S J (ed) Residential Schools and Indigenous Peoples: From Genocide via Education to the Possibilities for Processes of Truth, Restitution, Reconciliation, and Reclamation. Routledge, pp 113–140

Nordbäck C (2016) Försoning, erkännande och inklusion: Perspektiv på försoningsprocessen mellan Svenska kyrkan och samerna [Reconciliation, recognition and inclusion: Perspectives on the reconciliation process between the Church of Sweden and the Sami]. In: Dahlbacka I, Groop K, Dahlbacka J (eds) The Shifting Boundaries of Tolerance: Inclusion, Exclusion, and Religious Communities of Memory. Studies on Memory and Religion, pp 125–197

Norlin B, Lindmark D (2021) Generating and Popularising Historical Knowledge in a Reconciliation Process: The Case of the Church of Sweden and the Sami. In: Keynes M, Åström Elmersjö H, Lindmark D, Norlin B (eds) Historical Justice and History Education. Palgrave Macmillan, pp 131–151

Norlin B, Sjögren D (2016) Kyrkan, utbildningspolitiken och den samiska skolundervisningen vid sekelskiftet 1900: Inflytande, vägval och konsekvenser? [The Church, education policy and Sami school education at the turn of the 20th century: Influence, choices and consequences?]. In: Lindmark D, Sundström O (eds) De historiska relationerna mellan Svenska kyrkan och samerna [Historical relations between the Church of Sweden and the Sami]. Artos & Norma, pp 403–438

Norman-Hill R (2020) Australia's native residential schools. In: Minton S J (ed) Residential Schools and Indigenous Peoples: From Genocide via Education to the Possibilities for Processes of Truth, Restitution, Reconciliation, and Reclamation. Routledge, pp 66–94

Norstedt G (2016) Hur kyrkor och prästbord tog plats i det samiska landskapet [How churches and clergy took up space in the Sami landscape]. In: Lindmark D, Sundström O (eds) De historiska relationerna mellan Svenska kyrkan och samerna [Historical relations between the Church of Sweden and the Sami]. Artos & Norma, pp 823–854

Ojala C-G (2016) Svenska kyrkan och samiska mänskliga kvarlevor [The Church of Sweden and Sami human remains]. In: Lindmark D, Sundström O (eds) De historiska relationerna mellan Svenska kyrkan och samerna [Historical relations between the Church of Sweden and the Sami]. Artos & Norma, pp 993–1025

Oscarsson E-O (2015) "Kåtasystemet ägde det allra närmaste samband med lapparnas sedvänjor": Om det samiska motståndet och vittnesmål om missförhållanden på nomadskolan [About Sami resistance and testimonies of abuses at the nomad school]. In: Blind E, Huuva R-M (eds) "När jag var åtta år lämnade jag mitt hem och jag har ännu inte kommit tillbaka"—Minnesbilder från samernas skoltid ["When I was eight years old I left home and I have not yet returned"—Memories from Sami school days]. Verbum, pp 85–105

Oscarsson E-O (2016) Rastänkande och särskiljande av samer [Racial thinking and differentiating between the Sami]. In: Lindmark D, Sundström O (eds) De historiska relationerna mellan Svenska kyrkan och samerna [Historical relations between the Church of Sweden and the Sami]. Artos & Norma, pp 943–959

Partapuoli P J (2015) Arvet från det förflutna—kampen fortsätter [The legacy of the past—the struggle continues]. In: Blind E, Huuva R-M (eds) "När jag var åtta år lämnade jag mitt hem och jag har ännu inte kommit tillbaka"—Minnesbilder från samernas skoltid ["When I was eight years old I left home and I have not yet returned"—Memories from Sami school days]. Verbum, pp 229–235

Pettersson P (2000) Kvalitet i livslånga tjänsterelationer—Svenska kyrkan ur tjänsteteoretiskt och religionssociologiskt perspektiv [Quality in lifelong service relationships—The Church of Sweden from a service theoretical and religious sociological perspective]. Verbum

Raitio K, Allard C, Lawrence R (2020) Mineral extraction in Swedish Sápmi: The regulatory gap between Sami rights and Sweden's mining permitting practices. Land Use Policy 99. https://doi.org/10.1016/j.landusepol.2020.105001.

Regeringen [Government of Sweden] (2021) Kartläggning och granskning av den politik som förts gentemot samerna och dess konsekvenser för det samiska folket [Mapping and examination of the policy carried out towards the Sami and its consequences for the Sami people], Dir. 2021:10

Rosenfeld F (2010) Collective Reparation for Victims of Armed Conflict. International Review of the Red Cross 92:731–746

Shaw M N (2021) International Law, 9th edn. Cambridge University Press

Shelton D (2004) The World of Atonement Reparations for Historical Injustices. Miskolc Journal of International Law 1: 259–289

Shelton D (2008) Reparations for Indigenous Peoples: The Present Value of Past Wrongs. In: Lenzerini F (ed) Reparations for Indigenous Peoples: International and Comparative Perspectives. Oxford University Press, pp 47–72

Short D (2010) Cultural genocide and indigenous peoples: A sociological approach. The International Journal of Human Rights 14:833–848

Sjögren D (2017) Samerna och kyrkan som myndighet [The Sami and the Church as a government authority]. In: Lindmark D, Sundström O (eds) Samerna och Svenska kyrkan: Underlag för kyrkligt försoningsarbete [The Sami and the Church of Sweden: Foundation for church reconciliation work]. Gidlunds Förlag, pp 65–81

Smith N (2014) Political Apologies and Categorical Apologies. In: Mihai M, Thaler M (eds) On the Uses and Abuses of Political Apologies. Palgrave Macmillan, pp 32–51

Stoor K (2016) Svenska kyrkan och jojken [The Church of Sweden and the yoik]. In: Lindmark D, Sundström O (eds) De historiska relationerna mellan Svenska kyrkan och samerna [Historical relations between the Church of Sweden and the Sami]. Artos & Norma, pp 711–734

Sundström O (2016) Svenskkyrkliga förståelser av inhemsk samisk världsåskådning: En historisk översikt [Church of Sweden understandings of the indigenous Sami worldview: A historical overview]. In: Lindmark D, Sundström O (eds) De historiska relationerna mellan Svenska kyrkan och samerna [Historical relations between the Church of Sweden and the Sami]. Artos & Norma, pp 531–588

Svenska kyrkan [Church of Sweden] (2011) Rapport från Ságastallamat, en konferens om samerna och Svenska kykrkan, i Kiruna den 11-13 oktober 2011 [Report from Ságastallamat, a conference about the Sami and the Church of Sweden, in Kiruna 11–13 October 2011]. https://www.svenskakyrkan.se/filer/1374643/Rapport%20fr%c3%a5n%20Sagastallamat.pdf. Accessed 28 August 2023

Svenska kyrkan [Church of Sweden] (2022) Handlingsplan: Åtaganden kopplade till Svenska kyrkans ursäkt till det samiska folket 2022–2031 [Action plan: Commitments relating to the Church of Sweden's apology to the Sami people 2022–2031]. https://www.svenskakyrkan.se/filer/1374643/11183_SK22129_Handlingsplan_samiska_V4_Utskrift.pdf. Accessed 28 August 2023

UN Office of the High Commissioner on Human Rights (OHCHR) (2011) Guiding Principles on Business and Human Rights, HR/PUB/11/04

UNGA (2006) Basic Principles and Guidelines on the Right to a Remedy and Reparation for Victims of Gross Violations of International Human Rights Law and Serious Violations of International Humanitarian Law, UN Doc. A/RES/60/147

UNGA (2007) UN Declaration on the Rights of Indigenous Peoples, UN Doc. A/61/L.67

UNGA (2014) Report of the Special Rapporteur on the promotion of truth, justice, reparation and guarantees of non-recurrence, UN Doc. A/69/518

UNGA (2019) Report of the Special Rapporteur on the promotion of truth, justice, reparation and guarantees of non-recurrence, UN Doc. A/74/147

UNGA (2021) Report of the Special Rapporteur on the promotion of truth, justice, reparation and guarantees of non-recurrence, Fabián Salvioli, Transitional justice measures and addressing the legacy of gross violations of human rights and international humanitarian law committed in colonial contexts, UN Doc. A/76/180

UNSC (2004) The rule of law and transitional justice in conflict and post-conflict societies, UN Doc. S/2004/616

West H S (2020) Renegotiating Relations, Structuring Justice: Institutional Reconciliation with the Saami in the 1990–2020 Reconciliation Processes of the Church of Sweden and the Church of Norway. Religions 11. https://doi.org/10.3390/rel11070343

Winder N N (2020) Colliding Heartwork: The space where our hearts meet and collide to process the boarding school experience. In: Minton S J (ed) Residential Schools and Indigenous Peoples: From Genocide via Education to the Possibilities for Processes of Truth, Restitution, Reconciliation, and Reclamation. Routledge, pp 141–162

Öhman M-B (2016) Tyst om markfrågan i Svenska kyrkans "Vitbok" [Silence on the land issue in the Church of Sweden "White Paper"]. https://feministisktperspektiv.se/2016/10/25/tyst-om-markfragan-i-svenska-kyrkans-vitbok/ (link no longer active). Accessed 13 August 2023

Össbo Å (2014) Nya vatten, dunkla speglingar: Industriell kolonialism genom svensk vattenkraftutbyggnad i renskötselområdet 1910-1968 [New waters, dark reflections: Industrial colonialism through Swedish hydropower development in the reindeer husbandry area 1910–1968]. Institutionen för idé- och samhällsstudier, Umeå universitet

Össbo Å (2020) Från lappmarksplakat till anläggarsamhällen: Svensk bosättarkolonialism gentemot Sápmi [From Lappmark Statutes to Company Towns: Swedish Settler Colonialism towards Sápmi]. Historisk tidskrift 140: 420–443

Össbo Å (2021) "A constant reminder of what we had to forfeit": Swedish industrial colonialism and intergenerational effects on Sámi living conditions in the area of upper Stuor Julevädno. International Journal of Critical Indigenous Studies 14: 17–32

Part IV
Dutch Practice in International Law

Chapter 13
Finding the Truth but Ending the Conversation? How Dutch Civil Court Cases on the Srebrenica Genocide Shaped the Space for Reparation

Alma Mustafić and Niké Wentholt

Contents

Abstract Due to the presence of Dutchbat troops in July 1995, when over 8000 Bosniaks were killed, the Srebrenica genocide became a shared Bosnian-Dutch history. This chapter explores how civil court cases (Nuhanović; Mustafić; Mothers of

Both authors have equal authorship.

A. Mustafić (✉)
Research Groups Sustainable Communities and Access to Justice, Utrecht University of Applied Sciences, Padualaan 101, Utrecht, The Netherlands
e-mail: alma.mustafic@hu.nl

N. Wentholt
Citizenship and Humanisation of the Public Sector, University of Humanistic Studies, Kromme Nieuwegracht 29, Utrecht, The Netherlands
e-mail: n.wentholt@uvh.nl

O. Spijkers et al. (eds.), *Netherlands Yearbook of International Law 2022*, Netherlands Yearbook of International Law 53, https://doi.org/10.1007/978-94-6265-627-7_13

Srebrenica) by survivors and relatives shaped the space for reparation in the Netherlands. Departing from a sociological definition of genocide, this chapter arrives at a similarly broad and transformative conceptualisation of reparation as a spectrum (based on Lisa Laplante (Laplante, Cornell International Law Journal 48:513–578, 2015)). While court cases themselves can only be expected to address the narrow, left side of the reparation spectrum, their contributions to fact-finding and the conversation on responsibility can form the basis for a larger, politics- and society-driven reparation process. The chapter thus starts by studying plaintiffs' lived experiences of the court procedures vis-à-vis their needs and aims. While recognizing several instances of delay and denial, we acknowledge that the legal narratives and outcomes held significant reparation potential. However, studying the political and societal responses to the court cases, the chapter argues that this potential did not materialize. Most importantly, the political and societal emphasis is still on Dutchbat rather than on the Bosniak stories, thus blocking restorative and civic reparation. Therefore, we present initiatives by the Bosnian-Dutch community as 'interventions' in this stalling process. These initiatives re-imagine what reparation can be. We conclude that, through them, Dutch politics and society are given another chance to contribute to inclusive and transformative reparation for the shared history of the Srebrenica genocide.

Keywords Srebrenica · Genocide · Reparation · Transformative justice · Lived experiences

13.1 Introduction

13.1.1 Scene Dangerous Names

> Rizo: There are 8000 stones on a slope. I am one of those stones. Mustafić My parents' name. My name, your name. A name is the first in a long list of things you must learn about yourself. [...] I was killed by a story. I was killed because of my name. 2 Look....that's you...You were fourteen when I passed away. You're almost the same age as I was. When I... Yes, you thought you left that child behind, in Srebrenica. But you know. We all carry a child with us. One that keeps us awake. Whenever we try to forget who we once were. Burnout. Depression. PTSD. It is always the same child that asks for attention. It whispers. Very gently, but every second of your life. 'Do not forget me'.
>
> *This is the prologue scene of the theatre play 'Dangerous Names.' It is the first play in the Netherlands from the perspective of the Srebrenica survivors.*[1]

In July 1995, the Dutchbat battalion was present as part of the United Nations (UN) peacekeeping mission during the Srebrenica genocide. In the preceding years, Srebrenica had functioned as a United Nations (UN) 'safe haven' for Bosniak

[1] Mustafić and Jonkergouw (2020). Gevaarlijke Namen. Het Zuidelijk Toneel, Tilburg.

refugees. More than 8000 Bosniaks, mostly civilians, were killed by the Bosnian-Serb army around the area of the town of Srebrenica.

The genocide thus became a shared history of the Netherlands and Bosnia, especially when many survivors and relatives found a new home in the Netherlands. Some of them turned to Dutch political representatives to find answers to difficult questions of responsibility and reparation. But as these pleas often came with no response, Dutch civil court rooms became an important platform for the discussion of this shared history. Bosnians and Bosnian-Dutch citizens initiated three landmark cases against the Dutch state about the harm resulting from Dutchbat's conduct: respectively Hasan Nuhanović; Mehida, Damir, and Alma Mustafić; and the Foundation of the Mothers of Srebrenica ['de stichting Moeders van Srebrenica']. The cases were eventually all decided in favour of the plaintiffs and will be discussed in more detail later in this chapter.

While there has been, understandably, plenty of academic focus on analysing the significance of these legal breakthroughs,[2] we know less about the wider social impact of these court cases on the reparation process. Although court cases are, for good reasons, bound by legal rules, their impact on reparation exceeds the legal realm, as the walls of the courtroom are porous and facts, stories, and claims on responsibility penetrate into the realm of politics and society at large. As such, civil court cases set the scene for wider political and societal reparation. This chapter is interested in this latter, social dimension and asks the question how Dutch politics and society responded to the potential for reparation that was created through the civil court cases on Srebrenica.

This chapter investigates how the space for reparation was shaped in court rooms before, during, and after by focusing on the *lived experiences* of plaintiffs—the surviving relatives. We introduce a theoretical framework based on the work of Lisa Laplante to position the court cases on a spectrum for reparation.[3] We show that the court process was meaningful in terms of 'narrow' reparation. Additionally, the court cases held significant potential for 'wider' reparation, to be taken up by politics and society, through its contributions to truth-finding and for holding a state legally liable for its conduct towards citizens of another country. The second section of this chapter investigates the responses emanating from the court room procedures which were to have ramifications on Dutch politics as well as society at large. We argue that they largely did not take on this potential offered by the court cases for such wider process of reparation. This further enlarged the gap between what was and what could have been.

Thirdly, we present initiatives by the Bosnian-Dutch community as 'interventions' to make up for what was missing in the reparation process. Through an art movement, and theatre play, the Bosnian-Dutch community 'spoke back,' giving much more meaning to the idea of reparation. Where Dutch politics and society failed to maximise the potential of the court cases the first time around, they now have another chance to design and implement an inclusive and participatory reparation process

[2] See e.g. Rijnhout 2021 and Ryngaert and Spijkers 2019.

[3] Laplante 2015.

for the shared history of Srebrenica that both the Bosnian-Dutch community and Dutch society as a whole deserve. We depart from the observation that by both legal, societal, and moral norms it is remarkable that civil courts have been able to hold the Dutch state liable and thus accountable for its conduct during the Srebrenica genocide. Despite obvious legal limitations, the courts were able to address the collective and political nature of the genocide. The court cases have thus opened avenues for much wider reparation. Our investigation is about this *potential* and the response to this potential, not about the limitations of the court cases.

13.2 Theoretical Framework

In this chapter, we approach reparation as a broad, socio-legal process to address the injustice of the Srebrenica genocide. We argue for a broader understanding of genocide than the traditional legal one, and thus for a broader understanding of reparation for genocide than the legalistic one. After all, Jonassohn and Björnson already argued in 1998 that the legal definition of genocide was only a legal instrument and eventually a diplomatic compromise that cannot be used as a marker for scholarly research, as it insufficiently covers the reality of genocide.[4] According to this legal definition in the Genocide Convention, after Raphael Lemkin introduced the term in 1944,[5] genocide is a crime under international law and encompasses acts committed with the intent to destroy, in whole or in part, a national, ethnic, racial, or religious group.[6] We conceptualise genocide as proposed by various social scientists, specifically following the definition of Uğur Ümit Üngör, Professor of Holocaust and Genocide Studies at the University of Amsterdam and the Dutch Institute for War, Holocaust and Genocide Studies (NIOD):

> Genocide can be defined as a complex process of systematic persecution and annihilation of a group of people by a government... We can speak of genocide when individuals are persecuted and murdered merely on the basis of their presumed or imputed membership in a group rather than on their individual characteristics or participation in certain acts.[7]

What stands out in this conceptualization of genocide is the complexity around the offense at the state-level. The contrast between this 'social' and legal definition becomes particularly evident when classifying the Srebrenica genocide. The International Criminal Tribunal for the Former Yugoslavia (ICTY) categorizes only the events around Srebrenica in July 1995 as genocide,[8] Professor Üngör interprets

---

[4] Jonassohn and Björnson 1998, p. 133–135.

[5] Lemkin 2008.

[6] Convention on the Prevention and Punishment of the Crime of Genocide, 9 December 1948, 78 U.N.T.S. 277, art. 2.

[7] Üngör 2011, pp. 32–38.

[8] ICTY (2015) https://www.irmct.org/specials/srebrenica20/#:~:text=In%20July%201995%2C%20Srebrenica%20was,and%20elderly%20from%20the%20town. Accessed 16 September 2023.

all occurrences throughout the Bosnian War (1992–1995) as a process of genocide against Bosniaks as such.[9]

What can be seen as 'justice' in the case of genocide from a legal standpoint, is not necessarily justice when seen from a broader social perspective. Survivors and relatives can experience *legal justice* as *social injustice*—hence our specific attention for lived experiences. Through this broad social understanding of genocide, the plea for social injustice becomes particularly urgent. Bosnian-Australian genocide scholar H. Halilovich adds an eleventh stage to the well-known ten-stage understanding of genocide by Gregory H. Stanton:[10] triumphalism. In Bosnia and Herzegovina, killings are being glorified by celebrating acts of genocide, humiliating the survivors, or/and building monuments to the convicted war criminals.[11]

Because of Dutchbat's presence during the Srebrenica genocide, the Netherlands and Bosnia became entangled in the processes of genocide itself and justice for that genocide. Through our focus on how the court cases for the Srebrenica genocide related to the broader process of social justice and reparation, we facilitate a mutual understanding between the legal and social perspectives when addressing justice in such sensitive and grave matters as genocide. For this, we need a similarly broad, relational, and transformative definition of reparation.

While reparation is traditionally understood as the 'attempt to place a victim back in the position they would have been in had the harm not occurred,' this understanding has been impacted by achievements of transformative justice scholarship.[12] Transformative justice is defined as the 'transformative change that emphasizes local agency and resources, the prioritization of process rather than preconceived outcomes and the challenging of unequal and intersecting power relationships and structures of exclusion at both the local and the global level.'[13] Here the emphasis on relationality, process, and power resonates with our definition of reparation as *the process to remedy a harm in order to transform the social relations and power structures between all parties involved, to contribute to more dignified and equal relations.* Reparation is always a 'communal process' that thrives on inclusive dialogue.[14]

Lisa Laplante's model, see Fig. 13.1 below, originally designed for justice, helps to conceptualize the reach of this transformative understanding of reparation. It helps us pinpoint the transformative maturity of the reparation process on a scale from a 'narrow,' minimum approach to a 'broad,' maximum approach.

Let us first pinpoint the place of court cases on the scale of Laplante (Fig. 13.1). Civil court cases, as we understand them, represent a form of reparative justice. We conceptualize their contribution to reparative justice in two ways. First, they offer a

---

[9] Hannah Arendt Instituut (2022) https://app.livestorm.co/hannah-arendt-instituut/srebrenica-van-wij-zij-denken-tot-genocidair-geweld-en-ontkenning/live?s=36944a4d-610f-4fe5-bb03-dde891c2f969#/chat. Accessed 23 August 2023.

[10] Stanton 2017.

[11] Halilovich 2017.

[12] Leyh and Fraser 2019, p. 40.

[13] Gready and Robins 2014.

[14] Immler 2022, p. 20.

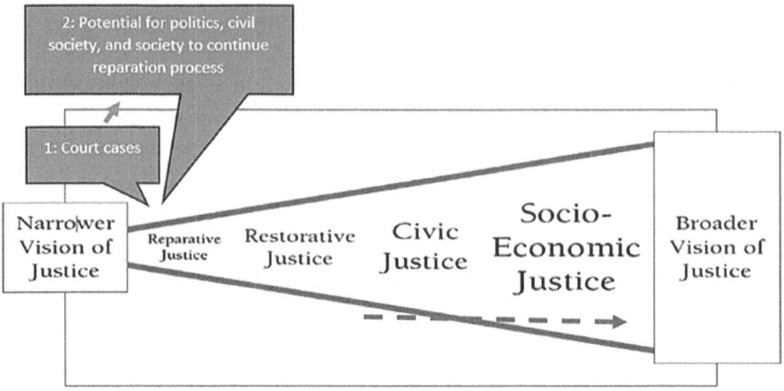

Fig. 13.1 Court cases on the continuum for justice and reparation. *Source* Cornell International Law Journal, Laplante 2015, with additions by the authors

platform for plaintiffs to voice their experiences and formulate their claims, where the defendant is forced to listen. Plaintiffs can potentially find 'narrative ownership' during the court process.[15] We thus centre on the lived experiences of plaintiffs as strategic actors who mobilize this 'public forum' of the law ('legal mobilization') in their wider search for reparation.[16] The second contribution of civil court cases to reparative justice is in their capacity to establish facts about the harm and, by establishing legal liability, helping to define relations and responsibility pertaining to the harm.[17] To better understand this second strand we focus on the legal outcomes and narratives, as socio-legal artefacts, produced through the court process.

These elements all contribute to reparative justice. But court cases are limited in what they can deliver. The onus is on politics and society to take up on their potential, through for example the facts established and the legal conclusions on liability and responsibility. Then, restorative justice can take shape, indicating reparation through the involvement of the community, in this case Dutch society. Civic justice is about the repair of trust between citizens and their government—the Bosnian Dutch community on the one hand and Dutch State on the other. For reasons of clarity and conciseness, we will not address socio-economic justice or reparation here.

This 'afterlife' of the court cases forms the focus of the second and third part of this discussion and is studied through a social-legal approach. The wide-ranging, multidisciplinary field of socio-legal studies enables us to study legal events and processes as social practices and to investigate their impact in societal terms. Law does not simply reflect and shape societal norms. Court cases are also relational as they 'inevitably affect human relationships.'[18] Court order reparations can 'remove the hindrances to justice by clearing the ground so that trusting relations can take

[15] Pemberton et al 2019, p. 405.

[16] McCann 2008, p. 522.

[17] Spijkers 2021, p. 121.

[18] Minow 2015, p. 1627.

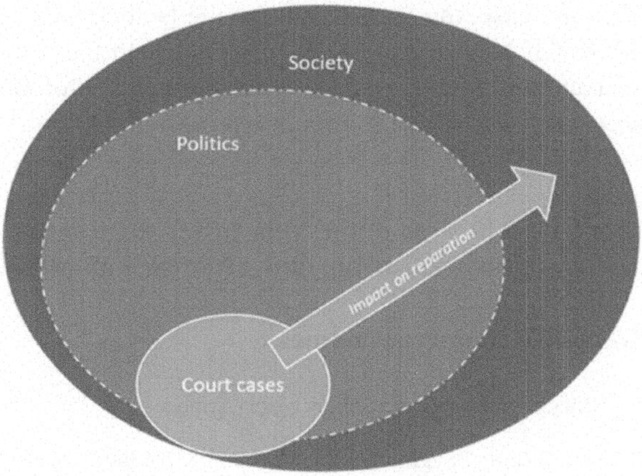

Fig. 13.2 Showing trajectory of court cases into politics and society. *Source* The authors

root.'[19] This relational approach to law sees the court cases as a potential starting point for a wider reparation process that politics and society can then take up.

The above model (see Fig. 13.2) reflects the 'levels' of the court cases' effect on reparation: we start with the experiences, process, and rulings of the court cases themselves. We then move to responses by politics, government and society at large. The effect of the court cases on reparation in these latter two levels are intertwined and represent the denominator of 'political and societal responses to the court cases.'

Some reflection on our positionality as co-authors is helpful in understanding our focus on relationality and lived experience. We met each other professionally over our shared interest in Dutch political and societal conversations on the Srebrenica genocide. Alma Mustafić as one of the co-authors of this chapter has direct experience as a plaintiff. We see this experience as a direct source of expertise, next to her professional knowledge as an educational specialist. Our professional lives intertwine but over and above that, taking part in expert meetings of our respective projects, we both recognise how much we value co-operation and exchange of knowledge that goes beyond academic boundaries.

13.2.1 Inside the Court Room: Legal Reparation for the Srebrenica Genocide

13.2.2 The Lead-up to the Court Case: Finding Information about the Missing People

Victims and survivors of human rights violations find themselves in court for different reasons. The common cause is injustice that has not been acknowledged. In the

[19] Leif Wenar, as cited in Kumar 2014, p. 200.

Mustafić-case, the family came to the Netherlands hoping that the Dutch State and the Dutch Ministry of Defence would help them find out what happened to their husband and father, since as a local employee of Dutchbat from 1994 onward, he was supposed to be, but was not, protected.

13.2.2.1 The Fate of the Men Inside the Compound: What Happened Before, During and After the Fall of Srebrenica

Scene 17b Dangerous names

Alma: Two Dutchbat soldiers enter. Armed.

Ray: (Facing the ground) You have to go. All the refugees have to go. You are the last ones left. You have to go.

Rizo: We have to go.

Mehida: Rizo, you are on Dutchbat's list. They can't do that!

Alma: We have to leave everything we could defend ourselves with.

Ray: Everything please.

Alma (hesitating) hands in the pocketknife.

Alma: We're walking outside. Dad presses my sister against him. We're silent. Then the Serbs hold him.

Mehida: No please. I need him. Please. I can't live alone with three children. Let him come with us. Please. Do you want to stay here or do you want to get your children to safety, he says. Please I beg you my husband is not a soldier. Walk on, he says, Give that child to her. Alma, keep your eyes in front of you!

Alma (looks back at Rizo)

Mehida: Don't look back Alma![20]

Rizo Mustafić was not the only missing person who tried to find protection. Tens of thousands of refugees had arrived in the safe area of Srebrenica over the years 1993–1995. By July 1995, the war had been raging for over three years. It had resulted in many deaths, forceful deportations and other war crimes, mostly by Bosnian Serb forces. UN troops, among them the Dutch battalion Dutchbat III, were present as peacekeeping forces in the town of Srebrenica.

In the weeks preceding the genocide, the situation had grown dire. The Bosnian Serb army had surrounded the enclave and there was a shortage of food, water, and medicines. After the Bosnian Serb army approached, many Bosniaks (+/− 25.000 mostly women with children and the elderly) sought refuge at the compound of Dutchbat. When, as the Dutch soldiers stated, the compound became overcrowded

---

[20] Mustafić and Jonkergouw (2020) See n.1.

(+/− 5.000 refugees entered the base), they closed the fence and refused the remaining 20.000 entry. Because of the decision to close the compound and being aware of numerous other massacres on their people during the war, many Bosniak men (+/−15.000) tried to flee through the mountains towards Bosniak-controlled areas. Approximately 20.000 refugees stayed around (but outside) the compound, hoping to get into the compound or otherwise to find protection from the Dutch UN troops. Those who sought refuge with the UN forces found themselves trapped: on one side, they faced the closed fence of the UN Dutch base, and on the other, advancing Bosnian Serb forces.[21]

General Mladić then ordered the deportation of all refugees in Srebrenica.[22] The Bosnian Serb army insisted that the citizens in the compound had to be handed over to them, stating that they wanted to 'evacuate' all refugees and 'interrogate' the Bosniak men, promising safe exit to Dutchbat and its employees, all operating under the UN flag. Before all remaining citizens were forced to leave the compound, (a choice that would later be contested in court) Dutchbat major Franken compiled a list of names of 239 men,[23] telling the Bosnian Serbs that 'these people now have a name. Do not forget that. We know who you are taking with you.'[24] Dutchbat eventually assisted with the separation of women, children, on the one hand, and boys and men on the other. The first group arrived in the town of Tuzla. The latter were all killed.[25] This decision of Dutchbat to force the refugees inside the compound to leave has been the focus of the three civil court cases.

13.2.2.2 Trying to Mobilise Political, Legal, and Societal Organisations to Find the Missing

From the time of the genocide right up to the present day, the main narrative in the Netherlands has been about the difficult situation the Dutchbat soldiers faced and not about the missing people of Srebrenica. The stories of the family Mustafić and Nuhanović show just how difficult it was to secure attention and support for the fate of the missing.

After a few months the family Mustafić managed to come to the Netherlands on their own. When they reached out to the Ministry of Defence to learn more about what happened to the father, the response was: 'Rizo Mustafić's name does not appear in our files.' And thus began the process of delay and denial. When the family showed pictures of him alongside Dutchbat soldiers, the family were told they needed an employment contract to prove that Rizo Mustafić was working for Dutchbat. Understandably the family could not bring a contract when fleeing Srebrenica. But then the family got a mysterious visit from a military officer. He handed a piece of

[21] Nuhanović 2007.

[22] UNGA 1999, pp. 74, 80.

[23] Sources differ on the exact number of names as many men were afraid to give their names.

[24] Koning (2000) http://retro.nrc.nl/W2/Lab/Srebrenica/000405a.html. Accessed 3 August 2023.

[25] Nuhanović 2007.

paper over to them and said: 'Your case is being discussed a lot within the military, you will need this' and then he swiftly disappeared.[26] This piece of paper was an employment contract for Rizo Mustafić. Despite this, the Dutch military still refused to enter into dialogue with the Mustafić family. The family Mustafić had hoped that their father might still be alive in a concentration camp like Šljivovica and Mitrovo Polje in Serbia, only to find out that he had been killed by the Bosnian Serb forces.

Hasan Nuhanović, who worked as translator for Dutchbat, has a very similar story to tell. His story confirms the uncooperative stance of the Netherlands/Dutch state and, as was the case with the family Mustafić, he ended up taking the Dutch State to court over the fate of his relatives. Hasan Nuhanović was put on the list of the local employees who were supposed to be protected, but his father, mother and younger brother were some of the last refugees forced to leave the safety of the Dutchbat compound.

Hasan Nuhanović spent seven years trying to find out what had happened to his family. He visited many international organizations, in search of his loved ones, but also in search of other missing people, especially the men who had stayed inside the Dutch compound and were then expelled from it. He first turned to the International Red Cross, where he was informed that he could only report his own family members as missing.[27] Trying to inquire after the fate of the others from the above-mentioned infamous 'Franken list,' he was told that the list had disappeared. Only after three months the list mysteriously appeared at the Dutch Ministry of Defence. Nuhanović remembered the moment he confronted the Dutch Minister of Defence Joris Voorhoeve: 'I put the list on the table and asked him if the Netherlands could help find these people.'[28] Both the Netherlands and the UN, where Hasan had also inquired, referred back to the Red Cross.

In his desperate search Nuhanović turned to the International Criminal Tribunal for the former Yugoslavia as well as the Dutch embassy in Bosnia: 'When will you find these people?' His specific request to the Dutch ambassador was to ask the representative of the Serb that the authorities in Bosnia, then Plavšić, should provide information about the missing people. Nuhanović recalls the ambassador answering that it was not a good moment because the West was helping Plavšić to stay in power, and they did not want 'to burden her with such questions.' Nuhanović, during his visit to Sarajevo, asked the Secretary-General of the UN the same question. Kofi Annan replied that he could not say anything before the official UN report on Srebrenica came out.[29] When this report came out in 1999, the situation about the role of Dutchbat in sending away the man from the compound was hardly mentioned.[30] Nuhanović once again

---

[26] Personal recollections Mehida Mustafić shared with author Alma Mustafić, various dates in February 2023, by telephone.

[27] Interview Hasan Nuhanović with author Alma Mustafić, 20 February 2023, online.

[28] Ibid.

[29] UNGA 1999.

[30] Ibid.; Nuhanović here refers to the brief description of how Dutchbat 'ordered [the men within the compound] to leave the compound and present themselves to the waiting Serbs,' UNGA 1999, p. 80.

turned his hopes towards the Netherlands. Their answer resembled that of Annan: he was to wait for the official report on Srebrenica, commissioned by the State and compiled by the Institute for War, Holocaust and Genocide Studies (NIOD). The family Mustafić and Nuhanović felt that the fate of their family members was simply not being heard.

13.2.2.3 Towards the Court Hearing

All this time, the idea of bringing the Dutch State to court had not been on the agenda. The Nuhanović and Mustafić family did not even know that this was not a possibility. The initial plan was to get the International Criminal Tribunal for the former Yugoslavia (ICTY) to prosecute Dutchbat commander Karremans and his deputy Franken. This meant that the idea of a legal court procedure was now an option. The ICTY tried the genocide's main perpetrators, resulting in several life sentences. Its impact has been widely researched.[31] Hasan Nuhanović submitted information related to the alleged criminal actions of Franken and Karremans to the ICTY. The answer from the ICTY was both disappointing but also encouraging. The ICTY did not see elements for a criminal prosecution of Franken, Karremans or other Dutchbat personnel, but 'that does not mean that Nuhanović should not seek justice at some other court,' as Nuhanović recalls.[32]

It was after this that the idea of suing the Dutch State was born. For Nuhanović this idea was strengthened after the publication of the state-commissioned NIOD report. In the NIOD report, Nuhanović read that his family had 'left' the Dutch compound. Both Nuhanović and the Mustafić family felt that the report was full of mistakes in its (mis)representation of the situation in Srebrenica, especially in relation to the fate of their relatives. The Dutch NGO PAX, then named IKV Pax Christi, concluded that the report was a 'bitter disappointment,' as 'once again Dutch responsibility is denied.'[33] It was then that he decided he needed the court room to find the truth about his family: 'If they can claim, if they can lie that we left the base voluntarily, when in fact they actively forced all those people to leave the base, then you cannot expect fair treatment. Then you have no choice but to get the truth out on the table in the courtroom.'[34]

With the help of PAX and well-known peace activist Mient Jan Faber, Nuhanović was advised by a Dutch lawyer that it was more likely that the Dutch State could be held responsible for the actions of the individuals than that the individuals themselves

---

[31] See for example: Orentlicher 2008.

[32] Interview Hasan Nuhanović with author Alma Mustafić, 20 February 2023, online.

[33] Van den Berg 2014b, p. 109.

[34] Interview Hasan Nuhanović with author Alma Mustafić, 20 February 2023, online. On pages 2130–2132 of the NIOD report, it is indeed described that his father Ibro 'decided' to leave the compound together 'with his wife and younger son.' According to the report, Ibro could have potentially stayed as he had been part of a special delegation thus receiving protection. But as Hasan's younger brother was forced to leave the compound, together with his mother, Ibro felt obliged to accompany them. NIOD 2002, pp. 2130–2131.

would be prosecuted.[35] This was the moment when the relatives of the Srebrenica victims realized that it was possible to hold the State accountable. This moment proved pivotal, not only for the family Mustafić and Nuhanović themselves, but also for the larger survivor community. The Nuhanović-Mustafić cases paved the way for the Mothers of Srebrenica to start a similar lawsuit against the Dutch State, presenting the fate of all husbands, brothers and sons who had been inside the compound. Just like Nuhanović and the Mustafić family, they had first tried many other platforms such as the Red Cross, Dutch Ministry of Defence, Ambassadors, the UN and the ICTY, before turning to the Dutch civil courtroom. From the Mustafić and Nuhanović testimonies it became clear that the political and societal story that led to the court cases, was not conducive to justice and an open and honest recognition. It was thus that the civil court became the place for Nuhanović to establish the facts about the fate of his family, to seek narrative ownership and to engage the Dutch State in a more honest conversation about their responsibility.

13.2.3 The Legal Process: Silencing and Denial in the Court Room

In the direct run-up to the court cases survivors felt that, even before the trial officially began, their dignity and that of their relatives was violated through the media. In 2002 the Mustafić family and Hasan Nuhanović, represented by human rights lawyer Liesbeth Zegveld, started the necessary preparations for the coming trial. The Mustafić family was living in the Netherlands, but Nuhanović had to come from Bosnia for this meeting. As soon as he landed at Schiphol airport, he was accosted by a camera and asked whether he wanted to sue the Dutch State for financial compensation. For seven years he only wanted to know what happened to his family and others who went missing, he wanted to have his story heard, and to seek a conversation about responsibility[36]—but the first question of the Dutch media was about financial compensation. Hasan Nuhanović was furious and answered: ‘Pass on my message to the Dutch people. If you, the Dutch people, decide to prosecute Franken and Karremans for their actions, I will immediately drop all the charges.’[37]

Plaintiffs felt that they were misunderstood and misrepresented in the court room and by Dutch media. At the first court hearing in 2005 a policeman with handcuffs was standing right behind Hasan Nuhanović, something highly unusual in a civil

[35] Riemersma 2015 https://www.vn.nl/hasan-nuhanovic-dutchbat. Accessed 25 July 2023.

[36] As also stated by his lawyer Liesbeth Zegveld in Zegveld (2014) https://www.volkskrant.nl/nieuws-achtergrond/regering-fatsoen-moet-je-doen~ba504bf6/. Accessed 4 September 2023.

[37] Interview Hasan Nuhanović with author Alma Mustafić, 20 February 2023, online. Nuhanović wished to see Karremans, Franken, and Oosterveen prosecuted in the Netherlands. Eventually, he and other survivors started a procedure to demand prosecution of these three military officials, but the court of justice in Arnhem ruled against prosecution.

case.[38] This created the idea that the plaintiffs were seen as violent, criminals or/and troublemakers. In an interview from 2014, Nuhanović reflected on how the state-commissioned Srebrenica report described him as 'a nervous young man. That is how I was portrayed to 16 million Dutch people.'[39]

Since Mehida Mustafić and Hasan Nuhanović did not speak the Dutch language, translation had to be arranged. However, the court did not consider language to be an issue even though the plaintiffs could not properly follow the trial. The plaintiffs' attorney tried to arrange for interpreters. However, the interpreters had to ask the State lawyers to slow down as they could not keep up with the translation. Their request to receive written texts to prepare for court was rejected. They themselves were asked to lower their voices when translating so as not to 'disrupt' the proceedings.[40] Regardless of the legal rules that judges and interpreters have to follow, it was often impossible for Hasan Nuhanović and Mehida Mustafić to follow the case, thus affecting their access to narrative ownership and hence the potential for satisfaction and reparation.

The most frustrating experience for the survivors, as they now share and have shared during the process, was the arrogance, ignorance, and abuse of legal power by the State lawyers, evident during the breaks of the official court process where lawyers tried to plant doubt, leave important details out, distort facts in time and place, deny other facts and sometimes even present lies as facts. By denying the lived experiences that survivors had been through, the implication from the State attorneys was that the plaintiffs were liars. For example, when the plaintiffs explained they were forced to leave the Dutchbat base, the State attorney insinuated that the refugees wanted to leave voluntarily. They (mis)used the video images where one could see the Bosniak refugees running to the busses, using this as evidence that they left 'voluntarily'. The plaintiffs' lawyer Zegveld later wrote in a newspaper article that the State would 'try everything to deny the facts.'[41] Outside the Dutch base Bosniak people were being murdered, raped, and subjected to other crimes. As they had been through hell and wanted to leave as quickly as possible, when they saw the busses, they ran in desperation towards them.

Inside the compound the situation was very different. Here the refugees were safe. People inside the base wanted to stay in this safe place but they were forced by Dutchbat to leave. To make sure that all the people would 'leave' the Dutch base, the refugees were 'escorted' to the main exit. Refugees walked slowly, they did not push or run. They knew that they would be in danger once they were outside the base. And yet, they found themselves sitting in a courtroom, listening to the State attorney distorting the facts and implying that the refugees wanted to leave the base. One of the State attorneys said: 'It's not like someone was holding a gun to your

[38] Ibid.

[39] Egmond 2014. Indeed, on page 2130 of the NIOD report, we find this literal description. NIOD 2002, p. 2130.

[40] Personal recollections Mehida Mustafić as shared with author Alma Mustafić, February 2023.

[41] Zegveld (2014); see n.36.

head.'[42] The attitude of the State lawyers was unbearable for the plaintiffs. The State attorneys deliberately made everything unnecessarily complex, implying that because of the chaotic situation, nobody could be held accountable. The plaintiffs were given insufficient speaking time to correct all the inaccuracies. Their lawyer wrote in outrage in a newspaper article that the State should change its 'crude' attitude towards the plaintiffs.[43]

13.2.4 Legal Narratives and Outcomes and Their Potential for Reparation

Nevertheless, the court processes and rulings created legal outcomes and narratives of the Srebrenica genocide that had an impact. Since there have been detailed legal and interdisciplinary analyses of the court rulings in the cases Mustafić, Nuhanović, and the Mothers of Srebrenica,[44] this chapter will only outline the most important elements of the ruling. Afterwards, it will analyse the potential of these narratives and outcomes for a broader reparation scenario.

In September 2013, in the Nuhanović and Mustafić cases, the Supreme Court ruled 'in two separate but parallel proceedings, that the State of the Netherlands had acted wrongfully when Dutchbat [...] sent Rizo Mustafić, his father and also the brother of Hasan Nuhanović, out of the United Nations compound.'[45] In July 2019, building upon the legal breakthroughs in these cases, the Supreme Court ruled in the case of the Mothers of Srebrenica that 'the Netherlands had acted wrongfully when the Bosnian Muslims, seeking protection from the advancing Bosnian Serbs, from inside the Potočari compound, were not given the choice by Dutchbat of remaining there. In so doing they were deprived of the 10% chance of not being exposed to inhumane treatment and execution by the Bosnian Serbs.'[46] In all three rulings, the Dutch State was ordered to provide compensation.

13.2.4.1 Potential of the Court Case: Getting the Facts Right about the Genocide

In many ways the court cases have delivered important legal breakthroughs in telling the story of Srebrenica. First, by following ICTY and International Court of Justice (ICJ) rulings, they confirmed that the killings constituted 'genocide of Bosnian

---

[42] Personal recollections of the author Alma Mustafić.

[43] Zegveld (2014); see n.36.

[44] These would include: Rijnhout 2021; Spijkers 2021; Van Dijck 2017; Ryngaert and Spijkers 2019.

[45] Spijkers 2021, p. 121.

[46] Spijkers 2021, p. 121.

Muslims,'[47] bringing this term into Dutch societal conversations where they had previously been referred to as 'massacre' or 'tragedy'—and sometimes still are.[48] Second, the court cases determined facts about the events and, most importantly, the Court of Appeal ruled in both the cases of Nuhanović and Mustafić that the Dutch State had committed a tort given that it had 'effective control,' over the compound.[49] This ruling applied also to the case of the Mothers of Srebrenica. In the case of Mustafić, the Court of Appeal concluded that 'the State acted wrongfully towards Mustafić by forcing him to leave the compound against his will. The Court also believes that Mustafić would still be alive (except for special circumstances that are not under discussion) if the State had not acted wrongfully towards him.'[50] The ruling then continued to set out in detail how Dutchbat could have ensured his safe evacuation, without risking the lives of Dutchbat soldiers or other evacuees. This was not only an important legal milestone in terms of defining the norm of diligent care for the State in cases of peacekeeping missions abroad, but also offered an important counterargument to the Dutch dominant political and societal narrative of the time which was that Dutchbat could not have acted differently.[51]

While understandable and even admirable from a legal point of view, this turn towards tort law to address a case of genocide stands in stark contrast to the broad, systematic definition of genocide that social science offers us. Otto Spijkers contrasts the 'typical tort' for, normally, quite straightforward wrongs like a 'fall on a slippery floor' with the use of this same legal frame for 'a failure to prevent the murder of hundreds of innocent civilians.' But he concludes, and we agree, that even such technical court rulings can carry potential for a wider discussion on political and

---

[47] Dutch Supreme Court (Hoge Raad der Nederlanden), *Mothers of Srebrenica Association et al. v. The Netherlands,* Judgment, 19 July 2019, ECLI:NL:HR:2019:1223, para 2.1.2.

[48] For example, Dutch regional broadcasting company RTV Drenthe published a radio interview and accompanying article with a Dutchbat veteran in which the word genocide was completely circumvented. The authors of this chapter contacted the broadcaster, asking for rectification, referring to the rulings in the Netherlands and at the ICTY. The broadcaster then adjusted the item, included the word genocide in the first paragraph and adding an historical overview including reference to the Supreme Court decision from. RTV Drenthe 2023, https://www.rtvdrenthe.nl/nieuws/15616615/na-28-jaar-terugkeren-in-srebrenica-een-reis-met-een-lach-en-een-traan. Accessed 31 July 2023.

[49] While the district court had ruled that nor the Dutch state nor the United Nations had 'effective overall control' over the territory in Bosnia, the court of appeal ruled later that the Dutch state in fact had 'effective control' over the alleged conduct of Dutchbat.' 's Gravenhage Court (Rechtbank 's Gravenhage), *Nuhanović v. The Netherlands,* Judgment, 10 September 2008, ECLI:NL:RBSGR:2008:BF0181, para 4.14.2; 's Gravenhage Court (Rechtbank 's Gravenhage), *Mustafć v. The Netherlands*, Judgment, 10 September 2008, ECLI:NL:RBSGR:2008:BF0182, para 4.14.2; 's Gravenhage Court of Appeal (Gerechtshof 's Gravenhage), *Nuhanović v. The Netherlands,* Judgment, 5 July 2011, ECLI:NL:GHSGR:2011:BR0133, para 5.20; 's Gravenhage Court of Appeal (Gerechtshof 's Gravenhage), *Mustafć v. The Netherlands,* Judgment, 5 July 2011, ECLI:NL:GHSGR:2011:BR5386, para 5.20.

[50] 's Gravenhage Court of Appeal (Gerechtshof 's Gravenhage), *Mustafć v. The Netherlands,* Judgment, 5 July 2011, ECLI:NL:GHSGR:2011:BR5386, para 6.14.

[51] This narrative was largely supported by the state-commissioned Srebrenica report, published in 2002, to the extent that this report was welcomed by many politicians as a 'full rehabilitation of Dutchbat.' Van den Berg 2014b, p. 111.

societal responsibility.[52] In the next section, we consider political apologies as a response to these court conclusions around liability.

Most importantly, the courts linked their highly technical narrative to human rights violations and the human stories and moral weight that inevitably accompany such harm. As Rianka Rijnhout has meticulously set out, this also led to many legal difficulties around the topic of partial liability. The courts now had to deal with the complexity of applying national law to human rights violations that may then potentially 'set precedents for 'more regular' tort law situations.'[53] The courts thus navigated a tough balancing act and also seemed to be aware of the societal consequences of the case and its rulings. In the above cited Mustafić case, after balancing the difficulties in coming to a legal conclusion about a precarious political and military situation, the Advocate General of the Supreme Court eventually formulated its task as follows:

> 'It does belong to the task of the judge to judge whether the commands from that time have led to a violation of universally applicable fundamental human rights, especially the right to life and the ban on inhuman treatment. When the judge would not be allowed to speak about that, lawlessness could fall upon us.'[54]

At the same time, the rulings regrettably also showed the shortcomings of the Dutch societal narratives which failed to reflect the lived realities of the plaintiffs. A good illustration of this is the courts' use of the term 'Bosnian Muslims,' rather than the more accurate and inclusive term 'Bosniaks' to refer to the people targeted by the genocide. This term locks people into a religious identity that is not necessarily shared by all Bosniak people. From our social definition of genocide, moreover, it deflects from, rather than contributes to justice for a crime that is based on the very reduction of people to a specific identity that would lead, consequently, to their annihilation. The terminology has been widely used in Dutch media, even before the court cases, to the extent that newspapers edit the term Bosniak into 'Bosnian Muslim' in the pieces they decide to publish.[55]

13.2.4.2 Potential of the Court Case: Understanding Responsibility

Plaintiffs, the Bosnian–Dutch community, and even to a large extent Dutch society, hoped that the court cases could provide more clarity about the exact responsibility of the State for the genocide. The language and technicalities of the legal narratives sometimes directly clashed with the lived experiences of the plaintiffs. This became especially apparent in the case of the Mothers of Srebrenica where the judges used a percentage argument to determine the extent of the liability of the Dutch State: the

---

[52] Spijkers 2021, p. 122.

[53] Rijnhout 2021, p. 135.

[54] Dutch Supreme Court (Hoge Raad der Nederlanden), *Mustafć v. The Netherlands,* Judgment, 6 September 2013, ECLI:NL:HR:2013:BZ9228, Judgment, para 5.40.

[55] Both authors have experienced this when submitting their written work to Dutch publication outlets.

Court of Appeal specified 30%, the Supreme Court 10%, which reflected their estimation of the chance that the men who were in the compound on 13 July 1995 would have survived if Dutchbat had offered them the choice to remain in the compound.[56]

Shortly after the Supreme Court ruling, the Mothers published on their website a short blog titled 'what does '10%' of a human life mean?' While the rulings consistently spoke of this legal aspect of liability, we see that from the perspective of the Mothers' lived experiences, this was seen as a statement of diminished responsibility: the blog continues to speak of the Dutch state being "10%' responsible,' even though the exact legal narrative would mean rather 100% responsibility for the 10% chance that these men had not been killed had Dutchbat acted otherwise. 'That might be the mathematics of the Dutch judiciary, but we cannot recognize this in whatever mathematics of humanity,' the blog concludes, illustrating very clearly the (understandable and perhaps unavoidable) disparity between the legal outcome and the real lived experiences of the plaintiffs.[57]We conclude that the legal justice for the Srebrenica genocide that the civil courts offered, could not deliver the broader conversation on responsibility, justice, and reparation that plaintiffs and the community desired. Using a vivid image, Čamil Duraković, the former Bosniak Mayor of Srebrenica in a tweet compared the ruling to a hypothetical situation where someone pushing a person from a 300 meter height, was only being held responsible for the 'first 100 meters of the deadly fall.'[58]

13.2.5 Politics and Society at Large: Responses to the Court Cases

According to Gijs van Dijck, 'the Srebrenica case illustrate[s] that tort law is not designed for repairing historic injustice.'[59] He attributes this to the discrepancy between legal process and real life experiences and needs, as 'plaintiffs were likely to have been seeking recognition, an acknowledgement, information about what happened and why, and the opportunity to have a voice.'[60] We cannot expect court cases to offer reparation in themselves. But we can expect politics and the broader society to act upon the courts fact-finding, clarifying relations and responsibility to continue a wider conversation about reparation. In the second section of this chapter, we zoom out to study the political and societal responses to the court cases.

---

56 For a more precise analysis of the legal meaning of these percentages, see: Ryngaert and Spijkers 2019, p. 549.

57 Pokret Majke enklava Srebrenica i Žepa 2019.

58 Durakovic (2019) https://twitter.com/camil_durakovic/status/1152162642590490624. Accessed 1 September 2023.

59 Van Dijck 2017.

60 Ibid.

13.2.6 Compensation: Making Meaning Out of Money

In all three cases, it was eventually ruled that the Dutch State was liable to damages suffered by the plaintiffs because of the conduct of Dutchbat. In 2015, thirteen years after the start of the court case, Nuhanović and Mustafić and the Dutch State reached an agreement about compensation, the extent of which is not publicly known.[61] But earlier in 2014, the Dutch government had announced publicly that it set the compensation at 20.000 euro. Nuhanović stated that this amount barely covers the 'direct material costs' of going to court and refused to accept it.[62] He moreover told Dutch media:

> 'The Dutch have to properly pay me, so that I can rest. That is what financial compensation is about: my recovery. A psychiatrist has diagnosed me with severe posttraumatic stress disorder [...] I do not want a new car; I want to heal and that costs money.'[63]

After the court cases, plaintiffs and human rights organizations emphasised the larger collective group of victims and the political and social impact of this legal, individual outcome of compensation. Jezerca Tigani from Amnesty International called the Supreme Court ruling on the Nuhanović and Mustafić cases:

> a historic victory for the relatives of those who were killed in this case, but also marks a symbolic step for the thousands of other victims [... The ruling] should pave the way for the Dutch government to provide full reparation—including compensation—to the relatives who brought this case, as well as other family members of victims of the Srebrenica genocide.[64]

These words of Tigani, emphasising 'reparation' alongside compensation, are taking us closer to Laplante's right side of the spectrum. However, the potential benefits of this 'symbolic step' were undermined by the unilateral, top-down communication from the State as experienced by the plaintiffs. Nuhanović stated there '[was] no communication between the Dutch state and me' when the compensation was offered. He concluded that the State feared court cases by other relatives, polarising the reparation process: 'so my success created *collateral damage* for myself.'[65]

A Mother of Srebrenica confirmed this when she referred to the compensation saying that 'there [was] no negotiation [... it was] more like an order.'[66] In the case of the Mothers of Srebrenica, a large-scale compensation scheme ('civielrechtelijke regeling') was set up in September 2021. The Ministry of Defence and the Ministry of Foreign Affairs appointed a Committee to execute this compensation scheme,[67]

---

61 Riemersma 2015.

62 Ibid.

63 Ibid.

64 Amnesty International (2013) https://www.amnesty.org/en/latest/press-release/2013/09/netherlands-supreme-court-hands-down-historic-judgment-over-srebrenica-geno/. Accessed 27 August 2023.

65 Riemersma 2015.

66 Koster and Grebo (2021) https://detektor.ba/2021/06/15/porodice-srebrenickih-zrtava-nezadovoljne-na-pocetku-procesa-isplate-odstete/. Accessed 12 September 2023.

67 Ministerie van Defensie 2021.

intending to compensate 'all damages the applicant has suffered as a consequence of the passing of the victim.'[68] It has since granted relatives a total of 8.7 million euros. The regulation stipulates the exact amounts of compensation for widows (15.000 euro) and 'other relatives' (10.000 euro). This followed from the 10% liability established by the court, thus calculating the total lump damages to 150.000 and 100.000 euro respectively. The scheme admits that 'a uniform regulation cannot do justice to all individual situations,' but argues that 'the benefits of such a uniform regulation significantly outweigh this downside.' Although it does not specify the exact calculation, the regulation claims that 'the State considers [...] it plausible that the damage of the relatives in most cases will not exceed these damage amounts.'[69] The reason for wanting to avoid the 'arduous road' of individual calculations[70] is understandable and arguably best for plaintiffs too, it also came at the cost of precision.

13.2.6.1 Repeating the Logic of the Harm through the Netherlands Compensation Committee Potočari

We want to zoom in here on the logics of inclusion and exclusion that were inherent in the compensation scheme. As discussed above, as the Bosnian Serb army was approaching, Dutch UN troops, closed off the compound when it became overcrowded. The fence that shielded off the compound became the demarcation line for Dutch liability. The Supreme Court ruled that the Dutch state was liable for the conduct of Dutchbat as it forced out the people inside the compound, who were subsequently killed. Any applicant thus must make it 'plausible' that their killed relative was present at the compound in the late afternoon of July 13.

The work of the Committee follows the logic of the court case, but as we argue, also replicates the logic of the harm of 1995 itself. As one survivor and relative Hava Avdić puts it:

> One of my uncles was on the other side of the fence, but he stayed in Potočari and was found [dead] there. However, the wire is relevant for the Dutch to tell who was a victim and who was not.[71]

The fence was of utmost importance in establishing liability. From the perspective of 'effective control,' a key point in the court case, the fence was of utmost importance to establish liability. Yet this legal logic, reproduced in the political and procedural logic of the compensation scheme, had nothing to do with the lived realities of the relatives. The fence originated from Dutchbat. From the lived experiences of the victims' relatives, the fence was already an injustice in 1995, and even more so today. Often, loved ones had tried to get inside the compound but were refused entry by the Dutch. What matters is that in the end, people who were killed after seeking

[68] Ibid.

[69] Ibid.

[70] Rijnhout 2021, p. 136.

[71] Koster 2023.

refuge in the compound, those outside of the fence, or those trying to flee through the woods (a choice made by many after they realized they could not find protection within the compound), were all victims of the same genocide.

Survivors and relatives point out this discrepancy between legal, political, and procedural logic (which they appear to clearly understand) and lived realities. Hava Gluhić for example states that: 'I agree that they [the Dutch battalion] were with so few people that they couldn't protect us. But they should have admitted the 10 per cent guilt for all [Bosniaks who tried to seek refuge at the compound]. That is the hardest part, because we were all together.'[72] The compensation Committee's Chair, Sylvia Wortmann, emphasises that rejecting such claims for people outside of the compound 'is really distressing.' Defending her work, she states that 'a line had to be drawn and the fence is that line. That's harsh, but if people don't find that right, it's not up to us. It's the decision of the Supreme Court. And within the limits of that decision, we as a Commission try to do what is just.'[73]

While reasonable from a legal and procedural perspective, from the lived experiences by survivors themselves, we see that this narrative mirrors the logic of the harm for which the Dutch state was found to be liable in the first place. After all, according to many survivors, it was the insistence on bureaucratic rules that had led Dutchbat to force Muhamed (and Ibro and Nasiha) Nuhanović and Rizo Mustafić and many others out, resulting in their killing. The Court of Appeal upheld by the Supreme Court, were clear in their ruling that Dutchbat could have given both men UN cards, even though they were not on the respective list, to help secure their safety.[74] Admittedly, Dutchbat's conduct for the situation of the men in the compound in the Mothers of Srebrenica case had been different, as well as regarding the people seeking protection outside of the compound, but for the survivors, the logic was the same. The fact that even a court of law concludes that Dutchbat could have diverted from the rules, adds to the irony that 25 years later, the Dutch State still deliberately chooses to keep to the narrowest reading of the Supreme Court ruling in executing the compensation scheme. From the perspective of survivors' lived experiences, the State is (again) hiding behind bureaucratic arguments. For the Bosnian-Dutch community specifically, this meant that the logic of the Committee harmed the potential for restorative and civic justice and reparation, as the State's conduct again mimicked that of 1995.

---

[72] Ibid.

[73] Ibid.

[74] In the Mustafić-case, the Court of Appeal concluded that: 'considering the great interests of Mustafic that were at stake, the possible risks that were related to taking Mustafić along with or without a UN-pass in reasonableness should not have resulted in the decision not to take him along. The Court admits that Dutchbat, given the earlier experiences, had to take into account that the convoy that would leave the compound would be thoroughly inspected by the Serbs. The Court also accepts that taking Mustafić along, who was not employed by the UN, would have implied a certain risk, but that this risk could have been reduced by making a UN-pass for him and by placing him on the list of local personnel, in so far as he did not appear on that list already.' s Gravenhage Court of Appeal (Gerechtshof 's Gravenhage), *Mustafć v. The Netherlands,* Judgment, 5 July 2011, ECLI:NL:GHSGR:2011:BR5386, para 6.18. For the Nuhanović case, considering Muhamed, the same reasoning was used. 's Gravenhage Court of Appeal (Gerechtshof 's Gravenhage), *Nuhanović v. The Netherlands,* Judgment, 5 July 2011, ECLI:NL:GHSGR:2011:BR0133, para 6.18.

This insight mirrors the influential work by Eelco Runia. Studying the state-commissioned study into Dutchbat's conduct shortly after Srebrenica, he found similar parallels between the work of NIOD on the one hand, and the bureaucracy of Dutchbat and Dutch politics during the fall of Srebrenica, on the other hand.[75] In this light, the following quote from survivor Hava Avdić is particularly striking: she called the Supreme Court decision and Committee's work 'a game with us who have survived and who are trying to remain dignified after so many years.'[76]

13.2.7 Apologies, Memory, and Education

Legal procedures, through their fact-finding and their contribution to the conversation about responsibility, often give rise to political apologies, commemoration activities and education around what constitutes harm. Such activities can contribute to restorative and civic justice, thus moving the reparation process towards the right side of Laplante's spectrum. The Dutch State remains actively involved in the commemoration of the Srebrenica genocide. Representatives are present during the annual commemoration in the Netherlands and recently have also attended the commemoration in Potočari, both on 11 July. The State, together with the organization PAX, has helped to establish the Memorial Centre Srebrenica, located in the former Dutchbat compound in Potočari. The State has also earmarked a 5-million-euro annual budget for activities and projects concerning Srebrenica.[77]

13.2.7.1 Political Apologies: Pushing the Question of Responsibility to the Margins

A first 'proto' apology from the Dutch State for its conduct during the Srebrenica genocide, came before the court cases. Prime Minister Wim Kok resigned from his position following the publication of the 2002 state-commissioned report on Srebrenica. While he stated that the 'government of the Netherlands, as a member of the international community, therefore failed as well,' survivors found this statement, according to experts, 'utterly unconvincing.'[78] Kok concluded that since the international community is 'faceless and cannot express its responsibility to the victims and survivors of Srebrenica[,] I can, and I do so now.'[79] The consequence of expressing this responsibility meant that he resigned, together with his cabinet, and thus there was no clear follow-up to this actually protracted question of responsibility. Elections were around the corner (adding to cynicism amongst the Bosnian-Dutch community

[75] Runia 2004.

[76] Koster 2023.

[77] Van den Berg 2014a, p. 17.

[78] Van den Berg 2014b, pp. 110, 114.

[79] Kok, as cited in Van den Berg 2014b, p. 111.

that Kok's resignation was mostly symbolic and strategic) and other issues soon overshadowed the conversation on Srebrenica. As Dion van den Berg concludes, the words were directed towards the Dutch public hoping for closure. Bosniak survivors and the Bosnian-Dutch community wanted an apology that would engage them in a dialogue on responsibility.[80] Kok's proto-apology had the chance to foster a sense of civic justice and reparation by reinforcing a trusting relationship between Bosnian-Dutch citizens and the State. But due to its limited wording and lack of follow through, the apology failed to bring the conversation on reparation to the right side of Laplante's spectrum.

For the two decades to come, the call for such a reparative apology remained unheard—until on 11 July 2022, the Dutch Minister of Defence Kajsa Ollongren offered 'deepest apologies' on behalf of the Dutch government as it had been part of the 'international community [that] failed in the protection of the people of Srebrenica.'[81] The apology had long been demanded by the Bosnian community, especially the Bosnian-Dutch community, and was welcomed by many. Kok's statement dates from far before the start of the court cases, while this apology followed the three cases' conclusion. It could moreover build on the 'closed door' apology to Nuhanović (while the Mustafić family did not befall such apology) by then Minister of Defence Jeanine Hennis-Plasschaert during the compensation negotiations after the 2013 Supreme Court ruling.[82] We can thus hypothesize that the facts and clarity produced in the court procedures positively impacted the Dutch state's apology.

However, the apologies came very late, did not refer to the court cases, and were partial, just like Kok's statement: the Dutch government apologized for having failed as part of the international community. While this is understandable historically and legally, it also externalized the responsibility and it did not correspond to the survivors' lived experiences. Moreover, the apology followed after years of, what the plaintiffs and other survivors perceived to be an unwillingness by the Dutch State and its representatives to enter into conversation and openly discuss questions of responsibility. This affected the credibility of the apology from the outset. For example, as concluded by Dutch NGO PAX, high-ranking military, Ministers and their officials were 'conspicuously absent' from dialogue activities between Dutchbat and Srebrenica survivors, despite clear invitations from both parties to be present.[83]

Perhaps most painfully to the relatives, Minister Ollongren's apologies came months after the Dutch State offered an official apology to Dutchbat.[84] This apology to Dutchbat, ushered in by the Prime Minister Mark Rutte, gave an outdated version of Srebrenica events, speaking about 'heartbreaking decisions' that had to be made

[80] Van den Berg 2014b, p. 114.

[81] Ollongren 2022.

[82] Ribbens (2022) https://www.nrc.nl/nieuws/2022/06/19/liesbeth-zegveld-rutte-had-eerst-excuses-moeten-aanbieden-aan-de-nabestaanden-a4133922. Accessed 25 July 2023; Riemersma 2015. Nuhanović recalls how the Minister apologised 'three or four times,' moreover interrupting the state lawyer who kept diminishing the story of Dutch responsibility.

[83] Van den Berg 2014a, p. 19.

[84] Maas (2022) https://www.volkskrant.nl/nieuws-achtergrond/in-diepste-excuses-van-kabinet-voor-srebrenica-spaart-het-kabinet-zichzelf-en-de-militairen~b393ffb9. Accessed 27 July 2023.

in a 'split second.'[85] This was hard to understand for many of Bosnian and Bosnian-Dutch community, as the court cases had carefully established that Dutchbat did have a choice. Formulations like these created polarisation as well as distrust between Dutchbat and the Bosnian-Dutch community and distrust for the Dutch State. They also distracted from the type of civic justice that could have been fostered through an inclusive reparation process. The plaintiffs' lawyer Liesbeth Zegveld concluded:

> our Prime Minister pretends that the ruling of the Supreme Court [referring to the 2013 ruling in the cases of Mustafić and Nuhanović] does not exist [...] Rutte could have apologized for sending Dutchbat without preparation. But he should also have said: 'the state and Dutchbat have made some serious mistakes, let us not forget.[86]

13.2.7.2 The Srebrenica Genocide in Dutch Education: The Dutch Perspective

Another opportunity for state-sponsored reparation following the fact-finding of the court cases lies in education. Since 2006, the Dutchbat mission in and events of Srebrenica have become part of the Dutch 'canon,' used in high school history teaching. 'Inclusion of an accurate account of the violations that occurred [...] in educational material at all levels' can, according to the UN-understanding of reparation, be a form of satisfaction[87] in fostering restorative and civic justice and reparation—sliding much more towards the right side of Laplante's spectrum. Professor of Holocaust Education Marc van Berkel concluded in his research on the canon, that it fails to mention the term genocide and is one-sided: it heavily focussed on Dutchbat rather than the Bosnian victims. Moreover, the war is labelled a 'civil war,' portraying the image of the war as an equal level playing field. This is far removed from the accepted historical assessment that it constituted a war of aggression and that the events of July 1995 constituted genocide and a joint criminal enterprise.[88] This detracts from the deliberately orchestrated nature of the genocide and harms the potential for satisfaction and wider reparation. It reiterates a narrative that has been dominant in extremist right-wing and nationalist discourse in Serbia and the Republika Srpska up until the present day and that adds to the 'triumphalism' stage of genocide. The court cases' contribution to fact-finding, and its conclusions on the

[85] Ribbens 2022.

[86] Ibid.

[87] UNGA 2005, pp. 8-9.

[88] Van Berkel 2020. This historical assessment has also been accepted in ICTY documents. In the Stanišić Simatović arrest for example, Brammertz concluded that 'the Trial Chamber found proven beyond reasonable doubt that, from at least August 1991 and at all times relevant to the crimes charged in the Indictment, a common criminal purpose existed to forcibly and permanently remove the majority of non-Serbs from large areas of Croatia and Bosnia and Herzegovina, through the commission of the crimes of persecution, murder, as well as deportation and inhumane acts (forcible transfer) charged in the Indictment.' United Nations International Residual Mechanism for Criminal Tribunals, *Appeal Judgement Summary for Jovica Stanišić and Franko Simatović*, Judgment (Appeals Chamber), 31 May 2023, para A.4 https://www.irmct.org/sites/default/files/case_documents/PR316e-S-S-Summary-Appeals-Judgement.pdf.

precise responsibility of Dutchbat and the Dutch State, deserve to be taken into the Dutch education system.

This prioritisation of Dutchbat over the Bosniak victims reflects a larger asymmetry in the societal narrative. On the 25-year anniversary of the genocide, for example, Dutch media made an extensive documentary about Dutchbat veterans. The documentary, called 'powerless mission of Dutchbat' was nominated for the highest journalistic price in the Netherlands.[89] While Dutchbat veterans were invited to a popular Dutch talk show to discuss this documentary, representatives of the Bosnian Dutch community were not.[90] As the Dutch commentator Chris Keulemans put it:

> We have turned Srebrenica into a Dutch ['Hollands'] trauma [...] The story since 1995 has been solely about us. But we do not talk about the actual, much larger trauma of the Bosnian Muslims [sic] who have to live with the memory of 8372 deaths.[91]

13.2.8 Responding to the Lack of Reparation: Initiatives by the Bosnian-Dutch Community

This chapter has so far argued that while the court cases represented important legal breakthroughs, their achievements were not taken up by Dutch politics and society and did not in the end advance the broader reparation process. The Dutch societal narrative is still mostly focussed on Dutchbat rather than the Bosniak victims—and Bosnians within the Netherlands and Bosnia are aware of this. Emir Suljagić, Director of the Srebrenica Memorial Centre, connected this one-sided story to the above-mentioned 'triumphalism' stage of genocide in a recent tweet: 'As long as they continue to place Dutchbat soldiers at the centre of their narrative of Srebrenica, Dutch society, and in particular the Dutch government, are colluding with the revisionist forces attempting to obfuscate the human cost of the Srebrenica.'[92]

Realizing the limitations of the legal route and its reluctant transfer into political and societal conversations, the Bosnian-Dutch community took various initiatives over the past 28 years to seek the type of broad reparation that would correspond to their lived experiences. Through our theoretical framework using the Laplante model, as represented in Fig. 13.3 below, we see these initiatives as an intervention (4) in the reparation process, which stalled (3) at the narrow end of the spectrum because political and societal responses (2) failed to take on the potential of court cases (1), which themselves can only be expected to contribute to reparative justice,

---

[89] Moorman (2021) https://www.volkskrant.nl/cultuur-media/nominaties-nipkow-schijf-bekendereschijf-gaat-naar-het-sinterklaasjournaal~b6bc9975/. Accessed 31 July 2023.

[90] BNNVARA (2020) https://www.npostart.nl/srebrenica-de-machteloze-missie-van-dutchbat/BV_101399454. Accessed 16 September 2023.

[91] Keulemans (2020) https://www.groene.nl/artikel/srebrenica-is-nederlandse-geschiedenis. Accessed 1 September 2023.

[92] Suljagić (2021) https://www.aa.com.tr/en/analysis/analysis-quo-vadis-aida-srebrenica-survivors-finally-telling-their-own-story/2150305. Accessed 1 September 2023.

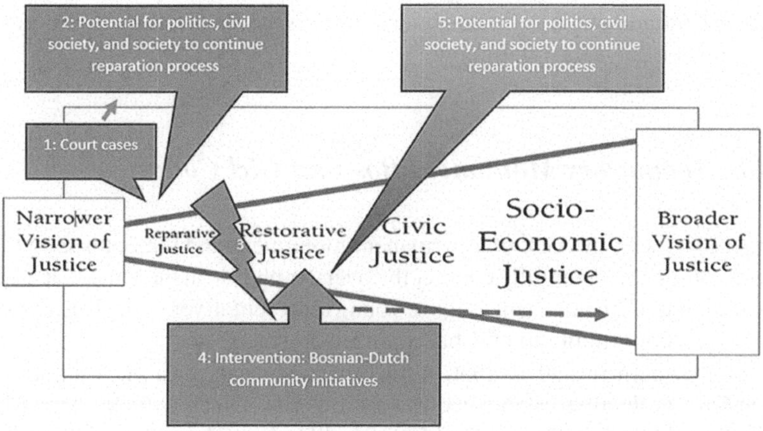

Fig. 13.3 Laplante's spectrum applied to the situation after the court cases. *Source* Laplante 2015

further along the spectrum. These initiatives (4) are potentially powerful as they give politics and society another chance (5) to take on the potential of these initiatives and move the reparation process to the broader, more transformative side of the spectrum.

13.2.9 Keeping Memory Alive

The Bosnian Dutch community organizes the annual Srebrenica commemoration, the first one being held on July 11, 1996, opposite the ICTY in The Hague. The participants walked from the tribunal to the World War II memorial next to the Peace Palace. A wreath was laid there, with a message cautioning about motives that lead to dehumanizing political systems and result in such atrocities. Since then, the commemoration relocated to the central square in the Hague, in front of the Netherlands Ministry of Defence. This location was chosen because the Bosnian community wanted to be more visible to both society and to the Dutch government, urging it to explore its responsibility.[93]

In the early years, the commemoration attracted only 20 participants. But over time it has grown into a recognizable event that attracts hundreds of people, Bosnian and Dutch, and hosts high-ranking speakers from politics and civil society.[94] Through this commemoration, the Bosnian Dutch community has tried to push the reparation process in the direction of restorative and civic dimensions, inviting speakers to honour and commemorate the victims and discuss what broad political and societal responsibility could look like. Their consistent calls to the Dutch State to erect

[93] See Srebrenica Herdenking, https://www.srebrenica-herdenking.nl/. Accessed 15 January 2025.

[94] For an archive of the commemoration up until 2005, see: https://www.srebrenica-herdenking.nl/. Accessed 15 January 2025.

a permanent monument for the genocide can be seen in the same light, but were unsuccessful for 26 years—until now.[95]

13.2.10 Temporary Monument Bosnian Girl Collective

This frustration with the lack of a permanent monument and the realisation that the commemoration could not fully counter the over-emphasis on the Dutchbat-narrative at the cost of that of Bosnian voices, gave young representatives of the Bosnian-Dutch community an opportunity to take back narrative ownership.

One of the main initiatives that bring Bosnian voices into the spotlight is the 'Bosnian Girl' collective, established by four Bosnian-Dutch women: Arna Mačkić, Daria Bukvić, Emina Ćerimović and Ena Sendijarević. The name of the collective refers to the internationally renowned artwork Bosnian Girl by the Bosnian artist Šejla Kamerić (Fig. 13.4 below). This artwork consists of a portrait of Kamerić, overwritten with graffiti texts from the UN compound in Potočari where Dutch soldiers were stationed. 'No teeth…? A moustache…? Smells like shit…? BOSNIAN GIRL!'. The young Dutch-Bosnian women transformed this image to highlight that Bosnian voices cannot be excluded when it comes to the genocide, thus advocating for a broader, more inclusive societal conversation on Srebrenica and reparation.

The collective launched a project and website called 'Srebrenica is Dutch history' to highlight this inclusive Bosnian-Dutch perspective on the genocide and thus broaden the reparation process.[96] Since a permanent monument was still lacking and the collective realized that a whole new generation had grown up since, they decided to take the lead themselves. For the 25 years Srebrenica genocide commemoration, Bosnian Girl created 25 portraits of Bosnian-Dutch men and women, all aged 25. They do not have memories of the war themselves, but they symbolize the connection between the Netherlands and Bosnia. The temporary monument of the Bosnian Girl collective, which attracted significant media attention,[97] was on display for three weeks and then journeyed through different cities in the Netherlands. Its attempt to broaden the spectrum for reparation and recognition was understood well, as is clear in the response of participant Lejla:

> My parents, who have experienced Srebrenica, still bear the pain. Also, because it is not part of Dutch history. […] The story has to be told. Otherwise, the generation that does not learn anything about it will soon be in charge- and fatal decisions will be made again.[98]

While the monument was temporary, its effect on the reparation narrative was significant. During the same commemoration of the 25 years genocide in 2020,

[95] Mustafić and Spijkers 2020.

[96] This website is Srebrenicaisnederlandsegeschiedenis.nl. Accessed 12 October 2023.

[97] Leeuwen (2020) https://www.volkskrant.nl/cultuur-media/anna-dasovic-deed-er-vier-jaar-over-de-beelden-van-dutchbatters-te-bemachtigen-en-dat-loonde-de-moeite~b4631309/. Accessed 7 September 2023

[98] Lejla (undated) https://srebrenicaisnederlandsegeschiedenis.nl/. Accessed 16 September 2023.

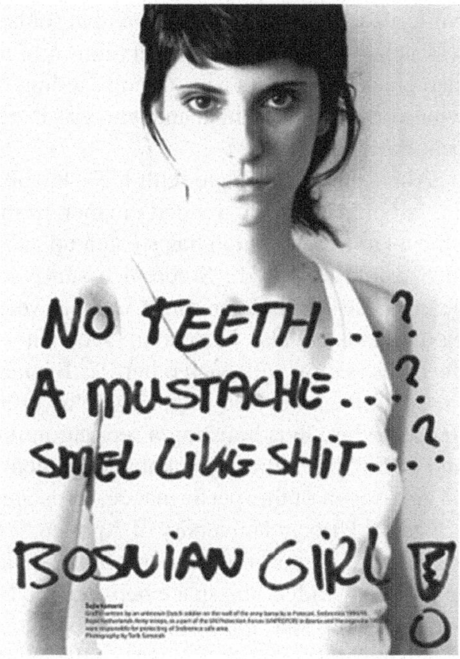

Fig. 13.4 Bosnian Girl artwork. Photography by Tarik Samarah, art by Šejla Kamerić, 2003.[99]

after the community had called for a permanent monument every year, and perhaps inspired by the temporary manifestation by Bosnian Girl, the Mayor of the Hague announced that a national monument for Srebrenica would be erected in the Hague, the City of Peace. Although this has not yet been realized, this promise signifies a move by Dutch authorities towards the right, broader end of the reparation spectrum. This is being supported by formal Dutch authorities and finally, the efforts of more than 25 years are bearing fruit.

13.2.11 Theatre Play 'Dangerous Names' and Education

The Bosnian-Dutch call for broader reparation was also expressed through theatre, most recently when Dutch producer Boy Jonkergouw and Srebrenica survivor Alma Mustafić co-created 'Dangerous names.'[100] Several theatre performances about Srebrenica genocide took place in the Netherlands in the past years, such as 'With eyes open' and 'Dark numbers'. All those performances were made from the perspective of Dutchbat veterans only. 'Dangerous names' was the first Dutch play to overcome this dichotomy by, taking on a perspective that was that of the Srebrenica survivors

[99] Leeuwen (2020); see n.97.

[100] Embrechts (2020) https://www.theaterkrant.nl/recensie/25-jaar-srebrenica-gevaarlijke-namen/boy-jonkergouw-theaterproducties-i-s-m-het-zuidelijk-toneel-en-pax/. Accessed 2 August 2023.

while also, literally, inviting Dutchbat soldiers onto the stage. For that reason the play was acknowledged as an 'intervention in a deadlocked debate.'[101] Alma Mustafić also plays the leading role, directly telling the story about her father, Rizo Mustafić, who worked for Dutchbat and who was handed over to the Serb militias by the Dutch peacekeepers.

Alma shares the stage with UN-Dutchbat veteran Raymond Braat, who, during the fall of Srebrenica, divided the men from the women. This meant that for the first time a Dutchbat veteran has spoken up and said loud and clear 'we knew that these men would be killed', Srebrenica survivors already knew this but they had never heard these words from any Dutchbat veteran. The play was well received in the Netherlands but also in Bosnia. One visitor commented that the play 'helps to open the conversation with each other.'[102] Bosnians in the audience articulated their relief in seeing their story on stage. The play brought veterans and survivors a step closer to each other, thus boosting a reparation process that is not defined by polarization and denial, but rather by acknowledgement of responsibility and inclusion.

As a result of this performance, a special honours module on Srebrenica has been created at Utrecht University of Applied Sciences (HU).[103] Srebrenica has also been included in the existing research line 'social impact of art and culture'.[104] In order to literally 'bridge' the space between the Bosnian and Dutch communities and thus arrive at a broader, more inclusive reparation process, the University also organizes excursions to Srebrenica as part of the Minor International Development Work. HU students call the trip 'a life changing experience.' They learn to understand specific challenges of rebuilding society and community after a war and genocide. The trip and module illuminate the complex and multifaceted nature of international development work, building commitment amongst students to advocate for community-level healing, human rights, social justice, and reparation on a global scale.[105]

13.3 Conclusion

In this chapter, we have studied how Dutch politics and society at large responded to the potential for reparation that was created through the civil court cases on Srebrenica. We have seen, from the perspective of their lived experiences, that plaintiffs turned to the court as a last resort. Both Nuhanović and Mustafić were faced with a political and a societal context that went against their search for justice, recognition,

[101] Immler et al. 2022, p. 358.

[102] Der Linde (2022) https://www.groene.nl/artikel/als-alma-mustafic-omkijkt. Accessed 1 September 2023.

[103] Genocide Srebrenica (undated) https://husite.nl/huhonours/genocide-srebrenica/. Accessed 11 September 2023.

[104] Mustafić et al. (2022) https://www.hu.nl/onderzoek/projecten/de-impact-van-theater-gevaarlijke-namen-srebrenica-25-jaar. Accessed 7 September 2023.

[105] HU (undated) https://husite.nl/minors/minors/international-development-work/. Accessed 11 September 2023.

and reparation. The court cases constituted important legal breakthroughs, achieved fact-finding, and opened up the conversation on responsibility.

The court cases thus held important potential, had the relevant political and societal actors taken up on this. However, this did not happen. Most strikingly, in its implementation of the compensation scheme for the Mothers of Srebrenica, the Dutch state reproduced the bureaucratic logic of inclusion and exclusion that caused Dutchbat's harmful and destructive conduct in the first place. The political apologies, commemoration, and education on Srebrenica similarly failed to give proper due to the achievements of the court cases, especially in terms of their contribution to fact-finding and to the conversation on political and social responsibility. Moreover they repeated the same-old emphasis on Dutchbat rather than the Bosniak victims and thus failed to contribute to an inclusive, broad reparation process.

Arguably, political and societal actors understand the court cases as an argument to slow down rather than accelerate the reparation process. Since the Dutch State has been held liable and some of the victims did receive some kind of financial compensation, the court cases are often seen as an 'end station' for Dutch responsibility. In the eyes of the survivors of Srebrenica and Bosnian-Dutch community, however, they are only a first step towards a much broader reparation process. Given that genocide is a complex and intentional process of destruction, it is logical that reparation of such a historical injustice is also a relational process that encompasses complex webs of responsibility. Since the Dutch State and society were directly present, Srebrenica is a shared history and the responsibility for the harm and the reparation is shared by us all.

The Bosnian-Dutch community responded to this incomplete and unsatisfactory reparation process through its own initiatives. In so doing it gave Dutch politics and society another chance to kickstart a more inclusive reparation process—one that leans much more towards the right side of the spectrum and promotes restorative and civic justice. This is a type of reparation that the Bosnian-Dutch community want to see and have now begun to build themselves, as shown through the annual commemoration, the initiative Bosnian Girl, and the theatre play 'Dangerous names.' The shared history of Srebrenica belongs to all of us. The genocide deserves the kind of reparation that only a society as a whole can give.

Scene Dangerous Names

Ray: It's taken me years Alma. But in a way I made my peace with it. I had to. And I have forgiven. I have even forgiven that motherfucker Mladic. I had to. But just because I forgive… doesn't mean I forget. To find peace…In myself.

Alma: You know Ray, you hurt me when you say that. Don't get me wrong, I'm very happy for you that you have found peace. I want that so badly. But how can I find peace if the bodies of our loved ones have not been put to rest, how can I find peace if Serbia continues to deny the genocide and their children glorify war criminals? How can we celebrate 76 years of freedom in Europe if we forget what happened 26 years ago in Europe? Never again. How many times are we going to say that? And every time it happens and we can learn from it, we look away.[106]

[106] Mustafić and Jonkergouw (2020), see n.1.

References

Egmond J (2014) Hasan Nuhanović: 'Ik blijf die lastpost uit Srebrenica.' Donaustroom 20 December 2014, https://www.donaustroom.eu/hasan-nuhanovic-ik-blijf-die-lastpost-uit-srebrenica. Accessed 1 July 2023.
Gready P, Robins S (2014) From Transitional to Transformative Justice: A New Agenda for Practice. International Journal of Transitional Justice 8: 339–61.
Halilovich H (2017) Globalization and Genocide. Global Encyclopedia of Public Administration, Public Policy, and Governance: 2493–2502.
Immler N (2022) De (Dia)Logics van Erkenning en Herstel. Het belang van geschiedenis voor rechtvaardigheid. Oratie. Universiteit voor Humanistiek, Utrecht.
Immler N, Driessen S, van Brenk J (2022) 'Bosnië is veranderd, terwijl wij zelf stil zijn blijven staan.' Terugkeerreis veteranen vanuit een relationeel perspectief. Militaire Spectator 191: 352–359.
Jonassohn K, Björnson K S (1998) Genocide and Gross Human Rights Violations. In Comparative Perspective. Transaction Publishers, New Brunswick/London.
Karčić H (2022) Torture, humiliate, kill: Inside the Bosnian Serb camp system. University of Michigan Press, Ann Arbor.
Koster M (2023) Netherlands Pays €8.7 Million to Srebrenica Victims' Relatives. BalkanInsight. https://balkaninsight.com/2023/01/04/netherlands-pays-e8-7-million-to-srebrenica-victims-relatives/. Accessed 20 February 2023.
Kumar R (2014) Why Reparations. In: Oberdiek J (ed) Philosophical Foundations of the Law of Torts. Oxford University Press, 193–213.
Laplante L J (2015) Just Repair. Cornell International Law Journal 48: 513–78.
Lemkin R (2008) Axis Rule in Occupied Europe: Laws of Occupation, Analysis of Government, Proposals for Redress. The Lawbook Exchange, Ltd.
Leyh B M, Fraser J (2019) Transformative Reparations: Changing the Game or More of the Same? Cambridge International Law Journal 8: 39–59.
Loth M (2020) How Does Tort Law Deal with Historical Injustice? On Slavery Reparations, Post-Colonial Redress, and the Legitimations of Tort Law. Journal of European Tort Law 11: 181–207.
McCann M W (2008) Litigation and Legal Mobilization. In: Caldeira G, Kelemen D, Whittington K (eds) The Oxford Handbook of Law and Politics. Oxford University Press, Oxford, 522–540.
Ministerie van Defensie (2021) Civielrechtelijke regeling ter uitvoering van het arrest van de Hoge Raad van 19 juli 2019 inzake Staat/Stichting Mothers of Srebrenica, Staatscourant van het Koninkrijk der Nederlanden. https://zoek.officielebekendmakingen.nl/stcrt-2021-27109.html. Accessed 13 March 2023.
Minow M (2015) Forgiveness, law, and justice. Calif. L. Rev., 103, 1615–1646.
Mustafić A, Spijkers O (2020) A Monument for Srebrenica in The Hague. Art and International Justice Initiative 25 October 2020, https://artij.org/en/blog.html. Accessed 12 March 2023.
NIOD (2002) Srebrenica. Reconstruction, Background, Consequences and Analyses of the Fall of a 'Safe' Area. https://www.niod.nl/en/publications/srebrenica. Accessed 20 July 2023.
Nuhanović H (2007) Under the UN Flag: The International Community and the Srebrenica Genocide. DES Sarajevo.
Ollongren K (2022) Toespraak van minister van Defensie Kajsa Ollongren bij Srebrenica-herdenking in Potočari, 11 July 2022. https://www.defensie.nl/downloads/toespraken/2022/07/11/toespraak-minister-kajsa-ollongren-bij-srebrenica-herdenking-in-potocari,. Accessed 10 February 2023.
Orentlicher D (2008) Shrinking the Space for Denial. The Impact of the ICTY in Serbia. Open Society Justice Initiative, New York.
Pemberton A, Aarten PG, Mulder E (2019) Stories as Property: Narrative Ownership as a Key Concept in Victims' Experiences with Criminal Justice. Criminology & Criminal Justice. 19:404–20.
Pokret Majke enklava Srebrenica i Žepa (2019) Šta znači '10 posto' od ljudskog života?, 14 October 2019, http://www.enklave-srebrenica-zepa.org/aktuelnosti.php. Accessed 21 March 2023.

Ribbens A (2022) Liesbeth Zegveld: Rutte had eerst excuses moeten aanbieden aan de nabestaanden. NRC 19 june 2022, https://www.nrc.nl/nieuws/2022/06/19/liesbeth-zegveld-rutte-had-eerst-excuses-moeten-aanbieden-aan-de-nabestaanden-a4133922. Accessed 25 July 2023.
Riemersma G (2015) Interview: Dutchbat-tolk Hasan Nuhanović. Vrij Nederland 25 juni 2025, https://www.vn.nl/hasan-nuhanovic-dutchbat. Accessed 25 July 2023.
Rijnhout R (2021) Mothers of Srebrenica: Causation and Partial Liability under Dutch Tort Law. Utrecht Journal of International and European Law 36: 127–140. https://doi.org/10.5334/ujiel.543
Runia E (2004) 'Forget about It': 'Parallel Processing' in the Srebrenica Report. History and Theory. 43: 295–320
Ryngaert C (2012) Tort Litigation in Respect of Overseas Violations of Environmental Law Committed by Corporations: Lessons from the Akpan v. Shell Litigation in the Netherlands. McGill International Journal of Sustainable Development Law and Policy 8: 245–60
Ryngaert C, Spijkers O (2019) The End of the Road: State Liability for Acts of UN Peacekeeping Contingents After the Dutch Supreme Court's Judgment in Mothers of Srebrenica (2019). Netherlands International Law Review, 66, 537–553.
Spijkers O (2021) Legal Monuments for Srebrenica in the Hague. Utrecht J. Int'l & Eur. L., 36, 118.
Stanton G (2017) Ten Stages of Genocide. http://www.genocide-watch.com/genocide/tenstagesofgenocide.html. Accessed 23 Augustus 2023.
UNGA (1999) Report of the Secretary-General pursuant to General Assembly resolution 53/35. The fall of Srebrenica, A/54/549.
UNGA (2005) Basic Principles and Guidelines on the Right to a Remedy and Reparation for Victims of Gross Violations of International Human Rights Law and Serious Violations of International Humanitarian Law, A/RES/60/147.
Üngör Ü (2011) Team America: Genocide Prevention? Genocide Studies and Prevention. 6 (1): 32–38.
Van Berkel M (2020) Veilig gebied? Srebrenica in het Nederlandse Onderwijs. PAX. https://paxvoorvrede.nl/wp-content/uploads/import/import/pax-rapport-srebrenica-in-het-nederlands-geschiedenisonderwijs.pdf. Accessed 10 February 2023.
Van den Berg D (2014a) Rekindling the National Debate. How Public and Private Recognition Can Shift the Dutch Discourse on Srebrenica.' Published on Dealing with the Past Balkan, accessed 7 July 2023: https://www.dwp-balkan.org/cms_dwp/userfiles/file/20110606%20Rekindling%20the%20National%20Debate%20-%20Dion%20vd%20Berg.pdf. Accessed 3 July 2023.
Van den Berg D (2014b) Rekindling the National Debate: How Public and Private Recognition Can Shift the Dutch Discourse on Srebrenica. In: van Liere L, Spronk K (eds) Images of Enmity and Hope: Texts, Beliefs, Practices. LIT Verlag, Berlin, 105–141.
Van Dijck G (2017) When Historic Injustice Meets Tort Law: the Case of the Srebrenica Genocide. Law Blogs Maastricht. https://www.maastrichtuniversity.nl/blog/2017/07/when-historic-injustice-meets-tort-law-case-srebrenica-genocide. Accessed 20 July 2023.
Woudwijk M, Wentholt N (2021) Het gesprek over Srebrenica is nu aan ons. Trouw 15 juni 2021, https://www.trouw.nl/opinie/het-gesprek-over-srebrenica-is-nu-aan-ons~bf5d4c00/. Accessed 15 March 2023.

Cases

's Gravenhage Court (Rechtbank 's Gravenhage), *Nuhanović v. The Netherlands,* Judgment, 10 September 2008, ECLI:NL:RBSGR:2008:BF0181.
's Gravenhage Court (Rechtbank 's Gravenhage), *Mustafć v. The Netherlands,* Judgment, 10 September 2008, ECLI:NL:RBSGR:2008:BF0182.

's Gravenhage Court of Appeal (Gerechtshof 's Gravenhage), *Nuhanović v. The Netherlands,* Judgment, 5 July 2011, ECLI:NL:GHSGR:2011:BR0133.
's Gravenhage Court of Appeal (Gerechtshof 's Gravenhage), *Mustafć v. The Netherlands,* Judgment, 5 July 2011, ECLI:NL:GHSGR:2011:BR5386.
Dutch Supreme Court (Hoge Raad der Nederlanden), *Mothers of Srebrenica Association et al. v. The Netherlands,* Judgment, 19 July 2019, ECLI:NL:HR:2019:1223.
Dutch Supreme Court (Hoge Raad der Nederlanden), *Mustafć v. The Netherlands,* Judgment, 6 September 2013, 12/03324, ECLI:NL:HR:2013:BZ9225.
United Nations International Residual Mechanism for Criminal *Tribunals, Appeal Judgement Summary for Jovica Stanišić and Franko Simatović,* Judgment (Appeals Chamber), 31 May 2023.

Niké Wentholt Part of the research which resulted in this publication was done with the Dialogics of Justice project (VI.C.191.051), financed by the VICI scheme of the Dutch Research Council (NWO).

Chapter 14
No 'Effective Remedy' with(out) National Tort Law—A Dutch Perspective on the Obstacles for Enforcement of the Right to a Remedy

Anneloes Kuiper-Slendebroek

Contents

Abstract The governing aspect of international human rights law depends on its interpretation and application by national courts. This chapter discusses the national private law enforcement of the Right to a Remedy (Art. 13 ECHR). When ECHR-rights are violated, individuals can ask for a remedy before a national court. Although national law is of vital importance for the application of international law, it is shown that national (case) law can also stand in the way of the effective application and enforcement of the right to a remedy. Cases in point are from the Dutch legal system, being one of the most progressive: ECHR-provisions can be applied over conflicting domestic law. Therefore, Dutch case-law on the right to a remedy was selected to examine the application and interpretation of international law by national courts. The

A. Kuiper-Slendebroek (✉)
Utrecht University, Utrecht, The Netherlands
e-mail: B.A.Kuiper@UU.nl

Utrecht Centre for Accountability and Liability Law (Ucall), Utrecht, The Netherlands

Empirical Legal Research into Institutions for Conflict Resolution (ERI), Utrecht, The Netherlands

Netherlands Institute of Human Rights (SIM) Utrecht, Utrecht, The Netherlands

O. Spijkers et al. (eds.), *Netherlands Yearbook of International Law 2022*, Netherlands Yearbook of International Law 53, https://doi.org/10.1007/978-94-6265-627-7_14

direct application of international law in Dutch case law shows the effects of international law in the domestic legal order. But it also becomes clear that the peculiarities of national tort law contain certain obstacles that can easily overlooked by international law (makers), and can stand in the way effectively remedying international human rights' violations.

Keywords Domestic law · Compensation · Human Rights · Right to a remedy · Tort law

14.1 Introduction

International law is ever dynamic. In the interaction between international and national law, the role of national courts is important. When international law is interpreted and applied by national courts, it can evolve further and confirm its relevance. On the other hand, national law can stand in the way of the right or successful implementation of international law. Especially the law of remedies has been characterized as 'a jurisprudence of deficiency, of what is lost between declaring a right and implementing a remedy'.[1] This characterization indicates the distance between 'the ideal and the real', between the aspired rights of international law and the mechanisms in national (tort) law that remedy the breach of these rights. National law is vital for, but can also stand in the way of, an effective remedy for the violation of international law, and more specifically: a remedy for the violation of fundamental human rights.

As is the case with most international law, the European Convention on Human Rights (ECHR)[2] counts on the implementation, enforcement and remediation of international right's breaches in the domestic legal order (Sect. 14.2.1). Primary responsibility for implementing and enforcing its rights and freedoms has been placed on national authorities of the Member States. Especially national courts play an important role for the protection of these fundamental rights by effectively implementing the ECHR. Central to the cooperative relationship between the ECHR and national legal systems is Article 13 ECHR:[3]

[1] Gewirtz 1983, pp. 585–587.

[2] European Convention for the Protection of Human Rights and Fundamental Freedoms ('ECHR'), Council of Europe, ETS No. 005, opened for signature 4 November 1950, entered into force 3 September 1953.

[3] Harris et al. 2018, p. 745.

> Everyone whose rights and freedoms as set forth in (the) Convention are violated shall have an effective remedy before a national authority notwithstanding that the violation has been committed by persons acting in an official capacity.[4]

For the cooperative relationship between ECHR and national law to succeed, the status and effect of the ECHR in national law is important. This cooperation depends on two aspects: the position of the ECHR in the domestic hierarchy of sources of law, prevailing over conflicting national laws, and the self-executing character of the ECHR rules and the direct enforcement of these rules by national courts.[5] As such, the Dutch legal system is viewed as one of the most progressive, because the Dutch Constitution holds the explicit rule that generally accords 'pre-eminence to the self-executing norms of international treaties over conflicting domestic law, even of constitutional rank'.[6] Due to recent changes, allowing Dutch courts to directly apply international law in tort law cases, the Dutch legal system should be even better equipped for the application of international law. Therefore, the Dutch system is subject of this chapter (Sect. 14.3.1). But despite this progressiveness, there are still elements in the interaction between international and national law, that challenge the effective enforcement of human rights law by Dutch courts. These challenges are examined in Sect. 14.3.2. And finally, where human rights are enforced through the open norms of tort law[7]—i.e. the positive obligations of the State to protect against the dangers of climate change (Articles 2 and 8 ECHR)—the application of remedies in national tort law is central to the cooperative relationship between international human rights treaties and the national legal system (Sect. 14.4.2). Here as well, there are obstacles found in the cooperation between Article 13 ECHR and Dutch tort law.

This chapter lays out the progress and obstacles for effective international law enforcement that are found in both the interaction between national and international law, and in the application of human rights through tort law. It does not aim to be exhaustive, but to paint a picture through typical Dutch court cases.

[4] The extent of Article 13 ECHR is further explained in Sect. 14.2.2.

[5] See also: Caligiuri and Napoletano 2010, pp. 125–127.

[6] Polakiewicz 1994, p. 184.

[7] Rijnhout and Emaus 2014. See also: More 1994, p. 82.

14.2 The ECHR and the 'Right to a Remedy'

14.2.1 System of the ECHR

The interpretation of treaties is governed by international (customary) rules, but whether and how treaties are implemented and applied in the national legal system is nationally regulated. The Vienna Convention on the Law of Treaties (VCLT)[8]—codification of customary law—only states that '[e]very treaty in force is binding upon the parties to it and must be performed by them in good faith'[9] and '[a] party may not invoke the provisions of its internal law as justification for its failure to perform a treaty'.[10] Thus, the implementation of treaties differs between States. Classically, States are presumed to have either a monistic or a dualistic approach towards international law.[11] Generally speaking, the monistic approach considers international and national law as part of the same legal system, while in the dualist approach international law and national law are two separate and distinguishable bodies of law.

In line with these international interpretation rules, the ECHR leaves it to contracting States to decide how to comply with their duties; by ratifying the ECHR, the contracting States only 'undertake to ensure that their domestic legislation is compatible with it'.[12] In monistic States such as Bulgaria and Romania, the ECHR-provisions are directly applied, while dualistic States like Norway and the United Kingdom have first implemented the ECHR in their national law.[13] This can be done either by adopting a law that refers to certain international human rights treaties saying they have to be regarded as domestic law,[14] or by rewriting the international human rights into national law.[15]

Regardless of being monistic or dualistic, the hierarchy of the ECHR in the national legal system is another point of relevance. In some States the Convention

---

[8] Vienna Convention on the Law of Treaties ('VCLT'), opened for signature 23 May 1969, Treaty Series, vol. 1155, entered into force 27 January 1980, p. 331.

[9] VCLT, above n. 8, art. 26.

[10] VCLT, above n. 8, art. 27.

[11] Although it is under discussion whether this distinction should still be made, due to the ongoing convergence of international and national law. See Nijman and Nollkaemper 2007, Von Bogdandy 2008.

[12] ECtHR, *Case of Paksas v. Lithuania*, Judgment, 6 January 2011, 34932/04, para 119.

[13] Norway: Act on Strengthening of the Status of Human Rights, entered into force 21 May 1999. The United Kingdom: An Act to give further effect to rights and freedoms guaranteed under the European Convention on Human Rights; to make provision with respect to holders of certain judicial offices who become judges of the European Court of Human Rights; and for connected purposes, 1998 c. 42, entered into force 9 November 1998.

[14] For example in Norway.

[15] Germany has included the international human rights in its Grundgesetz (Basic Law): Basic Law for the Federal Republic of Germany, entered into force 8 May 1949.

prevails above all other (conflicting) national laws,[16] in other States the ECHR is applicable at the level of statutory law, being superior to statutes, but inferior to the Constitution.[17] Although States are not obliged to incorporate the Convention into domestic law, there is a minimum requirement to safeguard its fundamental rights:

> the substance of the rights and freedoms set forth must be secured under the domestic legal order, in some form or another, to everyone within the jurisdiction of the Contracting States.[18]

In securing these rights and freedoms, Article 13 ECHR plays an important role. In the early years of the Convention, judges of the European Court of Human Rights (ECtHR or Court) described Article 13 ECHR as 'one of the most obscure clauses in the Convention', whose 'application raises extremely difficult and complicated problems of interpretation'.[19] Luckily, the European Court of Human Rights (Court) did embark upon the interpretation of Article 13 to ensure its application, because it is crucial to the functioning of the rights in the Convention. According to the Court, Article 13 of the European Convention on Human Rights (ECHR, Convention) is 'giving direct expression to the States' obligation to protect human rights first and foremost within their own legal system' and 'establishes' an additional guarantee for an individual in order to ensure that he or she effectively enjoys those rights'.[20] Furthermore, the object of Article 13 ECHR is 'to provide a means whereby individuals can obtain relief at national level for violations of their Convention rights before having to set in motion the international machinery of complaint before the Court'.[21] If such means would not be available, 'the effective functioning, on both the national and international level, of the scheme of human rights protection set up by the Convention is liable to be weakened'.[22]

With Article 13 ECHR, the national legal system is primarily responsible for providing an effective remedy in cases where ECHR-rights are breached. The Contracting States are required to secure the full enjoyment of these international human rights in their national legal systems. The right to a remedy is often addressed through the national tort law system, but there appear to be some hurdles in coming to its full potential. Neither one of the two European tort law harmonization projects—the Principles of European Tort Law[23] and the Draft Common Frame of Reference[24]—addressed the specific case of liability for human rights violations. It is therefore questionable whether the responsibility of Contracting States is met by

---

[16] As is – to a large extent – the case in the Netherlands (Sect. 14.3).

[17] As is the case in Germany.

[18] ECtHR, *Case of James and others v. the United Kingdom*, Judgment, 21 February 1986, 8793/79, para 84.

[19] ECtHR, *Malone v. the United Kingdom*, Partially dissenting opinion of Judges Matscher and Pinheiro Farinha, 2 August 1984, 8691/79.

[20] ECtHR, *Kudla v. Poland*, Judgment, 26 October 2000, 30210/96, para 152.

[21] Ibid.

[22] Ibid., para 154.

[23] European Group on Tort Law 2005.

[24] Von Bar et al. 2005.

addressing the right to a remedy through the national tort law system (Sect. 14.3.2). What the right to a remedy under Article 13 ECHR entails will be explained in the next section.

14.2.2 Right to a Remedy

The primary responsibility for implementing and enforcing the ECHR's rights and freedoms is laid at the national level by requiring a domestic remedy before a competent national authority.[25] In order to bring such a claim, the Court adopted a broad view:

> This provision, read literally, seems to say that a person is entitled to a national remedy only if a "violation" has occurred. However, a person cannot establish a "violation" before a national authority unless he is first able to lodge with such an authority a complaint to that effect. Consequently, (…) Article 13 requires that where an individual considers himself to be prejudiced by a measure allegedly in breach of the Convention, he should have a remedy before a national authority in order both to have his claim decided and, if appropriate, to obtain redress.[26]

Thus, Article 13 guarantees everyone whose rights and freedoms under the Convention have allegedly been violated an effective remedy before a national authority. Whether this claim to be the victim of a violation of the rights set forth in the Convention is arguable, it must be determined in the light of the particular facts and nature of the legal issue(s) raised.

As made clear by its opening words, Article 13 is not a freestanding right; it merely complements the other substantive clauses and can only be applied in combination with one or more articles of the Convention or its Protocols of which a violation has been alleged. The effectiveness of the remedy does not depend on the certainty of a favourable outcome for the applicant but is either preventing the alleged violation or its continuation, or providing adequate redress for any violation that has already occurred'.[27] In order to be effective, the remedy must be 'sufficient and accessible, fulfilling the obligation of promptness'.[28]

Effectiveness of the remedy required means it must be effective in practice as well as in law, although the scope of the obligation under Article 13 can vary depending on the nature of the applicant's complaint or the graveness of the other Convention rights that are (allegedly) breached.[29] For example:

> 'The Court considers that, in the case of a breach of Articles 2 and 3 of the Convention, which rank as the most fundamental provisions of the Convention, compensation for the

[25] ECtHR 2022, p. 8.

[26] ECtHR, *Klass and others v. Germany*, Judgment, 6 September 1978, 5029/71, para 64.

[27] ECtHR, *Kudla v. Poland*, Judgment, 26 October 2000, 30210/96, para 158.

[28] ECtHR 2022, p. 15.

[29] ECtHR, *Hasan and Chaush v. Bulgaria*, Judgment, 26 October 2000, 30985/96, para 98.

non-pecuniary damage flowing from the breach should, in principle, be available as part of the range of redress.'[30]

Even the prospect of not being able to claim the non-pecuniary damages suffered, because the relatives of the deceased individual whose rights had been violated have no legal standing before a court, can constitute a breach of Article 13.[31] In cases under Article 8 ECHR[32] or Article 1 First Protocol,[33] compensation for pecuniary damages alone might suffice for the purposes of Article 13—although there could be cases where compensation would be 'so derisory that it raises an issue as to the effectiveness of the redress'.[34] The timely payment of the compensation award is also an essential element of a remedy under Article 13.[35] In addition to the payment of compensation where appropriate, when authorities or 'agents of the State' are involved in the breach of Article 2 or Article 3, Article 13 entails

> a thorough and effective investigation capable of leading to the identification and punishment of those responsible and including effective access for the relatives to the investigatory procedure.[36]

This effective investigation should meet the standards given by the Court. The Court does however draw a distinction between the degrees of effectiveness of the remedies required in relation to the negative obligations—violation of substantive rights by the State or its agents—and the violation of positive obligations of the State—violation due to a failure by the State to protect individuals from acts of third parties. In the latter cases, 'a mechanism for establishing any liability of State officials or bodies for acts or omissions involving the breach of their rights under the Convention' should be available to the victim('s family).[37]

Thus, the right to an effective remedy under Article 13 ECHR entails both an effective mechanism for determining liability for breaches of Convention rights by being able to bring a case to court, as well as the granting of appropriate relief in cases where breaches are well-founded. This relief can consist of compensation for pecuniary damages as well as for non-pecuniary damages flowing from the breach, depending on the gravity of the rights breached.

By awarding monetary relief, Article 13 ECHR is closely linked to Article 41 ECHR that provides the Court with the possibility for awarding sums of money to

---

[30] ECtHR, *Paul and Audrey Edwards v. the United Kingdom*, Judgment, 14 March 2002, 46477/99, para 97.

[31] ECtHR, *Bubbins v. the United Kingdom*, Judgment, 17 March 2015, 50196/99, para 172.

[32] ECHR above n. 2, art. 8 entails the right and respect for private and family life.

[33] Protocol to the Convention for the Protection of Human Rights and Fundamental Freedoms, Council of Europe, ETS No. 009, opened for signature 20 March 1952, entered into force 18 May 1954. Art. 1 of this Protocol entails the right to protection of property.

[34] Harris et al. 2018, p. 750.

[35] ECtHR, *Öneryildiz v. Turkey*, Judgment, 30 November 2004, 48939/99, para 151-152.

[36] ECtHR, *Kilic v. Turkey*, Judgment, 18 June 2002, 25656/94, para 384.

[37] ECtHR, *Z. and others v. the United Kingdom*, Judgment, 10 May 2001, 29392/95, para 109. See also: ECtHR 2022, p. 21.

applicants by way of just satisfaction. It is not a main duty of the Court, but serves the Court's purpose to ensure observance by States of their obligations under the Convention. The wording of the article allows the Court discretion in deciding on the matter:

> If the Court finds that there has been a violation of the Convention or the Protocols thereto, and if the internal law of the High Contracting Party concerned allows only partial reparation to be made, the Court shall, if necessary, afford just satisfaction to the injured party.

The ECtHR indicated that the guiding principle for just satisfaction is 'equity', involving an objective consideration of

> what is just, fair, and reasonable in all circumstances of the case. [The Court's] non-pecuniary awards serve to give recognition to the fact that moral damage occurred because of a breach of a fundamental human right and reflect in the broadest of terms the severity of the damage.[38]

Other than the role of national courts, the role of the ECtHR under Article 41 '[is not] to function akin to a domestic tort mechanism court in apportioning fault and compensatory damages between civil parties'. The monetary compensation that is awarded by the Court under Article 41 ECHR functions as just satisfaction for the violation of the fundamental right. The next section reflects on the application of human rights by national courts through the national tort law system.

14.2.3 Remedies and Tort Law

When an individual wants to address a breach of their right(s) under the ECHR, they can instigate ordinary civil proceedings against the alleged tortfeasor.[39] The focus of this chapter are cases where the liability for (alleged) fundamental rights violations and the right to a remedy is then examined by a judge through the lens of the general provisions governing liability arising from an unlawful act, the general tort clause. To understand this channelling, the general idea of tort law is discussed in this section.

Tort law is built on the idea of reparation, prevention and risk spreading. Guiding principle for tort law is that a wrongdoer has an obligation to rectify the injury caused by the wrongful act. Although the principal aim is to restore the *status quo*, justice is mostly brought through the second-best option: compensation. The main function of tort law is to offer compensation to 'an aggrieved party who has suffered harm as a consequence of one's unlawful conduct or negligence'.[40] This compensatory justice aim is found in most tort law systems. Damages should thus reflect the loss and offer compensation for the loss suffered. Tort law can consist of only unwritten law or—as is the case in The Netherlands—be a mix between written and unwritten law. Because

[38] ECtHR, *Al-Skeini and others v. the United Kingdom*, Judgment, 7 July 2011, 55721/07, para 182.

[39] Generally, when criminal proceedings are in place, these human rights infringement claims can also be dealt with by the criminal court. However, the award of damages is usually reserved to the civil courts.

[40] Emaus 2016, p. 11.

of its unwritten nature, legal doctrine can play a role in the development of tort law. And through the open norms of tort law, recent developments in international law can also be taken into consideration.

The general provisions governing liability do carry certain requirements, such as an unlawful act, damage, a causal link between the damage and the unlawful act, and attribution of the unlawful act to the wrongdoer. Accountability can either arise both from legislation, and from an unwritten standard of care. The most general rule is that of culpability or negligence, which consists of an objective element—wrongfulness of the act or omission—and a subjective element—the tortfeasor must be to blame for the wrongful act or omission. Statutory duties and other written norms—i.e., human rights regulations—may shed light on the standard of care the tortfeasor's behaviour will be tested against. Via (treaty) interpretation, duties for the tortfeasor can be derived from provisions that expressly only grant rights to the claimant. When such international duties are indeed applicable on the tortfeasor, the requirement of relativity has to be tested, meaning that the standard breached must be intended to protect the person suffering. Thus, to establish civil liability, international provisions must be interpreted by the judge to determine the duties for the tortfeasor, the applicability on the relationship between tortfeasor and claimant, as well as fulfil the relativity-requirement to regulate the act through which the damage occurred.

When the infringement of a right is then established, legally relevant damages can be claimed. In most national tort law system, these claims carry the aim of financial compensation for harm resulting from that infringement. Financial compensation is often the second-best option in order to restore the applicant as far as possible in a situation equivalent to the one in which he or she would have been had there not been a breach, the first aim being that of returning (the claimant) to the situation as it was before the infringement. There must be a causal link between the wrongful act and the loss(es) claimed. Furthermore, a distinction must be made between personal injuries and property damages on the one hand, and purely economic losses on the other. Personal injuries can consist of physical or mental injuries, and the losses flowing therefrom. The physical or mental injury must represent an infringement of a legally protected interest. Purely economic losses can be compensated after assessing a broad range of requirements, ranging from protection in legislative measures to 'reasonable expectations'.[41]

14.3 Interaction between International Law and the Domestic Tort System

The remedying aspect of international human rights law depends largely on its interpretation and application by national courts. When international human rights are breached, individuals can only enforce the right to a remedy of Article 13 ECHR

[41] Thorson 2016, p. 265.

when national courts can apply this right. In this chapter, Dutch judgments on specifically selected topics relevant for this application and interpretation of international law are examined.

In Dutch civil law, the application of international law used to be subject to certain conditions that recently have been changed (Sect. 14.3.1). These new conditions provide for a more direct application of international law and a unique viewpoint on the effects of international law in the domestic legal order (Sect. 14.3.2). But even with this direct application of international law, the peculiarities of national tort law can lead to obstacles that are sometimes overlooked by international law (makers), but stand in the way of the effective protection of international human rights (Sect. 14.4).

14.3.1 Constitutional Guidelines and the Implementation of International Law

The relationship between international and national law in the Kingdom of the Netherlands[42] is described as 'deeply rooted in the monistic tradition'[43] and 'being very open to the application of international law in its domestic legal order'.[44] Although it is often categorized as being a monistic system, the term 'moderately monistic' would do it more justice.[45] The system is monistic because implementing legislation is not necessary for the legal force of treaties or resolutions by international organizations: they apply as soon as they are binding on the State from in international law point of view. As a result, not only treaty law, but all international law that binds the State is part of the national legal system and the executive branch and local governments are required to apply international (treaty) obligations. From the presumption that the State wants to fulfil its obligations under international law, rises the principle that national law may not be interpreted in conflict with international law. Therefore, Dutch courts interpret and apply national law as much as possible in a way that allows the State to comply with these obligations.

The 'moderate' side of Dutch monism emerges for example when a private party invokes treaty-law before a Dutch court: direct application of international law is then subjected to the conditions of Articles 93 and 94 of the Dutch Constitution (DC). According to Article 93, the court can only directly apply provisions of treaties or resolutions of international organizations when they have been published and 'may be

[42] The Kingdom of the Netherlands consists of the Netherlands located in Europe and the Netherlands Antilles and Aruba located in the Caribbean. Subject of international law is the Kingdom, which enters into treaties (although the territorial scope may be limited) and is responsible for the breach of treaty obligations. In this chapter, a reference to the Netherlands is a reference to the Kingdom.

[43] Fleuren 2010, p. 246.

[44] Nollkaemper 2009, p. 327.

[45] For example: Wildhaber 2007, p. 218.

binding on all persons by virtue of their contents'.[46] These provisions reflect the 'self-executing' character of treaties in Dutch law.[47] According to Article 94, provisions of international law suitable for direct application, can prevail over (conflicting) national legislation.

Article 93 and 94 DC give the court jurisdiction to determine whether international law provisions can be directly applied, allowing private parties to invoke these provisions. However, the legislator did not specify any criteria, but left it to the judiciary to determine whether a provision would qualify for direct application. Therefore, these criteria are developed in Dutch case-law. The Supreme Court has indicated several times that the first step in answering the question whether a treaty provision has direct effect, is to examine the intention of the parties for the treaty to be not directly applicable. If no such intention can be determined, the next step is exclusively based on the provision's content. In the *Spoorwegstaking* case, concerning the right to strike under Article 6(4) of the European Social Charter, the Supreme Court considered:

> '[U]nder Dutch law, only the content of the provision [is] decisive: either it obliges the Dutch legislature to enact national legislation with certain content or purport, or is it of such a nature that the provision can be directly applied in the national legal order as being objective law?'[48]

Both using the intention of the parties, as well as the content of the provision as criteria for direct application is in line with VCLT-interpretation rules, albeit a secondary interpretation method. However, for international treaty-provisions that start with a variation of 'The States Parties to the present Convention recognize the right of everyone to...'[49] or 'States Parties shall take all appropriate measures...'[50] followed by the protected rights in the treaty or the duties of the State. Thus, application of the *Spoorwegstaking* criteria led Dutch courts to the conclusion that, especially in cases where social human rights were invoked, the treaty-provision entailed an obligation for the State to enact national legislation with a certain content, the court being unable to directly apply the provision or the rights therein.[51]

Confirmation for this conclusion was often found in the Explanatory Memorandum to the relevant treaty, written by the Dutch government to explain its status. The use of a Memorandum in which the Government decides upon the purpose and scope of a treaty, is not a recognized source for the interpretation of international treaties. In 1998, the Dutch Government was addressed on this by the Committee on Economic, Social and Cultural Rights when a Dutch State representative informed the Committee on the workings of the Dutch system and its implications for the

---

[46] Fleuren 2010, p. 248. Alternate terminology: directly applicable, self-executing.

[47] Fleuren 2004, pp. 45–61.

[48] Supreme Court (Hoge Raad), *Spoorwegstaking*, Judgment, 30 May 1986, ECLI:NL:HR:1986:AC9402, para 3.2.

[49] International Covenant on Economic, Social and Cultural Rights, opened for signature 19 December 1966, 993 UNTS 3, entered into force 3 January 1976 (ICESCR), Article 11.

[50] Convention on the Rights of the Child, opened for signature 20 November 1989, Treaty no. 27531 (Treaty Series 1577), art 2, art. 27.

[51] Kuiper-Slendebroek 2017.

direct application of the International Covenant on Economic, Social and Cultural Rights (ICESCR):

> [E]conomic, social and cultural rights were principally oriented towards the obligations of the State. The (…) question of the effectiveness of steps taken to discharge an obligation was considered a matter for Parliament rather than for the judiciary. Of course, if the State failed to discharge its obligation altogether, an individual who believed that his or her human rights had been violated as a result could bring the matter before the courts. That did not mean, however, that all the provisions of the [ICESCR] could be regarded as self-executing.[52]

Thus, the representative of the Netherlands brought forward the Constitutional structure of the State to explain the role of the Parliament and the (lack of) direct application of human rights by the Dutch courts. In doing so, the provisions of internal law were indirectly used as justification for failure to perform the treaty. To this practice, the Committee reacted:

> [T]he Committee considers that, at a minimum, certain provisions of the [ICESCR] are potentially able to be directly applied both in law and in policy. It therefore cannot accept the assertion by the representative of the State party that for essentially technical reasons the [ICESCR] is not directly applicable.[53]

For decades, these 'technical reasons' were cause for Dutch courts to not (directly) apply treaty provisions, even when citizens claimed their (human) rights that lay embedded in these provisions.

The criteria for direct effect of treaties underwent a change in 2014, when the Dutch Supreme Court gave judgment on the protection from exposure to tobacco smoke as laid down in article 8(2) of the WHO Framework Convention on Tobacco Control (FCTC).[54] In cassation, the Dutch Government had pointed out that this provision was not sufficiently clear, only implied an obligation for the State and could therefore not be directly applied by the Dutch courts.[55] First, the Dutch Supreme Court explicitly examined Articles 93 and 94 DC in the context of the Vienna Convention on the Law of Treaties, thus recognizing the role of international interpretation rules in national law. According to the Supreme Court:

> What matters is whether the provision is unconditional and sufficiently clear to be applied as objective law in the national legal order.[56]

Thus, when a treaty provision is unconditional and sufficiently clear, Dutch courts can directly apply this provision. Its content can serve as an objective right, directly

[52] United Nations Economic and Social Council 1998, para 25.

[53] Ibid., para 177.

[54] World Health Organization Framework Convention on Tobacco Control, opened for signature 21 May 2003, entered into force 27 February 2005. Article 8(2) FCTC reads: Each Party shall adopt and implement in areas of existing national jurisdiction (...) the adoption and implementation of effective legislative (...) measures, providing for protection from exposure to tobacco smoke (...) in indoor public places and, as appropriate, other public places.

[55] Supreme Court (Hoge Raad), *Rookverbod*, Judgment, 10 October 2014, ECLI:NL:HR:2014:2928, para 3.4.

[56] Supreme Court (Hoge Raad), *Rookverbod*, Judgment, 10 October 2014, ECLI:NL:HR:2014:2928, para 3.5.2.

applicable in the context to which it is invoked, even where the Dutch Government has freedom to choose the policy or measures to be taken to achieve the intended result. The *Rookverbod* case created a new route for international provisions to have direct effect in concrete cases. This implies a more active role for the courts, who must check each specific case to see whether the invoked international provisions can be regarded as objective law and can thus be directly applied. In addition, the *Rookverbod* case created awareness amongst courts on the use of the international rules under the VCLT as grounds for the interpretation of international law, whether it would be directly applicable.

14.3.2 Interpretation of International Human Rights Law by Dutch Courts

The existence of any legal system depends on the social practice of 'legal officials', law-applying authorities operating within the legal system whose practices validate the system.[57] For the survival, effect, and prosperity of international human rights law, the recognition of law as such in social and therefore in judicial practice is crucial.

To apply an international treaty, national courts must interpret this treaty, ideally by using the VCLT-interpretation rules. But while the application of international law is largely dependent upon national courts, the VCLT rules—or their applicability—are not always known by the judges. As characterized by Peat:

> To be able to explain and justify one's proposed interpretation in terms of Articles 31 and 32 [VCLT] is to demonstrate membership of a group, to show that one is an international lawyer properly so-called.[58]

Well, not all national judges (or parliamentary representatives) are 'international lawyers properly so-called'. The examination in Sect. 14.3.1 showed that even in the Dutch monist system, the interpretation rules for international law are not always applied (right). Even in the application of the ECHR-rights, for which it is widely and long-time accepted they can be directly applied by Dutch courts, there are differences between Dutch courts. These differences can also have an impact on the correct enforcement of human rights and the right to a remedy and are therefore examined in this section.

In the *Rookverbod* case, the Supreme Court guided Dutch courts in the application of international law by expressly stating:

> The question to what extent a treaty provision has direct effect within the meaning of Article 93 and 94 DC, must be answered by an explanation thereof. This interpretation must take place on the basis of the criteria of Article 31, 32 and 33 VCLT.[59]

---

[57] Hernández 2022, p. 204.

[58] Peat 2022, p. 223.

[59] Supreme Court (Hoge Raad), *Rookverbod*, Judgment, 10 October 2014, ECLI:NL:HR:2014:2928, para 3.5.1.

Five years later, in December 2019, the Dutch Supreme Court issued the famous *Urgenda* case, extending the protection of fundamental rights under Article 2 and 8 ECHR to the threatening dangers of climate change. The Supreme Court did so by stating the VCLT-interpretation rules, while also referring to the common ground-method of the ECtHR:

> According to established ECtHR case law, the provisions of the ECHR must be interpreted and applied so as to make its safeguards practical and effective. According to the ECtHR, this "effectiveness principle" ensues from "the object and purpose of the Convention as an instrument for the protection of individual human beings". This also regards the application of Article 31(1) of the Vienna Convention on the Law of Treaties, which stipulates that a treaty must be interpreted in good faith in accordance with the ordinary meaning to be given to the terms of the treaty in the light of its object and purpose. According to ECtHR case law, an interpretation of the ECHR must also take into account the relevant rules of international law referred to in Article 31(3)(c) of the Vienna Convention on the Law of Treaties. (...) Furthermore, in accordance with Article 31(3), opening words and paragraph (b), of the Vienna Convention on the Law of Treaties, an interpretation of treaty provisions must take the Member States' application practice into account. (...) According to ECtHR case law, an interpretation and application of the ECHR must also take scientific insights and generally accepted standards into account.[60]

In the *Urgenda* case, the Supreme Court applied Articles 2 and 8 ECHR directly into the domestic legal system—i.e. not via the tort law system of article 6:162 DCC. The Supreme Court interpreted the meaning of these articles by examining ECtHR case-law, the context in which the articles were used before, and the most recent developments in ECHR case-law, and seemed quite confident on the position of the ECHR in the Dutch legal system:

> Pursuant to Articles 93 and 94 of the Dutch Constitution, Dutch courts must apply every provision of the ECHR that is binding on all persons. Because the ECHR also subjects the Netherlands to the jurisdiction of the ECtHR (Article 32 ECHR), Dutch courts must interpret those provisions as the ECtHR has, or interpret them premised on the same interpretation standards used by the ECtHR.[61]

The direct application of international law was re-arranged by the *Rookverbod*-criteria, and in *Urgenda* the Supreme Court used these criteria to apply the ECHR in a top-down manner where the international rule plays a leading role.

For the application of international law, top-down is not the only way: courts also apply international law 'bottom-up'. The starting point is then a national law provision, and courts check whether the minimum-criteria of these fundamental human rights are being met. An example in tort law is the *Groninger aardbeving* case, ruled by the Supreme Court in July 2019. In this case, the District Court of Assen asked the Supreme Court preliminary questions concerning the duty of care and accountability to the State of the damages resulting from gas drilling in the Province of Groningen:

---

[60] Supreme Court (Hoge Raad), *Urgenda*, Judgment, 20 December 2019, ECLI:NL:HR:2019:2006, para 5.4.1-5.4.3.

[61] Ibid., para 5.6.1.

> Under what circumstances can the State—also considering Art. 2, 3 and 8 ECHR—be held liable for earthquake damages on the grounds of Article 6:162 Dutch Civil Code?[62]

Before the District Court, plaintiffs had argued that the State had acted unlawful with regard to Articles 2, 3 and 8 ECHR within the general basis of liability arising from an unlawful act—Article 6:162 of the Dutch Civil Code (DCC). The Supreme Court could have identified the criteria of article 2, 3 and 8 and applied them to the case. Instead, the Supreme Court first determined the elements of unlawful acts that according to national law should be fulfilled, and then considers:

> In general, the question of whether an unlawful act or omission can be applied to the State, must be answered by taking into account the minimum requirements set by the relevant provisions of the ECHR and related jurisprudence of the ECtHR regarding acts or omissions of the State.[63]

The reference to indirect application—checking whether the minimum requirements set by the ECHR are taken into account when applying the Dutch liability-clause—is remarkable. In the *Urgenda* case, the Supreme Court expressly stated that every provision of the ECHR is directly applicable in the national legal system. This could be done to stay in line with the case-law of the ECtHR on Article 8 ECHR, where minimum levels of protection are also the Court's main consideration. However, in its case-law the ECtHR respects a margin of appreciation for the domestic interpretation and application of (Article 8) ECHR, while national courts are not required to hold this margin but can review the actions of their own State in a more intrusive manner than the ECtHR would. Furthermore, in the *Groninger aardbeving* case, the Supreme Court incorrectly translated the requirements of the ECHR that should be considered when applying the national factors of acts and omissions that lead to accountability. For example: the threshold to determine whether Article 8 ECHR is applicable in environmentally related cases—the *minimum level of severity*—is wrongly used by the Supreme Court to establish the infringement of the positive obligation under Article 8 ECHR.[64] This incorrect translation from the international to the domestic could be prevented by applying international law top-down, letting international law lead the way into the national system, instead of bottom-up, where international law is used as an operational aspect in the application of national law. In Dutch tort law cases, a similar operational issue can be detected with regards to Article 13 ECHR.

---

[62] Supreme Court (Hoge Raad), *Groninger aardbeving*, Preliminary Answer, 19 July 2019, ECLI:NL:HR:2019:1278, para 2.2.3.

[63] Ibid., para 2.7.8.

[64] Ibid., para 2.7.10.

14.4 Dutch Tort Law and the Right to a Remedy

In Sect. 14.3, the first requirement for the effective application of international law in the domestic order was examined: the self-execution of international provisions and their hierarchy over conflicting national law. Although direct application is the norm, it is not always applied and these differences lead to different interpretations of international (human rights) law. In this section, we zoom in further and the different applications and interpretations of Article 13 ECHR in national tort law will be examined. To establish the position and role of Article 13 in the Dutch tort law system, this system will be briefly explained (Sect. 14.4.1). Then Dutch case law on awarding damages for the breach of fundamental rights will be examined and the obstacles are pinpointed (Sect. 14.4.2). This cannot lead to a full picture, but the scenery will be painted with relevant case law.

14.4.1 Dutch Tort Law and Damages

The general basis for fault liability in Dutch tort law is Article 6:162 DCC, of which the first section reads:

> A person who commits a tort against another which is attributable to him, must repair the damages suffered by the other in consequence thereof.

Establishing fault liability requires a wrong, the attribution of this wrong, damage, causation, and a protected interest. The wrong is an unlawful act or omission, either in violation of a right, in violation of the law or in violation of the general duty of care, established according to unwritten law. Because of Articles 93 and 94 DC, the ECHR is directly applicable in the Dutch legal system, and its provisions have precedence over conflicting statutory provisions. For example: when State actors breach a duty under the ECHR, the criterion of an unlawful act or omission is in principle fulfilled because it falls under the second—an act or omission breaching a duty imposed by law—or third category—the infringement of unwritten rules (i.e. the duty of care) as was the case in *Groninger aardbeving*.[65] The result is similar: if a violation under the ECHR exists, then a 'wrong' exists, because the law or the duty of care has been violated.[66]

When the tortfeasor is successfully held liable for this wrong, and the causal connection between the act and the damages is established, the claimant has a right to claim for damages as stipulated in Article 95 DCC. Compensation can be claimed for pecuniary loss and for non-pecuniary loss, the latter only to the extent that the law confers a right to damages therefor. This legal basis can be found in article 6:106(1)(b) DCC:

---

[65] In cases of fundamental rights violations by non-state actors, the last category seems to be most relevant in practice. This will not be elaborated further for the purposes of this article.

[66] For a more exhaustive explanation of Dutch Wrongful Act Law, see Roorda 2022, pp. 246–253.

> The injured person has a right of compensation for damage that does not consist of material loss, assessed in conformity with the standards of reasonableness and fairness:
>
> (…)

b. if the injured person sustained physical injuries or if his honour or reputation is injured or if he is harmed otherwise in person'.

Equitable damages can be offered in several situations including the situation where the claimant is 'harmed otherwise in person'. Damages for fundamental rights violations are generally non-pecuniary and will therefore be based on Article 6:106 DCC. Non-pecuniary loss can thus be awarded, but under the conditions dictated in this article. The criteria for these damages are further developed in case law. In the next section, this development, and the effects on the right to a remedy will be examined.

14.4.2 The Right to a Remedy in Dutch Case Law

The basic principle in tort law is awarding compensation for damages once wrongful act, liability and extent of the damage are established. Regarding the violation of fundamental rights, another form of redress was added in Dutch case-law. In the landmark *Oudejaarsrellen* case,[67] the Supreme Court accepted 'rights vindication' as an independent function in addition to compensation for damages.[68] Although Article 13 ECHR was not mentioned explicitly, this judgement is a clear example of applying the right to a remedy where fundamental rights are breached. Although this is the way to go, it this addition came with its own framework and seems to not be applicable in every case concerning the violation of fundamental rights.[69]

14.4.2.1 Additional Requirements for Non-pecuniary Compensation

On New Year's Eve 1997, a family had called the police at least five times for assistance because their house was surrounded by about 65 rioters. Initially, the police decided not to act. After two more calls and a consultation with the mayor, the authorities called in the anti-riot squat to assist. After these events, the family claimed compensation from the authorities for non-pecuniary damages based on Article 6:106 (1)(b) DCC, stating they had suffered psychological harm as they experienced serious threats to their body and property during the night. According to the District Court, the negligence of the authorities did contribute to the claimants' experience of feeling unsafe in his own home. This feeling, however caused by the rioters, could have been

[67] Supreme Court (Hoge Raad), *Oudejaarsrellen*, Judgment, 9 July 2004, ECLI:NL:HR:2004:AO7721.

[68] See: Emaus 2016, p. 243.

[69] Supreme Court (Hoge Raad), *EBI-case*, Judgment, 15 March 2019, ECLI:NL:HR:2019:376.

absent or have lasted shorter if the police had acted immediately.[70] The District Court found that the right of personal integrity and safety of their own home—Article 8 ECHR—was seriously breached. This constituted a harm under Article 6:106 DCC and non-pecuniary damages were awarded. The Supreme Court affirmed this view, thus allowing a right to reparations for the violation of fundamental rights as such.[71]

Although in this case is an example where the serious violation of a fundamental right gave rise to compensation for non-pecuniary damages under article 6:106(1)(b) DCC, the focus shifts in later cases. In 2019, the *EBI* case was brought on by a claimant serving a life sentence. After complaining about his detention in the Extra Secure Prison (ESP, *EBI*), the Council for criminal law application decided that claimant should be transferred and was detained unlawfully for 350 days in ESP instead of in normal prison. It was thereby established that the State had acted unlawfully against the claimant and the Council awarded him a monetary compensation. In a civil law procedure, claimant claims compensation for non-pecuniary damages because of a violation of his person on the grounds of Article 6:106(1)(b) DCC. Both the District Court and the Court of Appeal reject his claim because there was no psychological damage.

In cassation, the claimant argues that in case of a violation of fundamental rights—Articles 3, 5 and 6 ECHR are mentioned—the damages suffered should be assumed, even if there is no question of (factually proven) immaterial damage as referred to in Article 6:106(1)(b) DCC. In his Advisory Opinion, the Advocate-General agrees with this argument, based on the ECHR and ECtHR case law:

> Undeniably, in the past two decades, not only in Dutch case law, but also under the influence of the ECHR and case law of the ECtHR, there has been an expansion of the cases in which a right to compensation exists. This development, both with regard to mental injury and the violation of fundamental rights as such, took place under the heading of personal attacks or, where developments in the context of the ECHR are concerned, falls within that framework. With regard to the latter, one could think, for example, of awarding punitive damages for exceeding the reasonable term for taking a judicial decision within the meaning of art. 6 ECHR. In addition to the fact of expansion, it is also important that this has been accompanied by a certain independence of the category of the violation of fundamental rights as such in relation to cases of mental injury. This development fits in with and is also fed by the idea that has become quite popular that punitive damages can not only fulfill a useful role in giving substance to rights and thus serve the interests of claimants, but (thereby) also support liability law as such in the context of the enforcement of rights and obligations.[72]

The Advocate General argues for an approach, where the violation of a fundamental right, regardless of its consequences, is sufficient to successfully claim reparation for damages due to a personal injury under Dutch liability law, i.e., Article 6:106 (1)(b) DCC. As was explained in Sect. 14.2.2, the case law on Article 13 ECHR substantiates this view.

[70] Supreme Court (Hoge Raad), *Oudejaarsrellen*, Judgment, 9 July 2004, ECLI:NL:HR:2004:AO7721, para 4.6.

[71] Emaus 2016, p. 244. This view was confirmed in Supreme Court (Hoge Raad), *Wrongful life*, Judgment, 18 March 2005, ECLI:NL:HR:2005:AR5213.

[72] Advocate General (Parket bij de Hoge Raad), *EBI-case*, Conclusion, 26 October 2018, ECLI:NL:PHR:20181295, para 3.7-3.8.

But the Supreme Court does not go along with this. Referring to its previous judgments, he reviews the grounds for non-pecuniary damage claims under Article 6:106(1)(b) DCC extensively:

> Cases of 'harmed otherwise in person' refer to psychological damage, if the injured party can provide sufficient concrete data from which objectively can be established that psychological damage has occurred. (...) In addition, the nature and seriousness of the breach of the norm and the consequences thereof for the injured party may mean that the person has been harmed in another way. (...) Where appropriate, the nature and seriousness of the breach of the norm may mean that the adverse consequences relevant in this context for the injured party are so obvious that an impairment in the person can be assumed.[73]

Exemplary for bringing forward this required objective proof for psychological damage, the seriousness of the breach and the consequences for the injured party, is the *Oudejaarsrellen* case, where the personal harm was due to the feelings of fear and insecurity about life and property, due to a very threatening situation, while the request for help was not answered. The Supreme Court considers:

> A violation of the person in another way as referred to in Article 6:106 (1)(b) DCC is not already set with the mere violation of a fundamental right.[74]

Not only the violation of the fundamental right, but also the nature and seriousness, as well as the consequences of this breach are found relevant by the court and must be made concrete by the claimant before non-pecuniary damages can be awarded. This is not in line with case law of the ECtHR: in case of violations of fundamental rights by the State, compensation should in principle be available as part of redress. The seriousness of the right(s) breached only effects the height of this compensation.[75] In Dutch tort law, the severity of the violation is used to determine whether these damages are at all compensable. Thus, national law adds requirements for compensating damages due to a human rights violation. This addition of (national law) requirements can leave the application of international human rights law insufficient. It can even be questioned whether this in itself constitutes a breach of Article 13, by not providing an effective remedy in cases where violations of human rights only lead to non-pecuniary damages.[76]

In the next section, it is shown that even when the ECHR and the right to a remedy are applied correctly on all required elements, the use of national law to fill in the blanks that are specific to the national system or are (intentionally) left open by international law may lead to an outcome that is unsatisfactory in light of its scope and purposes. Exemplary of this are the *Mothers of Srebrenica* case and the subsequent *Bosnian father* case.

---

[73] Supreme Court (Hoge Raad), *EBI-case*, Judgment, 15 March 2019, ECLI:NL:HR:2019:376, para 4.2.1.

[74] Ibid., para 4.2.2.

[75] And as to whether there should be a further investigation to bring tortfeasors to justice, see Sect. 14.2.2.

[76] Rijnhout 2020, pp. 202–204.

14.4.2.2 Compensation Consistent with ECHR, yet Not a Desired Outcome?

In the *Mothers of Srebrenica* case, claimants are mothers of Bosniak men, who were killed by Bosnian Serb forces in the Srebrenica genocide while Dutch armed troops (Dutchbat) were present in the region as part of the United Nations Protection Force. In the 2019 case before the Supreme Court, the Dutch State was held liable because Dutchbat acted wrongfully under Dutch tort law, and in violation of Articles 2 and 3 ECHR, by not offering the men inside its compound the choice of whether to remain in the compound.

Ultimately, it was not choice, but chance that defined the outcome of this case. The notion of 'partial liability' is used in Dutch tort law to redeem causal uncertainty and can either be applied when multiple potential causes exist but it is impossible to prove which factor caused the damage, or when it is uncertain whether the result would have been better in the hypothetical situation had the party responsible refrained from committing the wrong.[77] The latter is called 'loss of a chance' and was used in the *Srebrenica* case. Since uncertainty occurs in determining the damage, the lost chance of a better result is considered to be the damage. The question is thus what would have been the chance of survival: even if the Bosniak men would have been given the choice to stay on the compound, what would be the probability that they would have survived, or that Bosnian Serb forces would eventually have killed the Bosniak men? The Supreme Court considers:

> All in all, it must be ruled that the chance that the [Bosnian men], had they been offered the choice of remaining in the compound, could have escaped the Bosnian Serb forces, was indeed small, but not negligible.[78]

The Supreme Court estimated that probability in the light of all circumstances at ten percent, thus holding the State liable for ten percent of the damage.

According to the Supreme Court, the Dutch theory of loss of a chance can be applied in cases of human rights violations. It is however questionable whether both this application as well as the outcome will suffice as being an effective remedy, given the criteria under Article 13 ECHR. Firstly, the ECtHR holds that when a fundamental right is violated, especially Article 2 or 3 ECHR, the violation as such is grounds for compensation for damages resulting from the violation. Secondly, bearing in mind the aim of the ECHR to offer full compensation, 10% is a long way away from 100% and may not be an 'effective' remedy. From the viewpoint of national tort law, it can be argued that this 'partial liability actually creates the possibility of compensation notwithstanding uncertainty about the causal link between the wrong and the damage'.[79] This way, at least there is 10% compensation where otherwise there would have been 0% compensation.

[77] Rijnhout 2021, p. 130.

[78] Supreme Court (Hoge Raad), *Srebrenica-case*, Judgment, 19 July 2019, ECLI:NL:HR:2019:1223, para 4.7.9.

[79] Rijnhout 2021, p. 128.

To end on a happier note, there is a case in which the right to an effective remedy did prevail, showing that applying international law over conflicting national tort law is a possibility for the (Dutch) domestic system. In the *Bosnian father* case by the District Court of The Hague in 2020, the particularities of the ECHR were considered at crucial points in the case, especially where national law did not provide for an outcome that would fulfil the criteria of Article 13 ECHR's right to a remedy.

Claimant is the son of a Bosniak, who was not given refuge on the Dutchbat compound and died by the hands of Bosnian Serbs. The necessary facts were proven in court by using witnesses, and the State was held fully liable for damages arising out of the death of the father—still regarding the 10% as found by the Supreme Court in the *Srebrenica* case. Claimant wanted reparations for both pecuniary damages—which were awarded—and for non-pecuniary damages based on Articles 2 and 13 ECHR. Since 2019, the Dutch tort law system provides in Article 6:108 DCC for relatives of deceased injured persons to claim damages on the same grounds as the injured persons themselves would have had, would they still be alive. But because the Dutchbat case took place in 1995, this new provision was not applicable to the claimant. In its reasoning, the District Court considered that regarding Article 2, the ECtHR holds that in vertical relations between a State and its citizens,

> "compensation for the non-pecuniary damage flowing from the breach should, in principle, be available as part of the range of redress". (...) When there are no possibilities in national law to lay down a claim for non-pecuniary damages, the State infringes the relative's adequate right to a remedy under Article 13 ECHR in case of violation of the right to life.[80]

The court elaborated further on the purpose of Article 13 ECHR and how the diminishing practical effectivity of the ECHR should be prevented. It also considered the direct application of the ECHR via Articles 93 and 94 DC, the hierarchy of the ECHR above national (civil) law and—while referring to the case of *Edwards v. the United Kingdom*—explained:

> The court, which also has the obligation to ensure these rights, may not apply Dutch compensation law insofar as this conflicts with the ECHR and the jurisprudence of the ECtHR. The court must therefore verify whether there is such a conflict in this specific case.[81]

Consequently, the District Court examined Dutch tort law: Article 6:106 DCC gives no ground for non-pecuniary damages of the claimant, Article 6:108 does provide for this but is not applicable in this case. This led the court to find that the State acts unlawful against the claimant by not providing for an 'effective remedy' to claim non-pecuniary damages resulting from the dead of his father. For reference, the court turned to the case law of the ECtHR under Article 41 ECHR and found:

> the claimant's claim, which has not been disputed by the State and is clearly conceivable, permanent emotional damage resulting from the State's violation of Article 2 ECHR falls beyond reasonable doubt into the category for which the ECtHR awards compensation under this provision.[82]

---

[80] District Court the Hague, *Bosnian Father*, Judgment, 11 November 2020, ECLI:NL:RBDHA:2020:15220, para 2.22.

[81] Ibid., para 2.24.

[82] Ibid., para 2.27.

The court noted that in several cases under Article 41, the ECtHR awarded 'just satisfaction' without demanding proof of psychological harm. To be on the safe side—i.e. taking into account the Dutch *EBI*-case framework—, the court considered that in the present case there are not only some 'serious violations of fundamental rights', but also 'extremely harmful consequences' that are so obvious that an injury to the person can be assumed.[83] Claimant is awarded a sum that is in line with the just satisfaction awards of the ECtHR, albeit 10% due to the outcome in the *Srebrenica* case.

In the *Bosnian father* case, the District Court first addressed the relevant international legal requirements: applying interpretational rules and the right to a remedy under Article 13 ECHR. This is legitimized by the Articles 93 and 94 DC, where international law is given hierarchy above national (tort) law. When these requirements are placed within the framework of national tort law, two things stand out. Firstly, the national tort law system did not provide for a form of compensation that is in line with the ECHR. The court finds its way around this by addressing the hierarchy of ECHR. Secondly, the threshold in national tort law for (fully) compensating victims of fundamental rights violations is aimed at the causality between wrong and damage, while the ECHR awards damages for the violation as such. In this case, the District Court could not go against the Supreme Court and addressed this threshold. Nevertheless, it shows the possibility to apply Article 13 ECHR and offer compensation to victims, even when the nationally conceived thresholds of 'partial liability' and seriousness of the breach and severity of the consequences are not met.

14.5 Concluding Remarks

When international human rights are breached, the effectiveness of their protection is safeguarded with the remedies that are upheld at the national level. While States are free to decide upon their national implementation of international law, national courts play a large role in applying and thereby safeguarding and further developing international (human rights) law. Regarding the rights embedded in the Convention, their application in national tort law can largely be claimed to be successful. However, the remedies that are provided in the national tort law systems, not always coincide with the remedy that is envisioned by the ECHR.

In this chapter, both the national implementation of the ECHR as well as the role of the courts in ensuring the right to a remedy under Article 13 ECHR were examined, and obstacles were found in two categories. The first category of obstacles for a full enjoyment of the right to a remedy indeed lies in the application of international law in the national system. While Dutch law was the starting point for this research because it is one of the most progressive in its monist tradition, there are still cases where national law is put first while the ECHR should be in the lead. When international treaties or interpretational rules are overlooked by national law practitioners, this

[83] Ibid., para 2.29.

can become a problem when it leads to different outcomes between States or even between courts. Exemplary is the difference between the *Urgenda* case, where Article 2 and 8 ECHR were applied directly in Dutch tort law, while in the advisory opinion of the *Groninger Aardbeving* case the Supreme Court applied the ECHR bottom-up, by first addressing the requirements of national tort law and then checking whether and how these requirements would align with the requirements under the ECHR. Next to this—or because of this? —the Supreme Court misread the system of the ECHR and the less far-reaching elaboration of the ECHR became the standard. A similar bottom-up approach was taken in the *EBI* case, where the Supreme Court created a framework based on national tort law for compensating fundamental rights violations instead of taking the ECHR as its starting point. The mistranslation from the international to the domestic could be prevented by applying international law top-down, letting international law be the premise when building the national framework, instead of bottom-up, where international law is used as an operational aspect in the application of national law.

The second set of obstacles are found in the boundaries of tort law remedies and their peculiarities. Exceptions aside, national tort law comes with its own framework and requirements. These are often overlooked by international law (makers), but especially relevant for the private enforcement of international law via the national tort law system. Compensation for non-pecuniary damages is subject to certain limitations, which are also upheld with violations of fundamental human rights. Even when courts apply international law in a top-down manner, the outcome is subject to the requirements of national tort law and can lead to an outcome that is not in line with the aim of international law. For example, in the *Srebrenica* case, the violation of Articles 2 and 8 ECHR was established. These serious violations of fundamental rights should under the ECHR-system lead to full compensation. However, the Dutch doctrine of 'loss of a chance' limited this compensation to only ten percent in both the *Srebrenica*- and the *Bosnian father* case. The question is whether national law should have such a decisive mark on the outcome when claimants seek internationally regulated redress for violations of fundamental human rights. One might wonder what the outcome would have been when the reasoning of the District Court of The Hague was applied on the *Srebrenica* case, or even on the *EBI* case. The framework of national tort law creates obstacles for the full enjoyment of the right to a remedy under Article 13 ECHR. This can—at least partly—be corrected by (other) national courts, as shown in the *Bosnian father* case.

But let us not forget the role of the ECtHR, which can 'continue its proactive interpretation of Article 13 to encourage the introduction of effective domestic remedies.'[84] National (procedural) law requires definitions that can be directly applied by the judge, but clearcut definitions are not always given by international law. Without a clear definition—i.e., what constitutes an 'effective remedy'—it is left to national courts to interpret the meaning of the Convention, which can lead to different outcomes. But even with a clear definition, there is no guarantee for the

[84] Harris et al 2018, p. 763.

desired outcome, because human rights remedies are put through the compensation-system provided by national tort law. Until the aims of human rights law remedies are fully considered when applied through national tort law—either via direct application in a monistic system, or indirectly applied in a dualistic system—differences in the preferred outcome will still exist. That would be a real loss of a chance for international human rights law and its remedies.

References

Caligiuri A, Napoletano N (2010) The Application of the ECHR in the Domestic Systems. Italian Yearbook of International Law Online, vol. 20 issue 1, pp 125–159.

ECtHR (European Court of Human Rights) (2022) Guide on Article 13 of the European Convention on Human Rights; Right to an effective remedy. Council of Europe/European Court of Human Rights.

Emaus J (2016) Damages for Fundamental Rights Violations, Dutch Perspectives. In: Bagińska E (ed) Damages for Violations of Human Rights; A Comparative Study of Domestic Legal Systems. Springer International Publishing Switzerland, pp 241–258.

European Group on Tort Law (2005) Principles of European Tort Law, Text and Commentary. Springer Verlag, Vienna.

Fleuren JWA (2004) Een ieder verbindende bepalingen van verdragen. Boom Juridische Uitgevers.

Fleuren JWA (2010) The application of public international law by Dutch courts. Netherlands International Law Review, vol. 57, issue 02, pp 245–266.

Gewirtz P (1983) Remedies and Resistance. Yale LJ, vol. 92 no. 4, pp 585–681.

Harris D, O'Boyle M, Bates E, Buckley C (eds) (2018) Law of the European Convention on Human Rights. Oxford University Press.

Hernández G (2022) Law's Determinability: Indeterminacy, Interpretative Authority, and the International Legal System. Netherlands International Law Review. https://doi.org/10.1007/s40802-022-00222-0

https://www.un.org/esa/documents/ecosoc/docs/1999/e1999-22.htm. Accessed 14 September 2023.

Kuiper-Slendebroek BA (2017) Rechter over grenzen; de toepassing en interpretatie van internationaal recht in het Nederlands privaatrecht. Ipskamp Printing.

More D (1994) Human Rights from a Tort Law Perspective. Tel Aviv University Studies in Law, vol 12, pp 81–113.

Nijman JE, Nollkaemper PA (2007) New Perspectives on the Divide between National and International Law. Oxford University Press, Oxford.

Nollkaemper PA (2009) The Netherlands. In: Sloss D (ed) The Role of Domestic Courts in Treaty Enforcement, A Comparative Study. Cambridge University Press, pp 326–369.

Peat D (2022) Disciplining Rules? Compliance, the Rules of Interpretation, and the Evaluative Dimension of Articles 31 and 32 of the VCLT. Netherlands International Law Review. https://doi.org/10.1007/s40802-022-00220-2

Polakiewicz J (1994) The Implementation of the European Convention for the Protection of Human Rights and Fundamental Freedoms in the Field of Private Law. Tel Aviv University Studies in Law, vol 12, p 181–208.

Rijnhout R, Emaus JM (2014) Damages in Wrongful Death Cases in the Light of the European Human Rights Law: Towards a Rights-Based Approach to the Law of Damages. Utrecht Law Review, vol. 10, issue 3, pp 91–106.

Rijnhout R (2020) Van bijzonder letsel naar bijzondere normschendingen en *beyond*. Verkeersrecht, vol. 7–8, pp 194–206.

Rijnhout R (2021) Mothers of Srebrenica: Causation and Partial Liability under Dutch Tort Law. Utrecht Journal of International and European Law. https://doi.org/10.5334/ujiel.543.
Roorda L (2022) The Netherlands: A Wide Open Window for Human Rights Norms? In: Aristova E, Grusic U (eds) Civil Remedies and Human Rights in Flux: Key Legal Developments in Selected Jurisdictions. Bloomsbury Publishing Pic, pp 245–265.
Thorson B (2016) Damages for the Infringements of Human Rights Under Norwegian Law. In: Bagińska E (ed) Damages for Violations of Human Rights; A Comparative Study of Domestic Legal Systems. Springer International Publishing Switzerland, pp 259–288.
United Nations Economic and Social Council (1998) Report on the Eighteenth and Nineteenth Sessions, E/C.12/1998/SR.13.
Von Bar C, Clive E, Schulte-Nolke H (eds) (2005) Principles, Definitions and Model Rules of European Private Law; Draft Common Frame of Reference.
Von Bogdandy A (2008) Pluralism, direct effect and the ultimate say: On the relationship between international and domestic constitutional law. ICON-International Journal of Constitutional Law vol. 3–4, pp 397–431.
Wildhaber L (2007) The European Convention on Human Rights and international law. International & Comparative Law Quarterly, vol. 56, pp 217–232.

B.A. (Anneloes) Kuiper-Slendebroek is Assistant Professor at Utrecht University and researcher at the Utrecht Centre for Accountability and Liability Law (Ucall), the research cluster Empirical Legal Research into Institutions for Conflict Resolution (ERI) and the Netherlands Institute of Human Rights (SIM). Author owes gratitude to Rianka Rijnhout and Lucas Roorda for their comments on earlier versions of this contribution.

Table of Cases*

HYBRID COURTS AND TRIBUNALS

Special Courts

---

* The Table of Cases was compiled by Ms. M. Nanninga, Exter Indexing, Haarlem, The Netherlands, e-mail: info@exterindexing.com

O. Spijkers et al. (eds.), *Netherlands Yearbook of International Law 2022*, Netherlands Yearbook of International Law 53, https://doi.org/10.1007/978-94-6265-627-7

Tribunals

International Residual Mechanism for Criminal Tribunals

United States Military Tribunal at Nuremberg

INTERNATIONAL

Committee on Economic Social and Cultural Rights (CESCR)

Northern Ireland

High Court of Justice in Northern Ireland

Sweden

Swedish Supreme Court

United States (US)

District Court, S.D. New York

Index*

Page numbers in *italics* indicate figures. Court cases can be found in the separate table of cases

* The Index was compiled by Ms. M. Nanninga, Exter Indexing, Haarlem, The Netherlands, e-mail: info@exterindexing.com

O. Spijkers et al. (eds.), *Netherlands Yearbook of International Law 2022*, Netherlands Yearbook of International Law 53, https://doi.org/10.1007/978-94-6265-627-7

J

T

The manufacturer's authorised representative in the EU is Springer Nature Customer Service Centre GmbH, Europaplatz 3, 69115 Heidelberg, Germany. If you have any concerns regarding our products, please contact ProductSafety@springernature.com

Printed and bound by CPI Group (UK) Ltd, Croydon, CR0 4YY
30/09/2026
02225596-0011